W9-DEI-053

WITHDRAWN

hermeneia

**Hermeneia
—A Critical
and Historical
Commentary
on the Bible**

Old Testament Editorial Board

Frank Moore Cross, Harvard University, chairman
Klaus Baltzer, University of Munich
Paul D. Hanson, Harvard University
S. Dean McBride Jr., Union Theological Seminary in Virginia
Peter Machinist, Harvard University
Susan Niditch, Amherst College
Christopher R. Seitz, University of St.Andrews
Roland E. Murphy, O. Carm., emeritus

New Testament Editorial Board

Helmut Koester, Harvard University, chairman
Harold W. Attridge, Yale University
Adela Yarbro Collins, University of Chicago
Eldon Jay Epp, Case Western Reserve University
James M. Robinson, Claremont Graduate School

Ref.
220.7
H553

Shepherd of Hermas

A Commentary
by Carolyn Osiek

Edited by
Helmut Koester

**Fortress
Press**

Minneapolis

Shepherd of Hermas
A Commentary on the Shepherd of Hermas

Copyright © 1999 Augsburg Fortress

All rights reserved. Except for brief quotations in critical articles or reviews, no part of this book may be reproduced in any manner without prior written permission from the publisher. Write to: Permissions, Augsburg Fortress, Box 1209, Minneapolis, MN 55440.

Scripture quotations from the Revised Standard Version of the Bible are copyright © 1946, 1952, 1971 by the Division of Christian Education of the National Council of the Churches of Christ in the USA and are used by permission.

Scripture quotations from the New Revised Standard Version of the Bible are copyright © 1989 by the Division of Christian Education of the National Council of the Churches of Christ in the U.S.A. and are used by permission.

Cover and interior design by Kenneth Hiebert
Typesetting and page composition by
The HK Scriptorium

Library of Congress Cataloging-in-Publication Data

Osiek, Carolyn.
    Shepherd of Hermas : a commentary / by
Carolyn Osiek ; edited by Helmut Koester.
        p.   cm. — (Hermeneia—a critical and
historical commentary on the Bible)
    Includes bibliographical references and indexes.
    ISBN 0-8006-6063-3 (alk. paper)
    1. Hermas, 2nd cent. Shepherd Commentaries.
I. Koester, Helmut, 1926–   . II. Title. III. Series.
BS2900.H5084   1999
229'.93—dc21   99-21999
                                                    CIP

The paper used in this publication meets the minimum requirements of American National Standard for Information Sciences—Permanence of paper for Printed Library Materials, ANSI Z329.48–1984.

Manufactured in the U.S.A.   AF 1-6063

03   02   01   00   99   1   2   3   4   5   6   7   8   9   10

DEDICATION

To my religious community and my colleagues
in the Department of Biblical Literature and
Languages at Catholic Theological Union, Chicago,
who have encouraged me and waited patiently
for this for many years.

The Author

Carolyn Osiek is Professor of New Testament at Catholic
Theological Union, Chicago. Born in St. Charles,
Missouri, she attended schools in St. Louis and received
the doctorate in New Testament and Christian Origins
from Harvard Divinity School in 1978. She has served as
New Testament Book Review Editor for the *Catholic
Biblical Quarterly* and is past president of the Catholic
Biblical Association of America. She has served on
several committees of the Society of Biblical Literature
and has been the recipient of grants from the
Association of Theological Schools and the National
Endowment for the Humanities. She is author or editor
of many books and articles on the New Testament,
Apostolic Fathers, Early Church, and Feminist
Hermeneutics.

Contents
Shepherd of Hermas

■ **Introduction**

■ **Visions**

The name *Hermeneia*, Greek ἑρμηνεία, has been chosen as the title of the commentary series to which this volume belongs. The word *Hermeneia* has a rich background in the history of biblical interpretation as a term used in the ancient Greek-speaking world for the detailed, systematic exposition of a scriptural work. It is hoped that the series, like its name, will carry forward this old and venerable tradition. A second, entirely practical reason for selecting the name lies in the desire to avoid a long descriptive title and its inevitable acronym, or worse, an unpronounceable abbreviation.

The series is designed to be a critical and historical commentary to the Bible without arbitrary limits in size or scope. It will utilize the full range of philological and historical tools, including textual criticism (often slighted in modern commentaries), the methods of the history of tradition (including genre and prosodic analysis), and the history of religion.

Hermeneia is designed for the serious student of the Bible. It will make full use of ancient Semitic and classical languages; at the same time, English translations of all comparative materials—Greek, Latin, Canaanite, or Akkadian—will be supplied alongside the citation of the source in its original language. Insofar as possible, the aim is to provide the student or scholar with full critical discussion of each problem of interpretation and with the primary data upon which the discussion is based.

Hermeneia is designed to be international and interconfessional in the selection of authors; its editorial boards were formed with this end in view. Occasionally the series will offer translations of distinguished commentaries which originally appeared in languages other than English. Published volumes of the series will be revised continually, and eventually, new commentaries will replace older works in order to preserve the currency of the series. Commentaries are also being assigned for important literary works in the categories of apocryphal and pseudepigraphical works relating to the Old and New Testaments, including some of Essene or Gnostic authorship.

The editors of *Hermeneia* impose no systematic-theological perspective upon the series (directly, or indirectly by selection of authors). It is expected that authors will struggle to lay bare the ancient meaning of a biblical work or pericope. In this way the text's human relevance should become transparent, as is always the case in competent historical discourse. However, the series eschews for itself homiletical translation of the Bible.

The editors are heavily indebted to Augsburg Fortress for its energy and courage in taking up an expensive, long-term project, the rewards of which will accrue chiefly to the field of biblical scholarship.

The editor responsible for this volume is Helmut Koester of Harvard University.

June 1992

Frank Moore Cross
For the Old Testament
Editorial Board

Helmut Koester
For the New Testament
Editorial Board

Reference Codes

1. Sources and General Abbreviations

A	Athous Codex (*Facsimile of the Athos Fragments of the Shepherd of Hermas*, ed. Kirsopp Lake [Oxford: Clarendon, 1911])
AB	Anchor Bible
ABD	*Anchor Bible Dictionary*
Act. John	*Acts of John*
Act. Paul Thec.	*Acts of Paul and Thecla*
Act. Pet.	*Acts of Peter*
Act. Phil.	*Acts of Philip*
Acts Scil. Mart.	*Acts of the Scillitan Martyrs*
Act. Thom.	*Acts of Thomas*
AJP	*American Journal of Philology*
Ambrose	
Hex.	*Hexameron*
ANF	Ante-Nicene Fathers
ANRW	*Aufstieg und Niedergang der römischen Welt*
Ant	Antiochus of St. Sabbas (7th cent.), Πανδέκτης τῆς ἁγίας γραφῆς, quotations (Migne, Patrologia Graeca 89.1413–1855)
Apoc. Abr.	*Apocalypse of Abraham*
Apoc. Paul	*Apocalypse of Paul*
Apoc. Pet.	*Apocalypse of Peter*
Apoc. Zeph.	*Apocalypse of Zephaniah*
Ap. Const.	*Apostolic Constitutions*
Ap. John	*Apocryphon of John*
Apollodorus	
Bibl.	*Bibliotheca*
Asc. Isa.	*Ascension of Isaiah*
As. Mos.	*Assumption of Moses*
ASTI	*Annual of the Swedish Theological Institute*
Ath	Pseudo-Athanasius, Διδασκαλίαι πρὸς Ἀντίοχον, quotations (*Athanasii Alexandrini Praecepta ad Antiochum. Ad codices duos recensuit Guilielmus Dindorfius;* ed. Wilhelm Dindorf; Leipzig: T. O. Weigl, 1857)
Ath²	Pseudo-Athanasius, Paris codex 635 (*Athanasii Alexandrini Praecepta ad Antiochum. Ad codices duos recensuit Guilielmus Dindorfius;* ed. Wilhelm Dindorf; Leipzig: T. O. Weigl, 1857)
Athanasius	
Ad Afros episc. ep.	*Ad Afros episcopos epistula*
De decret. Nic. syn.	*De decretis Nicaenae synodi*
De incarn.	*De incarnatione verbi*
Ep. fest.	*Epistulae festales*
Athenagoras	
Leg.	*Legatio*
ATR	*Anglican Theological Review*
Augustine	
Conf.	*Confessions*
Aulus Gellius	
At. N.	*Attic Nights*
B	Bodmer Papyrus 38 (*Papyrus Bodmer XXXVIII. Erma: Il Pastore [Ia–IIIa visione]*, ed. Antonio Carlini [Bibliotheca Bodmeriana; Cologny-Genève: Fondation Martin Bodmer, 1991])
BA	*Biblical Archaeologist*
BAGD	Walter Bauer, *A Greek-English Lexicon of the New Testament*, ed. William F. Arndt, F. Wilbur Gingrich, Fredrick W. Danker (2d ed.; Chicago: University of Chicago Press, 1958)
2 Bar.	*Syriac Apocalypse of Baruch*
3 Bar.	*Greek Apocalypse of Baruch*
4 Bar.	*4 Baruch*
Barn.	*Letter of Barnabas*
BDF	F. Blass and A. Debrunner, *A Greek Grammar of the New Testament and Other Early Christian Literature*, ed. Robert W. Funk (Chicago: University of Chicago Press, 1961)
Bib	*Biblica*
BR	*Biblical Research*
BTB	*Biblical Theology Bulletin*
C¹	Akhmimic Coptic translation (*Les Pères apostoliques en copte*, ed. L. Théophile Lefort [CSCO 135–36; Louvain: Durbecq, 1952])
C²	Sahidic Coptic translation (*Les Pères apostoliques en copte*, ed. L. Théophile Lefort [CSCO 135–36; Louvain: Durbecq, 1952])
Caesarius of Arles	
Hom.	*Homiliae*
CAH	*Cambridge Ancient History*
Cassian	
Conf.	*Conferences*
CBQ	*Catholic Biblical Quarterly*
CBQMS	Catholic Biblical Quarterly Monograph Series
CC	Agreement of the two Coptic translations
CChr	Corpus Christianorum
CD	Cairo (Genizah) text of the *Damascus Document*
CH	*Church History*
Cicero	
Att.	*Ad Atticum*

CIL — *Corpus inscriptionum latinarum*

Clement of Alexandria
- *Ecl. proph.* — *Eclogae propheticae*
- *Excerp. ex Theod.* — *Excerpta ex Theodoto*
- *Paed.* — *Paedagogus*
- *Protrep.* — *Protrepticus*
- *Quis Dives* — *Quis Dives Salvetur*
- *Strom.* — *Stromata*

1 Clem. — *1 Clement*

2 Clem. — *2 Clement*

Columella
- *De arbor.* — *De arboribus*

Commodianus
- *Inst.* — *Instructiones*

ConBNT — Coniectanea biblica, New Testament

Corp. Herm. — *Corpus Hermeticum*

CSCO — Corpus Scriptorum Christianorum Orientalium

Cyprian
- *Ad Demtr.* — *Ad Demetrianum*
- *De hab. virg.* — *De habitu virginum*
- *De mortal.* — *De mortalitate*

DACL — *Dictionnaire d'archéologie chrétienne et de liturgie*, ed. Fernand Cabrol, Henri Leclerq, and Henri Marrou (15 vols.; Paris: Letouzey et Ané, 1907–1953)

Did. — *Didache*

Didasc. — *Didascalia Apostolorum*

Dig. — Justinian, *Digest*

Diogn. — *Epistle to Diognetus*

Dio Cassius
- *Epit.* — *Epitoma Historiae Romanae*
- *Hist.* — *Historiae Romanae*

Diodorus Siculus
- *Bibl. hist.* — *Bibliotheca historica*

E — Ethiopic translation (*Hermae Pastor. Aethiopice primum edidit et Aethiopica Latine vertit Antoninus d'Abbadie*, ed. Antoine d'Abbadie [Abhandlungen der Deutschen morgenländischen Gesellschaft 2.1; Leipzig: Brockhaus, 1860])

1 Enoch — *Ethiopic Enoch*

2 Enoch — *Slavonic Enoch*

3 Enoch — *Hebrew Enoch*

Ep. Apost. — *Epistula Apostolorum*

Epictetus
- *Diss.* — *Dissertationes*
- *Enchir.* — *Enchiridion*

Epiphanius
- *Pan.* — *Panarion*

ERE — *Encyclopedia of Religion and Ethics*

EThL — *Ephemerides theologicae lovanienses*

ÉThR — *Études théologiques et religieuses*

Eusebius
- *Hist. eccl.* — *Historia ecclesiastica*
- *Vit. Const.* — *Vita Constantini*

F — Eurydice Lappa-Zizicas, "Cinq fragments du *Pasteur* d'Hermes dans un manuscrit de la Bibliothèque Nationale de Paris," *RechSR* 53 (1965) 251–56

FRLANT — Forschungen zur Religion und Literatur des Alten und Neuen Testaments

Gos. Eg. — *Gospel of the Egyptians*

Gos. Pet. — *Gospel of Peter*

Gos. Phil. — *Gospel of Philip*

Gos. Thom. — *Gospel of Thomas*

Gos. Truth — *Gospel of Truth*

GRBS — *Greek, Roman, and Byzantine Studies*

GThA — Göttinger theologische Arbeiten

HDR — Harvard Dissertations in Religion

Hermas — *Shepherd of Hermas*
- *Vis.* — *Visions*
- *Man.* — *Mandates*
- *Sim.* — *Similitudes*

Hippolytus
- *Antichr.* — *De antichristo*
- *Ap. Trad.* — *Apostolic Tradition*
- *Ref.* — *Refutatio omnium haeresium*

HNT — Handbuch zum Neuen Testament

Horace
- *Sat.* — Horace, *Satires*

HTR — *Harvard Theological Review*

Ign. — Ignatius
- *Eph.* — *Letter to the Ephesians*
- *Magn.* — *Letter to the Magnesians*
- *Phld.* — *Letter to the Philadelphians*
- *Pol.* — *Letter to Polycarp*
- *Rom.* — *Letter to the Romans*
- *Smyrn.* — *Letter to the Smyrnaeans*
- *Trall.* — *Letter to the Trallians*

Int — *Interpretation*

Irenaeus
- *Adv. haer.* — *Adversus haereses*

JBL — *Journal of Biblical Literature*

JECS — *Journal of Early Christian Studies*

Jerome
- *Comm.* — *Commentarii*
- *De vir. ill.* — *De viris illustribus*
- *In Hab.* — *In Habacuc*

Jos. and As. — *Joseph and Aseneth*

Josephus
- *Ant.* — *Antiquities of the Jews*
- *Ap.* — *Contra Apionem*
- *Bell.* — *Bellum Judaicum*

JSPSS — Journal for the Study of the Pseudepigrapha Supplement Series

JTS — *Journal of Theological Studies*

Jub. — *Jubilees*

Justin
- *1 Apol.* — *First Apology*
- *Dial.* — *Dialogue with Trypho*

Keryg. Pet.	Kerygma Petri	Comm. Matt.	Commentarii in evangelium Matthaei
L[1]	"Vulgate" Latin translation (Hermae Pastor. Veteram Latinam interpretatione codicibus, ed. Adolph Hilgenfeld [Leipzig: Reisland, 1873])	Comm. ser.	Commentariorum series
		De prin.	De principiis
		Hom. in Jer.	Homiliae in Jeremiam
		Hom. on Josh.	Homilies on Joshua
L[2]	"Palatine" Latin translation (Hermae Pastor graece, addita versione latina recentiore e codice Palatino, ed. Oskar von Gebhardt and Adolf von Harnack [Patrum Apostolicorum Opera 3; Leipzig: Hinrichs, 1877])	OTP	James. H. Charlesworth, ed., The Old Testament Pseudepigrapha (2 vols.; Garden City, NY: Doubleday, 1988–1985)
		Ovid	
		Metam.	Metamorphoses
		OxCD	Oxford Classical Dictionary (ed. Simon Hornblower and Anthony Spawforth [3d ed.; Oxford/New York: Oxford University Press, 1996])
LCL	Loeb Classical Library		
LL	Agreement of the two Latin translations		
LPGL	A Patristic Greek Lexicon, ed. G. W. H. Lampe (Oxford: Clarendon, 1961–1968)		
		Pam	Amherst Papyrus 2.190 (The Amherst Papyri, ed. Bernard P. Grenfell and Arthur S. Hunt; London: Frowde, 1901)
LSJ	Henry George Liddell and Robert Scott, A Greek-English Lexicon (9th ed. Henry Stuart Jones; Oxford: Clarendon, 1940)		
		PG	Patrologia graeca=J.-P. Migne, Patrologiae cursus completus, series graeca (162 vols.; Paris: Migne, 1857–1866)
Lucian			
Hermot.	Hermotimus		
Lucius Annaeus Florus		PGM	Karl Preisendanz (ed.), Papyri graecae magicae (2 vols.; Leipzig: Teubner, 1928–1931)
Ep.	Epitome Historiae Romanae		
M	Michigan Papyrus 129 (A Papyrus Codex of the Shepherd of Hermas [Similitudes 2–9] with a Fragment of the Mandates, ed. Campbell Bonner [University of Michigan Studies, Humanistic Series 22; Ann Arbor: University of Michigan Press, 1934])	Phamb	Hamburg Papyrus (ed. Charles Wessely; Patrologia Orientalis 18 [1924] 472-77)
		Philo	
		Agric.	De agricultura
		Cher.	De cherubim
		Conf. ling.	De confusione linguarum
		Ebr.	De ebrietate
Martial		Fug.	De fuga et inventione
Epig.	Epigrammata	Migr. Abr.	De migratione Abrahami
Mart. Matt.	Martyrdom of Matthew	Op. mundi	De opificio mundi
Mart. Pol.	Martyrdom of Polycarp	Q. Exod.	Quaestiones in Exodum
Minucius Felix		Sacr. AC	De sacrificiis Abelis et Caini
Oct.	Octavius	Som.	De somniis
Nestle-Aland[26]	Novum Testamentum Graece, ed. Eberhard and Erwin Nestle, Kurt Aland, et al. (Stuttgart: Deutsche Bibelgesellschaft, 1979)	Spec. leg.	De specialibus legibus
		Vit. Mos.	De vita Mosis
		P.Iand.	Papyrus Iandanae 1. 4 (ed. Charles Kalbfleisch [Leipzig: Teubner, 1912])
NHLE	Nag Hammadi Library in English		
NHS	Nag Hammadi Studies		
NIGTC	New International Greek Testament Commentary	PL	J.-P. Migne, Patrologia latina
		Pliny the Elder	
NovT	Novum Testamentum	N. H.	Natural History
NovTSup	Novum Testamentum, Supplements	Pliny the Younger	
		Ep.	Epistles
NTApoc	New Testament Apocrypha, ed. Edgar Hennecke and Wilhelm Schneemelcher	PO	Patrologia orientalis
		Pol.	Polycarp
		Phil.	Letter to the Philippians
NTS	New Testament Studies	Polyaenus	
Odes Sol.	Odes of Solomon	Strat.	Strategemata
Origen		Polybius	
Comm. in Joh.	Commentarii in evangelium Joannis	Hist.	Historiae
Comm. in Rom.	Commentarii in Romanos		

Pontius		Suetonius		
Vit. Cyp.	*Vita Cypriani*	*Aug.*	*Augustus*	
POxy	*The Oxyrhynchus Papyri* (ed. A. K. Bowman et al.; vol. 50; Graeco-Roman Memoirs 70; London: Egypt Exploration Society, 1983)	*Claud.*	*Claudius*	
		Tib.	*Tiberius*	
		Sulpicius Severus		
		Chron.	*Chronica*	
PPrag	*Papyri Graecae Wessely Pragense (P.Prag. I)* (ed. Rosario Pintaudi et al.; Papyrologia Florentina 16; Florence: Gonnelli, 1988)	SVTP	Studia in Veteri Testamenti Pseudepigrapha	
		Tab. Ceb.	*Tabula of Cebes*	
		Tacitus		
Prot. Jas.	*Protoevangelium of James*	*Ann.*	*Annals*	
Ps.-Chrysostom		*Teach. Silv.*	*Teachings of Silvanus*	
Hom. on Matt.	*Homilies on Matthew*	TDNT	*Theological Dictionary of the New Testament*, ed. Gerhard Kittel and Geoffrey W. Bromiley (10 vols.; Grand Rapids, MI, and London: Eerdmans, 1964–1976)	
Ps.-Cyprian				
Adv. Aleat.	*Adversus Aleatores*			
PW	*Paulys Real-encyclopädie der classischen Altertumswissenschaft,* ed. Georg Wissowa et al. (Stuttgart: Metzler, 1894ff.)			
		Tertullian		
		Ad uxor.	*Ad uxorem*	
1QH	*Thanksgiving Hymns* from Qumran Cave I	*Adv. Marc.*	*Adversus Marcionem*	
		Apol.	*Apologeticum*	
1QS	*Community Rule,* Qumran	*De jejun.*	*De jejunio*	
1QSb	Appendix B (*Blessings*) to 1QS	*De monog.*	*De monogamia*	
RAC	*Reallexikon für Antike und Christentum*	*De orat.*	*De oratione*	
		De paen.	*De paenitentia*	
RB	*Revue biblique*	*De praes.*	*De praescriptione haereticorum*	
RechSR	*Recherches de science religieuse*	*De pud.*	*De pudicitia*	
RevQ	*Revue de Qumran*	*De spec.*	*De spectaculis*	
RH	*Revue historique*	*Exh. cast.*	*De exhortatione castitatis*	
RSPhTh	*Revue des sciences philosophiques et théologiques*	*Tg. Ps.-J.*	*Targum Pseudo-Jonathan*	
		T. Abr.	*Testament of Abraham*	
Rufinus		*T. 12 Patr.*	*Testament of the Twelve Patriarchs*	
Exp. symb.	*Expositio Symbolum Apostolorum*	*T. Ash.*	*Testament of Asher*	
S	Codex Sinaiticus	*T. Dan*	*Testament of Dan*	
Sᶜ	Corrections to Sinaiticus Codex	*T. Iss.*	*Testament of Issachar*	
SBLASP	Society of Biblical Literature Abstracts and Seminar Papers	*T. Jos.*	*Testament of Joseph*	
		T. Jud.	*Testament of Judah*	
SBLMS	Society of Biblical Literature Monograph Series	*T. Lev.*	*Testament of Levi*	
		T. Naph.	*Testament of Naphtali*	
SBLTT	Society of Biblical Literature Texts and Translations	*T. Reub.*	*Testament of Reuben*	
		t.Sanh.	Tosephta, tractate Sanhedrin	
SBT	Studies in Biblical Theology	*ThQ*	*Theologische Quartalschrift*	
SC	Sources chrétiennes	*TS*	*Theological Studies*	
SCO	*Studi classici e orientali*	TU	Texte und Untersuchungen zur Geschichte der altchristlichen Literatur	
SecCent	*Second Century*			
SEG	Supplementum epigraphicum graecum			
		VC	*Vigiliae christianae*	
Seneca		Vg.	Vulgate	
Ep.	*Epistulae morales*	Virgil		
Sib. Or.	*Sibylline Oracles*	*Aen.*	*Aeneid*	
SNTSMS	Society for New Testament Studies Monograph Series	*VT*	*Vetus Testamentum*	
		Vitruvius		
Soph. Jes. Chr.	*Sophia Jesu Christi*	*De agric.*	*De agricultura*	
SR	*Studies in Religion/Sciences religieuses*	WUNT	Wissenschaftliche Untersuchungen zum Neuen Testament	
StPatr	*Studia Patristica*	Xenophon		
Strabo		*Mem.*	*Memorabilia*	
Geog.	*Geographica*	ZNW	*Zeitschrift für die neutestamentliche Wissenschaft*	
StTh	*Studia Theologica*			

ZWTh   *Zeitschrift für wissenschaftliche Theologie*

2. Short Titles of Frequently Cited Literature

Audet, "Affinités"
> Jean-Paul Audet, "Affinités littéraires et doctrinales du Manuel de Discipline," *RB* 59 (1952) 219–38; 60 (1953) 41–82.

Aune, "Now You See It"
> David E. Aune, "Now You See It, Now You Don't! Ancient Magic and the Apocalypse of John," unpublished seminar paper, SBL, 1986.

Aune, *Prophecy*
> David E. Aune, *Prophecy in Early Christianity and the Ancient Mediterranean World* (Grand Rapids, MI: Eerdmans, 1983).

Bausone, "Aspetti"
> Carla Bausone, "Aspetti dell'ecclesiologia del Pastore di Hermas," *StPatr* 11=TU 108 (1972) 101–6.

Bobertz, "Role of Patron"
> Charles A. Bobertz, "The Role of Patron in the Cena Dominica of Hippolytus' *Apostolic Tradition*," *JTS* 44 (1993) 170–84.

Bonner, *Papyrus Codex*
> Campbell Bonner, *A Papyrus Codex of the Shepherd of Hermas (Similitudes 2–9) with a Fragment of the Mandates* (University of Michigan Studies, Humanistic Series 22; Ann Arbor: University of Michigan Press, 1934).

Brox
> Norbert Brox, *Der Hirt des Hermas* (Kommentar zu den Apostolischen Vätern 7; Göttingen: Vandenhoeck & Ruprecht, 1991).

Carlini, *Bodmer Papyrus*
> *Papyrus Bodmer XXXVIII, Erma: Il Pastore (Ia–IIIa visione)* (Bibliotheca Bodmeriana; Cologny/Genève: Fondation Martin Bodmer, 1991).

Carlini, "Erma"
> Antonio Carlini, "Erma (*Vis.* II 3.1) testimone testuale di Paolo?" *SCO* 37 (1987) 235–39.

Carlini, "Testimone e testo"
> Antonio Carlini, "Testimone e testo: Il problema della datazione di PIand I 4 del Pastore di Erma," *SCO* 42 (1992) 17–30.

Carlini, "Testuale e prescrizioni"
> Antonio Carlini, "Tradizione testuale e prescrizione canoniche: Erma, Sesto, Origene," *Orpheus* 7 (1986) 40–52.

Carlini, "Tradizione manoscritta"
> Antonio Carlini, "La tradizione manoscritta del Pastor di Hermas e il problema dell'unità dell'opera," in *Papyrus Erzherzog Rainer: Festschrift zum 100-Jährigen Bestehen der Papyrussammlung der Österreichischen Nationalbibliothek* (Textband; Vienna: Hollinek, 1983) 97–100.

Carlini, "Tradizione testuale"
> Antonio Carlini, "La tradizione testuale del Pastore di Erma e i nuovi papiri," in Guglielmo Cavallo, ed., *Le Strade del Testo* (Lecce: Adriatica Editrice, 1987) 23–43.

Cirillo, "Christologie pneumatique"
> Luigi Cirillo, "La christologie pneumatique de la cinquième parabole du 'Pasteur' d'Hermas," *Revue de l'histoire des religions* 184 (1973) 25–48.

Cirillo, "Erma e il problema"
> Luigi Cirillo, "Erma e il problema dell'apocalittica a Roma," *Cristianesimo nella Storia* 4 (1983) 1–31.

Clark, "Subintroductae"
> Elizabeth A. Clark, "John Chrysostom and the Subintroductae," *CH* 46 (1977) 171–85.

Crombie
> F. Crombie, "The Pastor of Hermas" (Introduction, translation, notes) (ANF; Edinburgh: T. & T. Clark, 1867) 2. 3–58. Introduction by A. Cleveland Coxe.

D'Alès, *L'édit de Calliste*
> Athémar D'Alès, *L'édit de Calliste. Études sur l'origine de la pénitence chrétienne* (Paris: Beauchesne, 1914).

Dibelius
> Martin Dibelius, *Der Hirt des Hermas* (HNT; Die Apostolischen Väter 4; Tübingen: Mohr/Siebeck, 1923).

Dibelius-Greeven, *James*
> Martin Dibelius, rev. by Heinrich Greeven, *James* (Hermeneia; Philadelphia: Fortress, 1976).

Dronke, "Arbor Caritatis"
> Peter Dronke, "Arbor Caritatis," in P. L. Heyworth, ed., *Medieval Studies for J. A. W. Bennett* (Oxford: Clarendon, 1981) 207–43.

Ford, "Liturgical Background"
> Josephine M. Ford, "A Possible Liturgical Background to the Shepherd of Hermas," *RevQ* (1969) 531–51.

Funk
> Francis X. Funk, "Hermae Pastor," *Patres Apostolici* (2 vols.; Tübingen: Laupp, 1901) 414–639.

Gamble, *Books and Readers*
> Harry Y. Gamble, *Books and Readers in the Early Church: A History of Early Christian Texts* (New Haven/London: Yale University Press, 1995).

Garrett, *Demise of the Devil*
> Susan R. Garrett, *The Demise of the Devil: Magic and the Demonic in Luke's Writings* (Minneapolis: Fortress, 1989).

Gebhardt-Harnack
> Oskar von Gebhardt and Adolph von Harnack, *Hermae Pastor graece, addita versione latina recentiore e codice Palatino* (Patrum Apostolicorum Opera 3; Leipzig: Hinrichs, 1877).

Giet, "De trois expressions"
> Stanislas Giet, "De trois expressions: 'Auprès de la tour,' 'la place inférieure,' et 'les premiers murs,' dans le *Pasteur d'Hermas*," *StPatr* 8=TU 93 (1966) 24–29.

Giet, Hermas
> Stanislas Giet, *Hermas et les pasteurs: les trois auteurs du Pasteur d'Hermas* (Paris: Presses Universitaires de France, 1963).

Goldhahn-Müller, *Die Grenze der Gemeinde*
Ingrid Goldhahn-Müller, *Die Grenze der Gemeinde: Studien zum Problem der zweiten Busse im Neuen Testament unter Berücksichtigung der Entwicklung im 2 Jh. bis Tertullian* (GThA 39; Göttingen: Vandenhoeck & Ruprecht, 1989).

Grobel, "Parable II"
Kendrick Grobel, "The Shepherd of Hermas, Parable II," in Richmond C. Beatty et al., eds., *Vanderbilt Studies in the Humanities* (Nashville: Vanderbilt University Press, 1951) 1. 50–55.

Grotz, *Entwicklung*
Joseph Grotz, *Die Entwicklung des Busstufenwesens in der vornicänischen Kirche* (Freiburg: Herder, 1955).

Hahneman, *Muratorian Fragment*
Geoffrey M. Hahneman, *The Muratorian Fragment and the Development of the Canon* (New York: Oxford University Press, 1992).

Hellholm, *Visionenbuch*
David Hellholm, *Das Visionenbuch des Hermas als Apokalypse* (vol. 1; ConBNT 13:1; Lund: Gleerup, 1980).

Henne, "À propos"
Philippe Henne, "À propos de la christologie du *Pasteur* d'Hermas," *RSPhTh* 72 (1988) 569–78.

Henne, "Canonicité"
Philippe Henne, "Canonicité du 'Pasteur' d'Hermas," *Revue Thomiste* 90 (1990) 81–100.

Henne, *Christologie*
Philippe Henne, *La christologie chez Clément de Rome et dans le Pasteur d'Hermas* (Paradosis, Études de littérature et de théologie anciennes 33; Fribourg: Éditions Universitaires, 1992).

Henne, *L'unité*
Philippe Henne, *L'unité du Pasteur d'Hermas* (Cahiers Revue Biblique 31; Paris: Gabalda, 1992).

Henne, "Pénitence"
Philippe Henne, "La pénitence et la rédaction du *Pasteur* d'Hermas," *RB* 98 (1991) 358–97.

Henne, "Polysémie"
Philippe Henne, "La polysémie allégorique dans le *Pasteur* d'Hermas," *EThL* 65 (1989) 131–35.

Henne, "Véritable christologie"
Philippe Henne, "La véritable christologie de la *Cinquième Similitude* du *Pasteur* d'Hermas," *RSPhTh* 74 (1990) 182–204.

Hilgenfeld
Adolph Hilgenfeld, *Hermae Pastor graece* (Leipzig: T. O. Weigl, 1866).

Hilhorst, "Hermas"
A. Hilhorst, "Hermas," *RAC* 108/109 (1988) 682–701.

Hilhorst, *Sémitismes*
A. Hilhorst, *Sémitismes et latinismes dans le Pasteur d'Hermas* (Graecitas Christianorum Primaeva 5; Nijmegen: Dekker and Van de Vegt, 1976).

Humphrey, *Ladies and the Cities*
Edith McEwan Humphrey, *The Ladies and the Cities: Transformation and Apocalyptic Identity in Joseph and Aseneth, 4 Ezra, the Apocalypse and the Shepherd of Hermas* (JSPSS 17; Sheffield: Sheffield Academic Press, 1995).

Jeffers, *Conflict at Rome*
James S. Jeffers, *Conflict at Rome: Social Order and Hierarchy in Early Christianity* (Minneapolis: Fortress, 1991).

Joly
Robert Joly, *Hermas le Pasteur* (SC 53 1958; 2d ed.; SC 53bis; Paris: Éditions du Cerf, 1968; reprint 1986).

Joly, "Milieu complexe"
"Le milieu complexe du 'Pasteur d'Hermas,' *ANRW* 2. 27.1 (1993) 524–51.

Koester, *Introduction*
Helmut Koester, "Apocalyptic Ordering of Christian Life: The Shepherd of Hermas," in idem, *Introduction to the New Testament*, vol. 2: *History and Literature of Early Christianity* (Berlin and New York: De Gruyter, 1982) 256–61.

Kraft, *Clavis*
Heinrich Kraft, *Clavis Patrum Apostolicorum* (Munich: Kösel, 1963).

Lake
Kirsopp Lake, "The Shepherd of Hermas" (*Apostolic Fathers* 2; LCL; Cambridge, MA: Harvard University Press, 1913) 1–305.

Lampe, *Stadtrömische Christen*
Peter Lampe, *Die stadtrömischen Christen in den ersten beiden Jahrhunderten* (WUNT 2. 18; 2d ed.; Tübingen: Mohr/Siebeck, 1989).

Leutzsch, *Wahrnehmung*
Martin Leutzsch, *Die Wahrnehmung sozialer Wirklichkeit im "Hirten des Hermas"* (FRLANT 150; Göttingen: Vandenhoeck & Ruprecht, 1989).

Liébaert, *Enseignements moraux*
Jacques Liébaert, *Les enseignements moraux des Pères Apostoliques* (Recherches et synthèses; Morale 4; Gembloux: Duculot, 1970).

Lightfoot
James B. Lightfoot, *The Apostolic Fathers* (London: Macmillan, 1889; reprinted Grand Rapids: Baker, 1981).

Luschnat, "Jungfrauenszene"
Otto Luschnat, "Die Jungfrauenszene in der Arkadienvision des Hermas," *Theologia Viatorum* 12 (1973–74) 53–70.

Maier, *Social Setting*
Harry O. Maier, *The Social Setting of the Ministry as Reflected in the Writings of Hermas, Clement and Ignatius* (Canadian Corporation for Studies in Religion, Dissertations SR 1; Waterloo, Ontario: Wilfrid Laurier University Press, 1991).

Malina, *New Testament World*
Bruce J. Malina, *The New Testament World: Insights from Cultural Anthropology* (rev. ed.; Louisville: Westminster John Knox, 1993).

Miller, "All the Words"
Patricia Cox Miller, "'All the Words Were Frightful': Salvation by Dreams in the Shepherd of

Hermas," *VC* 42 (1988) 327–38.

Miller, *Dreams in Late Antiquity*
Patricia Cox Miller, *Dreams in Late Antiquity: Studies in the Imagination of a Culture* (Princeton, NJ: Princeton University Press, 1994).

Mohrmann, "Les origines"
Christine Mohrmann, "Les origines de la latinité chrétienne à Rome," *VC* 3 (1949) 67–106, 163–83.

Moyo, "Angels and Christology"
Ambrose Moyo, "Angels and Christology in the Shepherd of Hermas" (Ph.D. diss., Harvard University, 1978).

Nijendijk, "Christologie"
Lambartus W. Nijendijk, "Die Christologie des Hirten des Hermas" (Th.D. diss., Rijksuniversiteit Utrecht, 1986).

Osiek and Balch, *Families*
Carolyn Osiek and David Balch, *Families in the New Testament World: Households and House Churches* (Louisville: Westminster John Knox, 1997).

Osiek, "Genre and Function"
Carolyn Osiek, "The Genre and Function of the Shepherd of Hermas," in Adela Yarbro Collins, ed., *Early Christian Apocalypticism: Genre and Social Setting* (Semeia 36; Decatur, GA: Scholars Press, 1986) 113–21.

Osiek, "Oral World"
Carolyn Osiek, "The Oral World of Early Christianity in Rome: The Case of Hermas," in Karl P. Donfried and Peter Richardson, eds., *Judaism and Christianity in First-Century Rome* (Grand Rapids: Eerdmans, 1998) 151–72.

Osiek, "Ransom"
Carolyn Osiek, "The Ransom of Captives: Evolution of a Tradition," *HTR* 74 (1981) 365–86.

Osiek, *Rich and Poor*
Carolyn Osiek, *Rich and Poor in the Shepherd of Hermas: An Exegetical-Social Investigation* (CBQMS 15; Washington, DC: Catholic Biblical Association, 1983).

Osiek, "Second Century"
"The Early Second Century through the Eyes of Hermas: Continuity and Change," *BTB* 20 (1990) 116–22.

Paramelle, "Hermas"
E. Paramelle and Pierre Adnès, "Hermas (Le Pasteur d')," *Dictionnaire de Spiritualité* (ed. M. Viller et al.; Paris: Beauchesne, 1969) 7. 316–34.

Pernveden, *Concept of the Church*
Lage Pernveden, *The Concept of the Church in the Shepherd of Hermas* (Studia Theologica Lundensia 27; Lund: Gleerup, 1966).

Peterson, "Begegnung"
Erik Peterson, "Die Begegnung mit dem Ungeheuer," in idem, *Frühkirche, Judentum, und Gnosis* (Freiburg: Herder, 1959) 285–309.

Peterson, "Beiträge"
Erik Peterson, "Beiträge zur Interpretation der Visionen im 'Pastor Hermae'," in idem, *Frühkirche, Judentum, und Gnosis* (Freiburg: Herder, 1959) 254–70.

Peterson, "Kritische Analyse"
Erik Peterson, "Kritische Analyse der fünften Vision des Hermas," in idem, *Frühkirche, Judentum, und Gnosis* (Freiburg: Herder, 1959) 271–84.

Poschmann, *Paenitentia Secunda*
Bernhard Poschmann, *Paenitentia Secunda: Die kirchliche Busse im ältesten Christentum bis Cyprian und Origenes* (Theophaneia 1; Bonn: Hanstein, 1940).

Poschmann, *Penance*
Bernhard Poschmann, *Penance and the Anointing of the Sick* (New York: Herder and Herder, 1964).

Rahner, "Penitential Teaching"
Karl Rahner, "The Penitential Teaching of the Shepherd of Hermas," *Theological Investigations* 15 (New York: Crossroad, 1982).

Reiling, *Hermas and Christian Prophecy*
J. Reiling, *Hermas and Christian Prophecy: A Study of the Eleventh Mandate* (NovTSup 37; Leiden: Brill, 1973).

Reitzenstein, *Poimandres*
Richard Reitzenstein, *Poimandres: Studien zur griechisch-ägyptischen und frühchristlichen Literatur* (Leipzig: Teubner, 1904).

Snyder
Graydon Snyder, *The Shepherd of Hermas* (ed. Robert M. Grant; Apostolic Fathers 6; Camden, NJ: T. Nelson, 1969).

Solin, *Griechische Personennamen*
Heikki Solin, *Die griechischen Personennamen in Rom: Ein Namenbuch* (3 vols.; Berlin/New York: De Gruyter, 1982).

White, "Interaction"
John Carroll White, "The Interaction of Language and World in the 'Shepherd of Hermas'" (Ph.D. diss., Temple University, 1973).

Whittaker
Molly Whittaker, ed., *Der Hirt des Hermas* (1956; 2d ed.; Die Apostolischen Väter 1; Berlin: Akademie-Verlag, 1967).

Wilson, *Reassessment*
J. Christian Wilson, *Toward a Reassessment of the Shepherd of Hermas: Its Date and Pneumatology* (Lewiston/Queenston/Lampeter: Mellen, 1993).

Young, "Being a Man"
Steve Young, "Being a Man: The Pursuit of Manliness in *The Shepherd of Hermas*," *JECS* 2 (1994) 237–55.

The traditional way of numbering the sections of *Hermas* was supplemented by a new consecutive system in Whittaker's critical edition of 1956. Since then, translators and commentators have chosen one or the other, or a combination of both. Here, both numberings systems are given in the translation, while all references in the commentary follow the traditional system.

The endpapers of this volume are from a ceiling painting in the Catacomb of San Gennaro, Naples, Italy. The young women portrayed are participating in the building of the tower (see *Similitudes* 9.3.4–5). The painting dates from the late second or early third century. The photo is courtesy of the Pontifica Commissione di Archelogia Sacra and used with permission.

1 Literary Character
1.1 History of the Text
1.1.1 Manuscript History

No other noncanonical writing was as popular before the fourth century as the *Shepherd of Hermas*. It is the most frequently attested postcanonical text in the surviving Christian manuscripts of Egypt well into the fifth century.[1] That it later became unknown in the East while continuing to be popular in the West in Latin translation through the Middle Ages, and that it is relatively unknown today in the churches either East or West, reflect differing responses to differing needs in differing times.

In the case of such a text that was not necessary to preserve carefully for its historical or literary character, but which was freely used in a variety of church settings, "it is doubtful whether there ever was an authoritative text after the writer's autograph copy had perished."[2] If the text was composed over a long period of time and on the basis of oral use, it is even doubtful whether the author had one authoritative text. The enormous variety of readings within a relatively small range of manuscripts witnesses to the diverse uses to which the text was put.

The Greek text was unknown in modern times until the discovery of Codex Athous. The text is preserved in four substantial manuscripts, none of them complete:

Codex Athous (A), dated to the fifteenth century, contains almost the entire text, from the beginning to the end of *Sim.* 9.30.3, thus about 95%.[3] The leaves were discovered in 1855 on Mt. Athos and the facsimile edition published in 1907.[4] The text was thought by many at first to be a retroversion from Latin, but only with the subsequent discovery of another Greek text in Codex Sinaiticus was A vindicated as an edition of the original Greek text.

Codex Sinaiticus (S), dated to the fourth century, was discovered by Tischendorf in the major New Testament manuscript at the Monastery of St. Catherine in Sinai. *Hermas* follows the *Letter of Barnabas* and breaks off four and one-half words into *Man.* 4.3.6; thus about the first quarter is preserved.[5]

Michigan Papyrus 129 (M), dated to about 250 CE and published in 1934, contains most of *Sim.* 2.8–9.5.1 with occasional lacunae, thus most of the third quarter of the text.[6]

Bodmer Papyrus 38 (B), dated to the late fourth or

---

1   E. Paramelle and Pierre Adnès, "Hermas (Le Pasteur d')," *Dictionnaire de Spiritualité* (ed. M. Viller et al.; Paris: Beauchesne, 1969) 7.316–34; Philippe Henne, *L'unité du Pasteur d'Hermas* (Cahiers Revue Biblique 31; Paris: Gabalda, 1992) 46.

2   Campbell Bonner, ed., *A Papyrus Codex of the Shepherd of Hermas (Similitudes 2–9) with a Fragment of the Mandates* (University of Michigan Studies, Humanistic Series 22; Ann Arbor: University of Michigan Press, 1934) 30.

3   Percentages here and following are estimates of A. Hilhorst, *Sémitismes et latinismes dans le Pasteur d'Hermas* (Graecitas Christianorum Primaeva 5; Nijmegen: Dekker and Van de Vegt, 1976) 15. See his useful discussion of MSS. and critical editions, pp. 15–18.

4   Kirsopp Lake, *Facsimiles of the Athos Fragments of the Shepherd of Hermas* (Oxford: Clarendon, 1907). For an account of the adventures between the discovery and publication, see Molly Whittaker, ed., *Der Hirt des Hermas* (1956; 2d ed.; Die Apostolischen Väter 1; Berlin: Akademie-Verlag, 1967) IX–XI.

5   Published by A. F. C. Tischendorf, *Hermae Pastor Graece. Ex fragmentis Lipsiensibus instituta quaestione de vero Graeci textus Lipsiensis fonte* (Leipzig: Hinrichs, 1856) and *Novum Testamentum Sinaiticum sive N. T. cum epistula Barnabae et fragmentis Pastoris*

ex Sinaitico codice (Leipzig: Brockhaus, 1863); facsimile edition by Kirsopp Lake, *Codex Sinaiticus Petropolitanus. The New Testament, the Epistle of Barnabas and the Shepherd of Hermas* (Oxford: Clarendon, 1911). The discovery of other leaves of the text was announced in 1983 but they are as yet unpublished (Antonio Carlini, "Tradizione testuale e prescrizioni canoniche: Erma, Sesto, Origene," *Orpheus* 7 [1986] 40–52 [44–45]). One leaf was photographically reproduced in *Sinai: Treasures of the Monastery of Saint Catherine* (ed. Konstantinos A. Manafis; Athens: Ekdotike Athenon, 1990) 368.

6   Bonner, *Papyrus Codex*. The editor points out (p. 20) that the carefully written text contains a surprising number of vulgarisms that do not appear in the Athous text, indicating that the later text has polished and refined awkward expressions that therefore must have come from the original author. On the other hand, nearly sixty years later, Antonio Carlini, ed. (*Papyrus Bodmer XXXVIII. Erma: Il Pastore [Ia–IIIa visione]* [Bibliotheca Bodmeriana; Cologny-Genève: Fondation Martin Bodmer, 1991] 17), points out on the basis of B that some readings of A are just as old as those of S.

early fifth century, bound with a previously unknown revelatory work entitled the *Vision of Dorotheus*,[7] contains *Visions* 1–3, and is more closely related to S than to A. It was published in 1991.[8]

In addition, there are approximately twenty-one Greek fragments known to date, depending on whether one counts individual fragments or discrete publications of fragments.[9] They include two miniatures intended to be worn as amulets or for handy reading,[10] and a small fragment of the *Mandates* published in 1912 as a "medical text"[11] but not identified as belonging to *Hermas* until 1979–80[12] and now tentatively dated to the early second century.[13]

Two complete Latin translations are invaluable where the Greek manuscripts are not extant except for a few fragments and quotes: *Sim.* 9.30.3–10.4.5. The Vulgate (L[1]), extant in several exemplars, is a translation usually considered very old, perhaps late second century; it was first published in 1873.[14] The Palatine (L[2]) is extant in two fifteenth-century manuscripts, Vat. Palatinus lat. 150 and Vat. Urbinas lat. 486, the latter a copy of the former; but the translation is thought to be of the fourth or fifth century; a critical edition was published in 1877.[15] L[1] is more closely related to A.[16]

An Ethiopic (E) translation of the fourth century is of questionable value because of its own theological tendencies, which play freely with the text, but its existence testifies to enlarged circles of interest in the book.[17] Fragmentary Akhmimic (C[1]) and Sahidic (C[2]), Coptic translations from the fourth and fifth centuries, and

7 André Hurst, Otto Reverdin, and Jean Rudhardt, ed. and trans., with appendix by Rudolph Kasser, *Vision de Dorotheus* (Papyrus Bodmer 29; Cologny-Genève: Fondation Martin Bodmer, 1984).

8 Antonio Carlini, *Bodmer Papyrus;* idem, "La tradizione testuale del Pastore di Ermo i nuovi papiri," in Guglielmo Cavallo, ed., *Le Stade del Testo* (Lecce: Adriatica Editrice, 1987) 29.

9 For instance, codex F contains five fragments (Eurydice Lappa-Zizicas, "Cinq fragments du *Pasteur* d'Hermas dans un manuscrit de la Bibliothèque Nationale de Paris," *RechSR* 53 [1965] 251–56). The count given here is of discrete publications. Most recent listings in G. H. R. Horsley and S. R. Llewelyn, eds., *New Documents Illustrating Early Christianity* (8 vols.; Sydney: Ancient History Documentary Research Centre, Macquarie University Press, 1981–98) 2. 160–61; Stuart Pickering, *The Shepherd of Hermas* (Papyrology and Historical Perspectives 4; Sydney: Ancient History Documentary Research Centre, Macquarie University Press, forthcoming).

10 Among Gospels and apocryphal works used for the same purpose: discussed in Harry Y. Gamble, *Books and Readers in the Early Church: A History of Early Christian Texts* (New Haven/London: Yale University Press, 1995) 236.

11 *Papyri Iandanae*, ed. Charles Kalbfleisch (Leipzig: Teubner, 1912) 1. 4 (pp. 12–13) and table III.

12 Independently and nearly simultaneously by J. Lénaerts, "Un papyrus du Pasteur d'Hermas," *Chronique d'Egypte* 108 (1979) 356–58; and M. Gronewald, "Ein verkannter Hermas-Papyrus (PIand. I 4=Hermae Pastor, Mand. XI 19–24; XII 1,2–3)," *Zeitschrift für Papyrologie und Epigraphik* 40 (1980) 53–54.

13 By paleographer Peter Parsons and others at an international congress of classical scholars in Dublin in 1984: letter to Bruce Metzger of October 28, 1985, partially quoted in Bruce Metzger, *The Canon of the New Testament* (Oxford: Clarendon, 1987) 63 n. 36. Antonio Carlini ("Testimone e testo: Il problema della datazione di PIand I 4 del *Pastore* di Erma," *SCO* 42 [1992] 17–30) does not quarrel with the date but discusses many examples of uncertain dating and warns repeatedly of the problems.

14 Adolf Hilgenfeld, *Hermae Pastor. Veteram Latinam interpretationem e codicibus* (Leipzig: Reisland, 1873).

15 Oskar von Gebhardt and Adolf von Harnack, *Hermae Pastor graece, addita versione latine recentiore e codice Palatino* (Patrum Apostolicorum Opera 3; Leipzig: Hinrichs, 1877); now available in a new edition with Italian translation: Anna Vezzoni, *Il Pastore di Erma: Versione Palatina contesto a fronte* (Il Nuovo Melograno 13; Florence: Casa Editrice Le Lettere, 1994). Additional fragments of the Palatine translation: Antonio Carlini, "Due estratti del *Pastore* di Erma nella versione Palatina in *Par. Lat.* 3182," *SCO* 35 (1985) 311–12; Anna Vezzoni, "Un testimone testuale inedito della versione Palatina del *Pastore* di Erma," *SCO* 37 (1987) 241–65.

16 Antonio Carlini, "La tradizione manoscritta del *Pastor* di Hermas e il problema dell'unità dell' opera," in *Papyrus Erzherzog Rainer: Festschrift zum 100-Jährigen Bestehen der Papyrussammlung der Österreichischen Nationalbibliothek* (Textband; Vienna: Hollinek, 1983) 97–100.

17 Antoine de Abbadie, *Hermae Pastor. Aethiopice primum edidit et Aethiopica Latine vertit Antonius de Abbadie* (Abhandlungen der Deutschen morgenländischen Gesellschaft 2. 1; Leipzig: Brockhaus, 1860). On its tendencies, see comments by Hilhorst, *Sémitismes*, 16.

Middle Persian and Georgian translations witness to the widespread popularity of *Hermas* in the early church.[18] A first attempt at a critical edition was tried by J. Cotelier in Paris in 1672, by aligning a Latin text with the known Greek fragments. A critical text was published in 1856,[19] but the Latin text was available only on the basis of a partially counterfeit copy of the Palatine text done by Constantin Simonides, who had taken three of the original nine leaves preserved, transcribed the rest, and made up what was lacking.[20] Several critical editions were done in the late nineteenth and early twentieth century.[21] Two critical editions are in use today,[22] those of Whittaker[23] and Joly.[24] Of the two, that of Whittaker is superior,[25] though Joly's is also partly commentary and therefore contains introductory essays.

1.1.2 Integrity of the Text

The complete text as given in the major manuscripts and translations now comprises five *Visions,* twelve *Mandates,* and ten *Similitudes. Vision* 5 is really an introduction to the *Mandates.* Some of the manuscript evidence, however, indicates that parts of the whole circulated independently. B has only *Visions* 1–3, though *Vision* 4 was probably also attached.[26] By contrast, M seems to have contained only *Vision* 5 through the end of the *Similitudes.*[27] A heads *Vision* 5 with ὅρασις ε (vision 5), following the sequence of terminology that was used with the four previous *Visions.* But S calls *Vision* 5 ἀποκάλυψις ε (revelation 5), using a different term for the chapter. The two published Latin versions now contain the whole text, but L¹ has at the beginning of *Vision* 5: *Visio quinta initium pastoris* ("vision 5, beginning of the shepherd"). L² has at the beginning of the chapter *Incipiunt pastoris mandata duodecim* ("[Here] begin the twelve commandments of the Shepherd"). Thus there is evidence even in the integral manuscripts that *Vision* 5 was seen as the beginning of a new section, and codices B and M confirm that the text sometimes circulated in two independent parts. The same may have been true in translation. The two Coptic versions seem not to have contained *Visions* 1–4.[28] Athanasius' festal letter 11 of 339 CE quotes *Man.* 1.1 as the beginning of Hermas' book.[29]

The end of *Mandate* 12 also apparently functioned in some editions as an introduction to the *Similitudes.* A marks *Man.* 12.3.4 with Ἀρχή (beginning), while E indicates that same place as "Beginning of the Similitudes,"

---

18 Details in Whittaker, XVIII, 116. Coptic versions in: L. Théophile Lefort, ed., *Les Pères apostoliques en copte* (CSCO 135–36; Louvain: Durbecq, 1952). The Georgian translation comprises *Vision* 5 and the *Mandates,* under the name of Ephrem! The translation is not directly from Greek, but from Arabic, thus witnessing to an unknown Arabic version: Bernard Outtier, "La version géorgienne du *Pasteur* d'Hermas," *Revue des études georgiennes et caucasiennes* 67 (1990–91) 211–16.

19 Rudolph Anger, *Hermae Pastor Graece* (Leipzig: T. O. Weigl, 1856).

20 Accounts in Whittaker, X, and Carlini, "Tradizione testuale," 25–26.

21 Adolf Hilgenfeld, *Hermae Pastor Graece* (Leipzig: T. O. Weigl, 1866); Francis X. Funk, "Hermae Pastor" (2 vols.; *Patres Apostolici;* Tübingen: Laupp, 1901); Auguste Lelong, *Le Pasteur d'Hermas* (*Les Pères apostoliques* 4; Paris: Picard, 1912); Kirsopp Lake, "The Shepherd of Hermas," *Apostolic Fathers* (LCL; Cambridge, MA: Harvard University Press, 1913) 2. 2.

22 Earlier editions from before 1934 are obsolete due to the absence of the M MS. Besides those already listed, they include Francis X. Funk, "Hermae Pastor," *Opera Patrum apostolicorum* 1 (Tübingen: Laupp, 1887).

23 First edition 1956; revised 1967.

24 Robert Joly, *Hermas le Pasteur* (SC 53, 1958; 2d ed., SC 53bis; Paris: Éditions du Cerf, 1968; reprint, with new appendix, 1986).

25 See Hilhorst's accurate critique of Joly's edition, *Sémitismes,* 18.

26 Carlini, *Bodmer Papyrus,* 12.

27 Bonner, *Papyrus Codex,* 8–9, 13.

28 The two Latin translations (LL) in *Visions* 1–4 come from different traditions, while after *Vision* 5, they are so closely related that L² can almost be thought of as a revision of L¹ (Carlini, "Tradizione manoscritta"; "Tradizione testuale," 25). C² is represented in two different volumes, the first containing the Apocalypse of John and the *Visions,* the second, the *Mandates* and the *Similitudes,* and the two volumes are in different written style: Enzo Lucchesi, "Le Pasteur d'Hermas en copte: Perspective nouvelle," *VC* 43 (1989) 393–96.

29 Henne (*L'unité,* 38–41) argues, however, that Athanasius means not the beginning of the text but of the teaching section, which is Athanasius' concern.

so that present *Similitude* 1 is really 2 in E, thus throwing off the entire numbering system in that version, which then does not give numbers to the last two *Similitudes*.[30] The alternative numbering of the *Similitudes* in some of the manuscripts is thought by some to indicate traces of editions in which the full text was not present. This arrangement, in turn, could indicate that the text was not originally published as a whole, but the parts were later combined.[31] This theory could support theories of multiple authorship. On the other hand, the fragmentation of an original text could have happened later because the whole text was too long and cumbersome.[32] Henne points out[33] that the earliest frequent users of *Hermas* in the East, Clement of Alexandria and Origen, quoted from all three sections, and that one of the earliest users in the West, Tertullian, quotes from both the *Visions* and the *Mandates,* that is, from both parts according to the supposed manuscript division discussed above. This would seem to be persuasive evidence that at the end of the second century the text was circulating as a unity in both Egypt and North Africa and that divisions occurred later. The earliest manscript evidence for division is M, dated by Bonner to about 250 CE.

1.1.3 Reception and Canonicity

Knowledge of the writing spread very quickly. By the end of the second century, it was known to Tertullian in Carthage and appreciated by Irenaeus in Gaul and Clement and later Origen in Egypt.[34] Contemporaneously, Irenaeus quotes *Man.* 1.1 once.[35] Other later Western users include Hippolytus,[36] Pseudo-Cyprian,[37] Commodian,[38] Pseudo-Pius,[39] Ambrose,[40] Jerome,[41] Augustine,[42] and Cassian.[43] After Clement and Origen, later Eastern users include Eusebius[44] and Athanasius.[45]

With the sole exception of Tertullian, all the authors listed above cite *Hermas* positively, though sometimes with hesitation. Tertullian had his own special problems with it because of his theological and ascetical tendencies. He cites the text three times. In the bizarre reference in *De orat.* 16, he refutes the argument of some that, because Hermas was praying seated on a couch in *Vis.* 5.1, that is the preferred position for prayer. While Tertullian uses *Hermas* neutrally here, the discussion indicates the high regard in which the text was held in his church. Later the Montanist Tertullian alludes to the author twice in *De pud.* 10 and 20 as "lover of adulterers" and "shepherd of adulterers" because of Hermas' posi-

---

30   Helpful table in Graydon Snyder, *The Shepherd of Hermas* (ed. Robert M. Grant; Apostolic Fathers 6; Camden, NJ: T. Nelson, 1969) 7; extensive discussion and suggested solutions in Henne, *L'unité,* 58–63.

31   The possible early dating of the fragment of *P.Iand.* 1. 4 to the beginning of the second century (see discussion above) could be evidence for early circulation of part of the text without the whole (Carlini, "Testimone e testo," 27–28).

32   The position of Henne, *L'unité,* 58–59. He also makes the point (p. 27) that use of the name Hermas by a later author presupposes knowledge of the *Visions*, since the name occurs only there. It is also possible, however, after the example of the Gospel of John, that the name could attach to another part of the work with no internal evidence to support it.

33   *L'unité,* 18–21.

34   Most of the references to quotations and allusions to *Hermas* by early church writers are collected by Whittaker, XIX–XX, and many of the texts by Henne, *L'unité,* 15–44, who gives a more complete list (e.g., seventeen for Clement as opposed to ten in Whittaker). To these lists must be added two papyrus witnesses: *POxy* 1.5, possibly a treatise of Melito on prophecy from the third, fourth, or fifth century that quotes a portion of *Mandate* 11; and

Michigan Papyrus 6427, a fourth-century prayer quoting *Man.* 1.1.

35   *Adv. haer.* 4.20.2.

36   As quoted in the *Liber Pontificalis:* Louis Duchesne, *Le liber pontificalis* (2d ed.; Paris: Boccard, 1955) 5.

37   *Adv. aleat.* 2.

38   *Inst.* 1.30.16.

39   No earlier than the fourth century. A strange allusion: Hermas' Shepherd figure instructed him that he was to celebrate Easter on Sunday! Nothing of the sort is found in any known edition. Text in Henne, *L'unité,* 22 n. 20; *PL* 130. 111C.

40   *Hex.* 3.12.50.

41   *Comm.* 1 on Hab 1:14; 2 on Hos 7:9.

42   Not cited by Henne but by Marcello Marin, "Sulla fortuna delle *Similitudini* III e IV di Erma," *Vetera christianorum* 19 (1982) 331–40 (336–38, 340 n. 35). Marin gives a total of seventeen possible references to *Hermas* in Augustine's works, thus raising questions about Jerome's remark (*De vir. ill.* 10) that the book *apud Latinos paene ignotus est* ("among Latins it is practically unknown").

43   *Conf.* 8.1; 13.12. This follows the list given in Henne, *L'unité,* 16–17, 22, based on that compiled by Harnack, who also listed Pontius *Vit. Cyp.* 6 for a quote from *Vis.* 3.1.4, which is apparently an error.

44   *Hist. eccl.* 3.3.6.

tion in favor of marital reconciliation even after divorce for adultery, if the adulterous partner repents.[46] In the first of these texts, Tertullian states that every church council had judged the writing *apocrypha et falsa*—which seems not to have been the case even in his own previous community.

The other probable outright rejection comes from the Coptic *Apocalypse of Peter* from Nag Hammadi, which calls someone named Hermas "the first-born of unrighteousness."[47] The discussion in the context is obscure and does not sound on casual reading like a direct attack on *Hermas*.[48] Nevertheless, the possible Egyptian origin of the *Apocalypse of Peter,* the popularizing theology of *Hermas* and its appeal to forgiveness of ordinary sins, and the immense popularity of *Hermas* in Egypt in the first centuries make the connection attractive.

With the growing rejection of Montanism in the early third century, *Hermas* was identified by some with that movement because of its visions, sexual ascesis, apocalyptic expectation, and perhaps because of the prominence of a female leadership figure (the woman church). Yet ironically, Tertullian had rejected *Hermas* as too liberal with respect to repentance when he became a Montanist. *Hermas* was sufficiently diverse and controversial to come under fire from both directions![49]

Use of allusions to a writing to support one's own arguments indicates a positive valuation of the quoted text. It could then be argued, of course, that the silence of other early church authors indicates their rejection of the text, but the argument from silence will always be indecisive. There is no doubt that at some times and places, *Hermas* was considered both scripture, that is, inspired, and canonical, part of the rule of faith sanctioned for liturgical use.[50] Irenaeus' quotation of *Man.* 1.1 in *Adv. haer.* 2.20.2 introduces it as χραφή, ordinarily understood as scripture, but the order of references (*Hermas,* Malachi, Paul, Jesus) indicates a recognition of the text as authoritative, even if it is not clear exactly how he would value its authority.[51] Eusebius' reference to Irenaeus' quote, however,[52] at a later time when the terminology was much more exact, indicates his belief that Irenaeus accepted *Hermas* as scripture.

The most enthusiastic early user of *Hermas* was Clement of Alexandria, who frequently quoted the text and explicitly referred to it as divinely inspired. Likewise Origen used it freely with scriptural arguments in his earlier years, becoming cooler toward it as time went on. But this could have resulted from his change of venue from Alexandria to Caesarea, where the text was not as well known or appreciated,[54] yet it was he who made the connection between the protagonist and the Hermas of Rom 16:14. Add to this the fact that, without any special comment, the *Letter of Barnabas* and *Hermas* were attached to Codex Sinaiticus, and a pattern emerges:

45   *De incarn.* 3.1; *De decr. Nic. Synod.* 4.3; 18; *Ad Afros episc. ep.* 5; *Ep. fest.* 11, 39.

46   *Man.* 4.1.6–8.

47   *NHLE* 78. 18–19. See brief discussion of the possible connection by Andreas Werner, *NTApoc* 2. 702.

48   But see the careful discussion in Klaus Koschorke, *Die Polemik der Gnostiker gegen das kirchliche Christentum* (NHS 12; Leiden: Brill, 1978) 54–60.

49   R. A. Lipsius, "Der Hirte des Hermas und der Montanismus in Rom," *ZWTh* 8 (1965) 266–308; 9 (1966) 27–81; 183–218; Luigi Cirillo, "Erma e il problema dell'apocalittica a Roma," *Cristianesimo nella Storia* 4 (1983) 1–31.

50   The two notions of scripture and canon are not exactly identical: see discussion in Lee M. McDonald, *The Formation of the Christian Biblical Canon* (rev. ed.; Peabody, MA: Hendrickson, 1995) 6–21. Henne gives three criteria for his discussion of canonicity ("Canonicité du 'Pasteur' d'Hermas," *Revue Thomiste* 90 [1990] 81–100 [81]): use in liturgical proclamation, belief that the text is inspired, and use of the text in theological discussions.

Accounts of the historical evidence in Carlini, "Tradizione testuale"; Henne, "Canonicité"; Robert M. Grant, "The Appeal to the Early Fathers," *JTS* n.s. 11 (1960) 13–24; idem, "The Apostolic Fathers' First Thousand Years," *CH* 31 (1962) 421–29; Henry Chadwick, "The New Edition of Hermas," *JTS* 8 (1957) 274–80.

51   See nuanced discussion of recent scholarship on the meaning of γραφή in these contexts, in Henne, "Canonicité," 82–83.

52   Eusebius *Hist. eccl.* 5.8.7.

53   Θείως τοίνυν ἡ δύναμις ἡ τῷ Ἑρμᾷ κατὰ ἀποκάλυψιν λαλοῦσα ("the power that spoke divinely to Hermas by revelation") *Strom.* 1.29.181.

54   J. Ruwet, "Les 'Antilegomena' dans les oeuvres d'Origène," *Bib* 23 (1942) 18–42 [33–35]; discussed in Henne, "Canonicité," 91.

Hermas was most highly valued early in Egypt, where more fragments of it have been found thus far than of any other noncanonical text. An exception to this pattern of Egyptian predilection is Pseudo-Cyprian's citation of *Sim.* 9.15.5-6 as *scriptura divina*. Another possible exception is the biblical list in the bilingual sixth-century Codex Claromontanus, a Western biblical manuscript[55] that inserts between Philemon and Hebrews a Latin stichometry of biblical books that ends with the *Letter of Barnabas,* the *Shepherd of Hermas,* the *Acts of Paul,* and the *Apocalypse of Peter.* It has been argued, however, that the list is quite independent of the biblical manuscript, is Eastern, and may date from as early as the third century.[56]

The famous *Muratorian Canon* is indicative of the opposite trend, toward dismissing the authoritative value of the text while retaining the book as useful for private reading. The date and provenance of the *Canon* have been much discussed in recent years, its reference to *Hermas* being the major criterion for dating the canonical list.[57] Whenever and wherever the *Canon* comes from, its rejection of reading *Hermas* in church is coupled with its approval of reading it privately. The stated reason for rejecting public use of the text, whether historical or not—that it was written recently by the brother of Bishop Pius—reveals an awareness of scripture as coming from another era. The real reason for the rejection

of *Hermas* in the list may be less the reasons stated than objections to its theological content.[58]

The movement toward canonical rejection was steady, while retention for private reading remained. No one seems to have known or cared about Tertullian's objections. Eusebius, Jerome, and Athanasius all acknowledge that *Hermas* is helpful reading; for Athanasius, the book is "most helpful" ($\dot{\omega}\varphi\epsilon\lambda\iota\mu\omega\tau\acute{\alpha}\tau\eta$), while Eusebius reports that for some it is essential ($\dot{\alpha}\nu\alpha\gamma\kappa\alpha\iota\acute{o}\tau\alpha\tau\sigma\nu$), though rejected by others. He seems influenced by Origen's ascription of the work to the Hermas of Rom 16:14.[59] Both Eusebius and Athanasius say that it is still used for catechesis.[60] Rufinus places it among books of the church, but not among canonical books, to be read but not to be used for theological discussion.[61] In the late fourth century, the Alexandrian theologian Didymus the Blind was still quoting it,[62] and Jerome reports that it was even read publicly in some Greek churches.[63] In Egypt at least, copies still circulated into the sixth century. Pseudo-Athanasius in the fifth or sixth century, and Antiochus of Mar Saba in Palestine in the seventh, could plagiarize it repeatedly without feeling the need to acknowledge sources, perhaps indicating a serious decline in use.[64]

From there, the Eastern trail grows cold until the discovery of Codex Athous of the fifteenth century. Not so in the West, however. Jerome would prove to be mistak-

---

55 Bruce M. Metzger, *The Text of the New Testament: Its Transmission, Corruption, and Restoration* (3d ed.; New York/Oxford: Oxford University Press, 1992) 51.

56 By Harnack: Gebhardt-Harnack, 49–50; *Geschichte der altchristlichen Literatur bis Eusebius* (2d ed.; Leipzig: Hinrichs, 1958) 55.

57 Older bibliography in Henne, "Canonicité," 85–86. Albert C. Sundberg ("Canon Muratori: A Fourth-Century List," *HTR* 66 [1973] 1–41) attempted to strike down the prevailing consensus of a Roman origin at the end of the second century. Wilhelm Schneemelcher (*NTApoc* 1. 27; "despite the erudition displayed and the extensive material worked over") and Everett Ferguson ("Canon Muratori: Date and Provenance," *StPatr* 17 [1982] 2. 677–83) cast serious doubts on Sundberg's arguments. Most recently, Geoffrey M. Hahneman (*The Muratorian Fragment and the Development of the Canon* [New York: Oxford University Press, 1992]) proposes not only a fourth-century dating but also an Eastern origin for the list and discredits all references to the origins of *Hermas* in it (pp. 34–72). See further

below in the discussion of the dating of *Hermas,* at 2.1.

58 For instance, Henry Chadwick ("A New Edition of Hermas," *JTS* 8 [1957] 274–80 [278–79]) suggests the attempt to discredit any kind of prophecy under the threat of Montanism. Likewise Cirillo ("Erma e il problema") sees the *Muratorian Canon's* rejection of both *Hermas* and the *Apocalypse of Peter* as part of the inevitable move to reject apocalypticism, both in Pharisaic Judaism, Hellenistic Judaism, and Christianity.

59 Eusebius *Hist. eccl.* 3.3.6; Jerome *De vir. ill.* 10; Athanasius *De incarn.* 3.1.

60 Eusebius *Hist. eccl.* 3.3.6; Athanasius *Ep. fest.* 39 (365 CE).

61 *Exp. symb.* 36.

62 References in Henne, "Canonicité," 94–95.

63 *De vir. ill.* 10: *apud quasdam Graeciae ecclesias etiam publice legitur.*

64 References in Whittaker, XIX–XX.

en that the book was hardly known in the West.[65] Besides heavy use by his contemporary Augustine, in the next generation John Cassian (who may have learned of it in the East) knew and quoted it.[66] The sixth-century Pseudo-Gelasian Decrees on books to be received and rejected assigned *Hermas* among books to be rejected, useful only to heretics and schismatics.[67] This distinct condemnation may have taken its toll on the popularity of the book by eliminating its use extensively.[68] Yet in the West, *Hermas* seems never completely to have disappeared. Small references appear in Prosper of Aquitaine, Bede, and others. Bibles circulated with apocryphal books accompanying canonical writings, *Hermas* being one of the apocrypha, in one case placed between Tobit and Maccabees, in another after the Wisdom of Solomon, and in a third between Psalms and Proverbs![69] First printed in 1513,[70] its influence has been traced in Boethius, Dante, and *Piers Plowman*.[71] Hildegard of Bingen (1098–1179), prolific abbess, poet, preacher, and visionary prophet, writes of the vision of a tower with different kinds of people within it, identified by their different appearances; the tower is the church.[72] The English mystic Francis Quarles (1592–1644), in his poem "Even Like Two Little Bank-Conjoined Brooks," writes of his union with Christ, "He's my supporting elm, and I His vine; Thus I my best beloved's am, thus He is mine," with possible reference to *Similitude* 2.[73] In more recent times, the psychoanalyst Carl G. Jung read the text and interpreted the relationship between Hermas and the woman church in terms of the male pursuit of the feminine archetype.[74] Even a disgruntled modern French priest reacting to the changes brought into the Catholic church by Vatican Council II could find in Hermas a worthy protagonist.[75]

1.1.4 Representation in Early Christian Art

There is only one sure depiction of a scene from *Hermas* in early Christian art, in the Catacomb of San Gennaro at Naples. The fresco, dated to the early third century and restored in 1985, adorns a ceiling in the upper gallery next to a picture of Adam and Eve and is framed in red. It depicts the young women bringing stones to build the tower (*Sim.* 9.2–3). Three women with bound hair and bare shoulders, in long dresses of dark colors, bring stones for the tower. The woman on the right carefully carries a square stone. Other stones lie around on the ground. The middle woman stands behind the tower and is either putting stones into its wall or handing them through a door that is not shown. The turreted tower is out of proportion to the women, who are almost as tall as it is. No one has raised any serious doubts that the painting does indeed depict the building of the tower

---

65 *De vir. ill.* 10.

66 *Conf.* 8.17; 13.12.

67 Carlini, "Testuale e prescrizioni," 46.

68 Discussed by Carlini, ibid., 46–49.

69 Ibid., 49–51.

70 By J. Le Fève d'Étaples; details in Norbert Brox, *Der Hirt des Hermas* (Kommentar zu den Apostolischen Vätern 7; Göttingen: Vandenhoeck & Ruprecht, 1991) 73 n. 13.

71 Theodore Bogdanos, *"The Shepherd of Hermas* and the Development of Medieval Visionary Allegory," *Orpheus* 22 (1975) 57–75.

72 *Scivias* 3.9. Identification of the tower as the church appears at 3.9.7. For discussion and other allusions in Hildegard, see H. Liebeschütz, *Das allegorische Weltbild der heiligen Hildegard von Bingen* (Leipzig: Teubner, 1930); Peter Dronke, "Arbor Caritatis," in P. L. Heyworth, ed., *Medieval Studies for J. A. W. Bennett* (Oxford: Clarendon, 1981) 207–43 (220–31); idem, *Women Writers of the Middle Ages: A Critical Study of Texts from Perpetua († 203) to Marguerite Porete († 1310)* (Cambridge: Cambridge

University Press, 1984) 161–70.

73 I owe this reference to John Strugnell. Here the influence may also come directly from Ovid or Catullus; see comment on *Similitude* 2.

74 *Psychological Types, Collected Works* (ed. William McGuire et al.; Bollingen Series 20; Princeton, NJ: Princeton University Press, 1971) 6.224–31, 238; paragraphs 381–91, 402, in the chapter entitled "The Worship of the Woman and the Worship of the Soul." See Robert Joly, "Philologie et psychanalyse: C. G. Jung et le 'Pasteur' d'Hermas," *L'antiquité classique* 22 (1953) 422–28. Joly is sharply critical of Jung's eisegesis and tendency to take all elements in the texts at historical face value.

75 Hermas, *Les prêtres, ont-ils perdu la mémoire?* (Paris: Éditions ouvrières, 1969). Writing in the name of Hermas, whom he places in the first century, the anonymous author writes seven letters of complaint.

from *Hermas*. Its appearance in the early third century in Campania fits well with the Roman origin of the book, and suggests a high authority for it in central Italy at the time.[76] Other depictions in art are less sure: a man looking at a tree that supposedly contains a vine,[77] a gem fragment of a man in a tunic under a willow tree,[78] a painting of a square rock with a door in the Catacomb of Callistus,[79] and a "coronation" scene from the Catacomb of Praetextatus that could represent *Sim.* 8.2.1.[80]

Aside from the possibility of narrative scenes from the book, there is the representation of the shepherd figure, ubiquitous in Greco-Roman pastoral scenes, often depictions of Orpheus and possibly of Hermes. This shepherd figure, particularly the *kriophoros,* bearing a lamb or goat on his shoulders, was gradually taken over into Christian art and at some point, though not necessarily early on, became Christ the shepherd. Transition points are not at all clear, and they lend themselves to overinterpretation or underinterpretation, depending on the mind-set of the interpreter.[81] Few have raised a question worth raising: could some of the earlier shepherd depictions in Christian contexts be Hermas' shepherd, and in fact, could Hermas' shepherd have helped to mediate the transition from Greco-Roman pastoral figure to Christ?[82] Unfortunately, given the poor state of preserved evidence that correlates early Christian literature and art, we will never know.

1.2 Literary Unity

The best historical evidence based on early use of the text indicates an initial unity that was later broken by circulation of separate sections independently (see above at 1.1.2). Throughout the modern history of scholarship, however, the question of single or multiple authorship has been asked not on the basis of early use but of internal evidence. It is obvious that *Visions* 1–4 constitute a literary unit in which the revelatory agent is the woman church, who will never appear again in the rest of the book. *Vision* 5, in which the Shepherd appears for the first time, is really an introduction to the *Mandates* and perhaps also to the *Similitudes,* not a conclusion to the *Visions.* Conclusions and new introductions are present in other places: *Sim.* 9.1.1 is a transition from a concluded section into something new; *Sim.* 9.33 is a conclusion; the beginning of *Sim.* 10.1 is again a transition into new material. These literary seams, the length of the whole, and the apparent changes of theme early prompted theories of multiple authorship. Adding to these factors were the three "historical" references: the Hermas of Rom 16:14, identified by Origen as the author of the book; the mention of Clement in *Vis.* 2.4.3, usually thought to be Clement of Rome; and the data of the *Muratorian Canon,* by which the author was the brother of Pius, a prominent Roman churchman of the middle of the second century, according to Eusebius. The time

76 Hans Achelis, *Die Katakomben von Neapel* (Leipzig: Hiersemann, 1936) 56, pl. 8, 10; Antonio Bellucci, "La notizia a Napoli del ΠΟΙΜΗΝ di Erma e la datazione delle piu antiche pitture del cimitero di S. Gennaro," *Atti del IV Congresso Nazionale di Studi Romani* (Rome: Istituto di Studi Romani, 1938) 1. 109–18. Umberto Fasola, *Le Catacombe di S. Gennaro a Capodimonte* (Rome: Editalia, 1975) 26–29. For Achelis (56), its appearance means that *Hermas* was considered canonical in third-century Campania, but Carlini (*Bodmer Papyrus,* 35–36 n. 73) raises the caution that artistic representations from biblical and other sources can appear together. Fasola (26) suggests *Sim.* 9.16.1–3 as reason for location of the picture in a burial context.

77 Achelis, *Die Katakomben von Neapel,* 56, pl. 11, interpreted by Peter Demetz ("The Elm and the Vine: Notes toward the History of a Marriage Topos," *Proceedings of the Modern Language Association of America* 73 [1958] 521–32 [524]) as elm and vine, but the picture is not clear.

78 *DACL* 6. 851 fig. 5114, doubted by Joly (107 n. 3)

and Brox (73).

79 *DACL* 6. 2286.

80 Paul Styger, *Die römischen Katakomben* (Berlin: Verlag für Kunstwissenschaft, 1933) 151, pl. 32; late second century; Michelangelo Cagiano de Azevedo, "La cosidetta 'coronatio' di Pretestato," *Studi sull' Oriente e la Bibbia offerti al P. Giovanni Rinaldi nel 60° compleanno da allievi, collaghi, amici* (Genoa: Editrice Studio e vita, 1967) 117–22.

81 A good example is the frequently reproduced *kriophoros* in classic style, Vatican Pio Cristiano Museum inv. no. 28590, that formed part of the Vatican Museum's U.S. exhibit in 1982. Other examples of ambiguity can be seen today in the Pio Cristiano collection. See Alejandro Recio Veganzones, "Iconografia en estuco del pastor en las catacombas de Roma," *Atti del IX Congresso internazionale di archeologia cristiana,* Rome, 1975 (Vatican City: Pontifical Institute of Christian Archaeology, 1978) 2. 425–40; Nikolaus Himmelmann, *Über Hirten-Genre in der antiken Kunst* (Abhandlungen der Rheinisch-Westfälischen Akademie der Wissen-

range being impossible for one person, the obvious solution in order to be able to take all three references as historical was multiple authorship over a period of some years.

1.2.1 Theories of Multiple Authorship

Already in 1858, H. W. Thiersch suggested dual authorship in the simplest way: the *Visions* were the work of the Hermas of Rom 16:14, the rest of a mid-second-century writer.[83] The next step was the realization of the difference between *Vision* 5 and what goes before, so that that chapter was detached from the other *Visions* and placed with what follows. In 1866, Hilgenfeld in his critical edition proffered a more complex theory of multiple authorship. First, *Hermas pastoralis* wrote *Vision* 5, the *Mandates*, and *Similitudes* 1–7 about 95 CE. Second, *Hermas apocalypticus* wrote *Visions* 1–4 about 117. Third, *Hermas secundarius*, the brother of Pius, wrote *Similitudes* 8–10 about 150 CE.[84] Later Dibelius tentatively offered stages of composition without identifying the various authors or the actual number of them: *Visions* 1–4; *Vision* 5 through *Similitude* 8; *Similitudes* 9 and then 10.[85]

More complex theories were still to come. In 1963 Stanislas Giet[86] proposed another three-author scheme. The first, author of *Visions* 1–4, wrote in the late first or early second century and was a contemporary of Clement of Rome, to whom the name of Clement in *Vis.* 2.4.3 does refer. The second, author of *Similitude* 9 on

the basis of the earlier *Visions*, was the brother of Pius in the middle of the second century. The third wrote everything else, *Vision* 5 through *Similitude* 8, and *Similitude* 10 a few years later. The advantage of both Hilgenfeld's and Giet's schemes is that they can include both the Clement reference and the data of the *Muratorian Canon*.

But the most complex theory was that of W. Coleborne in 1969 on the basis of linguistic analysis.[87] For him, six different authors or redactors contributed to the book. First, *Man.* 1–12.3.3 were written as paraenetic material. Then *Similitudes* 1–7 were added by another writer. A third editor filled in *Vision* 5 and the conclusion of the *Mandates, Man.* 12.3.3–6.5, to form a transition to the *Similitudes*. Fourth, another redactor added *Visions* 1–4. Fifth, another author added *Similitude* 8 to correct the adoptionist Christology of *Similitude* 5. Finally, *Similitude* 9 was added to enlarge on previous themes. *Similitude* 10, because the Greek is not preserved, could not be included in the method.

Defenders of the unity of the work under a single authorship have never been lacking, however, and have probably always been in the majority. Already in the 1880s there were objectors to Hilgenfeld on this issue.[88] Giet's most staunch opponent was Joly.[89] Nor has Coleborne's proposal met with any more enthusiasm.

---

schaften 65; Opladen: Westdeutscher Verlag, 1980) 134–56; Salvatore Di Cristina, "'Il pastore e il suo gregge.' Studio della metafora nella letteratura cristiana più antica" (thesis, Institutum Pastristicum Augustinianum, Rome, 1982); Paul C. Finney, *The Invisible God: The Earliest Christians on Art* (New York/Oxford: Oxford University Press, 1994) 188–90.

82 Jean de Savignac, "Quelques problèmes de l'ouvrage dit 'Le Pasteur' d'Hermas," *EThR* 35 (1960) 159–70 (167).

83 *Die Kirche im apostolischen Zeitalter* (Frankfurt am Main: Herder und Zimmer, 1852) 350–58. This and what follows here are summarized in J. Christian Wilson, *Toward a Reassessment of the Shepherd of Hermas: Its Date and Pneumatology* (Lewiston/Queenston/Lampeter: Mellen, 1993) 14–23.

84 Hilgenfeld, *Hermae Pastor Graece*, xxi–xxix. Other variations by I. Haussleiter (*Visions* 1–4 written later, at the end of the second century and pseudepigraphically attributed to the Hermas of Romans 16) and F. Spitta (the whole was a Jewish writing of mid-

first-century Palestine adapted by a Christian in mid-second-century Rome) are summarized in Wilson, *Reassessment*, 15.

85 Martin Dibelius, *Der Hirt des Hermas* (HNT; Die Apostolischen Väter 4; Tübingen: Mohr/Siebeck], 1923) 420–21.

86 "Les trois auteurs du Pasteur d'Hermas," *StPatr* 8=TU 93 (1966) 2. 10–23; idem, *Hermas et les pasteurs: Les trois auteurs du Pasteur d'Hermas* (Paris: Presses Universitaires de France, 1963).

87 "A Linguistic Approach to the Problem of Structure and Composition of the Shepherd of Hermas" (Ph.D. diss., University of Newcastle, 1965); article by the same name in *Colloquium* 3 (1969) 133–42; "The *Shepherd* of Hermas: A Case for Multiple Authorship and Some Implications," *StPatr* 10=TU 107 (1970) 65–70.

88 Zahn, Harnack, A. Link, and P. Baumgärtner; details in Wilson, *Reassessment*, 15–16.

89 Joly, 411; idem, "Hermas et le Pasteur," *VC* 21 (1967) 201–18; idem, "Le milieu complexe du

1.2.2 Return to Single Authorship

Most scholars today have returned to the single author hypothesis, though not without some hedging about "multiple sources," or "multiple redactions."[90] Few would suggest that one author wrote the whole book at the same time. There is nearly complete consensus that *Visions* 1–4 form a unity, and that *Vision* 5 belongs with what follows it. There has also been a strong prevailing judgment that *Visions* 1–4 are the oldest part of the book. After that, there is not as much agreement. Brox's proposal[91] of a single author in several redactional stages is attractive: first, *Visions* 1–4; second, *Vision* 5 through *Similitude* 8; and finally, *Similitudes* 9–10. *Sim.* 10.1.1–2 presumes knowledge of *Vis.* 5.1–3 and *Sim.* 10.3.1 presumes knowledge of *Sim.* 9.10–11, so that the final *Similitude,* as it now stands, could not have preceded either. Thus a theory of sequential composition in the order in which the parts are now arranged is the simplest solution.

The thematic unity of the book in spite of some divergences indicates a guiding hand throughout. The loose and fluid structure of the whole is best explained by the close relationship of the written text to the medium of oral performance.

1.3 Genre and Structure
1.3.1 Is Hermas an Apocalypse?[92]

Most who attempt an answer to this question end in some way by saying both yes and no. In the definition and survey of apocalyptic literature in *Semeia* 14, *Hermas* qualifies to be listed and discussed as a Christian apocalypse, and Adela Yarbro Collins in her contribution on *Hermas* in the same volume concludes that "there is no good reason to exclude it from the genre 'apocalypse,'"[93] an indication of others' attempts to do so, for example, Vielhauer/Strecker: "We should reckon the Pastor Hermae as falling in the genre of Apocalypse only in a non-literal sense, and must therefore designate it as a

'Pasteur d'Hermas,'" *ANRW* 2. 27.1 (1993) 524–51 [528–29].

90   Paramelle, "Hermas," 316; Lambartus W. Nijendijk ("Die Christologie des Hirten des Hermas" [Th.D. diss., Rijksuniversiteit Utrecht, 1986] 74, 175–80) proposes two authors, one editor; Joly, "Milieu complexe," 527–29; Bonner, *Papyrus Codex,* 13–14; Steve Young, "Being a Man: The Pursuit of Manliness in *The Shepherd of Hermas,*" *JECS* 2 (1994) 237–55 [238 n. 2]; Wilson, *Reassessment,* 22–23; Carla Bausone, "Aspetti dell'ecclesiologia del Pastore di Hermas," *StPatr* 11=TU 108 (1972) 101–6; Brox, 30–33; Harry O. Maier in *The Social Setting of the Ministry as Reflected in the Writings of Hermas, Clement, and Ignatius* (Canadian Corporation for Studies in Religion, Dissertations SR 1; Waterloo, Ontario: Wilfrid Laurier University Press, 1991) 58 proposes different stages of writing; perhaps another final editor; A. Hilhorst, "Hermas," *RAC* 108/109 (1988) 682–701 (682); Henne, *L'unité* and "Un seul 'Pasteur,' un seul Hermas," *RThL* 23 (1992) 482–88; Ingrid Goldhahn-Müller, *Die Grenze der Gemeinde: Studien zum Problem der zweiten Busse im Neuen Testament unter Berücksichtigung der Entwicklung im 2. Jh. bis Tertullian* (GThA 39; Göttingen: Vandenhoeck & Ruprecht, 1989) 243. In *Rich and Poor in the Shepherd of Hermas: An Exegetical-Social Investigation* (CBQMS 15; Washington, DC: Catholic Biblical Association, 1983) 7, I assumed Giet's theory as a basis for that study. I now think single authorship in several stages and redactions best fits the evidence.

91   Pages 26–28.

92   Further discussion on the whole topic in Carolyn Osiek, "The Genre and Function of the Shepherd of Hermas," in Adela Yarbro Collins, ed., *Early Christian Apocalypticism: Genre and Social Setting* (Semeia 36; Decatur, GA: Scholars Press, 1986) 113–21.

93   John J. Collins, ed., *Apocalypse: The Morphology of a Genre* (Semeia 14; Missoula, MT: Scholars Press, 1979) 74–75. So too Joly, 11. The now classic definition of an apocalypse given at the beginning of Collins' volume (p. 9) is: "a genre of revelatory literature with a narrative framework, in which a revelation is mediated by an otherworldly being to a human recipient, disclosing a transcendent reality which is both temporal, insofar as it envisages eschatological salvation, and spatial insofar as it involves another, supernatural world," with friendly amendment offered by David Hellholm: "intended for a group in crisis with a purpose of exhortation and/or consolation by means of divine authority" ("The Problem of Apocalyptic Genre" [SBLASP 1982] 169).

94   Philipp Vielhauer and Georg Strecker, *NTApoc,* 2. 599; cf. refs. in Brox, 36 n. 10; also Philipp Vielhauer, *Geschichte der urchristlichen Literatur* (Berlin/New York: De Gruyter, 1975) 522.

95   Brox, 37; Vielhauer/Strecker, *NTApoc,* 2. 593.

pseudo-apocalypse."[94] An intermediate position often taken is that it is an apocalypse in form but not in content.[95] Others recognize a certain difference from the usual apocalypse and apply qualifying adjectives.[96]

The book lacks, or plays down considerably, some of what are often considered essential elements of an apocalypse: detailed revelations about the world beyond and end-time catastrophes; historical speculations; pessimism about the outcome of this world; and pseudepigraphical character.[97] On the other hand, many writings accepted as apocalypses lack one or another of these characteristics. In the tables of characteristics of Christian apocalypses, *Hermas* ranks well.[98]

Hermas forces the question of the limits of apocalyptic genre. The long work is not of only one genre, and genres within it are not confined to parts with the most likely titles. There are visions, commandments, and parables throughout the text, though each predominates in the section by that name. The primary content of the *Visions* is revelations largely through the medium of verbal communication, though the image of the tower dominates. Here apocalyptic form and content are clearest, with otherworldly messages and eschatological warnings, but these in fact continue throughout the book. The commandments or teachings of the second part, the *Mandates,* is largely verbal as well, yet images and even revelations (*Mandate* 11) appear there. The third part, the *Similitudes,* is structured around images interpreted allegorically, but this section is also filled with commandments,[99] and many of the *Similitudes* end with prescriptive teaching.

Allegory is heavily used and favored by the author, yet allegory does not drive the book and the whole is not pure allegory, since the primary referent is Hermas himself, who is meant to be taken as a historical character, and the primary narrative is of his experiences, which are not allegorized in themselves.[100] The principal image of the *Visions,* the building of the tower, is an allegory of the community in its historical and eschatological aspects. Other aspects can develop into allegory, as when the rejuvenated woman church becomes a figure of the converted community in *Vis.* 3.10–13. The images in the *Similitudes* are explained directly as allegories, with a paraenetic purpose and context, but that is true of most allegory. Allegory and paraenesis are both present in apocalypses, but rarely to this extent.[101]

It is paraenesis that drives and unifies the whole, within an apocalyptic framework. The strongest current running through the entire book is concern for the life of the church, especially its suffering members, from the perspective of the world beyond. That life can only be improved and purified through the conversion and changed behavior of its members within a limited (but not specified) time frame. The content of the book is therefore largely apocalyptic paraenesis,[102] "parenetic salvation-judgment oracles" of the same form as those in Revelation 2–3,[103] with both space and time dimensions, within a framework of otherworldly revelation about the theological realities that engage the lives of the recipients. The Christian apocalyptic interest in paraenesis means that the social function of apocalypticism has

---

96 "Une apocalypse refroidie" ("a cooled-down apocalypse") (Joly, "Milieu complexe," 527); "une apocalypse morale" (Paramelle, "Hermas," 320); the "practical apocalypse" of a reformer (Kirsopp Lake, "The Shepherd of Hermas and Christian Life in Rome in the Second Century," *HTR* 4 [1911] 25–47).

97 Discussed by Brox, 36–37.

98 With 16 out of 28 in a listing where the average is 13.3: John J. Collins, ed., *Apocalypse: The Morphology of a Genre* (Semeia 14; Missoula, MT: Scholars Press, 1979) 104–5; cf. the table of characteristics comparing *Hermas* with Jewish apocalypses in Snyder, 8–9. Nevertheless, Snyder characterizes the book as "apocalyptic in form only" (p. 9) because it lacks historical, political, and theodictic content.

99 E.g., *Sim.* 6.1.1–4 is a little excursus on keeping the

commandments; 7.7 refers to commandments given in that context.

100 Roelof Van Deemter, *Der Hirt des Hermas: Apokalypse oder Allegorie?* (Delft: Meinema, 1929) 157.

101 Paraenesis is represented more strongly, for instance, in *2 Enoch* and *2 Baruch.*

102 What is said about Matt 6:19–34 is relevant here: it "functions to create in the reader an epistemological position within the Kingdom of God, a position from which the reader may seek that Kingdom and the righteousness that belongs to God" (Stephenson Humphries-Brooks, "Apocalyptic Paraenesis in Matthew 6:19–34," in Joel Marcus and Marion Soards, eds., *Apocalyptic and the New Testament: Festschrift for J. Louis Martyn* [JSNTSup 24; JSOT, 1989] 97).

103 David E. Aune, *Prophecy in Early Christianity and the*

changed in response to changed situations. The spirit of apocalypticism is no longer simply expectation of the eschaton, but a look backwards to what has already happened in Christ, who is present in the church speaking through the apostles and prophets. Christian apocalyptic therefore collapses the difference between this world and the world to come, so that there is only one time, the end time.[104]

It has become axiomatic that apocalyptic literature seeks to respond to a crisis, whether political, spiritual, or other.[105] That crisis need not be an externally imposed political one. A crisis can be perceived where there is none, but it can also exist alive and well with regard to internal matters like community division and loss of good spirit. This is the sort of crisis that we face in *Hermas*.

Apocalyptic form in *Hermas* is not an empty shell with false content. Form must be at the service of function. The form serves the function of Christian apocalypticism in that situation. "The function of apocalyptic literature is to shape one's imaginative perception of a situation and so lay the basis for whatever course of action it exhorts."[106] Hermas' strategy is to reshape the church by bringing listeners to the point of openheartedness in which they can change.

1.3.2 Structure
As has been pointed out above, the obvious three-part structure is very porous. Different genres are not clearly distinguished from one part to another, and what are called part of one can really be transition to another, as is the case with *Vision* 5. Another proposal would distinguish between *Visions* 1–4 in which Hermas' guide is the woman church, and the rest of the book in which he is led by the Shepherd, except for *Similitude* 10 in which the great angel himself steps in to interpret Hermas'

experience. By any account, the structure of the whole is very loose and difficult to grasp.

A concentric pattern is suggested by Philippe Henne[107] whereby the central block, *Vision 5–Similitude 8*, contains the core of the message, exhortation to repentance. This block is surrounded by the vision of the holy and pure tower (*Visions* 1–4) on one side and the historical and imperfect tower (*Similitudes* 9–10) on the other. Framing this whole picture are Rhoda the accuser (*Vis.* 1.1.5–6) and the great angel who declares Hermas' innocence (*Man.* 10.2.2). Such a sharp contrast between the two towers, however, is not justified, and the sheer amount of text is in no way balanced between the two. It is more a contrast of amount of detail. The contrast between Rhoda's accusation at the beginning and the angel's declaration of Hermas' innocence at the end, however, is striking.

Another more developed proposal, intriguing but not watertight, is made elsewhere by Henne,[108] that the key to understanding the structure is "allegorical polysemy" whereby successively different meanings are given to the same narrative element. Hermas has a pattern of beginning with cosmology and ending with soteriology. For instance, the earth is founded on water (*Vis.* 1.3.4); the first tower is built on water (*Vis.* 3.2.4); and the water is baptism (*Vis.* 3.3.5, 7.3). Another example is the twelve mountains (*Sim.* 9.1.4–10), which are twelve tribes (*Sim.* 9.17.1), which then become twelve kinds of believers (*Sim.* 9.17.4). Each level of meaning has its own coherence without comparison with other levels. Another example that does not follow the movement from cosmology to soteriology, but from ascesis to christology to soteriology, is *Similitude* 5, where the parable of the slave and vineyard (5.2) is applied first to fasting (5.3), then to the Son of God (5.5), and finally to the salvation of the

Ancient Mediterranean World (Grand Rapids, MI: Eerdmans, 1983) 299–310.

104 Elisabeth Schüssler Fiorenza, "The Phenomenon of Early Christian Apocalypticism: Some Reflections on Method," in David Hellholm, ed., *Apocalypticism in the Mediterranean World and the Near East* (Uppsala: Mohr, 1983) 295–316 (311–13).

105 Cf. David Hellholm's amendment to the Semeia 14 definition in n. 93 above; Adela Yarbro Collins, *Crisis and Catharsis: The Power of the Apocalypse* (Philadelphia: Westminster, 1984) 84–110; Osiek, "Genre," 116–17.

106 John J. Collins, *The Apocalyptic Imagination: An*

Introduction to the Jewish Matrix of Christianity (New York: Crossroad, 1984) 32.

107 *La christologie chez Clément de Rome et dans le Pasteur d'Hermas* (Paradosis, Études de littérature et de théologie anciennes 33; Fribourg: Éditions Universitaires, 1992) 151–54.

108 "La polysémie allégorique dans le *Pasteur* d'Hermas," *EThL* 65 (1989) 131–35.

109 Already Charles Taylor had the right idea: ". . . a work originally composed in two books by one and the same imaginative writer and teacher, every-

flesh (5.6–7). In many cases, however, the image has but one referent, given through allegorical interpretation.

These structural patterns do occur. Other examples are cited in the commentary. But no one to date has been able to demonstrate a consistent structural pattern throughout the book, and this is precisely why studying its structure is so frustrating. Inasmuch as there is an underlying pattern, it is that of *expansion* of images and interpretations to bring home the same point,[109] sometimes one following another in a related chain, as is the case for interpretation of the parable of the slave in *Similitude* 5, for example, or the parable of the willow sticks in *Similitude* 8 followed by the twelve mountains in the next. Sometimes, however, the elements are at a distance from earlier related units, as is the case with the retelling of the narrative of the tower in *Similitude* 9.

This loose structure is best explained as the result of the underlying oral patterns present in the original use of the text: as a basis for oral proclamation. Recent scholarship is coming more and more to understand the oral use of texts in early Christianity and its environment. Only a small percentage of the population was literate,[110] and the possession of literacy by a small usually male elite contributed to social power.[111] The interaction between literacy and prophetic authority must be taken account of in this context, with emphasis on those apocalyptic texts in which the recipient is told to, or the text says explicitly that he does, write down the revelation.[112] What gives Hermas his authority is the written revelation with its origin in heaven, source of all truth and accurate information.[113]

There was no smooth transition from orality to literacy in any society. Literate habits of thinking were already beginning in the Homeric era and were fully present in the classical period. Hellenistic Judaism took important strides toward literacy with its embrace of

---

where given to reiteration for the sake of emphasis, and not very methodical" (*The Shepherd of Hermas* [2 vols.; London: SPCK, 1903, 1906] 1. 22).

110 An accurate number will never be available; somewhere between 10% and 30% are the usual estimates. Scholars who study the Jewish and Christian populations tend to estimate higher because of the emphasis placed on, and unusual authority granted to, written texts in both traditions. This evidence of Jewish and Christian literacy stands in some tension with the generalized assumptions of historians who would play down the extent of literacy. Some recent scholarship includes: William V. Harris, *Ancient Literacy* (Cambridge, MA: Harvard University Press, 1989); Alan K. Bowman and Greg Woolf, eds., *Literacy and Power in the Ancient World* (Cambridge: Cambridge University Press, 1994; a series of responses to Harris); Gamble, *Books and Readers;* Werner Kelber, *The Oral and the Written Gospel* (Philadelphia: Fortress, 1983); Joanna Dewey, "Oral Methods of Structuring Narrative in Mark," *Int* 53 (1989) 32–44; idem, ed., *Orality and Textuality in Early Christian Literature* (Semeia 65; Atlanta, GA: Scholars Press, 1995). Much of the work on early Christian literature is based on the earlier work of Eric Havelock, Milman Parry, and Albert Lord on Homeric literature and of Walter Ong on linguistic structure and the transition from orality to literacy. Still valuable is Adolf von Harnack, *Bible Reading in the Early Church* (New York: Putnam, 1912), which collects massive data for Christian Bible reading, which must be interpreted with caution, since he did not adequately take into account oral means of disseminating teaching.

111 The introduction of literacy "usually involved the domination of the nonliterate segment of the population by the literate one, or even the less literate by the more. Where writing is, 'class' cannot be far away" (Jack Goody, *The Interface between the Written and the Oral* [Cambridge: Cambridge University Press, 1987] xv, also 161–64, 265). The same point is made about the ancient Mediterranean world by Mary Beard, "*Ancient Literacy* and the Function of the Written Word in Roman Religion," in J. H. Humphrey, ed., *Literacy in the Roman World* (Journal of Roman Archaeology Supplementary Series 3; Ann Arbor, MI: Dept. of Classical Studies, University of Michigan Press, 1991) 35–38 (56–58); and by Keith Hopkins, "Conquest by Book," ibid., 133–58 (142–43, 157). Joanna Dewey ("Textuality in an Oral Culture: A Survey of the Pauline Traditions," in idem, ed., *Orality and Textuality in Early Christian Literature* [Semeia 65; Atlanta, GA: Scholars Press, 1995] 37–65), argues that the possession of literacy was one of the contributing factors in the consolidation of power into the hands of a ruling male elite soon after the first years in early Christianity.

112 Rev 1:19; 2:1, etc.; *Vis.* 2.1.3–4; 5.5–6; *Sim.* 9.1.1; 10.1.1.

113 See Robin Lane Fox, "Literacy and Power in Early Christianity," in Alan K. Bowman and Greg Woolf, eds., *Literacy and Power in the Ancient World*

Hellenistic culture.[114] But none of this means that classical Greece or Hellenistic Judaism were literate societies. So too under imperial Rome and in the world of Hermas. The vast majority of people remained nonliterate; the situation is sometimes referred to as "residual orality," but this way of phrasing leaves the impression of a literate majority, which was not the case.

Not all students of the transition from orality to literacy in the ancient Mediterranean world take sufficiently seriously the ample studies on the differences between oral and literate thinking, already suggested by Eric Havelock more than thirty years ago.[115] It is not simply a question of whether one individual could read or not, or of what percentage of the population could read a civic inscription. There are varying degrees of literacy. The ability to write up a business receipt or tax record, affix one's signature to such a record, or to write or read a political slogan or a piece of social commentary on a Pompeian wall, does not indicate full literate thinking. The usual way to read in antiquity was by reading aloud or at least moving the lips, so that even individual reading was a partly oral process.[116] Not all levels of literacy are accompanied by the kind of abstract and synthetic thinking that comes with full literacy. From before the classical period there were educated elites and their secretaries who were engaged in fully literate thinking, but still well into the Christian era the majority of the population were not among them. The majority relied on oral delivery of information, and especially of extended teaching, whose thought processes bear different characteristics.

We must assume that most early Christian texts were dictated orally and intended to be proclaimed orally to a group of people. In most examples, one more or less finished text was sent off to be read in another context. When the text came from a revered figure, there is little likelihood that the written text itself would have been changed to reflect the ongoing interpretation of the community around it. Seldom are we able to see in the text the result of the interaction between written version and oral performance. But this is the key to grasping the structure of *Hermas*. The current consensus on authorship, of many revisions by a single author, needs to be supplemented with the understanding of how those many revisions took shape: through the pattern of oral proclamation and commentary, such as was usually done in worship assemblies. One author was able to expand indefinitely on his own work. Reader and commentator could be different people, so that not everyone involved in the process had to be able to read.[117] The text as it was eventually passed down into the third and fourth centuries is the result of a great deal of editing and expansion over a period of years by a single author or by others working in close association with him.

Hermas' authority in the community rests on his possession of a written text of revelation which he is to disseminate and himself proclaim with the presbyters (*Vis.* 2.4.3). All indications are that male literacy was higher than female; yet Grapte will receive a copy of the written text with which she is to exhort or admonish ($\nu o \nu \vartheta \epsilon$-$\tau \epsilon \hat{\iota} \nu$) the women's group. She can therefore presumably read, and perhaps her position as leader is closely relat-

---

(Cambridge: Cambridge University Press, 1994) 126–48. Both Rev 20:12 and *Vis.* 1.3 refer to a secret "book of life," "secret files," as it were, kept by "recording angels [who] were a constant, literate police force" watching Christians and keeping records. For Tertullian (*De spec.* 27) this is why Christians should not attend the games (p. 133). Cf. Matt 18:10; 1 Cor 11:10.

114 See Thomas E. Boomershine, "Jesus of Nazareth and the Watershed of Ancient Orality and Literacy," in Joanna Dewey, ed., *Orality and Textuality in Early Christian Literature* (Semeia 65; Atlanta, GA: Scholars Press, 1995) 7–36.

115 *Preface to Plato* (Cambridge, MA: Harvard University Press, 1963); followed by *The Literate Revolution in Greece and Its Cultural Consequences* (Princeton, NJ: Princeton University Press, 1982) and *The Muse Learns to Write: Reflections on Orality and Literacy*

from Antiquity to the Present (New Haven: Yale University Press, 1986).

116 Well known is Augustine's expression of surprise (*Conf.* 6.3.3) that Ambrose read without speaking the words. There is other evidence for silent reading as well, but it was probably not the norm: B. M. W. Knox, "Silent Reading in Antiquity," *GRBS* 9 (1968) 421–35; Michael Slusser, "Reading Silently in Antiquity," *JBL* 111 (1992) 499; Frank D. Gilliard, "More Silent Reading in Antiquity: *non omne verbum sonabat,*" *JBL* 112 (1993) 689–96; further refs. in Gamble, *Books and Readers*, 321–22 n. 1.

117 A glimpse of the process as it happens is afforded some six hundred years before in Neh 8:2–8, where Ezra presides over a worship assembly holding the scroll of the Law from which he first reads, then

ed to her ability to read. Yet her presentation of the text to her audience will be interpreted through her own teaching. The woman church too knows how to read (*Vis.* 2.1.3). Hermas' authority is confirmed in writing, but most of the process as described within the narrative is oral: the opening scenes of the *Visions* use personal figures to give oral instruction and communication; the woman church reads aloud to Hermas (*Vis.* 1.3.3–4), and only a year later does he receive a written text, which requires two weeks of prayer and fasting from him to be able to read (2.1.3–4; 2.2.1). The first written text is actually quite brief (2.2.2–3.4). At the appearance of the Shepherd, Hermas is commanded to write what he receives by oral dictation for the purpose of oral proclamation (5.5–6).[118]

Characteristics of oral style include: additive rather than subordinative structure; use of repeated traditional and circumlocutionary formulas; redundancy; traditionalism; practicality of examples; and situational, present-oriented consciousness and mode of delivery.[119] All are present in *Hermas*. The very structure of the book is additive, not subordinative: new images and above all, new interpretations, keep accumulating. This is why, for instance, the successively younger appearance of the woman church is not mentioned throughout her conversations with Hermas, until it is time to give an interpretation (*Vis.* 3.10), or why the four-legged couch upon which she sat now suddenly means the security of the four elements (3.13.3). The moral teaching is thoroughly traditional and in the *Mandates,* and even a number of times in the *Similitudes,* the familiar refrain which ends

many chapters, "Do this . . . (or avoid this . . .) and you will live to God, and all those who do these things will live to God," is in fact a recitational cue for group participation by completing the statement.[120] Usually the second person verbs switch to the plural only for this phrase, then return again to the singular afterwards. The listening audience is thus brought into the recitation to say the conclusion themselves and so reinforce the lesson. The direct connection with a listening audience is reinforced by use of the familiar address ἀδελφοί ("brothers [and sisters]"), a form of address much more common in paraenetic contexts, but here used only in the *Visions* in the context of revelation of a new vision.[121] The language is close to conversational street language.[122] The repetition of formulas and narration of detail in some of the revelations is heavily redundant, so that many of the sections make uninteresting reading to the modern reader used to synthetic and abstract presentation of ideas. Hermas has been criticized as a supposed apocalyptic writer for lack of sufficient eschatological speculation. The emphasis is rather on the significance of change in the present in order to affect the future. This present orientation is not overpowered by an imagined future.[123]

One consequence of this process of interaction between written text and oral proclamation is that after the author's first draft, there never was an original text, because the text went through many changes in the

---

Levites engage in spontaneous biblical commentary by interpreting it so that the people will understand. The reading and interpretation go on for hours, from early morning until midday. The people's reaction is sorrow until Ezra reassures them that it is time for rejoicing and feasting (vv. 9–12). For evidence on illiterate lectors, see Gamble, *Books and Readers*, 250 n. 31.

118 Cf. *Rev* 1:11, 19; *4 Ezra* 15.2; *2 Bar.* 50.1; 77.12, 19; 78.1; 86; 87.

119 Extended and specific characterization in Walter Ong, *Orality and Literacy* (New York: Methuen, 1982) 37–57 and elsewhere. Further discussion and examples from *Hermas* in Osiek, "The Oral World of Early Christianity in Rome: The Case of Hermas," in K. Donfried and P. Richardson, eds., *Judaism and Christianity in First-Century Rome* (Grand Rapids: Eerdmans, 1998) 151–72.

120 The concluding formula of all the *Mandates* except 1, 6, and 11, and of *Sim.* 5.1, 7; 6.1.4; 8.11.4 (see vv. 1, 3); 9.20.4, 22.4, 28.8, 29.3.

121 *Vis.* 2.4.1; 3.1.1, 4; 3.10.3; 4.1.1, 5, 8; its most frequent use is in the most apocalyptic chapter, *Vision* 4, the encounter with the beast. The form of address is ubiquitous in paraenetic writing, e.g., 1 Cor 10:1; 11:3; Jas 1:2, 16, 19; 2:1, 14; *1 Clem.* 4.7; 13.1; 33.1; 37.1; 38.3; Ignatius *Eph.* 16.1; *Rom.* 6.2; *Phld.* 3.3; *Barn.* 2.10; 3.6; 4.14, etc.

122 John Carroll White, "The Interaction of Language and World in the 'Shepherd of Hermas'" (Ph.D. diss., Temple University, 1973) 161–65.

123 Further discussion of *Hermas* and the characteristics of orality in Osiek, "Oral World."

hands of its author as he and perhaps his assistants or colleagues added more and more material as it developed in the interpretive process in which he and others were engaged on the basis of the text.[124]

1.4 The Characters

1.4.1 The Woman Church

It is not completely unusual in apocalyptic and allegorical writings to have mythological female guides and revelatory agents, even ones who become transformed into something else. The closest parallel that is often pointed out is *4 Ezra* 9.38–10.57, in which a mourning woman is changed into a great city. But the parallel is not that close. The woman does not lead or reveal anything to Ezra; rather, he reproaches her for seeming to be fixated on her own suffering instead of that of the people. She is then transformed into a great city, which in a later vision an angel identifies as Zion, just as "an attractive young man" in a dream reveals to Hermas that the woman of his visions is the church (*Vis.* 2.4.1).

However, in *Hermas* the character and role of the woman are quite different. She is the principal revealer in the *Visions*. She repeatedly charges Hermas to communicate the revelation that she has dictated to him (*Vis.* 2.2.6, 4.3; 3.8.11; 4.3.6). She encourages, cajoles, reproves, and loses her patience. Her revelations continue for some time even after she is identified as the church, an identification that she herself repeats (*Vis.* 3.3.3), though she is unwilling or incapable of directly explaining her own identity and rejuvenation process; for this, she relies on a "young man," an angel (2.4.1; 3.10.2).

Here, after preliminary visions as a woman, the figure is at the same time woman and tower: she interprets to Hermas the vision of the tower as it is being built, begin-

ning at *Vis.* 3.2.4. Thus she interprets herself, and appears under two aspects at the same time. Her transformation from old to young in *Vis.* 3.10–13 shows her intimate connection to the historical realities: her well-being rises or falls with that of the collective human membership of the church. Later, the woman church will also be identified with the Holy Spirit, the Son of God (*Sim.* 9.1.1), an identification that emphasizes the pneumatic or transcendent aspect of the church. This female guide has no true precedent in Western literature.[125]

1.4.2 The Shepherd

The Shepherd is the major guide and revelatory agent from *Vision* 5 onward. He is first of all a heavenly companion sent by one superior to himself (*Vis.* 5.2), not so much as guardian but as instructor. He directs, interprets and explains visions, and dictates teaching that Hermas is to pass on to the church. Indeed, the whole of the *Mandates* and much of the *Similitudes* consists of his teaching as dictated or spoken to Hermas. He is also identified several times as the angel of conversion (ὁ ἄγγελος τῆς μετανοίας), the spirit whose special responsibility is to oversee the process, a not uncommon angelic assignment.[126] At the end, he is again assigned to Hermas' house as protector and guarantee of prosperity (*Sim.* 10.2). The ubiquity of shepherd figures in Greco-Roman and early Christian art and imagination makes it difficult to establish parallels.[127] Eventually in early Christianity they assimilate into the figure of Christ the Shepherd, but not this early. The Shepherd here is probably not Hermas' heavenly double, and there is probably no direct influence of *Poimandres*.[128]

1.4.3 Other Characters

The cast of characters is long, and can be divided by sex, but also by the two categories of those who belong to

---

124 The suggestion of a predominantly oral base and oral process of composition for the text is not new. In the introduction to his translation, F. Crombie ("The Pastor of Hermas" [Introduction, translation, notes; ANF; Edinburgh: T. & T. Clark, 1867] 2. 3–58) 8 notes that James Donaldson, one of the general editors of the ANF, agrees with Crombie "that *The Shepherd* is a compilation, traditional, or reproduced from memory. He supposes its sentiments 'must have been expressed in innumerable oral communications delivered in the churches throughout the world.'" The quotation of Donaldson is from the *Theological Review* 14 (1877) 564.

125 See discussion below at *Vis.* 3.10.2–5.

126 *Vis.* 5.7; *Man.* 12.6.1; in *1 Enoch* his name is Phanuel. *Testament of Gad* 5.7–8 and *Joseph and Aseneth* 7(6) personify conversion, the latter as a virgin, while God is the father of conversion. Clement of Alexandria, in his charming story about the elder John, also uses the term, in probable dependence on *Hermas*, since he knew and valued it so well (*Quis dives* 42.18).

127 See Nikolaus Himmelmann, *Über Hirten Genre in der antiken Kunst* (Opladen: Westdeutscher Verlag, 1980).

Hermas' life-world, and those who are imaginary or personifications.

The female characters in Hermas' life world include Grapte, a literate church leader responsible for the instruction of widows and their children (*Vis.* 2.4.3). She receives one copy of the initial revelation with which to instruct her charges. Hermas' unnamed wife is the source of much of his trouble, because of her unrestrained tongue—a traditional female stereotype—and other unspecified transgressions, none of which, however, seems to be of a sexual nature (*Vis.* 2.2.3, 2.3.1). Rhoda, Hermas' former mistress, then crosses categories from real-life character to become part of the heavenly population as accuser, teacher, the first to proclaim healing through conversion, and the first heavenly figure to point him in the right direction, away from preoccupation with personal failings to concern with larger social and spiritual problems in the church (*Vis.* 1.1).

Besides the women of Hermas' life world, there are multiple female literary characters in groups. In the *Visions,* the woman church is once mistaken by Hermas for the Sibyl (2.4.1-2). Seven women (γυναῖκες, not virgins) are seven generations of virtues that uphold the tower (*Vis.* 3.8.2-8). In the *Similitudes,* their number has grown to twelve, who are now virgins (παρθένοι, *Sim.* 9.2.3), who stand guard at the gate of the tower and later participate in its ongoing construction (9.3, 4.8).[129] One of the most provocative scenes is that in which the Shepherd entrusts Hermas overnight to the virgins. They spend the night with him as brother, not husband, dancing, praying, and "dining on the words of the Lord" (9.10–11). The virgins are later idenitified as holy spirits, guardian spirits who carry the names of virtues (9.15.12), who will return to remain with Hermas on a permanent basis (*Sim.* 10.3.1-2; 4.5). Meanwhile, how-

ever, the twelve virgin virtues have been paralleled by twelve fierce-looking women in black clothing who are personified vices (*Sim.* 9.9.5, 15.3).[130]

While it is true that the female church gives way to the male Shepherd as revealer and in the later parts of the book no woman plays a major role,[131] still there can be no doubt that female persons and feminine imagery had a major effect on the author's imagination. One author who constructs Hermas' experience as guilt-ridden and ambiguous can still conclude that there is "a calm beauty in Hermas' symbolic Women, and it is this that makes his writing, for all its defects, unique in the early Church."[132]

Among the male characters of Hermas' life world are an otherwise unknown Maximus who has publicly apostasized in some way (*Vis.* 2.3.4). Given the import of the teaching that will later unfold, his apostasy might not be formal public denial, but the equivalent in compromising actions. Clement is an important figure in the Roman church, probably to be identifed with the man known to history as Clement of Rome.[133]

Among male literary figures are Eldad and Modat, pseudonymous authors of a lost apocryphal book,[134] to which is attributed the only direct quote from another work. Four, later six, young men escort the woman church in her appearances and carry her couch when necessary (*Vis.* 1.4.1; 3.1.6, passim).[135] They are soon identified as the first-created angels (3.4.1). They also participate in the building of the tower (3.1.7) and are joined by thousands of other men (3.2.5), who are also later identified as angels (3.4.2). When the image of the tower is resumed in *Sim.* 9.3.1, the six men return, now looking more like supernatural creatures, tall, wondrous, and similar in appearance (ὑψηλοὺς καὶ ἐνδόξους καὶ ὁμοίους τῇ ἰδέᾳ). The large group of other male

---

128 See further discussion below, Introduction 2.4 and at *Vis.* 5.1-2.

129 For a study of possible biblical allusions behind the twelve women carrying stones, see Oscar J. F. Seitz, "What Do These Stones Mean?" *JBL* 79 (1960) 247-54.

130 Cf. personified vices as mother and daughter in Achilles Tatius *Leucippe et Clitophon* 6.10.4-6.

131 Martin Leutzsch, *Die Wahrnehmung sozialer Wirklichkeit im "Hirten des Hermas"* (FRLANT 150; Göttingen: Vandenhoeck & Ruprecht, 1989) 184–85.

132 Herbert Musurillo, *Symbolism and the Christian*

Imagination (Baltimore/Dublin: Helicon, 1962) 39–40. See also Martha M. Smith, "Feminine Images in the Shepherd of Hermas" (Ph.D. diss., Duke University, 1979).

133 See further comment at *Vis.* 2.4.3.

134 Figures mentioned in Num 11:26–30. See note at *Vis.* 2.3.4.

135 At 3.1.6, the four seem to have turned into six, but at 3.10.1, the two groups of four and six are distinct, the four being the couch bearers and the six the builders.

builders have come with them. The six angels continue to supervise the building of the tower, and are the personal attendants of the lord of the tower when he comes to inspect it (9.6.1–2). Another lone angelic figure, a handsome young man, reveals to Hermas the true identity of the woman church and the reason for her aged appearance (*Vis.* 2.4.1). Later, another young man, not identified as the same one, appears to Hermas to interpret for him the meaning of the rejuvenation of the elder woman church in successive scenes (*Vis.* 3.10.7–12.4). The one sustained story-within-a-story is that of the vineyard owner with his son, slave, and advisors in *Similitude* 5. Finally, the great angel, perhaps to be identified with Christ, is the one who sends the Shepherd to be with Hermas, and who may be the same as the angel who distributes and inspects the willow branches in *Sim.* 8.1–2.

Among characters of uncertain sex can be included Hermas' children (*Vis.* 2.2.2–3, 3.1), the presbyters of the church (*Vis.* 2.4.3), and of course the many categories of persons who correspond to the various kinds of stones in the tower (*Vision* 3 and *Sim.* 9.3–16, 30–31), willow sticks (*Similitude* 8), and sheep and others from the various mountains (*Sim.* 9.17–29).

2 Historical Character

2.1 Place and Date

There can be little doubt that the geographical origin of *Hermas* is central Italy and probably Rome. Only Erik Peterson has objected, and his objections have not found favor with scholars.[136] References to Rome itself and the Tiber (*Vis.* 1.1–2) and to the Via Campana (*Vis.* 4.1.2) are local,[137] and no one has adequately explained why they would have been used if the book were written anywhere else. There are a number of allusions to viticul-

ture, which fit central Italy but could also come from other wine-growing regions. The description of vines grown on elm trees in *Similitude* 2, however, is most characteristic of central Italy.[138] The only geographical reference that is out of keeping with central Italy is Arcadia (*Sim.* 9.1.4), and this must be seen as mythological. The book originates in Rome and its environs, but the author is familiar with some of the surrounding rural area, not only the urban setting.

The date of the writing is a much more complex question. There are three pegs upon which all theories of the date hang: the Hermas of Rom 16:14, the reference to Clement in *Vis.* 2.4.3, and the *Muratorian Canon*. The Hermas of Rom 16:14 could have been alive no later than the end of the first century. Clement of Rome is usually considered to have been active at the end of the first century.[139] The *Muratorian Canon* dates the writing of *Hermas* much later by assigning it to the brother of Pius, who, according to Eusebius,[140] was prominent in the Roman church in the fourth decade of the second century.[141] All three references cannot be correct if a single author is involved, for the time range is over eighty years. While the *Muratorian Canon* is used as a point of reference for dating *Hermas,* its reference to *Hermas* is also used as a point of reference for dating the *Muratorian Canon,* so that a circular argument is involved. Moreover, the *Canon*'s reference to *Hermas* may be the device of a later document to make it seem earlier.

Origen is the first to opine that the Hermas of Rom 16:14 is indeed the author, but his is simply the expression of an opinion as part of his attempt to situate the book as early as possible, since he regarded it as inspired. Eusebius and Jerome follow him.[142] If Eusebius had known of the Muratorian identification of the author with the brother of Pius, he would have known

---

136 Peterson argues that the heavily Jewish influence of the commandment and parable motifs obviously come from a Palestinian ascetic milieu; all references to Rome are imaginary, and it is a methodological error to assume anything about Roman Christianity from *Hermas* ("Kritische Analyse der fünften Vision des Hermas," in idem, *Frühkirche, Judentum, und Gnosis* [Freiburg: Herder, 1959] 271–84 [275, 282]). More recently, Hahneman (*Muratorian Fragment*, 34–72) also proposes an Eastern origin and close relationship with Elchasai.

137 The two supposed references to Cumae in Campania, south of Rome (*Vis.* 1.1.3; 2.1.1) must be

abandoned; see refs. *ad loc.*

138 *Man.* 10.1.5; *Sim.* 2; 5.2; 9.26.4. The water pump used as an example in *Man.* 11.18 was used for watering fields, but also for urban fire engines. See comment below on *Similitude* 2, and Osiek, *Rich and Poor*, 146–53.

139 But this is scholarly convention: cf. Lawrence L. Welborn, "On the Date of First Clement," *BR* 29 (1984) 35–54.

140 *Hist. eccl.* 4.11.6.

141 *Pastorem vero nuperrime temporibus nostris in urbe Roma Hermas conscripsit sedente cathedra urbis Romae ecclesiae Pio episcopo fratre eius* ("Hermas wrote the

the chronological inconsistency with Origen's theory. This silence on Eusebius' part strengthens the argument that the *Muratorian Canon* is in fact a much later document, perhaps contemporary with or after Eusebius.

Some scholars reject the Muratorian witness altogether and opt for a very early dating.[143] The recent attempt to date *P.Iand.* 1.4 to the early second century on paleographical grounds would support this early dating.[144] Others dismiss the connection to Romans and sometimes even the reference to Clement, and opt for a later date with reliance on the *Muratorian Canon.*[145] Crombie suggests the charming but whimsical idea that Hermas and Pius of the second century were "elderly grandchildren" of Paul's Hermas, and that the early popularity of the book was due to its identification with the earlier Hermas as well as its staunch anti-Montanism, for which Crombie argues throughout his annotated translation.[146] Though there is no consensus on dating, the majority of scholars would situate the writing in the first half of the second century.

The references to Clement and to Pius need not be placed in an either/or antagonism. Whatever the reliability of the *Muratorian Canon,* and whatever it intends to say by *nuperrime* ("recently"), the two references are not totally incompatible. Copying and writing letters to other churches is not the job of one of the most important leaders of the community, but of a gifted scribe. If

the person known as Clement of Rome was a young secretary in the Roman church at the end of the first century, and Hermas was a young man at the time of the first visions, it is quite possible that he and a brother named Pius could still be alive but elderly toward the middle of the second century. The text could have been composed over a long period of years as interaction with audiences and expanded parts were added.

Besides the reference to Clement, other pieces of internal evidence are the passing allusions to "persecutions." They prove to be elusive, however. *Vis.* 2.2.7, 3.4 speak of the great tribulation that is coming, and the great beast of *Vision* 4 is given the same meaning. In both cases, the word used is $\vartheta\lambda\hat{\iota}\psi\iota\varsigma$, which can mean persecution but can also more likely mean eschatological distress or simply severe suffering, as it does only three verses prior to one of the warnings of future suffering.[147] *Vis.* 3.1.9 gives priority seating to "those who have suffered" for the name, while 3.2.1 lists what they suffered: beating, imprisonment, great affliction, crucifixion, and wild beasts, all of which sounds like the description of an all-out persecution, but it could refer to something not lived by the audience but remembered as the stuff of legend from such oral traditions as those behind the *Acts of Peter. Vis.* 3.5.2 assigns identification of the best stones for the building of the tower to those who have suffered for the name of the Lord. The same

---

Shepherd recently in our times while his brother Pius was sitting as bishop in the chair of the church of the city of Rome"); lines 73–77.

142 Origen *Comm. in Rom* 10.31 on Rom 16.14; Eusebius *Hist. eccl.* 3.3.6; Jerome *De vir. ill.* 10.

143 Among them, Wilson (*Reassessment*, 9–61: 80–100 CE after the Neronian persecution), but his interpretation is complicated by unhistorical assumptions about the early origins of the monarchical episcopate; Maier (*Social Setting*, 58) also dates the book to the late first century, as does James S. Jeffers, *Conflict at Rome: Social Order and Hierarchy in Early Christianity* (Minneapolis: Fortress, 1991), 106–12.

144 See above at 1.1.1; but also cautions in Carlini, "Testimone e testo."

145 A. Cleveland Coxe's introduction to *Hermas* (ANF 2. 3–5) dates the text to the age of Irenaeus, while the translator-editor Crombie in the same volume dates it to the time of Hadrian or Antoninus Pius. Dibelius (421–22) accepts the authenticity of the *Muratorian* reference and dates it to the third or fourth decade of the second century, as does Joly (14–15) and idem, "Milieu complexe," 527–29

(140–150 CE; the *Muratorian Canon* is the surest guide). Also rejecting the historicity of the Clement allusion are: James B. Lightfoot, *Apostolic Fathers* (1889; reprinted Grand Rapids: Baker, 1981) 1. 359–60; Christine Mohrmann, "Les origines de la latinité chrétienne" (*VC* 3 [1949] 67–106). Cirillo, ("Erma e il problema") argues throughout that *Hermas* belongs to the age of Montanism and was rejected for canonical status because of the church's fear of apocalyptic texts at that time. Brox too (15–16) sides with the *Muratorian Canon* and assigns a date of 140–155. Coxe's entire interpretation is flawed because of his reading of "canon law" into every aspect possible, e.g., Clement's role in *Vis.* 2.4.3 or "canonical hours" in 3.1.2.

146 Crombie, 4.

147 In *Vis.* 2.3.1, Hermas is told that his recent difficulties ($\vartheta\lambda\iota\psi\epsilon\iota\varsigma$) have resulted from his family's wrongdoing. In *Sim.* 7.3, the same word means purifying suffering in the present. The weak fall away in time of $\vartheta\lambda\hat{\iota}\psi\iota\varsigma$ (*Vis.* 3.6.5; *Sim.* 9.21.3).

identification is given to those whose sticks are immediately acceptable and who therefore are crowned and go at once into the tower, and to those of the eleventh mountain, where there is a long discussion and encouragement not to deny in present circumstances.[148] The memory of the local persecution under Nero in the sixties of the first century is likely, especially if, as tradition has it, both Peter and Paul perished in it.[149] Others have suggested a persecution under Domitian or Trajan, but the evidence for either is not strong.[150]

In light of the uncertainties, it is best to assume that the references to actual persecution, that is, "suffering for the name" and legal punishments, are part of a collective memory that projects the possibility of similar catastrophic events recurring. Most of the references to tribulation ($\vartheta\lambda\hat{\imath}\psi\iota\varsigma$), however, are either eschatological or meant with regard to present sufferings of loss of property and the like, seen in eschatological perspective. Hermas is more afraid of his listeners losing their faith than losing their lives.

The best assignment of date is an expanded duration of time beginning perhaps from the very last years of the first century, but stretching through most of the first half of the second century.

2.2 Social Context and Biographical Information

There is general consensus today that first- and second-century Roman Christianity was widely diverse both ethnically and theologically,[151] heavily influenced by a strong Jewish component,[152] predominantly Greek-speak-

---

148 *Sim.* 8.3.6–7; 9.28.

149 Tacitus *Ann.* 15.44.2–8; Suetonius *Nero* 16.2; *1 Clem.* 5–6; Eusebius *Hist. eccl.* 2.25.5–8.

150 A persecution under Domitian rests primarily on Melito's and Tertullian's passing comments that Domitian was the second after Nero to persecute Christians (*Apol.* 5.4–5; Melito quoted in Eusebius *Hist. eccl.* 4.26.9), Eusebius' echo of Tertullian, his assumption that John of Patmos was exiled under Domitian, and that Flavius Clemens and Domitilla were not simply Judaizers but Christians (*Hist. eccl.* 3.17–19; Dio Cassius *Epit.* 67.14). Evidence for a Domitianic persecution of Christians is assessed by Leonard L. Thompson, "A Sociological Analysis of Tribulation in the Apocalypse of John," in Adela Yarbro Collins, ed., *Early Christian Apocalypticism: Genre and Social Setting* (Semeia 36; Decatur, GA: Scholars Press, 1986) 147–74 (153–63); idem, *The Book of Revelation: Apocalypse and Empire* (New York/Oxford: Oxford University Press, 1990 [95–115, 133–37]); Maier, *Social Setting*, 79–80 n. 24. Evidence for a persecution under Trajan is Pliny *Ep.* 10.96–97 for Bithynia, with an implied readiness to apply the same standards elsewhere, and the likely death of Ignatius of Antioch during Trajan's reign. At issue with any so-called persecution before Decius is the question what exactly constitutes a persecution. A local uprising or a few isolated incidents do not necessarily imply a policy to eliminate Christians.

151 ". . . the history of the church of Rome of the first three centuries has a unique importance . . . the Christian community at Rome was not only one of the largest, but also was highly representative of the various currents of thought, tradition, and practice of the whole Christian church" (George LaPiana, "The Roman Church at the End of the Second Century," *HTR* 18 [1925] 201–77 [203]). Also Gustave Bardy, "Les écoles romaines au second siècle," *Revue d'histoire ecclésiastique* 28 (1932) 501–32; Peter Lampe, *Die stadtrömischen Christen in den ersten beiden Jahrhunderten* (WUNT 2. 18; 2d ed.; Tübingen: Mohr/Siebeck, 1989) 75–78, 203–95, 301–45; George LaPiana, "Foreign Groups in Rome during the First Centuries of the Empire," *HTR* 20 (1927) 183–403; Paul Minear, *The Obedience of Faith. The Purpose of Paul in the Epistle to the Romans* (SBT 2. 19; London: SCM, 1971) 8–21; Carolyn Osiek, "The Early Second Century through the Eyes of Hermas: Continuity and Change," *BTB* 20 (1990) 116–22.

152 Osiek, *Rich and Poor*, 111–21. Wolfgang Wiefel ("The Jewish Community in Rome and the Origins of Roman Christianity," in K. P. Donfried, ed., *The Romans Debate* [1977; reprinted Peabody, MA: Hendrickson, 1991] 85–101; original article, "Die jüdische Gemeinschaft im antiken Rom und die Anfänge des römischen Christentums. Bemerkungen zu Anlass und Zweck des Römerbriefs," *Judaica* 26 [1970] 65–88) argues that the expulsion of Jews from Rome under Claudius was the occasion for the building up of a more Gentile community in the city; but the extent of the "expulsion" is much questioned. Rome at this period was a strong center of Jewish life and learning: Harry Leon, *The Jews of Ancient Rome* (rev. ed.; Peabody, MA: Hendrickson, 1994) 35–38.

153 The Latinization of Roman Christianity was completed by the mid-third century, but was probably beginning by the late second century. The so-called Vulgate Latin translation of *Hermas* may date from that early time. The Latin influence in the Roman church at that time may have come from the church of North Africa, which by that time had changed

ing,[153] and drawing its membership almost exclusively from the nonelite classes of the city.[154] Within this context is to be found the more specific context of *Hermas.*

All evidence indicates a nonelite Greek-speaking context with limited literary education. Hermas belongs to "the common people" of the city.[155] The language and structure of the text are characteristic of a predominantly oral culture, in which paratactic aggregations, repetitions, and images from everyday life are common and do not distract, but rather strengthen the medium of communication. The text arose over the course of some years, with several editions, in a milieu and from a mind in which oral communication was the norm.[156]

Nonelite does not necessarily mean economically poor, however. The terminology for poverty in ancient Mediterranean languages has little correspondence with modern understandings of poverty, but has rather to do with maintenance of the status and honor, however limited, that the family claims to possess; without sufficient economic means, the family cannot maintain its claimed honor status. The church increasingly began to function as an economic unit, paralleling and eventually replacing the household as primary center of economic distrib-

ution. That process was in its early stages in the early second century as the church began to foster economic interdependence within its own ranks. This is precisely what was not happening with those perceived as wealthy who refused to associate with other Christians for fear their patronage would be presumed upon.[157]

It is fairly certain that Hermas identifies himself as a freedman in *Vis.* 1.1.1. A great deal is known regarding the economic mobility of freedpersons in the first centuries of the empire. Many remained in very modest circumstances, serving their former owners in the same jobs they had as slaves. Many also made a great deal of money in trade and commerce,[158] exactly what Hermas criticizes in the attitudes of his church members[159] and for which he is criticized himself by the woman church.[160] They also tended to socialize and form mutual aid associations with one another. If Hermas was a freedman, most of his associates were as well. He was probably a small craftsman[161] and/or businessman.[162] At a few years and one generation removed, we may have the type of Hermas in one Lucius Caecilius Jucundus, son of a freedman, wealthy businessman and creditor at Pompeii.[163] He owned a large house in the city, to which

---

over to Latin (Lampe, *Stadtrömische Christen,* 117–19; George LaPiana, *Il problema della chiesa latina in Roma* [Rome: Libreria di Cultura, 1922]; idem, *Le successione episcopale in Roma e gli albori del primato* [Rome: Libreria di Cultura, 1922] 17–24; Mohrmann, "Les origines," 67–106). *Hermas* does, however, show some influence of Latin: R. G. Tanner, "Latinisms in the Text of Hermas," *Colloquium* 4 (1972) 12–23; Brox, 43–45; Hilhorst, *Sémitismes;* Lampe, *Stadtrömische Christen,* 197.

154 George LaPiana, "The Roman Church at the End of the Second Century," *HTR* 18 (1925) 201–77; Osiek, *Rich and Poor,* 92–111.

155 Hilhorst, "Hermas," 686–87; Lampe, *Stadtrömische Christen,* 198–200.

156 See further 1.3.2 above; Osiek, "Oral World"; Lucretia B. Yaghjian, "Ancient Reading," in R. L. Rohrbaugh, ed., *The Social Sciences and New Testament Interpretation* (Peabody, MA: Hendrickson, 1996) 206–30.

157 *Vis.* 3.6.2; *Sim.* 8.8.1, 9.1; 9.20.2, 26.3. 9.20.2 says explicitly that they fear they will be asked for something, that is, that clientage will be more demanding than they desire.

158 Osiek, *Rich and Poor,* 127–32 and references there; John H. D'Arms, *Commerce and Social Standing in Ancient Rome* (Cambridge, MA: Harvard University

Press, 1981) esp. 97–148; Georges Fabre, *Libertus: Recherches sur les rapports patron-affranchi à la fin de la république romaine* (Collection de l'École française de Rome 50; Rome: École française, 1981). Tacitus (*Ann.* 13.26–27) reports a discussion under Nero of freedmen mistreating their patrons, and complains that freedmen cannot be distinguished as a class because that would reveal how many they are.

159 *Vis.* 3.6.5–7; *Man.* 3.5; 6.2.5; 10.1.4–5; *Sim.* 4.5–7; 8.8.1; 9.19.3, 20.1–2.

160 *Vis.* 3.6.7.

161 Joly, 17–21; Hilhorst, "Hermas," 683.

162 Jeffers (*Conflict at Rome,* 23) suggests that his business may be wine, since there are a good number of references to wine and viticulture (*Man.* 11.18, the siphon used to clean and water vines; 11.15; 12.5.3 on wine storage; *Sim.* 2 on viticulture with young elm trees; 9.26.4 on useless vines).

163 *CIL* 4.3340, probably son of a freedman, Lucius Caecilius Felix (*CIL* 10.891): Caroline E. Dexter, "The Casa di L. Cecilio Giocondo in Pompeii" (Ph.D. diss., Duke University, 1974) 187–223; Jean Andreau, *Les affaires de Monsieur Jucundus* (Collection de l'École française de Rome 19; Rome: École française, 1974). The well-known House of the Vettii at Pompeii, a house built for luxury entertaining, was also owned by two freedmen, A. Vettius

either he or his agents returned after the eruption of Vesuvius in August 79 CE in the vain attempt to retrieve his business records, stored in a wooden chest.[164] The chest contained 153 waxed tablets bound in diptychs and triptychs, receipts from 137 sales and 16 rents from 351 people, all but one transaction done between 52 and 62 CE, years before the eruption in 79 CE. The difference with Hermas, of course, is that he is a Christian who believes he has received a revelation to communicate to his church.

The church of early second-century Rome was characterized by considerable theological diversity, which grew as the century moved on. Depending on the date of the final edition of the text, it is possible that Valentinus, Cerdo, Marcion, and Marcellina had all arrived in Rome and were teaching there, as was Justin.[165] References to false, evil, and would-be teachers, and differences with regard to the mortality of the flesh indicate theological tensions in the church.[166] For the intellectually adventurous, it must have been an exciting place to be in the church. For Hermas, these theological disagreements were not at the center of concern. There is some reference to suffering and possible persecution, which should not be understood as the present situation of the community, but as a collective memory and eschatological forewarning.[167]

Though Hermas has very little to say about local church structure,[168] the assumption is that in early second-century Rome communities were still meeting in house churches, with occasional larger meetings of the whole assembly of a city.[169] By this time in Rome, that entire assembly must have been quite large, perhaps too large to meet all together. Hermas mentions various kinds of church leaders in several passages: apostles, overseers (ἐπίσκοποι), presbyters, teachers, and deacons, in a way that defies any kind of ordering.[170] These titles that at some point allude to church office refer to past situations, biblical allusions, and hypothetical roles. All terms are found in the Pauline letters, all but ἐπίσκοπος[171] in Romans or the Corinthian correspondence,[172] both of which were known in Rome.

The most specific reference is to a group of presiding presbyters of the church (πρεσβύτεροι προϊσταμένοι τῆς ἐκκλησίας) with whom Hermas is to proclaim to the church the message he has received (*Vis.* 2.4.3). Neither Clement nor Grapte seems to belong to this group of presbyters. This and several other similar passages that refer to presiders in the church are the only reliable statements from which to glean any information about actual church organization.[173] If from 2.4.3 it can be inferred that other references to presiders refer to this collegial group of presbyters, then they also appear at

---

Restitutus and A. Vettius Conviva. Evidence found in the house suggests that they may have been wine merchants (Lawrence Richardson, *Pompeii: An Architectural History* [Baltimore/London: Johns Hopkins University Press, 1988] 324).

164 The alternative is that ancient thieves came very soon after the catastrophe and tried to take it, thinking it contained treasure. The chest was found by excavators well above the floor level in the layers of volcanic ash that filled the house.

165 Eusebius *Hist. eccl.* 4.10–11; Irenaeus *Adv. haer.* 1.25.6; 27.2–3.

166 *Vis.* 3.7.1; *Man.* 11.1; *Sim.* 5.7.2; 8.6.5; 9.19.2–3, 22.1. See comment on *Sim.* 5.7.2.

167 See further under 2.1 above.

168 Unless his οἶκος ("household," "family") is a metaphor for a house church; see dicussion at 2.3 below.

169 On house churches, see Joan M. Peterson, "House Churches in Rome," *VC* 23 (1969) 264–72; Hans-Josef Klauck, "Die Hausgemeinde als Lebensform im Urchristentum," *Münchener theologische Zeitschrift* 32 (1981) 1–15; idem, *Hausgemeinde und Hauskirche*

im frühen Christentum (Stuttgarter Bibelstudien 103; Stuttgart: Katholisches Bibelwerk, 1981); Carolyn Osiek and David Balch, *Families in the New Testament World: Households and House Churches* (Louisville: Westminster John Knox, 1997).

170 *Vis.* 3.5.1 (apostles, overseers, teachers, deacons); *Sim.* 9.15.1 (prophets, deacons, apostles, teachers, in a clearly past context); 16.5 (apostles and teachers, who performed the "descent to hell"); 17.1 (apostles, implicitly the Twelve); 25.2 (apostles and teachers, in the past); 26.2 (deacons, but meant in a general sense of "ministers"); 27.2 (overseers [ἐπίσκοποι] and those who show hospitality—perhaps by hosting house churches).

171 Found only in Phil 1:1.

172 Ἀπόστολος many times; διάκονος in this sense Rom 16:1; 1 Cor 3:5; 2 Cor 3:6; 6:4; 11:23; διδάσκαλος 1 Cor 12:28, 29.

173 Another possible one would be the reference to "elders" (πρεσβύτεροι) who must sit before Hermas in *Vis.* 3.1.8, but the context here more likely means that the older should sit down first; see comment there.

Vis. 2.2.6 and 3.9.7. In both instances they are castigated for their transgressions. At 2.2.6 "to the leaders of the church" (τοῖς προηγουμένοις τῆς ἐκκλησίας) is addressed a solemn warning to change their ways. At 3.9.7–8 is addressed "to the leaders of the church who take the front seats" (τοῖς προηγουμένοις τῆς ἐκκλησίας καὶ τοῖς πρωτοκαθεδρίταις) the accusation of hardened hearts that carry poison. Just as in *1 Clem.* 44.4–5; 47.6 πρεσβύτεροι (presbyters or elders) and ἐπίσκοποι are synonymous, so too here many of the terms may apply to the same group of people, whose primary designation is probably presbyter. They may be the same as those viewed more positively in *Sim.* 9.27.2: overseers and hospitable persons (ἐπίσκοποι καὶ φιλόξενοι) who willingly gave hospitality to believers, especially the needy and widows.[174] Whatever the designation, it seems that there were recognized collegial leaders in the Roman church at the time, whose title was not exactly fixed. Hermas was not one of them, but his revelation gave him—at least in his own eyes—comparable status for its proclamation (*Vis.* 2.4.3). Inasmuch as prophecy was a recognized function in Hermas' church—and the Eleventh *Mandate* would suggest that it was—Hermas too may be considered a prophet in a general sense, since he meets the criterion of one who speaks only when the Spirit inspires him to speak rather than by consultation (*Man.* 11.5, 7–9).[175]

2.3 Historical Reliability

The portrayal of the central character Hermas is of a moderately wealthy freedman and householder with wife and probably grown children, whose family are causing him some kind of trouble by their behavior. He may be Jew or Gentile, and is influenced by literary and theological motifs from both traditions, which is not anomalous for second-century Roman Christianity.[176]

But is this portrait historical? A good number of scholars have assumed so. For some, Hermas is "the early Christian whom we know best after St. Paul."[177] A genuine spiritual experience lies behind the visions, and the family of Hermas are real people. Everything centers around the historical Hermas.[178] At the opposite extreme is Erik Peterson, for whom it is a methodological error to draw any conclusions about historicity from the text.[179] At least since Dibelius, strong doubts have been raised about the historical reliability of the biographical details. For Dibelius, there is no real biographical reliability. Hermas' family are the church, and his troubles with them are the personification of the whole community's way to salvation through sin, repentance, and grace.[180] Following this line of interpretation, Hermas is a real person but also a composite literary figure, as is his family.[181]

To pose the question so that the biographical information is either historical or not is probably to set up a

---

174 Maier (*Social Setting*, 62–64) suggests that each of these presbyters is in charge of a house church as patron and host.

175 This is a very debated point, since Hermas never is called a prophet nor claims to be one: on the negative side is Brox (20–22, 266), who also, however, gives a long list of those on the positive side. If Hermas' prophecy is "only a literary device," it is an imaginative depiction of how prophecy happened by one who is not personally involved (M. Eugene Boring, *The Continuing Voice of Jesus: Christian Prophecy and the Gospel Tradition* [Louisville: Westminster John Knox, 1991] 84–85).

176 One of the more unusual suggestions is that of Jean-Paul Audet ("Affinités littéraires et doctrinales du Manuel de Discipline," *RB* 59 [1952] 219–38; 60 [1953] 41–82) that Hermas is the descendant of a former Qumran member taken prisoner in 70 CE, enslaved, and brought to Rome.

177 Robin Lane Fox, *Pagans and Christians* (San Francisco: Harper and Row, 1986) 381–90.

178 At one extreme in this direction is Arthur W. Strock, "The Shepherd of Hermas: A Study of His

Anthropology as Seen in the Tension between Dipsychia and Hamartia" (Ph.D. diss., Emory University, 1984) 182–231. Similarly, Ake von Ström (*Der Hirt des Hermas: Allegorie oder Wirklichkeit?* [Arbeiten und Mitteilungen aus dem neutestamentlichen Seminar zu Uppsala 3; Uppsala: Wretmans, 1936]) argues on the basis of "modern psychology" that all of the visions are psychologically explainable and that the portrait of Hermas' family is totally plausible.

179 "Kritische Analyse," 275–77, 282–84.

180 Dibelius, 419–20, 449. See further discussion of the alternatives in Osiek, *Rich and Poor*, 8–10.

181 Kenneth W. Clark, "The Sins of Hermas," in A. Wikgren, ed., *Early Christian Origins: Studies in Honor of Harold R. Willoughby* (Chicago: Quadrangle, 1961) 102–19, reprinted in J. L. Sharpe, ed., *The Gentile Bias and Other Essays* (NovTSup 54; Leiden: Brill, 1980) 30–48.

false dichotomy.[182] A more nuanced interpretation would be that there is a basis of historicity upon which the author builds to emphasize his message. Thus the text contains a mixture of biography and literary reworking, so that the family becomes a literary mirror of the whole community.[183]

2.4 Sources and Influences

The attempt to determine literary sources for *Hermas* has been long and frustrating. No direct literary influence has ever been demonstrated to general satisfaction. Yet there are rich allusions that echo a variety of Jewish, Greco-Roman, and Christian writings. In an age of biblical scholarship when the establishment of literary sources was a greater priority, many of these were proposed as direct influences on the author. Today it is wiser to speak of general allusions and literary parallels.

Hermas' relationship with contemporary Judaism is certain but not clear.[184] Underlying the text is a Hellenistic Jewish tradition of moral teaching, much of it based on the Two Ways.[185] The Hebrew Scriptures are of course available, and there are occasional allusions especially to the Psalms and Wisdom literature, but no direct quotes. The one direct and explicit quote is from a lost apocryphal work, the Book of Eldad and Modad, later listed among the New Testament Apocrypha (*Vis.* 2.3.4).[186] The Two Ways teaching that underlies much of the moral instruction of the *Mandates* appears in one of its earliest forms in 1QS 4, but the Two Ways tradition is so widespread that direct influence is unable to be substantiated.[187] The Law, though probably alluded to in *Sim.* 5.6.3; 8.3.2–7, 6.2, is not the source of authority. Significantly, Hermas does not contend with and reject the claims of the Law as does Barnabas. Some of the foundation stones of the tower in the ninth *Similitude* are the biblical founders and prophets (9.15.4), and the church is composed of twelve tribes (9.17.1–4) who are not, however, only from Israel but from the entire world.[188] Several Jewish intertestamental writings contain similar images and allegorical motifs: mountains, plants, working angels, etc. No immediate interdependence with any of them can be securely established.

The ethical precepts of Pseudo-Phocylides, possibly contemporary to *Hermas,* offer some general parallels to the moral instruction of the *Mandates,* but no definite relationships.[189] Studies of possible relationships with

---

182 Young, "Being a Man," 241–42.

183 So Brox, 41–43; Lampe, *Stadtrömische Christen,* 182–88; Leutzsch, *Wahrnehmung,* 22. "Sexual sins are thus not the issue for Hermas, but sex serves by synecdoche to represent the disturbances of household management and church unity . . ." (Wayne A. Meeks, *The Origins of Christian Morality: The First Two Centuries* [New Haven: Yale University Press, 1993] 126). Another way to read that Hermas' family stands for the church is "mimetic appeal": readers are invited to see their own condition "mirrored" in that of Hermas (Patricia Cox Miller, *Dreams in Late Antiquity: Studies in the Imagination of a Culture* [Princeton, NJ: Princeton University Press, 1994] 142).

184 "Hermas pense en juif les dogmes chrétiens" ("Hermas thinks Christian teaching as would a Jew") (Pedro Lluis-Font, "Sources de la doctrine d'Hermas sur les deux esprits," *Revue d'ascétique et de mystique* 39 [1963] 83–98 [97]).

185 See discussion of Hermas' use of traditional Jewish material in Helmut Koester, *Introduction to the New Testament,* vol. 2: *History and Literature of Early Christianity* (2 vols.; Berlin and New York: De Gruyter, 1982) 2. 257–61. For further discussion of the Two Ways tradition, see section 3.3 below.

186 The two characters appear in Num 11:26–29. See references in Lake, 23; Snyder, 38; Brox, 103. The parallel passage in *1 Clem.* 23.3 and *1 Clem.* 11.2 is also thought by some to be taken from this writing (Martin Dibelius, *James* [rev. Heinrich Greeven; Hermeneia: Philadelphia: Fortress, 1976] 31 n. 102), as is the unknown scriptural quote in Jas 4:5 (ibid., 223 n. 82).

187 See section 3.3 below. Audet ("Affinités") argued for a Qumran origin for Hermas, but few have followed this lead, except recently J. Christian Wilson, *Five Problems in the Interpretation of the Shepherd of Hermas: Authorship, Genre, Canonicity, Apocalyptic, and the Absence of the Name "Jesus Christ"* (Mellen Biblical Press Series 34; Lewiston/Queenston/ Lampeter: Mellen, 1995) 38–50, going so far as to suggest what he readily admits is a fanciful reconstruction: that Hermas was brought up at Qumran and later lived in Rome.

188 See further Snyder, 13–14.

189 *The Sentences of Pseudo-Phocylides* is a collection of maxims that represents biblical ethics, but not cultic precepts, in Hellenistic language and form. The date range is first century BCE to first century CE: Pieter W. Van der Horst, *The Sentences of Pseudo-Phocylides. Introduction, Translation and Commentary* (SVTP 4; Leiden: Brill, 1978); idem, *Essays on the Jewish World of Early Christianity* (Göttingen: Vandenhoeck & Ruprecht, 1990) 19–62; idem, *OTP* 2. 565–82.

Qumran, in spite of numerous thematic similarities, come up just as short.[190] Such studies demonstrate that these writings and *Hermas* are part of the same thought world, where writers have similar ideals of human behavior and use similar images,[191] symbols, allegories, and examples to achieve similar ends. The author is deeply influenced by both biblical traditions and some strands of Hellenistic Jewish teaching.

The elements of similarity to Greco-Roman motifs are equally puzzling. Such literary allusions as Arcadia and the Sibyl could be had from idealized popular Roman art or literature.[192] There has long been effort to link *Hermas* with the *Tabula of Cebes,* with its allegorical interpretation of a painting that depicts women who represent virtues, a use of the common Hellenistic technique of ἔκφρασις (exposition by explanation of a scene or illustration).[193] Certainly the overall motif of *Tabula of Cebes* is reminiscent of limited parts of *Hermas* (notably *Vis.* 3.8; *Sim.* 6.2–4; 9.15), as is the continued pattern of

question and answer by which revelations are made. But the similarity is that of common genre, not literary dependence,[194] though it is possible, as Joly argues, that Hermas has read the *Tabula of Cebes.*[195]

Of equal interest in the attempt to trace influences in *Hermas* has been the *Corpus Hermeticum,* a collection of Hellenistic Egyptian mystical tracts from the late Hellenistic and early Roman periods, especially its first tractate, *Poimandres.* Richard Reitzenstein in 1904 suggested that Hermas had read an early edition of *Poimandres* and drew from it and the surrounding tradition the image of Hermes, whose home was Arcadia, as revealer and personal companion under the guise of a shepherd.[196] The similarities are intriguing, but the differences are also striking. In *Poimandres,* revelation comes to the recipient in a semiconscious waking state; in *Hermas,* in prayer or dream. There, the revealer is larger than life; here, the lord of the tower is of greatest stature (*Sim.* 9.6.1). There, the content of revelation is

---

190   See Audet, "Affinités"; Josephine M. Ford, "A Possible Liturgical Background to the Shepherd of Hermas," *RevQ* 6 (1969) 531–51; A. T. Hanson, "*Hodayoth* vi and viii and Hermas *Sim.* VIII," *StPatr* 10=TU 107 (1970) 105–8.

191   For example, the tower; cf. *Sib. Or.* 5.420–33; 7.71–73.

192   *Sim.* 9.1.4; *Vis.* 2.4.1. Audet, "Affinités," 80–81.

193   The *Tabula of Cebes* is probably a first-century CE work in the name of Cebes of Thebes, a student of Socrates. Its popularity in the second century is attested by allusions in Lucian (*De mercede conductis* 42; *Rhetorum praeceptor* 6) and Tertullian (*De praes.* 39). It employs the three genres of Socratic dialogue, ἔκφρασις (allegorical description), and ἐρωταποκρίσεις (question and answer in which an inferior questions a more knowledgeable character): John T. Fitzgerald and L. Michael White, eds., *The Tabula of Cebes* (SBLTT 24; Chico, CA: Scholars Press, 1983) 1–14; discussion of *Hermas* and the *Tabula of Cebes,* 17–20.

194   Earlier efforts to prove literary dependence: Charles Taylor, "Hermas and Cebes," *Journal of Philology* 27 (1901) 276–319; 28 (1903) 24–38, on the basis of an unpublished remark of J. M. Cotterill; Charles Taylor and J. M. Cotterill (deceased by this time), "Plutarch, Cebes, and Hermas," *Journal of Philology* 31 (1908–1910) 14–41. Taylor here edited notes of Coterill, expanding the search for parallels to Plutarch's *Moralia.* When St. George Stock ("Hermas and Cebes–A Reply," *Journal of Philology* 28 [1903] 87–93) exposed the

weaknesses of the argument, Taylor replied once more ("Note on Hermas and Cebes–A Reply," *Journal of Philology* 28 [1903] 94–98); also more recently, J. Schwartz, "Survivances littéraires païennes dans le 'Pasteur' d'Hermas," *RB* 72 (1965) 240–47; Robert Joly, *Le tableau de Cébès et la philosophie religieuse* (Collection Latomus 61; Brussels-Berchem: Latomus, 1963); idem, 51–53. Joly adduces other parallels not offered by Taylor: the use of book and baton by the interpretive guide; the firm seating of a principal female figure (but she is on a square rock in *Tab. Ceb.* 18.1, on a couch or bench with four legs in *Vis.* 3.1.4, 13.2); some common terminology; and a common motif of chastized sinners delivered up to a leading figure for salvation, saved by the intervention of μετάνοια (who, however, appears only here in *Tab. Ceb.* 10–11; cf. *Sim.* 6.3.3–6).

195   "Hermas chrétien a lu beaucoup de livres. S'imagine-t-on qu'il n'ait rien lu avant sa conversion?" ("The Christian Hermas read many books. Are we to suppose that he read nothing before his conversion?") Joly, 53. The argument continues that the *Tabula of Cebes,* since it deals with immortality, would have been popular especially with those asking religious questions. There is nothing in the text of *Hermas,* of course, that necessitates an author converted rather than born Christian. See too discussion in Hilhorst, "Hermas," 696–97.

196   *Poimandres: Studien zur griechisch-ägyptischen und frühchristlichen Literatur* (Leipzig: Teubner, 1904) 31–36.

cosmic mysteries of life and death; here, *Mandate 1* begins this kind of theme briefly, but the revelation moves quickly to the realm of moral instruction. *Poimandres* concludes with general wisdom teaching; *Hermas* gives specific wisdom teaching throughout. Further, there is the discrepancy between Hermes the revealer and Hermas the recipient, and the picture of Arcadia in *Hermas* is quite different from that in Hellenistic literature.[197] Moreover, the text of *Poimandres* as it has been preserved is usually dated contemporary with or slightly later than *Hermas*. There is insufficient evidence to conclude direct dependence of *Hermas* on *Poimandres,* though it cannot be excluded that the author may have either read some earlier version of the Egyptian tractate or heard allusions to similar material that influenced his choice of terms or images.

Christian sources are no clearer. Any similarity between parables in *Hermas* and those in the Gospels is better explained on the basis of a common oral tradition.[198] A recurring phrase, εἰρηνεύετε ἐν ἑαυτοῖς ("Be at peace among yourselves," *Vis.* 3.6.3, 9.2, 12.3; *Sim.* 8.7.2), echoes 1 Thess 5:13, but could be simply a liturgical or paraenetic refrain common to both texts. Common to *Hermas,* the Gospel traditions, and Paul is the language of the kingdom of God as a place to enter or dwell.[199] There are no explicit allusions or quotations from Synoptic or Pauline writings. The image of the Son of God as door or gate (πύλη) in *Sim.* 9.12.1 evokes John 10:9, though a different word is used there (θύρα).

Similarities with the Letter of James abound, and here the relationship is considerably more complex. An important factor is the common use of the word "double-minded" (δίψυχος). However, whereas it is one of the most frequently occurring words and concerns in *Hermas,* it appears only twice in James, once in a context that indicates the kind of vacillation, discouragement, and doubt that Hermas attributes to it (1:8),[200] and another in the context of a call to conversion for the person caught between the two spirits (4:8).[201] Another similarity is that both James and *Hermas* have a deep concern for the poor and needy and a mistrust of the rich, but in *Hermas* the mistrust of the rich is tempered by reminder and exhortation to their responsibility (*Vis.* 3.9; *Man.* 2.4; *Sim.* 2), whereas in James the condemnation of the rich is never compromised by a suggestion that they are important to the community.[202]

Yet another similarity is the concern about the interrelationship between faith and works, though the theme lacks in *Hermas* the vigor of debate that it has in Jas 2:14–26.[203] A similar concern is present, but is a common theme of Hellenistic Jewish ethos. A comparable expression about the indwelling spirit of God occurs in Jas 4:5 (quoted from an unknown scripture) and in *Man.* 3.1 and elsewhere in *Hermas.*[204] Brox gives an impressive list of similarities, but concludes, as do most others, that they are insufficient to prove literary dependence.[205] Both writings reflect the common world of Hellenistic Jewish moral instruction.

There has been great controversy over the literary relationship of *Hermas, Barnabas,* the *Didache,* and the *Doctrina Apostolorum,* with respect to their use of Two Ways moral instruction and the appearance of literary

197 See discussions in Harold R. Willoughby, *Pagan Regeneration: A Study of the Mystery Initiations in the Graeco-Roman World* (Chicago: University of Chicago Press, 1929) 199–202; Joly (48–51) and Snyder (17–18, with bibliography), and especially Hilhorst ("Hermas," 694–96).

198 Koester, *Introduction* 2. 258; idem, *Synoptische Überlieferung bei den apostolischen Vätern* (TU 65; Berlin: Akademie-Verlag, 1957). See the about-face of Joly, to the negative, from the first to the second edition of his commentary (46, 414–15).

199 E.g., Matt 19:24; Mark 9:47; Luke 13:29; John 3:5; *Sim.* 9.12.3–4, 8, 13.2, 15.2, 16.2–4, 20.2–3, 29.2.

200 Dibelius-Greeven (*James,* 31) consider *Mandate 9* to be the best commentary on Jas 1:5–8.

201 See sections 3.2 and 3.3 below.

202 Osiek, *Rich and Poor,* 32–38, 56.

203 Snyder (15) lists the principal locations in *Hermas*

that evoke James: *Vis.* 3.6.1; *Man.* 10.1.4–5; *Sim.* 8.9.1, 10.3, 19.2, 21.2.

204 Especially *Man.* 5.2.5–7; cf. Dibelius-Greeven, *James,* 223–24.

205 Pages 46–47. The same conclusion is reached by Dibelius-Greeven, *James,* 31–32.

206 F. X. Funk, "Die Doctrina apostolorum," *ThQ* 66 (1884) 381–402; idem, "Didache und Barnabasbrief," *ThQ* 87 (1905) 161–79.

207 By J. Armitage Robinson, *Barnabas, Hermas, and the Didache* (London: SPCK, 1920). His position was that *Barnabas* was the original Two Ways text. Any argument for one of these Christian texts as the original Two Ways text was later disproved by the discovery of 1QS at Qumran.

208 The history of the investigation is now conveniently summarized by John S. Kloppenborg in "The Transformation of Moral Exhortation in *Didache*

parallels. Most of the discussion has concerned not so much *Hermas* as the other three, where there are striking parallels, so much so that it has been argued both that the *Didache* is the original Two Ways text, on which *Barnabas* depends,[206] and vice versa,[207] and that the *Doctrina* is a Latin translation of the *Didache*.[208] The consensus now is that all depend on some earlier Two Ways document.

Whatever the relationship between *Barnabas* and the *Didache*, the Two Ways material in them and in *Hermas* is not of a kind of parallelism to suggest literary dependence, except in one instance, *Did*. 1.5 and *Man*. 2.4–6. There the sequence of three connections, at a few points with identical language, is notable. The context is exhortation to generosity to the needy. First, in different language, comes the appeal to give to all who ask, without discrimination. Then comes the reason: because God (*Hermas*) or the Father (*Didache*) wishes (good things) to be given to all from God's (or the giver's)[209] gifts. The third connection, in the same order, is that the giver is ἀθῷος ("innocent").[210] Within the passage, however, there is a great deal of verbal variance, while maintaining the same sequence of ideas. The best conclusion to draw is that there is a common written, or perhaps even oral, source behind the appearance of this one cluster of ideas in the two teachings on the Two Ways in these two otherwise quite different texts.

One more early Christian movement must be discussed in relationship to *Hermas*: that of Elchasai, of whom only fragmentary sources remain.[211] According to the remaining information given by Hippolytus, Epiphanius, and Eusebius, a man named Elchasai in the third year of Trajan (101 CE) began to proclaim in or near Parthia a new forgiveness of sin based on repeated baptism, in anticipation of some form of apocalyptic chaos. The original language of the preaching and written text was probably Aramaic.[212] Forgiveness of sin focused on adultery, fornication, and incest, but also included other sins. Apostasy was not one of them: as long as internal confession of the heart did not waver, external denial under pressure was understandable. Prayer should be done facing Jerusalem. At the time of Callistus, bishop of Rome (c. 220 CE), Alcibiades of Apamea, a disciple, brought the teaching of Elchasai to Rome, and c. 247, Origen spoke against its recent arrival at Caesarea.

Certainly there are some similarities with aspects of *Hermas*, even leading one scholar to conclude that Elchasai could actually *be* Hermas.[213] More likely, both are witnesses to currents of common Jewish-Christian traditions. Obviously the call to the possibility of a second forgiveness is shared by the two authors, though Hermas does not include further baptisms than an original one. The dismissal of public apostasy as an unforgiv-

1–5," in C. N. Jefford, ed., *The* Didache *in Context: Essays on Its Text, History, and Transmission* (NovTSup 77; Leiden/New York/Cologne: Brill, 1995) 88–109 (88–92).

209 Ἐκ τῶν ἰδίων can be understood either way. For the *Didache*, Jean-Paul Audet (*La Didachè: Instructions des Apôtres* [Paris: Lecoffre, 1958] 227) translates "ses propres dons" ("one's own gifts"); likewise Aelred Cody ("The *Didache*: An English Translation," in C. N. Jefford, ed., *The* Didache *in Context: Essays on Its Text, History, and Transmission* [NovTSup 77; Leiden: Brill, 1995] 5), "the gifts that have been freely given to them." Translators of *Hermas* have tended to take the other interpretation: "of his own bounties" (Lake, 73); "from his own gifts" (Snyder, 66); "was ja seine Gabe sind" (Brox, 193); "that his own gifts be given" (Osiek). Joly's translation is (perhaps deliberately) ambiguous: "de ses propres largesses" (149).

210 See discussion at *Man*. 2.4–5 below, where Greek terminology is given.

211 The sources are: Hippolytus *Ref*. 9.13–17; Epiphanius *Pan*. 19; 30; Eusebius *Hist. eccl*. 6.38 (testimony of Origen). For further discussion: Luigi

Cirillo, *Elchasai e gli elchasaiti: Un contributo alla storia delle comunità giudeo-cristiane* (Università degli studi della Calabria, Centro interdipartimentale di scienze religiose, Studi e Ricerche 1; Cosenza: Marra, 1984); Gerard P. Luttikhuizen, *The Revelation of Elchasai* (Texte und Studien zum Antiken Judentum 8; Tübingen: Mohr/Siebeck, 1985).

212 The Greek name Ἠλχασαί (Hippolytus) or Ἠλξαί (Epiphanius) derives from Aramaic חיל כסי, "hidden power." The written text was dedicated to the Σοβιαί, the "baptized," from צבע (Hippolytus *Ref*. 9.13.1). The special prayer in mystical words which followers were directed to say is readable from the middle outwards as an Aramaic acrostic meaning "I am witness over you on the day of the great judgment" (J. Irmscher in *NTApoc* 2. 689).

213 Hahneman, *Muratorian Fragment*, 38. The only way to reconcile this identification with the given chronology would be to place Hermas in the Eastern Mediterranean, which Hahneman does.

able sin seems to echo *Sim.* 9.26.5, in which forgiveness is held out to those who have done it but have kept their intentions pure.[214] The most interesting parallel is Elchasai's vision of the Son of God as an angel of great height.[215] He is accompanied by a female figure of similar height who is identified as the Holy Spirit, an aspect shared not with *Hermas,* but with *Asc. Isa.* 9.33–10.4,[216] and a parallel relationship implied between the two in *Sim.* 5.2.7.

Any possible direct contact between Hermas and Elchasai would be impossible on the basis of the given chronology and the usual assumptions about Hermas' location. If Hermas is in Italy and Elchasai's teaching did not reach there until the early third century, there is no possible connection. However, there is no way of knowing if the preserved information about the dissemination of Elchasai's teaching is correct. Why would it have taken over a century to reach Rome? There is every possibility—but no evidence—that in fact Elchasai's doctrines

may have reached Rome earlier. Given the echoes of the same motifs that arise in other works of the same period, however, it is equally feasible that we are dealing with popular religious symbols, spread throughout the Mediterranean in Jewish and Jewish-Christian circles more by oral teaching than by written documents. These motifs then surface here and there in the preserved documents that reflect what was being popularly taught and believed.

3 Theological Character

3.1 Metanoia

Though some have raised doubts,[217] most scholars conclude that μετάνοια is the major theme or concern in *Hermas.*[218] But much depends on what is understood by the term. One major line of interpretation assumes that behind the author's preoccupation lie the beginnings of a church discipline of penitence.[219] Such an assumption is unfounded. But to say that μετάνοια is the central

---

214 There is a subtle difference as given in Epiphanius *Pan.* 19.1.8–9, however. Hermas calls such apostates destroyers of their own souls, useless wild vines, certainly implying that sin is involved—yet there is the possibility of forgiveness if they have not denied from the heart (*Sim.* 9.26.3–5). Elchasai, at least according to Epiphanius, says that such denial is not a sin; but this could be Epiphanius' misunderstanding.

215 Hippolytus *Ref.* 9.13.1–3; cf. *Gos. Pet.* 40; *Sim.* 8.1.2; 9.6.1; sections 3.3 and 3.4 of the Introduction, below; comment below on 8.1.2.

216 The female gender of the Holy Spirit is not explicit in *Asc. Isa.,* but is not unusual in early Christian literature that originates in a Semitic language, in which the word for spirit is feminine. Cf. *Odes of Solomon* 19.2, 4–5.

217 Lage Pernveden, *The Concept of the Church in the Shepherd of Hermas* (Studia Theologica Lundensia 27; Lund: Gleerup, 1966) 298, in explicit reaction to Dibelius, 423; also Edith McEwan Humphrey, *The Ladies and the Cities: Transformation and Apocalyptic Identity in Joseph and Aseneth, 4 Ezra, the Apocalypse and the Shepherd of Hermas* (JSPSS 17; Sheffield: Sheffield Academic Press, 1995) 135–48, 155, with good survey of opinions.

218 The distribution of terms is as follows:

	Visions	Mandates	Similitudes
μετάνοια	7	15	33
μετανοεῖν	15	16	62
paenitentia			8
Total	22	31	103

Grand Total: 156

as counted by Ingrid Goldhahn-Müller (*Die Grenze der Gemeinde*), 245. The largest concentrations are in *Vision 3* (12 of 22), *Mandate 4* (20 of 31), and *Similitudes 8* and *9* (45 and 32 of 95, respectively). But this is not surprising: with the exception of *Mandate 4*, these are the longest sections of the book. General discussion in Dibelius, 510–13; Paramelle, "Hermas," 327–31; Snyder, 69–71; M. A. Molina, "La penitencia en el Pastor de Hermas," *Mayéutica* 6 (1980) 63–70; Brox, 476–85.

219 Pernveden, for instance, understands it so, even as he rejects it (*Concept of the Church*, 298). The major studies in this direction are: Adhémar D'Alès, *L'édit de Calliste. Études sur les origines de la pénitence chrétienne* (Paris: Beauchesne, 1914); Bernhard Poschmann, *Paenitentia Secunda: Die kirchliche Busse im ältesten Christentum bis Cyprian und Origenes* (Theophaneia 1; Bonn: Hanstein, 1940) 134–205; idem, *Penance and the Anointing of the Sick* (New York: Herder and Herder, 1964) 26–35; Joseph Grotz, *Die Entwicklung des Busstufenwesens in der vornicänischen Kirche* (Freiburg: Herder, 1955) 13–70; Karl Rahner, "The Penitential Teaching of the Shepherd of Hermas," *Theological Investigations* 15 (New York: Crossroad, 1982) 57–113; Goldhahn-Müller (*Die Grenze der Gemeinde*, 226–88), who breaks with the traditional interpretation.

message does not presuppose a discipline of penance; this distinction is often blurred by commentators.[220] The attitude of repentance is a fundamental Jewish and Christian value. It does not in itself require any ritual or ecclesiastical discipline of reincorporation.

Another problem involved is the theology of repentance in the early church. While 1 John 1:6–2:2 and 5:15–18 seem to equivocate over whether sin after baptism is forgivable, Heb 6:4–6 and 10:26–31 take the position that it is not. *Hermas* reaffirms the ideal that only those newly called, not the already baptized, have another chance (*Man.* 4.3.1–7). Previously, he had announced with heavenly authority the possibility of forgiveness for the baptized—but only once and in eschatological context (*Vis.* 2.2.4–5). If this teaching is seen as compromising the original disciplinary rigor of Hebrews, then *Hermas* can be seen as a step along the way of moral decline after the pristine earlier ideals. Alternatively, the author stands in a tradition that always offered repentance to the baptized, especially in eschatological perspective. He could also represent a middle position that uses eschatological expectation as the occasion to proclaim an exceptional "jubilee" release from sin.[221]

Hermas attempts, as does already the author of 1 John, to hold in tension the ideal that there be no necessity of forgiveness after baptism with the reality that there is.[222] The same teachers who teach no repentance after baptism to catechumens also preach repentance to baptized sinners, not by insincerity or deception, but by adjustment to this reality.[223] The church, all the while maintaining the integrity of baptism, did not wish to make baptism a greater obstacle to salvation.[224] The central problem is not one of church discipline, but of anthropology: the problem of the sinning Christian.[225] Seen in the perspective of those caught between ideal and reality, there is a tension but not a contradiction. The change envisioned is not a ritual or repetitive action, but a fundamental personal change.[226] Though it may have to be repeated, the underlying conviction is that it is permanent.

This is the reason why consistently throughout this commentary, the word $\mu\epsilon\tau\acute{\alpha}\nu o\iota\alpha$ is translated not by the usual "repentance" but by "conversion." The English "repentance," like the most frequent German translation "Busse,"[227] the French "pénitence,"[228] and even less so the Latin *paenitentia* (*Sim.* 9.33.3, etc.), does not convey

---

220　See discussion in Humphrey, *Ladies and the Cities*, 135, quoting two of the misconceptions, by Pernveden and Barnard.

221　The three alternatives and their advocates are laid out by Goldhahn-Müller, *Die Grenze der Gemeinde*, 241–42.

222　The position of Snyder, 69–71. See further comment below on *Vis.* 2.2.4–5; *Man.* 4.3.1–7.

223　Poschmann, *Paenitentia Secunda*, 165–66. There has long been a theory espoused by some (since first set forward by D'Alès, *L'édit de Calliste*, 52–113) that the no-repentance message was intended only for catechumens, the possibility of repentance only to baptized sinners. See discussion with bibliography in Snyder, 70, but rejected by him. Most recently, Henne (*L'unité*, 91–139) espouses a theory that some parts of *Hermas* are intended for catechumens and others for the baptized.

224　P. Battifol, "L'église naissante. Hermas et le problème moral au second siècle," *RB* 10 (1901) 337–51 [351].

225　Arthur W. Strock, "The Shepherd of Hermas: A Study of His Anthropology as Seen in the Tension bewteen Dipsychia and Hamartia" (Ph.D. diss., Emory University, 1984). For a brief discussion of the term in non-Christian literature, see John T. Fitzgerald and L. Michael White, *The Tabula of Cebes*

(SBLTT 24; Graeco-Roman Religion Series 7; Chico, CA: Scholars Press, 1983) 144 n. 40; 165 n. 105.

226　Rahner sums it up well: "Just as one cannot love truly without excluding in the act of love the thought that it could be revoked and come to an end, so one cannot repent of one's guilt before the unconditioned that is God if this sorrow is not intended as irrevocable and once and for all. Only from the outside and by one who is not involved can it be said that it could happen often" ("Penitential Teaching," 82–83).

227　"Bekehrung" is closer to the meaning of conversion as used here, but is seldom employed with regard to *Hermas*. Brox (484, following Hans A. Frei, "Metanoia im 'Hirten' des Hermas" [*Internationale kirchliche Zeitschrift* 64 (1974) 118–39, 189–202; 65 (1975) 120–138, 176–204] [65:183]) admits that "Busse" may be anachronistic and lead to misunderstanding, but does not offer an alternative. For Frei, $\mu\epsilon\tau\acute{\alpha}\nu o\iota\alpha$ is not a technical term for penance, but for the gift of God's mercy; its future orientation means taking on the search for holiness (64:189–202; 65:120–38).

228　Henne, too, recognizes that a better French word would be "conversion" (*L'unité*, 114).

the profound change of heart envisioned and pleaded for by Hermas. It is not a question of ritual or repeated action, not a discipline or an expectation, but personal and corporate transformation through the power of the good spirit, which necessitates new commitments for the future, not only the eschatological future, but the immediate historical future as well.[229] The best image for what the author intends is the old woman church who becomes younger as the process of transformation takes shape (*Vis.* 3.10–13). The narrative contains all the elements of surprise, delight, reenergizing, and future expectation.

The rejuvenated woman is the symbol of the whole church, which experiences conversion together. It is therefore incomprehensible that some commentators see in *Hermas* a move into individualist ethics, seemingly mistaking a move from public, national, and political to private, domestic, or nonpolitical for a move from communal to individualist.[230] True, the revelation is given to one person, but that characteristic is common to nearly all apocalyptic literature. The concerns are not with a broad sweep of history but with the daily life of the faithful. But the seer is deputed immediately to communicate the revelation to the church (*Vis.* 2.4.3). The paraenesis is consistently addressed to persons in the plural. The various visions of the church, from the tower and building stones to the twelve mountains, are of a collective society in which each unit is part of the whole. The concern for the doing of justice toward others recurs regularly. The very last admonition in the book is to help those who suffer (*Sim.* 10.2–4). The whole purpose of the book is the dissemination of a message of conversion to all believers. It is not a philosophical discussion on virtue, as is the case, for instance, with its probable contemporary, the *Tabula of Cebes*. Rather, it is a "how to" book of instruction for Christian believers in community.

The social function of *Hermas* is to maintain the close integration of Christian faith and life, to keep attitudes and especially behavior consonant with articulated beliefs. This is probably one reason that the book is long on ethical teaching and short on what is usually recognized as theology. In fact, the eclectic theology of the book reinforces the conviction of the author that the best theology is that written on the heart of believers and communicated through eyes, speech, hands, and feet. Without the message of the possibility of further conversion after that of baptism, there would be no incentive for the alienated to rejoin the community.[231] As it is, the author is able to realize his goal of reinforcing and re-creating the holiness of the community, especially in its members' dealings with each other. *Metanoia,* change of heart, makes that possible.

3.2 Dipsychia

Διψυχία ("double-soulness" or "doublemindedness") and its related verb and adjective occur 55 times in *Hermas*: διψυχία ("doublemindedness") 16 times, διψυχεῖν ("to be doubleminded") 20 times, and δίψυχος ("doubleminded") 19 times—as contrasted to a total of 10 times in all other early Christian literature up to this time.[232] The expression may derive from the Hebrew ולב

---

229 "La *metanoia*, que prêche le *Pasteur,* est un sentiment, une attitude, une activité complexe qui renferme en soi, avec le regret du passé et le ferme propos pour l'avenir, un changement d'âme, un renouvellement moral, une transformation de toute la vie. En un mot, c'est une vraie conversion" ("The *metanoia* that *Hermas* preaches is a conviction, an attitude, a complex activity that contains, along with past regret and a firm purpose for the future, a change of soul, a moral renewal, a transformation of the whole of life. In brief, it is a true conversion") (Paramelle, "Hermas," 328).

230 E.g., for Dibelius (485–86, 490) apocalyptic terrors are individualized and human fate is held in balance not at the end time but at an individual's death; so too Brox, 162, 168, 170–71, 471; Leutzsch, *Wahrnehmung,* 207.

231 Lampe, *Stadtrömische Christen,* 75–76.

232 Jas 1:8; 4:8; *Did.* 4.4 par. *Barn.* 19.5; *1 Clem.* 11.2; 23.2–3; *2 Clem.* 11.2 (a parallel to *1 Clem.* 23.3); *2 Clem.* 23.5; 19.2. Discussion in Oscar J. F. Seitz, "Relationship of the Shepherd of Hermas to the Epistle of James," *JBL* 63 (1944) 131–40; idem, "Antecedents and Signification of the Term ΔΙΨΥΧΟΣ," *JBL* 66 (1947) 211–19; "Afterthoughts on the Term Dipsychos," *NTS* 5 (1959–1960) 327–34; C. Gilmour, "Religious Vacillation and Indecision: Doublemindedness as the Opposite of Faith: A Study of *Dipsychos* and Its Cognates in the *Shepherd of Hermas* and Other Early Christian Literature," *Prudentia* 16 (1984) 33–42; Brox, 551–53.

233 1 Chron 12:33 (the LXX [v. 34] ἑτεροκλινῶς is difficult, but Vg. *in corde duplici* ["with double heart"]); Ps 12:2, LXX literally translated ἐν καρδίᾳ καὶ καρδίᾳ; Sir 1:28 LXX ἐν καρδίᾳ δισσῇ ("in double

לב,[233] which, however, seems to have more to do with human dealings with one another. In some of the Christian references the word group more closely approximates its meaning in *Hermas,* that is, having to do with one's relationship to God.[234]

Here, the key is the discussion in *Mandate* 9, where it becomes clear that for our author the struggle of the doubleminded is not the moral struggle between good and evil, as it is, for instance in *T. Ash.* 1–4, or between honesty and dishonesty, but between trust or lack of trust in God. It is "a divided allegiance . . . doubt, uncertainty with regard to God and salvation, and with regard to their own affairs."[235] The doubleminded one hesitates to ask anything from God because of previous sinfulness (v. 1), but is reassured that God does not keep grudges (vv. 2–3), and is encouraged to have the confidence to ask boldly and without hesitation (ἀδιστάκτως), the opposite of doublemindedness, and therefore to choose faith which has power and to abandon doubt which is powerless.[236] Doublemindedness is the fate of the person caught between the two spirits, not with a clear-cut distinction between good and evil, but in that the spirit at work in the doubleminded is a spirit of discouragement

and doubt.[237] This discouragement necessarily then overflows into the rest of one's life, causing disruptions such as dissension (*Sim.* 8.9.4) and unwillingness to act justly (*Sim.* 8.8.1–3).[238] But the starting point is not deeds; it is lack of trust in God. The doubleminded are drawn to the false prophet of *Mandate* 11 because they are kindred spirits: not demonic or evil, just earthly and empty.[239]

3.3 Pneumatology/Angelology and the Two Ways

The world of *Hermas* is inhabited by many spirits, both good and evil. For some, this is evidence of the pre-Christian or non-Christian origin of much of its teaching material.[240] The foundation for teaching on the two spirits is the Two Ways tradition of moral teaching. There is now consensus on the pre-Qumran Jewish origins of this tradition, probably with Iranian influence, though the more general theme of two paths, perhaps even of two spirits, is also known in Greco-Roman context.[241] The Two Ways theme is a "natural rhetorical device" that places patterns of behavior and values in sharp contrast to each other for the sake of highlighting the contrast. The typical pattern includes a sharply dualistic introduc-

---

heart") is probably the same. See also *1 Enoch* 91.4; *T. Ash.* 1.3–6.2; *T. Benj.* 6.5-7. In its Greek form, however, it may have originated in Christian use: Stanley Porter, "Is *dipsuchos* (James 1,8; 4,8) a 'Christian' Word?" *Bib* 71 (1990) 469–98.

234 Especially Jas 1:8; *1 Clem.* 11.2; 23.2–3; *2 Clem.* 11.2, 5.

235 J. Reiling, *Hermas and Christian Prophecy: A Study of the Eleventh Mandate* (NovTSup 37; Leiden: Brill, 1973) 22–32.

236 Dibelius-Greeven (*James,* 81) draw attention to other early Christian texts in which doubt about receiving from God is a hindrance to asking: Mark 2:5; 4:40; 5:34, 36; 9:23–24; Mark 11:23–24 par. Matt 21:21–22, and others.

237 See the next section.

238 Here it is similar to its use in *Did.* 4.4 par. *Barn.* 19.5, where doublemindedness is vacillation about doing good.

239 They have a "pneumatological affinity" (Reiling, *Hermas and Christian Prophecy,* 33).

240 For Dibelius (517–19), the teaching on the spirits is lightly christianized by adding the Lord to the good spirits and eventually combining all good spirits into one. Brox (217) thinks the teaching is not Christian in origin or quality. In these discussions, what constitutes "Christian" is rarely specified. It

usually means consonant with the canonical Gospels or Paul. Yet compare Luke 9:55–56 var.; Rom 8:15; 1 Cor 2:12; Gal 5:16–25, and in view of the later flowering of a Christian tradition of discernment of spirits, the teaching on the spirits in *Hermas* may be considered very Christian.

241 Charles Taylor, "The Two Ways in Hermas and Xenophon," *Journal of Philology* 21 (1893) 243–58; Pierre Boyancé, "Les deux démons personnels dans l'antiquité grecque et latine," *Revue de philologie, de littérature et d'histoire anciennes* 9 (1935) 189–202; Oscar J. F. Seitz, "Two Spirits in Man: An Essay in Biblical Exegesis," *NTS* 6 (1959–1960) 82–95; S. Vernon McCasland, "The Black One," in A. Wikgren, ed., *Early Christian Origins: Studies in Honor of Harold R. Willoughby* (Chicago: Quadrangle, 1961) 77–80; M. Jack Suggs, "The Christian Two Ways Tradition: Its Antiquity, Form, and Function," in D. E. Aune, ed., *Studies in the New Testament and Early Christian Literature: Essays in Honor of Allen P. Wikgren* (NovTSup 33; Leiden: Brill, 1972) 60–74; C. Haas, "Die Pneumatologie des 'Hirten des Hermas,'" *ANRW* 2. 27.1 (1993) 552–86. Pedro Lluis-Font ("Sources de la doctrine d'Hermas sur les deux esprits," *Revue d'ascétique et de mystique* 39 [1963] 83–98) at an earlier date argued for the Qumran origin of the teaching. For

tion, lists of vices and virtues, sometimes greatly expanded into commentary, and a concluding eschatological admonition.[242] The teaching form is a means of concretizing and legitimating a popular understanding of the divisiveness of human existence and moral choice. In some cases, it serves to delineate the social separation of believers from nonbelievers, as in 1QS 3.13–4.26, but in *Hermas* both spirits and thus both behavioral tendencies reside in believers, though the author would certainly expect the good spirit to dominate there. There is no way to tell whether the ethical teaching of the Two Ways is prior to its casting as the competition between spirits, but the earlier literary evidence points in that direction.[243]

The Two Ways moral tradition does not necessitate a teaching on two spirits. In Matt 7:13–14 the alternatives are simply set forth, and in *Didache* 1–6, for instance, the Two Ways teaching ascribes the tendencies toward good or evil to the hearts of the listeners.[244] But personification of the Two Ways as two spirits competing for the human heart is consonant with ancient anthropology and cosmology, and fills the need to attribute external personal causality to human tendencies, so that the responsibility of the individual becomes more diffused and generalized. Thus *Barn.* 18.1–2 assigns angels of light and darkness to preside over the Two Ways, and the *Community Rule* of Qumran (1QS 4.23) assigns the tendencies to two spirits resident in the human heart. Presiding over cosmic elements and human religious functions is a common use of angels in Jewish intertestamental literature.[245]

The distinction between spirits and angels in this context is a fine one, if it exists at all. In *Barn.* 18.1–2, the two angels in charge of the Two Ways seem external to humans, but in 1QS 4.23 the two spirits (רוחי) are resident in persons. In *Man.* 5.1–2, the indwelling spirits (πνεύματα) lead persons in one direction or the other; in *Man.* 6.2, they are angels (ἄγγελοι) of justice and evil; in *Man.* 12.1–3, the author speaks of good and evil desires that are the human responses to the operation of these spirits. Later, virtues personified as women are identified as holy spirits (*Sim.* 9.13.2, 15.2). Their negative counterparts, named as vices, should also be understood as moralized spirits (9.15.3). In *Hermas,* the human person is inhabited by one or other kind of spirit. Both cannot coexist in the same person (*Man.*

the Two Ways at Qumran, see 1QS 3.13–4.26. For its appearance in Philo, *Q. Exod.* 1.23; cf. *Sacr. AC* 20–34; Marc Philonenko, "Philon d'Alexandrie et l'instruction sur les deux esprits," in A. Caquot et al., ed., *Hellenica et Judaica: Hommage à Valentin Nikiprowetzky* זיל (Leuven/Paris: Peeters, 1986) 61–68. Willy Rordorf ("Un chapitre d'éthique judéo-chrétienne: les deux voies," *RechSR* 60 [1972] 109–28; ET "An Aspect of the Judeo-Christian Ethic: The Two Ways," in J. A. Draper, ed., *The Didache in Modern Research* [Leiden: Brill, 1996] 148–64), traces later use of the Two Ways as far as medieval monasticism. In rabbinic discussions, the two "impulses" (יצרים), the bad (יצר הרע) and the good (יצר הטוב), are inclinations in the human heart. Cf. *T. Ash.* 1–4; *T. Jud.* 20.1–2; *2 Enoch* 30.15.

242 M. Jack Suggs, "The Christian Two Ways Tradition: Its Antiquity, Form, and Function," in D. E. Aune, ed., *Studies in the New Testament and Early Christian Literature: Essays in Honor of Allen P. Wikgren* (NovTSup 33; Leiden: Brill, 1972) 60–74 (63–64). Compare Gal 5:16–25.

243 See Deut 30:15–20; Josh 24:15; Jer 21:8–10; Sir 15:16–17.

244 But the *Doctrina Apostolorum,* a Greek text preserved only in Latin translation that is in close literary relationship with the *Didache,* immediately adds after the initial introduction of the Two Ways that an angel is set in each way, one of good, the other of evil (*in his constituti sunt angeli duo, unus aequitatis, alter iniquitatis*). Text and introduction in Willy Rordorf and André Tuilier, eds., *La Doctrine des douze Apôtres (Didachè)* (SC 248; Paris: Éditions du Cerf, 1978) 203–10. Yet the fourth-century *Apostolic Constitutions,* with probable literary dependence on the *Didache,* does not (*Ap. Const.* 7.1–3, 18).

245 Angels are responsible for instruction (*1 Enoch* 60.10–11 and many other places); for intercession and mediation (*T. Lev.* 5.6; more refs. in *OTP* 1. 790 note d); for recording human deeds (*Apoc. Zeph.* 3.6–9); for punishment of people (*1 Enoch* 56.1; 66.1; *2 Enoch* 10.3; *T. Abr.* 12.1–3; *Apoc. Zeph.* 4.1–7; cf. *Sim.* 6.3.2; 7.1–2). Cf. Harald B. Kuhn, "The Angelology of the Non-Canonical Jewish Apocalypses," *JBL* 67 (1948) 217–32.

246 Hermas' idea of the indwelling spirits is one of the most "animist" or "materialist" interpretations of the presence of the spirits in the human person as in a container (e.g., *Man.* 5.2.5–7), reflective of popular Stoicism (José P. Martín, "Espíritu y dualismo de espíritus en el Pastor de Hermas y su relación con el judaísmo," *Vetera christianorum* 15 [1978] 295–345 [323–24]).

5.2.5–7). Persons are, therefore, the battleground between the two kinds of spirits and the proving ground of their effectiveness.[246]

Each kind of spirit yields a specific set of results in human behavior, and therefore by these results, it is clear which spirit is operative. This early Christian treatise on the discernment of spirits (*Mandates* 5–6 especially) is one of the most concrete.[247] The clearest sign of the presence of the good spirit is joy,[248] and of the evil spirit, sadness or discouragement (λύπη).

There are other spirits/angels besides those who inhabit people, however. The Shepherd is really an angel, the angel of conversion (ὁ ἄγγελος τῆς μετανοίας, *Vis.* 5.7; *Sim.* 9.14.3, 33.1). There is an angel of punishment (ὁ ἄγγελος τῆς τιμωρίας, *Sim.* 6.3.2; 7.1–2). The four, then six, young men who first accompany the woman church, then begin to build the tower (*Vis.* 1.4.1; 3.1.6–7), and later direct others in the building are the six chief angels who accompany the lord of the tower at his visitation (*Sim.* 9.6).[249] The mysterious "most-honored" angel, the great angel, is of supernatural height, a motif common to other Jewish and Jewish-Christian depictions of principal figures.[250] The name Michael is given only once to a figure possibly to be identified with this great angel, at least some of the time.[251]

The Holy Spirit is not always a distinctive figure, but one of the many good spirits of God. Translation may skew the meaning by capitalization when a more generic reference is intended. As in 1 Corinthians 2–3, it is difficult to know. In the Christian and possibly contemporary *Ascension of Isaiah,* the "angel of the Holy Spirit" joins Michael to assist Jesus at the resurrection,[252] and is a guide on the way for followers of Jesus to ascend to the triadic vision in heaven. This spirit is to be worshiped with Christ, but ultimately the Holy Spirit and Christ worship God together.[253] Since other angels are not to be worshiped, it can only be concluded that there the "angel of the Holy Spirit" is really the Holy Spirit itself.

In *Hermas,* there is a spirit that catches up the author in ecstasy (*Vis.* 1.1.3; 2.2.1), a holy spirit that inhabits the faithful (*Man.* 5.1.2, 2.5; *Sim.* 5.6.5–7) who is exhausted by sadness and bitterness (*Man.* 10.1.2, 2.1–6), and a divine spirit (τὸ πνεῦμα τὸ θεῖον) or holy spirit who is the inspiration of true prophecy (*Man.* 11.7–9, 12) and of apostles and teachers (*Sim.* 9.25.2). In some contexts, the term "holy spirit" is probably a general term for one of the many spirits that come from God and do God's work. There are other contexts, however, in which something more must be meant. Examples include *Sim.* 5.6.5, in which the preexistent Holy Spirit dwells in human flesh, or *Sim.* 9.1.1, where the Shepherd reveals that it was the Holy Spirit who spoke to Hermas in the form of the church. In these passages, a particular theological designation must be intended: that Spirit which is closest to God and is the most authoritative representative of God. This kind of ambiguity is not surprising in a text whose author seems to feel little need for theological consistency.

The world of *Hermas* is inhabited by hosts of intermediary spirits, as was common in popular Greco-Roman and Jewish cosmology of the time. Some of them

---

247 "Un petit traité du discernement des esprits, le plus ancien connu" ("a little treatise on the discernment of spirits, the oldest known") (Paramelle, "Hermas," 324). Further discussion: Gustave Bardy, "Discernement des esprits II. Chez les pères," *Dictionnaire de spiritualité* 3 (Paris: Beauchesne, 1957) 1222–91; Jean Daniélou, "Démon: démonologie chrétienne primitive," ibid., 154–89; Günter Switek, "'Discretio Spirituum.' Ein Beitrag zur Geschichte der Spiritualität," *Theologie und Philosophie* 47 (1972) 36–76; Joseph T. Lienhard, "On 'Discernment of Spirits' in the Early Church," *TS* 41 (1980) 505–29.

248 Some form of ἱλαρότης (joy) appears 33 times, its synonym χαρά three times, and its Latin synonym *gaudium* twice. Hermas, the woman church, hearers, people, sheep (*Sim.* 6.2.3), even plants (*Sim.* 9.1.8;

24.1), mountain (*Sim.* 9.1.10), and tower plaza (*Sim.* 9.10.3) rejoice at various points. For Hermas, sadness is unchristian (Brox, 248).

249 Compare Philo *Fug.* 18.94–95; *Migr. Abr.* 32.181.

250 *Sim.* 8.1.2 (see comment there); 9.6.1; see Ambrose Moyo, "Angels and Christology in the Shepherd of Hermas" (Ph.D. diss., Harvard University, 1978) 100–107.

251 See comment on *Sim.* 8.3.3. Michael is not to be identified with the Son of God: see Pernveden, *Concept of the Church,* 58–62.

252 *Asc. Isa.* 3.16–17. Compare *Gos. Pet.* 40.

253 *Asc. Isa.* 7.23; 9.18, 36, 40.

are messengers and intermediaries between God and humanity, often in very personal and individualized contexts, as is the case with some of the angelic characters in the text, especially the Shepherd. Many of these are called at one point or another "men" or "young men" rather than angels or spirits. Others are spirits that are capable of inhabiting persons and inspiring them—though not forcing them against their will—to act in a given way. Others are good spirits who are personifications of virtues, as are the twelve young women around the tower, or of vices, as are the women in black clothing, both groups usually referred to as "young women" or "women" in the ninth *Similitude*.[254] Given the way in which the whole text probably developed by oral, then written accretion, it is not to be supposed that the entire list of identifications of given characters was present in the mind of the author all at once; for example, the young women may have originally been intended to be only allegorical figures, then spirits, then personified virtues. To try to distinguish sharply between allegorical figures, spirits, and angels is to do violence to the elusive nature of the imagery.

A problem remains: the relationship of the Son of

God to the angelic population. To this we now turn.

3.4 Christology

The name Jesus never occurs in *Hermas,* and the title Christ appears only three times in very dubious manuscript variants,[255] though there are a number of references to "the name," either of God or of the Son.[256] The omission of the personal name or title is puzzling, and may occur because of reverential avoidance.[257] Throughout *Hermas,* however, there is an authority figure lurking in the background who is variously identified as the highest or the most distinguished angel (*Vis.* 5.2; *Man.* 5.1.7; *Sim.* 7.1–3; 9.1.3, etc.). At one point, but only one, the same figure seems to be identified as Michael (*Sim.* 8.3.3).[258] At other points, the supreme angelic figure seems to be identical with the Son of God. An angel christology would not be new: it has even been argued that it is the earliest Christology.[259] It is well known that Justin and others after him repeatedly exegeted passages of the Hebrew Scriptures by identifying Christ with biblical angelic appearances.[260] Hebrews 1–2 may be a repudiation of such a christology. Nevertheless, the position of Christ or the Son of Man with regard to the angels in

---

254 The young women who represent the good are called spirits, necessary for entrance into the reign of God (*Sim.* 9.13.2). Later, they are called by the names of virtues (9.15.2). In the next verse (9.15.3), the women in black are given the names of vices. If the women-virtues are spirits, it can be inferred that the women-vices are also.

255 *Vis.* 2.2.8; 3.6.6; *Sim.* 9.18.1.

256 See discussion at *Vis.* 2.2.8, below.

257 Suggested by J. Christian Wilson (*Five Problems in the Interpretation of the Shepherd of Hermas: Authorship, Genre, Canonicity, Apocalyptic, and the Absence of the Name "Jesus Christ"* [Mellen Biblical Series 34; Lewiston/Queenston/Lampeter: Mellen, 1995] 73–79) on the basis of Jewish custom and the cosmic role of the Son in *Sim.* 9.14.5.

258 This identification, however, comes only in the explanation of the vision of the cosmic tree, in which every element of the vision is assigned a correlation. The tree is already the law, and the law is the Son of God (which does not set the equation that the tree is also the Son of God). It is likely that the identification of the great angel with Michael applies only to this vision (*Sim.* 8.1–2). An identification of Michael with the Son of God is ably refuted by Giet (*Hermas,* 227–28) and Pernveden (*Concept of the Church,* 58–64); see comment below on *Sim.*

8.3.3. It is even possible that the identification of the great angel with Michael here is derived from oral performance: a momentary need to fill in a missing link with a familiar name, or a suggestion from the audience that then becomes part of the recitation.

259 By Martin Werner, *Die Entstehung des christlichen Dogmas problemgeschichtlich dargestellt* (1941; 2d ed., Bern and Tübingen: Haupt, 1953); shortened English version in *The Formation of Christian Dogma: An Historical Study of Its Problem* (London: Black, 1957). Rejections of Werner's thesis soon followed: W. Michaelis, *Zur Engelchristologie im Urchristentum: Abbau der Konstruktion Martin Werners* (Gegenwartsfragen biblischer Theologie 1; Basel: Majer, 1942); Joseph Barbel, *Christos Angelos. Die Anschauung von Christus als Bote und Engel in der gelehrten und volkstümlichen Literatur des christlichen Altertums* (1941; 2d ed., Bonn: Hanstein, 1964); John Reumann, "Martin Werner and 'Angel Christology,'" *Lutheran Quarterly* 8 (1956) 349–58. More positively inclined to accept the prevalence of early angel christology is Christopher Rowland, *The Open Heaven: A Study of Apocalyptic in Judaism and Early Christianity* (New York: Crossroad, 1982) 94–113. Those who rejected Werner's thesis that angel christology was the earliest christology admit

many apocalyptic texts is that of commander-in-chief.[261] In the *Ascension of Isaiah,* the Lord on his descent to historical birth takes the form of an angel at every heavenly level through which he passes (10.17–31). To say that he *takes the form of* an angel, which is actually what Justin also sometimes says, and to say that he *is* an angel is a very fine distinction.

The identification of Michael with the great angel is limited to one passage, and is much in doubt beyond that. But it is much debated whether the Son of God is to be identified with the great angel.[262] Rather than speak of identification, it is probably better to speak of angelomorphism,[263] which would be consonant with the *Ascension of Isaiah* and with Justin. Appearance under different forms is a common motif in *Hermas.* The Son of God appears in the form of an angel, just as the twelve holy spirits who personify virtues appear in the form of young women (*Sim.* 9.13.2), the angels who build the tower appear in the form of young men, or the Holy Spirit appears in the form of the church (*Sim.* 9.1.1).

With regard to the Son's relationship to the spirit world beyond the general question of angelomorphism, the starting point must be the words of the Shepherd in *Sim.* 9.1.1: "I want to show you whatever the Holy Spirit showed you, who spoke with you in the form of the church, because that spirit is the Son of God."[264] This is one of the most frustrating statements in the book. If we were to take it with complete literalness, the woman, the tower, the church, the Holy Spirit, and the Son of God would be all one and the same! But this kind of equation is not meant to be made. Such statements are not metaphysical but symbolic. *Sim.* 9.1.1 draws together the messages of the *Visions* with those of the *Similitudes.* Only by letting each passage and each image stand on its own, without assuming that comparisons made in one are valid in another, can we come to some glimpse of the whole.

The Son of God is the slave or servant (*Sim.* 5.5.2) who faithfully tends the vineyard, gives the law (5.6.3), and is rewarded by filial adoption. He is himself not only lawgiver but God's law given to the world,[265] imaged as a tree whose branches shade the nations that respond (*Sim.* 8.3.2). He is lord and inspector of the tower (*Sim.* 9.6–7). He is rock[266] and door in the rock, foundation of the tower-church and means of access through which all must enter. In that capacity, he preexists his creation (*Sim.* 9.12.2). When put together, this is an impressive list of biblically rooted titles, images, and affirmations about the character and work of the Son of God.

There is not total clarity on the distinction between Son of God and Holy Spirit, as there is in the *Ascension*

---

that this kind of christology did exist, and was a basis for later subordinationist christologies, especially Arianism.

260 Especially *1 Apol.* 62–63; *Dial.* 58; 61; 75–86; 113–14; 125–28; cf. *Gos. Thom.* 13. See Margaret Barker, *The Great Angel: A Study of Israel's Second God* (London: SPCK, 1992) 190–94; Loren T. Stuckenbruck, *Angel Veneration and Christology: A Study in Early Judaism and in the Christology of the Apocalypse of John* (WUNT 2; Tübingen: Mohr/Siebeck, 1995) esp. 138 n. 238; 209 n. 4; Jonathan Knight, *Disciples of the Beloved One: The Christology, Social Setting and Theological Context of the Ascension of Isaiah* (JSPSS 18; Sheffield: Sheffield Academic Press, 1996) 158–63. In Elchasai's vision, the revelation is communicated to him by an angel who is the Son of God, accompanied by a female figure of equal height who is the Holy Spirit (Hippolytus *Ref.* 9.13.1–3).

261 Matt 13:41; 16:27; 25:31; Mark 8:38; 13:27; Luke 9:26; 1 Thess 4:16; 2 Thess 1:7. Cf. Moyo, "Angels and Christology," 133; John J. Collins, "The Son of Man and the Saints of the Most High in the Book of Daniel," *JBL* 93 (1974) 50–66.

262 In the affirmative: Halvor Moxnes, "God and His Angel in the *Shepherd of Hermas,*" *StTh* 28 (1974) 49–56; in the negative: Giet (*Hermas,* 227–28); Pernveden (*Concept of the Church,* 58–64); Snyder (60–61); Moyo ("Angels and Christology," 58–59).

263 Brox, 490–92.

264 For Brox (486), on the other hand, the starting point is the role of the Son of God in the Fifth *Similitude.* But this is a self-contained story, with its own several applications. *Sim.* 9.1.1 is a revelatory statement that refers back to the revelatory agent of the *Visions,* and thus is more comprehensive.

265 See Justin *Dial.* 11; 12; 14; Pernveden, *Concept of the Church,* 42–52.

266 Compare Justin *Dial.* 113–114.

of Isaiah where they work side by side in a complimentary manner. In the parable of the Fifth *Similitude* and its interpretation, there is an awareness of a triad of Father, Spirit, and Son. They are distinct characters with quite different roles to play, slave/adopted son versus full son of the God-figure. Yet, according to the parable, the Holy Spirit is God's original son, the one later called Son of God, the son subsequently becoming the Spirit's brother by an act of God. In *Sim.* 9.1.1, the distinction between the two is blurred. Both are preexistent, agents of creation, at some times more distinct than others (*Sim.* 5.6.5 and 9.1.2).[267] More attention is usually paid, for external theological reasons, to the figure of the Son than to that of the Spirit. Yet the Spirit of God is in *Hermas* the prevailing, polymorphous presence, personified to an unusual degree. Pneumatology is more prominent than christology.

It is clear to the reader that speculative or systematic christology is not the author's goal. All attempts to reconstruct a systematic christology in *Hermas* falter.[268] As in Paul's Letter to the Philippians, christology is at the service of moral teaching and soteriology.[269] The figure of the Son of God is "ecclesio-centrically determined."[270] That is to say, christology is not a central concern, but it serves the paraenetic purpose of building up the church. Nevertheless, a text in which the Son of God preexists creation and appears prominently as servant exalted for his fidelity, as joint heir with the Holy Spirit, as sustainer of the universe, and as inspector of the tower-church, can hardly be said to have no significant christology.

3.5 Ecclesiology

Some would suggest that the two aspects of the church, the heavenly or ideal and the earthly or imperfect, are presented in distinctly different parts of the text: the heavenly origins of the church in *Visions* 1–2, the realized church in *Visions* 3–4;[271] or the ideal church in *Vision* 3 and the real church in *Similitude* 9.[272] Rather, both aspects of the church are represented throughout the ecclesial images. The church is both ideal and real at the same time; this is exactly the point and the particular insight of *Hermas*. At the same time that the church is an eschatological mystery, it is also a community of people, both living and dead (*Vis.* 3.5.1), of mixed spiritual quality, with need for improvement.[273] "Hermas gives us a double vision, always maintaining the tension between the divine and the mundane, the cosmic and the pedestrian, the pure and the tarnished."[274] The associations made in *Sim.* 9.1.1, of woman, tower, church, Holy Spirit, and Son of God, bring together the transcendent and historical aspects of the church.

The woman church can affirm her identity as church (*Vis.* 3.3.3) but must have angelic mediation to tell Hermas more or to explain anything about her (2.4.1; 3.10.7–12.4). The rejuvenation of the church that happens through conversion (*Visions* 3.10–13) is a way of expressing the reality of the body of Christ: what happens to the members affects the whole, as in Paul's message in 1 Cor 12:12–26. Hermas is instructed by the woman church who in the process is both heavenly revealer and the one who is rejuvenated through conversion. He is therefore taught not by the ideal, heavenly

267 For J. Christian Wilson (*Reassessment*, 132–33, 139), the distinction between the Holy Spirit and the Son is clarified in the Son's earthly life, that among Holy Spirit, Son, and church in the building of the tower and the life of faithful believers.

268 Nijendijk ("Christologie") argues for a unified christological portrayal of the Son of God as personification or representation of God on earth. That much can be admitted, but many other characters in the book have the same or similiar function.

269 Pernveden, *Concept of the Church*, 49; Brox, 494.

270 Pernveden, ibid., 71.

271 Ibid., 33 passim.

272 Numerous authors listed in Brox, 375–76, and S. Folgado Florez, "Sentido ecclesial de la penitencia en el 'Pastor' de Hermas," *La Ciudad de Dios* 191 (1978) 3–38 (20–21).

273 S. Folgado Florez, "Teoría teórico-descriptiva sobre

la Iglesia en el 'Pastor' de Hermas," *La Ciudad de Dios* 101 (1978) 217–46 [222–23]. See also idem, "La Iglesia anterior a los siglos en el 'Pastor' de Hermas," *La Ciudad de Dios* 191 (1978) 365–91. While some commentators see *Hermas* as part of the ongoing development of institutionalized church discipline (see comment on section 3.1 above), Patrice G. de Mestral ("The Heavenly Church in the Second Century: Delaying Factors in the Process of Institutionalization of the Church in the Second Century" [Ph.D. diss., Northwestern University, 1966]), under the influence of "early catholicism," sees *Hermas* as part of a second-century tradition of symbolic ecclesiology (with *Barnabas, Clement,* and some of the apologists) that impeded the development of institutionalization.

274 Humphrey, *Ladies and the Cities*, 146.

church in an isolated sense, but by the converting church, in process and on the way. He learns as much from the historical, imperfect church as he does from its idealized form, and he learns through its sufferings as well as its triumph.[275]

There are three principal images of the church: the tower (*Vision* 3; *Sim.* 9.2–9, 12–16, 30–31), the cosmic willow tree (*Similitude* 8), and the twelve mountains (*Sim.* 9.1, 17–29). The image of the willow tree is integrated into that of the tower inasmuch as the goal of inspection of the willow branches is to send their bearers to live in the tower. Each image serves as a symbol with its own integrity, yet each points in the same direction: there are different kinds of people, both more and less holy, who inhabit the church. Their interdependence is made clearest in the predominant image of the tower, first introduced in *Vision* 3 and taken up again, with some differences, in *Similitude* 9.[276] Only acceptable stones can go into the construction of the tower because the quality of each stone affects the whole.

For most commentators, the central message of the book is repentance or conversion. Pernveden argues against that trend, that participation in the mystery of the church is the central point.[277] His argument, however, is largely in reaction to the interpretation of *metanoia* as establishment of a discipline of penance. The confusion not only of terminology but of concepts and social contexts related to the terminology is at work here.[278] For Moyo, "[i]t is the theme of obedience, of righteous action which is the key to understanding *Hermas.*"[279] But this is precisely what full membership in the church demands, in the conviction of the author. Thus the discussion of the central theme can become circular. The later church discipline of penance is read into the text only by mistaken eisegesis; in this, some previous commentators have let their own context and presuppositions lead them into error. Nor is individual salvation the issue. Every admonition leads to collective behavior and responsibility. The book is a call to communal, ecclesial examination of conscience.[280] Though there is no ecclesiastical discipline of penance, conversion is situated in ecclesial context. To debate whether the central theme is conversion in the sense spoken of here, or the church as both ideal and fallible reality, leads nowhere. There is no reason for such conversion without the necessary context of the church as community in process of rejuvenation, and there is no full reality of the church in both its earthly and heavenly existence without the process of conversion. There is no conversion except in the church, and no church except of those on the way to conversion.

4 Conclusion

It is not the presence of Hellenistic materials in a Jewish-Christian book, nor the opposite, "but the blending of genuine Jewish-Christian elements with these unmistakable hellenistic elements which constitutes the milieu of Hermas."[281] All investigative roads lead to popular religion within a broad social base, equally open to both Jewish and Hellenistic influence, as the author's primary milieu and source of inspiration. Without *Hermas,* perhaps no one would have suspected this kind of popular

---

275 "The central and positive role given to the sufferings of the Church is the distinctive shift of emphasis which characterizes early Christian apocalyptic and which Hermas faithfully represents" (Richard J. Bauckham, "The Great Tribulation in the Shepherd of Hermas," *JTS* 25 [1974] 27–40 [40]).

276 For the differences, see comment on *Sim.* 2.1–2 below.

277 *Concept of the Church,* 298. Agreeing with him are José P. Martín, "Espíritu y dualismo de espíritus en el Pastor de Hermas y su relación con el judaismo," *Vetera christianorum* 15 (1978) 295–345 (339); Humphrey, *Ladies and the Cities,* 135.

278 See above, section 3.1. "In our opinion it is a misinterpretation to understand Hermas' essential importance as a founder figure in the history of the development of the system of penance. He did not intend to give any guide-lines for Church discipline as has sometimes been claimed. . . . [Hermas'] intention is . . . to awaken men [*sic*] to insight about their chance of still sharing in salvation in the Church from the evil age. His message is an expression of the Church's existence amongst men, which means that God's mercy embraces men" (*Concept of the Church,* 298). Pernveden's whole study is an appropriate reaction to the classifications of moralism and penitential discipline in which *Hermas* has been confined by some commentators.

279 "Angels and Christology," 20.

280 S. Folgado Florez, "Sentido ecclesial de la penitencia en el 'Pastor' de Hermas," *La Ciudad de Dios* 191 (1978) 3–38 (5).

281 Reiling, *Hermas and Christian Prophecy,* 26.

religion in Rome, though there are sure signs of it in other early Christian literature from elsewhere. With the advent of greater appreciation of popular religiosity and the role of orality in religious traditions, *Hermas* becomes a window on the world of everyday Christianity.

> He is in close contact with the Christian life as it was being lived by ordinary Church members in the Church of Rome and gives us a valuable insight into what people were thinking and the way they were behaving.[282]

If similarities can be detected between *Hermas* and James, *Barnabas,* the *Didache,* Elchasai, and the *Ascension of Isaiah,* it is difficult to see how it can be considered "not in the current" of Christian tradition.[283] It would seem that our notions of the Christian tradition need to be widened.

It is a mistake to look for perfect overall consistency in the text except in a few stylistic tendencies like oral patterns of repetition or polysemy. Each story or unit must be taken primarily on its own merits, with a glance to possible relationships with other passages, but without expecting overall consonance of details. It is not ideas or concepts that are at work here, but symbols and images, which are infinitely pliable. The perceived crisis is not in belief or teaching but in behavior and action. What is not pliable is the demand for change of heart and thus change of life. Perhaps those who find *Hermas* uninspiring do so because they know that, if we are to take it seriously, we too must change.

---

282 L. W. Barnard, "Hermas, the Church, and Judaism," in *Studies in the Apostolic Fathers and Their Background* (New York: Schocken, 1966) 151–63 (163).

283 "Le *Pasteur* appartient à la tradition chrétienne, mais il n'est pas dans le courant" ("The *Shepherd* belongs to the Christian tradition, but is not in the current" [Audet, "Affinités," 82]).

Shepherd of Hermas

1

Vision of Rhoda

1 [1]   1/ The one who raised me sold me to a certain Rhoda at Rome. Many years later, I became reacquainted with her and began to love her as a sister. 2/ After some time, as she was bathing in the river Tiber, I saw her, gave her my hand, and brought her out of the river. Seeing her beauty, I thought in my heart: "How happy I would be if I had such a wife, both in regard to beauty and manner." I wanted only this, nothing more.
3/ After some time, as I was on my way into the countryside and glorying in the greatness, splendor, and power of God's creatures, I became drowsy as I walked along. A spirit took hold of me and brought me through a place off the road, humanly impassable. It was very steep and eroded by running water. When I had crossed that stream I came to level ground and kneeling, I began to pray to the Lord and confess my sins.
4/ As I was praying, heaven opened, and I saw that woman upon whom I had set my heart, greeting me from heaven with: "Hello, Hermas!"
5/ Looking up at her, I said: "Lady, what are you doing here?" But she answered: "I was taken up in order to reproach you for your sins before the Lord." 6/ I said to her: "Will you now reproach me?" "No," she said, "but listen to what I am about to say to you. The God who dwells in the heavens and created what is from what is not and increased and multiplied it for the sake of God's holy church is angry with you because you sinned against me." 7/ I answered her: "Have I sinned against you? How? Or when did I say a shameful thing to you? Have I not always considered you as a goddess? Have I not always honored you as a sister? Why do you malign me, woman, with these evil and unclean charges?"
8/ Laughing she said to me: "The evil desire arose in your heart. Do you not think it is an evil thing if an evil desire arises in the heart of a just man? It is a sin, a great one," she said. "The just man has just intentions. So long as his intentions are just, his honor stands in heaven, and he finds the Lord well disposed to all his ventures. But those who intend evil in their hearts draw down upon themselves death and imprisonment, especially those who acquire the things this world has to offer and rejoice in their riches and do not take part in the goods of the world to come.
9/ The souls of those who have no hope will be filled with regret, yet they have given up on themselves and their true life. But you, pray to God, who will heal your sins and those of your whole household and of all the holy ones."

■ **1.1 [1]** The opening line gives quite a bit of autobiographical information about the author. "The one who raised me" (ὁ θρέψας με) identifies the author as a θρεπτός (=Latin *alumnus*), one picked up as a foundling and usually raised in the house as a slave, rather than a house-born slave (οἰκογενής=Latin *verna*). The custom of raising abandoned children in slavery was widely practiced in the Roman world.[1] Many girls so abandoned (fem. sing. θρεπτή, *alumna*) became slave-prostitutes, so much so that Justin (*1 Apol.* 27) assumes this fate for most abandoned girls. The legal discussions of the practice all assume parents' right to abandon unwanted children, but center on problems of inheritance and status should the child later be proved to have been freeborn. The author could have been sold either as a child or as a young adult to Rhoda, who may well have been a freedwoman herself. Of the nineteen Roman inscriptional examples of the name Hermas, six are certainly slave or freedman, one probably so, and in twelve cases the status is uncertain.[2] Under ordinary circumstances, however, the text probably necessitates that he was later sold again by Rhoda to another owner; otherwise, the close patron-client obligations that persisted upon manumission, normally including daily visits, would exclude a reacquaintance "many years later."[3] Such resale, however, is perfectly credible. Since at the time of the narrative the author seems to be a freedman, he presumably was manumitted by an owner subsequent to Rhoda. He may have been born and raised in Rome, or brought there later, perhaps when sold to Rhoda. Εἰς (in, to, or at) is often confused with ἐν in Hellenistic Greek.[4] The mention of the Tiber in the next verse and especially the commission to read the revelation "in this city" (*Vis.* 2.4.3) locate the delivery of the revelation in Rome.

The author's former relationship with Rhoda as slave to owner has passed not only to that of client to patron, but into something more. His loving her "as a sister" means with affection rather than erotic feelings; it probably also means as a fellow Christian (cf. Rom 16:1; 1 Tim 5:2; *Sim.* 9.11.3), since Rhoda will later reappear in his visions as a heavenly agent (vv. 4–9). The general assumption that Hermas' desire for Rhoda is only sexual may not be complete: such a liaison would mean status elevation for a freedman. In view of the fact that the desire for wealth and status is to be the central focus for sin (see 1.8 below), it must also be implied here.[5]

■ **1.2** If the previous details of the author's situation are credible, the same cannot be said for those of v. 2.[6] The idea of a woman accepting the assistance of her former slave while bathing is not unthinkable, given the known occurrences of romantic liaisons and even marriages between male freedmen and their female patrons, even though highly discouraged.[7] However, the bathing scene is universally recognized as being replete with erotic lit-

---

1   Plato *Meno* 85e; Pliny *Ep.* 10.65–66; Hippolytus *Ref.* 9.12; A. Cameron, "ΘΡΕΠΤΟΣ and Related Terms in the Inscriptions of Asia Minor," *Anatolian Studies Presented to William H. Buckler* (Manchester: Manchester University Press, 1939) 27–62; T. G. Nani, "Threptoi," *Epigraphica* 5–6 (1943–1944) 45–84; Beryl Rawson, "Children in the Roman *Familia*," in idem, ed., *The Family in Ancient Rome: New Perspectives* (Ithaca, NY: Cornell University Press, 1987) 170–200; John Boswell, *The Kindness of Strangers: The Abandonment of Children in Western Europe from Late Antiquity to the Renaissance* (New York: Pantheon, 1988) especially 60–75, 160–66.

2   Heikki Solin, *Die griechischen Personennamen in Rom: Ein Namenbuch* (3 vols.; Berlin/New York: De Gruyter, 1982) 1. 1104. Cf. Acts 12:13.

3   Though some freedmen, especially if their freedom was purchased by a third party, were more independent from their former owners. It has also been argued by Peter Garnsey ("Independent Freedmen and the Economy of Roman Italy under the Principate," *Klio* 63 [1981] 359–71) that some freed-

men who purchased their own freedom may have had such independence.

4   E.g., Mark 1:39; Hilhorst, *Sémitismes*, 25–26 n. 4, 27, 32.

5   Lampe, *Stadtrömische Christen*, 190 n. 223 (insight attributed to Gerd Theissen).

6   "That sexual promiscuity existed in the bathing establishments of Rome is undoubted (Juvenal *Satire* VI.419–25; Clement *Paed.* III.32–33), but that a Roman matron would have been bathing openly in the Tiber is incredible" (Snyder, 28).

7   Clement of Alexandria berates Alexandrian Christian women whose modesty protects them from free males not of the household, but who will strip before their male slaves at the baths (*Paed.* 3.5.32.3). Manumission of female slaves for marriage (*matrimonii causa*) with their male owners—but not the reverse—was common at least from the beginning of the Principate as witnessed by the *Lex aelia sentia* of 4 CE. "There was a distinct prejudice against a freeborn *patrona* marrying her own *libertus*. This is explicit in the legal sources as well. . . . even a

erary evocations, both Jewish and Greco-Roman, among them the biblical scenes of David and Bathsheba (2 Sam 11:2) and Susanna and the elders.[8] Thus its historicity is heavily in doubt. The introduction of literary motifs into the narrative need not negate the autobiographical setting.[9] Hermas disavows any deliberately adulterous thought, but compare Epictetus: "To-day when I saw a handsome lad or a handsome woman I did not say to myself, 'Would that a man might sleep with her,' and 'Her husband is a happy man,' for the man who uses the expression 'happy' [μακάριος as here] of the husband means 'Happy is the adulterer' also." [10]

■ **1.3** The temptation to reconstruct εἰς Κούμας ("to Cumae") here and at *Vis.* 2.1.1 with most of the older commentaries, based on L² here[11] and LL there,[12] and especially because of the later reference to the Sybil (*Vis.* 2.4.1), must be resisted not only because of the unlikelihood that such a long journey of over 130 miles would be envisioned[13] but also on the basis of the unanimous Greek manuscript evidence for εἰς κώμας ("to the countryside" or "small villages").[14] Being sleepy when seized by the spirit occurs elsewhere in revelatory literature.[15]

Being taken up by a spirit is recognizable visionary symbolism,[16] with a possible play on the Greek ambiguity of πνεῦμα as both "spirit" and "wind."[17] The presence of running water to cross is evocative of a liminal situation, but hardly here of the cosmic river or ocean, nor need ποταμόν ("river") be emended to τόπον ("place") on the basis of the L¹ reading, *locum*.[18] The level ground (τὰ ὁμαλά) may have overtones of place of salvation.[19]

---

patrona who was herself an ex-slave was not encouraged to marry her freedman" (P. R. C. Weaver, "Children of Freedmen [and Freedwomen]," in Beryl Rawson, ed., *Marriage, Divorce, and Children in Ancient Rome* [Oxford: Clarendon, 1991] 166–90 [180]). Nevertheless, even the random selection of inscriptions preserved in *CIL* 6 contains nine cases in Rome in which funerary monuments publicly proclaimed this supposedly socially unacceptable practice: 14014, 14462, 15106, 15548, 21657, 23915, 25504, 28815, and 35973.

8 Leutzsch, *Wahrnehmung*, 31–39, lists nine scenes in which a mortal man surprises a bathing goddess, eighteen pictures and washings of goddess statues, nine erotic scenes connected with bathing, and three biblical scenes. The liaison between Reuben and Bilhah (Gen 35:22) is blamed on his seeing her in her bath in *Jub.* 33.15; *T. Reub.* 3.10–15, suggesting to Peterson ("Kritische Analyse," 275) a Jewish rather than Greco-Roman background. Cf. Lampe, *Stadtrömische Christen*, 183–84.

9 See Introduction 2.2.2, 3.

10 *Diss.* 2.18.15, trans. LCL 1. 353.

11 L² *apud civitatem Ostiorum* ("to the city of Ostia"); L¹ reconstructed from the sound of *cum his cogitationibus* ("with these thoughts").

12 *Ad regionum Cumanorum* ("to the region of the Cumaeans").

13 Dibelius, 430–31; Snyder, 28.

14 Cf. Mark 8:27. Fullest discussion in Antonio Carlini, "Le passeggiate di Erma verso Cuma (Su due luoghi controversi del *Pastore*)," in S. F. Bondi et al., ed., *Studi in onore di Edda Bresciani* (Pisa: Giardini, 1986) 105–9. Carlini suggests the connection of κώμα ("countryside") with ἀγρός ("field") of *Vis.* 2.1.4 as site of revelations, as in *4 Ezra* 13.57.

15 E.g., *Corp. Herm.* 1.1. Whether this and all the visions are intended to be dreams or waking visions (cf. nighttime settings at *Vis.* 2.4.1; 3.1.2, 10.6; perhaps 5.1) is not important, since dreams were widely believed in antiquity to be revelations from beyond (Patricia Cox Miller, "'All the Words Were Frightful': Salvation by Dreams in the Shepherd of Hermas," *VC* 42 (1988) 327–38; idem, *Dreams in Late Antiquity*, 133.

16 Cf. *Vis.* 2.1.1; Ezek 2:2; 3:12, 14; 8:3; 11:1, 24; 43:5; *3 Bar.* 2.1; 3.1.

17 Dibelius, 432. For an allegorical interpretation of the impassable place, see Erik Peterson, "Die Begegnung mit dem Ungeheuer," in idem, *Frühkirche, Judentums, und Gnosis* (Freiburg: Herder, 1959) 285–309 (287–88 n. 8).

18 Cf. Erik Peterson, "Beiträge zur Interpretation der Visionen im 'Pastor Hermae,'" in idem, *Frühkirche, Judentums, und Gnosis* (Freiburg: Herder, 1959) 254–70 (266, 289); Brox, 81.

19 Compare further use of the term: *Vis.* 1.3.4; *Man.* 2.4; 6.1.2, 4; *Sim.* 9.10.1; and probably *Sim.* 9.33.3 (*exaequata sunt*); note progression from topographical to moral to soteriological use (Henne, "Polysémie"). Also, the "plain" (τό πεδίον) is an important location in *Sim.* 6.1.5; 7.1; 8.4.2; 9.1.4, 2.1, 6.6–7, 9.4, 29.4, 30.1. Cf. Brox, 495–500, Isa 40:3, where Symmachus has ὁμαλίσατε for LXX εὐθείας ποιεῖτε ("make smooth") the paths of the Lord. The word occurs fourteen times in Aquila, five in Symmachus, twice in Theodotion, and not at all in the LXX. J. Ramsey Michaels ("The 'Level Ground' in the Shepherd of Hermas," *ZNW* 59 [1968] 245–50) suggests connections between Symmachus and the Ebionites (Eusebius *Hist. eccl.* 6.17) and the possible connections of Hermas with the Elchasaites (see Introduction 2.2.4) might be

The acknowledgement of sin is Hermas' spontaneous response to theophany.[20]

■ **1.4** The earthly Rhoda is now the heavenly Rhoda, who greets him from the open heaven (cf. Ezek 1:1; Acts 7:56; Rev 4:1; compare Luke 1:28). The expression ἀνελήμφϑην ("I was taken up") would seem to suggest her previous death, but at any rate, she has become for Hermas a revelatory agent. Ἐπιϑυμέω ("desire," "set one's heart upon") can also mean "lust after," but Hermas denies that this is the case (1.2, 7). Her greeting contains the first mention of the author's fairly common and frequently servile Greek name.[21]

■ **1.5–6** Hermas' own sense of sinfulness and his perception of Rhoda form a delicate interplay: his defensiveness about the earlier encounter with her (1.1) leads to a preoccupation about it. She will take up the question later (1.8) for a more important purpose. Here she deflects it into a wider vision of God's greatness, using familiar biblical language.[22] That creation was made for the sake of the church, a teleology reserved in the NT for Christ (Col 1:16), is probably a Christian adaptation of the Jewish motif that the world was created for Israel.[23]

■ **1.7** In spite of his previous confession of sin in general, Hermas rejects the accusation that he has sinned against Rhoda. Ποίω τρόπω ("How?")[24] is to be preferred to ποίω τόπω ("Where?").[25] He protests his honorable treatment of her, stressing external conduct: speech, considered treatment, honor. Honoring her as a sister is understandable (cf. 1.1.1); considering her as a goddess seems "strikingly unchristian,"[26] but it need be no more than reverential. However, his address to her as γύναι ("woman") rather than κύριε ("lady") in the next question is rhetorical rather than reverent, evoking the literary scenes of male mortals' encounter with goddesses.[27]

■ **1.8** By contrast to external actions, Rhoda lays emphasis not on behavior but on the desires of the heart. To have something "arise in the heart" (ἀναβαίνειν ἐπὶ τὴν καρδίαν) is an "indirectly semitic"[28] expression that will recur frequently. Here as elsewhere (for example, *Vis.* 1.2.4; 3.7.2, 3; 3.8.4; *Man.* 6.2.5; 8.5; *Sim.* 9.19.3), ἐπιϑυμία ("desire" or "lust"), often labeled πονηρά ("evil"), connotes not only improper sexual desires, but greed as well (but see 1.4 above, where it does not connote evil desire). Here is the introduction of the second level of association in Hermas' call to conversion: from personal sin of lust and greed to communal and social sin. "The just man" here is ὁ ἀνὴρ δίκαιος, gender-specific; it will reappear in *Man.* 4.1.3; 11.9, 13, 14; *Sim.* 9.15.4. Members of the community addressed—or at least ideal members—are frequently called "the just ones," in both terrestrial and eschatological contexts,[29] an expression replete with biblical connotations.[30] Those who have the wrong attitude, especially because of the

---

traceable through such word usage. Further discussion in Peterson, "Begegnung," 289–91.

20 *Vis.* 2.1.2; 3.1.5; cf. Luke 5:8.

21 Thought by Origen (*Commentary on Romans* 10.31=*PG* 14. 1282) to be the Hermas of Rom 16:14, chronologically unlikely. Solin, *Griechische Personennamen*, 1. 338 lists five other examples in Rome, of whom two are slaves, including *CIL* 6.518, 20055, 23257; 9.6281; 14.6474; *PW* 8. 722.4; 12. 417.20; the variations Hermia, Herma, and Hermo are far more common. Documented elsewhere: SEG 26. 1403 (Pamphylia); 28. 1179 (a priest in Phrygia); 29. 1256 (Kyzikos); 30. 935 (Black Sea); 31. 1165 (Pisidia); Jean Rouffiac, *Recherches sur les caractères du grec dans le Nouveau Testament d'après les inscriptions de Priène* (Paris: Leroux, 1911) 91; James H. Moulton and George Milligan, *The Vocabulary of the Greek New Testament* (London: Hodder and Stoughton, 1930) *s.v.* For the difficulties of judging social status from names already at this period, see Osiek, *Rich and Poor*, 106–11.

22 "God who dwells in the heavens": cf. Pss 2:4; 122:1; Tob 5:17; *4 Ezra* 8.20. "Created what is from what is not": *2 Bar.* 48.8; *2 Enoch* 24.2; 2 Macc 7:28; Philo *Spec. leg.* 4.187; *Op. mundi* 81; Rom 4:17; *Man.* 1.1. "Increased and multiplied": Gen 1:22, etc.; *Corp. Herm.* 1.18.

23 Dibelius, 433. Cf. *4 Ezra* 6.55, 59; 7.11.

24 Majority of mss.; Funk, Whittaker, Dibelius.

25 S L¹; Lake, Joly, Brox.

26 Dibelius, 434. Further discussion with literature, Brox, 83. The strangeness of the reading provoked numerous attempts to interpret and alter: ϑυγατήρα ("daughter") A; *dominam* ("lady") E; omission of the statement entirely L².

27 See n. 8 above.

28 Hilhorst, *Sémitismes*, 159; cf. Luke 24:38; Acts 7:23; Isa 65:16 quoted in 1 Cor 2:9.

29 E.g., *Vis.* 1.4.2; 2.2.5; *Sim.* 3.2; 4.2; 8.9.1.

30 E.g., Matt 1:19; 13:17, 43, 49; Luke 14:14, as is Paul's preferred "the holy ones" (e.g., Rom 1:1; 1 Cor 1:2; Phil 1:1).

31 The ancient translations attempt unsuccessfully to interpret: *vagantur* ("they wander") L¹; *non resistent*

distraction of wealth, bring their own (spiritual) prison with them.

■ **1.9** This difficult verse seems to contain the contradictory elements of conversion and ultimate loss, and a number of possible interpretations have been tried.[31] The present translation follows Carlini: following the partially restored B reading $\mu\epsilon\tau(\alpha\mu\epsilon)\lambda\dot{\eta}\sigma\sigma\nu\tau(\alpha\iota)$ ("they will be filled with regret"), he argues in light of 2 Cor 7:8–10, where both $\mu\epsilon\tau\alpha\mu\dot{\epsilon}\lambda\omicron\mu\alpha\iota$ and $\mu\epsilon\tau\dot{\alpha}\nu\omicron\iota\alpha$ appear (as well as $\lambda\dot{\upsilon}\pi\eta$ ["grief"], a key word in *Hermas*), that the former lays more stress on regretful feelings, while the latter refers rather to concrete action.[32] They have given up the pursuit of what is best for them because of the attraction of worldly things.[33] The image of healing sin is biblical[34] and appears frequently in Hermas.[35] At the end of v. 9 occurs the first mention of Hermas' family or household ($\omicron\tilde{\iota}\kappa\omicron\varsigma$), which will continue to figure in his problems.[36]

---

hisdem luxuriis ("they do not resist these luxuries") L[2]; "they should repent" E. Dibelius rejects the reading of S, $\mu\epsilon\tau\alpha\nu\omicron\dot{\eta}\sigma\omicron\upsilon\sigma\iota\nu$ ("they will repent") on theological grounds; Hilgenfeld emends to $\mu\epsilon\tau\alpha\lambda\gamma\dot{\eta}\sigma\omicron\upsilon\sigma\iota\nu$ ("they will feel remorse"), but without textual grounds.

32 "Saranno colte da rimorso le anime di quanti non hanno speranza e hanno rinunciato a se stessi e alla loro vita" ("*METANOEIN* e *METAMEΛEΣΘAI* nelle visioni di Erma," in Sebastià Janeras, ed., *Miscellània papirologica Ramon Roca-Puig* [Barcelona: Fundació Salvador Vives Casajuana, 1987] 97–102). However, the other NT passage cited in support, the remorse of Judas ($\mu\epsilon\tau\alpha\mu\epsilon\lambda\eta\vartheta\epsilon\grave{\iota}\varsigma$, "being filled with regret") without mention of $\mu\epsilon\tau\dot{\alpha}\nu\omicron\iota\alpha$, "repentance" (Matt 27:3), may not bear the weight of the argument, given the fact that suicide as an honorable solution to disgrace may not indicate lack of repentance, contrary to the traditional interpretation of the fate of Judas: Annelies Moeser, "The Death of Judas Iscariot" (M.A. thesis, Catholic Theological Union, 1990). *Tab. Ceb.* 11.1 uses $\mu\epsilon\tau\dot{\alpha}\nu\omicron\iota\alpha$; 35.4 uses $\mu\alpha\tau\alpha\mu\dot{\epsilon}\lambda\epsilon\iota\alpha$. John T.

Fitzgerald and L. Michael White (*The Tabula of Cebes* [SBLTT 24; Chico, CA: Scholars Press, 1983] 144 n. 40; 165 n. 105) take them to be synonymous. The attempt of Otto Michel ("$\mu\epsilon\tau\alpha\mu\dot{\epsilon}\lambda\omicron\mu\alpha\iota$, $\dot{\alpha}\mu\epsilon\tau\alpha\mu\dot{\epsilon}\lambda\eta\tau\omicron\varsigma$," *TDNT* 4 [1967] 626–29) to argue that the NT maintains a clear distinction between $\mu\epsilon\tau\alpha\mu\dot{\epsilon}\lambda\omicron\mu\alpha\iota$ and $\mu\epsilon\tau\alpha\nu\omicron\dot{\epsilon}\omega$ while its Hellenistic environment does not (629) is largely unconvincing, though Johannes P. Louw and Eugene A. Nida (*Greek-English Lexicon of the New Testament Based on Semantic Domains* [New York: United Bible Societies, 1988] 31. 59; 25. 270) consider them entirely different, emphasizing feelings of regret for $\mu\epsilon\tau\alpha\mu\dot{\epsilon}\lambda\omicron\mu\alpha\iota$ and change of behavior for $\mu\epsilon\tau\alpha\nu\omicron\epsilon\hat{\iota}\nu$.

33 Cf. *Man.* 12.6.2; *Sim.* 9.26.4.

34 Cf. Deut 30:3; Jer 3:22; by implication, Matt 9:12 and par.

35 E.g., *Vis.* 1.3.1; *Man.* 4.1.11; 12.6.2; *Sim.* 8.11.3; discussion in Snyder, 31–32.

36 See comment on *Vis.* 1.3.1–2 below.

1 First Vision of the Woman Church

2 [2]   **1/ After she said these things, the heavens closed, and I was in complete shock and grief. I was saying to myself: "If this sin is on record against me, how can I be saved? How shall I atone to God for my past sins? In what words can I ask the Lord to be reconciled with me?" 2/ As I was reflecting on what had happened and discerning in my heart, I saw in front of me a large white chair made of snow-white wool. An older woman in a shining robe approached me with a book in her hands. She sat down by herself and greeted me: "Hello, Hermas." Sad and weeping, I said: "Hello, lady." 3/ She said to me: "Why are you so downcast, Hermas? The courageous, good-natured one who is always laughing—why are you so long-faced and not joyful?" I said to her: "On account of a wonderful woman who says I sinned against her." 4/ She said: "In no way should this happen to the servant of God! Though certainly it did enter your heart about her. It is an intention like this that brings sin to the servants of God. It is an evil and terrible intention against a distinguished and tested spirit for someone to lust after an evil deed, especially Hermas the continent, who abstains from all evil desires and is filled with simplicity and great innocence."**

■ **2.1–2 [2]** Just as the beginning of the vision was marked by the opening of the heavens (*Vis.* 1.1.4), its end is marked by their closing. Again Hermas retreats to bemoaning his own sinful state, and again in the following verses a heavenly apparition will attempt to broaden his awareness.[1] The recording of sin as well as of good deeds for future judgment is a common ancient Middle Eastern theme, especially in Jewish apocalyptic literature.[2]

The vision of Rhoda is followed in the same location by the second heavenly revealer figure, who will be the central revelatory character until the end of *Vision* 4. The white chair ($\kappa\alpha\vartheta\acute{\epsilon}\delta\rho\alpha$) upon which she sits down is usually understood as a throne or seat of teaching authority or judgment, or a Roman magistrate's seat.[3] Snow and wool are the two traditional images for great whiteness (Ps 51:7; Dan 7:9; Rev 1:14). The chair is not literally made of wool, but of some substance having the appearance of wool. Later (*Vis.* 3.1.4) the woman's seat will be made of ivory and spread with linen.

The older woman ($\gamma\upsilon\nu\grave{\eta}\ \pi\rho\epsilon\sigma\beta\hat{\upsilon}\tau\iota\varsigma$) will later be identified as the church. It is possible but not likely that she

1   For Miller (*Dreams in Late Antiquity*, 132), the rest of the book is the answer to Hermas' question, "How can I be saved?"

2   With positive ramifications, cf. *Vis.* 1.3.2; *Man.* 8.6; *Sim.* 2.9; 5.3.8. Further refs. in Dibelius, 436; Brox, 85; Snyder, 30; Joly, 81, 85. Imagining one is guilty of a crime and suffering the psychological consequences was apparently a kind of "psychotherapy" used by some mystery religions and later by philosophical schools: Georg Lusk, "The Doctrine of Salvation in the Hermetic Writings," *SecCent* 8 (1991) 31–41 (35–37).

3   Dan 7:9–10; Matt 19:28; 23:2; Rev 20:4; 21:5; Peterson, "Beiträge," 254–57; Leutzsch, *Wahrnehmung*, 60; taken as a sign of her dignity by Dibelius (436–51), followed by Brox (159), a viable interpretation but altogether different from that of 3.11.1–4.

4   With a play on her name and the church of Rome ($\text{P}\acute{o}\delta\eta$-$\text{P}\acute{\omega}\mu\eta$), so that Hermas' sin against her is symbolic of that against the church (George Tavard, *Woman in Christian Tradition* [Notre Dame: Notre Dame University Press, 1973] 51–53). Others assume a common identity for other reasons, e.g., psychological sublimation of erotic desire into spiritual quest (Carl G. Jung, *Psychological Types*

is Rhoda in another form.[4] The book in her hand contains the content of the coming revelation. The combination of shining garments, chair, and book evokes magical texts.[5] This first time she sits down alone while he remains standing, an indicator of their different status; later (*Vis.* 3.1.7) she will compel Hermas to sit beside her.

■ **2.3–4** The rather familiar greeting of a very disturbed recipient of revelation is not without precedent in apocalyptic literature (*4 Ezra* 5.16; Rev 1:17). The woman affirms Hermas' conviction of sin in the context of his otherwise steady intention to please God; the seriousness of sin is judged not by some external norm but by the sinner's conscience. The expression "servant(s) of God" (δοῦλος τοῦ θεοῦ) will appear in *Hermas* nearly

fifty times. It does not refer here to a group of ascetics in Hermas' community,[6] but to all Christians, perhaps an extension of biblical usage, notwithstanding its later use in ascetical circles[7] or the fact that Hermas is here called "the continent" (ὁ ἐγκρατής), also later a technical term for an ascetic. This word group is used in *Hermas* in a wide variety of contexts[8] and is more frequent in the *Mandates* and *Similitudes* than in the *Visions*. It occurs usually in contexts of warning or challenge to a less than perfect church, whereas the other frequent terms for church members, the "holy ones" or "chosen ones," occur only in the *Visions* (except *Sim.* 8.8.1) and in references to the ideal church.[9]

[Collected Works 6; Princeton, NJ: Princeton University Press, 1971]) 224–31, 238. But Hermas' relationships with the two of them, even though both are client to patron, are quite different.

5 Refs. in Peterson, "Beiträge," 257–58.

6 Peterson, "Kritische Analyse," 278.

7 Reiling, *Hermas and Christian Prophecy*, 32 n. 2; Carolyn Osiek, "Ransom," 371 n. 17; cf. *4 Ezra* 16.35; *Didasc.* 11=*Ap. Const.* 2.45.2, still as a general

term for Christians, but for ascetic groups, P. Brown, *Augustine of Hippo* (Berkeley/Los Angeles/London: University of California Press, 1967) 132–37.

8 E.g., *Vis.* 2.3.2; 3.8.4; *Mandate* 8.

9 Henne, "Pénitence," 371–72, esp. n. 38.

1 Family Problems and a Message of Judgment and Consolation

3 [3] 1/ "But this is not the reason that God is angry with you; rather, it is that you [sing.] must make your family, that has acted lawlessly against God and against you [pl.], their parents, mend their ways. Since you [sing.] love your children so much, you do not admonish your family, but let them become corrupted. This is why the Lord is angry with you, but will heal all the previous evil deeds in your family, since because of those sins and lawlessness you [sing.] have been corrupted by everyday affairs. 2/ But the great tenderness of the Lord has had mercy on you and your family, and will strengthen you and establish you in his glory. You, however, do not get careless, but take heart and strengthen your family. For just as the smith hammering at his work prevails over the object as he wishes, so too the righteous word spoken daily prevails over all evil. So do not leave off from admonishing your children, for I know that if they are converted with all their heart, they will be recorded in the books of life with all the holy ones." 3/ When she had finished these sayings, she said to me: "Would you like to hear me read?" I answered: "I would like that, lady." She said to me: "Then become a listener, and listen to the glories of God." I heard great and awesome things that I could not remember, for all the sayings were too frightening for human comprehension. So I remembered the last words, for they were helpful and easy: 4/ "Behold, the powerful God who created the world with great and invisible power and understanding, and by glorious design surrounded creation with beauty, and with powerful word established the heaven and founded the earth upon the waters, and with wisdom and foresight created the holy church, which he blessed. Behold, he alters the heavens, the mountains, the hills and the seas, and everything is being leveled for his chosen ones, so as to give them the assurance that was promised with great glory and joy, provided they keep the decrees of God which they received with great faith."

4 [4] 1/ So when she finished reading and rose from the chair, four young men came to take up the chair and went off toward the East. 2/ She called me, touched my chest, and said: "Did my reading please you?" And I said to her: "Lady, these last things please me, but the first things were very difficult." But she answered me: "These last things are for the just, while the first things are for the outsiders and apostates." 3/ While she was still speaking with me, there appeared two men who took her by the arms and they went away to the East, just like the chair. But she left in a joyful mood and said to me as she left: "Be of good courage, Hermas!"

■ **3.1–2 [3]** The woman revealer shifts the focus from Hermas' fixation on his own sin to his responsibility at the next wider level: his family. Οἶκος, usually to be understood as "household," involving a wider circle of relationships than the immediate family,[1] must here be translated rather as "family," given the immediate references to parents and children that follow. If this reference is autobiographical, it reveals the author as a householder[2] with adult children, who may or may not be living under the same roof. In Roman law, the *paterfamilias* (patriarchal head of the family) possessed *patria potestas*[3] by which he was responsible and prosecutable for the conduct, finances, and legal obligations of all sons and of all daughters married without *manus*[4] until his death, when sons were "emancipated" to take on similar responsibilities for themselves and the next generation, daughters by this time largely to be economically independent even if still nominally under a male guardian.[5] Thus the blame attributed to Hermas for his family's sin simply follows Roman legal custom.[6] Here and in *Vis.* 2.2.2–3, 3.1, Hermas' family is most easily understood in the literal sense. Other passages, however,[7] lend themselves more to the interpretation that Hermas' family is a cipher for the whole community. Their corruption "by everyday affairs" (ἀπὸ τῶν βιωτικῶν πράξεων) is best understood as related to business concerns, as will become clearer in subsequent references.[8] On "healing" rather than forgiveness, see above at 1.1.9.

The movement of the revelatory message now proceeds from confirmation of Hermas' own sense of sinfulness, to the wider horizon of his (and the readers') social responsibility, to the assurance of God's mercy and strengthening. The image of founding evokes biblical allusions to creation (see 2.4 below) and NT passages with figurative meanings similar to its use here (Matt 7:25; Col 1:23; Eph 3:17; 1 Pet 5:10), but the immediate context of the householder's desire that his house and family flourish should not be overlooked as well. In v. 2, the double invocation to Hermas not to get careless or slacken in his familial admonishment forms an inclusion around the supporting image of the blacksmith, making Dibelius' suggested emendation unnecessary.[9] The blacksmith image suggests a variant on Jeremiah's potter (Jer 18:1–4), but it is also known in Greco-Roman literature.[10] Turning to God with "all one's heart" (ἐξ ὅλης καρδίας) is a traditional biblical formula that will appear frequently throughout the book.[11] The conversion of Hermas' family will mean that they will share in the promise of eternal life accorded to those enrolled "in the books of life."[12]

■ **3.3–4** Everything in this first vision of the woman church until now has been introduction to the actual revelatory message. Hermas has been duly chastised by his

---

1   Different levels of meaning of οἶκος include habitation, material property, family and dependents, whether living in the house or not, including slaves (Leutzsch, *Wahrnehmung*, 52–53, need not raise so hesitantly the question of slaves in a Christian household; there is ample evidence of the fact). The meaning encompassed at times meanings of both the Latin *familia* and *domus* (Richard P. Saller, "*Familia, Domus*, and the Roman Conception of the Family," *Phoenix* 38 [1984] 336–55; Osiek and Balch, 6, 41–43).

2   Though as Lampe (*Stadtrömische Christen*, 185) points out, nothing definitive excludes that Hermas be a tenant rather than property owner.

3   J. A. Crook, "Patria Potestas," *Classical Quarterly* 17 (1967) 113–22; Richard P. Saller, "*Patria Potestas* and the Stereotype of the Roman Family," *Continuity and Change* 1 (1986) 7–22; William V. Harris, "The Roman Father's Power of Life and Death," in R. S. Bagnall, ed., *Studies in Roman Law in Memory of A. Arthur Schiller* (Leiden: Brill, 1986) 81–95.

4   Official and legal control of the person and her assets. Transfer of this control to the husband at marriage, common at an earlier period, was uncommon by this time, and so was maintained by the father, probably to prevent the transfer of property out of the family. Cf. *OxCD²* s.v. *manus* and *patria potestas*.

5   Alan Watson, *Roman Slave Law* (Baltimore/London: Johns Hopkins University Press, 1987) 116–117; Leutzsch, *Wahrnehmung*, 57–58.

6   Cf. *Sim.* 7.2.3.

7   *Vis.* 3.1.6; *Man.* 5.1.7; maybe *Sim.* 5.3.7.

8   E.g., *Vis.* 2.3.1; 3.11.3; *Man.* 6.2.5. Full list in Osiek, *Rich and Poor*, 39–46; discussion in Dibelius, 438.

9   David Hellholm, *Visionenbuch*, 131 n. 5. Greek μὴ ῥαθυμήσῃς ("do not slacken"); Dibelius (488) conjectures μὴ ἀθυμήσῃς ("do not be discouraged") on the basis of L¹ *noli vagari* ("do not wander off course") and E "do not be discouraged."

10 Refs. in Dibelius, 439.

11 Hilhorst, *Sémitismes*, 142–44.

12 See comment on 2.1 above.

own vision![13] She has confirmed Hermas' sense of his own sinfulness and widened it to the family dimension that he apparently had not thought of, and she has balanced that sense of sinfulness with the assurance of God's mercy and healing both for him and for his family. The developing familiarity of Hermas' relationship with his vision is indicated by her almost playful question and his response. True to the portrayal of his human weakness, when he has heard "the great and awesome [and presumably long] things"[14] that she has read, he forgets most of it, but remembers only the good part at the end. The message has been divided into one of judgment or challenge and one of consolation, typical of the revelatory structure throughout. On this first attempt, only the message of consolation is retained.

The brief quotation remembered by Hermas (v. 4) is a harmonious medley of allusions and reflections in biblical style, perhaps from a liturgical context. It moves from the Wisdom theme of God's designs in creation, to the level of the church, to the soteriological level with the promise to those who are faithful to God's decrees. The "powerful God" is literally the "God of powers," (ὁ θεὸς τῶν δυνάμεων, אלהים צבאות) the familiar "God of hosts" (for example, Ps 79:5, 8, 15 LXX; Ps 80:4, 7, 14 NRSV), a Jewish liturgical expression, but perhaps not without Stoic influence as well. The Greek manuscripts read here "the powerful God, *whom I love,* (who created the world) with great power . . ." instead of "with (great and) *invisible* power . . ." (ὅν ἀγαπῶ instead of ὁ ἀοράτῳ),[15] but this reading does not fit the semantic context. The foundation of the earth upon the primeval waters (Pss

24:1–2; 136:6, etc.) will later form part of the background for the church founded upon the water of baptism.[16] God created the church "with his own wisdom and foresight" (τῇ ἰδίᾳ σοφίᾳ καὶ προνοίᾳ) or "with powerful strength" (τῇ δυνάμει αὐτοῦ τῇ κραταίᾳ).[17] The leveling of irregular topography is important language elsewhere in the Bible and in *Hermas*.[18]

Departure of the Woman Church

■ **4.1–3 [4]** The woman church is accompanied by a number of young men, to be understood as angels; the use of such terminology for angels is common in the literature (for example, Mark 16:5; Luke 24:4; *Gos. Pet.* 36–39). The four who carry the chair evoke the angels of the four winds or four directions, just as the chair itself has four foundations (*Vis.* 3.13.3), while the two who take her by the arms, or elbows, serve in a supportive capacity (*Acts of Perpetua and Felicitas* 11.1; 12.3; esp. *Gos. Pet.* 39). The six will reappear with her later (*Vis.* 3.1.6).[19] The east is the natural origin of revelation and divine manifestation. Most temples, including that in Jerusalem, faced east, and most early Christian churches reversed the orientation so that door faced west and the congregation faced east. The woman's touching Hermas on the breast may be an act of empowerment,[20] but is more likely part of the familiar pattern of communication established between them. Again, the structure of the revelation is confirmed: first judgment, then consolation. The message of judgment is intended for both apostates and "outsiders" (ἔθνη), "the others" who are

---

13 Brox, 88–89.

14 The text of S (μεγάλως καὶ θαυμαστῶς) is corrupt, and several conjectures have been offered (Dibelius, 439–40; Joly, 84–85) to clarify the grammar and referent of the two adjectives. Either it is the things he hears that are great and awesome, or the glories of God in the preceding sentence, but not his hearing, adverbially modified.

15 Restored by Hilgenfeld and followed by Whittaker, from L¹ *invisibili.*

16 Further discussion and refs. in Dibelius, 440–41. For an analysis of the structure of the "hymn," see Philippe Henne, "Le péché d'Hermas" (*Revue Thomiste* 90 [1990] 640–51), 646–47.

17 The first reading S A in rare agreement against LL; L¹ *virtute sua potenti* ("with his powerful strength"), L² *potenti virtute* ("with powerful strength") now joined by B τη δυν[αμει α]του τη κρατ[αια]. Carlini

(*Bodmer Papyrus*, 68 n. 5) argues for the authenticity of LL B.

18 Ps 46:23; Isa 40:14; see note at *Vis.* 1.1.3.

19 Further discussion and refs.: Dibelius, 441–42; Peterson, "Beiträge," 260–65; Snyder, 33–34. Many suggested parallels are apotheosis scenes, which this is not. The difference must be kept in mind.

20 So Dibelius, 441, but not as clearly so here as, e.g., Rev 1:17–19.

21 Usually translated "heathen": for Greeks, non-Greeks; for Romans, non-Italians; for Jews, Gentiles; for Christians, pagans—a word that would be anachronistic here. Cf. BAGD² *s.v.* 2.

not us; thus here, those who do not share the same faith.[21] The woman church leaves in a cheerful mood (ἱλαρά), a state of mind characteristic of her and later of the Shepherd's teaching on virtue,[22] and encourages Hermas to "behave like a man" (Ἀνδρίζου), a gender-specific term not, however, limited to men.[23]

---

22 As an attribute of the woman church: *Vis.* 3.9.10, 10.4–5, 12.1, 13.1; in the teaching on virtue: *Man.* 2.4; 5.2.3; especially 10.3.1; etc.; also how Hermas is expected to be (*Vis.* 1.2.3). The word group is used thirty-three times, to describe not only Hermas and the woman church, but sheep (*Sim.* 6.2.3), angels and people (*Sim.* 8.1.17–18), plants (*Sim.* 9.1.8, 10), the shepherd and the visionary maidens around the tower (*Sim.* 9.9.6–7), passim; also χαρά in *Vis.* 1.3.4; 3.13.2; *Sim.* 1.10; *gaudium* at *Sim.* 9.31.4, 5; 10.4.3. Joy is a sign of life in the spirit of God. Cf. Dibelius, 534–35.

23 E.g., *Vis.* 3.8.4. Cf. *Sim.* 10.4.1 (*viriliter*); *4 Ezra* 10.32–33; *Mart. Pol.* 9.1; Steve Young, "Being a Man."

2
Second Vision of the Woman Church;
The Message Delivered in Writing

1 [5] 1/ As I was going into the countryside at about the same time as the previous year, while walking along I remembered last year's vision, and again the spirit seized me and took me away to the same place as the previous year. 2/ So when I came to the place, I fell on my knees and began to pray to the Lord and glorify his name because he had found me worthy and had made me aware of my previous sins. 3/ When I got up from prayer, I saw before me the same elder lady that I had seen the previous year, walking and reading from a little book. She said to me: "Can you proclaim these things to God's elect?" I answered her: "Lady, I cannot remember so much, but give me the little book so I can copy it." "Take it," she said, "and return it to me." 4/ I took it to a certain place in the field and copied it all letter by letter because I was having trouble separating the syllables. When I had completed the letters of the little book it was suddenly snatched out of my hand—by whom, I did not see.

■ **1.1–2 [5]** The first *Vision* has introduced the situation and the theme. Now the second will deliver the kernel of the heavenly message. A year has elapsed since the last revelation, and Hermas again finds himself outside the city in the country,[1] and again seized by the spirit and carried off.[2] The marking of the time and place of divine communications is characteristic of revelatory literature for the purpose of testimony and authentication.[3] Upon reaching the place, Hermas' response is the same as the year before, with one important difference: his prayer is now one of thanksgiving rather than confession.

■ **1.3–4** Rhoda will appear no more, but the elder lady will now become a frequent companion for the duration of the *Visions*. Her βιβλίον (scroll of substantial length, *Vis.* 1.2.2) is now a βιβλαρίδιον (paper or short document; cf. Rev. 10:2) which she finds interesting enough to be reading as she walks along. Though not called a letter, the text as later given (*Vis.* 2.2.2–3.4) contains a

personal message to Hermas, a public message, and directions to him for public proclamation. If it is a "heavenly letter," it is unique in being handed over for copying instead of being dictated (Rev 1:19; 2:1, etc.) or hidden for later discovery.[4] Having been unable to remember the whole message the first time (*Vis.* 1.3.3), he is given a second chance, this time by making a copy for himself.[5] This certainly implies that the text is not overly long, yet too long to remember. Hermas is at least basically literate, therefore, though he has difficulty separating the letters into words, since ancient manuscripts did not leave spaces between words, but depended on the reader to interpret. However, as the following text shows, his basic problem about understanding the message is less his inability to read its written form than his lack of enlightenment about its interpretation.[6]

---

1 On the conjectural emendation "going to Cumae," see comment on *Vis.* 1.1.3.

2 See comment on *Vis.* 1.1.3 above.

3 E.g., Dan 10:4; 2 Cor 12:2; Rev 1:10; *4 Ezra* 11.1; 13.1; 14.1; *T. Naph.* 6.1; *Vis.* 2.2.1, 4.2; 3.1.2; 4.1.1; Peterson, "Begegnung," 286.

4 Ezek 2:9–10; Joly, 90–91 n.1; Dibelius, 443, excursus on heavenly letters; Brox (96) insists the revelation

5 given here is a "book," not a "letter."

5 Cf. *Jub.* 32.25. Discussion and further examples in Peterson, "Beiträge," 259 n. 32.

6 "Thus part of Hermas' 'therapy'—his initiation into *metanoia*, repentance, and so into salvation—is literacy: he must learn to read the images of dream" (Miller, "All the Words," 331).

2

The Written Message Understood

2 [6] 1/ Fifteen days later, as I was fasting and greatly beseeching the Lord, the meaning of the writing was revealed to me. These are the things that were written: 2/ "Your offspring, Hermas, have renounced God, blasphemed against the Lord, and betrayed their parents by their great wickedness, and are known as betrayers of parents. Though their betrayal has not been to their benefit, but they have still added to their sins deeds of licentiousness and accumulated wickedness, so that their lawlessness has gone as far as it can go. 3/ But communicate this message to all your children and to your wife who from now on will be as a sister to you. She does not hold her tongue, with which she does evil. But when she hears this, she will hold back and receive mercy. 4/ After you have communicated to them these words that the master commanded me to reveal to you, then all the sins they previously committed will be forgiven as well as to all the holy ones who sinned, up to this day, if they are converted with all their heart and remove all doublemindedness from their heart. 5/ For the master has sworn upon his honor to his elect: if there is still sin once this day has been determined, there is no salvation for them. Conversion for the just has a time limit. The days for conversion of all the holy ones are complete; but for the outsiders conversion is possible until the last day. 6/ So you will tell the leaders of the church to straighten out their paths in righteousness, so that they might benefit fully from the promises in great honor. 7/ So hold on, you [pl.] doers of righteousness, and do not be doubleminded, so that you will be traveling companions with the holy angels. Blessed will be you who endure the coming great tribulation and will not deny their life. 8/ For the Lord has sworn on his son that those who deny their Lord have been disenfranchised from their life, that is, those who are about to deny in the coming days. But to those who previously denied, mercy has come to them because of great compassion.

3 [7] 1/ "But you [sing.], Hermas, no longer hold anything against your children, nor neglect your sister, so that they may be purified from their former sins. For they will be chastised with just chastisement, if you do not hold anything against them. Resentment is deadly [but forgiveness leads to eternal life]. But you, Hermas, have had your own serious tribulations on account of your family's transgressions, because you did not give them proper attention. But you neglected them and became overinvolved in your own evil affairs. 2/ But what saves you, besides your simplicity and great restraint, is that you have not distanced yourself from the living God. These things have saved you, provided that you endure, as they save all who behave accordingly and proceed in innocence and simplicity. These people will conquer every evil and survive into eternal life. 3/ Blessed are all who act justly. They will never perish. 4/ But say to Maximus: `Behold, tribulation is coming. Go ahead and deny again if you wish.' `The Lord is near to those who are open to conversion,' as it is written in the Book of Eldad and Modat, who prophesied to the people in the desert."

■ **2.1 [6]** Only after a prolonged period of prayer and ascesis does the meaning of the message come clear, "revealed" this time not directly by a heavenly agent but through inspiration in his own understanding. "Fifteen days" means two weeks;[1] the day on which the count began was included as the first day, contrary to modern Western custom. Originally an Eastern practice, νηστεία ("fasting"), practiced in Greco-Roman religion in the West by this period as purification before offering sacrifice and before approaching major oracles such as Claros and Didyma, can mean partial as well as total abstinence from food and/or drink. In the *Visions*, it is done as preparation for revelation. Later, it will have an ethical and social dimension (*Sim.* 5.1, 3).[2]

■ **2.2** The message, which begins in v. 2, moves in a triple cycle of the recognizable pattern of judgment and exhortation (2.2–3, 6, 8a) followed by encouragement (2.4–5, 7, 8b), and again the same pattern appears in 3.1–4: exhortation (3.1, 4a) and encouragement (3.2–3, 4b). In both sections the message moves from Hermas' family to the community at large. While it is possible to interpret in some passages that the family is only a cipher for the community, the literary structure here argues against

that interpretation (see comment on *Vis.* 1.3.1 above).

The accusations against the children are grave: renunciation, blasphemy, betrayal—all terms that could be related to political persecution but need not be in light of *Vis.* 1.3.1, where their sin has more to do with being overinvolved with practical affairs. However, *Vis.* 2.3.4, which seems to recall a time of persecution, must also be taken into account, . It may be that Hermas' children did not prove faithful under this trial *because* of their material interests. The Lord (κύριος) against whom they have sinned is God, not Christ (compare *Vis.* 1.3.1; 2.2.8).

■ **2.3** Hermas' new relationship to his wife as a "sister" cannot mean as a new Christian (1 Cor 9:5), for she has already been part of his Christian family problems (*Vis.* 1.3.1).[3] It can only mean sexual abstinence, and the directive is meant here for Hermas alone, not for all, as *Man.* 4.1 shows. The motive may be not so much asceticism as prophetic call, though *Man.* 4.4, following 1 Cor 7:8, 27, 40, leans more in the direction of asceticism with eschatological intent. The objection to the behavior of Hermas' wife is possibly to her ready and assertive speaking out, perhaps in the assembly (1 Cor 14:34–35; 1 Tim 2:11–16), or is due to the general male stereo-

---

1   Compare Daniel's fast of three weeks (Dan 10:2–3).
2   Cf. as ascesis and preparation for religious experience: *Vis.* 3.1.2; 10.6; Matt 4:2; Luke 2:37; 4:2; Acts 13:2; *4 Ezra* 5.13, 20; 6.31; 9.23–24 (partial fast); *2 Bar.* 5.7; 9.2; *Apoc. Abr.* 9; *Asc. Isa.* 2.11; Philo *Ebr.* 148–52; *Q. Exod.* 2.39; *Som.* 1.36; *Vit. Mos.* 2.69–70. Tertullian (*De jejun.*) wrote a whole treatise in defense of Montanist fasting as coordinate to prophecy, even suggesting in conclusion that thinner bodies will get through the "narrow gate" (Matt 7:13–14; Luke 13:24) and lighter bodies will rise from the tomb more easily! Fasting for the sake of charity: *Barn.* 3.3 (quoting Isa 58:4–10); *Didasc.* 19=*Ap. Const.* 5.1.3–4. Rudolph Arbesmann, "Fasting and Prophecy in Pagan and Christian Antiquity," *Traditio* 7 (1949–1951) 1–71; Bruce J. Malina, *Christian Origins and Cultural Anthropology*

(Atlanta: John Knox, 1986) 185–204. Whether for the purpose of ascesis and preparation for visions or for charity, fasting is a type of "communicative non-consumption" that signals "a request for status-reversal" (ibid., 204), whether of the faster or of other recipients of the benefits of fasting.
3   Dibelius, 444–45. But against Dibelius, it may have much to do with the eschatological vision of Mark 12:25 as developed in early Christian ascetical tradition. Hermas' consideration of Rhoda as a "sister" (*Vis.* 1.1.7) is partially related to the meaning here.
4   Leutzsch, *Wahrnehmung*, 172–74. Cf. Sir 26:27; 1 Tim 3:11; 5:13; Titus 2:3; Philo, *Spec. leg.* 3.171–74; Pol. *Phil.* 4.3; *Didasc.* 15=*Ap. Const.* 3.6.4 (though, as Leutzsch points out, sins of the tongue are not always gender-specific in the tradition).

typing of women as loose-tongued.[4] But given the restrictions placed on women by marriage, this may be less a reduction of her role than a freeing for new relationship.[5]

■ **2.4–5** After the judgment comes the promise of forgiveness, at the first level to Hermas and his family, then to all Christians "up to this day" ($\mu\acute{\epsilon}\chi\rho\iota$ $\tau\alpha\acute{\upsilon}\tau\eta\varsigma$ $\tau\mathring{\eta}\varsigma$ $\mathring{\eta}\mu\acute{\epsilon}\rho\alpha\varsigma$ v. 4), if their turning to God is with their whole heart.[6] The time that has yet to be has been determined (v. 5). This is an eschatological narrative time frame in which possible linguistic inconsistencies should not be pushed. The time of salvation is now (cf. Mark 1:15; Luke 4:21), yet it will not last forever—a warning that focuses the urgency of the message on the present. Later, the end of that time will be imaged as the completion of the tower (*Vis.* 3.8.9), after which change is not possible (*Vis.* 3.9.5; *Sim.* 9.32.1; 10.4.4). But the completion of the tower is also the end (*Vis.* 3.8.9). It is therefore not certain that the end of possible conversion for believers is something more proximate than the "end time,"[7] even though this creates more difficulty to explain how the outsiders seem to have more time. The answer lies not in chronological but in narrative theological structure: believers have the word of revelation already addressed to them in baptism, and repeated in Hermas' proclamation; the time for conversion is therefore the immediate present, whereas for unbelievers, it is the time in which they hear the message.[8] Verse 4 contains the first reference to "doublemindedness" ($\delta\iota\psi\upsilon\chi\acute{\iota}\alpha$), a major complaint whose relinquishing is here a condition for true conversion.[9]

■ **2.6–8** This is the first time that part of the revelatory message has been addressed directly to the leaders or presiders of the church ($o\mathring{\iota}$ $\pi\rho o\eta\gamma o\acute{\upsilon}\mu\epsilon\nu o\iota$ $\tau\mathring{\eta}\varsigma$ $\mathring{\epsilon}\kappa\kappa\lambda\eta\sigma\acute{\iota}$-$\alpha\varsigma$), signaled by the change from second person singular to plural in v. 7. This sudden switch from singular to paraenetic plural will occur frequently throughout the text, an indication of the wider audience participating in the oral proclamation. The structure of the prophetic oracle here consists of commisioning formula (v. 6), admonition (v. 7a), beatitude (v. 7b), conditional threat (v. 8a), and conditional promise (v. 8b).[10] The plural term for church leaders, probably synonymous with earlier $\pi\rho o\ddot{\iota}\sigma\tau\acute{\alpha}\mu\epsilon\nu o\iota$ ("presiders" or "leaders," Rom 12:8; 1 Thess 5:12) and $\pi\rho\epsilon\sigma\beta\acute{\upsilon}\tau\epsilon\rho o\iota$ ("elders"),[11] appears again at *Vis.* 3.9.7 linked and perhaps synonymous with $\pi\rho\omega\tau o\kappa\alpha\vartheta\epsilon\delta\rho\hat{\iota}\tau\alpha\iota$ ("those who hold the first place"). The plural and varying usage indicate a collegial form of church leadership by a group of elders, of which Hermas does not appear to be one.

The church leaders are exhorted against doublemindedness, which would bring about wavering in their firm endurance. If they endure, their $\pi\acute{\alpha}\rho o\delta o\varsigma$ ("entrance or journey") will be with the angels (also *Sim.* 9.24.4, 25.2), that is, their heavenly destiny is assured in company with the angels;[12] probably also that they will be escorted or conveyed to heaven by angels, a motif common enough in Greco-Roman apotheosis representations. A makarism (or beatitude) is pronounced on those who will "endure" ($\mathring{\upsilon}\pi o\mu\acute{\epsilon}\nu\epsilon\iota\nu$) in the coming "tribulation" ($\vartheta\lambda\hat{\iota}\psi\iota\varsigma$), recognizable apocalyptic language for the end time, which is not necessarily, however, totally separated from some historical catastrophe for the community (or for Hermas

---

5   The verse may reflect the early Christian custom of syneisaktism; see comment on *Sim.* 9.11.3.

6   On this expression as a biblical phrase, see Hilhorst, *Sémitismes*, 142–44. It is a favorite of Hermas, used eighteen times; cf. Matt 22:37; *2 Clem.* 3.4.

7   Against Brox, 100.

8   Further lengthy discussion in Dibelius, 416–17; Snyder, 36; Brox, 99–100; cf. Introduction 3.3.1.

9   See Introduction 3.3.2.

10   Aune, *Prophecy*, 300, 304.

11   Acts 14:23; 20:17 passim; Titus 1:5; Jas 5:14; 1 Pet 5:1; 2 John 1; 3 John 1; cf. esp. $o\mathring{\iota}$ $\kappa\alpha\lambda\hat{\omega}\varsigma$ $\pi\rho o$-

$\epsilon\sigma\tau\hat{\omega}\tau\epsilon\varsigma$ $\pi\rho\epsilon\sigma\beta\acute{\upsilon}\tau\epsilon\rho o\iota$ ("elders who preside well"), 1 Tim 5:17; *Vis.* 2.4.3; 3.1.8. The use of the term in *1 Clem.* 21.7, contrasted to the young, is more likely to mean aged persons than officeholders in its specific context.

12   These passages are often compared to *1 Enoch* 104.4; *2 Bar.* 51.5, 9, 12; *Mart. Pol.* 2.3 to demonstrate a belief that the faithful dead became angels (e.g., Lake 21, 215). The two refs. in *Hermas*, however, do not really say that, *1 Enoch* and *2 Baruch* are ambivalent, and even *Mart. Pol.* can be understood in the sense of Matt 22:30 and parr. But see *Acts of Paul and Thecla* 5; Lake, 21; Joly, 93 n. 3; Snyder,

himself, who has already had some of his own [Introduction 3.1, above]), as suggested by the topic of denial coming immediately upon it.

The question of what to do with apostates, a thorny problem in later centuries after widespread persecution, surfaces here. The oath taken by God on the son is unusual, a Christian adaptation of a Jewish motif[13] (see the more usual form above, v. 5). The two uses of κύριος ("Lord") in the same sentence are different: the first time it refers to God who swears the oath, the second time probably to Christ,[14] whose name was the testing ground for Christians under persecution—they, too, were pressured to swear an oath to renounce it.[15] There seem to be various levels of denial: neglect, doublemindedness, and outright apostasy. This will become clearer in later discussions of doublemindedness. The point here is that even for such denial in the past, there is forgiveness, while a solemn warning is issued against presuming on divine mercy in the same situation now and in the days to come.

ed back to Hermas himself and his family situation. His previously unmentioned negative treatment of his children and sister (=wife; see 2.3 above) is to be changed. It may not be so much a question of holding grudges (the usual understanding of μνησικακέω)[16] as of resenting the obligations, shame, and perhaps even unwanted legal attention forced on him by their misdeeds, which could have been prevented had he exercised proper vigilance instead of being involved in his own business affairs.

Hermas' fundamental faithfulness, however, has not been compromised, for he has not alienated himself, literally "apostasized" (ἀποστῆναι) from the living God (Heb 3:12), though probably not meant here in the technical sense. His fidelity is characterized by simplicity and great restraint (ἐγκράτεια), a term often in Christian literature meaning sexual continence, but used in *Hermas* with a far wider meaning (for example, throughout *Mandate* 8).

The Written Message Continued

■ **3.1–2 [7]** The revelatory message continues, now direct-

---

36–37; Brox, 101. For Charles Hill (*Regnum Caelorum: Patterns of Future Hope in Early Christianity* [Oxford: Clarendon, 1992] 86–87), there is a christological allusion here: since *Sim.* 9.12.8 says that even the angels must pass through the gate of the tower which is the Son of God, then those enrolled with the angels (*Sim.* 9.24.4; inaccurate reference in Hill) or passing with the angels (as here and *Sim.* 9.25.2) pass with them through this gate into the tower, and therefore to access to God.

13 Dibelius, 448.

14 Original reading of S Χριστόν ("Christ"); a twelfth-century correction aligns it with AL² κύριον ("Lord"); L¹ *filium* ("son"); missing B. Without question, the ms. tradition, whatever term is used, understands this as a reference to Jesus. Cf. *Vis.* 3.6.5 and esp. *Sim.* 9.13.2, but also 9.28.6: suffering in the name of God. Discussion in Nijendijk, "Christologie," 75–76; Snyder, 37–38. It is not clear how *kyrios* ("Lord") can be "not a Christological title in the Shepherd, but so nearly represents that presence of God which in the NT is the Son, that it can approximate a Christological meaning" (Snyder, 38). Cf. *Sim.* 9.14.5–6. Audet ("Affinités," 45–56) would deny any reference to Christ under the name of Lord.

15 Matt 10:22; 19:29; Jas 2:7; 1 Pet 4:14, 16; *Vis.* 3.1.9; *Sim.* 8.6.4; 9.19.,1; 28.3; *Acts Scil. Mart.* 5; *Mart. Pol.*

8.2; 9.2–3; Pliny *Ep.* 10.96.2, 5–6; Moyo, "Angels and Christology," 138–43.

16 Osiek, *Rich and Poor*, 61 n. 10. After "resentment is deadly" (μνησικακία θάνατον κατεργάζεται), B adds "but non-resentment gives eternal life" (τὸ δ᾽ ἀμνησίκακον ζωὴν αἰώνιον κατεργάζεται), which restores the Greek of L¹ *oblivio enim malorum vitam aeternam cooperatur* ("but forgetfulness of wrongs gives eternal life"). Antonio Carlini ("Erma [*Vis.* II 3.1] testimone testuale di Paolo?" *SCO* 37 [1987] 235–39) argues here a dependence on 2 Cor 7:10 as in *Vis.* 1.1.9; denied by Brox (102) on too little evidence: the juxtaposition of (κατ)εργάζεται alone; also by Joly (Carlini, ibid., 239 n. 12).

17 On occurrences of the name at all social levels: Osiek, *Rich and Poor*, 109.

18 Given in five canonical lists and known into the Middle Ages: E. G. Martin, *OTP* 2. 463–65; perhaps

■ **3.3–4** A second makarism (see above, 2.7) blesses those who do deeds of righteousness or justice, showing again the deeper concerns of the book. Δικαιοσύνη carries in English the meaning of both "righteousness," the inward attitude, and "justice," right behavior. In a deeply rooted Jewish or Jewish Christian ethic, consistency of attitude and behavior is expected. Thus, in Hermas' thinking, formal apostasy cannot be split off from the informal apostasy of everyday infidelity. Maximus (v. 4), unknown to us but undoubtedly an infamous object of shame in Hermas' community, is sarcastically singled out for a stinging taunt, and is the shining example of what not to do.[17] The quotation from the lost Book of Eldad and Modat (Num 11:26–30)[18] is the only attributed quote in *Hermas*. The address to Maximus is in prophetic oracle form: commission formula, conditional threat, and conditional promise.[19]

---

quoted in *1 Clem.* 23.3–4; *2 Clem.* 11.2–4 (Edgar J. Goodspeed, *A History of Early Christian Literature* [rev. Robert M. Grant; Chicago: University of Chicago Press, 1966] 89); perhaps an example of texts read in house churches (Leutzsch, *Wahrnehmung*, 71).

19   Aune, *Prophecy*, 300.

2

Identity of the Woman Church Revealed

4 [8] 1/ While I slept, a revelation came to me, brothers and sisters, from a handsome young man who said to me: "The elder lady from whom you received the little book—who do you think she is?" I answered: "The sybil." "Wrong," he said, "that is not who she is." "Then who is she?" I asked. "The church," he said. I said to him: "Then why is she elderly?" "Because," he said, "she was created before everything. That is why she is elderly, and for her the world was established." 2/ Later, I saw a vision in my house. The elder lady came and asked me if I had already given the book to the elders. I replied that I had not. "You have done well," she said. "I have words to add. When I have finished them all, they will be communicated through you to all the elect. 3/ So you will write two little books and send one to Clement and one to Grapte. Clement will send his to the other cities, for he is charged with this responsibility. Grapte will admonish the widows and orphans. But you will read it in this city with the presbyters who preside in the church."

■ **4.1 [8]** The location of Hermas' discovery of the meaning of the revelation (2.1b–3.4 above) is not specified, except that he was fasting and praying. That the next vision comes to him as a dream during sleep suggests that the location has been his home. The young man (angel) in this interpretive dream quizzes him on the identity of his heavenly revealer. Hermas' guess that she is the Sybil, undoubtedly the Cumaean one, has evoked much comment. It fits neatly with the reading that his first and second encounters with her happened on the road to Cumae (*Vis.* 1.1.3; 2.1.1). It is more difficult to interpret once that reading has been rejected.[1] Yet sybilline oracles had already been collected and institutionalized at Rome for several centuries by being kept in the temple of Jupiter; statues of the Sibyl may have been known at Rome in this period;[2] and Hellenistic Judaism had already been producing its own sybilline oracles for at least two centuries, soon to be joined by Christian redactors. *Hermas* is the earliest Christian reference to their popularity.[3] There are definite similarities between this woman and the Sybil: great age, seated position, holding a book, revealing hidden secrets, but the suggestion that Hermas' revealer was originally the Sybil has been rightly rejected. A more plausible possibility—but it remains only that—is that Hermas took the Sybil as model for the woman church.[4]

But Hermas is told by his interpreting vision that she is rather the church, created before everything else, and therefore elderly. Her primeval creation as end of all other creation is a wisdom motif already adapted to Jewish purposes,[5] and the personification of Israel, Jerusalem, or the church as a woman was already established.[6]

Instruction for Dissemination of the Message

■ **4.2–3** The next vision has a place but not a time

---

1 See comment on *Vis.* 1.1.3 above. A corruption of κώμας to κούμας is more readily understandable under the influence of this reference to the Sibyl, than the reverse.

2 Peterson, "Beiträge," 266–67, based on Longus *Pastorales* 2.23.1; Lactantius *Institutes* 1.6.12.

3 John J. Collins, *OTP* 1. 317–472; Alfons Kurfess, *NTApoc* 703–45. Their genre of apocalyptic framework for paraenetic content suggests a partial literary parallel to *Hermas*: John J. Collins, *Apocalypse: The Morphology of a Genre* (Semeia 14; Missoula, MT: Scholars Press, 1979) 46–47; 97–98.

4 Further discussion: Dibelius, 450–52; Brox, 104–6.

5 Prov 8:22–31; Sir 15:2–10; 24; 51:19–20; *4 Ezra* 8.52; *2 Bar.* 4.1–7; reserved for Christ in the NT: 1 Cor 8:6; Col 1:15–20. Creation of the world for the just

marker; it happens not out in the open like the first two, but in private, in his own house. The woman church indicates that the message is not complete, yet she does not add anything on the spot. The revelation will therefore remain free-flowing, added to from time to time. Her previous nudges in the direction of Hermas' duty to communicate the message (1.3; 2.3–4, 6; 3.6 above) now become quite specifically localized.

The debate has raged among scholars about this Clement: is he or is he not Clement of Rome, author of *1 Clement*?[7] Even if the two figures are identical, that does nothing to establish a monarchical episcopate at Rome at this early date; the end of v. 3 is very clear about church government.[8] Even if there were a single bishop in Rome at this time—though all evidence is to the contrary—sending someone else's letter to other churches would hardly be his task. The reference is more likely to the church secretary, perhaps a deacon. The figure of Clement was powerful enough in the early tradition to establish a long literary connection: not only *1 Clement*, but *2 Clement*, the *Clementine Romances*, and the *Recognitions*. Though the writing of *1 Clement* is generally dated to the 90s of the first century, there is nothing against an early second-century date, so that discrepancy of dating is not a problem.[9] Hermas' original community obviously knows who this person is supposed to be. If Clement of Rome is alive and functioning

as a kind of community secretary, this remark must refer to him.

If Clement is very well known, Grapte is otherwise unknown. Probably a widow and a freedwoman,[10] she holds responsibility for instruction of women and children who are not under male authority, a function entrusted to wise older women (Titus 2:3–4). She is perhaps a deacon charged with religious instruction (1 Tim 3:11; *Sim.* 9.26.2).[11]

The local church other than Grapte's flock are to receive the message directly from Hermas as he takes an unaccustomed place with the presbyters who lead the church. The supposition that at this period there were numerous house churches in Rome that came together occasionally for common worship leads to the question whether "the church" of which these presbyters are in charge is a local house church with collegial leadership, or the totality of the Christians in the city.[12] The international scope of Clement's charge suggests that the latter is the case. Hermas' authority to proclaim his message is now legitimated at the highest level and is to be communicated at the highest level of Christian assembly in the city. The wording suggests that neither Clement nor Grapte nor Hermas belongs to the usual group of presbyters.

---

or for Israel: *4 Ezra* 7.10–11; 9.13; *As. Mos.* 1.12–13. Pernveden, *Concept of the Church*, 24–25.

6 *4 Ezra* 9.38–10.57; Eph 5:23–33; Rev 21:2; *2 Clem.* 14.1–2.

7 Survey of opinions in Brox, 107–8.

8 Eusebius' identification of Clement as bishop of Rome from 93 CE is anachronistic (*Hist. eccl.* 3.15, 34).

9 Dating of *1 Clement* has depended heavily on Eusebius' connection with Flavius Clemens and the family of Domitian (*Hist. eccl.* 3.16–18), but could be anywhere from 80–140 CE: Lawrence L. Welborn, "On the Date of First Clement," *BR* 29 (1984) 35–54; Barbara E. Bowe, *A Church in Crisis: Ecclesiology and Paraenesis in Clement of Rome* (HDR 23; Minneapolis: Fortress, 1988) 1–3. Recently Jeffers, *Conflict at Rome*, has focused on the historical and archaeological evidence for Clement's connections with the Flavius Clemens family.

10 The name is frequent in Rome: of fifty-four occurrences in four centuries, sixteen are slaves and freedwomen, five probably freedwomen, and thirty-

three uncertain (Solin, *Griechische Personennamen*, 3. 1171–73).

11 Wilson (*Reassessment*, 33 n. 90) makes the unprovable but charming suggestion that Clement and Grapte were a couple "serving in equivalent ecclesiastical offices" like Aquila and Priscilla.

12 See comment on 2.6, above. Each house church may have been governed by its host and *paterfamilias* (or *materfamilias*: Acts 12:12; 16:40; Col 4:15), head of the household in which it met, with the title of presbyter (2 John 1:1; 3 John 1:1), who then represented that group in a council of presbyters for the whole city. Out of this leadership council was to evolve eventually a presbyter-bishop of the whole: Maier, *Social Setting*.

3

Building of the Tower

1 [9] 1/ This is what I saw, brothers and sisters. 2/ When I had fasted a great deal and asked the Lord to show me the revelation he had promised to show me by means of the elder lady, that very night the elder lady appeared to me and said: "Since you are so needy and eager to know everything, go into the field where you linger, and at about the fifth hour I will appear to you and show you what you must see." 3/ I asked her: "Lady, to what part of the field?" "Wherever you want," she answered. I found a lovely secluded spot. But even before I had told her the place, she said: "I will be there, wherever you want." 4/ So I went, brothers and sisters, into the field and watched the time and went to the place I had determined for her to come. I saw an ivory couch set up, on the couch a linen pillow, and a piece of good linen covering it. 5/ When I saw all this set out, but no one there, I was seized with terror and began trembling and my hair stood on end. I was panic-stricken because I was alone. When I came to myself and took courage, remembering God's glory, falling on my knees I once again acknowledged my sins to the Lord as before. 6/ Then she came with the six young men for escorts that I had seen before, and she stood by me listening as I prayed and acknowledged my sins to the Lord. Finally she touched me and said: "Hermas, stop concentrating on your sins, and ask instead about justice, so you can take something of it back to your household." 7/ She raised me by the hand, led me to the couch, and said to the young men: "Go and build." 8/ After the young men had gone away and we were left alone, she said to me: "Sit here." I said to her: "Lady, let the elders sit first." "Do what I tell you and sit," she said. 9/ Then when I wanted to sit on the right side, she would not let me, but with her hand directed me to sit on the left side. Since I withdrew into myself and was miffed that she would not let me sit on the right side, she said to me: "Are you upset, Hermas? The place on the right side is for others, those who have already been approved by God and have suffered for the name. You have a long way to go to sit with them. But continue in your simplicity as you are doing and you shall sit with them, and so shall all who act accordingly and endure what they have endured."

2 [10] 1/ "What have they endured?" I asked. "Listen," she said. "Beatings, imprisonment, great tribulations, crucifixions, wild beasts for the sake of the name. This is why those people are at the right hand of holiness, whoever suffers for the name, but for the rest there is the left side. To both, however, those who sit on the right and those who sit on the left, will come the same gifts and the same promises, except that those seated on the right have a certain honor. 2/ You want very badly to sit on the right side with them, but you have too many failings. You will be cleansed of

60

your failings, though, and all those who are not doubleminded will be cleansed of all sins up to today." 3/ Having said this, she wanted to leave, but falling at her feet I begged her by the Lord to show me the vision she had promised. 4/ Once again she took me by the hand, raised me up, and made me sit on the couch on the left while she sat on the right. Lifting a shining rod she said to me: "Do you see something great?" I answered: "Lady, I see nothing." She said to me: "Look, do you not see in front of you a large tower being built upon water with shiny square stones?" 5/ The tower was being built in a square by the six young men who had come with her. But about ten thousand other men were carrying stones, some from the depth of the sea, some from land, which they were delivering to the six young men who were taking and building with them. 6/ All the stones that were dragged from the depths they placed in the building, for they were shaped to fit right into joint with the other stones, so they adhered to one another so well that the joints did not show. The building of the tower seemed to be of one stone. 7/ Of the other stones brought from dry ground, some they threw away and some they put in the building. Still others they broke up and threw away far from the tower. 8/ But there were many other stones lying around the tower that they did not use for the building. Some were scaly, others had cracks, others were broken off, others were white and round, and did not fit into the building. 9/ I saw other stones cast far away from the tower that fell on the road and did not stay there, but rolled off onto rough ground. Others were falling into fire and burning up; others were falling near water and could not roll into the water even though they wished to keep rolling into the water.

The Woman Church and Her Attendants

■ **1.1–2 [9]** The Greek manuscripts number this as the third vision.[1] Again, as in *Vis.* 2.2.1, Hermas has fasted and prayed in preparation for a revelation that comes to him at night, presumably in a dream. The promise of the Lord to show Hermas more revelations is not recorded

---

1 Peterson ("Begegnung," 285) would make the numbering of the visions secondary on the basis that there are really more than three apparitions of the woman church, so that the opening lines resemble Dan 8:1 LXX: ὅρασιν ἦν εἶδον ἐγὼ Δανιήλ ("the vision that I, Daniel, saw"). But, as Brox points out (111–12), the author himself numbers the visions of the woman church in the narrative of the third *Vision* (11.2; 12.1; 13.1 [the last misprinted in Brox as 21.1 by slippage into the alternate numbering system]). Further discussion in Hellholm, *Visionenbuch,* 131 n. 10. Antonio Carlini ("Un accusativo da difendere [*Hermae Pastor, Vis.* III 1,1; *Vis.* IV 1,1]," *SCO* 38 [1988] 511–12) makes the credible suggestion that both here and at *Vis.* 4.1.1, the original text read ὅρασιν ἦν εἶδον, ἀδελφοί ... ("the vision I saw, brothers and sisters ...") without the numbering which now makes S ὅρασις γ(δ) ἢ εἶδον (vision 3 [4] [nominative] "that" [accusative] "I saw") grammatically awkward.

in the text, unless it is meant to be the follow-up on the woman church's statement (*Vis.* 2.4.2) that she has more to add to the written message. If that is what he is expecting, he will have a long time to wait, perhaps until 3.9. The next revelations will be visual and verbal but not written. The woman church's descriptions of Hermas are so many (at least literary) self-portraits.[2] Her description of him as "needy" (ἐνδεής) uses a favorite word of the author which has acquired for him a positive meaning in keeping with his later message of simplicity and identification with the poor.[3]

A field as place of revelation is not unknown (*4 Ezra* 9.26; 10.53 [where the vision of a woman has just turned into a city!]; 12.51; 13.57; 14.37), but Hermas' relationship to it has been interpreted at both extremes. On the one hand, Peterson would banish the difficult *hapax legomenon* ὅπου χονδρίζεις ("where you are farming"), thus doing away with Hermas' ownership of land.[4] On the other hand, Lampe would make of the field Hermas' business of growing spelt for brewing, enabling him to have the "self-sufficiency" (αὐτάρκεια) that he preaches in *Sim.* 1.6![5] The translation here follows the majority of manuscripts with χρονίζεις. The fifth hour is late morning.[6]

■ **1.3–6** The direct address to an audience (v. 4) reminds us that the text is intended for performance. Hermas' description of the linen-covered ivory couch or bench that he sees set up in the field evokes similarities to divination contexts in the magical papyri, and uses three Latin loanwords: συμψέλιον[7]=*subsellium* ("bench" or "couch," replacing the καθέδρα of *Vis.* 1.2.2; cf. 3.1.7,

2.4, 10.1, 5, 13.3); κερβικάριον=*cervical* (head pillow); λέντιον=*linteum* ("linen cloth"), not an unusual phenomenon in a Latin-speaking environment.[8] Hermas' response of fright to this awesome sight, including hair standing on end, is the expected reaction to the presence of the numinous.[9] The first reaction of terror is followed by Hermas' characteristic response to the presence of the supernatural: focus on sin (*Vis.* 1.1.3; 2.1.2).

The six young men are the same four angels who carried the chair and the two who escorted the woman church in her first appearance (*Vis.* 1.4.1, 3). As in that appearance, she again touches Hermas to establish contact, and as in 1.3.1, more forcefully here draws his attention away from his preoccupation with personal sin[10] toward his social responsibility, in the first instance in his own household as model for a wider perspective.[11]

■ **1.7–9** The woman church's directive to the angels to "go and build" is the beginning of the major motif of the third *Vision*, the building of the tower. While they begin the construction, this strange interlude takes place, in which Hermas is invited to sit with the woman on the couch, but is then told not to sit where he wants to. When first invited to sit, he demurs saying that the πρεσβύτεροι should sit first. The Greek word can mean either "elder persons" or "presbyters." Most commentators take the latter meaning, sometimes even to the point of seeing here a tension between presbyteral and prophetic authority (the latter represented by Hermas), or between the office of presbyters and the charismatic authority of martyrs, for whom the right side is reserved (v. 9). At the opposite extreme, Lake takes the statement

2 Compare *Vis.* 1.2.3; 3.3.1; 3.8.9; etc.

3 Cf. *Man.* 8.10; Osiek, *Rich and Poor,* 64–68.

4 "Beiträge," 287–91. Only S contains this otherwise unattested word, accepted by Lake and Whittaker; BS^cAL[2] follow a reading χρονίζεις ("stay," "pass time"), also better supported by L[1] *vis* ([where you] "wish"). Dibelius' suggestion (455) that the S reading is an otherwise unknown variant on χονδρεύω ("raise wheat" or "make groats") is more likely than Peterson's emendation to διορίζεις ("choose," "single out," as in v. 3); so too Brox (112 n. 4), but the majority witness is superior (Carlini, *Bodmer Papyrus,* 76). For Peterson, the field may even be an allegorical Garden of Eden!

5 *Stadtrömische Christen,* 186.

6 Also a time marker for visions in some magical papyri: Brox, 112.

7 S; or συμψέλλιον AB. Both spellings attested:

8 Carlini, *Bodmer Papyrus,* 76; BAGD[2] *s.v.*

8 Cf. Hilhorst, *Sémitismes,* 165–68, 184. Use of Latin loanwords does not imply Latin as the writer's native language; cf. same in Gospel of Mark. Refs. to magical papyri: Peterson, "Beiträge," 254–57. See comments on *Vis.* 1.2.2 above.

9 E.g., Job 4:15 LXX; Virgil *Aen.* 4.279: "his hair stood up in terror and the voice clave to his throat" (LCL 1. 415); Peterson, "Beiträge," 266 n. 68.

10 S translates literally "Stop asking about all (πάντα) your sins"; A "Stop asking again (πάλιν) about your sins," a preferred reading that would echo ἐξωμολο-γούμην τῷ κυρίῳ πάλιν τὰς ἁμαρτίας μου ("I once again acknowledged my sins to the Lord") at the end of v. 5. L[1] followed by E has caught the idea with a different word, *tantum* ("so much").

11 See comment on *Vis.* 1.3, 4 above.

as merely a gesture of respect: "elders first," which does not make the passage unintelligible,[12] but probably makes most sense; the woman church has been described as an older person (πρεσβῦτις *Vis.* 1.2.2; πρεσβυτέρα 2.4.1, 2; 3.1.1), and she is the only one present here. While grammatically possible (both terms are used later for female presbyters), the meaning here is hardly that she is a presbyter in the church. If presbyters are intended, once again we have confirmation, as in *Vis.* 2.4.3, that Hermas is not one of them.[13]

Sitting on the right side of a presiding dignitary is a mark of greatest prestige, and on the left secondary.[14] By trying to sit on the right, Hermas is not trying to take the place of the presbyters, for, even if they figure in this passage, there is no indication that they belong there; nor is he trying to usurp the position of the martyrs, for he has to be told that the right side is their place. Rather, he is making the foolish assumption that as recipient of her revelation he belongs there, and the woman church subjects him to a moment of humiliation to remind him that he can claim no privilege (cf. 2.2 below). But in the next breath she encourages him and the readers to continue along the way. The name for which the martyrs have suffered (also at 2.1 below) is the name of Christ, even though the manuscript evidence reveals theological confusion, and notwithstanding the honor given to the name of God in Judaism.[15]

First Glimpse of the Tower

■ **2.1–2 [10]** The recital of the martyrs' sufferings cannot be taken as a historical account of things Hermas has

seen. A simple acquaintance with a text like 2 Maccabees or Heb 11:33–39 could produce such a list, yet it undoubtedly evokes some known past history, though not in detail: perhaps the Neronian persecution, probably confined only to Rome[16] or the events alluded to in *1 Clem.* 1.1; 5; 6 (which may be the same). Crucifixion (σταυρός=*crux*) and condemnation to wild animals in the amphitheater (θηρία=*bestiae*) were normal Roman modes of punishment for lower-class persons, or *inferiores*.[17] There can be no doubt that this recitation of torture and execution refers to some kind of political persecution to the point of capital condemnation.

The place of the martyrs is on the right side of God's throne, the place of highest honor. It is the right side of "holiness" (ἁγίασμα), a Jewish euphemism for the presence of God (compare Mark 14:62: at the right hand of the "power"), perhaps originally in reference to the altar of the Jerusalem Temple, but then adapted to mean the heavenly throne.[18] The text is testimony to the early beginnings of the cult of martyrs. The use of left and right here is not part of Two Ways theology as is, for instance, Matt 25:33–46, for those on the left side receive everything the same except for special honor. Rather, it is a way of speaking borrowed from throne-room practice to signify the special honor given to martyrs.[19] For the time frame presumed in v. 2, see comment on *Vis.* 2.2.5 above.

■ **2.3–5** Hermas has been expecting another revelation since 1.1. The ivory couch, the woman church, and her escorts are all preparation. When she now starts to leave, he is not about to let her get away. She raises him

---

12 Against Brox, 114 n. 11.

13 Lake, 29 n. 1; Brox, 114–15.

14 Cf. 2.1 below; *Asc. Isa.* 7; 11:25–33; also Matt 20:21 par. Mark 10:37; Matt 25:33; Ps 110:1 and numerous christological passages inspired by it, e.g., Matt 26:64 and parr.; Mark 14:62; Acts 2:33; 5:31; Rom 8:34; Eph 1:20; Heb 1:3; Polycarp *Phil.* 2.1; *Apoc. Pet.* 6; *Sib. Or.* 2.243; quoted in *1 Clem.* 36.5; *Barn.* 12.10. Cf. David M. Hay, *Glory at the Right Hand: Psalm 110 in Early Christianity* (SBLMS 18; Nashville/New York: Abingdon, 1973).

15 Against Brox, 115. Both S μου τοῦ ὀνόματος ("for my name") and AL²E τοῦ ὀνόματος αὐτοῦ ("for his name") must be incorrect; only BL¹ are without qualifier. Both Whittaker and Joly omit the possessive adjective. The same ambiguity occurs elsewhere when "the name" is without qualifiers, e.g., 2.1 below. Cf. *Sim.* 8.10.3; 9.13.2, 28.3–6; Ignatius *Eph.*

3.1. See comment on *Vis.* 2.2.8. But see 5.2 below.

16 Tacitus *Ann.* 15:44.2–8.

17 Martin Hengel, *Crucifixion in the Ancient World and the Folly of the Message of the Cross* (Philadelphia: Fortress, 1977) 22–63; Osiek, "Ransom," 377–79.

18 Brox, 116. Eusebius, *Hist. eccl.* 7.15.4 uses it of the sanctuary or altar in a Christian church in his account of the martyrdom of Theoteknos.

19 Compare *Asc. Isa.* 7.15, 30, 34, where the glory of those angels on the right side of God's throne is greater than that of those on the left.

up by the hand,[20] and with both of them sitting on the couch in the positions she had assigned, she waves a magic wand[21] to open up the vision. Still, he needs two attempts to see it. The vision of the tower which then stretches out before him is the central image of the book, incorporating the eschatological, paraenetic, and ecclesiological content that will be gradually unfolded in the form of verbal instruction. The church as building has a previous history,[22] as does the tower as symbol of strength and duration.[23] Its use as antidote to the Tower of Babel (Genesis 11) does not seem to be at work here.[24] Given the literary background and the natural symbolism suggested by the familiar material reality, the choice of the image is not surprising. The emphasis laid upon it will be the process of its building as eschatological timekeeping and the participation of all sorts of members. Connections with myths of the heavenly city or heavenly Jerusalem should not be pushed too far with regard to the tower; it is precisely its presence in time

and history that is stressed in the ensuing narrative.[25] The foursquare design of the tower is to be expected both as symbol of solidity and for its cosmic significance.[26] The six young men (angels) who accompanied the woman church now have a key role in the building process; they will later be identified as foundations of creation (4.1).

■ **2.6–9** The detailed descriptions of the various kinds of stones mark the beginning of the allegory that will be explained after the description is completed. All the stones taken from the water are immediately useful and shaped to fit with one another, while those from dry ground have various problems, each of which will later have an application. The description of the stones that fall and lie around in unwanted places (vv. 8–9) may draw upon local quarrying methods.[27]

---

20   Compare *4 Ezra* 10.30.
21   A familiar instrument in magical divination, also portrayed in some early Christian painting in the hand of Moses striking the rock (see *Sim.* 9.6.3) or parting the Red Sea, and Jesus multiplying loaves, changing water to wine at Cana, and raising Lazarus. For Dibelius (458) definitely a magical accessory; for Brox (118) either that or a teacher's pointer as in *Tab. Ceb.* 4.2; for Peterson ("Beiträge," 260) a magic wand that is connected with the teacher's staff.
22   1 Cor 3:9–17; extended by Ignatius (*Magn.* 9.1–2) into an allegory of stones (Christians), hoist (the cross), and rope (the Holy Spirit).
23   Cant 4:4; 7:5; Mic 4:8; 1QSb 5.23–24; 1QH 7.8; *1 Enoch* 87.3; 89.50. Cf. Cirillo, "Erma e il problema," 9–11.
24   But it probably is in *Sib. Or.* 5.424–28 where the tower stretches over many stadia, touches the

clouds, and is visible to all, so that east and west are united in praise of God. Compare refs. to a heavenly human or angelic figure whose height reaches to the heavens, at *Sim.* 8.2 with further refs.; 9.6.1.
25   Against Dibelius, 459; with Snyder, 42–43.
26   13.3; Ezek 43:16; Rev 21:16; *Tab. Ceb.* 18.1–3.
27   Kirsopp Lake ("The Shepherd of Hermas and Christian Life in Rome in the Second Century," *HTR* 4 [1911] 25–47) tells of seeing the quarrying of stones between Frascati and Grotta Ferrata for the building of the electric railway, by quarrying on a precipice and allowing the stones to fall into a chute whose trajectory was not always accurate (29).

3

Explanation of the Tower

1/ When she had shown me these things, she was in a hurry to leave. I said to her: "Lady, what good is it to me to have seen these things and not know the meaning?" She answered: "You are a mischievous fellow, wanting to know what the tower means." "Yes, lady," I answered, "so I can report to my companions and they may be more joyful, and when they hear these things they will know the Lord with full honor." 2/ She said: "Certainly many will hear, and some of them will rejoice while others mourn. But even these, if they hear and be converted, will rejoice. So listen to the parables of the tower. I will reveal everything to you. Then do not bother me anymore about revelations. The revelations are finished and completed. But you will not stop asking for revelations, since you are shameless. 3/ The tower that you see being built is I myself, the church, who appeared to you both now and before. Ask whatever you want about the tower and I will reveal it to you so that you may rejoice with the holy ones." 4/ I said to her: "Lady, since you once found me worthy to reveal everything to me, on with the revelation." She said to me: "Whatever is given to you to be revealed, will be revealed. Only may your heart be turned to God and do not be doubleminded about what you see." 5/ I asked her: "Why was the tower built upon the water, lady?" "As I told you before," she said, "[you are mischievous about the writings] and you are inquiring carefully. By inquiring you will find the truth. So listen to why the tower was built on water: because your [pl.] life was saved and will be saved through water. The tower has been founded by the word of the almighty and glorious name, and is sustained by the unseen power of the master."

1/ I answered her: "Lady, this thing is great and marvelous. Who are the six young men who are building the tower, lady?" "These are the holy angels of God who were created first, to whom the Lord turned over all his creation, to increase, build up, and govern all creation. So through them the construction of the tower will be completed." 2/ "And who are the others who are bringing stones?" "They are also angels of God, but these six are superior to them. The construction of the tower will be brought to completion and all of them together will rejoice around the tower and will glorify God because the building of the tower has been finished." 3/ I asked her: "Lady, I would like to know the destiny of the stones and their import." She answered me: "It is not that you are more worthy than all others that it should be revealed to you. There were others before you and better than you to whom these visions ought to have been revealed. But that God's name might be honored, it was revealed and will be revealed to you because of the doubleminded who debate in their hearts whether things are like this or not. Tell them that all these things are true and nothing of this is beyond the truth, but everything is firm, reliable, and established.

5 [13] 1/ "Now listen about the stones that go into the building. Those that are square and white and fit into their joints are the apostles and overseers and teachers and deacons who proceed mindful of the dignity of God, who have governed and taught and served the elect of God in holiness and dignity, some of whom have fallen asleep and some of whom are still alive. They were always in harmony with each other and were in peace with one another and listened to each other. That is why their joints fit with one another in the building of the tower." 2/ "And who are those drawn from the depths and placed in the tower, whose joints fit together with the other stones already built into it?" "These are they who have suffered for the name of the Lord." 3/ "But I would like to know, lady, who are the other stones brought from dry land?" "Those that go into the building unhewn are those whom the Lord approved because they proceeded in the uprightness of the Lord and carried out his commandments." 4/ "And who are those that are brought and placed in the building?" "They are new in the faith and faithful. They are being admonished by the angels to do good, and for this reason no evil was found in them." 5/ "Who are those they were rejecting and throwing away?" "These are the ones who have sinned and wished to be converted. This is why they have not been thrown very far from the tower, because they will still be useful in the building, if they are converted. So those who are about to accept conversion, if they do so, will be strong in the faith if they do so while the tower is still being built. But if the building is finished, there will no longer be a place for them, but they will be cast out. But at least they have this advantage, that they lie alongside the tower.

6 [14] 1/ "Do you want to know who are those who are being broken up and thrown far from the tower? These are the sons and daughters of lawlessness. Their faith was hypocritical and everything evil never left them. That is why for them there is no salvation, since they are not useful because of their wickedness. That is why they were broken up and thrown far away because of God's anger which they provoked. 2/ But of the many others that you saw lying around and not going into the building, the scaly ones are those who have known the truth but did not persevere in it nor continue to cohere with the holy ones. Therefore they are unuseful." 3/ "Who are the ones with the cracks?" "These are the ones who hold things against each other in their hearts and are not at peace among themselves, but put on the appearance of peace; when they are away from each other, the evil remains in their hearts. These are the cracks that the stones have. 4/ The stunted ones are those who have believed and for the most part live justly, but still have a measure of

evil. That is why they are stunted and not completely developed." 5/ "Who are the ones, lady, that are white and round and do not fit into the building?" She answered me: "How long will you be stupid and mindless, asking everything and understanding nothing? These are the ones who have faith but also have wealth of this world. When tribulation comes, because of their wealth and their business affairs, they deny their Lord." 6/ I answered her: "Lady, then when will they become useful for the building?" She said: "When their wealth that seduces them is cut off, then they will be useful to God. Just as the round stone cannot become square unless something of it is cut off and discarded, so those who are rich in this world, unless their wealth is cut off from them, cannot become useful to the Lord. 7/ Learn this first from your [sing.] own case: when you were rich you were useless, but now you are useful and worthwhile for life. Be [pl.] useful to God, for you [sing.] are taken from the same stones.

7 [15] 1/ "The other stones that you see thrown far from the tower, falling onto the road and rolling off the road onto rough ground, these are the ones who have believed, but because of their doublemindedness they leave their true road. They think they can find a better road, and so they wander astray and are miserable on rough ground. 2/ Those who fall into the fire and are burned are those who completely apostasize from the living God and conversion no longer even occurs to them because of their depraved licentiousness and the evil things they have done. 3/ Do you want to know who are the ones who are rolling near the water but cannot be rolled into the water? These are the ones who have heard the word and want to be baptized in the name of the Lord. Then when they remember the purity of truth, they change their minds and return to their evil desires." 4/ So she finished the interpretation of the tower. 5/ Still shameless, I asked her if all those stones that had been thrown away and did not fit into the tower really had the opportunity for conversion and a place in this tower. "They will have the chance for conversion," she said, "but they cannot fit into this tower. 6/ They will fit into another much inferior place, and this after they have been tormented and have filled up the time of their sins. But then they will be changed to a different place because they had a part in the righteous word. Then it will happen that they will be taken out of the torments in which they were placed because of their evil deeds. But if it does not enter their heart to be converted, they will not be saved because of their hardness of heart."

The Tower Built on Water Is the Church

■ **3.1–2 [11]** As earlier at 2.3, the woman church tries to leave without explaining to Hermas' satisfaction. This time she has given him a vision but without interpretation. The question-answer pattern, a familiar device in revelatory literature, will remain throughout the book as the principal means of explanation of the various images presented. Her comments that often meet his insistent and stereotypical questioning put him clearly in the position of client petitioner to patron, but with a particular edge. Sometimes her reaction is encouraging (3.5), sometimes rather harsh (8.9), here somewhat playful. While on the surface her responses are often unflattering, in fact they function to portray the author as persistent and courageous in spite of the obstacles she tries to set up.

Hermas shows in v. 1 his awareness that the visions are not for him alone, but for the community, that "they may be more joyful" ($\iota\lambda\alpha\rho\acute{\omega}\tau\epsilon\rho\omega$), and Hermas along with them (v. 3); compare *Vis.* 1.2.3 for Hermas himself and 1.4.3; 3.9.10 for the woman church. Joy ($\iota\lambda\alpha\rho\acute{o}\tau\eta\varsigma$, $\chi\alpha\rho\acute{\alpha}$) is the sign of God's favor (*Man.* 10.3). The mixed reactions of rejoicing and mourning (v. 2) are familiar responses to apocalyptic revelation (for example, Matt 24:30; Luke 21:23, 28; John 16:20–22; 1 Cor 7:30–31). There is an apparent tension at the end of v. 2 between the woman church's statement that revelations are now completed, and her next statement that Hermas will continue asking for more. On one hand, this continues the literary device of Hermas' persistence. But it also contributes to the ongoing continuation of the eschatological moment, which cannot be pinned down in historical time. In a sense, the revelation of the tower is the ultimate revelation and the centerpiece of the book. It does visually what the call to conversion does verbally. All subsequent revelations, whether visual or verbal, are only further developments of the central message of the tower in process of being built.

■ **3.3** Here the explanation of the vision of the tower begins; it will continue through 7.6. The female personification of a city or community is commonplace in OT prophetic literature. The roughly contemporary *4 Ezra* 10:25–54 is often quoted as a parallel, in which a mourning woman talking with Ezra is suddenly changed into a city, which, as the angel Uriel explains to him later, is Jerusalem. But there are many differences. This is a tower, not a city, and the woman church does not *change into* the tower, but she *is* both woman and tower at the same time, and for this there are no parallels. That the interpreting figure interprets a vision which is at the same time herself is quite unique.[1] Perhaps the building of the tower was originally a depiction of the creation of the world, secondarily applied to the church,[2] but not necessarily; the church is at the same time transcendent wisdom figure and eschatological finality.[3] Here is one of the best and most central examples of the polyvalence of *Hermas'* symbols.

■ **3.4–5** Hermas' self-conscious comment about his worthiness to receive the revelation is balanced by the woman's wry comment a little later that his worthiness has nothing to do with it (4.3); he is chosen for the sake of others. The condition for him is to be openhearted and not doubleminded, in this case, hesitant or skeptical about what he sees.

Verse 5 contains a complicated textual problem. ABL[1] add the words in brackets ($\pi\alpha\nu o\hat{\upsilon}\rho\gamma o\varsigma$ $\epsilon\hat{\iota}$ $\pi\epsilon\rho\grave{\iota}$ $\tau\grave{\alpha}\varsigma$ $\gamma\rho\alpha\varphi\acute{\alpha}\varsigma$), omitted by many text critics and commentators as haplography, but retained by Dibelius, Snyder, Joly, and Brox on the grounds that the sentence makes no sense without it: the woman had not told Hermas previously why the tower was built on water, though she had called him mischievous ($\pi\alpha\nu o\hat{\upsilon}\rho\gamma o\varsigma$) about his inquiries (3.1). But how do the scriptures ($\tau\grave{\alpha}\varsigma$ $\gamma\rho\alpha\varphi\acute{\alpha}\varsigma$) enter in? Dibelius reconstructed the original as: "You are mischievous about inquiries, you inquire carefully, and by inquiring you will find . . ." ($\pi\alpha\nu o\hat{\upsilon}\rho\gamma o\varsigma$ $\epsilon\hat{\iota}$ $\pi\epsilon\rho\grave{\iota}$ $\tau\grave{\alpha}\varsigma$ $\epsilon\kappa\zeta\eta\tau\acute{\eta}\sigma\epsilon\iota\varsigma$ $\kappa\alpha\grave{\iota}$ $\epsilon\kappa\zeta\eta\tau\epsilon\hat{\iota}\varsigma$ $\epsilon\pi\iota\mu\epsilon\lambda\hat{\omega}\varsigma$ $\epsilon\kappa\zeta\eta\tau\hat{\omega}\nu$ $o\hat{\upsilon}\nu$ $\epsilon\upsilon\rho\acute{\iota}\kappa\epsilon\iota\varsigma$). But Joly, rejecting Dibelius' solution as too complicated, preferred to keep "scriptures," arguing that it was an early introduction into the text at a time when *Hermas* was considered Scripture, then removed later.[4] However, as Joly argues, $\alpha\grave{\iota}$ $\gamma\rho\alpha\varphi\alpha\acute{\iota}$ at this early date need not mean Scripture, but could refer to the written portion of the revelation given to Hermas (*Vis.* 2.1, 4).

Creation was founded upon the waters (*Vis.* 1.3.4),[5] as was the tower that is the church, the firstborn of cre-

---

1 Dibelius, 463.
2 Koester, *Introduction*, 258–59.
3 See comment on *Vis.* 2.4.1. Cirillo ("Erma e il problema," 10–15) gives a helpful survey of biblical and intertestamental affinities, but without taking sufficient note of the differences.
4 To complicate matters further, the reference to "scriptures" was taken by Tischendorf as partial

ation (*Vis.* 2.4.1), as is the life of the Christian in baptism (1 Pet 3:20–21). All three levels of meaning are present under the symbol of water. While the primeval waters are plural, both here in v. 5 and later in *Sim.* 9.16.2–6, the water of baptism is singular.[6] The "almighty and glorious name" is here the name not of Christ but of the creator God of unseen power,[7] a traditional Jewish expression.

The Tower Built by Angels

■ **4.1–2 [12]** The question-and-answer format of the revelation continues. The six primary angels are the ones who previously escorted the woman church and carried her chair (*Vis.* 1.4.1, 3; 3.1.7, 2.5), and are generally understood to be those first created and responsible for cosmic supervision in Jewish apocalypticism[8]—except that they are usually seven, not six. The seventh chief angel, the greatest of them all, will appear later as Michael (*Sim.* 8.3.3), as the greatest of the seven (*Sim.* 9.6.1), and finally as the "lord of the tower" (*Sim.* 9.7.1), a christological figure.[9] The job description of the six angels is to foster and take charge of creation, and therefore of the tower as its first component. What would otherwise be a protological function becomes eschatological as well because it includes the completion of the tower. Thus all the angels in the vision (2.5 above), under the direction of the six, participate in the eschatological process.

■ **4.3** Hermas asks to know the ἔξοδος ("end" or "goal")[10] of the stones and their δύναμις (lit. "power," but probably something more like "meaning" is intended here).[11] The woman church's warning to Hermas that his worthiness has nothing to do with his role as recipient of revelation continues the literary motif of disparaging remarks about him, but is also reminiscent of Deut 7:7.

The name of God here makes clear that the honorable name upon which the tower was founded (3.5) is also that of God. The doubleminded are not singlehearted or singleminded, necessary attitudes for the author of Deuteronomy (Deut 6:5). They cannot let go of their doubt and believe with all their heart, but must always debate at some level.[12]

Excursus: The Explanation of the Stones in Vision 3

The stones that go into the making of the tower and those rejected for the building are first listed in 2.4–9, but the explanation is given in 5.1–7.3. Both are schematized below, using the structure suggested by Grotz with slight adaptations.[13]

Description: 2.4–9	*Explanation:* 5.1–7.3
A. 2.4 square stones	5.1 apostles, overseers, teachers, deacons
B. 2.6 stones from the deep	5.2 martyrs
C. 2.7 from the dry land	5.3–6.1
1. 2.7b put into the building	5.3 the just
	5.4 neophytes
2. 2.7a thrown away	5.5 about to do penance
3. 2.7c thrown far and broken	6.1 sons and daughters of unrighteousness, hypocrites
D. 2.8 stones lying unused	6.2–5
1. 2.8a scaly	6.2 unfaithful to the truth and hypocritical
2. 2.8b cracked	6.3 not disposed to peace
3. 2.8c stunted	6.4 attached to evil[14]
4. 2.8d white and round	6.5 have faith and wealth

---

proof that A was a retroversion into Greek from the Latin, *scripturas* having been substituted for *structuras* ("buildings") by a copyist, but such has not proven to be the case. Full discussion in Dibelius, 464; Joly, 108–9; Hilhorst, *Sémitismes*, 3–4; Hellholm, *Visionenbuch*, 131–32; Brox, 127.

5   Cf. Gen 1:9; Exod 20:4; Pss 24:2; 136:6; 2 Pet 3:5.

6   Henne, "Polysémie," 131.

7   4.3 below; see comment on *Vis.* 1.3.4.

8   *1 Enoch* 90.20–22; *2 Enoch* 19.

9   See comment on passages above, on *Sim.* 5, and discussion on christology, Introduction 3.3.4.

10   Διαφορά A ("difference" or "distinction") is also a

possible reading.

11   Of meanings listed in BAGD *s.v.*, any of five is possible: (1) power inherent in a thing; (2) a particular ability; (3) meaning (cf. 1 Cor 14:11); (6) personal spirit or angel; (7) what gives power; also at 8.6–7.

12   Compare *Did.* 4.4 par. *Barn.* 19.5, a similar saying differently worded, in different contexts, suggesting multiple developments of a traditional topos. For later uses in the context of prayer, see Brox, 238 n. 8.

13   Grotz, *Entwicklung*, 16–17; also given in Henne, "Pénitence," 360–61.

14   A misprint in Grotz, *Entwicklung*, 17, identifies these as 6,5 instead of 6,4.

E. 2.9 stones thrown far away
   1. 2.9a falling on rough ground
   2. 2.9b falling in the fire
   3. 2.9c at edge of water

7.1-3
   7.1 wander from the faith
   7.2 definitively separated
   7.3 hesitating about baptism because of moral demands

Dibelius saw the connection between C3 and E: both were thrown far away from the tower.[15] Poschmann groups all rejected stones together (C3–E3).[16] Grotz and Henne distinguish group D, those lying close to the tower, from group E, which are violently thrown away, Grotz noting too that all in groups A–C3, even though very different, have passed through the hands of the builders, as distinct from the rest.[17] For Henne and Brox,[18] C2 is a generic statement later diversified in D1–3, and C3 likewise in E. That is, the stones rejected but not thrown far away from the tower (C2=5.5) are the same as those that are scaly, cracked, stunted, and white and round (D1–4=6.2-5, where they are expanded into several types); the stones rejected and thrown far away (C3=6.1) are the same as those falling on rough ground, into fire, and near but not in water (E1–3=7.1-3).

The problem with this layered structure is that in the initial recital of the different kinds of stones that Hermas sees (2.4–9), they are all described serially, even if not in a logical order: bright square stones put into the building (2.4); stones from the deep put right away into the building (2.6); other (ἕτεροι) stones from the dry ground, of which some are thrown away (2.7a), some put into the building (2.7b), some broken and thrown far away (2.7c); other (ἄλλοι) stones lying around the tower unused because they are scaly, cracked, stunted, or rounded (2.8a–d). Still others were thrown far away, onto the road and rough ground, into fire, and to the edge of the water (2.9a–c). The initial passage does not imply such a structure in which one description is an overall category for others that will return in more detail later. Given the nature of allegory as point-for-point correspondence, it seems less complicated to assume that each piece of the description stands on its own as an

image of a particular kind of Christians and their fate.

At the highest level of the structure, there are three categories of stories: church leaders who act rightly (A); martyrs, stones from the deep (B); all other stones from dry land (C–E). Some of the third category, those from the dry land, fit right into the tower: the approved and righteous, and the neophytes (C0–1).[19] Others cannot be used immediately because of their unconverted sinful ways (C2). Others cannot be used at all because of their wickedness (C3). Others are in an uncertain state, lying around the tower, because of various conditions (D1–4), and still others are in more desperate straits (E1–3). The main focus is on those stones not handled by the builders, but lying around the tower (Hermas among them), whose truth, charity, and faith are weak:

(2.4/5.1 ideal church leaders
2.6/5.2 martyrs from the deep)
From dry land (A–C handled by the builders):
A. 2.7b/5.3–4 approved and neophytes
   B. 2.7a/5.5 thrown not far away; sinned but wished to repent
      C. 2.7c/6.1 rejected and broken; children of lawlessness
         D. (not handled by builders, but lying around)
            1. 2.8a/6.2 scaly stones, incomplete in truth
            2. 2.8b/6.3 cracked stones, incomplete in charity
            3. 2.8c/6.4 stunted stones, incomplete in faith
            4. 2.8d/6.5–6 incomplete in faith because of wealth
(C'–A' thrown away, thus handled by builders)
      C'. 2.9a/7.1 stones fallen on rough ground, doubleminded
   B'. 2.9b/7.2 stones rolled into fire, apostates
A'. 2.9c/7.3 stones rolled near water, hesitant about baptism

Seen this way, it is the problem stones of D that need most attention, those wavering and in need of "cleaning up their act." This perspective is quite consonant with the tone of the rest of the *Shepherd*. Yet surprisingly, the chance of conversion is offered to all (7.5–6). It is only the refusal of some to accept it that condemns them.

15 Dibelius, 468.

16 *Penance*, 154.

17 Grotz, *Entwicklung*, 16–19; Henne, "Pénitence," 363. However, those stones in E (7.1-3) have also passed through the builders' hands, since they have been thrown away.

18 Norbert Brox, "Die weggeworfenen Steine im Pastor Hermae Vis III,7,5," *ZNW* 80 (1989) 130–33.

19 Henne ("Pénitence," 364) in fact suggests an emendation to Grotz' schema to make those tested and approved a separate category from the neophytes.

20 A common ancient euphemism for death: Sir 46:19; Acts 7:60; 1 Cor 15:6; *1 Clem.* 44.2; Ignatius *Rom.* 4.2; also in *Man.* 4.4.1; *Sim.* 9.16.3, 5, 7; BAGD *s.v.* κοιμάω 2; κοίμησις 2.

21 "Bishop" would be an anachronistic translation at

General Explanation of Types of Stones

■ **5.1 [13]** The first group of stones that fit easily into the tower are those in leadership positions in the Christian community who have served well in their roles, some from the past (those who have "fallen asleep")[20] and some from the present: "apostles" (ἀπόστολοι), "overseers" or "bishops"[21] (ἐπίσκοποι), "teachers" (διδάσκαλοι), and "ministers" or "deacons" (διάκονοι). Curiously, when the same functions are repeated in verbal form (having governed=ἐπισκοπήσαντες; having taught=διδάξαντες; having served=διακονήσαντες), the function of apostle is omitted, which may indicate that this is the single title no longer used in the Roman church, an assumption borne out by the apostles' appearance elsewhere in *Hermas* as figures from the past (*Sim.* 9.15.4, 16.6, 17.1, 25.2). Strangely missing completely is the function of prophet, perhaps because it was not the title of a "religious specialist" (Reiling), or because Hermas wants to distance himself from what he considers the practice of false prophecy.[22] The order of mention among the four groups, once apostles have been given primacy of place, may be less an indication of relative ranking than of alliteration.[23] The motif of group harmony is important to Hermas and will occur repeatedly (for example, 6.3; 9.2, 10). Here their common agreement and mutual consideration of one another are the reason for their allegorical perfect fit as stones in the tower. In fact, the same verb that here describes their human behavior, συνεφώνησαν ("they were in harmony," literally, with the same voice), will be used in the next verse for the martyrs as an architectural term. This description of idealized church leaders will not inhibit strong criticism later of those who do not live up to the ideal (9.7 below). Indeed, this first part of the description may be not so much the ideal church over against the real, imperfect church[24] as the consideration of that part of the church that does live up to the ideal, here, those church leaders who do what they are supposed to do.

■ **5.2–4** The stones dragged up from the depths in v. 2 (first described in 2.6) also fit immediately into the tower because they are martyrs. Nothing more need be said as justification. The only surprise is that they are not mentioned first, in view of their honored place at the right hand in 1.9; 2.1. As stones they fit so well because their joints fit together (συμφωνοῦντες), the same word used to describe the behavior of church leaders in v. 1. The depth from which they are taken is likely the realm of death.[25] The name for which they have suffered is that of "the Lord," that is, here, Christ.[26]

The stones that go into the building unhewn (v. 3; cf. 2.7) are simply those who have always been pleasing to God and thus, even though they are not perfectly square like the first group (v. 1), have no need of adjustment. The fourth group (v. 4) is composed of neophytes who respond to the angelic exhortation and refrain from evil.[27]

■ **5.5** Here begins the explanation of those stones not immediately acceptable. The first group consists of the baptized who have sinned since baptism, as contrasted to the neophytes of v. 4. They are aware of their sin and

---

this point if a single monarchical bishop is understood; but see Phil 1:1 for an earlier reference to ἐπίσκοποι (pl.) as collegial local leaders, probably as here synonymous with presbyters (compare Acts 20:17, 28 where the two terms apply to the same group). Ἐπίσκοποι occurs elsewhere in *Hermas* only in *Sim.* 9.27.4, where it is linked with hospitality. Here its appearance may reflect the same misquote of Isa 60:17 as *1 Clem.* 42.4–5, where the LXX's ἄρχοντες and ἐπίσκοποι have become Clement's ἐπίσκοποι καὶ διάκονοι, possibly under the influence of such traditions as are reflected in Phil 1:1; 1 Tim 3; *Did.* 15.1.

22 Aune, *Prophecy,* 209–10. But see *Sim.* 9.15.4 and comment on *Mandate* 11.

23 Dibelius, 466; Brox, 131.

24 Dibelius, 466.

25 Dibelius, 467.

26 So AB; "God" S. See comment on 1.9. "The Lord": Lake, Dibelius, Whittaker, Hellholm, Brox; "God": Snyder, Joly (113 n. 1) based on the argument of Audet ("Affinités," *RB* 60 [1953] 41–82 [53]) that "God" as the more difficult reading must be original, "the Lord" a christianization of the text. But suffering for the name of Christ is characteristic of martyrdom literature; see note on 2.2.8 above. The S reading may have been influenced by 4.3, a psalm quotation not in a context of suffering.

27 Most commentators (except Lake, 38) accept the AL¹E reading διότι οὐχ εὑρέθη ἐν αὐτοῖς πονηρία ("for this reason no evil was found in them") against the SL² omission of the negative, which would not fit the organization of the explanation thus far: those who have a place in the building without qualification.

wish to change their life, but have not yet done so, or have not yet completed the process. Their position on the ground but near the tower promises the possibility of being placed in the tower;[28] therefore, their present position may be temporary, depending on whether or not they really do accept conversion. It is up to them. While much of the allegory of the tower seems predetermined, this group witnesses to the real fluidity of the image and the place of human freedom within it. The situation of those outside the tower but near it will later be developed with more complexity (for example, *Sim.* 9.4.8, 6.5, 8; 7.1–7). Once again the warning is issued that the time for conversion does not last forever. To push this fixed end of the conversion period too literally in Hermas' time frame is pointless. *The accent is not on chronology but on the immediacy of the call to conversion.*

Explanation of the Rejected Stones

■ **6.1–4 [14]** Here begins the explanation of the problem stones of 2.8. The first group of those completely rejected are broken and thrown away (v. 1). As "sons and daughters of lawlessness" (υἱοὶ τῆς ἀνομίας),[29] they are the only ones explicitly to provoke God's wrath because they professed faith but lived unfaithfully, never really distancing themselves from their evil ways. They are different from the doubleminded, frequently admonished elsewhere. This group does not hesitate between good

and evil; they are not torn between alternatives. They are set in their hypocritical ways. The stark denial of salvation to them stands in sharp contrast to the way in which final salvation is held out to others, such as in 5.5 above (but compare *Vis.* 2.2.5). This is the only group of stones that the builders themselves break before throwing away (2.7), symbolic of their irreversible rejection. They are perhaps even meant to be excluded from the final allowance of salvation with conversion (7.5–6).

The scaly stones (v. 2) started out right, knowing the truth, but did not continue consistently according to it, and most important, they have not been faithful to their social responsibilities as Christians.[30] This unusual use of the verb κολλᾶσθαι ("to adhere, attach") will later go to the heart of Hermas' complaint about the quality of community life.[31] The theme of being "unuseful" (ἄχρηστοι) will be picked up again at vv. 6–7 below. The cracked stones (v. 3) are an apt image for those who cannot let go of resentments[32] and therefore cannot keep peace with each other (μὴ εἰρηνεύοντες ἐν ἑαυτοῖς),[33] even though they put on a semblance of it when together, literally, "having a peaceful face" (πρόσωπον εἰρήνης ἔχοντες). But the heart does not match the exterior, a fundamental Jewish paraenetic objection. The stones that are maimed or underdeveloped (οἱ κεκολοβωμένοι, v. 4) are also an apt image for what they represent: those who gave every promise of continuing in good faith but

---

28 If converted, they will be "useful" (εὔχρηστοι); see below 6.6–7.

29 A "genealogical metaphor" from a Semitic semantic field, though the construction is not unknown in Hellenistic Greek; cf. Hilhorst, *Sémitismes*, 144–47. Compare ὁ υἱὸς τῆς ἀπωλείας ("the son of destruction" [Judas], John 17:12); the same expression preceded by ὁ ἄνθρωπος τῆς ἀνομίας ("the person of lawlessness" [the eschatological opponent], 2 Thess 2:3).

30 The last part of the sentence, "nor continue to cohere with the holy ones" (μηδὲ κολλώμενοι τοῖς ἁγίοις) is missing in SBL²E; rejected by Lake, Carlini; accepted by Whittaker, Dibelius, Joly, Hellholm, Snyder. Carlini includes it in a number of examples of the tendency of AL¹ to interpolation for more expansive explanation ("Tradizione manoscritta," 100; "Tradizione testuale," 31). The expression recurs in similar but more strongly worded contexts in *Sim.* 8.8.1, 9.1, 20; 9.26.3 (compare *1 Clem.* 46.4, without the socioeconomic context), but that could also argue for interpolation here,

where it fits the context more awkwardly. Brox (134, 137) rightly rejects Dibelius' suggestion (468, 470) that not remaining in the truth means joining mystery cults (also 7.1 below) in favor of a socioeconomic interpretation, or what the author would consider heterodoxy, especially 7.1.

31 See references in previous note; cf. Osiek, *Rich and Poor*, 121–25; Bausone, "Aspetti." Used elsewhere as expression of church as community: Acts 9:26; 10:28; Rom 12:9; 1 Cor 6:16; *Did.* 3.9; 4.2; *1 Clem.* 15.1; 30.3; 46.4–5.

32 Ἔχειν κατά ("hold against"): cf. Matt 5:23; Mark 11:25; Rev 2:4, 14, 20; Ign. *Trall.* 8.2; *Sim.* 9.23.2. Synonym for μνησικακία (*Vis.* 2.3.1; *Man.* 8.3, 10; 9.3; *Sim.* 9.23.4.

33 Compare 1 Thess 5:13: εἰρηνεύετε ἐν ἑαυτοῖς ("keep peace with each other"); Mark 9:50: εἰρηνεύετε ἐν ἀλλήλοις; Rom 12:18; 2 Cor 13.11. Cf. 5.1 above; 9.2, 9; 12.3; *Man.* 2.3; *Sim.* 8.7.2 below.

have not completely rid themselves of evil and therefore never grew to complete size.[34]

■ **6.5–6** The exasperation of the woman church's reaction to Hermas' question about this final group of possibly useful stones serves to draw attention to the answer, more extended than most of the previous single explanations, a signal that this category is important. It is the only group since the first one of church leaders (5.1) whose color is given;[35] it is in fact the place where Hermas himself belongs and serves as example (v. 7). These are rich Christians who have the wealth of this world[36] along with their faith, and in time of tribulation,[37] when forced to choose between faith and prosperity, make the wrong choice. The Lord they deny is Christ.[38] Making rich people useful to God is like trying to fit round stones into square holes; they must be trimmed into squares first, an illustrative image of the dangers of riches, a major early Christian theme and one that will play a large part in the development of Hermas' message.[39] He will return to this specific image in *Similitude* 9.[40]

■ **6.7** A sudden change to the second person singular signals a piece of autobiographical information inserted by way of example. Hermas had previously suffered some kind of reversal of fortune, somehow connected with the misbehavior of his family (*Vis.* 2.3.1), either as a direct result (for example, because of their squandering of money without his adequate supervision), or as divine punishment for their misdeeds.[41] This reversal of fortune is again introduced here in a play on the words "useless/useful" ($\check{\alpha}\chi\rho\eta\sigma\tau\sigma\varsigma/\varepsilon\check{v}\chi\rho\eta\sigma\tau\sigma\varsigma$) reminiscent of Phlm 11. The beginning of the next sentence is an exhortation in the second person plural, and the last part of the sentence is an interpretive headache, probably corrupt in most MSS.[42] The gist of it appears to be that Hermas and/or others addressed belong to the group in v. 6, that is, faithful Christians who are vulnerable to defection because of their wealth.

More Stones Rejected—But Not Absolutely

■ **7.1–4 [15]** The final series of three kinds of stones are those thrown far away from the tower, and therefore with slim hopes of salvation; they correspond to those stones described in 2.9 above. The first group (v. 1) are very close to those in 6.2: they have come to faith but do not continue on the straight path, this time because of

---

34 A very similar expression appears in the prayer over the faithful in *Ap. Const.* 8.11.4: that none be stunted or incomplete ($\kappa o\lambda o\beta\grave{o}\varsigma$ $\mathring{\eta}$ $\mathring{\alpha}\tau\varepsilon\lambda\acute{\eta}\varsigma$).

35 In the similar allegory of the stones in *Similitude* 9, color will play a larger part (e.g., 9.6.4; 8.2, 5, 7).

36 "Of this world" is part of a lacuna in A and a homoioteleuton in S. Usually restored $\tau o\tilde{v}$ $\alpha\mathring{\iota}\tilde{\omega}\nu o\varsigma$ $\tau o\acute{v}\tau o\upsilon$ from LL *huius seculi*, but now to be restored as $\tau o\acute{v}\tau o\upsilon$ $\tau o\tilde{v}$ $\alpha\mathring{\iota}\tilde{\omega}\nu o\varsigma$ from B, the sole Greek witness to the text (Carlini, *Bodmer Papyrus*, 52, 88).

37 $\Theta\lambda\tilde{\iota}\psi\iota\varsigma$: eschatological tribulation or historical persecution, or the overlay of one on the other, or simple reversal of fortune: its use in *Vis.* 2.3.1 for what Hermas has suffered because of his family seems to demonstrate that the word does not always carry one of the first two meanings. But see comment on *Vis.* 2.2.7; 3.4 above.

38 Cf. *Vis.* 2.2.8; *Sim.* 9.21.7–8. Dibelius is correct (469) that here "their Lord" is Christ and in v. 6, God—the clearest illustration that the word can mean both and must be interpreted from context. In the last line of v. 6, A actually reads $\chi\rho\iota\sigma\tau\tilde{\omega}$ ("Christ") against all other readings of $\kappa\upsilon\rho\acute{\iota}\omega$ except B $\vartheta\varepsilon\tilde{\omega}$ ("God"). Both exceptions are to be rejected. Cf. Carlini, *Bodmer Papyrus*, 89.

39 Cf. Osiek, *Rich and Poor*, especially 51–52.

40 9.9.1–3, 30.4–5, 31.1–2.

41 Lampe (*Stadtrömische Christen*, 189) makes much of this: Hermas' financial reversal through persecution is a lesson about how the Christian life should really be, not in total deprivation but not in abundance of wealth, either.

42 $\kappa\alpha\grave{\iota}$ $\gamma\grave{\alpha}\rho$ $\sigma\grave{v}$ $\alpha\mathring{v}\tau\grave{o}\varsigma$ $\chi\rho\tilde{\alpha}\sigma\alpha\iota$ $\mathring{\varepsilon}\kappa$ $\tau\tilde{\omega}\nu$ $\alpha\mathring{v}\tau\tilde{\omega}\nu$ $\lambda\acute{\iota}\vartheta\omega\nu$ A; missing in S; *nam et tu ipse ex eis lapidibus fuisti* ("for you yourself were from these stones") L¹; *et tu autem utilior de ipsis lapidibus eris* ("for you too will be more useful from the same stones") L²; *nam et tu ipse ex illis lapidibus es (eris)* ("for you yourself are [will be] from these stones") E. The translations reveal the uncertainty of verb tense to be understood in the present middle deponent of $\chi\rho\acute{\alpha}o\mu\alpha\iota$ ("use"), but are united in taking it not in a passive sense ("you are used") but as an active equivalent of the verb "to be." Full discussion of possibilities in Brox, 136–37; Carlini, *Bodmer Papyrus*, 89. A very different, much simpler, and perhaps preferable text in B: $\kappa\alpha\grave{\iota}$ $\gamma\grave{\alpha}\rho$ $\mathring{\varepsilon}\kappa$ $\tau\tilde{\omega}\nu$ $\alpha\mathring{v}\tau\tilde{\omega}\nu$ $\lambda\acute{\iota}\vartheta\omega\nu$ $\mathring{\varepsilon}\sigma\tau\varepsilon$ ("but you [pl.] are from the same stones") preserves the plural of the first part of the sentence but raises the question who are the other people who are suddenly addressed.

doublemindedness. Here even more than in 6.2, some form of heterodox belief or worship may be envisioned, since they choose what they think to be something better, though it is more likely that they leave the community altogether.[43] The use of the "way" or "road" (ὁδός) for faith is traditional,[44] as is fire for the place of punishment for sinners in apocalyptic symbolism (v. 2).[45] Those who fall into the fire are "apostates" (οἱ ἀποστάντες, literally, those who withdraw or separate themselves) "from the living God"[46] εἰς τέλος (either "completely" or "finally").[47] The third group (v. 3) can only be catechumens or those attracted to becoming so, who have undergone some instruction[48] and have expressed a desire for baptism "in the name of the Lord."[49] But they backslide[50] when the obligations of the faith are made clear to them. "The purity of truth" (ἡ ἁγνότης τῆς ἀληθείας) is obscure; it probably means the call to keep chastity (not celibacy) or at least moral integrity.

■ **7.5–6** These two verses are full of difficulties. Which stones are intended by "all these stones that had been thrown away," but which will still have the chance for conversion, even if not for a place in the tower? If it means those in 7.1–3, then being thrown away, even into fire (v. 2), does not mean permanent rejection.[51] If it means those thrown far from the tower (6.1), then the statement there that these have no salvation is contradicted here, for even though they do not fit into the tower, if they accept the call of conversion, they do have salvation in a lesser place. The most likely referents are those not thrown far away (5.5), who sinned but wish to repent; but they are described at some distance from

these verses in the text. Verses 5–6 could refer not to the stones thrown far away (6.1; 7.1–3), but only to those thrown *not* far away from the tower (5.5, 6.2–6).[52] This solution, however, besides positing an overly complicated interpretive structure (see excursus), also necessitates a most unlikely consequence: that Hermas himself will not fit into the tower, for he is identified in 6.7 with the group in 6.5–6. All are presumably baptized Christians, with the exception of the wishy-washy catechumens of v. 3. The woman church's offer of the possibility of conversion must refer to all the stones not immediately used in the tower, that is, all from 5.5–7.3, even to those in 6.1, for whom there is no salvation only because they have refused it.

The complex relationships described here were probably never meant to be completely consistent as an overall system. In the process of repeated proclamation, each kind of stone targets some group, real or hypothetical, in the community, and the list of different groups was enlarged with repetition. The chance for conversion still held out to all here is one of a continuing string of illustrations of the central intention of the author: not to condemn or classify, but to encourage to conversion. Though the tower is the church, it is not coextensive with all baptized Christians. The place available outside the tower is not temporary, a place of penance until the persons there are ready to be included in the tower, but a permanent lesser place for those whose repentance

---

43 Which would seem to rule out some form of Gnosticism at this early date when Gnostics were unlikely to be entirely separate (Leutzsch, *Wahrnehmung*, 75).

44 John 14:6; Acts 2:28; 19:9, 23; 22:4; 24:14; 2 Pet 2:2, 15.

45 Matt 3:10 par. Luke 3:9; 3:12 par. Luke 3:17; Matt 5:22; 7:19; 18:8–9 par. Mark 9:43, 47; 2 Pet 3:7; Jude 7, 23; Rev 14:10; 17:16; 18:8; 19:20; 20:10, 14, 15; 21:8.

46 Heb 3:12.

47 Compare *Sim.* 8.6.4; 9.19.1; John 13:1.

48 Cf. Mark 4:14–20.

49 Cf. *Did.* 9.5. The name intended here may be Jesus; cf. Acts 2:38; 10:48; 19:5. See comment on 2.2.8 and 3.1.9 above. But Audet ("Affinités," 45–56) rejects any reference to Jesus under the name *Lord* in *Hermas*, even here, recalling the trinitarian bap-

tismal formula (Matt 28:19; *Did.* 7.1) as adequate explanation. In light of such passages as *Sim.* 9.12.4–5 and 13.3, however, it does seem that baptism in the name of Jesus is envisioned.

50 Literally, they "repent" or "are converted" (μετανοοῦσιν), an example of negative and nontechnical use of the word.

51 There is no conversion for apostates in *Sim.* 9.19.1; but compare the strange wording of 8.4 that seems to suggest they had the chance for conversion but did not take it, as does the wording here. But both here and in *Sim.* 8.4 there is a ring of finality that must mean the reference is only to those apostates who did not later accept conversion and reconciliation.

52 Norbert Brox, "Die weggeworfenen Steine in Pastor Hermae Vis, III, 7,5," *ZNW* 80 (1989) 130–36," and Brox, 138–39.

came too late.[53] While this idea of hierarchical placing of the saved is strange to modern readers, it would be quite comprehensible to status-conscious ancient Greco-Romans.

The placing of the various groups outside the tower is eschatological, as is the tower itself, in the sense that we are speaking here not of distinctions made in the historical Roman church of Hermas, much less of an anachronistic reference to the position of penitents in the narthex of the church.[54] Nor does the text say anything about the practice of ecclesiastical excommunication.[55] But the eschatological structure could be suggested by the general societal sensitivity to social stratification, especially as present in meal customs, the common meal being a core experience of Christian community. That is, though exclusion from the tower into a less honorable place is not a description of church life, the motif is not alien to, and could be suggested by, what every male contemporary knew who had ever hoped to be invited to dinner by a patron as sign of social advancement, only to find himself assigned to a place less honorable than he had expected, and what every woman outside the status elite experienced in the ambiguity of gender roles. While often sporting the ideology of parity, Greco-Roman social meals were inevitably exercises in social hierarchy.[56] The relative placement of guests was a matter of utmost sensitivity and importance. Something of

the sort must have been operative at Christian community meal assemblies as well. In Christian house church gatherings, social stratifying must not have been entirely absent,[57] and the approval or disapproval of the host or hostess for the behavior of certain members must have been reflected in their assigned places. In the social structure of salvation, it is not birth or wealth that determines status, but willingness to accept the call to conversion offered to all, who can only bring ruin on themselves by refusal. That responsibility is put squarely on the shoulders of the hearers themselves.[58]

It is not clear whether the torment that must afflict these late arrivals to conversion is in this life or the next. Hermas has already endured suffering ($\vartheta\lambda\hat{\iota}\psi\iota\varsigma$, Vis. 2.3.1) which, while historical, has made him useful for the tower (6.7), and therefore has eschatological value as well. The same possibility is held out to others (6.6). Perhaps just such human suffering and reversal is intended here for those who come late to conversion, too late to fit into the tower. More likely, some kind of eschatological punishment is in view. The Greek text of the third sentence of v. 6 is difficult, seeming to say that they will be removed from their torment because of their evil deeds, but the meaning must be as translated here.[59]

---

53 With Brox, 141; Henne, "Pénitence," 369; against Poschmann, *Paenitentia Secunda*, 156. Contrast *Sim.* 9.4.8, 6.5, 8, 7.1.

54 So D'Alès, *L'édit de Calliste*, 62; Poschmann, *Paenitentia Secunda*, 195–96; rejected by, among others, Giet, "De trois expressions."

55 Grotz, *Entwicklung*, 20–23; rejected by Rahner ("Penitential Teaching," 105–9).

56 Matt 23:6; Luke 14:7; 20:46; John D'Arms, "The Roman *Convivium* and the Idea of Equality," in Oswyn Murray, ed., *Sympotica: A Symposium on the Symposion* (Oxford: Clarendon, 1990) 308–20; idem, "Control, Companionship, and *Clientela*: Some Social Functions of the Roman Meal," *Echos du monde classique* 3 (1984) 327–48.

57 Compare the widely accepted interpretation of 1 Cor 11:17–34 from this perspective: Gerd Theissen, *The Social Setting of Pauline Christianity:*

Essays on Corinth (Philadelphia: Fortress, 1982) 153–62.

58 Poschmann, *Paenitentia Secunda*, 154–56. Henne ("Pénitence," 371) suggests that the explanation of the tower in *Vision 3* is intended for catechumens. The culminating example of those who are on the brink of baptism (7.3) certainly makes such an intended audience plausible.

59 SB: $\kappa\alpha\grave{\iota}\ \tau\acute{o}\tau\epsilon\ \alpha\grave{\upsilon}\tauο\hat{\iota}\varsigma\ \sigma\upsilon\mu\beta\acute{\eta}\sigma\epsilon\tau\alpha\iota\ \mu\epsilon\tau\alpha\tau\epsilon\vartheta\hat{\eta}\nu\alpha\iota\ \grave{\epsilon}\kappa\ \tau\hat{\omega}\nu\ \beta\alpha\sigma\acute{\alpha}\nu\omega\nu\ \alpha\grave{\upsilon}\tau\hat{\omega}\nu,\ \delta\iota\grave{\alpha}\ \tau\grave{\alpha}\ \check{\epsilon}\rho\gamma\alpha\ \grave{\alpha}\ \grave{\eta}\rho\gamma\acute{\alpha}\sigma\alpha\nu\tau\omi\ \pi\omi\nu\eta\rho\acute{\alpha}$ ("and then they will be removed from their torments because of the evil deeds they did"). AL¹E attempt a longer explanation, giving for the second part of the sentence: $\grave{\epsilon}\grave{\alpha}\nu\ \grave{\alpha}\nu\alpha\beta\hat{\eta}\ \grave{\epsilon}\pi\grave{\iota}\ \tau\grave{\eta}\nu\ \kappa\alpha\rho\delta\acute{\iota}\alpha\nu\ \alpha\grave{\upsilon}\tau\hat{\omega}\nu\ \tau\grave{\alpha}\ \check{\epsilon}\rho\gamma\alpha\ \grave{\alpha}\ \grave{\eta}\rho\gamma\acute{\alpha}\sigma\alpha\tau\omi\ \pi\omi\nu\eta\rho\acute{\alpha}$ ("if it enters into their heart [about] the evil deeds they did").

3 The Seven Women Who Support the Tower

8 [16] 1/ When I stopped asking her about all these things, she said to me: "Would you like to see something else?" I was eager to see it, and became excited at the prospect. 2/ She looked at me smiling and said to me: "Do you see seven women around the tower?" "I see them, lady," I said. "The tower is being sustained by them according to God's command. 3/ Now listen to how they work. The first one who is clasping her hands together is called Faith. Through her the elect of God are saved. 4/ The other one who is girded and acts like a man is called Restraint; she is the daughter of Faith. Whoever follows her will be blessed in life and will refrain from doing evil, believing that the one who refrains from all evil desires will inherit eternal life." 5/ "But who are the others, lady?" "They are daughters of one another. They are called Simplicity, Knowledge, Innocence, Reverence, and Love. When you do all the works of their mother, you can live." 6/ "I would like to know, lady, what kinds of power they have." "Listen," she said, "to the kinds of power they have. 7/ Their powers are sustained by one another, and they follow one another in birth order. From Faith is born Restraint, from Restraint Simplicity, from Simplicity Innocence, from Innocence Reverence, from Reverence Knowledge, from Knowledge Love. Their works are pure, reverent, and godly. 8/ Whoever is devoted to these women and can embrace their works shall have a dwelling in the tower with God's holy ones." 9/ I asked her about the times, whether the end time was already here. She raised her voice and cried out: "Senseless person! Do you not see the tower still being built? Whenever the construction of the tower is completed, that is the end. But it will be built quickly. Do not ask me anything else. Let this reminder suffice for you [sing.] and the holy ones, along with the renewal of your [pl.] spirits. 10/ But these things were not revealed only for you [sing.], but for you to interpret them all, 11/ after three days—for you must understand first. I direct you first, Hermas, to say all these words I am about to tell you into the ears of the holy ones, so that hearing and doing them they might be cleansed of their wickedness, and you with them."

■ **8.1–2 [16]** In contrast to the usual mode of communication in the revelatory process in which Hermas asks and the woman church answers, or when occasionally he is annoyingly persistent (for example, 3.1, 4; v. 9 below), here it is she who offers more. Her smile is consistent with her usual patience and joyful mood (*Vis.* 1.1.8; 4.3) and a recognizable motif in heavenly revelations.[1] While the six angels build the tower, the seven women (a cos-

---

1   Brox, 143.
2   See comment on 4.1 above; Emiel Eyben, "Roman Notes on the Course of Life," *Ancient Society* 4

(1973) 213–38 (227–29). Their number will grow to twelve, accompanied by twelve vices, in *Sim.* 9.15.2.
3   E.g., Matt 15:19; Mark 7:21–22; 1 Cor 5:10–11;

mologically significant number)[2] support and sustain it. Under the guise of the catalog of virtues personified in these seven women (γυναῖκες, not παρθένοι ["virgins" or "maidens"]), the paraenetic level of interpretation of the tower is introduced. The catalog of virtues or vices is a traditional paraenetic form.[3] Treatises on virtues and vices are common in Greco-Roman paraenetic literature.[4] The personification of virtues and vices in feminine form is traditional in Greco-Roman mythology and numismatics, and their family relationships also appear in an important contemporary comparison, the *Tabula of Cebes* 20.3.[5] What is unique, however, is the association of personified virtues in female form connected with the building of a tower.[6] In one sense, this section could stand independently of the previous vision of the building of the tower, and could therefore be an interpolation in the text; but it is also closely related to the central message of the tower, and is probably originally an oral, and later literary expansion that further

extends its symbolism.[7]

■ **8.3** To Hermas is explained the ἐνέργειαι ("working")[8] of the seven women.[9] The list begins with "faith" (πίστις) and ends with "love" (ἀγάπη), two of the primary triad of virtues.[10] Faith is depicted "clasping hands" (ἡ κρατοῦσα τὰς χεῖρας), a phrase that has brought much puzzlement. Since she is the agent of salvation, some have thought she was holding the hands of the other women-virtues, or of the elect of God; still other possibilities have been suggested.[11] The best, however, is that of Carlini, on the basis of the similar expression κρατεῖν τοὺς ἀντίχειρας ("to clasp opposite hands") in the magical papyri: Faith clasps her own hands together in front of her in an apotropaic gesture of defense. Thus, through her vigilance in warding off evil, the elect of God are saved.[12]

■ **8.4–5** The second woman (v. 4) is wearing a heavy belt, as a man would for a journey or battle, and has other stereotypically masculine characteristics, such as

---

6:9–10; Gal 5:19–23; Eph 4:31–32; 2 Tim 3:2–5; Jas 3:17; *Barn.* 20.1–2; *Man.* 8.3–5; in overlapping chains: 2 Pet 1:5–7; *Man.* 5.2.4. Cf. Hans D. Betz, *Galatians* (Hermeneia; Philadelphia: Fortress, 1979) 281–83, and further literature cited there. Note the connection between tower and virtues in John Cassian *Conferences* 9.2, 3, a possible allusion to *Hermas*; a tower built on rock with our virtues will withstand passion, persecution, and demons.

4   E.g., *Corp. Herm.* 1, 13; *Tab. Ceb.* Compare seven virtues in *Corp. Herm.* 13.8.

5   See also virtues as sisters of each other and daughters of God in *Ep. Apost.* 43, 45.

6   The only approximation, though quite different, is *Sib. Or.* 7.71–73: τρεῖς δ' αὐτῷ πύργους μέγας Οὐρανός ἐστήριξεν, ἐν τῷ δὴ ναίουσι θεοῦ νῦν μητέρες ἐσθλαί, Ἐλπίς τ' Εὐσεβίη τε Σεβασμοσύνη τε ποθεινή ("Great heaven established three towers for him [Christ]/in which the noble mothers now live:/hope and piety and desirable holiness"). Text J. Geffcken, *Die Oracula Sibyllina* (GCS 8; Leipzig: Hinrichs, 1902) 137; trans. Charlesworth, *OTP* 1. 411–12.

7   So too Dibelius, 471.

8   "Working, operation, action; way of working" BAGD[2]; "functions" (Snyder, 50); "Wirkweisen" (Brox, 143).

9   Parts of the end of v. 2 through v. 5 are freely cited by Clement of Alexandria *Strom.* 2.12.55.3–4 (*PG* 8.992–93).

10 1 Thess 1:3; 2 Cor 13:13; see esp. Ign. *Eph.* 14.1: ἀρχὴ μὲν πίστις, τέλος δὲ ἀγάπη ("the beginning

is faith, the end is love").

11 Dibelius (473) proposes, without MS. evidence, the emendation ἑτέρας for χεῖρας, thus "who supports the others": called "une audace qui n'est pas nécessaire" ("an unnecessary audacity") by Joly (120–21), who translates "qui de ses mains domine (les autres)" ("who with her hands controls the others")—the same interpretation as Dibelius' without the textual emendation; likewise, "Who governs (the others) by gestures" (Snyder, 50). For further documentation of suggestions, see Brox, 143–44.

12 Antonio Carlini, "La rappresentazione della ΠΙΣΤΙΣ personificata nella terza visione di Erma," *Civiltà classica e cristiana* 9 (1988) 85–94. Magical papyri cited are *PGM* 4.2328; 36.162; 69.3; 70.6 (translated "holding your thumbs" in Hans D. Betz, ed., *The Greek Magical Papyri in Translation* [Chicago/London: University of Chicago Press, 1986] 1. 80, 273, 297). Also cited by Carlini is the legend of the delay of the birth of Hercules by the same magical gesture, and its popularity among women: Antoninus Liberalis 29; Ovid *Metam.* 9.298–30: *et digitis inter se pectine iunctis* ("with her fingers interlocked," trans. Frank J. Miller [LCL 2.24–25]); Apollodorus *Bibl.* 2.4.5, with note by James G. Frazer on use of the gesture in women's folklore (LCL 1. 166 n. 2); Pliny *N. H.* 28.59 (17): *digitis pectinatim inter se inplexis* ("with the fingers interlaced comb-wise," trans. W. H. S. Jones, LCL 8. 42–43). Further bibliography in Hans D. Betz, "Fragments from a Catabasis Ritual in a Greek Magical Papyrus," *HR* 19 (1980) 290 n. 14.

strength and assertiveness.[13] Her name, Ἐγκράτεια, is best translated as "Restraint" or "Moderation" (Snyder gives "Self-control"), rather than "Continence" (per Lake), for it does not bear in *Hermas* the technical sense of sexual continence or celibacy that it would soon acquire in early Christianity. Rather, it is an essential and important consequence of Faith that expresses much of what Hermas will later have to say about the authentic Christian life. *Mandate* 8 will be entirely devoted to its explication. This verse is full of the language of discipleship: the one who follows her will be "blessed" (μακάριος) and inherit eternal life.

The other five virtues (v. 5) are less emphasized, and when the list is later expanded to twelve (*Sim.* 9.15.2), some of their names will change. The majority of manuscripts lists them in the order given, slightly differently than in v. 7 where Knowledge comes after Reverence.[14] The disparity is not significant except possibly for textual reconstruction. That Faith is first the mother only of Restraint (v. 4), then of all the virtues (v. 5), is not a contradiction. Such allegorical relationships are arbitrary, and the language of filiation makes of any ancestor a mother or father.[15]

■ **8.6–8** Hermas asks to know about the "power" (δύναμις)[16] of the women, that is, how they function (cf. *Sim.* 9.13.2, 7). There is no inherent theological theory behind the given order of virtues, which is somewhat arbitrary after the first two. The point is their mutual relationship, in which they form a chain or wreath or circle dance,[17] or even a set of female caryatids as base of the tower.

■ **8.9** The usually patient woman church loses her patience for a moment at Hermas' failure to understand the eschatological import of the ongoing construction of the tower, already partially explained at 4.2; 5.5: a

rhetorical device to draw attention to what she is about to say. The end will come when the tower is completed; the relationship between the two events is left vague. One may be the cause or sign of the other, or perhaps they are two ways of speaking of the same event. This passage stands in some tension with *Vis.* 2.2.5 in which the time for conversion of believers is limited, while that for outsiders lasts until the last day; but it is consistent with 3.5.5, in which the time for conversion of imperfect believers—even to get a place near but outside the tower—continues while the tower is still in process of construction. The solution to this apparent inconsistency cannot lie in chronological sequences.[18] The emphasis is on the speediness of the construction, and thus the urgency for conversion while there is still time. The "renewal of your spirits" (ἡ ἀνακαίνωσις τῶν πνευμάτων ὑμῶν)[19] that is possible as response to this call to conversion is one of the signs of the reality and nearness of the eschaton.

■ **8.10–11** The charge to hand on everything revealed to him was hinted at in *Vis.* 2.1.3, formalized in 2.4.3, and Hermas has been frequently reminded of it (3.3.1; 4.3). Once again (v. 10) that message is stressed. The breaks in meaning between the two verses are difficult, and the text may be corrupt. Everything in v. 11 from "I direct you first, Hermas, these words I am about to tell you" (ἐντέλλομαι δέ σοι πρῶτον, Ἑρμᾶ, τὰ ῥήματα ταῦτα ἅ σοι μέλλω λέγειν) clearly refers to the next section. But "after three days, for you must understand first" (μετὰ τρεῖς ἡμέρας νοῆσαι σε γὰρ δεῖ πρῶτον) could belong

---

13 See comment on *Vis.* 1.4.3.

14 BSL² and Clement of Alexandria (*Strom.* 2.12 [55] 3–4) give the list in this order; AL¹ bring the list in v. 5 into line with that of v. 7, either an argument for the reliability of A (Dibelius, 472) or, more likely, a correction, in any case one of many examples of the agreement of BSL² against AL¹ (Carlini, *Bodmer*, 93).

15 For faith as mother, probably an adaptation of wisdom as mother (Wis 7:12; Sir 15:2), cf. Polycarp *Phil.* 3.3; *Acts of Justin* 4.8; Joseph C. Plumpe, *Mater Ecclesia: An Inquiry into the Concept of the Church as*

Mother in Early Christianity (Studies in Christian Antiquity 5; Washington, DC: Catholic University Press, 1943) 19–22.

16 Or "meaning" (see comment on *Vis.* 3.4.3), but the rest of the description through v. 7 lends itself better to this translation.

17 Brox, 145–46, evoking Philo *Vit. Mos.* 2.7 on the relationship of virtues to one another. On the catena as a literary form, see Dibelius-Greeven, *James*, 94–99.

18 See comment and further refs. at *Vis.* 2.2.5.

19 Compare 13.1; *Sim.* 8.6.3; 9.14.3; Rom 12:2 (renew-

with the future revelation[20] or with what went before.[21] If the three-day reference is taken to refer to the future revelation and the full text is authentic, there is an awkwardness about the repetition of "first."[22] The present translation takes the problem statements to refer to what went before: Hermas is given a three-day delay to ponder the revelation before communicating it to others. The last sentence of v. 11 refers to the new teaching that the woman church is about to deliver, and should really stand at the beginning of chapter 9.

---

al of mind); 2 Cor 4:16 (of the inner person); Col 3:10 (of the new person); Tit 3:5 (of spirit); *Barn.* 6.11 (of all).

20 So Dibelius, 474; Whittaker, 15; Hellholm, *Visionenbuch*, 121, 133–34 n. 15.

21 Lake, 48–49; A. Puech, "Observations sur le Pasteur d'Hermas," in *Studi dedicati alla memoria di P. Ubaldi* (Milan: Università cattolica del Sacro Cuore Press, 1937) 83–85, noted by Whittaker[2], 117; accepted by Joly, 122–23; Snyder, 50; Brox, 147. Hellholm (133–34) objects to this reading that the three-day delay would contradict the twenty-day lapse of *Vis.* 4.1.1 and destroy the characteristic system of time markers in this section. The twenty-day reference at the beginning of *Vision* 4, however, is unrelated, and the three-day delay here is similar to the fifteen-day delay in *Vis.* 2.2.1, after which Hermas understands the revelation.

22 SL[1] omit ἐντέλλομαι δέ σοι πρῶτον ("I direct you first"), which leaves out the main verb and can hardly be correct; but B conveniently omits only this second πρῶτον ("first"), thus smoothing out the awkwardness.

3   A Wisdom Paraenesis

9 [17]   1/ "Listen to me, children. I raised you in great simplicity, innocence, and reverence by the mercy of the Lord who gave you justice drop by drop, that you might be justified and sanctified from all evil and from all deviousness. But you do not want to cease from your evil. 2/ But now listen to me, be at peace among yourselves, look after one another and help one another, and do not only help yourselves to the best of God's creatures, but share them with the needy. 3/ For some are becoming ill from too much eating and damaging their flesh while others who have no food are damaging their flesh by not having even necessary food, and their body is perishing. 4/ So this lack of mixing is dangerous to you who have and do not share with the have-nots. 5/ Look to the coming judgment. Let those who have an abundance seek out the hungry while the tower is not yet finished. For when the tower is finished you will want to do good but will not have the chance. 6/ Look to it, you who live it up in your wealth, lest the needy cry out, and their cry rise to the Lord, and you and your goods will be locked out of the door of the tower. 7/ So now I say to the leaders of the church and those in seats of honor: Do not become like concocters of poison. Poisoners carry their drugs in containers, but you carry your drug and your venom in your heart. 8/ You are hardened, and do not want to cleanse your hearts and blend your good sense into a clean heart, that you might receive mercy from the great king. 9/ So see to it, children, lest these dissensions of yours defraud your life. 10/ How do you intend to discipline the Lord's elect if you do not accept discipline? So discipline one another and be at peace with each other, so I can stand joyfully before the Father and give account for you all to your Lord."

■ **9.1 [17]** The chapter is a prophetic oracle, delivered orally, not for dictation, in paraenetic wisdom form.[1] The woman church speaks as mother who instructs her children in virtue, a wisdom motif.[2] But from v. 3 on, the pointed social critique is more characteristic of prophetic literature and goes to the heart of the social content of Hermas' message. There seems to be no special reason why these three particular virtues are singled out except that they are at the center of the seven in the previous chapter.[3] The verb στάζω ("drop, let fall, shed drop by drop")[4] implies a slow, steady application. For

resistance to wisdom's teaching: Matt 23:37 par. Luke 13:34.

■ **9.2** The exhortation to "be at peace among yourselves" is a recurring concern of Hermas, one of the litmus tests of true Christian living,[5] and the paraenesis of mutual care is traditional.[6] The second part of the sentence contains the difficult expression ἐκ καταχύματος ("from the soup or broth," translated here as "the best"), undoubtedly a proverbial expression whose exact mean-

---

1   For its oracle structure, see Aune, *Prophecy*, 301–2.

2   Prov 8:32; Wis 7:12, 21; 8:7; Sir 15:2, and esp. 4:11: "Wisdom instructs her children"; Luke 7:35.

3   8.5, 7: in the same consecutive order in v. 7 and AL[1] of v. 5; cf. *Man.* 2.1.4.

4   LSJ *s.v.*; Jer 42:18; 44:6 LXX.

ing is unknown.[7] In the given text and the present translation, it refers to what "you" have, but the suggestion has been made that it refers rather to what is shared with the needy.[8] The recurring Jewish and Christian concern about socioeconomic responsibility appears explicitly here for the first time, though the concern about the danger of wealth has already been introduced (*Vis.* 1.1.8; 3.6.6–7). Hermas' most common word for the needy is ὑστερούμενοι, introduced here.[9]

■ **9.3–4** Two traditions cross in these verses. The concern about damage caused to the body by unhealthy overindulgence is primarily Stoic;[10] the concern about the damage done by deprivation, though it also appears in Stoic reflection from the perspective of the responsibility of those well-off, is primarily Jewish and Christian. The introduction of the Stoic theme need not mean the use of an independent source; popular Stoic wisdom was commonplace in this period and often used by Christian writers. The lack of sharing among haves and have-nots, ἀσυνκρασία (lit. "unmixing"), otherwise unattested, from συνκεράννυμι ("mix, blend"; cf. v. 8) is closely related to Hermas' later complaint about the rich who do not associate with the poor.[11]

■ **9.5–8** The theological ambience has moved from wisdom (vv. 1–2) to philosophical-ethical (vv. 3–4) to apocalyptic. The warning about the coming judgment recalls the threat of persecution or eschatological tribulation (*Vis.* 2.2.7; 3.4), and the reminder about the tower contextualizes this message within the eschatological framework of the third *Vision* (v. 5). The motif of the needy crying out to God who will exact justice (v. 6) echoes a well-founded biblical tradition.[12]

The leaders of the church (οἱ προηγούμενοι) refer straightforwardly to those already mentioned;[13] those in the first seats (οἱ πρωτοκαθεδρίται) are probably synonymous with the first group as an alternate title[14] or, less likely, a sarcastic term for would-be ecclesiastical climbers or social elites conscious of their status,[15] though the echo of the Gospel critique may be present. The challenge addressed first to all Christians is narrowed at this point to those in positions of leadership and authority, who have the responsibility to encourage and discipline others (v. 10) and are more capable of influencing others by what they say and do. These church leaders are compared to magicians or sorcerers who mix magic ingredients, such as those described in

5   6.3; v. 10 below. Cf. Mark 9:50; 1 Thess 5:13.

6   E.g., *Man.* 8.10; Rom 15:7; Acts 20:35; Jas 1:27; 1 Pet 5:2 var. The use of the first verb of caring, ἐπισκοπέω ("look after") here, in *Man.* 8.10, James, 1 Peter, and even Ignatius *Rom.* 9.1 would suggest as early translation of ἐπίσκοπος not "overseer" but "responsible caregiver."

7   Dibelius' suggestion (475) that it means *Überfluss* ("abundance, superfluity") is otherwise unattested but widely repeated (e.g., BAGD² *s.v.*; LPGL *s.v.*).

8   Dibelius made the widely accepted suggestion, on the basis of L¹ *nolite . . . percipere. abundantius etiam imperite egentibus,* that the text read not μὴ μόνοι τὰ κτίσματα τοῦ θεοῦ μεταλαμβάνετε ἐκ καταχύματος, ἀλλὰ μεταδίδοτε καὶ τοῖς ὑστερουμένοις ("do not only take for yourselves 'from the soup,' but share with the needy"), but that words 7–11 should read in order 7–10–8–9–11: μεταλαμβάνετε, ἀλλ᾽ ἐκ καταχύματος μεταδίδοτε ("do not only take for youselves [of God's creation], but share from [your] abundance with the needy"). But the emendation is not necessary, as the given translation shows.

9   Also vv. 4, 6; *Man.* 2.4; 8.10; *Sim.* 5.3.7; 9.27.2. Cf. Osiek, *Rich and Poor,* 66 n. 27.

10   References in Dibelius, 475. See listing of overindulgence in food and drink in catalogs of vices in *Man.*

6.2.5; 8.3; 12.2.1.

11   See comment on *Vis.* 3.6.2; *Sim.* 8.8.1, 9.1; 9.20.2, 26.3; Osiek, *Rich and Poor,* 123–25.

12   E.g., Exod 22:23, 27; Deut 24:15; Ps 79; Jas 5:1–6; *1 Enoch* 91–105; Dibelius-Greeven, *James,* 235–40; Osiek, *Rich and Poor,* 15–38.

13   The same term in *Vis.* 2.2.6; Clement and Grapte and the presiding elders in 2.4.3; perhaps 3.1.8, but not according to the interpretation given there.

14   Here, though less likely in 1.8 and *Man.* 11.1, there may be reference to a seating arrangement for assemblies of the community; also in Rev 4:4; Ignatius *Magn.* 13.1; *1 Clem.* 40.3; 41.2; surely in *Didasc.* 2.57–58 (Connolly 12); but most of this is highly conjectural. See Maier, *Social Setting,* 103, 140–42 n. 113.

15   Cf. Matt 23:6; Mark 12:39; Luke 11:43; 20:46; Irenaeus *Adv. Haer.* 4.26.3; interpreted this way by L¹: *qui amatis primos consessus* ("you who love to sit first"), probably under the influence of the NT texts; this interpretation raised but rejected by Funk, 371–72; Dibelius, 476. Brox, 151, takes the second term as a warning to church leaders.

the magical papyri who carry their potions in boxes, whereas the magic concoctions of the church leaders are carried within themselves. False teaching has been suggested as the referent,[16] but the whole passage is embedded between two similarly worded appeals to harmony (vv. 2, 10) and just before a warning against dissension (v. 9). Their social practice seems more at fault than their teaching: neglect of the poor and contentiousness among themselves, which also harms the rest of the community (compare *Sim.* 9.31.5–6). They are accused of deliberate hardheartedness, a familiar biblical condemnation,[17] and a turning away from "the great king," an unusual expression in *Hermas*[18] which, with the equally unusual use of Father for God in v. 10, suggests a literary source.

■ **9.9–10** The address to "children" reminds us at the end of the speech that the speaker is the church as mother (v. 1), though here attention is narrowed to the leaders. The perennial problem raised here is that of the discipline and ongoing "formation" ($\pi\alpha\iota\delta\epsilon\acute{\iota}\alpha$) of church leaders, in the double sense of their own attention to living virtuously and the process of calling them to correction when necessary. They are to look to each other for such mutual correction. Again comes the appeal to be at peace with one another, in the familiar refrain of v. 2,[19] instead of living in "dissensions" ($\delta\iota\chi o\sigma\tau\alpha\sigma\acute{\iota}\alpha\iota$).[20] The woman church desires again to be "joyful" ($\iota\lambda\alpha\rho\acute{\alpha}$)[21] when she can give a good report to "the Father," not a typical name for God in *Hermas*,[22] as she "stands" ($\sigma\tau\alpha\vartheta\epsilon\hat{\iota}\sigma\alpha$) before him, evoking the role of the principal angels.[23]

16   Snyder, 51–52. But in *Odes Sol.* 22.7 poison symbolizes the power of opposition; in *Did.* 2.2; 5.1; in *Barn.* 20.1 using it is despised or forbidden. In Ignatius *Trall.* 6.2 $\varphi\acute{\alpha}\rho\mu\alpha\kappa o\nu$ is false teaching, but in *Eph.* 20.2, the one bread of the Eucharist is the $\varphi\acute{\alpha}\rho\mu\alpha\kappa o\nu$ $\grave{\alpha}\vartheta\alpha\nu\alpha\sigma\acute{\iota}\alpha\varsigma$ ("medicine of immortality"); cf. Eph 19.3, and Francis C. R. Thee, *Julius Africanus and the Early Christian View of Magic* (Hermeneutische Untersuchungen zur Theologie 19; Tübingen: Mohr/Siebeck, 1984) 322–23.

17   E.g., Ps 95:8; Heb 3:7–8; church leaders as lovers of money: *Asc. Isa.* 3.24–25.

18   Cf. Ps 47:3; Matt 5:35; *Did.* 14.3 (Mal 1:14 and possible influence of Matt 5:35).

19   Also 5.1; 6.3; 12.3; *Man.* 2.3; *Sim.* 8.7.2.

20   Also associated with lack of mutual peace in *Man.* 2.3 and *Sim.* 8.7.2.

21   For the importance of joy, see comment on *Vis.* 1.4.3.

22   Appearing elsewhere only in *Sim.* 5.6.3–4 and 9.12.2 in relation to the Son; see comment on "the great king" in v. 8.

23   Dibelius (477) recalls the representative role of Michael (Dan 12:1; *1 Enoch* 20.5; but also Raphael in Tobit 12:15; Gabriel in Luke 1:19; Rev 8:2). Aune (*Prophecy*, 302–3) takes this statement to be spoken by the Son of God, who is later identified with the church (*Sim.* 9.1.1).

3

Transformation of the Woman Church

10 [18]   1/ When she finished talking to me, the six young men who were building came and took her away to the tower, and another four took up the couch and took it to the tower as well. I did not see the faces of these men because they were turned away. 2/ But as she was leaving I asked her to give me a revelation about the three forms in which she had appeared to me. She answered: "You must ask someone else to reveal this to you." 3/ For at first, last year, brothers and sisters, I had seen her rather old and sitting in a chair. 4/ In the next vision, her face was younger but her flesh and hair were older and she spoke to me standing. She looked more joyful, though, than before. 5/ In the third vision, she was much younger, very lovely, and only her hair looked older. She was completely joyful, and seated on a couch. 6/ I was quite depressed about this, wanting to understand the revelation. In a night vision, I saw the elder lady say to me: "Every request requires humility. So fast, and you will receive what you ask from the Lord." 7/ I fasted one day, and that very night I saw a young man who said to me: "Why are you always seeking revelations in prayer? Look out lest all this seeking injure your health. 8/ These revelations are enough for you. Would you be able to take stronger revelations than you have seen?" 9/ I answered: "Sir, I only ask for a full revelation about the three forms of the elder lady." He answered me: "How long will you [pl.] be senseless? But your doublemindedness makes you senseless, and your not having your heart turned to the Lord." 10/ I answered back: "But from you, sir, we will know these things more clearly."

11 [19]   1/ "Listen," he said, "about the [three] forms you [sing.] seek. 2/ Why did she first appear to you older and seated in a chair? Because your [pl.] spirit is older and already fainting away, and has no power because of your softness and doublemindedness. 3/ Just as older people, no longer having any hope of rejuvenation, look forward to nothing but their sleep, so you too who have become softened by everyday concerns have given yourselves over to apathy and have not cast your cares upon the Lord. Your intent has been shattered and you have grown old in your sadness." 4/ "Then I would like to know why she was sitting in a chair, sir." "Because every weak person sits out of weakness in order to support the bodily weakness. You [sing.] have the meaning of the first vision.

12 [20]   1/ "In the second vision you saw her standing with younger-looking face and more joyful than before, but her flesh and hair were older. Listen," he said, "to this parable as well. 2/ Someone who is older has already abandoned hope because of weakness and poverty, and looks forward to nothing but the last day of life. Then, this person suddenly received an inheritance, and upon hearing of it, rose up, rejoiced, and got stronger. Such a one no longer lies prone, but

stands up, is renewed in the very spirit previously destroyed by the former deeds, and no longer
sits, but takes on courage. So too you [pl.], hearing the revelation [that the Lord revealed to you].
3/ Because he had compassion on you and
renewed your spirits, you have put aside your
soft ways and strength has entered into you and
you were empowered in the faith. The Lord, seeing you made strong, rejoiced. This is why he
showed you the building of the tower, and will
show you other things if you remain at peace
among yourselves with all your heart.

13 [21] 1/ "In the third vision, you [sing.] saw her young,
happy, and lovely in appearance. 2/ It is as if
some good news should come to someone living
in sadness, and this person at once forgets the
former sadness and focuses on nothing but the
news just heard, and is strengthened from then
on for doing good. Such a person's spirit is
renewed because of the joy received. So too you
[pl.] have received renewed spirits by seeing
these good things. 3/ You [sing.] saw her sitting
on a couch, a secure position, for a couch has
four legs and thus stands securely. So too the
world is supported by four elements. 4/ Those
who are converted will become completely new
and securely founded—those who are converted
with all their heart. You have the entire revelation; do not ask anything more about a revelation. If anything else is needed, it will be revealed
to you."

Hermas' Request for an Explanation

■ **10.1 [18]** When her discourse is completed, she leaves,
as in 2.3; 3.1. Whereas she began with six angel assistants (four to carry the chair and two as escorts, *Vis.*
2.4.1, 3; 3.1.6), the six have now increased to ten, six
escorts and another four to carry the chair. While she
was talking with Hermas, the original six had been busy
building the tower (3.1.7, 2.5). Now they come back with
their further four companions to take the woman church
to the tower; the church to the church. A rational conun-
drum is really a set of meaningful symbols: the young
men/angels (4.1–2) increase as their work continues; the
woman returns to the place she really belongs, unifying
the revelatory, prophetic church with the historical,
eschatological structure that is being built. Why the
angels (presumably but not certainly only the last-men-
tioned four) turn their faces away is not clear; the usual
connection with theophanic glory does not seem present
here.

■ **10.2–5** A whole new allegory is introduced here, but
one integrally dependent on what has gone before. As in
Vis. 2.4.1, a revelation about the woman church's identity or appearance must be made not by her but by an
angel in a dream-vision (v. 7). Three visions are numbered in the narrative, even though, strictly speaking,
there have been several more. The enumeration of three
refers to the three major events in which the woman
church is central.[1] In the first vision (1.2.2), she is
described as πρεσβῦτις ("elderly"), but in the second
(2.1.3) and third (3.1.2) visions, nothing is said about her
appearing younger; in fact, she is still called πρεσβυτέρα
("older" or "elder") in 3.1.2 and even here in v. 6, a title
which, like its masculine counterpart, can refer to either
age or authority. If the present text is seen as an integral
part of the narrative, perhaps this is an indication that
the title in 3.1.2 refers to honor rather than age. But the
theme of her rejuvenation is introduced for the first
time here, and could be secondary, but is more likely an

---

1 For Alistair Kirkland ("The Literary History of the
   Shepherd of Hermas Visions I to IV," *SecCent* 9
   [1992] 87–102), the excess of visions is indication of

ms. rearrangement. The original order would be:
the present *Vision* 1; *Vision* 2 (the tower); *Vision* 4.

expansion and development of the image,[2] though her change from καθέδρα ("chair," 1.2.2) to walking (2.1.3) to συμψέλιον ("couch," 3.1.4) does not contradict the rejuvenation theme and is carefully repeated here (vv. 3, 5). Here her sitting in a chair in the first vision (v. 3; 11.2) is attributed to age, not dignity, probably a reinterpretation.[3] The change of term for what she sits on, therefore, is not accidental; later (13.3), the couch will symbolize security.

The rejuvenation theme as set forth in these chapters has no true precedents or contemporary parallels, though polymorphism is common.[4] Ezra's vision of the mourning woman transformed into the heavenly city with its point-by-point explanation (*4 Ezra* 10.25–54) is often cited, but this is transformation along the line of the feminization of Jerusalem in biblical literature, not rejuvenation. Whether some background may have been supplied by the three statues of the Sibyl supposedly erected in the Roman Forum,[5] or early extrabiblical midrash on Sarah,[6] this is the first true instance of the feminine rejuvenation theme, later attested in Roman literature,[7] one of the "archaic photo-images in the collective unconscious (which) correspond to the language of

dreams."[8] The combination of white hair with a youthful face (v. 5) is later attested for a vision of God.[9]

■ **10.6–7** A supporting dream of the woman church (v. 6) urges him to prepare for the revelation of her metamorphosis by fasting and prayer, which he does for one day (v. 7), in great contrast to his previous fifteen-day fast,[10] before the revelation is given to him. Ταπεινοφροσύνη ("humbling"), originally associated more with oppressive socioeconomic humiliation, has acquired in this vocabulary the sense of mortification, a more general term for a humble attitude that is acted out by prayer, fasting, penance, and almsgiving.[11] The young man's reproach is by now recognizable as part of the dialogical pattern, a rhetorical device that draws attention to the message.[12] The reproach, however, contains a colloquial expression, ὑπὸ χεῖρα (here translated "always") whose meaning is unclear.[13] What is the danger to Hermas' health (literally, to his flesh) is equally unclear: perhaps that he will neglect a normal life while he is intent on having a revelation. The warning can hardly be directed at his fasting, since the woman church told him to do so (v. 6).

■ **10.8–10** The angel's pronouncement and question (v. 8) are teasers that function literarily to encourage further

---

The current *Vision* 2 and the couch episode of *Vis.* 3.1.1–4 are later or from another author.

2 So too Dibelius (477), on the basis of similar style, literary unity, and the integration of this motif later in 4.2.2.

3 See comment on *Vis.* 1.2.2.

4 E.g., *Ap. John* 2, 10; *Act. John* 87–89; *Act. Pet.* 20, 21; *Act. Thom.* 11; *Acts of Perpetua and Felicitas* 10.7; vision of Quintilla of Christ as a woman: Epiphanius *Pan.* 49.1; discussion and further references, Brox, 155; Jean-Daniel Kaestli, *Acta Johannis* (CChr Series Apocrypha; Turnhout: Brepols, 1983) 466–93, especially 472 n. 1. On the rejuvenation of individual literary characters, however, see Otto Luschnat, "Die Jungfrauenszene in der Arkadienvision des Hermas," *Theologia Viatorum* 12 (1973/74) 53–70 (54–56).

5 References in Peterson, "Beiträge," 267.

6 References in Ford, "Liturgical Background."

7 Claudian on the goddess Natura, Rutilius Namatianus, et al.; Ernest R. Curtius, *European Literature and the Latin Middle Ages* (Bollingen Series 36; New York: Pantheon, 1953) 103–5. The suggested parallel from the perhaps contemporary Lucius Annaeus Florus *Ep.* 1 Introd. 8 (see Brox, 158) concerns the rejuvenation of Rome after four successive stages of life, beginning with the age of the kings

and culminating in old age during the period after Augustus, then revived by military renewal under Trajan: the Roman people "grew old and lost its potency" (*quasi consenuit atque decoxit*) but under Trajan "again renewed its vigour with youth as it were restored" (*quasi reddita iuventute reviruit*, trans. Edward S. Forster [LCL; Cambridge: Harvard University Press, 1966] 8–9). But this is hardly a parallel, since Rome is not explicitly personified nor does it undergo successive stages of rejuvenation.

8 Curtius, *European Literature and the Latin Middle Ages*, 105.

9 *Acts of Perpetua and Felicitas* 12.3.

10 *Vis.* 2.2.1; on the significance of fasting as preparation for religious experience, see comment there. In 3.1.2., he fasts an indefinite πολλάκις ("often").

11 Compare *Man.* 4.2.2; *Sim.* 5.3.7 (also associated with fasting); 7.4, 6; 8.7.6. Its meaning in Col 2:18 is unclear. Cf. Osiek, *Rich and Poor*, 66 n. 27; BAGD² *s.v.*

12 E.g., 8.9 above.

13 See the same expression in *Vis.* 5.5; *Man.* 4.3.6. The meaning is probably something between "continually" and "occasionally"; cf. Dibelius, 478.

pursuit by Hermas (v. 9), who defines the limits of what he now wishes to know. He addresses the angel as κύριε ("sir"), the normal address of respect, and the masculine counterpart to the way he addresses the woman church (κύρια). Inexplicably, in the middle of a sentence in v. 9, the angel's addressee becomes second person plural until the end of the verse, a slippage into prophetic address to the listening community behind the revelation. The slippage, unanimously attested in the manuscripts, is not accidental, for the speaker remains plural in v. 10, but the text is unusually awkward.[14] The last part of the angel's reproach, "not having your heart turned to the Lord," is thought by some to echo the liturgical response immediately preceding the preface of the Roman eucharistic liturgy.[15] It could well be that a familiar liturgical response comes readily to the mind of the writer. Hermas has the last word (v. 10), a masterpiece of respectful manipulation after the angel's resistance, giving the impression that Hermas is less intimidated by the angel's scolding than involved in a playful word game.

The Aged Church

■ **11.1–2 [19]** The explanation of the three[16] forms of the woman church unfolds. Each successive form matches a diagnosis of the church as historical, an imperfect community of people. The analogy is ingenious but stands in flat contradiction with *Vis.* 2.4.1, where the church was aged because of her primacy in creation. Here instead she appeared older first as sign of the bodily weakness of the elderly (vv. 2, 4). Rather than contradiction, how-

ever, it is really a different use of the same image but one that need not be entirely cut off from the former one. The difference corresponds to the pattern of successive overlays of meaning assigned to the same image, from cosmological (2.4.1 in this case) to soteriological levels.[17] The church is both transcendent, heavenly figure and real, historical assembly of imperfect people. Nowhere in *Hermas* is that paradox, a foundation of early Christian ecclesiology, clearer than here. Except at the end of 12.3, consistently in these chapters the "you" who seeks to understand the interpretation of the vision is the singular Hermas, while the "you" who undergoes transformation is the plural community.

■ **11.3–4** In v. 3, "the elderly" (οἱ πρεσβύτεροι) abandon hope of life and await only their "sleep" (κοίμησις), a common expression for death, especially in Jewish and early Christian funerary inscriptions. The hopelessness of the aging process in a society with very low life expectancy and little protection against disease is accurately reflected in these lines. Attitudes toward aging differed as they do today, according to life experience.[18] The community is "softened" (μαλακισθέντες)[19] by daily, worldly, or business concerns (τῶν βιωτικῶν πραγμάτων), the same thing for which Hermas has been reproached by the woman church in *Vis.* 1.3.1; 2.3.1 in connection with the misdeeds of his family, thus showing the coherence between Hermas' family situation and that of the church in general. This coherence, however, need not mean that the family is only a literary device to represent the whole community.[20] They have given themselves to ἀκηδία (here translated "apathy"), indif-

---

14 Compare e.g., *Vis.* 2.2.7; 3.3.5; 11.1–2 below.

15 Funk, 375; Dibelius agrees (479). Ironically, the text to which Dibelius refers is *Ap. Const.* 8.12.5: Ἄνω τὸν νοῦν ("Lift up the mind [not heart]"), to which the congregation responds: Ἔχομεν πρὸς τὸν κύριον ("We have [them lifted up] to the Lord"). Closer to home is Hippolytus, *Ap. Trad.* 4.3: Ἄνω τὰς καρδίας ("Lift up your hearts"), with the same response; restored from Sahidic version, *Ap. Canons of Hippolytus*, and *Ap. Const.* cited above (Gregory Dix, ed., *The Treatise on the Apostolic Tradition of St. Hippolytus of Rome* [London: SPCK, 1968] 7).

16 Τριῶν ("three") only in A and inserted as correction in S.

17 Henne, "Polysémie," 133–34. Brox remains unconvinced (156–57).

18 Moses I. Finley, "The Elderly in Classical Antiquity," *Greece and Rome* 28 (1981) 156–71. Not surprisingly,

poets tended to consider adolescence the prime of life; but for philosophers and theologians like Seneca, Augustine, and Jerome, the prime was old age when the mind is at its apex: Emiel Eyben, "Roman Notes on the Course of Life," *Ancient Society* 4 (1973) 213–38.

19 While the verb μαλακίζομαι means primarily to soften through weakness, the word group carries contemptuous overtones of luxury (compare Luke 7:25), undoubtedly intended here and in 11.2; 12.3 (μαλακίαι, "soft ways"), and of effeminacy, probably not intended here (1 Cor 6:9). A, which avoids the word in both 11.2, 3 (though not in 12.3), may have found it awkward for the latter meaning. Cf. BAGD² and LSJ *s.v.* μαλακίζομαι, μαλακός.

20 So Dibelius, 479–80 and throughout his interpretation.

ference, boredom, or neglect[21] rather than placing their worries in God (οὐκ ἐπερίψατε ἑαυτῶν τὰς μερίμνας ἐπὶ τὸν κύριον).[22] The scriptural allusion is awkward, for in this context it seems less to mean that they are overly worried and not sufficiently trusting in God (the context in the psalm), than that they are not sufficiently concerned about what is important, and so *should* be more worried about the things of God.[23]

Second Stage of Rejuvenation

■ **12.1–3 [20]** The second vision of the woman church presented her walking and reading the message that she was about to reveal (*Vis.* 2.1.3). Now it is explained (v. 1) that her rejuvenation was at a midpoint there. Whereas the analogy in the first phase (11.3–4) was that of the aging process, this one (v. 2) is the realistic concern about inheritance, a preoccupation among Romans of financial means.[24] While a younger person might expect an inheritance, an older person who is poor has given up hope of ever becoming rich this way. Yet if it unexpectedly happens, such a person has a new lease on life and becomes almost another, younger person.[25] The proclamation (v. 3) that God has had mercy (ἐσπλαγχνίσθη)

uses a word group that with this meaning is characteristic of post-LXX Jewish and early Christian literature, often with eschatological overtones, and appears frequently in *Hermas*.[26] Unexpectedly, the second person plural is maintained through the end of the chapter, so that it is "you" plural to whom the tower was revealed, rather than the singular referring to Hermas, another slippage between the narrative single recipient and the plural audience for whom the message is intended. The passage ends with another echo of 1 Thess 5:13.[27]

Final Stage of Rejuvenation

■ **13.1–2 [21]** The final explanation really contains two analogies, like the explanation of the first vision (11.1–4): the youthfulness of the woman (vv. 1–2) and her sitting on the couch (vv. 3–4). In the final phase of transformation, the woman church is young, beautiful, and joyful—the feminine ideal (v. 1).[28] The analogy (v. 2) is not a continuation of the financial windfall from 12.2, but a new though similar example: the change that happens to one who is depressed,[29] then receives unanticipated good news and is changed into a very different person. The spirit of such a person is renewed (as in

---

21 Lake's translation "worry" (57) makes sense with what follows but is not consonant with the word's general meaning elsewhere, though it can also have the seemingly opposite meaning of "anxiety." Cf. Ps 118 (LXX 119):28; Sir 29:5; Isa 61:3; Cicero *Att.* 12.45.1; Lucian *Hermot.* 77. In later Christian monasticism, the word will become a major topos as the great enemy and deadly sin of the zealous monk (see LPGL *s.v.*). It is also something akin to λύπη, a later great concern (*Mandate* 10).

22 An exact paraphrase of the terminology of Ps 55:22 (54:23 LXX); cf. 1 Pet 5:7, of which the quote here shows no influence.

23 The same allusion to Ps 54:23 is used more gracefully in *Vis.* 4.2.4, 5.

24 See, e.g., Richard P. Saller, "Roman Heirship Strategies in Principle and in Practice," in David I. Kertzer and Richard P. Saller, eds., *The Family in Italy from Antiquity to the Present* (New Haven: Yale University Press, 1991) 26–47.

25 Dibelius (480) claims it as a traditional topos, yet can cite only three examples: Epictetus 2.7.9; 4.13.22 (passing remarks); Horace *Sat.* 2.3.142–57. To them could be added Matt 21:38 par. Mark 12:7; Luke 12:13. Cf. the common NT use of the image for salvation, e.g., Rom 8:17; Gal 3:29; Heb 6:17.

The words in brackets at the end of the verse are omitted by BS.

26 Πολυσπλαγχνία ("great compassion"): *Vis.* 1.3.2; 2.2.8; 4.2.3; *Man.* 9.2; *Sim.* 8.6; πολύσπλαγχνος ("very compassionate"): *Man.* 4.3.5; *Sim.* 5.4.4; 7.4; σπλαγχνίζομαι: *Man.* 4.3.5; 9.3; *Sim.* 7.4; 8.6.3; 11.1; 9.14.3 (of God); *Sim.* 6.3.2; 9.24.2 (σπλάγχνον) ("of people"). The use of σπλάγχνον ("compassion") and its derivatives is also a tendency of *T. 12 Patr.* with possible literary influence on *Hermas*: Helmut Koester, "σπλάγχνον κτλ.," *TDNT* 7 (1971) 548–59.

27 Compare 5.1; 6.3; 9.2, 10; *Man.* 2.3; *Sim.* 8.7.2.

28 White ("Interaction," 145–50) suggests a psychosexual interpretation whereby rejuvenation means return to presexual infancy. The interpretation is possible in *Sim.* 9.11.5 but, as he admits, it does not work here, for the woman church in her youngest phase is not an infant; on the contrary, she is nubile. But for White, this is the sign that she cannot continue as guide because she is now too dangerous to Hermas, even as Rhoda was in *Vis.* 1.1, and so had to be replaced by the old woman church.

29 The sadness spoken of here (λύπη) is not just a natural feeling, but a pervasive and destructive state: see *Mandate* 11.

12.3); the vision of the good things awaiting those whose hearts are converted has the same effect. This same renewal of spirit was the promised sign that the eschatological announcement of the tower is both true and urgent (8.9). This spiritual renewal, described in a kind of proleptic aorist (also 12.2–3) that anticipates the proclaimed conversion, is the experiential evidence of what is taking place.

■ **13.3–4** The last analogy integrates soteriological meaning with the earlier cosmic explanations of the church through the polyvalent symbol of sitting. Whereas her position seated in a chair was presumably originally a sign of her superior status and authority,[30] then a sign of the weakness of old age (11.1–2, 4), now her sitting on the couch is a sign of strength. Only the "chair" (καθέδρα) of the first vision, however, is used to mean both dignity (assumed from the context but not stated in 1.2.2) and weakness (explicitly stated in 11.1–4). The third vision of the woman church depicts her seated on

the "couch" (συμψέλιον), which is not explained as sign of weakness.[31] Rather, the foursquare couch means firm foundations upon the primeval cosmic elements or the four corners of the universe.[32] The proleptic past-tense description of the converted (12.2–3; v. 2 here) gives way in v. 4 to the future tense for the promise of renewal in a triple repetition of completeness as the explanation comes to an end: they will be made wholly new (ὁλοτελῶς νέοι ἔσονται), those who are converted with whole hearts (οἱ ἐξ ὅλης καρδίας μετανοήσαντες), and with that, you have the whole revelation (ἀπέχεις ὁλοτελῆ τὴν ἀποκάλυψιν). With a sense of completeness, the third *Vision* comes to an end. The final sentence, however, leaves the reader prepared for more.[33]

---

30   See comment on *Vis.* 1.2.2[. But it need not be so; cf. examples in LSJ *s.v.*

31   The *subsellium*, a common Roman piece of furniture, was often connected with those of inferior position, esp. to those sitting on a *cathedra*. The change of seating is curious; only on the *subsellium* is Hermas invited to sit with her. Cf. E. Hüber (?), "Subsellium," PW 24 (1931) 502–4. (The abbreviation of author's name at the end of the article is "Hug," which does not correspond to any author listing.)

32   Ezek 1; Rev 4:6–8; Philo *Cher.* 127; Josephus *Ant.* 3.183; Diogenes Laertius 7.137; cf. BAGD² *s.v.* στοιχεῖον 2. The suggestion of Charles Taylor and J. A. T. Robinson (Snyder, 54) that Hermas refers to the four Gospels as does Irenaeus (*Adv. Haer.* 3.11.8) is fanciful; Irenaeus uses the four directions and four winds for his comparison. Both draw on a

common tradition for their own purposes. Even more fanciful is Taylor's later connection ("Hermas and Cebes," *Journal of Philology* 27 [1901] 276–319 [289–90]) of the tripod of the Sibyl (confused with the church in *Vis.* 2.4.1), added to the bipod younger woman (3.12.1), to reflect the riddle of the Sphinx! The mature woman who stands on a firm square rock in *Tab. Ceb.* 18.1, 3 is mildly reminiscent of this scene but not really a parallel (Joly, 51).

33   Twenty words, or about four MS. lines before the end, at τεθεμελιθμένοι ("securely founded"), MS. B breaks off, but the text undoubtedly continued through *Vision* 3 and probably contained the whole of *Vision* 4 on the two lost central leaves of the codex (Carlini, *Bodmer Papyrus*, 2).

4

Vision of the Beast

1 [22] 1/ What I saw, brothers and sisters, twenty days after the last vision, was an omen of the coming tribulation. 2/ I was going into the country by the Via Campana. The place is easily reached at about ten stadia from the public road. 3/ As I was walking alone, I thought it fitting that the Lord complete the revelations and the visions shown to me through his holy church, so as to strengthen me and give conversion to his servants who have been made to stumble, so that his great and honorable name might be glorified because he found me worthy to show me his wonders. 4/ As I was glorifying and thanking him, something like the echo of a voice answered me: "Do not be doubleminded, Hermas." I wondered to myself: "How can I be doubleminded when I have been so firmly grounded by the Lord and seen such glorious things?" 5/ Advancing a little further, brothers and sisters, I saw a cloud of dust that seemed as high as heaven, and I began to wonder: "Is a herd of animals coming and raising dust?" It seemed just a stadion away. 6/ When the dust cloud got bigger and bigger, I suspected it was something supernatural. The sun came out a bit and I saw a huge beast like some sea monster, with fiery locusts coming out of its mouth. The beast was about a hundred feet long and had a head like a pottery urn. 7/ I began to weep and ask the Lord to deliver me from it. I remembered the word I had heard: "Do not be doubleminded, Hermas." 8/ So, clothed with the faith of the Lord, brothers and sisters, and mindful of the great things he had taught me, I took courage and gave myself over to the beast. The beast charged as though it could destroy a city. 9/ I approached it, and the monster, big as it was, stretched itself out on the ground and stuck out nothing but its tongue, and did not even move until I had passed it by. 10/ The beast had four colors on its head: black, then the color of fire and blood, then gold, then white.

2 [23] 1/ When I had passed by the beast and gone about thirty feet, a dressed-up young woman met me, as if coming forth from a bridal chamber, completely in white, with white sandals, veiled to the forehead, with a band around her head, and her hair was white. 2/ Knowing from the previous visions that it was the church, I was all the more joyful. She greeted me: "Hello, fellow." I greeted her back: "Hello, lady." 3/ She answered me: "Did anything meet you?" I said: "Lady, a beast so big it could destroy peoples, but by the power and compassion of the Lord, I escaped it." 4/ "It is well that you escaped it," she said, "because you cast your care upon the Lord and opened your heart to the Lord, believing that you could be saved by no other than the great and glorious name. Therefore, the Lord sent his angel in charge of the beasts, whose name is Thegri, who shut its mouth so that it might not hurt you. You have escaped great tribulation because of your faith and because when you saw such a huge beast, you did not become doubleminded. 5/ Now go and explain to the Lord's elect ones these wonderful things of his, and tell them that this beast is an omen of the great tribulation that is coming. If then you [pl.] are prepared in advance, and are converted with all your heart to the Lord, you will be able to escape it, if your heart becomes cleansed and blameless, and you serve the Lord blamelessly for the rest of the days of your life. Cast your cares upon the Lord, who will set them straight. 6/ Believe in the Lord, you doubleminded, who is all-powerful and can avert his wrath from you, and send plagues upon you, the doubleminded. Woe to those who hear these words and disobey; it would have been better for them not to have been born."

3 [24]   1/ I asked her about the four colors that the beast had on its head. She answered me: "Again you [sing.] are curious about these things." "Yes, lady," I said. "Tell me what they are." 2/ "Listen," she said. "The black is this world in which you [pl.] live. 3/ The color of fire and blood means that this world must be destroyed by blood and fire. 4/ The gold portion is you who have fled from this world. Just as gold is tried by fire and becomes useful, so also you who live among them are being tested. Those who endure and are consumed by flames will be purified by them. As gold drops off its dross, so you will let fall all sadness and anguish, and you will be purified and become useful for the building of the tower. 5/ The white part is the world that is coming, in which the elect of God will live, for those chosen by God for eternal life will be spotless and pure. 6/ You [sing.], therefore, do not cease speaking into the ears of the holy ones. You [pl.] have the omen of the great tribulation to come. But if you wish it to be so, it will come to nothing. Remember what has already been written." 7/ When she had said these things, she left, and I did not see where she went because there was a noise and I turned around out of fear, thinking that the beast was coming.

The Beast Passes

■ 1.1 [22] As at the beginning of *Vision* 3, the Greek MSS. give the numbering, taken by Peterson to be secondary, by Hellholm and Brox to be authentic.[1] The new narrative begins after a period of twenty days, which does not contradict the three days of *Vis.* 3.8.11, intended to give time for the absorption and understanding of the mes-

sage before its proclamation. The marking of time is characteristic of the connectors in the *Visions* and of apocalyptic narrative in general.[2] The frightful vision of the beast to come is identified beforehand, the only vision in which this has happened; usually Hermas must ponder and/or be told the meaning of his visions. The beast is a τύπος ("type," "figure," or "model")[3] of the

---

1   Peterson, "Begegnung," 285; Hellholm, *Visionenbuch*, 134 n. 17, 131 n. 10; Brox, 162–63.

2   *Vis.* 2.1.1, 2.1; 3.8.11; see comment on 2.1.1 above.

3   An important concept in early Christian biblical theology; see BAGD[2] *s.v.*, esp. 6.

coming ϑλῖψις ("tribulation," "suffering," "trouble").[4] While the word can simply refer to any kind of trouble, in apocalyptic literature it most often carries the meaning of eschatological tribulation, or affliction that is ordered to the eschaton. Clearly here it refers to some major trial, whether historical or mythological.[5] This brief, fast-moving narrative contains an unusual number of connectors to an envisioned audience by means of the address, "brothers and sisters" (ἀδελφοί) in vv. 1, 5, 8.

■ **1.2** Hermas is going out into the countryside or to "the field," probably intended to be the same place that was previously the site of a vision, whether or not the land belongs to him or he works it;[6] in any event, a specific place is envisioned. This time, the place markers are much more definite: ten stadia (1.2 Roman miles; 1.85 km.; 1.15 English miles) off the public road, the Via Campana, which ran from Via Portuensis at the south end of Trastevere to the Campus Salinarum, the salt

marshes on the right bank of the Tiber.[7] The Greek MSS. read that the place is easily reached (ῥαδίως δὲ ὁδεύεται ὁ τόπος).[8] Rather than a return to the difficult location of *Vis.* 1.1.3, the easy accessibility of this place stands in contrast to it, for the events here, though frightening, will be far more encouraging.[9]

■ **1.3** Hermas is deep in prayer as he walks along alone (v. 3), asking for a completion of the revelations and visions, even though in *Vis.* 3.13.4 the angel has already declared them complete. However, the last line of that verse left an opening for more, promising that if there were need, more would come. Once he has gotten accustomed to receiving visions, Hermas often asks for them, a literary signal that one is about to happen.[10] Three reasons are given for his desire: first, to strengthen him; second, as in *Vis.* 3.3.1, to benefit others in the community; third, to glorify God. Those persons about whom he is concerned are the ἐσκανδαλισμένοι ("those who have been made to stumble"), perhaps those with serious

---

4   S alone omits the whole phrase: εἰς τύπον τῆς ϑλίψεως τῆς ἐπερχομένης ("an omen of the coming tribulation"), which Peterson argues is authentic, the others having slipped it in from 4.3.6; all others, however, accept the phrase as original here, Hellholm (*Visionenbuch*, 134 n. 18) explaining well the omission through homoioteleuton from the line above. Peterson's variant reading of A in the plural (τῶν ϑλίψεων τῶν ἐπερχομένων) was apparently based on a faulty text: Hellholm, ibid.; Joly, 145. Cf. Matt 24:21; Mark 13:24–25; Rev 7:14; *Sib. Or.* 3.183.

5   See further comment on 2.5. below.

6   *Vis.* 3.1.2. See further comment there.

7   The very ancient Via Campana, probably improved ca. 350 BCE at the time of the founding of Ostia, meandered along the north bank of the Tiber; after crossing the Tiber at Rome, it continued north as the Via Salaria. After the founding of Portus by Claudius, the new Via Portuensis went more directly there from Rome and absorbed much of the traffic. The Via Campana passed the site of the well-known cult of the Arvales Brothers, though very little is known of the details of the cult. See *CIL* 6. 2107, 3.14; 29772; 10250; Suetonius *Aug.* 94.7; Aulus Gellius *At. N.* 7.7.8; Pliny *N. H.* 18.2.2; Thomas Ashby, *The Roman Campagna in Classical Times* (London: Ernest Benn, 1927) 29–30, 219; Raymond Chevallier, *Roman Roads* (rev. ed.; London: B. T. Batsford, 1989) 66–67; John Scheid, *Romulus et ses frères: Le collège des frères Arvales, modèle du culte publique dans la Roma des Empereurs* (Rome: École

Française de Rome, 1990). This road is to be preferred to that of the same name between Capua and Neapolis, nowhere near Rome. Lampe (*Stadtrömische Christen*, 30, 33–34) notes the proximity of the road to that quarter of Rome likely to have contained one of the largest gatherings of both Jews and Christians at that period. Peterson ("Begegnung," 287), takes the A variant καμπηνή as an adjective related to καμπή ("winding"), referring not to the Via Campana but to a winding, rough path off the public road.

8   Though LL seem to imply the opposite: *raro* ("scantily [traveled]"); E *vasta* ("unoccupied"), suggesting just the opposite of "easily"; hence the suggested restoration σπανίως ("seldom") for ῥαδίως. Besides picking up this restoration, Peterson ("Begegnung," 288) also gratuitously emends δὲ ὁδεύεται to διοδεύεται, thus "the place is seldom traveled through," to bring it into closer parallel with the rough level ground of *Vis.* 1.1.3. A number of further forced details lead to an unsustainable overall interpretation: see the thorough critique by Brox, 164–66.

9   So too Brox, 164.

10   Cf. *Vis.* 3.1.1, 3.1, 10.2, 6–10.

behavioral problems described in *Vis.* 3.5.5; 6.2–6, especially those in 3.5.5 who have the desire to be converted.[11] The motive of the glory of God is expressed in a psalmic refrain, and Hermas' rejoicing in God's finding him worthy is part of the praise of God.[12]

■ **1.4** In answer to his prayer of glory and thanksgiving, Hermas hears not a perfectly distinct voice, but an echo (ὡς ἤχος φωνῆς)[13] that encourages him against doublemindedness, the curse of Hermas' community. Up to this point, the diagnosis of doublemindedness has been applied to Hermas himself only once, and that in a similar context: preparation for a vision (*Vis.* 3.3.4). In both cases the exhortation functions not as a reproach for past behavior, but as warning and strengthening for what is to come (cf. v. 7), and gives its own clue to the meaning of doublemindedness: here, lack of faith and the courage that flows from it. An unidentified heavenly voice is a common motif in visionary literature.[14]

■ **1.5–6** Hermas has wondered (v. 4) why the question of his doublemindedness has even been raised, and he does not have long to find out, for he sees[15] a large dust cloud coming at him from the other direction (v. 5), of the kind one would expect from a large herd of animals.[16] Its estimated distance is a stadion (625 Roman feet or one-eighth of a Roman mile; 607 English feet or just over one-tenth of an English mile). As it grows larger and larger (v. 6), he realizes this is no ordinary dust cloud, but something θεῖον, that is, from the extraterrestrial realm. The cloud has obscured the sun, evoking the cosmic eschatological clouds of smoke and locusts that appear elsewhere in apocalyptic terror scenes, especially

accompanying a frightening beast such as this.[17] The beast (θηρίον) is compared to a κῆτος, a sea monster or Leviathan, the LXX's word for Jonah's whale and Job's Rahab.[18] The anomaly of a sea monster on a dusty Italian road is more understandable if it is kept in mind that this is meant to be merely a comparison, based on the common qualities of enormous and awesome bulk and movement.

The description of the beast's head is problematic: every manuscript is slightly different, but all mean either a pottery vessel or something made of the same material.[19] It is doubtful that Daniel's statue with clay feet (Dan 2:32–43) is related, since there the pottery signifies weakness, which it surely does not here. Since no material comparison is given for the rest of the body (in contrast to Daniel's gold, silver, bronze, and iron), the pottery could in fact connote unusual hardness for part of an animal's body. However, most commentators correctly take the analogy to refer to shape or size rather than material. The head is compared to a large upsidedown ceramic urn, with narrow neck and wide protruding body (the beast's head).[20] For the meaning of the beast, see 2.5 below.

■ **1.7–10** In his fear of the beast heading straight for him (v. 7), he remembers the directive given him in advance by the mysterious voice (v. 4), and realizes that faith in the Lord[21] protects him like armor[22] and is the source of his courage to face the beast head-on. The encounter turns out to be nothing dangerous, for the beast behaves

---

11   See *Man.* 8.10, where an important work of mercy is the acceptance and help of this group.

12   E.g., Ps 86:9, 12; compare *Vis.* 2.1.2.

13   *Not* "as an echo of *my* voice" (as Lake translates, 61).

14   E.g., the rabbinic *bat-qol*; Matt 3:17 par. Mark 1:11; John 12:28; Rev 6:6; 19:1; 21:3; *Gos. Pet.* 41; *Act. Thom.* 158; *Act. Joh.* 18; Peterson, "Begegnung," 293; Snyder, 56; Brox, 167.

15   The expression καὶ ἰδοὺ βλέπω ("and behold I see") used here, in v. 6, and *Sim.* 9.6.1 to announce a vision (ἰδού also at *Vis.* 1.3.4; 2.3.4; 3.2.4; *Sim.* 7.4), is probably an echo of biblical Greek (e.g., Dan 8:5 LXX), but the influence of the Latin *ecce* cannot be ruled out (Hilhorst, *Sémitismes*, 153–55).

16   Κτήνη: usually translated "cattle," but it could be a herd of any animals (LSJ s.v. κτῆνος), more likely sheep or goats, on a dusty unpaved side road used only by farmers and herders.

17   E.g., Dan 7:3–7; Rev 9:2 (esp. the fiery locusts); 11:7; 16:13. Though this beast is not called a dragon, the mythological dragon of apocalyptic literature is closely related. Peterson ("Begegnung," 298–300) gives a number of comparative features of this narrative with (probably fourth- or fifth-century) *Act. Phil.* 102–5, concluding that there is no evidence of direct dependence, but a common source.

18   Jonah 2:1, 2, 11; Job 9:13; 26:12.

19   S καίραμος (κέραμος); Sᶜ καιράμιον; A κεράμιον; L¹ *vas urnale*; L² *laguenam*; E *lagenam* (from Greek λάγηνος).

20   Further discussion in Dibelius, 483; Peterson, "Begegnung," 294–95; Brox, 167–69.

21   Τοῦ κυρίου: that is, in God; AL¹ var. God (θεοῦ).

22   A Pauline image: 2 Cor 5:3; Gal 3:27; Eph 4:24; Col 3:10, 12; with explicit metaphor of armor: Rom

more like a pet dog than a monster.[23] Hermas will not know until 2.4 below that his escape is due to angelic intervention.[24] By way of afterthought, he notes that the beast carried four colors on its head.[25] The symbolic use of colors in apocalyptic literature is traditional, especially black, red, and white, with a variant fourth color.[26] Though the apparition of the beast was announced as a vision (v. 1), there is a direct quality to the narrative that makes it different from previous visions, as if Hermas and the beast are really face-to-face. "Real world" and visionary world overlap.[27]

The Woman Church Explains the Beast

■ **2.1–2 [23]** The mood very suddenly shifts (v. 1) when, not thirty feet down the road (compare the hundred-foot length of the beast!), Hermas encounters quite a different apparition: a "young woman" (παρθένος) clothed entirely in white, with white hair, a band around her head,[28] and a veil extending down her forehead.[29] Certainly in light of tradition already established in the NT, the tendency to leap to bridal imagery is understandable, but care must be taken not to overinterpret in this direction.[30] The quotation from Ps 19:5 (LXX 18:6)

refers not to a bride but to the sun compared to a bride-*groom*, not going into, but coming out of a bridechamber, exulting after having consummated the marriage.[31] Rather than being maladjusted biblical application, it is meant only to hint at bridal imagery as the logical outcome of the woman church's rejuvenation, and in fact to suggest just as much her buoyant attitude.[32] It does not portray her as bride of Christ.[33] Except for the psalm allusion, spousal language for the woman church is completely lacking, here as everywhere else. Verse 1 is the first time in the *Visions* that she is called παρθένος ("young woman" or "virgin"), and it refers more to her rejuvenation than to her marital state. She is not so much an image of the end time[34] as of what the church can become if its members accept the challenge of transformation. In spite of her changed appearance, Hermas recognizes her as the church (v. 2), and they exchange a familiar greeting (*Vis.* 1.2.2).

■ **2.3** The verse seems almost playful. The woman church, immediately on the heels of the beast, asks tongue in cheek if he passed anything on the road, and his response is that of a child describing a monster from his imagination. Hermas recognizes here that he got

---

13:12; Eph 6:11, 14; 1 Thess 5:8; *1 Clem.* 30.3; Ignatius *Pol.* 1.2. Cf. Ps 131:9; *Man.* 1.2, 4; 5.2.8; 10.3.1; etc.; esp. *Man.* 9.7, 10; *Sim.* 6.1.2.

23 Compare *Acts of Perpetua and Felicitas* 4.4–7. Peterson ("Begegnung," 301–2) sees this as based rather on motifs of baptism and heavenly ladder ascent (ignoring Gen 3:15).

24 See also *Man.* 12.4.6, 7; 6.1.

25 Brox (170) complains of the clumsiness of inserting these details at this point, but Dibelius (484) rightly notes that the colors could only be seen up close, and offers Rev 9:7–10 for comparison.

26 E.g., Zech 1:8; 6:1–6; Rev 6:1–8; also used in astrology and in correlation with the four elements, winds, and directions; references in Dibelius, 484–85.

27 Brox, 169.

28 A μίτρα, often translated turban, but more likely a band tied around the head and catching the hair in back, commonly worn by girls; a snood (BAGD *s.v.*; LSJ *s.v.* μίτρα II); Varro *De lingua latina* 5.29.130; Jdt 16:8; Bar 5:2. The passage can be understood without reference to the headdress of the Jerusalem high priest, Roman women of ill repute, or effeminacy (Giet, *Hermas,* 18 n. 3). Further discussion in Joly, 425–36; Brox, 171–72.

29 Except for the headband, this dress seems to fit what we know of the Roman bride (see Leutzsch,

Wahrnehmung, 175 and references), though she lacks the *flammeum,* the flame-colored veil worn by some brides. For Dibelius (486) and Joly (136–37), this is because she is a heavenly, not an earthly bride; but compare the approximately contemporary picture of a reluctant bride in the "Aldobrandini Wedding" mural in the Vatican Museum (reproduced in Paul Veyne, ed., *A History of Private Life from Pagan Rome to Byzantium* [Cambridge, MA/London: Harvard University Press, 1987] 1. 35, and elsewhere). Other than the headband, she matches Hermas' description exactly.

30 2 Cor 11:2; Eph 5:25–33; Rev 21:2. Hegesippus speaks of the early church as virgin unviolated by heresy, in probable dependence on 2 Cor 11:2 (Eusebius *Hist. eccl.* 3.32.7; 4.22.4); perhaps too the Inscription of Abercius 11; *Acts of the Martyrs of Lyon and Vienne* 45 refers to the church as virgin mother. The image is already present in early Christian imagination, but it is only hinted at here.

31 But compare Sir 15:2.

32 Compare *Vis.* 1.4.3.

33 With Brox, 172; against Snyder, 57 et al.

34 Dibelius, 487.

through safely only by God's power and great compassion (πολυσπλαγχνία).[35]

■ **2.4–6** These verses form a double sequence of instructions on how to escape the beast. Verse 4 addresses Hermas through allusion to Ps 55:22 (54:23 LXX), "Cast your care upon the Lord,"[36] directed in the singular to him, followed by approval of his opening his heart to the Lord; he has been able to escape the "great tribulation" (μεγάλη θλῖψις) through the action of the angel Thegri, because of his faith and the correlative absence of doublemindedness. The same promise is present on the communal level: vv. 5b, 6 address the community in the plural with an invitation to be converted with full heart to the Lord, using the same psalm allusion, this time in the plural, and ending with the appeal against doublemindedness. Centered between the two sides of the inclusion lies the repeated explanation (from 1.1) that the beast is a "type" or omen "of the great tribulation to come" (τύπος ἐστὶν θλίψεως τῆς μελλούσης τῆς μεγάλης).

Thegri is otherwise unknown in early Jewish or Christian angelology. His invisible action in 1.9 (Hermas has to be informed of it here) echoes that of the angel of Dan 6:22–23.[37] Angels in charge of beasts and cosmic powers is a traditional motif,[38] but Thegri is a mystery. Suggested identifications have ranged from alteration to Segri, with an etymology in the Hebrew word סגר (to

close, as in Dan 6:23),[39] to the adaptation of a Turco-Mongolian word for a nature god, *tengri*.[40] A satisfactory answer has yet to be found.[41] But what is the "great tribulation to come," escape from which is the major preoccupation in these chapters?

Excursus: The "Great Tribulation to Come"

The great tribulation is something life-threatening that can only be escaped through faith in God's help. In Hermas' encounter with the beast, he has already escaped it—or begun to escape it—(μεγάλην θλῖψιν ἐκπέφευγας, perfect tense, v. 4).[42] The encounter with the beast uses apocalyptic symbols but does not develop them in the direction of description of end-time events, except in the brief explanation of the four colors in 3.2–5. For once the author, who otherwise enjoys long allegorical applications, does not develop each element at length. The locusts originally coming out of the beast's mouth (1.6) disappear with no further ado, unless the veiled threat of plagues in v. 6 is meant to refer to them.[43] The stress is rather on how to escape: through faith, doing away with doublemindedness. Despite the beast's fearsomeness, for those who follow the revealer's directions, it will not be the terrible thing it threatens to be (3.6).

If the great tribulation is historical, it is the anticipation of some kind of persecution, perhaps based on memory of a past one.[44] If accounts of the Neronian persecution, however local and brief, are authentic, surely that memory would have lingered in

---

35 See note on *Vis.* 3.12.3 for the significance of this word. Brox's observation (172) that the woman church's role in *Vision* 4 has undergone a "mutation" from her role in the first three *Visions*, being no longer revealer, but rather interpreter of visions, is inexact: in the first *Vision* she is also interpreter of the vision of Rhoda (1.2–3). Here she is interpreter of the vision of the beast. Rather, her role as interpreter frames that of revealer.

36 See also *Vis.* 3.11.3.

37 *Hermas*: ἐνέφραξεν τὸ στόμα αὐτοῦ, ἵνα μή σε λυμάνῃ ("he shut its mouth so that it might not hurt you"); Dan 6:23 (Theodotion): ἐνέφραξεν τὰ στόματα τῶν λεόντων, καὶ οὐκ ἐλυμήναντό με ("he shut the mouths of the lions and they did not harm me"); cf. Heb 11:33. The influence of Daniel, especially chaps. 10–12, is pervasive in *Vision* 4; cf. Angelo P. O'Hagan, "The Great Tribulation to Come in the Pastor of Hermas," StPatr 4=TU 79 (1961) 305–11 (309); R. J. Bauckham, "The Great Tribulation in the Shepherd of Hermas," JTS 25 (1974) 27–40 (38).

38 E.g., Rev 7:1; 14:18; 16:5; *1 Enoch* 20.1–7; 40.9–10;

Jerome *In Hab.* 1.12 (an angel named Tyri, charged with reptiles, in a disapproved apocryphal book); discussion and references, Peterson, "Begegnung," 298; Brox, 173.

39 By J. R. Harris, 1920; references and discussion in Snyder, 58; Brox, 174.

40 J. R. Krueger, "A Possible Turco-Mongolian Source for Θεγρί in Hermas' The Pastor," AJP 84 (1963) 295–99.

41 Further discussion and suggestions: Crombie, 18 n. 10; Brox, 173–74. Brox (174 n. 22) notices that Heinrich Kraft (*Clavis Patrum Apostolicorum* [Munich: Kösel, 1963] 214), for no apparent reason, reverses the third and fourth letters of the name and lists it alphabetically under Θεργί.

42 Hilhorst (*Sémitismes*, 59) takes this passage as an example of perfect tense used according to classical rules, thus with effect continuing into the present.

43 Snyder's suggestion (58) of relating them to the locust plague and call to conversion in Joel 1:1–2:11; Rev 9:3–5 is possible but without evidence, since they do no damage here.

44 So Snyder (23–24, 57–58), placing the writing dur-

the Roman church.[45] Other suggestions are the power of the demonic[46] or Gehinnom, as either hell or "purgatory."[47] But notions of Gehinnom as place of eternal punishment are common but imprecise at this period,[48] and evidence for belief in a place of temporary purification for the just after death is slim.[49] Rather than a post-death experience, the encounter with the great tribulation seems to be more thisworldly; in individual terms, not a passing of the soul through the dangerous journey after death, but something to be grappled with here and now,[50] though the eschatological dimension is also both present and important.[51]

Three different meanings of ϑλῖψις ("tribulation") can be distinguished in *Hermas*: the painful results of sin in everyday setbacks (*Vis.* 2.3.1; *Sim.* 6.3.3–6; 7.3–7); the result of persecution, including suffering that does not result outright in martyrdom (*Vis.* 2.3.4; 3.2.1, 6.5; *Sim.* 9.21.3); the "great coming tribulation" (*Vis.* 2.2.7; 4.1.1, 2.4–5, 3.6).[52] But the different uses should not be kept too distinct. *Sim.* 6.3.3–6; 7.3–7 speak of suffering in life as serving the purifying function of leading to conversion. But this suffering is also part of the transformation that must take place in preparation for participation in the building of the tower, sign of movement toward the end time.[53] It would be a mistake to see setbacks in life, like those of Hermas in *Vis.* 2.3.1; 3.6.7, as disconnected from the larger vision of suffering and tribulation. It is all of a piece, leading to the final consummation.

The promise here in v. 5 that preparation, conversion, and purification of the heart will make possible escape and continuance in God's service "for the rest of the days of your life" does not rule out an eschatological meaning to the great tribulation, as if it referred univocally to a designated moment beyond which mortal life does not continue.[54] Such a linear

interpretation of apocalyptic eschatology does not do justice to its many dimensions. Nor does it take them adequately into account to reduce Hermas' great tribulation to an apocalyptically coded warning against the temptation to doublemindedness.[55] The faithful escape through endurance (*Vis.* 2.2.7): escape and enduring are not contradictory, and only by putting these two concepts together does it become evident that escape in the great tribulation does not mean escape from suffering, but from the ultimate misfortune of alienation from God, for the doubleminded incur God's wrath (2.6).

The description of the great tribulation that is nearest the mark is that of R. Bauckham: "an impending persecution which he (Hermas) understands as part of a larger eschatological event,"[56]—but understanding "persecution" very broadly. A perception of crisis based on both the experience of suffering and a heightened awareness of the need for conversion from present directions; an explanation for present suffering; some kind of persecution, which need not be understood here as formal action of imperial authority, though that is not excluded: these elements combine with apocalyptic imagery in such a way that they are no more separable than they are in Synoptic apocalyptic accounts of the destruction of Jerusalem.[57]

Verses 5–6 are in the form of a prophetic oracle, containing a commissioning formula (v. 5a), a conditional promise (v. 5b), an admonition (vv. 5c–6a), and a conditional threat in the form of a "woe" saying (v. 6b). This final woe, like beatitudes elsewhere in prophetic oracles,[58] "functions as a legitimation formula in that it associates an eschatological sanction with the value,

ing the reign of Trajan; also Dibelius, 422; Hilhorst, "Hermas," 689 (under Trajan or Hadrian).

45   Tacitus *Ann.* 15.44.2–8; Suetonius *Nero* 16.2; Eusebius *Hist. eccl.* 2.25.5–8; Sulpicius Severus *Chron.* 29.3; perhaps *1 Clem.* 1.1; 5.1–6.2; *Vis.* 2.3.4.

46   Susan R. Garrett, *The Demise of the Devil: Magic and the Demonic in Luke's Writings* (Minneapolis: Fortress, 1989) 105.

47   Peterson, "Begegnung," 295–305; Angelo P. O'Hagan, "The Great Tribulation to Come in the Pastor of Hermes," *StPatr* 4=TU 79 (1961) 305–11 (307); rightly critiqued by Snyder, 56–57; Brox, 168, 176.

48   E.g., *4 Ezra* 7.75–115; *1 Enoch* 10.13–14; 21; 22.10–14; 26, 27; as eternal fire: *Sib. Or.* 1.103; 2.305.

49   2 Macc 12:38–45; 1 Pet 3:19; 4:6 (situation of being held, but not necessarily in suffering); maybe Matt

12:32, *1 Enoch* 18.14–16; *t. Sanh.* 13.3 (Shammai); Joachim Jeremias, "ᾅδης," *TDNT* 1 (1964) 146–49; "γέεννα," ibid., 657–58.

50   Peterson, 301; Brox, 170.

51   Aune, *Prophecy,* 303–4; 437 n. 38.

52   As outlined by Brox, 175; see also 471–76.

53   See comment on 3.4 below.

54   Against Peterson, "Begegnung," 303–4; Snyder, 58.

55   Brox, 177.

56   "The Great Tribulation in the Shepherd of Hermas," *JTS* 25 (1974) 27–40 (32).

57   Matt 24; Mark 13; Luke 21. Cf. Osiek, "Genre and Function," 116–18.

58   E.g., *Vis.* 2.2.7.

truth, and necessity of obeying the prophetic words with which it is associated."[59] The origin of the "woe" form is probably Latin, but its use here is biblical.[60] The play on the two present participles for "hear" and "obey" (ἀκούσασιν, παρακούσασιν) is lost in translation. The final words of v. 6 recall Matt 26:24 par. Mark 14:21, one of the few possible Synoptic allusions in *Hermas*.

The Four Colors

■ **3.1–5 [24]** Hermas asks (v. 1) about the four colors on the beast's head (1.10), and being told by the woman church that he is curious (περίεργος) does not dissuade him from being persistent.[61] Black, red, and white are traditional apocalyptic colors.[62] The fire and blood (v. 3) represented by the color red introduce a typical catastrophic apocalyptic vision, but one that is unusual in *Hermas*.[63] The gold color (v. 4) is the faithful who have "fled from this world," a mark of identification that alludes to the complex question of the relationship of Christians to the world; this rather negative, blanket description will be nuanced elsewhere.[64] The motif of the just being tried by suffering as gold is refined in fire is a common wisdom theme and an apt comparison, for in the refining process what is of value (what is useful) is separated from the unuseful dross.[65] The reader of Tacitus' account of Nero making torches of Christians to illuminate his gardens for night visitors would not find the association difficult to make, nor would the readers of *Hermas* if Tacitus preserves a historical memory.[66]

The "them" among which or whom the faithful live (οἱ κατοικοῦντες ἐν αὐτοῖς) is ambiguous.[67] If the referent is the inhabitants of the world, which is most likely, the statement reinforces the ambiguity of the position of Christians who have both fled from the world and continue to live in it. Again, as in *Vis.* 2.2.7 and 2.5 above,

the survivors are those who endure or remain (οἱ μείναντες S; οἱ ἐμμείναντες A with slightly more emphasis). The anomaly of remaining or enduring and fleeing or escaping simultaneously is not a contradiction but a paradox. Purification means casting off sadness and anguish, as gold casts off dross. This "sadness" (λύπη) is closely associated with doublemindedness, and will be used extensively in *Mandate* 10. The effect of the purification that comes through suffering is, in terms of the tower of *Vision* 3, to become stones useful for its construction (3.6.6). Thus the apocalyptic image of the beast in *Vision* 4 is connected with the eschatological image of the building of the tower in the previous *Vision*. Whiteness (v. 5) means both the coming world or age (αἰών) and those who will inhabit it. The title, the "elect" or "chosen" of God, is a favorite name for Christians in the *Visions* only,[68] but the concern about Christians being purified (καθαρός) is ubiquitous.[69]

The fact that the beast bears all of this meaning on its head is problematic: the problem also carries its resolution, in a veritable cacophony of symbols that fly by as fast as the beast itself. This very fact, however, indicates that the beast is not univalent. It cannot mean only persecution or the eschaton or the trials of daily living. The great tribulation, terrible as it may seem, carries upon itself the promise of breakthrough and transformation. The fourfold fate of God's chosen ones is all of a piece, and in the very endurance of its terrible aspects comes the escape into eternal life.

■ **3.6** The seer is exhorted once again (v. 6) to communicate what he has seen, referring not only to the immediately previous interpretation, but to the whole revelation, while the plural exhortation at the end of the verse, to remember everything previously written, can refer to the whole revelation only by slippage between

---

59 Aune, *Prophecy*, 304.

60 Cf. *Sim.* 9.31.5. The Greek οὐαί is in pronunciation closer to Latin *vae* than to Hebrew אוֹי or הוֹי which it translates in the LXX, where it is much more frequent than in nonbiblical Greek and acquires its meaning here: Hilhorst, *Sémitismes*, 179–82; A. D. Lowe, "The Origin of *ouai*," *Hermathena* 105 (1967) 34–39.

61 Compare *Vis.* 3.2.3, 3.1, 6.5, 8.9; see comment on 3.3.1.

62 See comment on 1.10 above.

63 Cf. Rev 6:4; 2 Thess 1:8 (in the context of suffering and vindication of the just); 2 Pet 3:7, 10.

64 Cf. *Sim.* 1; 2 Pet 2:20.

65 Prov 17:3; 27:21; Job 23:10; Sir 2:5; Wis 3:6; 1 Cor 3:15; 1 Pet 1:7; implicit in 2 Pet 3:10–13; maybe Mark 9:49.

66 *Ann.* 15.44.6–7.

67 Lake (67) takes it to mean "fire and blood" in an awkward construction; Dibelius (489–90) assumes the referent is the inhabitants of this world (v. 2), a rough editing job having introjected v. 3 to confuse the reference.

68 *Vis.* 1.5.3; 2.1.3, 2.5, 4.2; 3.5.1, 9.10; 4.2.5; only indirectly in *Sim.* 9.9.3.

69 S, probably through haplography, reads: "The white

the oral and written modes presumed in the narrative. If taken literally, it could refer only to those parts of the revelation that Hermas was commanded to write: *Vis.* 2.1.3, 2.2–4. The sudden change from singular admonition to plural address in the same verse indicates both prophetic self-consciousness and awareness of the levels of communication within the written text. The community is always present in Hermas' experience.[70] Between the singular exhortation to Hermas and the plural one to the community is the reminder once again that the beast and their own destiny as portrayed in the four colors on its forehead are meant to make them aware of both present and coming crisis. But the promise that, according to their will, it will come to nothing, literally, "If you wish, it will be nothing" ($\dot{\epsilon}\grave{\alpha}\nu$ $\delta\grave{\epsilon}$ $\vartheta\epsilon\lambda\acute{\eta}\sigma\eta\tau\epsilon$, $o\dot{\upsilon}\delta\grave{\epsilon}\nu$ $\check{\epsilon}\sigma\tau\alpha\iota$),[71] is problematic in an apocalyptic framework in which the end-time struggle will be harrowing even for believers.[72]

The promise, however, is not made facilely, but rather is consonant with the markedly hopeful tone of the whole work, which aims not so much to frighten but to encourage to action and change. If the listeners accept the message and experience a change of heart, the terror of the crisis can be overcome through faith. Prophetic critique and apocalyptic determinism are melded for the author's purpose, and while there is a historical component to the threat, its full dimensions escape the bounds of history.

■ **3.7** Typically, having delivered her message, the woman church disappears, this time for the last time. Hermas misses her disappearance because he has turned around in fear in response to a noise ($\psi\acute{o}\varphi o\varsigma$)[73] behind him that might be the beast returning. Or, by an alternate reading, there was a cloud ($\nu\acute{\epsilon}\varphi o\varsigma$)[74] that hid her from his sight as she disappeared. The cloud would carry familiar connotations of the numinous, and could be both explanation and means of her disappearance, but it does not explain why Hermas turned around in fear or thought the beast was returning, unless it is to be understood as a dust cloud ($\kappa o\nu\iota o\rho\tau\acute{o}\varsigma$) as in 1.5, but that is not the word used. On the other hand, the "noise" explains both Hermas' failure to see her disappear and his fear of a return of the beast.[75] The ending is abrupt and unfinished, like the ending of the *Similitudes.*

---

part is the world that is coming, in which the elect of God will live for eternal life." The copyist's eye dropped from $\vartheta\epsilon o\hat{\upsilon}$ ("of God") in one line to the same word in the next.

70　This fact makes strange the interpretations that would see here an individualizing of eschatology (e.g., Dibelius, 485–86; Brox, 162, 168, 170–71). See further discussion in Introduction 3.3.1; 3.3.5.

71　A $\dot{\epsilon}\sigma\tau\iota$ ("is").

72　This is the final indicator for Brox (179) that the great tribulation cannot be eschatological, but must refer only to the difficult necessity of conversion and purification of heart, and that such a statement can appear only in a "pseudo-apocalypse"—though it is not clear exactly what that is.

73　AL[1]E reading, accepted by Dibelius, 490; Crombie, 18; Brox, 179, et al.

74　SL[2] reading, accepted by Lake, 66; Whittaker, 22; Snyder, 60; Joly, 140.

75　Also to be preferred as *lectio difficilior*: Hellholm, *Visionenbuch*, 134 n. 19; compare *Jos. and Asen.* 17.8.

5 Introduction to the Shepherd, the Mandates, and the Similitudes

[25] 1/ As I prayed at home sitting on the dining couch, some man came in, splendid to see, dressed like a shepherd, covered with a white goatskin, with a sack on his shoulder and a staff in hand. He greeted me and I greeted him back. 2/ He sat down beside me right away and said to me: "I have been sent by the most distinguished angel to live with you [sing.] for the rest of the days of your life." 3/ I thought he was there to test me, and I said: "So who are you? For I know," I said, "to whom I have been given over." He said to me: "You do not recognize me?" "No," I said. "I am the Shepherd to whom you have been given over." 4/ While he was still speaking, his appearance changed, and I recognized the one to whom I had been given over, so that I was suddenly thrown into confusion; fear seized me and I was completely broken up with regret that I had answered him so badly and stupidly. 5/ But he answered me: "Do not be overwhelmed with confusion, but take strength in my mandates which I am going to command you. For I have been sent," he said, "to show you again everything you saw before, the important points that are helpful for you. First of all, write my commandments and parables. Beyond that, you will write as I show you. This is why," he said, "I am telling you to write the mandates and the parables first, so that you can read them right away and keep them." 6/ So I wrote the mandates and the parables as he commanded me. 7/ Therefore, if you [pl.] hear them, keep them, go forth in them, and do them with a pure heart, you will receive from the Lord everything he promised you. But if you hear and are not converted, but continue in your sins, you will receive just the opposite from the Lord. All these things the Shepherd commanded me to write, for he is the angel of conversion.

■ **1–2 [25]** There is general agreement that the Book of Visions really ends with *Vision* 4, and that *Vision* 5 is the introduction to the *Mandates* and *Similitudes* that will follow. That this has long been seen is witnessed by the titles given to this chapter in the manuscripts and translations.[1] This in itself is no evidence of different authorship or that the *Visions* circulated independently, but M

and the Coptic translations seem not to have contained the *Visions*, and B to have contained only *Visions* 1–4.[2] At the same time, there are elements of continuity, especially the similarity of revelatory structure: description of revealer and mutual greeting (v. 1); the identification of a new revealer (vv. 2–3); strengthening and promise of future revelations (v. 5); the change to plural address

1 The early ms. of S Ἀποκάλυψις εʹ (Revelation 5), as opposed to AE ὅρασις εʹ (*Vision* 5), S's name for *Visions* 2–4, may indicate an original difference in the titles, smoothed out later in A, which consistently calls *Visions* 1–5 by the same title. But L[1] *visio quinta. initium pastoris* ("*Vision* 5. Beginning of the Shepherd") and L[2] *incipiunt pastoris mandata duodecim* ("The twelve mandates of the shepherd

begin.") clearly show a separation before this title.

2 Peterson, "Kritische Analyse," 271 n. 1; Bonner, *Papyrus Codex*, 9, 13; Carlini, *Bodmer Papyrus*, 12; idem, "Tradizione testuale," 33–34. B breaks off in the middle of *Vis.* 3.13.4; it is only conjecture that it also contained *Vision* 4, necessitating a lost leaf in the center of the codex.

and conditional promise of results for obedience and threat for disobedience (v. 7).[3] Within the revelatory scene itself, the structure is also familiar: nonrecognition of apparition (vv. 1–2); questioning and recognition (vv. 3–4a); fearful reaction (v. 4b); reassurance and instructions from the apparition (v. 5).

The text opens in the setting of Hermas' home, a link with previous visions (*Vis.* 2.4.1; 3.1.2), as well as with *Sim.* 6.1; 10, which have the same revelatory setting. Thus *Vision 5–Similitude 10*, taken as a whole, begin and end with revelations in his house. While the two previous settings in the house (*Vis.* 2.4.1; 3.1.2) depict nocturnal dream visions, however, this one does not. Since there is no mention here either of sleep or of nighttime, the κλίνη upon which Hermas sits is best understood not as a bed but as a dining couch, the setting being not bedtime but mealtime as context for magical divination.[4] Thus the usually cited parallels are not cogent.[5] Tertullian's citation and exegesis of this passage against those who followed this text as literal and authoritative by sitting after praying demonstrates, besides the authority of the text as scripture in North Africa at the time, that the first sentence was understood to mean that the

vision of the shepherd happened *after* Hermas had prayed and sat down, but this is not a necessary interpretation of the Greek tenses.[6]

Whatever the relative verb tenses, the setting for the entry of the shepherd suggests a meal held for the purpose of summoning a πάρεδρος δαίμων ("assistant deity")—not that that is the Christian Hermas' intention, but that this is the familiar setting, and this is in fact what happens.[7] The scene is perhaps even an antidivination, a reversal of the usual expectation, given Hermas' abhorrence of divination,[8] for he does nothing to conjure the shepherd's appearance except provide the setting. The spirit who appears will be more than a helper; rather, he is revealer, guardian, and one who holds authority over Hermas (vv. 3–7). In spite of his humble and appropriately pastoral clothing, the shepherd is described as "splendid to see" (ἔνδοξος τῇ ὄψει), an indication of his extraterrestrial status. The exchange of greetings is characteristic of Hellenistic revelatory texts, as is the appearance of the revelatory agent described simply as "he came in" (εἰσῆλθεν).[9] That the revealer

---

3   Brox, 181.

4   With David Aune, "Now You See It, Now You Don't! Ancient Magic and the Apocalypse of John" (unpublished seminar paper, SBL, 1986) 16–17, in relation to Rev 3:20, where the magical context is less certain; against Patricia Cox Miller, "'A Dubious Twilight': Reflections on Dreams in Patristic Literature," *CH* 55 (1986) 153–64 (159). Peterson ("Kritische Analyse," 272–76) places the context as that of magical divination, but explicitly rejects the dining couch as a possibility, probably because of his mistaken interpretation of Hermas as an "ascetic" (274).

5   *1 Enoch* 83.3; *4 Ezra* 3.1 seem to be night settings; *4 Ezra* 5.14 is a bad dream; the closest is Ezek 8:1, in which the author has a vision while sitting at home, but in company of others.

6   *De orat.* 16 uses two pluperfect subjunctives: *Cum adorassem et assedissem super lectum* ("When I had prayed and was seated on the couch"). But the two Greek aorist participles, προσευξαμένου . . . καθίσαντος ("praying . . . sitting") need not be construed as expressing past time in relation to the aorist main verb, εἰσῆλθεν ("came in") (BDF §339). Tertullian's sarcasm in the continuing passage goes on to say that if the passage is to be taken literally as directive rather than narrative, it would be against

scripture (i.e., Hermas) to pray sitting in a *cathedra* or a *subsellium* rather than a *lectum* (bed or dining couch). It is interesting that he picks out precisely the two other objects of sitting present in the *Visions* (1.2.2, 4.1; 3.1.4, 10.1).

7   The magical papyri use the term δαίμων ("deity, spirit") interchangeably with god or angel (cf. vv. 2, 7), as one who is revealer and companion, e.g.: *PGM* 1 passim, especially 1–3, 24 (he will eat and sleep with you after being brought in at a meal); 37–39; 42–44; 80–91; 166–72; 186 (only you will see him). Compare *Gos. Thom.* 61.1. The procedure for obtaining such a guide includes abstinence, sacrifice, and invocation. With the appearance of the δαίμων, there is a greeting (v. 1b), questioning its name (v. 3a), dining together (v. 2a), discussion, and dismissal (Aune, "Now You See It," 15).

8   *Man.* 11.2–6.

9   Peterson, "Kritische Analyse," 274–75 with references; cf. Luke 1:28; *Vis.* 1.1.4–5; 2.2.

sits with him (v. 2) is also familiar in the literature of divination,[10] as is his mission of permanent accompaniment.[11]

Here the shepherd is introduced for the first time; he will continue as the chief revelatory agent and interpreter throughout the book. While earlier interpreters such as Reitzenstein argued for dependence on the *Poimandres,* the similarities are few and today are thought to derive from a common background.[12] The shepherd is himself the "angel of conversion" (ὁ ἄγγελος τῆς μετανοίας, v. 7), sent by the highest or most honored angel (ἀπὸ τοῦ σεμνοτάτου ἀγγέλου). The complex angelology of Hermas depicts the highest angel as identifiable either with Michael or with Christ, or with both.[13]

■ **3–4** Hermas thinks (v. 3) the shepherd-angel is there to try or test (ἐκπειράζειν) his faith and endurance (not tempt him to do evil).[14] The question, "Who are you?" with the answer, "I am. . . ." is a typical revelation pattern of speech.[15] But that Hermas knows "to whom he has been given over" appears with no preparation or explanation. Previous angels that have served communicational functions (*Vis.* 2.4.1; 3.10.7) have had no protective role. The text presumes a belief in custodial angels, either personally assigned or responsible for certain affairs in human life, as distinct from those charged with cosmic powers or whole nations, a belief that already appears in the NT and intertestamental literature.[16] But why this angel should be recognized as a shepherd is inexplicable in what has previously been said. The model may be partially Hermes,[17] but the image has surely been given greater christological import.[18]

While the angel is still speaking, his appearance changes (ἔτι λαλοῦντος αὐτοῦ ἠλλοιώθη ἡ ἰδέα αὐτοῦ), enabling Hermas to recognize the shepherd as his guardian (v. 4). While intriguing, Dibelius' suggestion that he recognizes the angel as an image of himself, his heavenly counterpart, is not convincing, for nothing explains why he would recognize himself as a shepherd.[19] Nor, in spite of the similarity of language, does this change seem to be of the same kind caused by the revealer's wrath in *Man.* 12.4.1. Rather, this is the kind of transformation in an epiphany narrative that enables deeper recognition of the true identity of the revealed person.[20] That this is the deepening of a theophanic

10 Peterson, "Kritische Analyse," 273–74, 276 n. 22; cf. *Vis.* 3.2.4; *Sim.* 5.1.1; 6.1–2; 10.1.1.

11 E.g., *PGM* 1.165–66; cf. *Man.* 12.6.1.

12 Richard Reitzenstein, *Poimandres: Studien zur griechisch-ägyptischen und frühchristlichen Literatur* (Leipzig: Teubner, 1904) 11–13; Dibelius, 492; Snyder, 61.

13 Cf. *Man.* 5.1.7; Dibelius, 491; Brox, 186; Introduction 3.3.4.

14 So Peterson, "Kritische Analyse," 278 n. 30. To test or try: Matt 4:7 par. Luke 4:12 (LXX Deut 6:16); Luke 10:25; 1 Cor 10:9.

15 Exod 3:13–14; Acts 9:5; *Corp. Herm.* 1.2.

16 See comment on Thegri in 4.2.4 above for cosmic responsibility. For guardian angels of humans: Matt 18:10; Acts 12:15; *3 Bar.* 12.3; *Tg. Ps.-J.* Gen 33:10; 48:16; Gerhard Kittel, "ἄγγελος," TDNT 1 (1964) 74–87 (86). Michael is already assigned to guard Israel in Dan 10:13, 21, and other nations as well in *1 Enoch* 20.5. On the basis of this suggestion, on the authority of Dibelius, Joly (49–50), and *Act. Thom.* 54, 57, Dronke ("Arbor Caritatis," 221–22) concludes that the Shepherd as Hermas' guardian angel resembles Hermas, and that is why he is recognized immediately—but in fact, Joly does not agree with this line of interpretation.

17 For Hermes as shepherd see references in Dibelius, 496; S. Eitrem, "Hermes" PW 8 (1913) 738–92

(775), but this attribution for Hermes was not widespread.

18 Rightly underlined by Snyder, 60–61; cf. John 10:11–16; Heb 13:20; 1 Pet 2:25; 5:4; *Mart. Pol.* 19.2. Shepherds, both as pastoral figures and gradually as christological symbols, are ubiquitous in early Christian art. Tertullian *De pud.* 7, 10 makes clear that Christ is known as shepherd and alludes to cups bearing this image used by Christians.

19 Dibelius, 495. Unconvinced too is Snyder, 61–62. Acts 12:15, however, certainly suggests Peter's angel as a heavenly double, showing the existence of such a belief in early Christianity; Hans Conzelmann, *Acts of the Apostles* (Hermeneia; Philadelphia: Fortress, 1987) 95 cross-references to this passage in *Hermas.* Cf. also Wilhelm Bousset, *Die Religion des Judentums im späthellenistischen Zeitalter* (3d ed.; HNT 21; Tübingen: Mohr/Siebeck], 1926) 324, but with very little evidence cited.

20 Luke 24:31; John 20:14,16; esp. *4 Ezra* 10.25 (evoking fear); *Corp. Herm.* 1.4: τοῦτο εἰπὼν ἠλλάγη τῇ ἰδέᾳ ("As he was saying this, his appearance changed").

experience is confirmed by the reaction of fear and regret.

■ **5–7** The shepherd's reassurance (v. 5) is also typical of the revelatory narrative structure. The S reading μὴ συν-χύνου ("do not be overwhelmed with confusion") is preferable to A μὴ αἰσχύνου ("do not be ashamed or embarrassed") as *lectio difficilior.* After speaking words of reassurance, the shepherd repeats (v. 2) and enlarges on his mission to Hermas: to review the highlights (τὰ κεφάλαια)[21] of the previous revelations. Taken literally, there is little in the *Mandates* and *Similitudes* that actually repeats or summarizes material from the *Visions.* The meaning is that the essentials will now be conveyed in different language and different images, but the message is the same; thus continuity is maintained with what went before.

The command to write the commandments and parables[22] places the rest of the teaching of the book, interrupted intermittently by narrative, into the literary genre of oral dictation, different from the delivery of a written message in *Vis.* 2.1.4. Verse 6 is in fact the summary of the rest of the book except for the supporting story line. The conditional promise and threat that occupies most of v. 7 can be construed either as Hermas' commentary on the eschatological value of what he writes or as the shepherd's summary. The final sentence identifies the shepherd as the "angel of conversion," that is, the one in charge of the primary import of that message, and establishes further links with what is to follow.[23]

---

21 For use of this term as summary or resumé, see Peterson, "Kritische Analyse," 277 n. 25.

22 Or mandates and similitudes (ἐντολαὶ καὶ παρα-βολαί), from which the following two sections take their names.

23 *Man.* 12.4.7; *Sim.* 9.1.1, 14.3, 23.5, 24.4.

Mandate 1

1 Faith in God

[26] 1/ **First of all, believe [sing.] that God is one, who created everything and maintained it, and who made everything to be out of what was not, who contains everything but alone is not contained. 2/ So believe in him and fear him, and in your fear exercise restraint. Observe these things and you will throw off from yourself every evil and be clothed with every just virtue, and you will live to God, if you observe this commandment.**

The twelve *Mandates* both build upon one another and recapitulate the fundamentals. Their teaching progresses from the basics to a rather sophisticated discernment of spirits, the first such Christian treatise in a tradition that was later to become significant in the history of spirituality. *Mandates* 1–5 set out the foundational virtues of faith, simplicity, fear of the Lord, and restraint (ἐγκρά-τεια). *Mandates* 2–5 develop the elementary virtues: simplicity, love of truth, chastity, and courageous endurance. *Man.* 6.1.1 repeats the triad of 1.2, faith, fear of the Lord, and restraint, which are then further developed in *Mandates* 6–8 but within the perspective of the discernment of spirits, a perspective assumed from *Mandate* 3 on. *Mandate* 8 is the fullest treatment of doublemindedness, an ongoing concern in the entire book. *Mandates* 9–12.2 are the spiritual teaching of a deeper wisdom by which Christians can know under the power of which spirit they are living. Finally, 12.3–6 undermines with relentless logic any objection that this way is too difficult. The author's teaching on true spirituality is illustrated along the way with simple concrete examples drawn from everyday life: wormwood in honey (5.5); vinegar in wine (10.3); empty wine jars (11.13, 15); stones and water pumps (11.18). Always the aim is the formation of the Christian community along the lines of Jewish wisdom paraenesis.

Mandate 1

■ **1 [26]** The *Mandates* open with a very brief but very significant introduction that affirms the centrality of monotheistic faith as the foundation of all faithful living, a statement that endeared this section to later heresiologists.[1] Only this first *Mandate* opens with no form of address,[2] thus further emphasizing the importance of the message and revealing the desired transparency of the narrative setting: though most of the teaching that follows is addressed to Hermas in the singular, it is a rhetorical singular meant to apply to all hearers. The narrative setting is oral teaching, with no command to write or communicate the message to others. But obviously the teaching is not intended for the author alone; the hearers are already presumed as silent witnesses and recipients of the revelation.

God is affirmed as creator of all things out of nothing, a familiar Hellenistic Jewish creedal formula.[3] The formula, "containing all but alone uncontained" (πάντα χωρῶν, μόνος δὲ ἀχώρητος), is the earliest Christian use of an idea drawn from Hellenistic philosophy that was soon to appear frequently among Christians, both

---

1   E.g., quote by Irenaeus *Adv. haer.* 4.20.2, passage quoted again from Irenaeus by Eusebius *Hist. eccl.* 5.8.7.
2   Brox, 191.
3   E.g., God as creator of all: Eph 3:9; from nothing: 2 Macc 7:28; Wis 1:14 (but cf. 11:17); Philo *Spec. leg.* 2.225; 4.187; *Vit. Mos.* 2.267; Rom 4:17; *2 Clem.* 1.8. Adelin Rousseau and Louis Doutreleau, eds., *Irénée*

de Lyon: Contre les hérésies livre I (SC 263; Paris: Éditions du Cerf, 1979) 276–78 suggest that ποιή-σας ἐκ τοῦ μὴ ὄντος εἰς τὸ εἶναι τὰ πάντα ("he made everything to be out of what was not"), especially for Irenaeus, expressed causality: "he made everything out of nothing *in order that it might be*" (cf. Brox, 192 n. 8; context in Wis 1:14).

Valentinian Gnostics and orthodox alike.[4] Though it was understood philosophically and cosmically by most later commentators, nevertheless the added comment in the Latin translations reveals an anthropological interpretation as well: *qui nec verbo (verbis) definiri nec mente concipi potest* ("which neither can word[s] contain nor mind conceive").

■ **2** The principal virtue of faith is repeated and, in contrast to v. 1, can here be understood not only as belief but also trust, the balancing quality to the second fundamental virtue of fear of the Lord that is added to it. This is the Jewish notion of a healthy respect and reverence for the power and holiness of God.[5] Together, faith and fear (=reverence) form the appropriate relationship of human persons to God. What flows from this right relationship is ἐγκράτεια (self-control, restraint in regard to those things that will disrupt the balance). Though the word sometimes focuses on sexual continence and asceticism in Christian texts, and will later be a technical term for celibacy, it is not so here.[6] Living in these virtues, and thus keeping them as commandments brings life. Already in v. 2 the "two ways" of evil and justice are juxtaposed in the apodictic statement that is the guiding principle of the *Mandates*: if you keep these commandments, you will be able to follow the right way and then ζήσῃ τῷ θεῷ ("you will live to [or for] God"). This frequent expression[7] concludes every *Mandate* except 5 and 11. While it certainly has eschatological meaning, it also carries the promise of earthly blessing, and is one of the factors in *Hermas'* paraenesis that joins the two dimensions. Not primarily a baptismal category, it nevertheless is a way of speaking of the continuation of baptismal blessedness restored with conversion. It is partially the opposite of "dying to God,"[8] but occurs far more frequently. Inasmuch as it means the ongoing life of faith and joy that the Christian experiences with conversion and that will continue in eternal life, "live to God" is the better translation, or "live in the eyes of God";[9] inasmuch as it also means how one lives the converted way of life, "live for God" is better.[10]

---

4 Examples of Valentinian use: *Eugnostos* 73.7–9 par *Soph. Jes. Chr.* 96.1–3; *Gos. Truth* 22.25; attribution by Epiphanius *Pan.* 31.5.3. By the orthodox: *Kerygmata Petrou*; Athenagoras *Leg.* 10.1; Irenaeus *Adv. haer.* 2.1.2–5; Origen *Comm. in Joh.* 1.103; 32.16.187; *De prin.* 1.3.3; 2.1.5; Athanasius *De incarn.* 3.1–2; Augustine *Conf.* 1.2. Further references and discussion in Dibelius, 497–98. Full investigation and references, including earlier beginnings of the idea in Philo: William R. Schoedel, "Enclosing, Not Enclosed: The Early Christian Doctrine of God," in idem and Robert L. Wilken, eds., *Early Christian Literature and the Classical Intellectual Tradition: In Honorem Robert M. Grant* (Théologie historique 53; Paris: Beauchesne, 1980) 75–86; cf. idem, "Gnostic Monism and the Gospel of Truth," in Bentley Layton, ed., *The Rediscovery of Gnosticism* (Leiden: Brill, 1980) 379–90 (380–81). 1 Cor 1:28 and *Sim.* 9.14.5 use the same idea differently.

5 "The beginning of wisdom" (Ps 111:10); better than riches and strength, a garden of blessing (Sir 40:26–27); one of the virtues of a royal figure (Isa 11:3); faith and fear of the Lord together (Isa 50:10); Acts 9:31; Rom 3:18 (Ps 36:1); 2 Cor 5:11.

6 *Mandate* 4 does not envision celibacy; *Mandate* 8 uses the word neutrally as self-restraint. See Snyder, 63.

7 It occurs twenty-nine times beginning here, eighteen of them in the *Mandates*, with an additional nineteen references lacking the object (four in the *Mandates*). Cf. Gal 2:19.

8 *Sim.* 8.6.4; 9.28.5.

9 Joly, 145 n. 4.

10 Cf. Snyder, 63–64; F. Barberet ("La formule ζῆν τῷ θεῷ dans le Pasteur d'Hermas," *RechSR* 46 [1958] 379–407) argues for dependence on Ezekiel and for a translation "in regard to God."

Simplicity

[27]   **1/ He said to me: "Have simplicity and be innocent, and you will be like little children who do
not know the evil that ruins human life. 2/ First
of all, do not slander anyone, nor listen willingly
to one who does. Otherwise, you the listener will
be guilty of the sin of the slanderer, if you believe
the slander that you hear, for by believing it, you
too will hold something against your brother or
sister. 3/ Slander is an evil thing; it is an unstable
demon, never at peace, but always at home in
dissension. So distance yourself from it and you
will always have harmony with everyone. 4/ Put
on reverence, in which there is no evil stumbling
block, but in which everything is smoothed out
and joyful. Do good, and from your labors that
God has given you, give simply to all in need, not
distinguishing to whom to give and to whom not
to give. Give to everyone, for God wishes that his
own gifts be given to everyone. 5/ For those who
receive will render account to God why and for
what purpose they took it. Those who took while
in distress will not be judged, but those who
took out of hypocrisy will pay the price. 6/ The
giver is blameless, and has received from God a
ministry to perform and does it blamelessly without distinguishing to whom to give and to whom
not to give. This ministry carried out with simplicity is honorable before God. So the one who
thus carries out this ministry with simplicity will
live to God. 7/ So keep this commandment as I
have said it to you, so that your conversion and
that of your household may be found in simplicity, innocent, pure, and spotless."**

■ **1–3 [27]** Simplicity (ἀπλότης) and innocence (ἀκακία), two of the virtues from *Vis.* 3.8, are connected here (v. 1) with the childlike absence of evil. They also appear together in *Sim.* 9.24.1–3. Whereas *Gos. Thom.* 37 associates being childlike with restored sexual innocence, here it is rather innocence of speech (absence of slander) and of intention in giving.[1] Both terms are recurring virtues in paraenetic contexts,[2] and words already used to describe Hermas himself.[3] The teaching against slander is harsh, implicating hearer as well as speaker (v. 2). Slander is identified as a δαιμόνιον, which in Jewish and Christian texts had already come to mean an evil spirit;[4] another step is taken here toward the later teaching on the two spirits. This "demon" is given a vivid character description (v. 3).

■ **4–5** Like simplicity and innocence, reverence (σεμνότης) also appears as one of the women sustaining the tower in *Vis.* 3.8, and is connected with simplicity and innocence in 3.9.8. Here simplicity is intimately connect-ed with the virtue of generosity and the problem of giv-ing to those who might be deemed unworthy to receive; it is the spirit in which one should give without regard to

---

1   *Gos. Thom.* 22 associates childlikeness with entry into the kingdom of God (cf. Matt 18:3; Mark 10:15).

2   Ἀπλότης: Matt 6:22 par. Luke 11:34; Rom 12:8; 2 Cor 8:2; 9:11, 13; 11:3; Eph 6:5; Col 3:22; and esp. *T. 12 Patr.* (references in Brox, 194); ἀκακία: Heb 7:26; *1 Clem.* 14.4, 5; *Did.* 3.8.

3   *Vis.* 1.2.4; 2.3.2; 3.9.1 (both together); see also 3.1.9.

4   Originally a lesser deity, sometimes connected with affliction or vengeance, and sometimes an evil spir-it even outside the Jewish and Christian context: cf. LSJ, BAGD *s.v.*

the recipient, who is accountable to God.[5] The principles laid down here spring not so much directly from social concern as from the traditional obligation of those who can give to the needy, and the necessity of giving alms for the life of faith (v. 4); but of course, the responsibility of those who can give is part of the larger plan of help for those who need it. Verses 4b–6a have close parallels in *Did.* 1.5;[6] the problem of their literary relationship remains unsolved, though the *Didache* passage seems more concerned with an actual abusive situation. Probably both draw on a common paraenetic source.[7]

■ 6 This ability and obligation to give without question is in v. 6 twice called a service or ministry (διακονία), as it is later in *Sim.* 1.9, indicating not office but a special function in the church, to be explored in greater detail in *Similitude* 2.

■ 7 The concluding verse recapitulates the theme of the section (as it does in *Man.* 3.5; 4.4.3; 9.12; 10.3.4), with the exhortation to keep the commandment, as in every *Mandate* except 1; 6; 11. It is worth repeating that the command to keep simplicity and innocence focuses not on chastity but on charity in both speech and deed; this is the meaning of being pure and spotless (καθαρά καὶ ἀμίαντος).[8] Hermas' family or household (οἶκος) has reappeared, reinforcing for Dibelius the theory that they are symbol of the community that is called to the same conversion as Hermas.[9] Rather, they are a reminder that all hearers of the revelation are responsible for family relationships as well as themselves.

---

5   Cf. *Didasc.* 17=*Ap. Const.* 4.3.2.

6   The closest verbal parallels are: *Man.* 2.4: πᾶσιν γάρ ὁ θεὸς δίδοσθαι θέλει ἐκ τῶν ἰδίων δωρημάτων ("God wishes that his own gifts be given to everyone") with *Did.* 1.5: πᾶσι γὰρ θέλει δί-δοσθαι ὁ πατὴρ ἐκ τῶν ἰδίων χαρισμάτων ("the Father wishes that his own gifts be given to every-one"); *Man.* 2.6: ὁ οὖν διδοὺς ἀθῷός ἐστιν ("the one who gives is without blame") with *Didache*: μακάριος ὁ διδοὺς κατὰ τὴν ἐντολήν· ἀθῷος γὰρ ἐστιν ("blessed is the one who gives according to the commandment, for that one is without blame"). But the topic of discussion is clearly the same. The "commandment" to which the *Didache* refers could be Luke 6:30, Acts 20:35, or *Mandate* 2, depending on the literary relationship of the last with the *Didache*.

7   The theory of the dependence of the *Didache* on *Hermas* (J. Robinson) is based largely on this text, but it has also been argued that *Did.* 1.3b–2.1, in spite of being an interpolation, represents an earlier form of the sayings to which *Hermas* refers from

memory, especially because of the blessing/woe pattern in the *Didache* that is not in *Hermas*: Jean-Paul Audet, *La Didachè: Instructions des Apôtres* (Paris: Lecoffre, 1958) 163–66, 261–65; Helmut Koester, *Synoptische Überlieferung bei den Apostolischen Vätern* (TU 65; Berlin: Akademie-Verlag, 1957) 230–36; Bentley Layton, "The Sources, Date and Transmission of Didache 1:3b–2.1," *HTR* 61 (1968) 343–83; Kurt Niederwimmer, *The Didache* (Hermeneia; Minneapolis: Fortress, 1998) 81–82.

8   The same words in Jas 1:27 also refer to generosity to the needy. The text here varies in the MSS.; L¹ *et cor mundum habe*, L² *et cor tuum sit mundum et indeficiens apud deum* led Hilgenfeld to conjecture: καὶ ἡ καρδία σου καθαρὰ καὶ ἀμίαντος ("your heart pure and spotless"); compare *Vis.* 3.9.8; 4.2.5; 5.7; Matt 5:8; 1 Tim 1:5; 2 Tim 2:22; 1 Pet 1:22.

9   Dibelius, 501. Cf. *Vis.* 1.1.9, 3.1–2; 2.3.1; 3.1.6.

3

Truth

[28] Again he said to me: "Love truth, and let every truth come out of your mouth, so that the spirit that God has placed in this flesh be truthful in the sight of all people, and thus the Lord who dwells in you will be honored; for the Lord is truthful in every word, and with him there is nothing false. 2/ But those who lie disavow the Lord and commit fraud against the Lord by not returning the deposit they received. For they received a spirit with no falsehood. If they render a spirit of falsehood, they have defiled the commandment and committed fraud." 3/ Hearing this I cried copiously. Seeing me crying, he said: "Why are you crying?" "Because, sir," I said, "I do not know if I can be saved." "Why?" he said. "Because, sir," I said, "never yet in my life have I said a true word, but have always dealt deceitfully with everyone, and passed off my lying as truth with everyone. No one ever contradicted me, but relied on my word. Now, how, sir," I said, "can I live after having done these things?" 4/ He said, "Your thinking is good and true, for you must live in truth as God's servant, and a bad conscience must not dwell with the spirit of truth, nor must sadness overtake a reverent and truthful spirit." "Never before, sir," I said, "have I heard such words so clearly." 5/ "Well, you hear them now," he said. "Keep them, so that even the former lies you used in your business affairs might become truthful, and even trustworthy. For even they can become trustworthy. If you keep these commandments and speak the whole truth from now on, you will be able to gain life for yourself. Whoever hears this commandment and moves away from the evil of lying will live to God."

■ **1–2 [28]** Concomitant with simplicity and innocence (v. 1) is the directness that comes from not only living, but loving truth.[1] The spirit placed by God in "this flesh" is the human spirit that supports the presence of God, but that is to be in perfect communion with the indwelling holy spirit which inspires to do good.[2] The banking metaphor of v. 2 pits the lover of truth, who returns the deposit intact, against the liar who makes it defiled and thus of lesser value. The deposit, rendered $\pi\alpha\rho\alpha\vartheta\eta\kappa\eta$ in 1 Tim 6:20; 2 Tim 1:12, 14 (and preserved in v. 14 by the indwelling holy spirit), is here

$\pi\alpha\rho\alpha\kappa\alpha\tau\alpha\vartheta\eta\kappa\eta$, an atticism unusual in this literature.

■ **3–4** It is perhaps the financial implications of the metaphor that cause the businessman Hermas to overreact as he does (see v. 5)! Such exaggeration in revelatory scenes, however, has good precedent.[3] Rather than breaking the flow of the chapter, these verses add narrative flavor by engaging the attention and affect of the hearer.[4] Just as "living to God," or simply "to live" here (v. 3) means both right relationship now and ultimately eternal life, so Hermas' question about being saved carries both dimensions. He is encouraged by the Shepherd

---

1   Compare Eph 4:25; *T. Dan* 2.1; contrast *T. Reub.* 3.9 ("love truth," but against sexuality and women); *Did.* 5.2 par. *Barn.* 20.2 (the way of darkness includes "haters of truth, lovers of lies" [$\mu\iota\sigma\upsilon\tilde{\upsilon}\nu\tau\epsilon\varsigma$ $\dot{\alpha}\lambda\dot{\eta}\vartheta\epsilon\iota\alpha\nu, \dot{\alpha}\gamma\alpha\pi\tilde{\omega}\nu\tau\epsilon\varsigma \psi\epsilon\tilde{\upsilon}\delta o\varsigma$]).

2   See comment on *Man.* 5.2 below; also the unknown scriptural allusion in Jas 4:5 to God's longing for the indwelling spirit; discussion in Dibelius-

Greeven, *James*, 223–24.

3   E.g., Isa 6:5; Jer 1:6.

4   Dibelius (503) calls attention to the alliteration through paronomasia in $\pi\dot{\alpha}\nu\tau o\tau\epsilon$ $\pi\alpha\nu o\dot{\upsilon}\rho\gamma\omega\varsigma$ $\ddot{\epsilon}\zeta\eta\sigma\alpha$ (LLE); or $\dot{\epsilon}\lambda\dot{\alpha}\lambda\eta\sigma\alpha$ (S) $\mu\epsilon\tau\dot{\alpha}$ $\pi\dot{\alpha}\nu\tau\omega\nu$ ("I have always dealt deceitfully with everyone"); cf. BDF §488.1.

(v. 4) to be fully aware of his shortcomings in the area of honesty in relationships. The difficulty of a bad conscience and sadness coexisting with a good spirit will be further elucidated in *Mandate* 5. His "bad conscience" (πονηρὰ συνείδησις) should not be understood in the modern individualist sense, but as the attempt to align behavior and self-image with public image—exactly the issue at stake here in his public trustworthiness (end of v. 3) and dishonesty in business (v. 5).[5] Hermas' response at the conclusion of v. 4 is not to be construed that he is hearing the problem raised for the first time,[6] but that he is understanding it at greater depth, with the kind of heart listening that is necessary for conversion.

■ **5** The Shepherd's response confirms this: now that Hermas truly understands the import of this issue of integrity, he has no excuse for not changing his behavior. The possibility of his former lies becoming trustworthy is puzzling. The simplest explanation is that he is to restore whatever damage he has done to others by his dishonesty, thereby (as well as by his honesty from now on) establishing coherence between his self-image and his public honor.[7] What is more, he may even be called on to make good on his false promises.[8] Divine forgiveness is of course included (*Vis.* 2.2.4–5).

---

5   Cf. Bruce J. Malina, *The New Testament World: Insights from Cultural Anthropology* (rev. ed.; Louisville: Westminster John Knox, 1993), 51–52; Krister Stendahl, "The Apostle Paul and the Introspective Conscience of the West," *HTR* 56 (1963) 199–215, reprinted in idem, *Paul among Jews and Gentiles* (Philadelphia: Fortress, 1976) 78–96.

6   The connection of truthfulness and business: so Dibelius, 503.

7   Compare Luke 19:8.

8   "Hermas having made untrue statements in the course of business must try so to act that his statements will be justified in fact; for instance, if he had made extravagant promises he must fulfil them" (Lake, 77).

4 Chastity and Adultery

1 [29] 1/ "I command you," he said, "to keep chastity and not let anything enter your heart about someone else's wife, or about sexual immorality, or any similar evil deed. For if you do this, you commit a great sin. But if you just remember your own wife, you will never sin. 2/ If this lust arises in your heart, you will sin, or if another such evil desire arises, you will sin. This lust is a great sin to the servant of God. The one who does this evil deed brings death upon himself. 3/ So you be careful: abstain from this lust. Where reverence dwells, lawlessness should not arise in the heart of a just man." 4/ I said to him: "Sir, let me ask you about a few things." "Speak," he said. "Sir, if a man has a believing wife in the Lord and finds her in some adultery, does the man sin by continuing to live with her?" 5/ "As long as he does not know," he said, "he does not sin. But if he knows about her sin, and the woman does not have a change of heart, but remains in her adultery, and the man continues to live with her, he is guilty of her sin and participant in her adultery." 6/ "Then what, sir," I said, "should the man do if the woman remains in this passion?" He said, "He should divorce her and live alone. But if he divorces the woman and marries another, he too commits adultery." 7/ "But sir," I said, "what if after being divorced, the woman has a change of heart and wants to return to her own husband, should she not be taken back?" 8/ "Certainly," he said, "and if the man does not take her back, he sins and incurs for himself great sin, for one must take back the one [masc.] who has sinned and undergone a change of heart—not often, however, for to the servants of God, there is one chance for conversion. So because of the possibility of change of heart, the man ought not to marry. The same principle applies to both woman and man. 9/ Not only," he said, "is it adultery to defile one's flesh, but whoever does things similar to what the outsiders do commits adultery. So if anyone remains in such deeds and does not change, stay away from such a person and do not live with him or her; otherwise, you will be a participant in his or her sin. 10/ That is why you [pl.] have a command to remain apart, whether man or woman, because in such situations a change of heart is possible. 11/ So," he said, "I am not giving an excuse for the matter to end like this, but a reason whereby the sinner should sin no more. As for the previous sin, there is one who can bring healing, the one who has charge of everything."

Remarriage

The structure of the fourth *Mandate* is problematic: chapters 1 and 4 deal with chastity and questions of marital discipline typical of the early church, but chapters 2 and 3 deal more generally with the principal theme of conversion. It has been suggested that the two middle chapters were originally a continuation of *Vision* 5 before its two last verses. The motif of the spirit sent to abide with Hermas (*Vis.* 5.2) is continued (*Man.* 4.2.1), as is the identification of the Shepherd as "angel of conversion."[1] The present position of these two chapters seems out of place and is undoubtedly not their original location, unless the intention was to locate the questions of marital discipline squarely within the realm of conversion, or to present marriage questions as a "case analogy" for conversion.[2] The structure as it now stands is as follows:[3]

Chastity	Conversion
1. general principle (1.1–3)	
2. applications	
a. adultery (1.4–11)	
	1. introduction (chap. 2)
	2. body: unique chance for conversion (chap. 3)
b. widowhood (4.1–2)	
3. conclusion (4.3)	3. conclusion (4.4)

■ **1.1–3 [29]** The commandment to chastity (ἁγνεία) means marital fidelity, not celibacy, and is a traditional paraenetic topos.[4] While some of these discussions are explicitly gender-inclusive (for example, 4.4.1; 5.2.2), this one proceeds in the usual androcentric mode, considering only the male perspective; the subject is explicitly a "just man" (ἀνὴρ δίκαιος) in v. 3; only in vv. 8, 10, almost by way of afterthought, does it become clear that the same approach applies to wronged wives. By this time divorce under Roman law was easy and common for both sexes, and the law applied only to citizens. The whole chapter follows the Jewish and Roman legal assumption that illicit sexual intercourse constitutes adultery only if a married woman is involved. Desire for the wife of another, at the most basic level, violates one of the biblical commandments (Exod 20:17). Other unspecified forms of sexual immorality (πορνεία) would include prostitution but not be limited by this narrower meaning of the word.[5] The injunction to remember one's own wife (when tempted toward another) is straightforward and appealingly relational rather than legalistic.

Possibly, but not surely, one should see a relationship of this passage to Hermas' presenting problem with Rhoda (*Vis.* 1.1.5–8; 1.2.4). Just as his experience with wealth is an example from which all can learn (*Vis.* 3.6.7), so too his ambiguous relationship with Rhoda can be seen as illustrative of what not to do. But the point is not made explicit as in the case of wealth, and therefore no attention is called to it. The directive of the woman church that his wife now be to him "as a sister" (*Vis.* 2.2.3) undoubtedly means celibacy, but as the special situation of one called to an all-absorbing mission. The paraenesis on chastity here covers the basics for everyone, and the marriage discipline envisions the normativity of marriage; all of the latter is narrated in the third person. The seeming distinction made in v. 2 between the "great sin" of lustful curiosity or desire and the deadly sin of carrying it through to action[6] should probably not be pushed too hard as difference, but only as degree of escalation.

■ **1.4–5** The bulk of the chapter deals with various aspects of male responsibility for female adultery, a typical preoccupation of a Roman *paterfamilias* (householder) whose honor is compromised by the behavior of the women of the house. Verses 1–2 speak quickly of desire for another's wife, without calling it μοιχεία (adultery), then pass to πορνεία (fornication or prostitution; Latin *stuprum*), which in Roman law is not adultery on the part of a married man if the woman is not in a legal marriage. Thus Hermas follows the legal terminology by introducing adultery (v. 4) as the infidelity of a wife, that can be shared in by the husband who knows but continues to live with her. The first part of v. 5 begs the question: the husband ignorant of the wife's adultery could be ritually defiled by association and dishonored by others' knowledge of the fact, but would not be faced with a decision whether or not to divorce her. This principle does, however, imply that sin must be conscious and deliberate. Only marriage among Christians is envisioned here. The "believing wife in the Lord" (γυνὴ πιστὴ ἐν κυρίῳ) could be translated "wife faithful in the

1	Suggested by Spitta: discussion in Dibelius, 504–5.
2	So Snyder, 67; for Dibelius (504–5) the central message of a second chance is located here because money (3.5) and sex are the primary problems around which the need for conversion arises.
3	Outline adapted from Henne, "Pénitence," 371.
4	*T. Reub.* 4.5; a major concern of *T. Jos.*; 1 Tim 5:2; *1 Clem.* 21.7; 64.1; *Barn.* 19.4. The word ordinarily

does not mean celibacy, but see Polycarp *Phil.* 5.2.

5	A and S both render here πονηρία ("evil"), but the reading must be rejected in favor of LLE Ath and corrections to S πορνεία, especially since πονηρία occurs again at the end of the sentence.
6	Dibelius, 505; Brox, 204; Grotz, *Entwicklung*, 29–30. Compare 1 John 5:16–17.
7	E.g., 1 Cor 4:17; 7:39. Because this is a recognized

Lord" but Christian usage elsewhere suggests that simply a Christian is meant.[7]

■ **6** Up to the point of divorce (v. 6a), the procedure follows the *Lex Julia de adulteriis coercendis* (18 BCE), whereby an adulterous wife must be divorced and accused in the courts rather than privately punished (a wife cannot bring a charge of adultery against her husband, however)—though nothing is said here about prosecution.[8] But v. 6b departs decisively from the Roman law in forbidding the remarriage that Roman law required or strongly compelled, to age sixty for men and fifty for women, and even calling a man who did so an adulterer, thus no doubt setting up considerable conflict for citizen Christians caught in this situation. The last sentence of v. 6 is a close parallel to the Synoptic saying, especially Matt 19:9. It demonstrates that the tradition represented by Matt 5:32; 19:9 was interpreted, at least here, as divorce meaning separation without remarriage.[9]

■ **1.7–8** The reacceptance of an adulterous woman by her former husband flatly contradicts the *Lex Julia*, which prohibits it. If we assume that a duly promulgated law was usually enforced (an assumption not always warranted), this passage is either directed at noncitizens, to whom marriage legislation did not apply, or else it would put citizens in violation of the law. There is warrant, however, for assuming that Roman family law was enforced only when advantageous. In v. 8 for the first time it becomes clear that these principles apply to women as well as to men. The wife's acceptance of a penitent husband would be much more culturally acceptable, and in fact reinforced, than the reverse. But the object of the second part of the first sentence in v. 8 switches suddenly to the generic masculine (see translation), suggesting that a more general principle of church policy about reconciliation of repentant sinners is being applied to this particular case.[10]

Such reacceptance from either partner is not an open door, however. The text wavers between "not often" ($\mu\grave{\eta}$ $\dot{\epsilon}\pi\grave{\iota}$ $\pi o\lambda\grave{\upsilon}$ $\delta\acute{\epsilon}$) and "one conversion" ($\mu\epsilon\tau\acute{\alpha}\nu o\iota\acute{\alpha}$ $\dot{\epsilon}\sigma\tau\iota\nu$ $\mu\acute{\iota}\alpha$), the latter perhaps an editorial addition that brings the discussion into the overall eschatological framework of the proclamation of conversion.[11] Here we see for the first time why this whole discussion of marriage has arisen. While the call to conversion is general and intended principally as the seeking of forgiveness from God (cf. v. 10), mutual forgiveness is also an essential part of the process. It is interesting that the motivation for remaining unmarried after divorcing an adulterer here and in v. 10 is not the indissolubility of the marriage bond, but the possibility of a change of heart on the part of the one dismissed; the implication almost seems to be that if it were not for that contingency, it would be permitted to marry another. It was this passage that turned a previously admiring, now rigorist, Tertullian against *Hermas*, "lover" and "shepherd of adulterers."[12]

Whether the principles laid down here reflect the thinking of one author, or commonly accepted notions in the Christian community of this time and place, or an already developed church discipline of readmission of

---

expression, the Lord here is probably Christ (against Brox, 205).

8 See Leutzsch, *Wahrnehmung*, 185–90; less enthusiastic about the connection is Brox, 205–6. The usual penalty for an adulterous citizen wife was exile, confiscation of one-third of her property and half her dowry. Pliny (*Ep.* 6.31.4–6) describes a similar case: Galitta, wife of a tribune, *et suam et mariti dignitatem centurionis amore maculaverat* ("defiled both her and her husband's honor by her affair with a centurion"). The *Leges Juliae de adulteriis coercendis* and *de maritandibus ordinibus* (both 18 BCE) and the *Lex Papia Poppaea* (9 CE) together constitute the Augustan marriage legislation that brought much of marriage custom under civil law, encouraged marriage and reproduction, and put restrictions on the rights of husbands and fathers to punish adulterous wives and daughters, as well as the amount of confiscated

property they could gain by accusing them. Cf. *OxCD*² 602–4; Hugh Last, *CAH* 10 (1934) 443–56.

9 K. Lake, "The Earliest Christian Teaching on Divorce," *Expositor* 7 (1910) 416–27; argued otherwise by C. W. Emmet, "The Teaching of Hermas and the First Gospel on Divorce," *Expositor* 8 (1911) 68–74. It cannot be assumed from this, however, that 1 Cor 7:12–16 was also understood to prohibit remarriage, since there it is the case of a Christian married to a non-Christian.

10 See comment on v. 9.

11 Giet's argument (*Hermas*, 24 n. 2; 191) that "one conversion" does not refer to a number of times, but to unity and continuity of the reality, is rejected by Joly (430) and Brox (206 n. 10), but is worth consideration.

12 *De pud.* 10.11; 20.2.

sinners after repentance, has been much debated.[13] The terminology of reacceptance, παραδέχεσθαι (literally, just "acceptance") in other contexts implies ecclesial policy.[14] But there is nothing in the text that suggests anything other than a private family arrangement, and Hermas can speak of public church proceedings when he wishes (*Vis.* 2.4.2–3). Roman family events were instinctively private affairs, notwithstanding the Augustan legislation, and it is doubtful to what extent at this early period the larger church may have been involved. The whole passage has more of an official tone than the rest of the paraenesis, but that is typical of discussions of marriage and divorce because of the legal aspects of the topic.[15]

■ **1.9–10** Verse 9 seems to interrupt the flow of the argument, which would continue smoothly from v. 8 to v. 10. It introduces a different but related problem, not mixed marriage[16] but some kind of pagan practice on the part of a Christian marriage partner, generally interpreted as relapse into worship of other gods, with appeal to the biblical use of adultery as metaphor for idolatry.[17] If the separation of the faithful person from one who does this also refers to marital separation, then we are given a sec-

ond reason for the breakup of a marriage, and, by implication, a second situation in which reconciliation might be had with a repentant partner. One wonders, however, whether in the context of marital chastity there is not more involved in doing "things similar to what the outsiders do" (τὰ ὁμοιώματα τοῖς ἔθνεσιν), perhaps homosexuality or promiscuity. The absolute language of separation in this case, contrasted to the insistence on taking the sinner back in v. 8, may refer not only to marital practice but to church excommunication. Like the general statement in the middle of v. 8 (see comment above), a wider policy about separation from Christians involved in unacceptable behavior seems to be applied here.

■ **1.11** Verse 11 is a reminder that the point of the proclamation of the possibility of conversion and a new beginning is not to assuage the conscience of the sinner with the assurance that there will always be such a possibility. That, of course, is always a danger with a less than rigorist approach. Only past sin is candidate for forgiveness, and even that is not automatic, but according to the power and will of God, whose forgiveness is experienced as healing.[18]

---

13 Discussion and references in Brox (207), who is also doubtful of a developed church discipline at this point.

14 E.g., Ignatius *Smyrn.* 4.1; compare ἐπιδέχεσθαι with the same meaning in 3 John 9.

15 E.g., compare Matt 5:31–32 or 19:3–9 with their contexts.

16 So Henne, "Pénitence," 372.

17 E.g., Jer 2:2; 3:8–11; 5:7–9; Ezek 16; 23; Hos 2:1–7; 3:1–4.

18 Compare 3.3 below; Rom 6:1; Gal 5:13. On forgiveness as healing, see comment on *Vis.* 1.1.9.

4   Reminder about Conversion

2 [30]   1/ I asked him again: "Since the Lord has considered me worthy to have you live with me always, still put up with a few words from me, because I do not understand at all and my heart has become hardened by my former deeds. Inform me, because I am very stupid and understand nothing at all." 2/ He answered me: "I am in charge of conversion, and I give understanding to all who experience conversion. Or does it not seem to you," he said, "that conversion itself is understanding? Conversion is great understanding. The sinner understands that he or she has done evil in the sight of the Lord, awareness of the deed arises in the heart, and the sinner experiences conversion and no longer does evil but entirely good, and has a humbled and tested soul, because of the sin. So you [sing.] see that conversion is great understanding." 3/ "This is why, sir," I said, "I inquire so carefully from you about everything: first, because I am a sinner, so that I can know what I must do to live, since my sins are many and varied." 4/ "You will live," he said, "if you keep my commandments and continue in them, for whoever hears these commandments and does them will live to God."

3 [31]   1/ "Still, sir," I said, "I have more to ask." "Speak," he said. "I have heard from some teachers, sir, that there is no other conversion possible than the one when we descended into the water and received forgiveness of our previous sins." 2/ He said to me: "You heard well. That is right. The one who has received forgiveness of sins should never have been sinning again, but should remain in purity. 3/ But since you ask such careful questions, I will also show you this, not so as to give an excuse to those who will believe or to those who are now coming to faith in the Lord. Those now coming to faith and future believers do not have conversion from sins, but forgiveness of former sins. 4/ For those called before these days, the Lord has appointed the chance for conversion. The Lord knowing the heart and having foreknowledge of everything, knew human weakness and the shrewdness of the devil, that he would do something bad to the servants of God and do them evil. 5/ Being full of compassion, the Lord had compassion on his handiwork and provided this chance for conversion, and authority over this conversion was given to me. 6/ But I tell you," he said, "after that great and holy calling, anyone who is tempted by the devil and sins has only one chance for conversion. If such a one sins and changes again repeatedly, it is of no profit to that person, who will barely live." 7/ I said to him: "I have been brought to life by hearing this from you so clearly. I know that if I no longer continue in my sins, I will be saved." "You will be saved," he said, "and so will all who act this way."

■ **2.1 [30]** Hermas the client works his patronage relationship (v. 1) in the by now recognizable way that provides narrative interlude as preparation for important communication that lies just ahead. He reminds the Shepherd of his role as spirit-companion (*Vis.* 5.2) and instructor. Instead of Hermas' heart being hardened (πεπώρωται), the alternate reading of SL² πεπήρωται (maimed, disabled) is possible but less likely, considering the biblical familiarity of the other expression.[1] The play on conversion as understanding (σύνεσις) begins in v. 1. Lack of understanding and hardened heart are two aspects of the same problem. His hardened heart is both cause and result of wrongdoing, as is his lack of understanding. Misdirected will and insight reinforce each other for evil.[2]

■ **2.2–4** The Shepherd holds responsibility for conversion (v. 2; *Vis.* 5.7), and in that capacity, gives understanding to those who enter into his process. The identification of conversion and understanding is an important indicator of the moral theology of *Hermas*. It is not that "doing penance" is a smart thing to do, but that the open heart is an understanding heart, which necessarily changes actions from evil to good. The inner response of the former sinner is to "humble and test the soul"[3] (ταπεινοῖ τὴν ἑαυτοῦ ψυχὴν καὶ βασανίζει) as attempted redress of the wrong of sin. In what this self-inflicted humbling and testing consists is not clear. *Sim.* 7.4 speaks of a process undergone before full forgiveness of sin can be completed, consisting of testing, humbling, and afflictions, the last-named not self-imposed, whereas the first two are, as here.[4] If the personal internal turmoil of

regret is meant, the use of βασανίζειν ("worry") in *Sim.* 9.9.3 is a milder comparison, and "humbling oneself" would mean stirring up a grateful response to God's mercy.[5] If something more formal is intended by way of discipline, as is usually understood, then fasting, prayer, and almsgiving are probabilities.[6] Hermas "inquires carefully" (ἐξακριβάζομαι) about the material revealed to him; this word family occurs at critical points where a deepening of understanding is called for.[7] The chapter closes with the usual formula.

Possibility of a Second Chance

■ **3.1–2 [31]** This chapter is one of the clearest in setting forth Hermas' teaching on second conversion and forgiveness of sin after baptism. On the identity of "some teachers" (τινὲς διδάσκαλοι, v. 1), there has been much speculation. There is no evidence that they are members of heretical groups, but it is not clear whether they represent mainstream thinking in the Roman church or a minority opinion. Their teaching that there is no possibility of forgiveness after baptism echoes Heb 6:4–6, though the terminology is completely different; it is not a case of textual influence but of common teaching. Baptism as descent into the water and ascent from it is traditional and suggestive of the actual manner in which it took place.[8] Hermas' revealed teaching is not in opposition to that of these teachers, but in complementarity, for the Shepherd immediately affirms their position (v. 2) before going further; this is very important to note. For the one who has received the forgiveness of sin (ἄφεσις ἁμαρτιῶν) in baptism, it is imperative not to

---

1 E.g., Exod 4:21; 7:3, 22; 8:19; 9:12,35; 10:1; Ezek 3:7; Prov 17:20; 28:14; Sir 3:26–27—always with the word group σκληρός, however.

2 Compare 10.1.3–6 below.

3 Ψυχή (here translated "soul") and καρδία ("heart") are used "quasi-pronominally" in *Hermas* in the biblical sense of person as center of experiences and feelings, corresponding to the LXX translation of שׁפֶנ (Hilhorst, *Sémitismes*, 137–42).

4 The βάσανος ("testing," "torment") word group is used in this self-inflicted manner only here and in *Sim.* 7.4. Elsewhere (*Vis.* 3.7.6; *Sim.* 6.3.1, 4, 4.1–4, 5.1–7; cf. *1 Clem.* 6.1; *2 Clem.* 10.4; Ignatius *Eph.* 8.1) it is synonymous with suffering, afflictions, setbacks, or persecution (examples given in 6.3.4), except in *Sim.* 9.9.3 where Hermas asks the Shepherd why he torments himself, meaning worry

(σεαυτὸν βασανίζεις). "Doing acts of penance," therefore, is not a strong theme in the book.

5 So Willem C. van Unnik, "Zur Bedeutung von ταπεινοῦν τὴν ψυχήν bei den apostolischen Vätern," *ZNW* 44 (1952–1953) 250–55.

6 There is a close LXX association between ταπεινοῦν τὴν ψυχήν ("to humble one's soul or self"), or similar expressions, and fasting or some kind of penance: Lev 16:29, 31; 23:27, 32; Jdt 4:9; Ps 34:13; Isa 58:3, 5; *Barn.* 3.1 (quoting Isa 58:5); probably Phil 4:12. Cf. Hilhorst, *Sémitismes*, 139–42; BAGD² *s.v.* ταπεινόω 2c. On fasting, see note on *Vis.* 2.2.3.

7 Again in 3.3, 7 below; *Vis.* 3.10.10; *Man.* 3.4; *Sim.* 9.1.3, 5.5, 6.3, 13.6: Henne, "Pénitence," 373.

8 Also *Vis.* 3.7.3; *Sim.* 9.16.

have been sinning again (ἔδει . . . μηκέτι ἁμαρτάνειν). This is the fundamental call and expectation upon which all the rest is based.

■ **3.3–4** Hermas is very much aware of the possible inconsistency between vv. 1–2 and what follows. It involves the tension between the ideal of the moral life and reality that is less than ideal, a tension already dealt with by Paul and the author of 1 John.[9] For Hermas, the second chance applies only to the baptized who have previously sinned, but not to those who might want to use this second chance as a cushion against future sin. This potential for misuse is the perennial problem with a doctrine of mercy and reconciliation. It is possible that the same teachers who preached only one remission of sin in baptism to catechumens (v. 1) also preached further forgiveness to baptized sinners.[10] Pushing this too far creates a double standard, but not pushing it far enough creates intolerable rigorism and exclusion.

The seeming contrast in the last sentence of v. 3 between ἄφεσις ("forgiveness") of sin in baptism and μετάνοια ("conversion") from postbaptismal sin is a terminological difference that will later be more important, but is not significant for Hermas and is not maintained in 4.4.[11] All is encompassed in the foreknowledge of God, "knower of the heart" (καρδιογνώστης),[12] about human weakness and the devil's power.

■ **3.5–7** Not only God's foreknowledge, but especially

that God is so very compassionate (πολύσπλαγχνος οὖν ὢν κύριος ἐσπλαγχνίσθη, v. 5),[13] is the key to the proclamation of a second chance. The invitation or calling (κλῆσις, v. 6)[14] is another name for the initial conversion and acceptance of baptism,[15] after which only one more chance is extended to those already baptized and having sinned again afterwards. But those who would abuse the chance by repeated sinning and expectation of forgiveness will find that it does not work for them, and they will with great difficulty (δυσκόλως) "live," that is, "live to God," prosper spiritually and be saved[16]—not that it will be impossible,[17] but that they will barely sneak through. This one small admission, repeated in different contexts a few other times,[18] in effect undermines a literal interpretation of the message of "only one more chance," suggesting once again that we are not dealing with rules of church discipline, but with an urgent appeal to respond to God's mercy. As in 3.4, Hermas' response in v. 7 reveals that it is not a question of new information, but of new understanding for himself that he must also communicate to others.

---

9 Cf. discussion of conversion in Introduction 3.3.1.

10 Poschmann, *Paenitentia Secunda*, 159–68; idem, *Penance*, 29, following the suggestion first made by D'Alès. Calling the double message a pedagogical device, however, is probably going too far. Poschmann's position has been sharply criticized, e.g., by Joly (156–67). Remaining in baptismal innocence was considered the norm, not the exception; Tertullian (*De paen.* 7) wanted to keep any word of postbaptismal remission of sin away from catechumens for precisely this reason. Certainly *Mandate* 4 is intended for baptized sinners, but Henne's view that it is aimed at the newly baptized who are already sinners ("Pénitence," 370–76) is too specific.

11 So too Snyder, 72; Brox, 212.

12 Cf. Acts 1:24 (the Lord Jesus); 15:8 (God); indirectly, 1 John 3:19–20, and even John 2:25.

13 On the significance of the word group, see comment on *Vis.* 3.12.3.

14 In the middle of the fifth word of v. 6, the major Greek MS. of the text, S, unfortunately comes to an end. The one or two further leaves discovered at St. Catherine's in 1975 await publication.

15 As in v. 4 above; compare 1 Cor 7:17–24; other possible interpretations in Brox, 213.

16 For the significance of this idea, see comment on 1.2 above.

17 So Dibelius, 510; against him, Poschmann, *Penance*, 30–31 n. 39; Brox, 213; and all contemporary translations. The word is used elsewhere in the same sense: 9.6; 12.1.2; *Sim.* 8.10.2; 9.20.2; compare especially 23.3 with Matt 19:23, par Mark 10:23; Luke 18:24.

18 References in previous note.

4

Widowhood and Remarriage

4 [32] 1/ I asked him again: "Sir, since you put up with me once, show me this, too." "Speak," he said. "Sir," I said, "if a woman or a man falls asleep and the other marries, the one who marries does not sin, right?" 2/ "The other does not sin," he said, "but by remaining single, that one acquires greater status and great honor before the Lord, but does not sin even by marrying. 3/ So preserve chastity and reverence, and you will live to God. Whatever I tell you or will tell you, observe from now on, from the day on which you were given over to me, and I will dwell in your house. 4/ There will be forgiveness for your previous transgressions if you keep my commandments, just as there will be forgiveness to all who keep these my commandments and continue in this purity."

■ **4.1–2 [32]** The discussion in v. 1 takes up where 1.11 left off, with one further question about marriage practice. The teaching on remarriage in widowhood follows closely that of Paul in 1 Cor 7:39–40. The language is so different that no literary dependence can be claimed, but *1 Clement* shows that 1 Corinthians was known very early in Rome, so that the Pauline text may well be the direct or indirect inspiration. There is no connection with the command that Hermas' wife be to him "as a sister" (*Vis.* 2.2.3), except in the same general direction toward sexual asceticism. But the discussion here is about remarriage, not altering the marriage relationship. As in 1.1 and 1 Corinthians 7, the ordinary way is marriage, and it is carefully stated (v. 2) that there is no sin in a second—or presumably even more—marriage in widowhood. But doing more than the ordinary leads to celibacy.[1] The fact that the question is even being raised both in 1 Corinthians 7 and here means that these passages reflect an early stage of the development of Christian mistrust of second marriages[2] and the ascetic valuing of celibacy.[3]

■ **4.3–4** These concluding verses refer not to what went immediately before, but to all the commandments in general, especially that of purity, as enunciated in 1.1.

Observance of what the Shepherd says as condition for his remaining in Hermas' house (v. 3) seems on the surface to contradict the unconditional promise to the same effect made in *Vis.* 5.2, and if that scene is understood as having happened well in the past, there is an apparent contradiction with "from now on" ($\dot{\alpha}\pi\dot{o}$ $\tau o\hat{v}$ $\nu\hat{v}\nu$) as starting point for the time of obedience, perhaps signaling an interpolation.[4] But there are no time markers here, and the point is that the present moment is always the moment of grace. For the same reason, the Shepherd now urges Hermas on with the promise to live in his house, not as a threat of the opposite, but as encouragement, which is extended to all in v. 4, according to the usual structure of the closing of a *Mandate.* Clearly v. 4a is speaking in the singular to the baptized Hermas as representative of all the faithful referred to in the plural in v. 4b. Yet the forgiveness of previous transgressions is $\pi\alpha\rho\alpha\pi\tau\dot{\omega}\mu\alpha\sigma\iota\nu$ $\ddot{\alpha}\phi\epsilon\sigma\iota\varsigma$, not $\mu\epsilon\tau\dot{\alpha}\nu o\iota\alpha$, so that, while a distinction between them is possible in 3.3, this verse shows that the two terms can be used interchangeably.

---

1 Compare *Sim.* 5.3.3.

2 E.g., 1 Tim 3:2; Tertullian *De monog.* 16.3; *Exh. cast.* 1.

3 E.g., Ignatius *Smyrn.* 13.1; *Pol.* 5.2; Justin *1 Apol.*

1.15, 29; Minucius Felix *Oct.* 31.5; Athenagoras *Leg.* 33.3; Tertullian *Apol.* 9.19; *De monog.* 3; Cyprian *De hab. virg.* 21; *Apost. Const.* 6.17.

4 Dibelius, 513–14.

5   Two Ways of Being

1 [33]   1/ "Have courage," he said, "and understanding, and you will have power over all evil deeds and do everything that is just. 2/ If you are courageous, the holy spirit that dwells in you will be pure, not overshadowed by another, evil spirit, but living openly, it will rejoice and be happy along with the vessel in which it resides, and it will minister to God in great joy, having within it a sense of well-being. 3/ But if any bad temper comes in, immediately the holy spirit, which is sensitive, feels claustrophobic since the place is not clean, and wants to get out, for it feels suffocated by the evil spirit, not having room to worship God as it wants, for the place is contaminated by the bad temper. The Lord is present in patient endurance, but the devil in bad temper. 4/ If both spirits live together, it is unhelpful for that person in whom they live. 5/ If you take just a little wormwood and put it in a jar of honey, is not all the honey made good for nothing? So much honey is ruined by such a little piece of wormwood, and does it not ruin the sweetness of the honey, so that it no longer has the same attraction for the master because it has become bitter and it has lost its usefulness? But if wormwood is not put into the honey, it will be sweet and useful to the master. 6/ You see that patient endurance is sweeter than honey and useful to the Lord, and he dwells in it. But bad temper is bitter and useless. If bad temper mixes with patient endurance, the endurance is contaminated and its prayer is no longer useful to God." 7/ "I would like to know, sir," I said, "how bad temper works, so I may guard against it." "Certainly," he said, "if you do not guard against it, you and your household, you will have eliminated all your hope. But be on guard against it; I am with you. Likewise all who refrain from it, who will be converted with all their heart: I will be with them and shield them, for all of them have been justified by the most reverend angel.

2 [34]   1/ "Now listen," he said, "to how bad temper works, how evil it is, how it ravages the servants of God with its work, and how it deceives them away from justice. But it does not deceive those who are full of faith, nor can it work on them, because the power of God is with them. It deceives the spiritually empty and doubleminded. 2/ When it sees such persons in peace, it insinuates itself into the heart of such a person, and out of nowhere the man or woman becomes bitter about business matters, or about food or something petty, about some social connection, or reciprocity appropriate to one's status, or such stupid things. These kinds of things are stupid, empty, meaningless, and useless for the servants of God. 3/ But courageous endurance is great and firm, and has lasting power, is sturdy and expansive, joyful, happy, unconcerned, honoring God at every moment, with nothing bitter in it, always remaining meek and gentle. So courageous endurance abides with those of mature faith. 4/ But bad temper is, first of all, stupid, lightweight, and silly. Then from silliness comes bitterness, from bitterness passion, from passion anger, from anger rage. Then rage itself, gathering in all of these, becomes a great and incurable sin. 5/ When all these spirits live in one vessel, where the holy spirit also dwells, the vessel cannot contain them all, but overflows. 6/ The sensitive spirit, unused to living with an evil spirit or with hardness, distances itself from that person and seeks to live with gentleness and quiet. 7/ Then when it stays away from the person in whom it was dwelling, that person is emptied of the just spirit, and from then on that person is filled up with evil spirits and is disoriented in actions, led here and there by the evil spirits, and completely blinded from any good thoughts. This is what happens to all the bad-tempered. 8/ So refrain from bad temper, be clothed with patient endurance and oppose bad temper and bitterness, and your place will be with the holiness that is beloved of the Lord. So see to it lest you neglect this commandment. If you master this commandment you will also be able to keep the other commandments that I am about to impart to you. Become strong and powerful in them, and may all who wish to continue in them become thus strengthened."

Courage

■ **1.1–2 [33]** The fifth *Mandate* contrasts two opposite qualities, μακροθυμία ("courage") and ὀξυχολία ("bad temper"). The first carries the combined meaning of patient endurance or long-suffering, and magnanimity or greatheartedness. It is the ability to direct one's desire consistently toward the good over the long haul. It is more than the passive endurance connoted by the English "long-suffering," but implies as well the energy to embrace the good in the face of setbacks.[1] It has been previously used by the woman church to describe Hermas himself.[2] The second is its opposite. If patience is emphasized as the meaning of μακροθυμία, then ὀξυχολία could mean something like "angry outbursts,"[3] but the practical examples in 2.2 suggest something

more insidious that eats away at a person's faith, freedom, and goodwill. *Man.* 10.1 will link it with double-mindedness and sadness as the three major corrupters of faith. The suggestion on the basis of 10.1 that ὀξυχολία originally formed the topic of its own commandment is unnecessary:[4] that verse simply singles out the major vices discussed up to that point. Understanding has previously been associated with conversion (4.2.1–2), and will be later identified as a characteristic of the person in whom the Lord dwells (10.6). The promise of having power over (κατακυριεύειν) evil deeds speaks not only of human choices but also of triumph over demonic power.[5]

Verse 2 introduces the two kinds of indwelling spirits, good and evil, which are the root causes for two differ-

---

1   "Courage" is Lake's translation (see note, 87); partially equivalent to Latin *longanimitas,* whereby most translations emphasize more the element of endurance: "patience" (Joly, Crombie, Snyder); "long-suffering" (Lightfoot); "long-suffering, patience" (LSJ *s.v.*); "patience, steadfastness, endurance" (BAGD² *s.v.* 1); "Geduld" (Dibelius, Brox). For biblical use of the word, see F. F. Bruce,

Galatians (NIGTC; Grand Rapids: Eerdmans, 1982) 253.

2   *Vis.* 1.2.3.

3   So Crombie; "angry temper" (Lightfoot); "ill temper" (Lake, Snyder); "un accès de colère" (Joly); "Jähzorn" (Brox).

4   Dibelius, 514.

5   Cf. *Man.* 7.2; 12.4.7, 6.2–4; Garrett, *The Demise of the*

ent kinds of human behavior, though, as becomes clear—and this is the whole point of the teaching on discernment of spirits in the *Mandates*—the person is still responsible for which kind of spirit predominates in him or her. In spite of the capitalizing of "holy spirit" in most translations, it is not clear that the one spoken of here is identifiable with *the* Holy Spirit as usually understood in Christian sources (in fact, 2.5 assumes a difference), though the whole attempt to distinguish one good spirit from another and from the "spirit of God" begs the question and would have been beside the point for Christian writers at this period, when many Jewish and Jewish-Christian believers found spirit possession, either good or bad, as a viable way to explain the otherwise inexplicable changes and contrasts in human behavior.[6] The image of vessel or instrument (σκεῦος) for the human person, especially but not exclusively its material aspect, is fairly common.[7]

■ **1.3–4** The anthropomorphism of the sensitive holy spirit that feels suffocated when forced to share its dwelling with the evil spirit of bad temper (v. 3) could well be inspired by the stifling, poorly ventilated close quarters of three- to five-story apartment houses, or *insulae*, in which most of the urban underclass of a Roman city lived, as testified by the archaeological remains of Ostia and Herculaneum. While τρυφερός usually means delicate, dainty, fastidious, even effeminate, that is surely not

its meaning here, unless it is meant as a parody to emphasize the inability of this spirit to abide with an evil spirit; but the use of the word elsewhere[8] in *Hermas* suggests more a spiritual sensitivity, an "allergy"[9] reaction to evil, or an unwillingness to endure it. The curious concurrence of the verbs ἀποστῆναι ("get out") and πνίγεται ("felt suffocated") in v. 3 and in 1 Sam 16:14 LXX in a very similar context[10] may be a coincidence, or a witness to the common vocabulary of the tradition of spirit possession.[11] The greatest problem, however, is not for the spirits but for the person in whom this competition takes place (v. 4): it is unhelpful (ἀσύμφορον, the same expression in 3.6 for the behavior of the person who sins and tries to change repeatedly) and even evil. What is surprising and without adequate precedent is the lack of competitiveness on the part of the good spirit.

■ **1.5–6** A practical example that may have been a known proverb (v. 5) illustrates the unhappy mix of good and bad spirits: a little of the bad stuff can ruin the whole of the good stuff.[12] The editorial addition of the master's pleasure[13] to the parable gives it theological contextualization and situates its purpose here.[14] Honey unmixed with wormwood, and patient courage unmixed with bad temper, are sweet and therefore "useful" (εὔχρηστος), just as those become whose wealth is cut off from them (*Vis.* 3.6.6–7), as compared with bad temper, which, even

Devil, 157 n. 30; Francis C. R. Thee, *Julius Africanus and the Early Christian View of Magic* (Hermeneutische Untersuchungen zur Theologie 19; Tübingen: Mohr/Siebeck, 1984) 324.

6 See further, Introduction 3.3.3. Attempts to make it all consistent breed frustration. As Brox remarks (218), Hermas presupposes a tolerant reader.

7 *T. Naph.* 8.6; 2 Cor 4:7; 1 Pet 3:7 (wife); vessel of the spirit: *Barn.* 7.3; 11.9. Cf. BAGD² *s.v.*

8 Besides again of the holy spirit (5.2.6), the word is used of the angel of justice (6.2.3) in paratactic apposition with "meek" and "tranquil"; and of the young women around the door in the rock (*Sim.* 9.2.5), where the more usual meaning, "delicate," could be applied. Cf. LXX: Isa 58:13 of the Sabbath; Susanna 31 of Susanna, both obviously positive appelations.

9 Brox, 219.

10 First noticed by Helmut Opitz, *Ursprünge frühkatholischer Pneumatologie. Ein Beitrag zur Entstehung der Lehre vom heiligen Geist in der römischen Gemeinde unter Zugrundlegung des 1 Clemens-Briefes und des*

"Hirten" des Hermas (Theologische Arbeiten 15; Berlin: Evangelische Verlagsanstalt, 1960); cf. Joly, 431; Brox (without attribution), 219 n. 4. The difference is that in 1 Samuel the evil spirit is "from the Lord," a quite different kind of pneumatology than here.

11 Not the good spirit (grammatically possible) but the place is defiled by the evil spirit of bad temper: with Brox (219), against Joly (165 n. 3), *Sim.* 5.6.5 and 5.7.4 notwithstanding.

12 Compare 1 Cor 5:6; other references in Dibelius, 515; Brox, 219. Wormwood was later a favorite of ascetics to spoil the taste of food and thereby lessen enjoyment of it.

13 "Master" (δεσπότης) is a frequent term for God, already in *Vis.* 2.2.4, 5; 3.3.5, and frequently hereafter: Kraft, *Clavis,* 98.

14 Much of the text of v. 5 is corrupt in A, the sole Greek MS. for this portion, but is reconstructed from the translations and homily 110 (*PG* 89.1772) of the seventh-century monk Antiochus; see notes in Lake, 88; Whittaker, 29.

in small amounts, renders the courage as "useless" (ἄχρηστος) as the wealth.[15] The power of intercession (ἔντευξις) of the courageous and patient person also becomes useless, because it is compromised.[16]

■ **1.7** The form of v. 7a may seem like the beginning of a new commandment, but is better seen as a transition into the next one, since v. 7b contains the usual ending formula that broadens the address from Hermas to all who hear and obey, including once again his household. The last phrase has a peculiarly Pauline ring: all have been justified (ἐδικαιώθησαν) by the great angel,[17] but it is not to be understood in the Pauline way. Rather, it is the reward to all who are faithful in deeds of justice, beginning with the elimination of bad temper.[18]

Bad Temper

■ **2.1–5 [34]** The opening general statement about the evil power of bad temper to destroy believers is qualified by its inability to be effective in those who are full of faith because of God's power at work in them,[19] while those filled with doublemindedness and self-preoccupation allow room for it to enter. This verse introduces the image of emptiness with regard to those who are inhabited by evil spirits, an image that will be much played upon later, especially in *Mandates* 11; 12.5.[20] Verse 2 is central to the teaching on the discernment of spirits: to be under the control of an evil spirit does not have to

mean the dramatic signs of demonic possession, for it can happen in everyday affairs. Yet the language is forceful: the evil spirit tries to push its way in (παρεμβάλλει) if it can. The effect is bitterness (πικρία), not loss of temper; an enduring negativity, not a violent outburst. The manifestation of this bitterness happens over ordinary business concerns (ἕνεκεν βιωτιῶν πραγμάτων)[21] or other petty occasions. Concern about friendship, though, is not as trivial as it might sound; it would have to do with status and patronage.[22]

The description of μακροθυμία ("courageous endurance," v. 3) is a catalog of virtues, some of which emphasize a strength that stands in some tension with the sensitivity of the good spirit in 1.3; 2.5, unless that sensitivity is understood, not as an inability, but as an unwillingness to cohabit with an evil spirit. Verse 4 is a catalog of vices in an escalating chain formula familiar in early Christian paraenesis.[23] Verse 5 echoes 2.5.[24]

■ **2.6–8** Verses 5, 7 speak of the holy spirit in the singular, evil spirits in the plural, perhaps a mark of Christianization of previous material, but v. 6 speaks of the evil spirit in the singular as well. There is probably nothing significant in the number of evil spirits. Verse 6 contrasts the sensitivity or softness of the good spirit with the "hardness" (σκληρότης) of the evil spirits, again giving a hint as to what τρυφερός ("soft, sensitive") means here: positively soft as opposed to negatively hard.[25] This

---

15 Important terms in regard to the prolonged metaphor of the building of the tower; cf. *Vis.* 3.5.5; 4.3.4; *Sim.* 9.15.6, 26.4.

16 Intercession is a key factor in *Similitude* 2, and perhaps synonymous for the service (λειτουργία) that the good spirit is unable to perform in v. 3. See *Man.* 10.3.2.

17 On the identity of the great angel, see Introduction 3.3.3, 3.3.4.

18 Compare *Corp. Herm.* 13.9: ἐδικαιώθημεν, ὦ τέκνον, ἀδικίας ἀπούσης ("we have been justified, child, since injustice has left us").

19 Power "of God" Ath¹ L¹; "of the Lord" Ath² L²; "my power" A; Whittaker: τοῦ κυρίου ("of the Lord"), but "of God" is consistent with "servants of God" at the beginning of the verse.

20 Also 12.2.1, 4.5; *Sim.* 6.2.1 A only; 9.19.2, 22.3.

21 Or "about business affairs": compare *Vis.* 1.3.1; 2.3.1; 3.11.3; *Man.* 3.5; 6.2.5; *Sim.* 4.5–7; 8.8.1–2. See comment on *Vis.* 1.3.1.

22 On the overriding concern for status in Roman male society, see Peter Garnsey and Richard Saller,

The Roman Empire: Economy, Society, and Culture (Berkeley/Los Angeles: University of California Press, 1987) 118–23; Andrew Wallace-Hadrill, "The Social Structure of the Roman House," *Papers of the British School at Rome* n.s. 43 (1988) 43–97; idem, *Houses and Society in Pompeii and Herculaneum* (Princeton, NJ: Princeton University Press, 1994) 3–16.

23 E.g., 2 Pet 1:5–7.

24 *POxy* 3526, a small fragment containing only 5.2.3b–6.1.2a, reads here: οταν γαρ παντα τα πνευματα εν ενι αγγιω κατοικη ουκετι το πνευματα το αγιον χωρει εκεινο το αγγιον αλλ᾽ υπερπλεοναζει ("when all [supported by EL¹] the spirits dwell in one vessel, the holy spirit can no longer contain that vessel, but it overflows"), considered by the editor to be "defensible, if not preferable," but nowhere else is there question of the holy spirit containing, rather than dwelling in, the human vessel (*POxy,* 16).

25 See comment on 1.3 above.

softness is not a lack of strength. The two concepts are envisioned in semimaterial terms, like the image of lack of room in the human vessel for too many spirits, but this is not a crude or naive materialism. The contrasts of soft-hard and the identification of the "soft" spirit with strength caution against assuming too much materiality in the ideas. The person who allows the evil spirits to chase out the good spirit becomes full of evil spirits but is in fact, therefore, empty because lacking in personal strength to withstand their destructive effects.[26] Verse 8 concludes the chapter with the usual commandment to stay away from the vice (compare 1.7), but adds that keeping this commandment is a key to keeping all the rest—another hint of how deeply set is the spirit of resentment envisioned here by bad temper. It is an atti-tude that poisons a person's ability to respond to the invitation to a spirit-oriented way of life.[27] Bad temper is called the worst spirit, not in a prioritized way but as one of the triad of the worst (10.1.2). Ironically and perhaps deliberately, the commandment that has spoken of the spirit as soft and sensitive ends with encouragement to be strong, another clue that here softness or sensitivity is not weakness.

---

26 While A reads "led here and there by the evil spirits," Ath[2] has "by evil persons" ($\dot{\alpha}\nu\vartheta\rho\acute{\omega}\pi\omega\nu$), undoubtedly an interpretation but a suggestive one.

27 After "if you master this commandment" (v. 8b), POxy 3526 adds above the line: "you will be able to live" ($\delta\upsilon\nu\eta\ \zeta\eta\sigma\alpha\iota$), the familiar refrain otherwise lacking here.

6 Discernment of Spirits

1 [35] 1/ "I commanded you," he said, "in the first commandment to keep faith, fear, and restraint." "Yes, sir," I said. "But now," he said, "I want to show you their power, so you can understand something of their power and how they work. They work in two ways: the right way and the wrong way. 2/ You, trust in the right way and do not trust in the wrong way. The right way has a straight path, but the wrong way a crooked path. But you, walk on the straight and smooth path and leave the crooked path alone. 3/ The crooked path has no thoroughfare, but only rough ground and many obstacles, and is jagged and thorny, dangerous to travelers on it. 4/ But those who go the right way walk smoothly and without obstacle; it is neither jagged nor thorny. So you see that it is better to go this way." 5/ "It is a pleasure, sir," I said, "to go this way." "Go ahead," he said, "and whoever turns to the Lord with a whole heart will go this way.

2 [36] 1/ "Now listen," he said, "about faith. There are two angels with a person, one that is right and one that is evil." 2/ "So how am I to know, sir," I said, "the workings of each, since both angels live with me?" 3/ "Listen," he said, "and you will understand them. The angel of right is sensitive to shame, meek and tranquil. When that angel enters your heart, it immediately speaks with you about justice, about purity, about reverence, about contentment, and about every right deed and every honorable virtue. When all of this enters your heart, you know that the right angel is with you. These are the works of the right angel. Believe in it and its works. 4/ Now look at the works of the angel of evil. First of all, it is bad-tempered, and bitter and stupid, and its works are evil, undermining the servants of God. When this one enters your heart, know it from its works." 5/ "How am I to recognize it, sir?" I said, "I do not understand." "Listen," he said. "When bad temper or bitterness overcomes you, you know it is in you; then come desire for doing more business, for extravagant food and drink, reveling, varied and unnecessary delicacies, lust for women, avarice, arrogance, pride, and whatever else goes along with them. So when these things enter your heart, you know that the angel of evil is in you. 6/ So when you recognize its deeds, stay away from it and do not trust it at all, because its works are evil and inappropriate for the servants of God. Now you have the workings of both angels; understand them and trust in the angel of right. 7/ But keep your distance from the angel of evil, because its teaching is evil in every action. Even though a man be completely faithful, if the thinking of that angel enters his heart, that man or woman is bound to sin somehow. 8/ And again, even though a man or woman be really evil, and the work of the right angel enters their heart, he or she will necessarily do some good. 9/ So you see that it is good to follow the angel of right but stay away from the angel of evil. **10/ This commandment clarifies the things of faith, so that you might trust in the works of the right angel, and when you do them, you will live to God. But believe that the works of the angel of evil are troublesome, and by not doing them, you will live to God."**

Two Ways

■ **1.1 [35]** This chapter serves as introduction to the teaching on the three major virtues of faith, fear of the Lord, and restraint, already introduced in *Man.* 1.2, to which the opening lines of this verse explicitly refer, and to be further developed in *Mandates* 6.2; 7; and 8, respectively. *Mandates* 6–8 are thus a literary unit related to *Mandate* 1. It is unnecessary to posit *Mandates* 2–5 as an insertion, since their material is groundwork for what follows here.[1] The chapter also introduces more explicitly the "two-way" theology that has been implicit in the description of the two kinds of spirits dwelling in human persons (especially developed in *Mandate* 5). Now, besides the two kinds of spirits, there are two ways of working (ἐνέργειαι), already familiar terminology, though not in the dual sense as laid out here.[2] The three principal virtues will be contextualized within the two-way theological system: two kinds of faith (6.2); two kinds of fear (7); two kinds of restraint (8). Verse 1 includes only the two ways of working; v. 2 brings in the "two ways" proper; chap. 2 describes the "two angels," bringing the whole system back more closely to the two kinds of spirits with which it began in *Mandate* 5. The adjectives "right" and "wrong" (δίκαιος, ἀδίκαιος) in the last sentence of v. 1 modify not persons but the "ways" (ὁδοί) that will be introduced in the next verse.

■ **1.2–5** Two-way paraenetic theology has roots in both Greek and Jewish moral traditions.[3] It externalizes the same idea that the teaching on the two kinds of indwelling spirits internalizes. While the question of different sources must be examined, it is not a question of different concepts or worldviews; all arise from an anthropological dualism that ascribes the experience of good and evil to external causality. What is unusual here (but shared with *Barn.* 20.1, though not as developed there) is that the wrong way is the harder one, beset with obstacles to the traveler (v. 3), whereas ordinarily if the two ways are described in physical or imaginative, rather than only moral terms, the wrong way seems more attractive.[4] The contrast between the rough going (ἀν-οδία)[5] of the wrong way and the smooth path (ὁμαλή)[6] of the right way (vv. 2–3) is just the opposite, perhaps for the paraenetic purpose of impressing or frightening an audience that would be quite familiar with the rough road conditions they would have to endure on foot when traveling off the few principal roads of the imperial system.[7] The opening exhortation of v. 2 (compare vv. 6, 7, 10) contains both the ideas of "believing in" and "trusting in"; one believes a teaching but trusts or relies on a path. It is the poverty of other languages, including English, that forces a decision in translation, whereas the Greek word can contain both meanings at the same time.[8] The concluding exchange (v. 5) expresses Hermas' acceptance of the right path and the usual

---

1 Discussion in Brox, 224.

2 *Vis.* 3.8.3; *Man.* 5.1.7; 2.1.

3 See further Introduction 3.3.3. Cf. especially *T. Ash.* 1.3–5, for Dibelius (520) the key ("Leitgedanke") of this passage: "two ways, . . . two mind-sets, two lines of action, two models, and two goals. Accordingly, everything is in pairs, the one over against the other. The two ways are good and evil" (*OTP* 1.816–17). Certainly the motif and the worldview are the same.

4 E.g., Sir 21:10; Matt 7:13–14; Xenophon *Mem.* 1.20–34. In *Tab. Ceb.* 16.3–5, the right way that is at first precipitous, after a little effort becomes beauti-

ful and smooth (ὁμαλή).

5 The same word used to describe the place of the initial vision in *Vis.* 1.1.3; of ground near the tower in *Vis.* 3.2.9, 7.1.

6 A clearly positive term for Hermas, whether used literally (*Vis.* 1.1.3 [see comment there]; *Sim.* 9.10.1) or figuratively (*Vis.* 1.3.4; *Man.* 2.4); J. Ramsey Michaels, "The 'Level Ground' in the Shepherd of Hermas," *ZNW* 59 (1968) 245–50; Brox, 495–500.

7 For Joly (171), this is because Hermas describes them in eschatological perspective.

8 Opting for "believe": Dibelius, 521; Lake, 95; Brox, 222 and comment, 225; "trust": Lightfoot, 428;

broadening of the promise to the plural; consonant with the image of way or road, it uses the biblical language of proceeding or walking (πορεύεσθαι),[9] and of conversion with a whole heart.

Two Angels

■ **2.1–2 [36]** The instruction on faith is the occasion to present the next step in the Two-Ways teaching. The two workings or two ways of the previous chapter are here personified as two accompanying "angels" (ἄγγελοι, v. 1), one that moves a person to justice (δικαιοσύνη) and the other to evil (πονηρία). While the two spirits of *Man.* 5.1.3 and 2.5 are spoken of as dwelling within the person, the two angels live with μετὰ τοῦ ἀνθρώπου . . . κατοικοῦσιν (vv. 1–2); but the difference is not deliberate, for in vv. 3–4, both angels enter the heart. Very similar to the two angels described here, and usually cited, is *T. Jud.* 20.1–2: "two spirits (πνεύματα) await an opportunity with humanity: the spirit of truth and the spirit of error. In between is the conscience of the mind which inclines as it will."[11]

■ **2.3–5** These verses contain the heart of Hermas' teaching on discernment of spirits, a tradition that has been of continuing importance in Christian spirituality.[12] The good spirit or angel is τρυφερός[13] καὶ αἰσχυντηρός, here translated together as "sensitive to shame," a positive quality that is the complement of being honorable and sensitive to the honor of others.[14] This good spirit "speaks" in the human heart of desirable qualities in the form of a catalog of virtues, the last of which is αὐτάρκεια (contentment), the Stoic virtue of self-sufficiency or independence from entangling relationships. In Christian usage, it has already come to mean making do with the minimum and peaceful acceptance of whatever comes.[15] It is not that, having recognized the presence of the angel of right, one will then behave in this

way, but rather that, when a person acts according to these qualities, that behavior is the sign of the presence of the good angel, who is therefore to be trusted. This is the whole point of the tradition of discernment of spirits: the spirits are known by their effects.

The same is true of the spirit, or angel, of evil (vv. 4–5). To the angel itself (v. 4) are ascribed the negative characteristics of bad temper, bitterness, and stupidity, the first two already key vices in this discussion (cf. v. 5). When the person is under the control of these inclinations, that is the sign of the presence and control of the spirit of evil, recognized by its effects or works.[16] As a literary device toward further elucidation, Hermas asks for more explanation (v. 5), and what follows is more detailed than the description of the effects of the good spirit, in line with the paraenetic and especially deterrent purpose of the text.[17] Bad temper and bitterness are the major clues. From them flow a series of vices, most of them recognizable paraenetic elements, some already familiar from a similar list in 5.2.2; see also 12.2.1. The first, ἐπιθυμία πράξεων πολλῶν, is to be understood as business affairs, not just "many deeds" (Lake) or "many affairs" (Snyder)[18] in the context of this major concern throughout the whole book.[19] The description of banquet revelry is more expanded here than in 5.2.2 or 12.2.1; the extravagance of Roman banquet scenes lies in the background. In contrast to the two other such lists that are explicitly gender-inclusive, this one is androcentric: ἐπιθυμίαι γυναικῶν (desire for women). The inclination to these material aspects of overindulgence, plus the attitudinal vices of avarice, arrogance, pride, and the like, are the sure signs of invasion by the spirit of evil.

■ **2.6–9** The distance that the believer should keep from the power of this spirit (v. 6) is accomplished by separation from its effects, or actions and attitudes. The spirit

Crombie, 24; Snyder, 76; Joly, 173. Dibelius' complaint (521–22) that 2.1–9 have nothing to do with faith as first introduced in *Man.* 1.1 seems to disregard this fact.

9   E.g., Deut 5:33; 8:6; 10:12; 11:22; Prov 1:15; 2:13; Ps 32:8; 81:13.

10   E.g., Jer 24:7; Joel 2:12; *Vis.* 1.3.2; 2.2.4; 3.12.3, 13.4; 4.2.5; *Man.* 5.1.7.

11   Trans. H. C. Kee, *OTP* 1. 800.

12   The first sentence of the verse ends with "you will understand them" (συνιεῖς αὐτάς) A; "understand" (imperative sing.) LL; omitted in E. Editors and translators are divided, though the meaning is not

altered; Lake (96–97) gives A text and LL translation!

13   On the difficulty of understanding the use of this word, see comment on *Man.* 5.1.3.

14   Malina, *New Testament World*, 44.

15   Cf. *Sim.* 1.6; 2 Cor 9:8; Phil 4:11; 1 Tim 6:6; Osiek, *Rich and Poor*, 53–55; Leutzsch, *Wahrnehmung*, 203–4. On the whole list, compare Phil 4:8.

16   Cf. Matt 7:16; 1 John 4:1–6.

17   Dibelius, 522.

18   Lake, 97; Snyder, 77; also opting for a business connotation is Brox, 223.

that leads to such deeds can be neither believed, nor trusted—both senses of πιστεύειν are operative here. Verses 7b–8 could be understood deterministically: even a faithful[20] person under the influence of the evil angel must commit some sin (δεῖ τὸν ἄνδρα ἐκεῖνον ἢ τὴν γυναῖκα ἐξαμαρτῆσαί τι), while a basically evil person under the influence of the good angel will necessarily do some good thing (ἐξ ἀνάγκης δεῖ αὐτὸν ἀγαθόν τι ποιῆσαι). But v. 9 makes clear that the choice is a human one; by avoiding evil deeds and attitudes, one does not give occasion to the evil spirit to gain the upper hand. Though there is no suggestion of a baptismal context here, the whole chapter is reminiscent of later baptismal instructions and renunciation formulas, especially the structure of doing good and avoiding evil, with examples of each. They differ decisively from this passage, however, in their assumption that the evil spirits resident in the nonbaptized are driven away by exorcism, baptism, and renunciation, while for Hermas they continue to hover, harass, and potentially invade the baptized.[21] Our passage, however, is more sophisticated than a simple baptismal instruction. It is a manual or set of guidelines for ongoing Christian life.

■ **2.10** Commentators have a more difficult time relating all of this to faith[22] than does Hermas, for whom the whole discussion has seemingly clarified the topic. Again, if the two dimensions of faith—belief and trust—are held together, there is no problem. Belief in God (*Man.* 1.1) is inseparable from trust in the spirit that directs the heart to God, and therefore from acting according to that spirit; this is the whole meaning of traditional Jewish-Christian theology and ethics. In spite of the natural attractiveness of the works of evil, the Christian must believe that they do not lead to God, and therefore not trust them. Literary parallelism would suggest here that the structure would be: believe in the good angel, do not believe in the bad angel. But the overall structure of two kinds of everything takes precedence, so that belief or trust is commanded in regard to both angels, but of different kinds: one directed to the things of God, the other against the things of evil. That the grammatical form of imperative command is not as clear here as at the end of most of the *Mandates* is inconsequential, though the absence of the usual pluralizing in the last sentence is noteworthy.

---

19   See comment on *Vis.* 1.3.1; Osiek, *Rich and Poor,* esp. 41–44.

20   Πιστότατος ("most faithful") A; *felicissimus* ("most happy") L¹; πιστός ("faithful") Lake (98) on the basis of L²E *fidelis,* but the A reading is to be preferred as parallel to the textually unquestioned πονηρότατος ("most evil") in v. 8.

21   Henry A. Kelly, *The Devil at Baptism: Ritual, Theology, and Drama* (Ithaca, NY, and London: Cornell University Press, 1985) 40–48, 74–75. Clement of Alexandria *Excerp. ex Theod.* 77.1 may be the earliest evidence of baptismal exorcism: ἀποτασσομένων ἡμῶν ταῖς πονηραῖς Ἀρχαῖς ("[in

baptism] we renounce the evil powers"), (SC 23, 201). On the basis of the word ἀποτάσσεσθαι ("separate," "say farewell") in v. 9, Dibelius (528) also associates discussions of renunciation of worldly things in: Justin *1 Apol.* 1.49.5; *Dial.* 119.6; Clement of Alexandria *Protrep.* 101.2. Already in *Barn.* 16.7–10, the remission of sins drives out the demons.

22   E.g., Dibelius, 523; Brox, 228.

7 Fear of the Lord

[37] 1/ "Fear the Lord," he said, "and keep his commandments. By keeping God's commandments, you will be powerful in every deed, and your deeds will be uncompromised. By fearing the Lord, you will do all things well. This is the fear that you must fear, and so be saved. 2/ But do not fear the devil. By fearing the Lord, you will have power over the devil, because he has no power in himself. Where there is no power, neither is there cause to fear. Everyone who has power is feared, and one without power is scorned by all. 3/ But fear the works of the devil because they are evil. Since you fear the Lord, fear the works of the devil and do not do them, but distance yourself from them. 4/ There are two kinds of fear. If you wish to do evil, fear the Lord and you will not do it. And again, if you wish to do good, fear the Lord and you will do it, for the fear of the Lord is strong, great, and honorable. So fear the Lord and you will live to him. As many as fear the Lord by keeping his commandments will live to God." 5/ "Why, sir," I said, "did you say about those who keep his commandments: `They shall live to God'?" "Because," he said, "all creation fears the Lord, but does not keep his commandments. So of those who fear the Lord and keep his commandments, life before God belongs to them. But as for those who do not keep his commandments, there is no life in them."

■ 1–3 [37] Explanation of the triad of faith, fear of the Lord, and restraint (*Man.* 1.2) continues with the second, fear of the Lord. The opening statement of the commandment is a paraphrase of Qoh 12:13 LXX. Verses 1–4 play on the relationship of fear and power, and at the same time, on the two meanings of fear, finally said outright at the beginning of v. 4: the terror of avoidance and the awe of respect for the power of God.[1] Unfortunately, the same word covers both distinct meanings, and this adds to the confusion of a chapter that tries to incorporate too many different ideas in too few words. The person who lives in respect of God is powerful (v. 1), even over the devil (v. 2),[2] who has no power of his own, and therefore is not to be feared.[3] The contest for power and honor, played out in the male social hierarchy of the culture, is projected as well into the cosmic realm, where divine and demonic power battle for control of human beings. Though most of the discussion about that struggle thus far has been described in terms of good and evil spirits, the devil has put in two previous appearances.[4] Here the struggle for power is plainly between God and the devil, but with very uneven odds in favor of God; in fact, for the person who keeps the commandments, the battle is already over. Verses 1–2 speak of the fear of reverence, which should be directed to God but not to the devil.[5] But v. 3a refers to the fear of avoidance, which *should* be directed toward the evil works of the devil.

---

1 The latter meaning as used here is primarily biblical, e.g.: Isa 11:3; Qoh 5:6; 7:19; 8:12; frequently in Sirach (always using the word group φόβος and always translating the Hebrew word group ירא); and common in early Christianity, e.g., Phil 2:12; *Did.* 4.9; *Barn.* 10.11.

2 Κατακυριεύσεις τοῦ διαβόλου ("you will conquer the devil"), suggestive of magical power; see comment on *Man.* 5.1.

3 Cf. 12.4.6–7; 5.2; 6.1–4; Matt 10:28 par. Luke 12:4–5.

4 *Man.* 4.3.4, 6; 5.1.3.

5 For fear of the devil, see *Man.* 12.4.6–7, 5.2, 6.1–4.

■ **4–5** The two kinds of fear (v. 4) continue the dual structure that has been maintained throughout *Mandates* 5–8. Again, both meanings are juxtaposed. The fear of the Lord that keeps someone from doing evil is desire to avoid judgment,[6] but the fear of the Lord that enables one to do good is reverence. The end of v. 4 would be a natural ending to the chapter, in conformity with the usual concluding formula. Verse 5 continues the discussion in dialogical form to put in one more point. All creation may fear the Lord, but if this fear does not inspire obedience to God's commands, it is not the true biblical "fear of the Lord" but terror of judgment. In the mystery of human evil, this fear is not sufficient to compel sinners to obedience.

---

6   Compare Rom 13:3–4, and especially 7.

8   Restraint

[38]   1/ "I told you," he said, "that the creatures of God are of two kinds, and restraint is also of two kinds. From some things one must refrain, from others not." 2/ "Tell me, sir," I said, "from which things one must refrain, and from which not." "Listen," he said. "Refrain from evil and do not do it. Do not refrain from good, but do it. If you refrain by not doing good, you commit a great sin. If you refrain by not doing evil, you do a great work of justice. So refrain from all evil by doing good." 3/ "Which, sir," I said, "are the evils from which one must refrain?" "Listen," he said, "from adultery and fornication, from lawless drunkenness, from the evil of luxury, from overeating and extravagant wealth, boasting, arrogance, and pride, and from lying, slander, and hypocrisy, resentment and blasphemy. 4/ All these deeds are the most evil in human life. From these deeds the servant of God must refrain. The one who does not refrain from these cannot live to God. Now listen to what follows." 5/ "Sir," I said, "are there still more evil deeds?" "Yes, many more," he said, "from which the servant of God must refrain: theft, lying, robbery, bearing false witness, covetousness, lust, deceitfulness, vanity, pride, and everything like them. 6/ Don't you think these things are evil?" "Very evil for the servants of God," I said. "The one who serves God must refrain from all of these. Refrain from all of them, so that you might live to God and be registered with those who refrain from them. So the things from which you must refrain are these. 7/ But listen to the things from which you must not refrain, but do: do not refrain from the good, but do it." 8/ "Show me the meaning of the good things, sir," I said, "so that I might continue in them and serve them, and by doing them be saved." "Listen," he said, "to the works of goodness that you must do, and not refrain from. 9/ First of all, faith, fear of the Lord, love, harmony, right speaking, truth, and patience; there is nothing better than these in human life. Anyone who observes them and does not refrain from them is blessed in life. 10/ Then listen to what comes next: to minister to widows, to look after orphans and the needy, to ransom from distress the servants of God, to be hospitable (for in hospitality is found the doing of good), to resist no one, to be gentle, to become poorer than everyone, to reverence the aged, to practice justice, to preserve brotherhood, to put up with insult, to endure patiently, not to carry resentment, to comfort the spiritually burdened, not to reject those who have been made to stumble in the faith but to convert and encourage them, to admonish sinners, not to oppress debtors and the poor, and anything else similar to these. 11/ Do you think these are good?" he said. "What could be better than these, sir?" I said. "Then continue in them," he said, "and do not refrain from them, and you will live to God. 12/ Keep

this commandment: if you do good and do not refrain from it, you will live to God, and all who do the same will live to God. Again, if you do not do evil but refrain from it, you will live to God, and all will live to God who keep these commandments and continue in them."

■ **1–2 [38]** The third member of the triad faith, fear, and restraint is introduced with the (rather late in coming)[2] comment that everything in God's creation comes in pairs, perhaps inspired by Sir 33:14–15; 42:24.[3] Just as faith-trust and fear have two aspects, so too does "restraint" (ἐγκράτεια), understood here as a general virtue of appropriate self-control, common to both Jewish and Greco-Roman moral teaching as well as Christian.[4] It does not here carry the later Christian specific meaning of celibacy. The "doubleness" motif is adapted to the virtue of restraint more smoothly than to the previous ones: one is to refrain from doing evil, but not refrain from doing good. This apparently simple formula contains one of the complexities of Jewish-Christian moral teaching, more relevant today than ever: that sin of omission is as great as sin of commission.[5]

■ **3–6** In dialogue form, Hermas is instructed about the evil deeds from which one[6] must refrain, given in two lists. Evidence that the two catalogs of vices are fully independent is the repetition of "lying" (ψεῦσμα in v. 3, ψεῦδος in v. 5).[7] In the first list in v. 3, items two to five are characteristic concerns of Hermas regarding wealth, luxury, and overindulgence.[8] Their very recurrence in many paraenetic passages indicates a deliberateness of intention. The others in the first list in v. 3 and all in the second list in v. 5 are traditional.[9] The connector between the first and second lists comes at the end of v. 4 with the allusion to "what follows" (τὰ ἀκόλουθα; compare beginning of v. 10), already a connector in Hellenistic moral teaching between the most important principles and secondary ones.[10] If the two lists here are examined in that light, more emphasis is placed on those in the first list, which addresses primarily questions of material lifestyle and lack of charity, two concerns already known to be present in the book.[11] Hermas' question in v. 5 seems forced, but it is part of this connective structure. The second list "covers" any possibility of incompleteness by adding "and everything

1   For an extensive study of the structure and character of this chapter, especially v. 10, see Osiek, *Rich and Poor*, 58–77.
2   Brox, 232: "ungeschickt spät placiert."
3   Suggested by Dibelius, 525, with wrong chapter reference for the first.
4   Cf. *4 Macc* 5.34; Acts 24:25; Gal 5:23; 2 Pet 1:6; *1 Clem.* 35.2; 62.2; 64.1; *2 Clem.* 15.1; *Tab. Ceb.* 20.3 and negatively, 23.2; Epictetus 2.20.13; *Corp. Herm.* 13.9; as sexual continence but not celibacy, *T. Naph.* 8.8; as marital chastity, Polycarp *Phil.* 4.2; probably already as the charism of celibacy, *1 Clem.* 38.2. Cf. Jacques Liébaert, *Les enseignements moraux des Pères Apostoliques* (Recherches et synthèses; Morale 4; Gembloux: Duculot, 1970) 204.
5   The fifth sentence of v. 2 which makes this statement is restored from LLE, having been omitted by A, presumably by homoioteleuton (Whittaker, 34), but it is not impossible to imagine that it was omitted precisely because of the difficulties it implies. However, the next sentence is omitted by L[1], while this fifth sentence is not.

6   ἡμᾶς ("we") A; με ("I") L[2]E; L[1] omits the pronoun. Most editors and translators go with A (Funk, 328 in brackets; Whittaker, 34; Joly, 178; Snyder, 80; Brox, 231), which breaks the usual pattern in the *Mandates* of a single addressee until the conclusion, but could still be original as the "we" of the church (see Brox's argument, 233). Dibelius (526) omits the pronoun.
7   Repetition of similar motifs in different places within the same writing is a characteristic of paraenetic genre: Dibelius-Greeven, *James,* 11.
8   Compare *Vis.* 3.9.3–6; *Man.* 5.2.2; 6.2.5; 12.2.1.
9   Dibelius (526) attempts to work out a pattern of doublets in the grammatical forms of the first list—a structure that he concludes is too artful to be original with Hermas!
10 Dibelius (526) refers to Epictetus 4.8.12, where the fundamental principles (τὰ τοῦ λόγου στοιχεῖα) precede those that follow.
11 On material lifestyle, see material on rich and poor; on lack of charity: *Vis.* 3.5.1, 6.3, 9.2, 10, 12.3.

like them" (ὅσα τούτοις ὅμοιά εἰσιν, end of v. 5; compare end of v. 10). On being registered with the living, see comment on *Vis.* 1.2.1.

■ **7–9** The second half of the chapter concerns the second aspect of restraint. It consists of instruction on the activities from which one must not refrain, the omission of which is just as great a sin as the commission of those things condemned in the first part (v. 2). Just as an imperative command *not* to do evil frames the two lists of vices (vv. 2, 6), so here (v. 7) and in v. 11, a positive command *to do* good deeds frames the two lists of virtues. Hermas asks (v. 8) for an explanation of the δύναμις (lit. "power") of the good deeds.[12] The list (v. 9) begins with the first two of the overall triad around which *Mandates* 6–8 are organized; the third is the very one under expansion in this chapter, and so need not be mentioned. The others are traditional except for ῥήματα δικαιοσύνης ("works of justice"), a Hebraic construction influenced by the LXX,[13] probably meaning the opposite of lying, slander, hypocrisy, etc., that appear in the lists of vices in vv. 3, 5. Just as the superlative is used to emphasize the evil of some vices (v. 4; 10.1.2), so it is used here (and in v. 11) to emphasize the goodness of these virtues, supplemented by a makarism pronounced on the one who does them.[14]

■ **10–12** The second list of virtues in v. 10 is unusual: it consists not of linked words but of infinitive clauses, and not of abstract qualities but of very concrete and socially oriented practices. Like the second group of vices (end of v. 4), they are introduced as "the things that follow" (τὰ ἀκόλουθα), and the care taken to formulate them indicates that they are hardly secondary in importance; nor are they "evangelical counsels"[15] over and above what is commanded. They form part of the content of the command given in v. 7, part of the content from

which one is not to refrain, under pain of great sin (v. 2). The first list of virtues in v. 9 represents those that are of foundational importance. The second in v. 10 is a program of community responsibilities that flow from them. The *Mandates* continually drive home the point that virtuous living is not isolated or abstract, but very practical. This verse is quite in keeping with that point, and with the spirit of Jewish and early Christian ethical thinking.

Some of the exhortations of v. 10 represent traditional duties in Jewish and early Christian paraenesis: to help widows and orphans, to practice hospitality, or to honor the aged, for example. Others have to do with community solidarity, a major preoccupation of the book: practicing justice, preserving the bond of fellowship, bearing patiently with trials.[16] Others have to do with organized activity on behalf of those in need, either coordinated by church leaders or practiced independently by patrons who can afford to do so: consideration for poor debtors, ransoming Christians from distress. The latter is part of a long Christian tradition that in this context must mean buying out those imprisoned for the faith or enslaved in oppressive situations.[17] "To become 'poorer' than all" (ἐνδεέστερον γίνεσθαι πάντων ἀνθρώπων) is a call to model oneself after God's lowly ones in the manner of the "pious poor."[18]

The final two verses (vv. 11–12) sum up the structure and thought of the chapter and conclude with the usual formula.

---

12 For the translation "meaning," see *Vis.* 3.4.3; possibly also 8.6 and elsewhere; BAGD² *s.v.* 3.

13 Hilhorst, *Sémitismes,* 111–13.

14 A prophetic pattern of speech; other makarisms: *Vis.* 2.2.7, 3.3; 3.8.4; *Sim.* 2.10; 5.3.9.

15 K. R. Jachmann, cited in Brox, 234.

16 Documentation in Osiek, *Rich and Poor,* 61–64, and on hospitality, Brox, 235.

17 Osiek, "Ransom," 371–73.

18 Osiek, *Rich and Poor,* 64–67; Dibelius-Greeven, *James,* 39–45; also *Man.* 11.8.

9   Doublemindedness

[39] 1/ He said to me: "Get rid of doublemindedness from yourself and do not be doubleminded at all, to ask anything from God, wondering to yourself, `How can I ask and receive anything from the Lord, since I have sinned so much against him?' 2/ Do not think this way, but turn with all your heart to the Lord and ask from him without doubting, and you will know his great compassion, that he will never abandon you, but will fulfill your soul's petition. 3/ For God does not keep resentments the way people do, but is himself without resentment, and has mercy on what he has made. 4/ So you, cleanse your heart from all the madness of this world and from what was described to you before. Ask of the Lord, and you will receive everything, and you will lack nothing that you have asked for, if you ask of the Lord without doubting. 5/ But if you doubt in your heart, you will receive nothing that you asked for. Those who doubt God are the doubleminded, and they will obtain nothing that they asked for. 6/ But those who are mature in faith ask everything, trusting in the Lord, and they receive it because they asked without doubting, not doubleminded at all. Every doubleminded person who is not converted will be saved only with difficulty. 7/ So cleanse your heart from doublemindedness, put on faith which is strong, and believe in God, that you will receive everything you ask. If sometimes you ask something of the Lord and receive what you asked somewhat slowly, do not be doubleminded because you do not get your soul's request quickly. It is surely because of some temptation or transgression of which you are ignorant that you receive your petition slowly. 8/ So do you not cease from asking your soul's request, and you will receive it. But if you become discouraged and doubleminded while asking, blame yourself and not the giver. 9/ Look to this doublemindedness: it is evil and senseless and uproots many from the faith, indeed even those who are very faithful and strong. This doublemindedness is the daughter of the devil and does much harm to the servants of God. 10/ Disdain doublemindedness and you will conquer it in every action; put on strong, powerful faith. For faith promises all and brings all to completion, while doublemindedness, which does not even trust in itself, fails in everything it does. 11/ So you see, then," he said, "that faith is from the Lord above and is very powerful, but doublemindedness is an earthly spirit from the devil that has no power. 12/ So you, serve the faith that has power and you will live to God, and everyone will live to God who has the same attitude."

■ **1–3 [39]** The ninth *Mandate* belongs with the fifth and tenth in unity of theme (see 10.1.1), treating bad temper, doublemindedness, and sadness, respectively. *Mandates* 6–8 on the virtues of faith, fear of the Lord, and restraint seem to have been inserted into this sequence. Yet *Mandate* 5 is also about the virtue of courageous endurance as well as the vice of bad temper, so the distinction between those *Mandates* that deal with vices and those with virtues is not completely clear. This chapter centers on doublemindedness (διψυχία), a favorite term for Hermas, a word group that appears over fifty times—though the argument could be made that the real theme of the chapter is the generosity of God. Only here is doublemindedness discussed directly, and contrary to its probable meaning in most other contexts, here it is directly associated with doubt in prayer of petition.[1] The chapter consists of vv. 1–3, 7–12 on the vice of doublemindedness, interrupted by vv. 4–6, a discourse on the importance of trusting prayer.[2] The interruption of vv. 4–6 may indicate an interpolation into an original commandment (Dibelius); or the treatment of doubt at beginning and end may serve to frame the central and more important section on confident prayer. Another aspect of the structure of the chapter is repeated movement from doubt to assurance: vv. 1–4; 5–7a; 7b–8a; 8b–12. The command to get rid of doubt is not hard-hearted in the face of human fear; rather, the fearful and doubting are repeatedly reassured of God's goodness and mercy. The whole chapter could be seen as commentary on the theology behind Mark 11:24; Matt 7:7–11; 21:22; John 14:13–14; 15:7; Jas 1:7–8.

The literary relationship of *Hermas* to James is more of a question here than anywhere. Especially vv. 1–3 appear frequently in patristic commentary on Jas 1:7–8.[3] In spite of the close similarities, however, no certain literary relationship can be established. Rather, we are dealing with a common background of Jewish-Christian instruction against doubt and in favor of confidence in prayer.

Verse 1 begins with one of the customary commandment formulas of the *Mandates*.[4] Doubt arises first from the fear of unworthiness in regard to sin.[5] The instruction is probably less autobiographical than a rhetorical singular intended for all hearers. The admonition to get rid of doubtful feelings (v. 2) and turn to the Lord with a full heart is one of Hermas' favorite ways to invoke traditional language to carry his central invitation to conversion. This turning to the Lord is to be done ἀδιστάκτως ("without doubting"), an unusual word that is for Hermas another way to express the opposite of doublemindedness.[6] Another favorite expression in v. 2 is εὐσπλαγχνία,[7] God's great mercy, the remembrance of which is the remedy for doubt, because God will not abandon those who trust.[8] One of the ways in which God is different from humanity is in being ἀμνησίκακος ("without resentment"), whereas μνησικακία ("harboring resentment") is a deadly failing.[9]

■ **4–6** The double invitation to purify the heart (vv. 4a, 7a)[10] frames two reminders to ask "without doubting" (ἀδιστάκτως, vv. 4b, 6), in the center of which lies the

---

1 For further discussion see Introduction 3.3.2.

2 Dibelius, 529. The literary coherence of this chapter lends itself to structural analysis. Brox (237) proposes a different structure, a series of commands: confident prayer (vv. 1–5); doubt contrasted with faith (vv. 6–7a, 10–12); resistance to the threat of doubt (v. 9); all interspersed with guidance in temptation to doubt (vv. 1, 3, 5, 7, 8). Still another suggestion is that of Arthur W. Strock, "The Shepherd of Hermas: A Study of His Anthropology as Seen in the Tension between Dipsychia and Hamartia" (Ph.D. diss., Emory University, 1984) 261–71: the commandment to remove doublemindedness (vv. 1–3); the struggle between faith and doublemindedness (vv. 4–10); conclusion (vv. 9–12). Dibelius' structure is most convincing.

3 Discussion and references in Dibelius, 527–28; Dibelius-Greeven, *James*, 31 n. 103. "*Herm. mand.* 9 is the best interpretation of Jas 1:5–8 imaginable" (ibid.). For the literary relationship with James, cf. ibid., 3, 31–32, 45.

4 Also *Man.* 10.1.1, 2.5, 12.1.1.

5 Cf. *Vis.* 1.2.1; a related but slightly different question in *Sim.* 4.6.

6 Another favorite word of Hermas that occurs nowhere else in early Christian literature up to this point, except here and vv. 4, 6; *Sim.* 2.5, 7; 8.10.3; 9.24.2, 29.2; see Osiek, *Rich and Poor*, 84 n. 23.

7 The preferred reading from *POxy* 1783, over variant forms of the same word group, given its frequency in *Hermas*; see comment on *Vis.* 3.12.3.

8 Reading ἐγκαταλείψει ("will [not] abandon") with *POxy* 1783, against ἐγκαταλίπη ("would [not] abandon") A and most ancient quoters of the text; with Joly (182), against Whittaker (36).

9 Cf. esp. *Sim.* 9.23.4, 32.5, also *Vis.* 2.3.1 with comment; *Man.* 8.3, 10.

10 Another familiar expression: *Vis.* 3.9.8; 4.2.5; 5.7; *Man.* 12.6.5; *Sim.* 4.7; 5.1.5; 6.3.6; 7.5–6; 8.3.8, 6.2.

twofold description that summarizes the teaching of the whole chapter (vv. 5b, 6a): those who doubt (the doubleminded) will not receive what they ask, while those who ask in complete faith will. The Christian is invited to purify the heart from the madness of the world and the words previously spoken (ἀπὸ πάντων τῶν ματαιωμάτων τοῦ αἰῶνος τούτου καὶ τῶν προειρημένων σοι ῥημάτων), two things that on first glance do not seem quite parallel. Later passages give some hints about what constitute the madness: inappropriate desires, excesses in food, luxury, and housing, and fasting apart from just deeds.[11] The previously spoken words can only refer to the descriptions of vices in the last chapters. The one who asks with purified heart (v. 4) will receive all without fail (ἀνυστέρητος),[12] as will those who are mature in faith (ὁλοτελεῖς, v. 6). But the doubleminded person who does not undergo some kind of conversion can hardly be saved (δυσκόλως σωθήσεται). This last saying raises for some the specter that Hermas would concede minimal salvation even to those who are not converted. However, that is not the emphasis. The accent is on the difficulty, but not impossibility, of salvation under these conditions, and therefore the need to act differently—not on the slim possibility on the other side that someone will sneak through. It is not so much a soteriological as a paraenetic issue.[13]

■ **7–8** The second invitation to purification of heart

(v. 7) is followed by the exhortation to be clothed or armored in faith (ἔνδυσαι δὲ τὴν πίστιν),[14] and to exercise that faith-trust. A seemingly vicious circle is presented: the doubleminded will not receive what they ask (v. 5), but not receiving leads to the temptation to be doubleminded (v. 7); in any shape or for whatever reason, doublemindedness must be resisted. Explaining why petitions are not granted is the thorniest problem in any theology of prayer as confident petition, and various answers are given. Here the only explanation is surely (πάντως)[15] the (unacknowledged) sin of the petitioner, temptation yielded to. The distinction between temptation and assent to it is not carefully drawn in an anthropology that predates analytical psychology,[16] so that unconscious sin is possible.[17] Petition for one's desire is to continue without ceasing (v. 8), in the spirit of Luke 18:2–8. Since good prayer of petition will include a plea for the forgiveness of sin, the only real obstacle is discouragement that leads to doubt, that is, doublemindedness.[18]

■ **9–10** The commandment against doublemindedness is reformulated[19] as a danger even to those who think they are rooted in strong faith. Among other things, it is ἀσύνετος ("senseless, stupid"), whereas μετάνοια ("conversion"), which strengthens in faith, is great σύνεσις ("understanding," 4.2.2). It is also the "daughter[20] of the devil," not to be understood in the same way as the

11 *Man.* 11.8; 12.2.1, 6.5; *Sim.* 1.1; 5.1.4, 3.6; 6.2.2.

12 Literally, "without need," but the meaning is "lacking in nothing that is asked for"; contrast the introduction in Ignatius *Smyrn.*, used of the church of Smyrna.

13 Compare similar sayings: 4.3.6; 12.1.2; *Sim.* 8.10.2; 9.20.2=Matt 19:23 and parr.; 9.23.3.

14 A frequent metaphor with Pauline connotations; cf. v. 10; 1.2, 4; 5.2.8; 11.4; etc., and comment on *Vis.* 4.1.8.

15 "In every case," Lake, 109; Snyder, 82; "invariably," Crombie, 26; "de toute façon" ("in any case"), Joly, 185; "mit Sicherheit" (surely), Brox, 236, with discussion, 239. Cf. use of the same word in *Vis.* 1.2.4 in a similar context. The idea is that of a "given," a strong affirmation; perhaps the opposite of δυσκόλως (see comment on v. 6 above).

16 Compare 6.2.7.

17 As in *Vis.* 1.1.7–8. This seems to contradict *Man.* 4.1.5, where a person ignorant of the adultery of a spouse is not guilty of sin, but there the ignorance is of the other's actions, not of one's own motivation.

18 To be "doubleminded" (διψυχεῖν) is the same as to "doubt" (διστάζειν); compare vv. 5a, ἐὰν δὲ διστάσῃς ("if you doubt") and 8b, ἐὰν δὲ ἐκκακήσῃς καὶ διψυχήσῃς ("if you become discouraged and doubleminded").

19 It is unclear why Dibelius (531) thinks that only here does doublemindedness formally become a vice, heretofore only an obstacle to prayer; it is already formally renounced in v. 1.

20 Θυγάτηρ ("daughter") Ant. LLE; ἀδελφή ("sister") A (unlikely and the only witness); ἔκγονος ("offspring") Athanasius *Nic. Synod.* 4.3 (not ἔγκονος as in Brox, 240 n. 11).

interwoven family relationships of the virtues,[21] or even of the sibling relationship of the three vices in 10.1.1–2, but as the Semitic (and sometimes also Greco-Roman) way of expressing connection.[22] Once again (v. 10) the power of faith is invoked as armor against the power of evil.[23] The personification of faith which promises everything and delivers on all promises is a "mild suggestion" of 1 Cor 13:7 based on the rhetorical repetition of πάν-τα ("all").[24]

■ **11–12** Verse 11 sets up in a clearer way the already familiar contrast (7.2) between the power of God and the impotence of the devil, now as ἄνωθεν ("above") versus ἐπίγειον ("earthly"), in preparation for the contrast between true and false prophecy in *Mandate* 11.[25] Doubt, because it is of the devil, is powerless, while faith, being of God, is strong. The obsession with power is not just rhetoric; it stems from a lively belief in external causality and the ability of unseen beings, whether good or evil, to affect human destiny. It is integral to the discernment of spirits, the central dynamic of the *Mandates*.

21   *Vis.* 3.8; *Tab. Ceb.* 20.

22   As in "sons of evil"; cf. Hilhorst, *Sémitismes,* 144–47.

23   As in v. 7; see comment on overcoming the devil in semi-magical context (5.1).

24   Dibelius, 531. Given that *1 Clement* evidences knowledge of 1 Corinthians, it is not unlikely that the resemblance is more than coincidental.

25   *Man.* 11.7, 11. Compare Jas 3:15; John 3:12 τὰ ἐπίγεια/τὰ ἐπουράνια ("the earthly/heavenly things"); v. 31 ἄνωθεν/ἐκ τῆς γῆς ("above/from the earth"). The contrast is a Greco-Roman commonplace: Wayne Meeks, "The Man from Heaven in Johannine Sectarianism," *JBL* 91 (1972) 44–72 (53).

10 Sadness

1 [40] 1/ "Get rid of sadness from yourself," he said, "because it is a sister of doublemindedness and bad temper." 2/ "How is it their sister, sir?" I said. "For it seems to me that bad temper is one thing, doublemindedness another, and sadness still another." "You are thick-headed, fellow," he said. "Don't you understand that sadness is worse than all the spirits and most ruinous to the servants of God, the most destructive of all the spirits to the human person, and wears down the holy spirit—but saves again?" 3/ "I am thick-headed, sir," I said, "and do not understand these parables. How it can wear down, but save again, I don't know." 4/ "Listen," he said, "those who have never searched for truth nor inquired about divine matters but only believed, who are embroiled in business deals, wealth, friendships with outsiders, and many other worldly affairs—those who are caught up in these things do not understand divine parables. They are obscured by these matters and compromised, and become barren. 5/ Just as good vineyards when neglected become barren due to thorns and many kinds of weeds, so too faithful people who fall into these many affairs described above deviate from their purpose and understand nothing about justice, but when they hear about divine and true things, their mind stays on their business affairs and they understand nothing at all. 6/ But those who fear God and inquire about divine and true things, with the heart oriented to the Lord, quickly take in and understand everything said to them because they have the fear of the Lord in them. For where the Lord dwells, there is great understanding. So adhere to the Lord, and you will take in and understand everything.

2 [41] 1/ "Listen now, foolish one," he said, "how sadness wears down the holy spirit, and again saves. 2/ When the doubleminded person takes on any project, and it fails because of his or her doublemindedness, sadness itself enters into the person and saddens the holy spirit and wears it down. 3/ Then again when bad temper adheres to a person for any reason, that one becomes very bitter, and again sadness enters the heart of the bad-tempered person, and that one is saddened by the deed and has a change of heart because he or she did evil. 4/ Therefore, this sadness itself seems to bring salvation because the person repented of the evil deed. Both situations sadden the spirit: doublemindedness because it did not achieve its purpose, and bad temper saddens the spirit because it did evil. Both sadden the holy spirit, doublemindedness and bad temper. 5/ So get rid of sadness from yourself and do not afflict the holy spirit that dwells in you, lest it implore God about you and leave you. 6/ For the spirit of God given to this flesh will put up with neither sadness nor oppression.

3 [42] 1/ "Therefore, put on joyfulness, which is always attractive and acceptable to God, and luxuriate in it. Every joyful person does good, intends good, and scorns sadness. 2/ But the sad person always does evil, first, because he or she saddens the holy spirit that is given to the joyful person; second, he or she saddens the holy spirit by acting lawlessly, neither praying nor acknowledging the Lord. The prayer of the sad person has no power anywhere to ascend to the altar of God." 3/ "Why," I said, "does the prayer of the sad person not ascend to the altar of God?" "Because," he said, "sadness presides in that person's heart. The sadness gets mixed up with the prayer and will not let the pure prayer rise to the altar. Just as vinegar and wine mixed together do not yield the same pleasure, so sadness mixed with the holy spirit does not yield the same prayer. 4/ So cleanse yourself from this evil sadness and you will live to God, and all will live to God, those who throw off sadness from themselves and put on real joyfulness."

Distractions from God

■ **1.1–3 [40]** The third vice to be driven out (v. 1) is λύπη ("sadness"), like the virtues of *Vis.* 3.8 linked in sibling relationship, here with doublemindedness and bad temper in a "trinity of bad spirits"[1] and a triad of teaching about them: *Mandates* 5; 9; 10. Hermas' rhetorical question (v. 2) occasions the affirmation of sadness as worse than all the other evil spirits (=vices), an identification that by now is apparent in the teaching on the spirits. But bad temper was called the worst of them in 5.2.8—a rhetorical flourish in both passages, not meant as absolute rank, but to place both among the worst. Here, however, the accumulated terrible statements lend added weight to the negative evaluation, even to the point that sadness not only destroys persons but exhausts the holy spirit as well. The sadness envisioned here is a prevailing discouragement that, like bad temper and doublemindedness, undermines the action of God; it can be likened to the later import of ἀκηδία ("boredom," "listlessness").[2] The most troublesome piece of v. 2, however, is slipped in at the end: in spite of being so destructive, sadness still saves. Verse 3 simply repeats the same information.

The text with which commentators place this statement in dialogue is 2 Cor 7:8–11, where Paul speaks of two kinds of "sadness" (λύπη): that which is of God, which produces conversion (ἡ γὰρ κατὰ θεὸν λύπη μετάνοιαν . . . ἐργάζεται), and that which is of the world, which produces death (ἡ δὲ τοῦ κόσμου λύπη θάνατον κατεργάζεται), and they sometimes conclude that, because Hermas does not seem to make the same distinction, his theology on the subject is "unchristian."[3]

■ **1.4–5** The answer to Hermas' dilemma of v. 3 will be delayed until the next chapter. Inserted between (vv. 4–6) is an interesting digression not directly on sadness, but on understanding—Hermas' last subject in v. 3. Those who are too heavily involved with their business, wealth,[4] and friendship with outsiders[5] have no time or desire to deepen their faith by understanding τὰς παραβολὰς τῆς θεότητος (literally, "parables of the godhead"; perhaps "wisdom of things divine"). The contrast is between matters of the world and matters of

---

1   Liébaert, *Enseignements moraux*, 209. Λύπη also appears in the list of vices in *Sim.* 9.15.3; cf. *Corp. Herm.* 6.1; 13.7; *T. Dan* 4.6 (as source of anger and lying).

2   So too Brox (248–49). See comment on *Vis.* 3.11.3.

3   So Dibelius, 531–32, with discussion of its non-Christian origin in Iranian sources. Both 2 Cor 7:10 and Hermas' discussion were influential in later

       patristic thinking: cf. LPGL *s.v.* λύπη.

4   Though vv. 4–6 ostensibly have nothing to do with the topic of sadness, cf. the connection between wealth and the sadness caused by a challenge about it: Mark 10:22 par. Matt 19:22, ἀπῆλθεν λυπούμενος ("he went away sad" [because of his many possessions]); par. Luke 18:23, where the rich offi-

God.[6] Those caught up in worldly concerns are not entirely without faith, but their faith lacks the important dimension of continuing theological inquiry. They are like neglected vineyards (v. 5): even the vines that still try to grow and produce fruit are hindered by thorns and weeds.[7] The praise for theological curiosity here, which Hermas obviously exemplifies, does not conflict with commandments to simplicity and belief (such as *Mandates* 1; 2) or against doubt (*Mandate* 9), or the reminder that humanity can have only limited understanding of God (*Sim.* 9.2.6–7); nor is it evidence of Gnosticism; the goal is not even knowledge, but understanding (v. 6). It simply indicates the author's conviction that worldly distractions block the full life of faith, and that that life necessarily includes the desire to understand more about the things of God. It also indicates the approval of "lay theology," the absence of assignment of theological knowledge to the religious professional.

■ **1.6** The summary of the teaching in vv. 4–5 relates understanding to fear of God[8] in a chiastic structure that frames the central statement, the heart directed to the Lord, with the seeking of truth on one hand, knowledge and understanding on the other, both enclosed by fear of the Lord. "Understanding" ($\sigma\acute{\upsilon}\nu\epsilon\sigma\iota\varsigma$) is a sign of the Lord's presence, and those who "adhere to the Lord"[9] recognize that. The final commandment of the chapter is not the negative avoidance of sadness (which will come in 2.5), but the positive movement toward a closer relationship with God.

Sadness Wears Out the Holy Spirit

■ **2.1–4 [41]** The question left behind at 1.2–3 in favor of the digression on understanding is now taken up (v. 1). The doubleminded person (v. 2) is not successful because of the fatal flaw of lack of unified vision and purpose; doubt is always the inhibitor (also 9.10). The sadness of failure wears down the human spirit that cannot shake it off because of doublemindedness, lack of clear faith. It also restricts the indwelling divine spirit which cannot act freely in that person. But there is another way in which sadness can work. For example, bad temper can also produce sadness (v. 3), but this time it is a sadness that works toward salvation because it aids the process of conversion from evil (v. 4). So sadness can work both ways, depending on the response of the person to the spirits. But—going back to the previous point—both doublemindedness and bad temper sadden and restrict the holy spirit.[10]

Verses 1–4 contain two overlapping themes, not well sorted out. The two kinds of sadness are introduced rather roughly into the middle of a treatment of the effects of the three vices, sadness, doublemindedness, and bad temper, perhaps as an attempt to maintain the twofold pattern from *Mandates* 6–8, or better, perhaps because the idea of two kinds of sadness was so well known from 2 Cor 7:10 that the author feels he cannot *not* include it. If it were not for the introduction of bad temper at the beginning of v. 3 (which needs to be seen by way of example as used in the sentence, though it still confuses the issue), vv. 1–4a would be a clearer explanation of the two kinds of sadness.[11]

■ **5–6** Verse 5 begins with the usual summation of the commandment at hand and takes up again (from 5.1.3, 2.5–6) the anthropomorphism of the vulnerable good spirit, this time oppressed not by the bad indwelling spirit but directly by a person under its influence, oppressed to such an extent that it will ask God for deliverance from this intolerable situation (compare 5.2.7). Comparison of this text with those cited from *Mandate* 5 con-

---

cial is $\pi\epsilon\rho\acute{\iota}\lambda\upsilon\pi\sigma\varsigma$ ("very saddened") by the challenge to sell his possessions.

5 Concerns of status and patronage; cf. 5.2.2; *Sim.* 8.9.1–3.

6 Compare the "faith from above," from the power of God, and the doublemindedness from below in 9.11.

7 The weeds and thorns in the vineyard may have a foundation in Gospel material (e.g., Mark 4:7), but the moral application of agricultural images, especially the vineyard, is so ubiquitous that nothing could be proved with regard to sources.

8 Cf. Prov 1:7 par. Ps 111:10 (LXX 110:10).

9 Sir 2:3. $Ko\lambda\lambda\acute{\eta}\vartheta\eta\tau\iota$ $\tau\hat{\omega}$ $\kappa\upsilon\rho\acute{\iota}\omega$; the verb $\kappa\sigma\lambda\lambda\hat{\alpha}\nu$ is also an important indicator for social teaching; cf. comment on *Vis.* 3.6.2; also *Sim.* 8.8.1, 9.1.

10 Cf. Eph 4:30: $\mu\grave{\eta}$ $\lambda\upsilon\pi\epsilon\hat{\iota}\tau\epsilon$ $\tau\grave{o}$ $\pi\nu\epsilon\hat{\upsilon}\mu\alpha$ $\tau\grave{o}$ $\acute{\alpha}\gamma\iota\sigma\nu$ $\tau\sigma\hat{\upsilon}$ $\vartheta\epsilon\sigma\hat{\upsilon}$ ("Do not sadden the holy spirit of God" [by bitterness ($\pi\iota\kappa\rho\acute{\iota}\alpha$) and other vices]).

11 For Liébaert (*Enseignements moraux*, 209), Hermas never succeeds in reconciling sadness as part of the trinity of bad spirits with its positive quality that leads to amendment of life, a conflict between the systematic structure imposed on the material and a fact of experience.

firms that, however much some of this discussion about two kinds of indwelling spirits may sound deterministic,[12] the real determination depends not on the spirits but on the human person. Verse 6 reaffirms the realistic incarnational aspect of the belief in indwelling spirits.[13]

The Benefits of Joy

■ **3.1 [43]** The third chapter is a rather straightforward teaching on the quality of joy and the destructiveness of sadness, which is now once again, according to its original valuation before 2.3–4, only negative. The opening commandment to "put on joy" employs the now familiar image of clothing or armor.[14] The hearer is to enjoy it fully (ἐντρύφα, another positive use of the τρυφή word group),[15] since it is highly favored by God and inspires to good deeds.[16] The alliteration caused by repetition of the word ἀγαθά ("good things") and the play on the verbs φρονεῖν ("have an attitude") and καταφρονεῖν ("have a negative attitude") is mostly lost in translation: the joyful person ἀγαθὰ ἐργάζεται καὶ ἀγαθὰ φρονεῖ καὶ καταφρονεῖ τῆς λύπης.

■ **3.2** What seem like universals at the end of v. 1 and in the first sentence of v. 2 ("every person . . . always") are simply generalities based on experience: spiritual joy leads to good behavior, while discouragement and sadness lead to selfishness, which leads to ἀνομία ("lawlessness"), a not infrequent term for evil, with biblical

roots.[17] The effect of the presence of the holy spirit is joy; this effect is blocked by sadness, and the saddened and discouraged person gets into a vicious circle: the person's sadness and discouragement "rub off" on the holy spirit, who is thus saddened and frustrated, and frustrating the holy spirit is not a good thing to do; but the sadness also leads to further evil attitudes and deeds, which further sadden the holy spirit. The outcome is that the sad person is unable to pray either prayer of intercession or of praise (μὴ ἐντυγχάνων μηδὲ ἐξομολογούμενος[18] τῷ κυρίῳ). The prayer of the discouraged person, like that of the rich person,[19] lacks the necessary power to ascend to the heavenly altar.[20]

■ **3.3–4** The heaviness of sadness and discouragement is emphasized by the image of sadness having "settled in" (ἐγκάθηται) in the heart so as to render it impure. The simile of vinegar in wine, like that of wormwood in honey (5.1.5), is a practical illustration that has gotten slightly muddled in the explanation, for it is not sadness that prays, but the person, or, better still, the holy spirit. The chapter concludes with the commandment to purify or cleanse oneself[21] from sadness, but as it began, to be clothed in joy. While most of the chapter seems taken up with the effect of sadness, it is a countereffect to joy, the real emphasis.[22]

---

12   E.g., 6.2.7–8; see comment there.
13   Compare *Man.* 3.1; *Sim.* 5.7.1–2; but see *Sim.* 5.6.5.
14   See comment on *Vis.* 4.1.8.
15   See comment on 5.1.3.
16   This second sentence for Dibelius (534) cannot be a Christian rule, perhaps because it does not follow the Pauline principle.
17   E.g., Matt 7:23; 23:28; Rom 6:19; Titus 2:14; *Barn.* 4.1; *1 Clem.* 8.3; *Vis.* 2.2.2; 3.6.1, 4; *Sim.* 7.2; 8.10.3.
18   Rightly understood by most commentators not as confession of sin, but of praise; cf. Ps 7:18, etc.; *Sim.* 2.5; in contrast to *Vis.* 1.1.3; 3.1.5–6; *Sim.* 9.23.4.
19   *Sim.* 2.5.
20   On the adaptation of the LXX θυσιαστήριον

("altar") of Jerusalem to the heavenly altar, see Hilhorst, *Sémitismes,* 159 n. 3; also Heb 13:10; Rev 6:9; 8:3.
21   Compare 9.11.
22   Later Christian moral literature seems to have largely abandoned ἱλαρότης for the preferred word for joy, χαρά, which remained a key virtue. E.g., Ps.-Chrysostom *Serm.* 18 (*PG* 61.735): ὅπου χαρά, λύπη οὐ πάρεστιν· ὅπου χαρά, εὐφροσύνης σύμβολα ("Where there is joy, sadness is not present; where there is joy, there are signs of good cheer").

11   Discernment of Prophecy

[43]   1/ He showed me people sitting on a bench, and another person sitting in a chair. He said to me: "Do you see those sitting on the bench?" "I see them, sir," I said. "They are the faithful," he said, "and the one sitting in the chair is a false prophet who is ruining the mind of the servants of God; he ruins that of the doubleminded, but not the faithful. 2/ Those who are doubleminded approach him as a soothsayer and ask him what will happen to them. That false prophet, who has in himself nothing of the power of God's spirit, speaks with them according to their inquiries and their evil desires, and fills their souls according to their own wishes. 3/ Since he is empty, he gives empty answers to empty people, too. Whatever he is asked, he plays to the person's emptiness. Of course, he says some things that are true, for the devil fills him with his own spirit so that he might be able to break down some of the just. 4/ Those who are strong in the faith of the Lord, clothed with the truth, do not adhere to such spirits but refrain from them. But those who are doubleminded and constantly changeable practice divination just like the outsiders and bring greater sin upon themselves, that of idolatry. The one who inquires of a false prophet about any situation is an idolater, empty of the truth, and a fool. 5/ Every spirit given by God is not questioned, but since it has the divine spirit, it says everything on its own accord because it is from above, from the power of the divine spirit. 6/ But the spirit that is consulted and speaks according to human desires is earthly, lightweight, without power, and does not speak at all unless consulted." 7/ "How, sir," I said, "is anyone supposed to know which of them is a prophet and which a false prophet?" "Listen," he said, "about both of the prophets, and what I am about to tell you is how you will discern the prophet from the false prophet. You can tell the one who has the spirit of God by the way of life. 8/ First, the one who has the spirit from above is meek and tranquil and humble, and refrains from every evil and mad desire of this world, and makes oneself poorer than everyone else, answers nothing to anyone when consulted, nor speaks alone; nor does the holy spirit speak when a human person wants, but such a prophet speaks only when God wants the prophet to speak. 9/ So when the person who has the spirit of God enters the assembly of just men who believe in the divine spirit, and prayer is made to God by the assembly of those men, then the angel of the prophetic spirit that rests upon that person fills the person, who, being filled with the holy spirit, speaks to the whole crowd as the Lord wishes. 10/ Thus the divine spirit is revealed. Such is the power of the Lord with regard to the divine spirit. 11/ Listen now," he said, "about the spirit that is earthly, empty, and has no power, but is stupid. 12/ First, the person who pretends to have a spirit exalts oneself and

wants to take precedence, and is soon reckless, shameless, chattering, living in luxurious habits and many other deceitful ways, and accepts payment for prophecy; in fact, without payment, there is no prophecy. Could the divine spirit accept payment and prophesy? It is inconceivable that a prophet of God could do this, but the spirit of such prophets is of the earth. 13/ Then, it does not even come near the assembly of just men, but flees from them. It adheres rather to the doubleminded and empty, and prophesies to them in a corner, and deceives them by saying everything according to their own desires in empty fashion—for it is answering empty people. An empty vessel put with other empty ones is not broken, but is compatible with them. 14/ But when it enters an assembly full of just men who have the divine spirit, and entreaty is made by them, that person is emptied and the earthly spirit flees from him or her in fear, and that person is rendered speechless, completely shattered, unable to say anything. 15/ If you arrange wine or oil in a storeroom and put in an empty pottery jar, then want to empty the storeroom, the jar you put in empty you will find still empty. So too the empty prophets that go in among just spirits are found to be exactly the way they came. 16/ You have the way of life of both prophets, so discern from the works and the way of life the person who claims prophetic inspiration. 17/ But you, trust in the spirit that comes from God and has power. Do not trust for anything the spirit that is earthly and empty, because there is no power in it; it comes from the devil. 18/ Listen to the parable I am going to tell you. Take a stone, throw it up to the sky, and see if you can touch it. Or again, take a water pump and squirt it up to the sky and see if you can bore a hole in the sky." 19/ "Sir," I said, "how can these things be? Both things you have said are impossible." "Just as these are impossible," he said, "so is it impossible to empower feeble earthly spirits. 20/ Take hold of the power that comes from above. The hailstone is an insignificant kernel, but when it falls on someone's head, what pain it causes! Or again, take the drop that falls from the roof tile onto the ground and makes a hole in the stone. 21/ So you see that the littlest things from above that fall upon the earth have great power; just so, the divine spirit that comes from above is powerful. So trust in this spirit, but avoid the other one."

The eleventh *Mandate* continues the doublet pattern that has run throughout the *Mandates* in various ways, and continues and develops in a new way the theme of the discernment of spirits by contrasting true and false prophets, the latter effective only with the doubleminded. Thus the chapter is as much about doubleminded-ness as it is about prophecy. However, its content is invaluable witness to the ongoing importance of prophecy in at least some churches in the early second century, and perhaps to the consonance of Christian interest in prophecy and the general renaissance of oracular prophecy at the time. Rather than a sign of the decline of early Christian prophecy, as has been suggested,[1] the chapter is testimony to its vitality and the ongoing search for viable criteria. The problem here is not prophecy, which is taken for granted, not argued for or against. The problem is the discernment of prophecy and the establishment of norms for that discernment, which indicates a thriving prophetic activity. The content of prophetic oracles is not really dealt with, only the question of authenticity. As is so often the case, what we would most like to know is not discussed because it was not the problem.[2] This chapter more than any other raises the question of *Hermas'* relationship with, and later use by, Montanism. Certainly the text is too early to be a Montanist document, and it was not sufficiently ascetic to pass muster for Tertullian, but among modern scholars it has been passed off as both Montanist and anti-Montanist.[3]

In form, the chapter is an instructional vision rather than a commandment, until vv. 16–17 and the familiar ending of v. 21. There is general agreement that the chapter can be divided into three main parts: vv. 1–6, 7–16, 17–21,[4] but no such agreement as to the detailed structure.

1a	introduction
1b–3	initial critique of the false prophet
4	two kinds of response
5–6	two kinds of prophetic spirits
7–8	character of the true prophet
9	how the true prophet works
10	conclusion for the true prophet
11–13a	character of the false prophet
13b	empty jar example
14	empty prophet
15	empty jar example further developed
16	conclusion of discussion of criteria
17	commandment
18–19	examples of stone and water pump
20	examples of hail and water
21	commandment repeated

■ **1 [43]** It is difficult to determine whether this section is meant to be a real scene interpreted or a vision shown by the revealer. Its opening line, "he showed me" (Ἔδειξέ μοι), is a characteristic apocalyptic vision opener,[5] yet it is doubtful, because of the realistic and extended description that follows, whether this is a true vision like the building of the tower or an appearance of the Shepherd, or a situation in which Hermas finds himself and receives a running subsurface explanation as he observes it.[6] The scene presented in v. 1 suggests either the synagogue or the schoolroom model.[7] Reiling correctly observes that the συμψέλιον here is no longer the couch, locus of authority or of magical divination, as in *Vis.* 3.1.4, but the subordinate seating of a group of people, as with the stone benches that lined the walls of schoolrooms[8] or sometimes of synagogues. The place

---

1. Dibelius (539) under the influence of the *Frühkatholizismus* model prevalent in his generation. For the opposite view, see Reiling, *Hermas and Christian Prophecy*, 10, 73–79. Other witnesses to the continuing importance of prophecy in the "mainline" churches include Justin *Dial.* 82.1; Irenaeus *Adv. haer.* 2.32.2. For Jean de Savignac ("Quelques problèmes de l'ouvrage dit 'Le Pasteur' d'Hermas," *EThR* 35 [1960] 159–70 [162–64]) the chapter demonstrates the central position of prophecy in Hermas' church as in that of the *Didache*.

2. See the interesting and extended attempts of Aune (*Prophecy*, 299–310) to characterize and give examples of the various possible kinds of prophetic oracles in *Hermas*. A dim view of such attempts is taken by Brox (259–60), who rejects them as unconvincing.

3. E.g., Crombie consistently (over)interprets an anti-Montanist polemic. For a detailed summary, see Brox, 267–68.

4. Dibelius, 536; Reiling, *Hermas and Christian Prophecy*, 28–30.

5. E.g., Jer 24:1; Rev 4:1; other examples, Reiling, *Hermas and Christian Prophecy*, 28 n. 2.

6. Compare the opening of *Similitude* 2, a clearer example of the latter; or *Sim.* 3.1; 4.1, less clear examples, as contrasted to the surrealist imagery of *Sim.* 8.1.

7. For Peterson ("Kritische Analyse," 283) the combination of the two: a synagogue school.

8. E.g., that of the side room referred to as the "Mithraic school" and presumed to be part of the Mithraeum complex under San Clemente in Rome.

of authority here is taken by the one on the "chair" ($\kappa\alpha\vartheta\acute{\epsilon}\delta\rho\alpha$), also symbol of authority, especially in school settings.[9] It is probably not a bishop's throne,[10] and the scene proposed here may be not a public worship setting, but rather a private one of group consultation, "a gathering of clients of the Christian *mantis* for an oracular séance."[11] Dibelius[12] aptly remarks on the double meaning of "faithful" ($\pi\iota\sigma\tau o\acute{\iota}$) in v. 1: the first time, it seems a general term for Christians, even without the definite article; the second time, in a sentence added perhaps by way of afterthought or clarification, the same term distinguishes the "good" Christians from the doubleminded, whose minds are being ruined by the false prophet.[13]

■ **2** In spite of Dibelius' lengthy attempt to associate his title of soothsayer in v. 2 with the contemporary fascination with the $\mu\acute{\alpha}\gamma o\varsigma$ ("magician"),[14] the critical editions resolutely read $\mu\acute{\alpha}\nu\tau\iota\varsigma$ ("diviner") in the uncertain text of A that preserves only the first three letters of the word.[15] The previous discussion of the presence of both good and bad spirits in the baptized (especially *Mandate* 6) makes it likely that both the false and true prophet are Christian.[16] The false prophet is not directly called a soothsayer, which here carries negative connotations; it is the attitude of those who consult him upon whom Hermas' condemnation comes down even harder that so characterizes him: the charge of idolatry is reserved for them, not for him (v. 5). Nor is the soothsayer accused of false teaching, and so cannot be called a heretic.[17] The reputation of the $\mu\acute{\alpha}\nu\tau\iota\varsigma$ in biblical and Christian sources is mixed; sometimes the term is closely associated with that of $\pi\rho o\varphi\acute{\eta}\tau\eta\varsigma$ ("prophet"), and may have been a figure officially resisted but privately popular, as is depicted here: "a 'small time' diviner."[18] The accusation that the false prophet says what his clients want him to say is a common critique of Greco-Roman oracular prophecy.[19]

■ **3** The wordplay on emptiness is consonant with the spatial language used elsewhere about spirit possession, especially 5.1.3, 2.5, and a sarcastic contrast to the way in which the false prophet "fills" the souls of the credulous with his own words (v. 2) and the devil "fills" the false prophet with diabolic spirit (end of v. 3), just as the person from whom the good spirit has fled is both empty and becomes full of evil spirits.[20] In this case, to be full is to be empty. The wordplay is enhanced by the triple meaning of the $\kappa\epsilon\nu\acute{o}\varsigma$ ("empty") word group in Greek and many other languages: materially empty or hollow; vain or fruitless; and exhausted or forsaken.[21] Irenaeus' report of Marcosian prophets may have this passage in the background, for the same attribute is

9 Reiling, *Hermas and Christian Prophecy*, 30–31; cf. the woman church's seat that changes to a chair in *Vis.* 1.2.2. Just such a chair is typical of school settings, but also of the synagogue: cf. the stone chair found in the synagogue of Ostia.

10 Rightly rejected by Eric G. Jay, "From Presbyter-Bishops to Bishops and Presbyters" (*SecCent* 1 [1981] 125–72 [145–46]), who does, however, see the gathering in *Mandate* 11 as a "coterie" of opposition.

11 Aune, *Prophecy,* 227 and 413 n. 226.

12 Page 536.

13 Compare 2 Pet 2:1. While the false prophet described in this chapter is grammatically masculine, early Christian prophets could also be female, whether true (Acts 21:9) or false (Rev 2:20).

14 Pages 536–37; followed by Snyder, 86–87. Compare Matt 2:1; Acts 13:6; the figure of Simon, etc.

15 L² *divinum*; L¹ *divinum spiritum*. Compare LXX Josh 18:22 (Balaam, negative); 1 Sam 6:2 (Philistines who speak the truth); Mic 3:7 (negative); Zech 10:2 (powerless Israelite diviners); Acts 16:16 (a girl with a divining spirit); Josephus *Ap.* 1.257–59; *Bell.*

1.79–80 (positive or neutral).

16 The term $\psi\epsilon\upsilon\delta o\pi\rho o\varphi\acute{\eta}\tau\eta\varsigma$ ("false prophet") seems to have been coined by the LXX, and thus continued in Christian Greek: J. Reiling, "The Use of ΨΕΤΔΟΠΡΟΦΗΤΗΣ in the Septuagint, Philo and Josephus," *NovT* 13 (1971) 147–56.

17 Against, Brox, 252. Dibelius (538–39), Reiling (*Hermas and Christian Prophecy,* 65–66), and Leutzsch (*Wahrnehmung,* 75–76) question whether this figure can be called a Gnostic, and all rightly answer in the negative.

18 Reiling, *Hermas and Christian Prophecy,* 34 n. 4; 73–96.

19 David Aune, "*Herm. Man.* 11.2: Christian False Prophets Who Say What People Wish to Hear," *JBL* 97 (1978) 103–4, in correction of Reiling (*Hermas and Christian Prophecy,* 37), for whom such an accusation is a "Hebrew-Christian judgment on divination."

20 *Man.* 5.2.7; cf. 5.2.1; 12.4.5, 5.2–4; *Sim.* 6.2.1; 9.19.2, 22.3.

21 Cf. LSJ, BAGD² *s.v.*; Brox, 254. Compare *4 Ezra* 7.25.

ascribed to them.[22] While the terminology is widely used in metaphorical senses, the particular way in which it is used here is uncommon.[23]

The second sentence of v. 3 could be understood in several different ways: ὃ γὰρ ἐὰν ἐπερωτηθῇ, πρὸς τὸ κένωμα τοῦ ἀνθρώπου ἀποκρίνεται. Whatever the false prophet is asked, he answers according to the emptiness of the person who asks;[24] or, according to his own emptiness; or, according to basic human emptiness in the absence of the divine spirit. In this worldview, the false prophet does not just concoct oracles like Lucian's *Alexander*; the prophetic gift is real, but from and allied with the wrong source. The ability of the false prophet to say true things is not surprising in view of the cultural belief that all spirits have access to information about human lives; in the Christian context, the difference lies in what they choose to do with it. Those spirits not allied with the true God are demonic, and thus will use their ability against God's servants.

■ **4** The first kind of response to the enticement of divination is from those who cannot be broken down by the evil spirit because they are strong in faith, and therefore not doubleminded. The first sentence of v. 4 is full of favorite terminology: ἰσχυροί . . . ἐν τῇ πίστει ("strong in faith");[25] ἐνδεδυμένοι τὴν ἀλήθειαν ("clothed with the truth");[26] κολλᾶν ("to adhere," in a relational sense);[27] and refrain (ἀπέχειν).[28] The second sentence describes the second kind of response by using language connected with the key notion of conversion: μετανοεῖν ("to change," "be converted"). The doubleminded do so often (πυκνῶς μετανοοῦσι): either they go through the actions of true conversion without lasting results (as in *Vis.* 1.1.9), or else the verb occurs here in one of its rare appearances with the more general meaning of changing one's mind, being changeable (as in *Vis.* 3.7.3). The

accusation of the sin of idolatry is one of the most serious that could be made. Significantly, it is directed not toward the false prophet, but toward those who consult him. As exemplified in this verse, bad spirits are usually spoken of in the plural, the good spirit in the singular.[29] Divination can be had about any kind of decision or question (περὶ πράξεώς τινος) affecting one's life.[30]

■ **5–6** The contrast between the spirit from God and that from elsewhere is cast here in the spatial framework of the two-level worldview predominant in antiquity. What is from above (ἄνωθεν) is necessarily superior to what is from the earth (ἐπίγειον).[31] The application to the functioning of prophecy is that all prophetic communication from the divine spirit comes not through human questioning or prompting, but directly and unplanned from the power of God. By contrast, the prophetic spirit that comes not from heaven but from earth and speaks through the false prophet is powerless to speak unless prompted.

■ **7–8** Now comes the central question, already partially answered: how to tell the two kinds of prophets apart (v. 7)? The author does not specify "true" prophet, who is simply a "prophet" (προφήτης) as distinguished from a "false prophet" (ψευδοπροφήτης). Obviously from what has just been said, one great difference is whether or not the prophet gives oracles to consulters, and this is Hermas' special bête noire. But there is yet another, time-honored criterion by which to test or discern (δοκιμάζειν) the true prophet, the criterion that places this discussion firmly within the early Christian tradition of discernment of prophecy: from the prophet's way of life

22 Irenaeus *Adv. haer.* 1.13.2–4; cf. 1.7.2 (Reiling, *Hermas and Christian Prophecy,* 41, 94, 103). Both reports characterize the prophet as "empty." Brox (252) considers direct dependence unlikely because of the differences in the two passages, but there are also similarities, e.g., that the prophet sent by God speaks only when God wants (compare v. 8).

23 Further discussion in Reiling, *Hermas and Christian Prophecy,* 38–41.

24 Translation: "according to the emptiness of the man who asked" (Snyder, 87); "selon la vanité de son interlocuteur" (Joly, 193); and most translations.

25 Compare *Vis.* 3.5.5 (not of those faithful from the

beginning, but of those who will be converted!); *Man.* 9.10.

26 On use of clothing language, see note on *Vis.* 4.1.5.

27 See discussion and note on *Vis.* 3.6.2.

28 Part of the repeated pattern of paraenesis in the *Mandates,* especially *Mandate* 8; but see also *Vis.* 1.2.4; 3.8.4.

29 Brox, 255.

30 For examples of the kinds of questions brought to Greco-Roman oracles, see Lucian *Alexander* 24–30, 48–54.

31 Compare *Man.* 9.11; Jas 1:17 and esp. 3:15; John 3:3, 12, 31.

(ἀπὸ τῆς ζωῆς).[32] The true prophet is exemplified by a catalog of virtues (v. 8a), among which are that he or she is meek and humble (πραῢς καὶ ἡσύχιος), as is the good angel (*Man.* 6.2.5), and excels in humility characterized as spiritual need of God, thus being "poorer" than anyone else (ἑαυτὸν ἐνδεέστερον ποιεῖ πάντων τῶν ἀνθρώπων).[33] This humility stands in contrast to typical descriptions of false prophets as "full of themselves" (v. 12),[34] whereas the true prophet is full of the holy spirit (v. 9). But again the original criterion from v. 5 is repeated: the true prophet refuses consultation and speaks only when inspired by God to speak.[35] Just as for 1 John it is incarnational Christology, for Hermas the ultimate test is this. This last part of v. 8 is in modified chiastic structure.[36]

■ **9–10** Another difference is what happens in the Christian assembly with the presence of the true prophetic spirit as contrasted with that of the spirit of false prophecy. The term for the Christian assembly here is unusual: the "synagogue (assembly) of just men" (συναγωγὴ ἀνδρῶν δικαίων, also vv. 13, 14). The use of "synagogue" for a Christian assembly is rare but attested, even relatively late and in distinctly non-Jewish Christian settings, so that nothing can be inferred from it about a Jewish source.[37] The use of the gender-specific ἀνήρ ("man") in the phrase, especially when the generic ἄνθρωπος ("human being") has just been used for the

person entering, is more puzzling, and must indicate a technical phrase whose origin, however, is unknown.[38]

In spite of the insistence throughout this chapter on the free action of the holy prophetic spirit in true prophecy, as contrasted to the oracular consultation of false prophecy, it does seem that something is done in the assembly to set the context for prophetic activity. When a group of just people of faith assembles and engages in intercessory prayer, true prophecy can happen—but only as God wishes. The freedom of God's prophetic spirit is still carefully preserved. The "angel of the prophetic spirit"[39] is generally identified with Ramiel, the angel in charge of prophetic visions, though no name is suggested here.[40] However, the interchangeability of angel and spirit in the pneumatology of the *Mandates* makes it unclear whether a specific angel is meant, like the "angel of conversion" in *Vis.* 5.7 (who is also the Shepherd), or whether this is only another set of terms for the spirit of God, who is the spirit of true prophecy in 11.5.[41] The "filling" of the person by the prophetic holy spirit continues the metaphor of emptiness and fullness carried on throughout the chapter.

The description given here raises the question whether it is a case of recognized "professional"

---

32 Besides this text, the other best discussions of the discernment of prophecy in early Christianity are: Matt 7:15–23; 1 John 4:1–3; *Didache* 11; *Act. Thom.* 79. With the exception of 1 John for whom the criterion is christological orthodoxy (and perhaps already 1 Cor 12:3), all others hold ethical responsibility as the major criterion of the true prophet. Discussion of these texts in Aune, *Prophecy*, 222–29.

33 Cf. comment at *Man.* 8.10 with further references.

34 Contrast Acts 8:9, and other examples given by Dibelius, 540.

35 Compare Irenaeus *Adv. haer.* 1.13.3: λαλοῦσιν ἔνθα καὶ ὁπότε θεὸς βούλεται, ἀλλ' οὐχ ὅτε Μάρκος κελεύει ("they speak where and when God wants, not when Marcus commands").

36 A οὐδὲ καταμόνας λαλεῖ ("neither does it speak alone")
    B οὐδὲ ὅταν θέλῃ ἄνθρωπος λαλεῖν ("nor when someone wants it to speak")
    C λαλεῖ τὸ πνεῦμα [τὸ] ἅγιον ("does the holy spirit speak")
    A' ἀλλὰ τότε λαλεῖ ("but it speaks")

B' ὅταν θελήσῃ αὐτὸν ὁ θεὸς λαλῆσαι ("when God wants it to speak")

37 E.g., Jas 2:2; Heb 10:25; Ignatius *Pol.* 4.2; Justin *Dial.* 63.5; Dionysios of Alexandria quoted in Eusebius *Hist. eccl.* 7.9.2; 11.11, 12, 17; *Act. Pet.* 9; assemblies of Shenoute's Coptic monks in the fifth century; an assembly of Marcionites in Lebaba, 318–19 CE. Cf. Dibelius-Greeven, *James*, 132–34.

38 Compare the similar "generation of just men" (γενεὰ ἀνδρῶν δικαίων) in *Sim.* 9.15.4.

39 *POxy* 1.5 L²E ἄγγελος τοῦ πνεύματος τοῦ προφητικοῦ (translation as given); A ἄγγελος τοῦ προφήτου ("angel of the prophet"); L¹ *nuntius sanctus divinitatis* ("holy angel of divinity").

40 *2 Bar.* 55.3; 63.6; *4 Ezra* 4.36 (Syr.); *1 Enoch* 20.8.

41 Or this figure, as well as the Shepherd, could be patterned on the "accompanying spirit" (πάρεδρος δαίμων), as ascribed by Irenaeus to the false prophecy of Marcus, though no such explicit connection is made by Hermas (Reiling, *Hermas and Christian Prophecy*, 87–91); Garrett, *Demise of the Devil*, 119–20 n. 30. See comment on *Vis.* 5.2.

prophets or rather the exercise of prophetic charismatic gifts by anyone in the community. The principle is clear that true prophecy is exercised only in the context of the community and only when the holy spirit wills. This does not clarify, however, who the true prophets are. Even though the terminology for true prophets is sometimes inexact as here, it seems likely from v. 7 that there are persons recognized as having the gift of prophecy, though the exercise of that gift resides in the community and may not be limited to such persons, any more than it is in 1 Cor 12–14.[42]

■ **11–12** Having described how the true prophetic spirit works in the legitimate Christian gathering, the author now contrasts how the spirit of false prophecy works. The catalog of vices applied to the false prophet in v. 12 and corresponding to the catalog of virtues for the true prophet in v. 8 is preceded by a few negative words, all of which have previously appeared, tossed in the direction of the false spirit itself in v. 11.[43] But the real criteria apply to the false prophet (v. 12), who is just the opposite of the humble true prophet of v. 8: proud and luxurious. His desire for precedence ($\pi\rho\omega\tau\sigma\kappa\alpha\theta\epsilon\delta\rho\iota\alpha$, literally, "to be seated first") may just mean prominence,

but in *Vis.* 3.9.7 it seems to mean desire for leadership and authority in the community, and could mean the same here.[44] The exercise of prophetic gifts, especially for personal guidance of community members through divination, could have been quite an enhancement for leadership positions.[45] The general sense of the description is traditional, though some of the terms are unusual.[46] Love of luxury ($\tau\rho\upsilon\phi\eta$) is for Hermas a sure sign of possession by a bad spirit.[47] The final proof is taking payment for prophecy: no money, no prophecy, something unimaginable for true prophets.[48] This seems to refer to the acceptance of direct payment and gifts for the prophecy, or perhaps even setting a fee, as was often done in oracular consultation.[49]

■ **13–15** The next two verses describe the behavior of the false prophet in relation to the common assembly. On the surface, the opening statements of the two verses seem to contradict each other: the false prophet avoids

---

42 In partial agreement with Brox (258–60); in partial disagreement with Reiling (*Hermas and Christian Prophecy*, 124–27), for whom there is no prophetic order in Hermas' church, but in complete agreement with his position that Hermas' theology of the presence of the holy spirit in the church "is not fundamentally different from that of the apostolic and early post-apostolic times" and "represents primitive Christian experience" (127). The meaning of *POxy* 1.5 containing comment on *Man.* 9.9–10a is obscure but relevant to this question and the interpretation of the text, and of the place of prophecy in the early church. See text and discussion in Reiling, 125 n. 2, and H. Paulsen, "Papyrus Oxyrhynchus I.5 und die ΔΙΑΔΟΧΗ ΤΩΝ ΠΡΟΦΗΤΩΝ," *NTS* 25 (1979) 443–53.

43 Reiling (*Hermas and Christian Prophecy*, 41–47) need not fret over the "logical impossibility" of the expression "empty spirit." "Empty" is consistently used in this chapter as a metaphor for powerless and futile (see comment on v. 3). The explanation that a human spirit is intended here (Brox, 260) is less satisfactory.

44 Cf. Irenaeus *Adv. haer.* 4.33.6, which assumes that the false prophet is in it for personal enhancement and gain.

45 For another opinion and further references, see

Brox, 260–61.

46 Reiling (*Hermas and Christian Prophecy*, 91–94) would see in the further associations of the terms $\iota\tau\alpha\mu\sigma\varsigma$ ("reckless"), $\alpha\nu\alpha\iota\delta\eta\varsigma$ ("shameless"), and $\pi\sigma\lambda\upsilon\lambda\alpha\lambda\sigma\varsigma$ ("talkative") suggestions of improper lack of restraint, as well as further evidence of the dependence of Irenaeus' Marcosian description on this chapter.

47 *Man.* 6.2.5; 8.3; 12.2.1; *Sim.* 6.2.1, 2.

48 In spite of the tradition that those who work for the gospel have a right to support from it (Luke 10:7; 1 Cor 9:13–14; 1 Tim 5:17–18). But this principle does not apply if these prophets are not in some way recognized as ministers who devote a considerable amount of time to the church.

49 Discussion in Reiling, *Hermas and Christian Prophecy*, 53–54. Compare the criteria for true and false prophets in *Didache* 11, which are more detailed and yet more ambiguous: here, too, the major criterion is behavior ($\alpha\pi\grave{o}$ $\tau\hat{\omega}\nu$ $\tau\rho\acute{o}\pi\omega\nu$, 11.8), which is to be according to the "ways of the Lord." The examples are: overstaying a welcome (11.5–6); ordering a meal and eating it; not living consistently with one's own true teachings (11.10); and asking for money for oneself, though asking for bread is acceptable (11.6), or asking money to be given to the needy (11.12).

the assembly[50] (v. 13), but enters it (v. 14). The first statement describes habitual behavior and associations; the second, what happens when he finds himself there anyway. The associations of the false prophet are with the "losers," for which Hermas' keyword is "empty," to whom he prophesies "in a corner" (κατὰ γονίαν), that is, in private or in secret, as contrasted to the open and public way in which the true prophet operates.[51] Again, the play on the emptiness of the false prophet versus the fullness of the true one enables the understanding of the first of a series of practical examples in v. 13b: empty pottery storage jars, or amphorae, stacked together do not break, presumably because they are all of the same weight and mass. They belong together, or more literally, make the same sound upon impact (συμφωνοῦσιν ἀλλήλοις).[52] Empty belongs with empty; they deserve each other.

However, the false prophet does eventually enter the common assembly where the true spirit of prophecy is active (contrast v. 9). Here the false prophet, full of the empty spirit of the devil, is in effect exorcised and left empty and speechless through the power of the holy spirit that is present. As in the human person in *Man.* 5.2.5–7, so also in the community assembly there is no room for both spirits in one container.

The second illustrated example takes up where the first left off (end of v. 13) with a commonsense observation. The first example illustrated the fact that empty belongs with empty. The second uses the case of one empty amphora placed among many that are full: the fullness of the others does not fill the one empty one. In spite of the obviousness of the example, it speaks loudly of the sharp division seen here between the power of good and the resistance to it on the part of evil. There is no common meeting ground.

■ **16–17** The conclusion to this part of the teaching reiterates the lesson of v 7: discern true from false prophets by their actions and way of life (δοκίμαζε οὖν ἀπὸ τῶν ἔργων καὶ τῆς ζωῆς), and put trust in the one who passes this test. For a similar structure, compare *Man.* 6.2.6.[53] The one who claims prophetic inspiration claims to be πνευματοφόρος ("bearer of spirit"), a familiar grammatical construction, but used only here with πνεῦμα ("spirit"). Its closest comparison in Christian literature is Ignatius of Antioch's self-ascribed appellative Θεοφόρος ("bearer of God"),[54] though there is no suggestion here that the expression is a proper name. Verse 17 is in familiar commandment form and could be the conclusion of the chapter without the sequel before the final conclusion (vv. 18–21). The verse packs in most of the opposition terms that have built the contrast in this chapter: power/from God, earthly/empty/powerless/from the devil (compare v. 3).

■ **18–19** Two series of two examples each make up the postscript after the first conclusion in v. 17. The first two (v. 18) concern the direction upwards, beginning from the earth, where the earthly, empty, false spirit must begin. The water pump in the example is the σίφων or *ctesibica machina,* carried on the shoulders and used by viticulturalists to water vineyards, but especially by *vigiles* (firefighters) in urban fire control.[55] Hermas' befuddlement (v. 19) highlights the contrast: both things are impossible (ἀδύνατα). The double meaning of the Greek word, "impossible" and "powerless," enables the play on impossible/powerless examples of impossible/powerless spirits.

■ **20–21** By contrast, that which comes from above, even if it seems small and insignificant like hail or a drop of water (v. 20), is actually quite powerful. On impact hail causes pain in the head out of proportion to its size, and

50 On the peculiar expression "assembly of just men" in vv. 13–14, see comment on v. 9.

51 Though divination is not usually associated with private occasions. Secrecy may also be part of the association carried by the term, as well as lack of credibility; cf. Reiling, *Hermas and Christian Prophecy,* 54–55, for further examples.

52 Joly, 197 n. 3. Since the issue here is true and false prophetic speech, the more literal meaning may be more apt.

53 But Hermas is fond of double comparisons: *Vis.* 3.2.1; *Man.* 5.1.4; 10.2.4; 11, 19; *Sim.* 2.7, 9; 5.7.4; 6.4.3.

54 Ignatius *Eph.* inscription; cf. William R. Schoedel, *Ignatius of Antioch* (Hermeneia; Philadelphia: Fortress, 1985) 36–37.

55 LSJ *s.v.*: siphon, waterspout, fire engine, and phallus. Two *siphonarii* were assigned to each Roman cohort of *vigiles.* Cf. Hero of Alexandria *Pneumatica* 1.28; Vitruvius *De agric.* 10.7; Pliny *Ep.* 10.33.2; further discussion and refs., Reiling, *Hermas and Christian Prophecy,* 56 n. 4; Gustav Hermansen, *Ostia: Aspects of Roman City Life* (Edmonton: University of Alberta, 1981) 207–25.

the slow persistence of water can wear through rock. The play on "above" and "below" (vv. 5–6) is again the basis of the comparison. The end of the simile is puzzling, for it assigns the divine spirit with the *least significant* things from above (τὰ ἄνωθεν ἐλάχιστα) that have a great effect. But for Hermas the holy spirit is not the driving force of Luke's Pentecost narrative, even though words like "power" (δύναμις) are applied to it; in fact, it flees when too much pressure is applied (*Man.* 5.1.3, 2.6)! It is rather a steady, quiet inspiration toward the good. At all events, Hermas' analogies are sometimes not to be pushed too far. The chapter closes with one of the familiar double commandment structures.[56]

---

56   Compare *Mandates* 8.12; 9.12.

12 Discernment of Desires

1 [44] 1/ He said to me: "Get rid of all evil desire from yourself, and put on the desire that is good and reverent, for if you are clothed with that desire, you will despise the evil desire and bridle it as you wish. 2/ For evil desire is wild and difficult to tame. It is fearful, and its wildness is very wearing on people. Especially if a servant of God falls into it without being aware, he or she can be extremely exhausted by it. It exhausts those who are not clothed with good desire, but embroiled in this world. These it hands over to death." 3/ "Which, sir," I said, "are the works of evil desire that hand people over to death? Tell me so that I can avoid them." "Listen," he said, "by which works evil desire kills the servants of God.

2 [45] 1/ "Taking precedence is desire for someone else's wife or husband, as well as for extravagant wealth, mad overeating and drinking, and many other stupid luxuries, for all luxury is stupid and empty for the servants of God. 2/ These desires are evil and kill the servants of God. This evil desire is the daughter of the devil. One must therefore stay away from evil desires, so that by staying away you [pl.] may live to God. 3/ But whoever are ruled by them and do not resist them will perish in the end, for these desires are deadly. 4/ But you [sing.], put on the right desire, and armed with the fear of the Lord, resist them. The fear of the Lord dwells in the good desire. If the evil desire sees you armed with the fear of the Lord and resisting it, it will flee to a distance out of sight from you, out of fear of your armor. 5/ So you, when you have conquered and have been crowned with victory over it, move toward the right desire, and handing over to it the victory you have achieved, serve it according to its wishes. If you serve the good desire and submit to it, you will be able to overcome evil desire and subdue it as you wish."

Rejection of Evil Desires

■ **1.1–3 [44]** The sections here are awkwardly divided. After an introduction (1.1), 1.1–3.1 treat of the two kinds of desire, good and evil, another use of the extended "two ways" structure that runs throughout the *Mandates*. The structure would be clearer if 1.1–2.3, on evil desire, constituted chapter 1, followed by 2.4–3.1 as chapter 2. Chapter 3 should begin at 3.2, which initiates an epilogue. Desire ($\epsilon\pi\iota\vartheta\upsilon\mu\iota\alpha$) is usually understood negatively, especially under Stoic influence.[1] But in Jewish-Christian context, Hermas realizes that not all desire is bad. This dualism of desires could well correspond to the good and bad יצר (desire or impulse) of Jewish two-ways moral teaching. Two images run through vv. 1–3: clothing or arming, and taming. The first is by now familiar language in *Hermas*.[2] The second employs in v. 1 $\chi\alpha\lambda\iota\nu\alpha\gamma\omega\gamma\epsilon\hat{\iota}\nu$, restraint and guiding of a horse through the bit, a metaphor often used of controlling the passions or the body.[3] In v. 2 the same idea is continued with a slight switch in metaphor: now passion is no longer a horse to be guided and controlled, but a fierce and dangerous wild animal that is not really

---

1   Also used this way in 8.5. For similar use in Philo, see references in Dibelius, 544.

2   See comment on *Vis.* 4.1.8.

3   Compare Jas 1:26; 3:2; BAGD *s.v.*; Dibelius-Greeven, *James*, 121, 184.

expected to submit to human control. Verse 3 is the familiarly phrased question that will lead to an explanation from the Shepherd about evil desire and how it is manifested.

Sample of Evil Desires

■ **2.1–3 [45]** The list of deadly evil desires (v. 1) seems fixated on the basics of adultery (using gender-inclusive language), food, and material possessions.[4] After the more subtle earlier teaching on the discernment of spirits in *Mandates* 5–11, this seems like "back to basics." A very similar description is given as the effect of bad temper in *Man.* 6.2.5. The diabolic filiation of evil desire (v. 2) is a small echo of more extended filiation patterns already familiar from previous passages.[5] The transition to a plural commandment at the end of v. 2 comes as a surprise, but it occurs for the familiar formula that usually ends a commandment: the promise of life toward God. The singular resumes in v. 4. The usual pattern in the *Mandates* inserts a plural commandment only at the end of a chapter. Its appearance here strengthens the

supposition that v. 3 should be the end of the first chapter. The expression $\epsilon i \varsigma \ \tau \acute{\epsilon} \lambda o \varsigma$ in v. 3 could mean that those who succumb to evil desires will perish "finally" or "completely."[6]

■ **2.4–5** These two verses are guided by the metaphor of clothing or arming as preparation for battle[7] and the military victory that follows.[8] The enemy is evil desire, and the armor is the fear of the Lord, the right kind of fear,[9] by which the believer can rout and conquer evil desire and be crowned with victory ($\sigma \tau \epsilon \varphi \alpha \nu \omega \vartheta \epsilon \acute{\iota} \varsigma$, v. 5), joining those who have merited their crown through suffering.[10] Good desire is personified as ruler and object of service, for the symbol of victory gained is handed over to it[11] and Hermas is to submit to it ($\dot{\upsilon} \pi o \tau \acute{\alpha} \sigma \sigma \epsilon \iota \nu$, the familiar NT language of submission)[12] so as to make evil desire submit to him. This idea stands in contrast to its opposite, allowing oneself to be a "slave of desire," a familiar rhetorical topos.[13] The text of the first part of v. 5 is uncertain, but the meaning seems to be rendered faithfully by the attempted reconstructions.[14]

---

4 This does not, however, lead to the conclusion that the instruction is only for the socially unimportant because it includes nothing about honor and status (Dibelius, 544). Other lists in 6.2.5, 8.3; 10.4, 5.2.2 include such concerns.

5 Doublemindedness is also daughter of the devil (*Man.* 9.9) and sister of sadness and bad temper (10.1.1); for relationships on the good side, cf. *Vis.* 3.8.5; *Tab. Ceb.* 16, 18, 21. Metaphors of filiation are known in both Jewish and Greco-Roman literature; cf. Hilhorst, *Sémitismes*, 144–47.

6 Use of the same expression in *Vis.* 3.7.2; *Sim.* 8.6.4; John 13:1 is equally ambiguous: in a process mode in which there is room for change until the eschatological end, as here, the two meanings are not that far apart. On the basis of the Ethiopic translation, Hilhorst (*Sémitismes*, 153) suggests that the original reading here was $\vartheta \alpha \nu \acute{\alpha} \tau \omega \ \dot{\alpha} \pi o \vartheta \alpha \nu o \tilde{\upsilon} \nu \tau \alpha \iota$ ("they die the death") as in *Sim.* 8.7.3.

7 Compare the clothing imagery in 1.1, which may be just that, or putting on armor for the struggle as here.

8 The predominant motif is military (compare Eph 6:10–17), but possibly an athletic victory is also combined into the symbols in v. 5; cf. 1 Tim 4:8; Dibelius, 545.

9 As opposed to fear of the devil (cf. *Mandate* 7).

10 *Sim.* 8.2.1; 3.6; compare Jas 1:12; Rev 2:10.

11 Compare 1 Cor 15:28; Rev 4:4,10. For Walter

Grundmann ("$\sigma \tau \acute{\epsilon} \varphi \alpha \nu o \varsigma$, $\sigma \tau \epsilon \varphi \alpha \nu \acute{o} \omega$," TDNT 7 [1971] 615–36 [633 with n. 98]), this passage is "a Christian version of the offering of the crown to the god in antiquity" (noticed by Brox, 274), but if the gesture really symbolized worship, it is doubtful that Hermas would have used it in this context. The use of crowns in Greco-Roman antiquity for athletes, banqueters, soldiers, and even prisoners of war on the slave block was so common, and the literature so extensive, that it is difficult to pinpoint the exact context. Cf. BAGD *s.v.*; Fiebiger, "Corona," PW 4 (1901) 1635–43; Ganszyniec, "Kranz," PW 11 (1922) 1588–1607.

12 E.g., Luke 2:51; 10:17; Rom 10:3; 13:1; 1 Cor 14:32; Col 3:18; Eph 5:21; 1 Pet 2:13.

13 References in J. Albert Harrill, "Ignatius, *Ad Polycarp* 4.3 and the Corporate Manumission of Christian Slaves," *JECS* 1 (1993) 107–42 (115 nn. 30–31). See especially Titus 3:3; Ignatius *Pol.* 4.3.

14 Lake (128) followed by Joly (200) suggests in A's lacuna before $\sigma \tau \epsilon \varphi \alpha \nu \omega \vartheta \epsilon \acute{\iota} \varsigma$ ("having been crowned"), $\nu \iota \kappa \acute{\eta} \sigma \alpha \varsigma \ \kappa \alpha \acute{\iota}$ ("having conquered and . . .") as opposed to the older emendation of G. Hollenberg, $\nu \tilde{\iota} \kappa o \varsigma \ \lambda \alpha \beta \acute{\omega} \nu \ \kappa \alpha \acute{\iota}$ ("having received the victory and . . ."), followed by Funk and Whittaker. For other minor differences of reconstruction in the sentence, see Dibelius, 545; Whittaker, 43; Brox, 275.

12 Concluding Instructions on the Commandments

3 [46] 1/ "I would like to know, sir," I said, "how I should serve the good desire." "Listen," he said, "act with justice and virtue, truth and fear of the Lord, faith and meekness, and all good qualities like these. Doing this, you will be a pleasing servant of God and you will live to God." 2/ Thus he finished the twelve commandments and said to me: "You have these commandments; continue in them and encourage the listeners, so that their conversion may be pure for the rest of the days of their life. 3/ Carefully complete this ministry that I am giving you and work at it steadily. You will be well received by those who are about to be converted and they will be convinced by your words. I will be with you and will compel them to take you seriously." 4/ I said to him: "Sir, these commandments are great, beautiful, honorable, and capable of gladdening the heart of the person who can keep them. But I do not know if these commandments can be kept by someone, because they are very difficult." 5/ He answered me: "If you presume they can be kept, you will keep them easily and they will not be difficult. If you already take it to heart that they cannot be kept by anyone, you will not keep them. 6/ Now I say to you: If you do not keep them, but neglect them, you will not have salvation, neither your children nor your household, because you have already decided for yourself that these commandments cannot be kept by anyone."

4 [47] 1/ He said these things to me very angrily, so that I was confused and quite afraid of him, for his appearance was changed, so that a person could not bear his wrath. 2/ But when he saw me completely disturbed and confused he began to speak to me more gently and joyfully, and said: "You silly, thick-headed, doubleminded fellow, don't you know the glory of God, how great, strong, and wondrous it is, since he created the world for humanity and all creation submits to humanity, to whom God has given every authority to rule everything under heaven? 3/ If then," he said, "the human person is lord of all God's creatures and rules them all, isn't it also possible to rule over these commandments?" He said, "The person who has God in one's heart can rule over all things and all of these commandments. 4/ But those who have the Lord on their lips while their heart is hardened and they are far from the Lord, for them these commandments are difficult and cumbersome. 5/ So you [pl.] who are empty and lightweight in the faith, put the Lord in your heart and you will know that nothing is easier or sweeter or tamer than these commandments. 6/ Return, you who continue in the commandments of the devil that are difficult, bitter, wild, and licentious, and do not fear the devil who has no power against you. 7/ I will be with you, the angel of conversion who rules over him. Do not fear him and he will flee from you."

5 [48] 1/ I said to him: "Sir, listen to a few words of mine." "Say whatever you want," he said. "A

150

person is eager to keep the commandments of God," I said, "and there is no one who does not entreat the Lord to be strengthened in his commandments and submit to them. But the devil is relentless and oppresses them." 2/ "He cannot," he said, "oppress the servants of God who hope in God with all their heart. The devil can wrestle with them but cannot throw them to the mat. If you resist him, he will flee from you conquered and shamed. But those who are empty fear the devil as if he had any power. 3/ When someone fills a quantity of pottery vessels with good wine, among them a few partially empty, he approaches the pots and gives no attention to the full ones because he knows they are full; rather, he focuses on those partially empty for fear that they have soured, for those partially empty quickly sour, and the taste of the wine is ruined. 4/ Just so, the devil approaches all the servants of God by tempting them. Those who are full of faith resist him with strength and he leaves them, not finding any place to enter. Then he goes to those partially empty, finds room to enter, and so does what he wants with them, and they become subject to him.

6 [49]   1/ "I, the angel of conversion, say to you [pl.]: do not fear the devil. For I was sent to be with you who are converted with all your heart and to strengthen you in the faith. 2/ Trust in God, you who have given up on your life because of sins and added to your sins, thus burdening your life, because if you turn to the Lord with your whole heart, do justice the remaining days of your life, and serve him correctly according to his will, your previous sins will be healed and you will be empowered to conquer the works of the devil. Do not fear the devil's threat at all; he is as weak as a tendon of a corpse. 3/ Listen to me and fear the one who can do everything, save and destroy; keep these commandments and you will live to God." 4/ I said to him: "Sir, now I have been empowered in all the right ways of the Lord, because you are with me. I know that you will shatter all the devil's power, and we shall rule over him and overcome all his works. And, sir, I hope to be able to keep these commandments that you have stipulated, with the Lord's strengthening." 5/ "You will keep them," he said, "if your heart is undefiled toward the Lord, and all who cleanse their hearts from the crazy desires of this world will keep them and will live to God."

■ 3.1 [46] This verse is really a conclusion to the discussion of the good desire that began at 2.4, and parallels the question put by Hermas to the Shepherd concerning evil desire at 1.3. The answer there was more extended (2.1–3). Here both question and answer are contained in the same verse. Whereas the answer in regard to evil desire was not expressed by a list of abstract vices, but rather by specific prohibitions about sex, food, and luxury, here the answer is expressed in a list of virtues and ends with the usual formula about life toward God. The first two qualities, justice and virtue ($\delta\iota\kappa\alpha\iota o\sigma\acute{u}\nu\eta$ $\kappa\alpha\grave{\iota}$

ἀρετή), constitute the overall category[1] of which the others (truth, fear of the Lord, faith, and meekness) are examples, with the generalized exhortation to do other deeds like these as conclusion.

■ **3.2–3** From this point until the end of the *Mandates* at 6.5, there are no more commandments introduced; this section forms an epilogue[2] or conclusion to all of the *Mandates*. Verses 2–3 are a final exhortation, followed by the question of the difficulty of keeping them (v. 4) and a long response with intermediate comment (5.1) and concluding comment (6.4) by Hermas. Both A and E considered the end of v. 3 to be the end of the *Mandates*,[3] even though the following material obviously relates to them. The commandments are numbered as twelve (v. 2), though there are of course many subcommandments within the twelve chapters, and in some, it would be difficult to say exactly which is the major commandment.

Hermas' responsibility to proclaim the commandments to others is called a "ministry" (διακονία), a remarkable expression that associates his charge with the growing terminology and practice of service in the early church, probably in a nontechnical sense, though the diaconal function undoubtedly existed in the Roman church at the time. Precisely because it is necessary to state that Hermas is to proclaim his message with the presbyters,[4] he is probably not one of them. That he may have been a deacon is possible, but this passage does not confirm it. The Shepherd's promise that Hermas will be well received by his hearers who are open to conversion, and that they will be persuaded to believe his words by a power from outside themselves, is the promise of prophetic efficacy.

■ **3.4–6** Hermas' very query about the difficulty of keeping the commandments (v. 4) shows his own incipient doublemindedness, which explains why it causes such a dramatic reaction on the part of the Shepherd (4.1–2).[5] The reference to "gladdening the human heart" is applied to the Law in the Psalms,[6] and the allusion here suggests a relationship between the two realms of commandments. In fact, the whole approach to the commandments in this chapter, though different in terminology, is reminiscent of Deuteronomy 30.[7] The rhetorical contrast all in one verse about the reception of the commandments is extreme: on the one hand, they are "great, beautiful, and honorable" (μεγάλαι καὶ καλαὶ καὶ ἔνδοξοι), and, on the other, they are difficult (σκληραί), from most uses of the word, "harsh, unpleasant" rather than conceptually difficult.[8]

The answer to Hermas' objection (v. 5) is a piece of psychological wisdom whose language may be inspired by Stoicism,[9] but whose lesson is universal: preconceptions determine outcome. The solemn warning (v. 6), though given in the singular, is meant for all, and is one of the clearest statements in the book that action must be consistent with faith. Once again Hermas' family enters the scene, as in *Vis.* 1.3.1; 2.2.3; *Man.* 2.7. The distinction between children and household here emphasizes Hermas' position as a Roman householder responsible not only for adult children but also for everyone else living under his roof.

---

1 Compare *Man.* 6.2.3.
2 Dibelius (546), for whom this section was inserted when the *Mandates* and *Similitudes*, originally joined (see *Vis.* 5.6), were separated.
3 A inserts Ἀρχή ("beginning") before v. 4; E inserts *finita sunt mandata duodecim. Initium similitudinum. Similitudo prima* ("The twelve mandates are ended. Beginning of the similitudes. First similitude"). For Joly (432), the copyists of A and E were deceived into thinking the *Similitudes* began here by the language of the beginning of v. 2. His suggestion, however (13) that the first *Similitude* contains no parable and really belongs to the conclusion of the *Mandates*, does not help, but Snyder (6–7) suggests that the *Similitudes* did indeed begin here originally, the example of the pottery vessels in 5.3 being the original first parable, modified when *Similitude* 9 was later inserted. Unless more insertions are

posited, however, it is then difficult to explain the continued discussion of keeping the commandments in 6.3–5. But even well into the *Similitudes*, Hermas is still worrying about keeping the commandments (*Sim.* 6.1).
4 *Vis.* 2.4.3.
5 Snyder, 90–91; Pierre Battifol, "Hermas et le problème moral au second siècle," *RB* 10 (1901) 337–51 (346).
6 Ps 18:9 LXX; cf. Ps 103:15 regarding bread and wine.
7 Especially Deut 30:6, 11, 15, 17–18, 20.
8 Compare 4.4: σκληρός καὶ δύσβατος, the latter meaning "difficult to get through."
9 Πρόθεσις ("prejudgment"), according to Dibelius (547), but the examples given (Epictetus 2.8.29; 4.6.26) are not compelling.

Conquest of the Evil Spirit

■ **4.1–3 [47]** The anger of the Shepherd (v. 1) can be compared to *Vis.* 3.8.9, in which the woman church seems to lose patience with her pedestrian recipient just before revealing an important part of the message. But here immediate reassurance and comfort (v. 2) follow, even though the epithets applied to Hermas are not complimentary. When Hermas is called doubleminded, however, it is not to be taken in the same way as in the case of those condemned or more seriously challenged for it. One almost gets the impression that these epithets are addressed to Hermas in a teasing way. The expression "his appearance was changed" ($\dot{\eta}$ $\mu o\rho\phi\dot{\eta}$ $\alpha\dot{\upsilon}\tau o\hat{\upsilon}$ $\dot{\eta}\lambda\lambda o\iota$-$\dot{\omega}\vartheta\eta$) echoes other appearance narratives,[10] so that not only the change to anger is intended here, but some kind of supernatural transformation that accents the centrality of the message to follow.[11] It begins with a reminder of the theme of Ps 8:6: creation has been placed by God under human dominion (v. 2), and continues with a clever bit of rhetoric (v. 3): cannot the one who has been set as master of everything else also master these commandments? The argument employs a play on words between $\kappa\acute{\upsilon}\rho\iota o\varsigma$ ("lord," "master") and $\kappa\alpha\tau\alpha\kappa\upsilon\rho\iota\epsilon\acute{\upsilon}\epsilon\iota\nu$ ("to master," "control"),[12] completed by the Shepherd's assurance at the end (v. 7) that he is the one who controls the devil ($\dot{o}$ $\kappa\alpha\tau\alpha\kappa\upsilon\rho\iota\epsilon\acute{\upsilon}\omega\nu$ $\alpha\dot{\upsilon}\tau o\hat{\upsilon}$).[13]

■ **4.4–7** In contrast to those who have the Lord in their heart and are thus able to keep the commandments (v. 3), those with hardened hearts who profess faith with their lips (v. 4) but have not taken it to heart[14] find the commandments too much; here they are $\sigma\kappa\lambda\eta\rho\alpha\grave{\iota}$ $\kappa\alpha\grave{\iota}$ $\delta\acute{\upsilon}\sigma\beta\alpha\tau o\iota$ ("harsh and difficult to carry through").[15] Verses 5–7 are an appeal in the plural addressed to the hearers. The use of "empty" ($\kappa\epsilon\nu o\acute{\iota}$) is surprising here (v. 5), given the total disdain with which it is used of false prophets and their followers in *Mandate* 11; apparently, even for them there is hope of change. Being empty and lightweight in faith is the opposite of being "full of faith,"[16] and the exhortation sounds quite active: not to invite God or the good spirit into your heart, but "Put the Lord into your heart" ($\vartheta\acute{\epsilon}\sigma\vartheta\epsilon\ldots\tau\grave{o}\nu$ $\kappa\acute{\upsilon}\rho\iota o\nu$ $\dot{\upsilon}\mu\hat{\omega}\nu$ $\epsilon\grave{\iota}\varsigma$ $\tau\grave{\eta}\nu$ $\kappa\alpha\rho\delta\acute{\iota}\alpha\nu$), so as to recognize that the commandments are not difficult at all, but rather easy to carry out.[17]

The last verses of chapter 4 through the end of *Mandate* 12 frequently discuss the efforts of the devil against the forces of good. The language and the thought world behind it presuppose an agonistic spirit world in which invisible forces of good and evil are engaged in a war, whose battleground extends into human hearts and motivations. The language bears similarities to that of magical divination, in which potentially malevolent spirits are subjugated and made to serve human purposes. At the same time, these passages give a good review of traditional Jewish and Christian moral teaching about the devil. The argument here is that of appearance contrary to fact: the commandments of God seem difficult, but are really easy (v. 5); those of the devil are the really difficult ones (v. 6), with negative adjectives heaped up to describe them. This is the first mention of commandments of the devil, but not of his powerlessness.[18] The Shepherd's self-identification as

---

10 Of the revealer: *Vis.* 5.4; *4 Ezra* 10.25; Luke 9:29 and parr. Of the recipient of revelation, but using the same verb as here: Dan 5:6, 9–10 (Belshazzar's reaction to the wall writing); 7:28 (Daniel's reaction to a revelation).

11 At the end of v. 2, A inserts apparently by error a long Wisdom prayer acknowledging God as creator of the universe. It bears no relationship to its context except as extended second person comment on the third person creation theme at the end of v. 2. Text in Lake, 130–31; Whittaker, 44.

12 Joly, 205 n. 2. The argument is that of Sir 15:14–20, which is itself an echo of Deuteronomy 30. See note on 3.4 above. The language of struggle and dominance (e.g., $\kappa\alpha\tau\alpha\kappa\upsilon\rho\iota\epsilon\acute{\upsilon}\epsilon\iota\nu$ ["overcome"] and $\kappa\alpha\tau\alpha\delta\upsilon\nu\alpha\sigma\tau\epsilon\acute{\upsilon}\epsilon\iota\nu$ ["oppress"]) is related to that of the effort to control demons in the magical texts:

13 Garrett, *Demise of the Devil*, 157 n. 30.

14 The language of control is very important in this context. See its recurrence in the summary at 6.4; comment below on 4.4–7.

14 Isa 29:13.

15 So A; Ath[2] $\delta\upsilon\sigma\kappa\alpha\tau\acute{o}\rho\vartheta\omega\tau o\iota$ ("difficult to keep straight") would also fit.

16 *Man.* 5.2.1; 12.5.4.; Brox, 278.

17 Cf. Matt 11:29–30; 1 John 5:3.

18 *Man.* 7.2, and later 12.5.2; 6.1–4.

angel of conversion (ὁ ἄγγελος τῆς μετανοίας)[19] is accompanied by the theophanic promise[20] to be with all who aspire to the commandments of God rather than those of the devil, and the promise that the devil will flee from those who know better than to fear him.[21] Verses 4.7 through 6.1 form an inclusion of which most is located in chapter 5. The promise of the supporting presence of the angel of conversion and the directive not to fear the devil (4.7; 6.1) frame the objection that the devil is powerful but not against the faithful (5.1–2; 5.4). In the center, only the empty, like partially empty wine jars, fear the devil (5.2b–3).

Parable of the Jars

■ **5.1–2 [48]** Verse 1 is the fourth intervention of Hermas in this conversation, twice before to ask about the works of bad and good desire (1.3; 3.1), and once to question whether the commandments are not too difficult to keep (3.4). This time the objection concerns the power of the devil to subject the believers to trial, notwithstanding the assurance that has just been given that the devil is powerless against those who fear only God (4.6–7). Here the devil himself is σκληρός ("harsh," "bitter"), not only his commandments. The image in v. 2 comes from the sport of wrestling. But the Shepherd assures Hermas (v. 2), according to traditional demonology, that the devil cannot win against the faithful person who resists, only against the empty—or, as the following example would have it, the partially empty.[22]

■ **5.3–4** The final everyday example of the *Mandates*[23] continues the tendency to use material space as image

for a site of spiritual activity. In this case, wine jars are the material objects used. Those full and sealed will continue to store well, but those that have been opened to the air risk turning sour. Those jars not full are ἀπόκενα, usually meaning completely empty, but the sense of the example demands the meaning "partially empty,"[24] for if they were completely empty, there would be no wine in them to turn sour. The example is only that, an example, not an allegory: the devil does not correspond to the wine steward, but more attention is to be focused on those jars not full. That is where the problem will lie. Those that are full leave no room[25] for the devil to enter, but those that are partially empty have space for him to enter and enslave them. What they are not full of is faith; they are the doubleminded.

Encouragement to Conquer the Devil

■ **6.1–2 [49]** Two inclusive structures form chapter 6, the first overlapping with a larger inclusion from 4.7.[26] It consists of vv. 1–2, in which the admonition not to fear the devil (vv. 1a, 2b) frames the appeal to full conversion and promise of the healing of sin (v. 2). The appeal in v. 2 is to faith as trust, the opposite of doublemindedness. Even those who through sin have apparently given up their chances (lit., given up their life, ἀπεγνωκότες τὴν ζωὴν ὑμῶν, a play on the meaning of "life"),[27] if they turn to the Lord with a full heart,[28] can be healed. Not only is the devil then powerless, but those who experience full conversion will have complete power over his effects. Thus the power of conversion and thus the startling but reassuring image of the devil as impotent as

---

19 *Vis.* 5.7.
20 Exod 3:12; Isa 43:2; Acts 18:10; see also 6.1 below.
21 *Man.* 5.2; James 4:7; *T. Dan* 5.1; *T. Iss.* 7.7; *T. Naph.* 8.4.
22 L[1] adds the following helpful comment at the end of v. 2: *diabolus autem temptat servos dei, et si invenerit vacuum, exterminat* ("But the devil tempts the servants of God, and if he finds something empty, he wipes it out").
23 The others at 5.1.2, 5; 11.13, 15, 18, 20.
24 As understood by L[1] and Origen (*Comm. Matt.* ser. 59; GCS 58, 135.25) as *semiplenas* ("half full"), perhaps rendering ὑπόκενα. "Empty," Crombie, 29; "Half empty," Lake, 135; "(halb)leere," Dibelius, 548; "pas tout à fait pleines," Joly, 207; "not full," Snyder, 92; "(halb) leer," Brox, 270.
25 Compare 5.2.5, where there is not enough room in one vessel for both kinds of spirits.
26 The promise of presence on the part of the Shepherd (the angel of conversion) appears here for the third time, after *Vis.* 5.2, 7; *Man.* 4.7 (see comment there).
27 For the same expression, see *Vis.* 1.1.9 and comment there (where the image of healing as forgiveness of sin also appears); *Sim.* 9.26.4.
28 Jer 24:7; Joel 2:12.

the tendon of a corpse (ἄτονος γάρ ἐστιν ὥσπερ νεκροῦ νεῦρα).

■ **6.3–5** The second inclusive structure is composed of the repeated formula "live to God" (ζῆν τῷ θεῷ, vv. 3, 5), which frames a summary of the whole epilogue, indeed of all the *Mandates*: the power of the commandments, control of the devil's power,[29] and hope in the ability, with the help of God, to keep the commandments (v. 4).

Rather than fear the devil, who is really powerless (v. 3), believers should fear the one who has real power to save and destroy, God.[30] This fear of the Lord is lived out in keeping the commandments. The final promise (v. 5) sums up the content of the positive aspect of conversion: the purification of desire is the task of the life of faith, and the pure of heart shall see God.[31]

---

29 Note again (see comment on 4.4–7) the language of conflict and victory in regard to the devil: "to break up" (συγκόπτειν), "overcome" (κατακυριεύειν), and "overpower" (κατισχύειν).

30 Luke 6:9; Jas 4:12; cf. Matt 10:28; Luke 9:24.

31 Matt 5:8.

Similitude 1

1

A Tale of Two Cities

[50] 1/ He said to me: "You [pl.] know that you, the servants of God, live in a foreign land, for your city is far away from this city. So if you are aware of your own city in which you are about to live, why do you arrange for fields, costly arrays, buildings, and silly housing arrangements? 2/ The one who sets up these things in this city does not expect to return to one's own city. 3/ You stupid, double-minded, unfortunate person, do you [sing.] not see that all these things are alien and under the control of someone else? The lord of this city will say: `I do not want you to live in my city, so leave this city, because you do not use my laws.' 4/ Then you who have fields and houses and many other possessions, when he throws you out, what will you do with field and house and all the rest that you have prepared for yourself? For the lord of this land rightly says to you: `Either use my laws or leave my land.' 5/ Then what will you do, since you have a law in your own city? Because of your fields and the rest of your possessions, will you completely deny your law and proceed according to the law of this city? Watch out lest it be futile to deny your law, for if you wish to go back to your city, you will never be received back, because you have denied the law of your city and will be shut out of it. 6/ So you, watch out: as one living in a foreign place, arrange no more for yourself than what is necessary and be ready, so that when the master of this city wants to expel you for resistance to his law, you will leave his city and go out to your own city and use your own law gladly and without harm. 7/ Watch out, then, you [pl.] who serve the Lord and hold him in your heart. Do the works of God, remembering the commandments and promises made by God, and trust that God will keep them if his commandments are kept. 8/ So instead of fields, buy suffering souls, as each one can, and take charge of widows and orphans and do not neglect them, but spend your wealth and all possessions that you have received from God for such fields and houses. 9/ This is why the Master has made you wealthy, in order to carry out these ministries for him. It is much better to buy such fields, possessions, and houses, which you [sing.] will find in your city when you arrive there. 10/ This wealth is full of beauty and happiness; it brings no sadness or fear, but rather joy. So do not deal with the wealth of outsiders. It is unhelpful for you [pl.], the servants of God. 11/ Deal with your own wealth, in which you can rejoice, and do not imitate or touch what is alien, or even desire it, for it is evil to desire what is alien to you. Just do your [sing.] own work, and you will be saved."

The *Similitudes* or parables are already verbally linked to the *Mandates* in *Vis.* 5.5, and again at *Sim.* 9.1. Thus the two sections together constitute the revelation of the Shepherd, in contrast to *Visions* 1–4, which are the revelation of the church. Further evidence of the close connection of *Mandates* and *Similitudes* is the speech of the Shepherd at the opening of *Similitude* 1 without introduction. There is ample concern for the keeping of the commandments in the *Similitudes* (especially *Sim.* 5–9),[1] and parabolic material occurs in the *Mandates*. While some of the *Similitudes* are sustained metaphors or allegories, for example, the first and the second, some also contain extended didactic dialogues. The distinctions are not hard and fast, therefore; they are literary divisions rather than genre delineations. In the manuscript tradition, there was understandably some confusion about exactly where the second division began,[2] and about the numbering of the *Similitudes*.[3] But this evidence that stands in contradiction to the present arrangement is probably secondary.

1–2 [50] This parable of the two cities is the author's clearest articulation of his view of the Christian's place in society. Its "homiletic" style[4] of plural address in v. 1, alternating with the rhetorical singular in vv. 3–6, 9b, 11b, sets a challenging tone that forces reflection on the tension between eschatology and historical rootedness. The idea that Christians live in the world as if in a for-

eign land is already a traditional eschatological motif,[5] inherited from the Platonic and Stoic philosophical tradition, and perhaps also from the Jewish diaspora experience.[6] Whether the present city is Rome[7] or the world in general, the lord of the city the Roman emperor or the devil (v. 3),[8] depends on whether a political critique is meant, which seems unlikely, though the threat of martyrdom or at least economic persecution cannot be excluded in v. 3, and it is not totally out of the question that memories of clashes between Roman Jews and the government under Tiberius and Claudius are invoked.[9] The emphasis of the argument is not on the evil of this city but on the contingency of Christians' existence in it and the greater allegiance they owe to the other city which is their own—the eschatological one, represented now by the church.[10] The rhetorical question at the end of the verse includes real estate property and the flaunting of wealth ($\pi\alpha\rho\alpha\tau\acute{\alpha}\xi\epsilon\iota\varsigma$ $\pi o\lambda\upsilon\tau\epsilon\lambda\epsilon\hat{\iota}\varsigma$),[11] the "conspicuous consumption" necessary to maintain social status and therefore honor—one of the author's major themes.[12]

Verse 2 warns that the tension between the two cities leads a person to prefer one over the other: the one who would settle in comfortably here[13] either "cannot" or, better, "does not anticipate"[14] to return to one's true city.

1   *Sim.* 1.7; 5.1.5; 3.3, 5, 5.3; 6.1.2–4, 6.2; 7.6–7 (this and 8.11.3–4 sounding very much like the conclusion of a *Mandate*); 8.3.8, 6.6, 7.5–6, 8.2, 11.3–4; 9.1, 14.5, 23.2, 29.2, 33.3, 10.1.2–3, 2.4, 3.1, 4; 4.1.

2   See comment on *Man.* 12.3.3.

3   Most clearly set out by Snyder, 6–7.

4   Brox, 284.

5   E.g., especially Phil 3:20; Heb 11:13–16; 12:22–24; 13:14; also John 14:2–3; Eph 2:19; 1 Pet 1:1, 17; 2:11; *1 Clem.* prescript; Polycarp *Phil.* prescript; *Mart. Pol.* prescript; *2 Clem.* 5–6; *Diogn.* 5.4–5, 9; 6.7–8.

6   Suggested by Dibelius (550), with reference to Philo *Conf. ling.* 76; *Cher.* 120; *Agric.* 65. See extensive discussion and further references in Dibelius, 550–51; Leutzsch (*Wahrnehmung*, 192–210) minimizes Platonic-Stoic influence and stresses Jewish motifs (e.g., *Sib. Or.* 5.159–60, 414–46; *4 Ezra* 3.1–2, 28, 31; *2 Bar.* 11.1–2; 67.1–9; Rev 12; 14:8; 16:17–21; 17:1–21:27).

7   Zahn (*Der Hirt*, 121–24, cited in Joly, 210–11 n. 2, 432–33) entertains this judgment as "pas interdit"

("not forbidden"), but seems to prefer a more allegorical interpretation; Snyder's opinion (94–95) following Zahn that the two cities are church and state is anachronistically institutionalized.

8   Dibelius, 551.

9   Under Tiberius, 19 CE: Dio Cassius *Hist.* 57, 17, 5a; Tacitus *Ann.* 2.85; Josephus *Ant.* 18.81–84; Suetonius *Tib.* 36; cf. Seneca *Ep.* 108.22. Under Claudius, prohibition of assembly: Dio Cassius *Hist.* 60.6.6 (probably in 41 CE); expulsion: Suetonius *Claud.* 25.4 (probably in 49 CE).

10   While to characterize the opposition as that between church and state is overdrawn, both the presence of the church as alternative community and its transcendent symbols of the woman and the tower from the *Visions* represent the preferred city.

11   An unusual use of $\pi\alpha\rho\acute{\alpha}\tau\alpha\xi\iota\varsigma$, normally meaning a battle array (cf. LSJ *s.v.*), but used similarly in Aschines *In Ctesiphontem* 1; Demosthenes *Contra Leocharem* 3 (cited by Dibelius, 551).

12   Osiek, *Rich and Poor*, especially 39–57.

13   $E\iota\varsigma$ $\tau\alpha\acute{\upsilon}\tau\eta\nu$ $\tau\grave{\eta}\nu$ $\pi\acute{o}\lambda\iota\nu$: "into" this city, or simply

■ **3** The vehemence and number of the epithets underscore the emphasis placed on the lesson given here.[15] Accumulating earthly wealth is one of the best ways to demonstrate doublemindedness. The branding of such things as "alien" ($\grave{\alpha}\lambda\lambda\acute{o}\tau\rho\iota\alpha$) and under another's authority is part of the traditional contrast[16] and is consonant with the author's dualism already developed in the *Mandates*. The identity of the lord of this city need not be decided between the Roman emperor and the devil, nor are the laws of this city to be identified with Roman law.[17] In spite of the "commandments of the devil" followed by some,[18] Hermas is more optimistic about the presence of God's spirit in the world and in Christians than to imply here that the devil controls the world. Rather, this is a point at which the story is more parable than allegory, so that a strict correspondence of every character need not be found. In the story world, cities have rulers and laws,[19] which lend themselves easily to the flow of the story.[20] The conflict between concerns of this world and those of the next is then cast in terms of the ruler's right to insist on obedience to the local laws.

■ **4–5** The metaphor of competing laws continues. Some kind of persecution may be envisioned,[21] but nothing of its specific nature can be inferred from the story. The point is the sheer vanity of amassing worldly treasure when a choice for one world or the other, each with its own value system, looms ahead. Denial of one's own law or values (v. 5) is $\grave{\alpha}\sigma\acute{v}\mu\varphi o\rho o\nu$ ("unprofitable," "inexpedient," "unwise"), a surprisingly mild term to use here, but its occurrence elsewhere in *Hermas* indicates a more serious meaning.[22] The story line about the hearers' true citizenship requires that their city be their place of origin, to which they will someday wish to return. This is not to be allegorized into a Gnostic theology of heavenly origins, but is rather an acknowledgment of the true home of Christians.

■ **6–7** The triple exhortative warning, $\beta\lambda\acute{\epsilon}\pi\epsilon(\tau\epsilon)$ ("see to it," "take heed"), that began in the middle of v. 5 continues at the beginning of vv. 6 and 7. Verse 6 recalls the motif of v. 3, the inevitability of expulsion from the city in which Christians are not citizens. Once again, the emphasis is placed on the hindrance of too many possessions in that crucial moment. Readiness requires limitation of possessions to what is adequate, and nothing more. The redoubled expression $\tau\grave{\eta}\nu\ \alpha\grave{v}\tau\acute{\alpha}\rho\kappa\epsilon\iota\alpha\nu\ \tau\grave{\eta}\nu\ \grave{\alpha}\rho\kappa\epsilon\tau\acute{\eta}\nu$ ("the sufficient sufficiency")[23] adds emphasis. The Stoic virtue of $\alpha\grave{v}\tau\acute{\alpha}\rho\kappa\epsilon\iota\alpha$, independence based on minimal needs, is adapted here;[24] vv. 8–9 will suggest the best way of disposing of unnecessary goods, so that the ideal of spiritual freedom and that of social responsibility are brought together in a distinctively Jewish and Christian way. The one who follows these instructions will not be weighted down with possessions, but can easily make the transition from one city to the other.[25] The beginning of v. 7, the third "see to it" exhortation, resumes the second person plural from v. 1 and situates the correct response not according to the "law" ($\nu\acute{o}\mu o\varsigma$) terminology of the chapter but according to that of the *Mandates*, commandments ($\grave{\epsilon}\nu\tau o\lambda\alpha\acute{\iota}$).

■ **8–9** The preferred use of money is works of charity, by which wealth given by God is used in the intended way.

---

14 "in," given the propensity of Hellenistic Greek in general and Hermas in particular to substitute $\grave{\epsilon}\nu$ ("in") for $\epsilon\grave{\iota}\varsigma$ (see comment on *Vis.* 1.1.1).

14 $\Delta\acute{v}\nu\alpha\tau\alpha\iota$ A ("to be able"), but the LL *cogitat* ("intend") and E "wish to" verify Ant. $\pi\rho o\sigma\delta o\kappa\tilde{\alpha}$ ("anticipate," "expect to"), which better fits the author's intent as well. So too Joly, 210–11; Snyder, 94.

15 Compare the Shepherd's exasperation in *Man.* 12.4.2, where two of the same epithets, $\check{\alpha}\varphi\rho o\nu$, $\delta\acute{\iota}\psi v\chi\epsilon$ ("stupid," "doubleminded"), also occur.

16 Compare Epictetus *Discourses* 3.22.38, but especially *Enchir.* 1.1–4; *2 Clem.* 5.5–6.

17 See comment on v. 1, above.

18 *Man.* 12.4.6–7, appealed to by Brox (286).

19 Not a classical Greek democracy, but a Hellenistic monarchy is envisioned here: Leutzsch, *Wahrnehmung*, 201.

20 Compare the use of God's law in *Sim.* 8.3.

21 *Vis.* 3.2.1; 6.5 make this likely.

22 Compare *Man.* 4.3.6; 5.1.4, 2.2; 6.2.6.

23 "A sufficient competence," Lake, 141; "(no) more than is necessary to be self-sufficient," Snyder, 95; "rien de plus que le strict nécessaire," Joly, 213; "nicht mehr als den ausreichenden Unterhalt für dich," Brox, 284.

24 Compare *Man.* 6.2.3; 2 Cor 9:8; Phil 4:11; 1 Tim 6:6; cf. Osiek, *Rich and Poor*, 53–55; Leutzsch, *Wahrnehmung*, 203–5.

25 Either "unhindered and gladly" ($\grave{\alpha}\nu\nu\beta\rho\acute{\iota}\sigma\tau\omega\varsigma\ \kappa\alpha\grave{\iota}\ \grave{\alpha}\gamma\alpha\lambda\lambda\iota\omega\mu\acute{\epsilon}\nu\omega\varsigma$ A) or "unhindered, rejoicing" (*sine iniuria hilaris* [$\grave{\alpha}\nu\nu\beta\rho\acute{\iota}\sigma\tau\omega\varsigma\ \grave{\alpha}\gamma\alpha\lambda\lambda\iota\acute{\omega}\mu\epsilon\nu o\varsigma$] LLE).

The first level of meaning of ἀγοράζετε ψυχὰς θλιβομένας ("purchase oppressed souls") relates to simple helping of those in need, as suggested by the following allusion to widows and orphans, the classic objects of charity.[26] It may mean further the ransoming of prisoners[27] and/or the providing of funds for the manumission of Christian slaves. The dominant metaphor in the statement is purchase, however, so nothing definite can be construed about these practices here.[28] Verse 9 states the main point of the chapter: wealth in itself is from God, and therefore good, but it is given for a definite social purpose, not to be enjoyed selfishly. This central statement (v. 9a) is enclosed by allusions to the more valuable kind of property (vv. 8b, 9b). Deeds that fulfill this divine purpose are services or "ministries" (διακο-

νίαι). The syntax is especially rough here, for the sentence begins with plural address and ends in the singular, with the plural resumed in v. 10.

■ **10–11** While material wealth brings worry and concern about security, this kind of wealth is life-giving[30] and free of sadness (λύπη). Verse 10b sets the opposition in different terminology: the (material) wealth of the outsiders versus your own (spiritual) wealth. Its unhelpfulness for believers (v. 10c) is the end of the thought unit and perhaps the original end of the chapter. Verse 11 introduces a new and extraneous exhortation against covetousness and theft. Thus the first *Similitude* ends with a commandment not unlike those that frequently appear in the *Mandates*.

26   Jas 1:27; *Man.* 8.10; *Sim.* 5.3.7; further references in Dibelius, 527; Osiek, *Rich and Poor*, 62 n. 13. See the use of the metaphor of buildings for charity in *Act. Thom.* 19–25.

27   Ignatius seems to allude contemporaneously to just this practice in the Roman church, which he does not want in his case (*Rom.* 1.2; 2.1; 4.1); cf. Osiek, "Ransom," 381–82.

28   Osiek, "Ransom," 371–72. But compare the more specific exhortation in *Man.* 8.10; see comments there.

29   Compare *Man.* 2.6; *Sim.* 2.7 with economic meaning for Christians in general; *Sim.* 26.2; 27.2 for designated church leaders.

30   Literally, "beautiful and joyful" (καλὴ καὶ ἱλαρά), as is fasting in *Sim.* 5.3.8; Lake's ἱερά here ("holy," "sacred," 140) is a misprint.

31   Therefore perhaps to be contrasted to the extended treatise on sadness in *Mandate* 10.

2   **Elm and Vine**

[51]   1/ As I was walking in the country taking notice of an elm and a vine and thinking about them and their fruits, the Shepherd appeared to me and said, "What are you pondering within yourself regarding the elm and the vine?" "I am thinking, sir," I said, "that they are well fitted to one another." 2/ "These two trees," he said, "are a symbol of the servants of God." "I would like to know," I said, "the symbol of these trees of which you speak." "Do you see," he said, "the elm and the vine?" "I see them, sir," I said. 3/ "This vine," he said, "bears fruit, but the elm is a barren tree; but this vine, if it does not grow up the elm, cannot bear much fruit lying on the ground, and the fruit it bears, it bears rotten when it does not hang upon the elm. But when the vine is cast upon the elm, it bears fruit both from itself and from the elm. 4/ So you see that the elm gives much fruit, not less than the vine, but rather more." "How, sir, is it more?" I said. "Because," he said, "the vine hanging upon the elm gives fruit that is plentiful and good, but when it lies on the ground it bears little and rotten fruit. So this parable refers to the servants of God, poor and rich." 5/ "How, sir?" I said, "Show me." "Listen," he said. "The rich person has money, which is poor in the sight of the Lord, and is distracted about wealth. Such a person's petition and praise are therefore very small in the sight of the Lord, and what he or she has is weak and small and has no holy power. So when the rich person relies upon the poor person and supplies to him or her what is needed, the rich person believes that whatever is done to the poor will be able to find its reward from God; for the poor person is rich in prayer of petition and praise, and his or her intercession has great power before God. Therefore the rich person supplies everything to the poor one without hesitating. 6/ So the poor one, sustained by the rich, prays to God in thanksgiving for the one who gives; and the rich person is continually concerned about the poor, that the poor may continue unceasing in life, for the rich one knows that the prayer of the poor is acceptable and rich in the sight of the Lord. 7/ So both together complete the work: the poor person works at intercession, being rich in this gift received from the Lord, and returns it to the Lord who sustains him or her. Likewise the rich person, with the wealth received from the Lord, supports the poor without hesitation. Now this work is great and right before God, because this rich one understands about wealth and has used the gifts of the Lord for the poor and accomplished the ministry rightly. 8/ Thus to human eyes the elm seems not to bear fruit, but they do not know that when drought comes the elm which has water nourishes the vine, and the vine having an uninterrupted flow of water produces double fruit, both for itself and for the elm. Likewise the poor by interceding for the rich before the Lord supply what is lacking to their

wealth, and again the rich by furnishing to the poor what they need supply what is wanting to their souls. 9/ So both are partners in the work of justice. Therefore the one who does these things will not be abandoned by God but will be enrolled in the books of the living. 10/ Blessed are those who have possessions and understand that their wealth is from the Lord; for the one who understands this will also be able to render some good service."

■ 1 [51][1] The structure of the chapter is complex and not altogether clear. Verses 1–4c, 8a contain the description or parable proper; vv. 4d–7, 8b–10 the application.[2] In contrast to the first *Similitude* on one hand, which employs a metaphor without visual representation, and symbolic visions like that of the tower in *Vision* 3 on the other, which derive their meaning from a vision, the parable of the elm and the vine is a real and not unusual sight from which springs a symbolic interpretation mediated by the Shepherd who appears *in situ*. Though the elm and the vine are presented in the singular, the intended setting is undoubtedly an *arbustum*, a vineyard in which vines are supported by young elm trees specially trimmed for the purpose. This method of viticulture was common in central Italy, where it is still sometimes used, especially in private settings.[3] The method was fully described by Pliny the Elder[4] and Columella,[5] and was a motif used by Roman writers for romance, marriage, and divorce;[6] it appears in later Christian writers,

in probable dependence on *Hermas*.[7] Hermas sees the vine either wound around or tied onto the elm branches. Both because of the agricultural need to match the same level of maturity on the part of both elm and vine, and because of the known literary use of the motif for human relationship, it is not surprising that he observes their close and fitting relationship.

■ 2–3 The Shepherd introduces in v. 2 the application that is the teaching of the chapter: the two elements are a "type" ($τύπος$) of believers. The pattern of question and answer familiar from the *Visions* proceeds. The supposed barrenness of the elm that bears no visible or edible fruit (v. 3) is an obvious contrast to the lush grapevine that produces one of the staples of the Mediterranean diet. The focus on the fruit, and especially on the cooperation of both to bear better fruit, is the insight of Hermas.[8]

■ 4 Through the cooperation of elm and vine—and with a little rhetorical exaggeration[9]—the elm can be said to

1   Most MSS. read here either "another parable" or "second parable" (L²); only E has "beginning."

2   Simpler outline in Dibelius, 553: vv. 1–4 parable; vv. 5–7 application; vv. 8–10 epilogue; but the chapter is more complicated than that. Cf. further structural suggestions in Osiek, *Rich and Poor*, 142–45, including an elaborate chiastic pattern developed by Kendrick Grobel, "The Shepherd of Hermas, Parable II," in Richmond C. Beatty et al., eds., *Vanderbilt Studies in the Humanities* (Nashville: Vanderbilt University Press, 1951) 1.50–55.

3   I have seen it in private gardens several times on back roads in Lazio and Umbria.

4   *N.H.* 17.35.19 passim.

5   *De arbor.* 16.

6   E.g., Ovid *Metam.* 14.661–68; Catullus 62.48–57.

7   Clement of Alexandria *Strom.* 6.15.19; Origen *Hom. on Josh.* 10.1; Commodianus *Inst.* 1.30.15–16; Ps.-Chrysostom *Hom. on Matt.* 13; perhaps Caesarius of Arles *Hom.* 24. Discussion in Peter Demetz, "The Elm and the Vine: Notes toward the History of a

Marriage Topos," *Proceedings of the Modern Language Association of America* 73 (1958) 521–32; Osiek, *Rich and Poor*, 78–90, 146–53; J. A. McGuckin, "The Vine and the Elm Tree: The Patristic Interpretation of Jesus' Teachings on Wealth," *Studies in Church History* 24 (1987) 1–14; Leutzsch, *Wahrnehmung*, 113–26. Grobel's argument ("Parable II") that this parable is conclusive evidence of the central Italian origin of *Hermas* cannot be sustained (Hilhorst, *Sémitismes*, 13; Leutzsch, *Wahrnehmung*, 113). Yet this form of viticulture was certainly characteristic of, if not unique to, central Italy.

8   Leutzsch, *Wahrnehmung*, 123. In spite of the awkwardness of the Greek, οὐ δύναται καρποφορῆσαι πολὺ ἐρριμμένη χαμαί in the second sentence of v. 3 must mean that the vine "cannot bear much fruit, lying on the ground," that is, πολύ ("much") must modify "bear fruit" rather than "lying on the ground"; see Brox, 293 n. 4 for discussion and rejection of the alternative.

9   Brox, 293.

bear more fruit than the vine because it is the agent or facilitator of the vine's production (v. 4). The final statement of v. 4 is really the introduction to the application that occupies the remainder of the chapter. While the potential application to the servants of God has already been introduced in v. 2, the naming of poor and rich appears here for the first time, and with terminology not typical of *Hermas* as a whole.[10] The traditional and majority interpretation has been to allegorize the parable in such a way that the elm symbolizes the rich and the vine, the poor, but it is sometimes argued that the reverse is intended.[11] Different parts of the chapter lend themselves better to one interpretation than to the other, and probably neither was intended to be the only one. Exact correspondence of terms is not the point of

the teaching, but mutual help and dependence.[12]

■ **5–6** The distraction afforded by wealth impoverishes the prayer of the rich[13] so that it is weak, small, and without power.[14] However, the rich, relying[15] on the effective and traditional[16] power of the prayer of the poor, find that their prayer is supplemented by that power. In response, the rich unhesitatingly[17] provide everything needed by the poor. This idea is reinforced in v. 6 by describing the concern with which the rich care for the poor so that the poor will continue in life (ἵνα ἀδιάλειπτος γένηται ἐν τῆ ζωῆ[18] αὐτό). There is certainly an appeal to the self-interest of the rich here: it is to their advantage to keep the poor happy so that they will continue their effective intercession for the rich. This is a spiritualization of the institution of patronage:

10 The common words for "poor," πτωχός (vv. 4) and πένης (all other references in the chapter), do not appear elsewhere in *Hermas,* while πλούσιος, the most common word for "rich," is used elsewhere only in *Sim.* 9.20.1–2, though its cognates occur elsewhere (cf. Osiek, *Rich and Poor,* 83–84). Some difference was understood between the two words for "poor," though the difference was often blurred as here: the πτωχός lived in want and dependence on others, while the πένης by working hard could be independent yet have the bare necessities: cf. ibid. n. 24 and refs. there, esp. Aristophanes *Plutus* 552–64.

11 Most recently by Brox, 294. Detailed discussion of the difficulties of this position in Osiek, *Rich and Poor,* 85–86.

12 "The fact that the correspondences are neither immediately apparent nor explicitly stated, gives rise to three observations: (1) that we have here more truly a parable form than . . . allegory . . . , (2) that interdependence is the point stressed, not correlation of symbols; (3) that the mutual dependence of rich and poor envisioned by the author is enhanced by the very ambiguity of the text" (Osiek, *Rich and Poor,* 86). Dibelius' remark (556) that this chapter encourages a reward-profit ethic which moves it on toward "early catholicism" is wide of the mark in regard to the author's intention.

13 Ἔντευξις καὶ ἐξομολόγησις (prayer of intercession and praise, as in *Man.* 10.3.2, not confession of sin as in *Vis.* 1.1.3; 3.1.5).

14 The third term is debated. Ανου (A), abbrev. for ἀνθρώπου ("human"), can hardly be right. *POxy* α(. .)ν has given rise to various conjectures: ἄλλην ("other") Lake (144); Whittaker (text, 48); ἀρχήν ("beginning" or "authoritative") Joly (216, 433) after conjecture by Whittaker—a good fit into the space

in *POxy* but difficult of meaning, since the word is not otherwise attested adjectivally; ἄνω ("from above") Tischendorf et al.; ἄγνην ("holy") Dibelius (555), which would correspond to L[2] *apud Dominum* ("before the Lord"); ἄνουν ("without understanding") Giuseppe Sgherri, "Textkritische Bemerkungen zu Hermas 51,5" (*VC* 31 [1977] 88–93). The author's earlier suggestion, μεγάλην ("great," Osiek, *Rich and Poor,* 139 n. 2), makes most sense in context and would be echoed by its opposite, the prayer of the poor with great power, at the end of the same verse, but does not fit the space left in *POxy.* Here the translation follows Dibelius, as corresponding to L[2].

15 Ὅταν . . . ἐπαναπάῃ ("when they rely" rather than "rest"), *POxy,* reflected in most versions, accepted by Dibelius (555); Lake (144); Whittaker (49); cf. similar use in *Did.* 4.2. Ἀναπλῆ A ("fulfill"), followed by L[1], is obviously wrong, and has given rise to multiple conjectures: cf. Dibelius, 555; Osiek, *Rich and Poor,* 139 n. 3.

16 E.g., Exod 22:21–27; Deut 24:13, 15; Sir 4:6; 35:12–15; Jas 5:4; *Vis.* 3.9.6.

17 Ἀδιστάκτως ("without hesitation or doubt"), the opposite of doublemindedness, and an expression not used outside *Hermas* in early Christian literature. Compare *Man.* 9.2, 4, 6; *Sim.* 2.7; 8.10.3; 9.24.2, 29.2, and the verbal μὴ διστάζων ("without hesitating") in *Man.* 2.4. See comment on *Man.* 9.2.

18 Dibelius (556) conjectures here ἐντεύξει and proposes the meaning of "unneglected" rather than "unceasing" for ἀδιάλειπτος, so that the phrase would read "so that the poor one is not neglected (or not disturbed by need) in prayer." But compare use of the same word in v. 8, where the vine has water supplied by the elm ἀδιάλειπτον, surely with the meaning of continual, unceasing.

the *obsequium* and *operae* owed by the client to a patron takes the form of intercessory prayer. The further question raised by this text is whether the mutual relationship is to be worked out somehow at the communal church level or in individual patron-client relationships; that is, whether the Roman church at this time had already extensively centralized its charity distributions, or whether the initiative was left to individuals. In the absence of corroborating evidence for large-scale organization of relief efforts in early second-century Rome, it is better to assume that wealthy Christians are being urged not only to contribute to the common fund, which undoubtedly existed in some form,[19] but also to take on patronage relationships with poorer members of the community,[20] a practice which seems to have continued in Rome well into the third century.[21]

■ **7** The most important point of the chapter is stated in v. 7 and again in v. 9: both rich and poor have an important part to play for each other and in the living of the Christian life. If Hermas seems slightly biased toward the poor as having the better part,[22] he could hardly have done otherwise in light of the strong biblical tradition of God's preference for the poor.[23] What is new to that tradition, almost revolutionary, is that here the stereotyped antagonism between the two groups is overcome in a complementarity of roles.[24] The key to the success of the model is not only the cooperation of each side to make its contribution, but the "understanding" (σύνεσις) of the rich (both here and in v. 10) that this is the reason for their wealth, a lesson already given in 1.9, also, as here and v. 10, under the title of the διακονία ("ministry," "service") of the rich. God has made them wealthy in order that they might help the poor. Thus the

two biblical traditions, that of the spiritual power of the poor with God over against the wicked rich, and that of the obligation of the rich to share their wealth with those in need, are brought together.

The point has been made in v. 7, and a fitting conclusion reached. The parable resumes briefly, almost as an afterthought, with the new observation that the elm appears not to bear fruit, but its root system collects moisture that sustains the vine through the long, dry Mediterranean summer; this is in fact one of the major reasons for the agricultural practice of planting them together. By way of application, each group complements or fulfills the "purpose" (πληροφοροῦσι) of the other: the poor by praying for the rich bring full circle the good accomplished by their wealth, while the rich by helping the poor enable them to use their spiritual resources in favor of the rich.[25]

■ **9-10** The opening of v. 9 repeats that of v. 7 in very similar language. Added to it here is the promise of enrollment in the book of life.[26] Verse 10 is the closest thing to a makarism for the rich that early Christianity has to offer—not for the rich per se, of course, but for those with understanding about the right use of wealth. Their contribution is more than responsibility; it is raised to the level of "ministry" (διακονία, v. 7; 1.9; here in verbal form: διακονῆσαι). Instead of being criticized, the aware wealthy of Hermas' community are given an essential role to play. Hermas seems not to agree with *Tabula of Cebes* 39-41, where wealth is of no advantage because it does not help to lead a good life and must have been acquired by evildoing. The paraenesis of the chapter is surely addressed primarily to the wealthy, thus indicating a substantial group in the community.[27]

---

19 See already in other places: Acts 4:35; 2 Corinthians 8-9; Ignatius *Pol.* 4.1, 3; implied in 1 Tim 5:3-8; *Did.* 13.3-4; a little later explicit in Rome, Justin *1 Apol.* 1.77.6.

20 Suggested by Leutzsch, *Wahrnehmung*, 123-26; doubted by Brox, 293 n. 3.

21 Hippolytus *Ap. Trad.* 27-28. Cf. Charles A. Bobertz, "The Role of Patron in the *Cena Dominica* of Hippolytus' *Apostolic Tradition*," *JTS* n.s. 44 (1993) 170-84.

22 So Brox, 295-96.

23 Dibelius-Greeven, *James*, 39-45; Osiek, *Rich and Poor*, 15-38.

24 The closest to this idea that is earlier or contemporary is *1 Clem.* 38.2: ὁ πλούσιος ἐπιχορηγείτω τῷ πτωχῷ, ὁ δὲ πτωχὸς εὐχαριστείτω τῷ θεῷ, ὅτι

ἔδωκεν αὐτῷ διʼ οὗ ἀναπληρωθῇ αὐτὸ τὸ ὑστέρημα ("Let the rich one supply what is needed to the poor and let the poor one give thanks to God who has given him or her one through whom what is lacking may be furnished"). Yet the active role of the poor toward the rich is not developed; see discussion in Osiek, *Rich and Poor*, 79-83.

25 The meaning of the last point is difficult because the majority mss. (only M is ambiguous with]υχας) read πληροφοροῦσι τὰς ψυχὰς αὐτῶν ("complement," "fulfill their souls"). Lake's conjecture, εὐχάς ("prayers"), is easier but unattested.

26 See comment on *Vis.* 1.2.1; 3.2.

27 Further discussion, Osiek, *Rich and Poor*, 87-88.

3 Winter Trees

[52] 1/ He showed me many trees without leaves, but they all seemed dry to me; they were all the same. And he said to me: "Do you see these trees?" I said, "Sir, I see that they are all the same, and dry." He answered me: "These trees that you see are those who live in this world." 2/ I said: "Sir, then why do they seem dry and all the same?" He said, "Because neither the just nor sinners are distinguishable as such in this world, but they are all alike. This world is winter for the just, and they are not distinguishable among the sinners with whom they live. 3/ Just as the trees that shed their leaves in winter look alike, and it cannot be determined which are dry and which alive, so too in this world neither the just nor sinners can be distinguished, but all look the same."

■ **1–3 [52]** In contrast to the metaphor without a vision in the first *Similitude* and the application of meaning to an everyday sight in the second, the opening here and in the next chapter uses the revelatory formula ἔδειξέ μοι ("he showed me").[1] The vision has two parts, comprising the third and fourth *Similitude,* both based on the seasonal appearance of deciduous trees. A more extended allegory on the same image will be carried throughout the eighth *Similitude.* This first part describes their appearance in winter, while the next takes place in spring. The content of the image would be more meaningful in a more northern climate where the seasonal change is more dramatic, rather than in the Mediterranean, where not all trees are deciduous; it must certainly indicate a latitude not much further south than

Rome, where the effect of the change of seasons is still quite noticeable in trees. The point of the parable is that all trees in the sample look alike, whether they are dead or seasonally dormant. The equation of living in this world and looking dry is not apparent to Hermas, for he must ask *why* the trees look dry (v. 2). The answer is that life in this world is winter for the just, meaning not hard, cold, or forbidding, but a condition in which they do not stand out as different from others.[2]

---

1 Compare *Man.* 11.1; see comment there.
2 Compare Matt 13:24–30 (Dibelius, 558); Tertullian *Apol.* 41.3; Cyprian *Ad Demtr.* 19; *De mortal.* 8; *Diogn.* 5; 6.1–4 (Joly, 219; Brox, 299), to which could be added Matt 5:45. Most commentaries earlier than Dibelius also referenced Origen's comment on Matt 24:32–33 (*Comm. ser.* 53) with explicit reference to *Sim.* 3.2: *saeculum praesens hiems est justis* ("this world is winter for the just"); cf. Marcello

Marin, "Sulla fortuna delle *Similitudini* III e IV di Erma," *Vetera Christianorum* 19 (1982) 331–40 (336); this author draws attention to seventeen references in Augustine that seem to be based on *Similitudes* 3 and 4, thus putting into question the accuracy of Jerome's statement (*De vir. ill.* 10) that *Hermas* was almost unknown among Latin writers (*apud Latinos pene ignotus*)—or questioning Jerome's knowledge of Augustine's writings.

4

Summer Trees

1/ Again he showed me many trees, some budding and some dry, and said to me: "Do you see these trees?" I said: "Sir, I see some budding and some dry." 2/ He said: "These budding trees are the just who are about to live in the world to come. For the world to come is summer for the just but winter for sinners. So when the Lord's mercy will shine forth, then those who serve God will be distinguishable, as will everyone. 3/ Just as in summer the fruit of each tree is distinguished and they are recognized by their species, so the fruit of the just will be distinguished, and all shall be known, thriving in that world. 4/ But the outsiders and sinners, the dry trees that you saw, will be seen as dry and fruitless in that world and will be burnt like wood and so be distinguished, because their behavior was evil during life. Sinners will be burnt because they sinned and were not converted. The outsiders will be burnt because they did not know their creator. 5/ So be fruitful so that your fruit will be known in that summer. Refrain from many business enterprises and you will not sin, for those who do much business also sin much, by being totally involved about their business and not about serving their Lord. 6/ So how can such a person," he said, "who does not serve the Lord, ask for anything from the Lord and receive it? The ones who serve the Lord will receive what they ask, but those who do not will receive nothing. 7/ Anyone who has only one business can also serve the Lord, for this person's attention will not be corrupted away from the Lord, but he or she will serve the Lord with pure attention. 8/ So if you do this, you will be able to bear fruit for the world to come, and whoever does this will bear fruit."

■ **1–4 [53]** The season has shifted to spring with its budding trees (v. 1), though the binary juxtaposition winter/summer is used, corresponding to the eschatological binary juxtaposition of present world/world to come (v. 2).[1] For the just, the season of the world to come has changed to summer; for sinners, it is still winter, but the *meaning* of the season has changed. Winter no longer means a common situation in which all are unrecognizable from one another (3.3), but eschatological hard times[2] in which the wicked and unbelievers will be shown up as dry and fruitless[3] and thus burnt (v. 4), an outcome that would normally happen in summer, not winter. The paradox of reversal is at work: what is supposed to be summer is really winter for sinners. The

---

1   Compare the same juxtaposition in *Vis.* 4.3. A similar metaphor, but one using sowing/reaping terminology, occurs in *Gos. Phil.* 2.52.25–30 (noted by Brox, 298): "Those who sow in winter reap in summer. The winter is the world, the summer the other eternal realm (aeon). Let us sow in the world that we may reap in summer" (*NHLE* 142). Joly (221 n. 2) calls attention to the present participial use, so

that the correct translation is really "the world that is arriving"; eschatology is imminent.

2   Dibelius, 558.

3   The image of bearing or not bearing fruit is a commonplace that will also appear at vv. 5, 8; cf. especially Matt 3:10; 7:17–19; 12:33; 21:19; Luke 13:6–9; Jude 12; Ignatius *Eph.* 14.2; Polycarp *Phil.* 1.2; *Barn.* 11.11.

apocalyptic character of the parable is brought out in these two chapters up to 4.4 by the continuity of the word φαίνομαι ("display," "make clear"), rendered by the verb "to distinguish" in the translation (3.2, 3; 4.2, 3, 4). Just as the budding of some trees in spring distinguishes live from dead, so in the world to come, the difference will become clear, when the summer sun, that is, God's mercy, shines on them (v. 2).[4] The burning of the dry trees includes both believers who sinned and did not have a change of heart (the principal target audience of *Hermas*) and unbelievers who failed to recognize God the creator—that is, those who, having recognized God, did not change their way of life accordingly (v. 4).[5]

■ **5–8** Verse 5 turns to exhortation to fruitfulness, followed by the characteristic concerns of Hermas: the bearing of good fruit is made impossible by total involvement in business concerns. The fact that one business is all right (v. 7) is of major importance for understanding the ethics of the author. Asceticism and escape from the world are not advocated, but rather, a moderate use of worldly goods that does not distract and absorb the attention of the user.[6] Relying on wealth and business for happiness is a form of doublemindedness, a major obstacle to receiving what is asked for in prayer (v. 6).[7] Those who do not fall into this distraction will also be able to understand the things of God (v. 7), having an uncompromised mind (διανοία).[8] Verse 8 ends the topic with casuistic command and promise similar in form to the typical ending of most of the *Mandates*. The central message of Hermas is reiterated here. In spite of the true heavenly identity of Christians developed in the first *Similitude*, they are to live normally in this world, yet with a spiritual freedom that leaves them unencumbered with excess baggage on the way to the next.

---

4   Cultic soteriological language (Dibelius, 558–59); cf. Titus 2:11; 3:4; perhaps also Eph 5:14.
5   Rom 1:20; *Sim.* 9.17–18.
6   Cf. *Vis.* 1.3.1; 2.3.1; 3.6.5, 11.3; *Man.* 6.2.5; 8.3; 10.1.4; 12.2.1; *Sim.* 9.31.2; etc.; Sir 38:24. Discussion in Osiek, *Rich and Poor*, especially 47–50, 125–26. The idea is old: Democritus, *Peace of Mind*: "If you want to enjoy peace of mind, do not get involved in too many activities," quoted in association to *Herm. Sim.* 4.5 as "this precept transformed into a Christian command" in Werner Jaeger, *Early Christianity and Greek Paideia* (Cambridge, MA: Harvard University Press, 1961) 9.
7   Compare *Man.* 9.4–8.
8   Compare *Man.* 10.1.5–6.

5

True Fasting

1 [54]   **1/ As I was fasting, sitting on a certain mountain thanking the Lord for everything he had done with me, I saw the Shepherd sitting next to me and saying: "Why have you come here so early?" I said: "Sir, because I have a station." 2/ He said: "What is a station?" "I am fasting, sir," I said. But he said: "What kind of fast is this that you [pl.] are doing?" "I am fasting as I usually do," I said. 3/ "You do not know how to fast to God," he said, "and this useless fast you are doing is no fast at all." "Why do you say this, sir?" "I tell you," he said, "that this fast you think you are doing is not really a fast. But I will teach you [sing.] a fast that is acceptable and complete to God." "Yes, Lord," I said, "you will render me fortunate to know the kind of fast that is acceptable to God." "Listen," he said. 4/ "God does not want such a silly fast. Fasting to God this way, you accomplish nothing for justice. Fast to God this way: 5/ do no evil thing in the course of your life, but serve the Lord with a pure heart. Keep his commandments, proceed according to his regulations, and let no evil desire arise in your heart. Trust in God, that if you do all this, fear God, and refrain from every evil deed, you will live to God. If you do these things, you will perform a great fast that is acceptable to God."**

Structure

The fifth *Similitude* has been the object of much attention, mostly because of the christological material that it contains. It is first of all about fasting, just as Philippians 2 is primarily about community unity. In both cases, however, more attention has been given by interpreters to its Christology. Despite the complexities of its problems, the structure is fairly straightforward. However the different elements are related to each other, there are three applications or levels of interpretation of the original bipartite parable.

1   On true fasting
2   A parable in two parts
        a) vv. 1–8: The slave becomes joint heir
        b) vv. 9–11: The slave's generosity to fellow slaves

3   First, parabolic explanation concerning fasting
4   Transition to second explanation
5   Second, allegorical explanation concerning salvation
6.1–4a Christ's role in salvation
6.4b–8 Third explanation: flesh-spirit relationship, with Christ as example
7   Paraenetic conclusion on honoring the flesh[1]

Probably the original interpretation was that of fasting, developed from the story by analogy. Then the christological potential was seen and developed secondarily by means of allegory.[2] Finally, the third interpretation about the flesh-spirit relationship was attached to the christological allegory but developed analogically rather than allegorically.

---

1   This outline does not differ substantially from that of Dibelius (564–65), also adopted by Henne (*Christologie*, 160–61), except that Dibelius sees 5.2–6.3 as an allegory applied to the *work* of Christ (and not adoptionist), and 6.4–8 as an allegory applied to the *person* of Christ (binitarian and adoptionist).

2   Nijendijk (*Christologie*, 86–92) proposes that the original interpretation was eschatological, with the

parable consisting of 2.2–8, and the interpretation of 4.1–5.2a, 3b; 6.4–8; and chap. 7. For him, the secondary interpretation was christological, at which time the rest of the parable (2.9–11) was added. The interpretation with regard to fasting came third, since 1.3–4 forbids fasting, while chap. 3 takes it for granted (but see comment on 3.5

■ **1.1–2 [54]** The chapter opens in a specified narrative setting. Hermas has taken his place on a mountain and is engaged in fasting and prayer of praise and thanksgiving (εὐχαριστῶν). In this and the next verse, the customary roles are reversed: usually the rhetorical device is so structured that Hermas asks annoying questions in order to elicit the Shepherd's teaching, but here the Shepherd asks naive questions of Hermas, who explains. Early morning is a familiar time for prayer in Jewish tradition.[3] A mountain is a frequent biblical setting as the site for prayer, for fasting less so. But if mountain (ὄρος) can be understood more generally as an isolated place away from human habitation, the parallels are more recognizable.[4] Hermas replies to the Shepherd's question by saying that he has a "station" (στατίων, the Latin loanword *statio*), about which the Shepherd seems to know no more than modern readers, an indication that the term is probably new in Hermas' church and must therefore be explained. The passage witnesses, along with *Did.* 8.1,[5] to the custom of personal fasting at this period, for Hermas indicates a regular practice on his part (v. 2), and the *Didache* indicates a regular disciplinary practice acquired from Judaism. The next Latin Christian writer to use the term στατίων is Tertullian, who, under the influence of the ideology of Christians as God's *militia*, suggests its evolution from Roman military terminology, an interpretation that is usually considered secondary.[6] The sudden transition to the plural in the Shepherd's second question in v. 2 continues through the first part of v. 3, and throws the challenge with regard to fasting practice to the listeners.

■ **1.3–5** The next statement of the Shepherd reveals why the rhetorical device of questioning was reversed in the previous verses. The Shepherd has questioned Hermas with supposed ignorance about his ascetic practice in order to introduce a critique of that practice that will expand Hermas' awareness of true disciplinary practice. Fasting as isolated and isolating ascetic practice is criticized in vv. 4–5 in a manner reminiscent of Isa 58:3–14: it is only valuable within a social context of relief of the needy and just practices. But this is not a condemnation of the practice of fasting as such, only an adjustment to put it in proper context, as will be evident at 3.5–8.[7] The teaching in v. 5 with its concern for observance of the commandments in purity of heart sounds like a lost fragment from the *Mandates,* even to the familiar refrain, ζήσῃ τῷ θεῷ ("You shall live to God").[8] The last whole sentence in v. 3 is missing in AL¹E, but present in M Pamb L²CC.[9]

---

below), and fasting is not mentioned anywhere else in *Similitude* 5.

3   Gen 19:27; Exod 24:4; Ps 92:2; Sir 39:5; Mark 1:35; Luke 4:42.

4   Suggested by Hilhorst, *Sémitismes,* 173–74: Moses on Mt. Sinai (Exod 34:28); Daniel at the Tigris (Dan 10:2–4); Jesus in the desert (Matt 4:1–2; Luke 4:1–2); *Prot. Jas.* 1.4; etc.

5   "Do not fast with the hypocrites on Mondays and Thursdays, but you fast on Wednesdays and Fridays" (Αἱ δὲ νηστεῖαι ὑμῶν μὴ ἔστωσαν μετὰ τῶν ὑποκριτῶν. νηστεύουσι γὰρ δευτέρᾳ σαββάτων καὶ πέμπτῃ· ὑμεῖς δὲ νηστεύσατε τετράδα καὶ παρασκευήν). For fasting in preparation for a vision, see comment on *Vis.* 2.2.1.

6   Tertullian *De orat.* 19; *De jejun.* 10; *Ad uxor.* 2.4; and elsewhere. Christine Mohrmann, "Les origines" (74–78) and "Statio" (*VC* 7 [1953] 223–45), argued from this and the other Latin loanwords in the text that Hermas was Latin-speaking, a view not now commonly accepted. After extensive discussion, Hilhorst (*Sémitismes,* 168–79) summarizes the scholarship on the origin of the term for Christian fasting into three possibilities: 1) from a Semitic word for standing, possibly the Mishnaic term עמד translated into the Latin of Greek speakers in a Latin environment; 2) a Latin loanword into a Semitic language, and from there into Christian Greek; 3) origin in a Latin milieu by Jews or Christians familiar with the biblical expression עמד לפני יהוה ("stand before the face of the Lord"), translated into Latin as *stare ante faciem Domini,* the verb then nominalized as *statio.* Hilhorst opts for the third possibility. Synder's translation (100) reflects the military association: "I am on guard duty"; to which the Shepherd responds in v. 2: "What . . . is the guard?"

7   Against Hilhorst, *Sémitismes,* 173, 178.

8   E.g., *Man.* 1.2; 3.5; 4.1.1, 2.4; 6.2.10; 8.12; 12.6.5.

9   L²CC begin the sentence with *et dixi ei* ("and I said to him"), based on a misreading of καί ("and") for ναί ("yes") (Dibelius, 561).

5   Parable of the Son, Slave, and Vineyard

2 [55]   1/ "Listen to the parable I am about to tell you about fasting. 2/ A certain person had a field and many slaves, and in a part of the field, cultivated a vineyard. The owner chose a slave who was trustworthy and pleasing to him, and when about to leave, the owner called him and said to him: `Take charge of this vineyard that I planted, build an enclosure for it, and, until I come, do nothing else to the vineyard. Keep this command of mine and you will have your freedom from me.' Then the owner of the slave went away. 3/ When the owner had gone, the slave enclosed the vineyard. When he had finished enclosing it, he saw that the vineyard was full of weeds. 4/ He deliberated to himself, saying: `I have completed the lord's command. Now I will dig up this vineyard, and it will look better when it is dug; without weeds it will give better fruit, since the weeds will not be choking it.' So he dug up the vineyard, and pulled out all the weeds that were in it. That vineyard improved and was thriving without weeds choking it. 5/ After a while, the owner of the slave and the vineyard returned and went to the vineyard. Seeing the vineyard nicely enclosed and even dug and weeded, and the vines thriving, he was extremely happy about what the slave did. 6/ Calling his loved son whom he held as heir, and his friends whom he held as advisors, he told them what he had commanded the slave and what he found achieved. These congratulated the slave according to the testimony given by the owner. 7/ He said to them: `I promised freedom to this slave if he kept the commandment I gave him. He kept my commandment and added good work to the vineyard, and so has pleased me greatly. In return for this work he has done, I want to make him joint heir with my son, for he appreciates the good and did not neglect it, but completed it.' 8/ The son of the owner was pleased with this opinion, that the slave should be joint heir with the son. 9/ After several days the householder prepared a banquet and sent him much food from it. But the slave took the food sent from the owner, kept only what he needed, and distributed the rest of it to the other slaves. 10/ His fellow slaves were very happy to receive the food and began to intercede on his behalf, that he might find great favor with the owner because he had treated them this way. 11/ The owner heard all this and once again rejoiced over his behavior. Calling his friends and his son together once more, the owner told them what the slave had done with the food that he had received. They were even more pleased that the slave would be joint heir with the son."

■ **2.1–4 [55]** The central piece in *Similitude* 5 is the parable that now ensues, and it is clear from the introduction in v. 1 that its primary and original meaning is intended to be a lesson about true fasting as generosity and willingness to serve. Later, other interpretations will be added. The vineyard (v. 2) is a familiar setting, and this

170

parable is reminiscent of several biblical stories,[1] yet it has its own unique development. A key difference is that most of the familiar vineyard stories are parables of destruction with unhappy outcomes, whereas this one has a happy ending.

The "trustworthy and pleasing" slave (δοῦλόν τινα πιστότατον καὶ εὐάρεστον)[2] is a familiar motif, but considered a rare and valuable asset. Seneca makes the distinction between the slave who does what is demanded and the one who voluntarily does more—exactly the point in this parable—and goes on to argue that, if masters become angry when a slave does less, they should also then show gratitude for more.[3] The owner assigns responsibility for the vineyard to the faithful slave with the command either to enclose it for protection or to stake the vines: the verb χαρακεῖν can mean either.[4] The admonition to follow instructions "until I come" (ἕως ἔρχομαι) carries eschatological connotations that cannot be developed in the christological interpretation because of different allegorical correspondences, but that nonetheless have general significance within the eschatological context of the whole document. In view of the owner's later pleasure that the slave did more (v. 5), the further instruction to do no more than fence or stake the vineyard must be understood as concession rather than command. However, the slave does not stop with the mere minimum, but goes on to weed the vineyard, so that it is greatly improved.

■ **2.5–8** As Dibelius remarks,[5] the son and friends show up somewhat by surprise and have little to do with the story. The friends/advisors may be an allusion to the family council of a *paterfamilias*, or the emperor's inner circle, the *amici augusti* ("friends of Augustus"),[6] or his coterie of clients. They do serve, however, as witnesses for a *manumissio inter amicos*, a legal form of manumission of slaves for which such witnesses are necessary.[7] This is what seems to be happening in v. 7. In this case, legal adoption as heir is added as an extra reward, also legally possible. That the son should be happy about sharing the inheritance with a former slave, however (v. 8), would be unlikely.[8] This is a narrative element that would have been as surprising to second-century hearers as to modern ones. Here the story could end.

■ **2.9–11** Instead of living happily ever after, the characters continue to act, in what could well be a sequel added later,[9] perhaps in response to the need in a proclamatory context to continue the story. From a great banquet, the owner sends food to the slave, not a gesture of condescension, but of honor to a social inferior. The slave now proves himself not only trustworthy and responsible beyond normal expectations, but also extraordinarily generous to his fellow slaves, after the manner of unanimous Jewish-Christian social teaching to share with the needy, but especially *Sim.* 1.8–11. Just as there (*Sim.* 1.6)

---

1 Especially Isa 5:1–11; Mark 12:1–12, par. Matt 21:33–46 and Luke 20:9–19; but also Matt 13:24–30; Matt 24:45–51, par. Luke 12:41–46; Mark 13:34; Matt 25:14–30; Luke 12:27; *Gos. Phil.* 52.2–15. The suggestion that this parable may be a Gnostic story, perhaps even from Valentinus himself, is unlikely: Leutzsch, *Wahrnehmung*, 75.

2 A adds ἔντιμον ("esteemed") instead of αὐτῷ ("to him"), and omits the next word, ἀποδημῶν (Berlin Papyrus 13272 [O. Stegmüller, *Aegyptus* 17 (1937) 456–59]) or ἀποδημήσων (restored from L and E; ἀποδ- M) ("going away"). See complete discussion in Bonner (*Papyrus Codex*, 47), and Dibelius' surprisingly accurate conjecture from the versions without benefit of better Greek MSS. (562).

3 *De beneficiis* 3.21–22. On the faithful slave, see Moses I. Finley, *Ancient Slavery and Modern Ideology* (New York: Penguin, 1983) 103–4; cited in Leutzsch, *Wahrnehmung*, 145. For an extended exposition on the social context of the parable, see ibid., 144–54.

4 Cf. LSJ *s.v.*; Henne, *Christologie*, 192. Both the verb and the noun χάραξ can refer to a military stockade or siege wall (1 Kgs 21 [20]:12; Isa 29:3; 37:33; Ezek 4:2; 21:22; 26:8; Qoh 9:14; 4 Macc 3:12; Luke 19:43), but also the city wall (Jer 39 [32]:2) or vineyard stakes as here (Isa 5:2). A vineyard enclosure is usually a φραγμός (Num 22:24; Prov 24:46 [31]; Ps 79 [80]:12; *Sim.* 9.26.4), but the same word can also mean part of the city wall (1 Kgs 11:27; Ps 88 [89]:40). Isa 5:2 LXX uses both terms in a way that seems to assign φραγμός to the enclosure fence and χάραξ to the stakes: φραγμὸν περιέθηκα καὶ ἐχαράκωσα καὶ ἐφύτευσα ἄμπελον (The owner "enclosed with a fence and staked and planted a vineyard").

5 Page 563.

6 Henne, *Christologie*, 175.

7 Leutzsch, *Wahrnehmung*, 148.

8 Leutzsch (*Wahrnehmung*, 148 n. 70) recalls other, NT slave-son relationships in John 8:35–36; Mark 12:1–12; Gal 3:26–4:11—all antagonistic.

9 The judgment of Dibelius, 564; Brox, 306.

the Christian is to keep only what is reasonably necessary (τὴν αὐτάρκειαν τὴν ἀρκετήν σοι) and give the rest to the needy, so here the slave keeps from the gift of food what he needs (τὰ ἀρκοῦντα αὐτῷ ἦρε, v. 9) and distributes the rest. The favorite slave and his fellow slaves begin to live out the lesson of *Similitude* 2: just as the rich provide for the poor who then intercede for the rich with their prayer, so here the slave who has just become rich in freedom and potential inheritance provides for those less fortunate, who, in return, pray for him (v. 10). Finally in v. 11, they do live happily ever after.

5

More on True Fasting

3 [56] 1/ I said: "Sir, I do not know these parables nor can I understand them unless you explain them to me." 2/ "I will explain it all to you," he said, "and everything that I will say to you I will show you. Keep the commandments of the Lord, and you will be pleasing to the Lord and recorded in the number of those who keep the commandments. 3/ If you do any good thing beyond the commandment of God, you will achieve for yourself greater honor, and you will be even more honorable with God than you were going to be. So if you keep the commandments of God and add on these services besides, you will rejoice, if you keep them according to my commandment." 4/ I said to him: "Sir, whatever you command me, I will keep, for I know that you are with me." "I will be with you," he said, "because you are so eager to do good, and I will be with all who are so eager. 5/ This fast, keeping the commandments of the Lord," he said, "is extremely good. So this is the way you will keep this fast that you are about to do. 6/ First of all, keep from every evil utterance and evil desire, and purify your heart from all the silliness of this world. If you keep these things, this fast will be complete for you. 7/ This is what you will do: after completing what has been written, on the day you fast, taste nothing but bread and water, calculate the price of the food you were going to eat, and give it to a widow or orphan or needy person, and thus you will practice humility, so that from your practice of humility the recipient may have fullness of well-being, and intercede for you to the Lord. 8/ If you complete the fast this way, as I commanded you, your sacrifice will be acceptable to God, and this fast will be recorded for you, and the service so done is beautiful, full of joy, and pleasing to the Lord. 9/ So you will observe these things with your children and your whole household, and if you observe them, you will be blessed. And whoever hears and does them will be blessed, and whatever they ask of the Lord they will receive."

■ **3.1–2 [56]** This chapter is the explanation of the parable as parable, whereas chapter 4 will allegorize it and therefore move off into a different interpretation. As simple parable, the story has a major point as illustration of proper fasting: like the slave of the parable, the believer needs to do much more than commanded, by way of anticipating the good and thinking of others. The ascetic practice of food deprivation is minimal performance which must be seen as part of a much larger picture that necessitates generosity of heart, especially to the needy. The chapter begins with the familiar banter between Hermas and the Shepherd. Unlike 1.1–2 where the roles were reversed, here Hermas has returned to the role of questioner and supplicant for further explanation. Most of the last sentence of v. 2 is missing in A, but restored from LL and partial preservation in M. Being enrolled in the records of the faithful (v. 2, 8) provides the promise of eternal life.[1]

---

1   See *Vis.* 1.3.2 and comment on 1.2.1.

■ **3.3–4** Verse 3 seems to contrast the commandments of God, the basic observances, with the commandment of the Shepherd, the extra ones, but the contrast is only rhetorical. For Dibelius, the contrast here between minimal observance and the way of greater honor is unlike the situation described in *Man.* 4.4.2, where the minimum is purity of heart and the greater honor is ascribed to celibacy.[2] The two situations certainly differ in that celibacy is the way for the few, while here the greater honor of doing more is open—and really expected—of every believer. But the challenge is the same: doing more brings greater honor and reward. The word translated "service" here and in v. 8 is λειτουργία, a term normally meaning some kind of official religious act. Here it means fasting in the wider sense. L[1] has understood it this way by translating *statio*. The Shepherd's promise to be with Hermas and all who have the same willingness (v. 4) echoes his original promise of presence in *Vis.* 5.2. The generalizing to all at the end of the verse is the familiar ending of many of the *Mandates*.

■ **3.5–7** Verses 5–6 underline one of the major lessons of the *Mandates*: that purity of heart is a prerequisite for faithful Christian life. The approval of fasting here is not in contrast to the Shepherd's seeming contempt for Hermas' way of fasting in 1.3–5. Here, the practice of fasting is put in proper context. The appeal to "what has been written before" (τὰ προγεγραμμένα) at the beginning of v. 7 most likely refers to the commandments of God (vv. 3, 5) rather than to a previous part of the revelation as in *Vis.* 2.1.3.[3] Fasting with bread and water, and sometimes with salt or vegetables added, was frequently the content of early Christian fasting.[4] The priority of charity over asceticism is a firmly entrenched Jewish and Christian value,[5] and the practical motive of saving

money which is then given to the needy is taken a step further in later tradition by the encouragement of fasting *in order to* raise money for charity if one does not otherwise have it to give.[6] This focus of the outcome of asceticism on the needy (v. 7) confirms most directly the teaching of *Man.* 8.10 (with exactly the same three kinds of neediness) and *Sim.* 1.8, but indirectly, the continued concern of the author for appropriate interaction between poor and rich. The practice of humility (ταπεινοφροσύνη) has been previously associated with fasting.[7] "Have fullness of well-being" is literally "have a filled soul" (ἵνα . . . ὁ εἰληφὼς ἐμπλήσῃ τὴν ἑαυτοῦ ψυχήν), meaning not psychic or spiritual, but physical nurture.[8] The willingness of the recipient of charity to pray for the giver continues the teaching of *Sim.* 6–8, also exemplified in the story here.[9]

■ **3.8–9** The sacrificial language of v. 8 is unusual. Θυσία ("sacrifice") appears only here in *Hermas*; δεκτή ("acceptable") has been connected with the right kind of fasting,[10] so that both the sacrifice and the "service" (λειτουργία)[11] here refer to the practice of true fasting. The joy which comes with its exercise parallels that which in *Sim.* 1.10 accompanies the wise use of wealth. Thus this lesson on fasting reinforces and complements those on responsible use of riches in *Similitudes* 1 and 2. The text does not support an interpretation of institutionalization of charitable giving, but the encouragement of a practice probably at this period carried on both by individual patronage and by a centralized collection of funds for distribution.[12] The conclusion in v. 9, like 1.5, sounds more like the conclusion of a *Mandate*.

---

2   Pages 565–66.
3   Τὰ προγεγραμμένα ML[1]; γεγραμμένα A. L[2] and Brox (313) see an inconsistency here by assuming that the previous oral instructions are meant. L[2] corrects to *quae audisti* ("what you heard").
4   Tertullian *De jejun.* 9.13; *Act. Paul Thec.* 25; *Act. Thom.* 20; other references in Dibelius, 567.
5   E.g., 1 Pet 4:8 and *2 Clem.* 16.4, both quoting Prov 10:12.
6   *Didasc.* 19 par. *Ap. Const.* 5.1.3. The believer either calculates (συμψηφίσας; same term at *Vis.* 3.1.4) the amount of money (Ath[2]) or gets an idea of it (συνοψίσας, MA, thus the better ms. evidence), but the end meaning is the same.

7   See comment on *Vis.* 3.10.6.
8   Prov 6:30; *Sim.* 2.8; Brox, 313.
9   5.2.10.
10 5.1.3, 5. Cf. Phil 4:18; especially Sir 35:6 in its context of the necessary connection between doing justice and performing acceptable sacrifice.
11 See also v. 3b above.
12 Against Leutzsch, *Wahrnehmung*, 136; with Brox, 313. For the early origin of a weekly collection for the needy, 1 Cor 16:1. Nor is this a doctrine of redemptive almsgiving set in tension with the fully atoning death of Christ; against Roman Garrison, *Redemptive Almsgiving in Early Christianity* (JSNTSup 77; Sheffield: JSOT, 1993) 86–94; 117–24.

5

Explanations of the Parable

4 [57]   1/ I begged him quite a bit to unravel for me the parable of the field and the owner and the vineyard and the slave who enclosed the vineyard, and the walls and the weeds pulled up from the vineyard, and the son and the friends who served as counselors, since I understood that all these things were a parable. 2/ Answering, he said: "You are extremely bold with your questions. You should not ask anything at all, for if it needs to be explained to you, it will be explained." I said to him, "Sir, whatever you show me and do not explain, I will have seen for nothing, since I do not understand what it is. Likewise, if you tell me parables and do not resolve them for me, I will have heard them from you for nothing." 3/ He said to me again, "Whoever is God's servant and has the Lord in one's heart seeks understanding from God and receives it and can resolve every parable, and the Lord's words spoken in parables are known to that one. But those who are insecure and lazy in prayer equivocate about asking the Lord. 4/ For the Lord is totally compassionate and gives unequivocally to all those who ask. But you, since you have been empowered by the noble angel, having received from him so many effects of prayer, and since you are not lazy, why do you not ask understanding and receive it from the Lord?" 5/ I said to him, "Sir, while I have you with me, I must seek from you and ask you. You show me everything and talk with me. But if I saw or heard these things without you, I would have asked the Lord for an explanation."

5 [58]   1/ "I just told you," he said, "that you are mischievous and brash, asking for explanations of the parables. But since you are so persistent, I will explain for you the parable of the field and all the rest that follow, so that you can make them known to everyone. So listen now and understand them," he said. 2/ "The field is this world. The lord of the field is the one who created all things and brought them to completion and empowers them. The son is the Holy Spirit. The slave is the Son of God. The vines are this people, which he planted. 3/ The walls are the holy angels of the Lord who sustain the people of the Lord. The weeds rooted up from the vineyard are the lawless deeds of the servants of God. The foods that he sent to him from the banquet are the commandments that he gave to the people through his son. The friends and counselors are the holy angels who were created first. The absence of the master is the time remaining until his arrival." 4/ I said to him, "Sir, this is all great, wonderful, and noble. So how, sir," I said, "could I have understood these things? Nor could anyone else, however wise, understand them. But still, sir," I said, "explain to me what I am about to ask you." 5/ "Ask if you want anything," he said. "Why, sir," I said, "is the Son of God in the parable presented in the manner of a slave?"

6 [59]   1/ "Listen," he said, "the Son of God is (not) presented in the manner of a slave, but with great

power and authority." "How, sir?" I said, "I do not understand." 2/ "Because," he said, "God planted the vineyard, that is, created the people and turned them over to his son. And the son appointed the angels over them to take care of them. He himself purified their sins by laboring hard and with exhaustive efforts. For no vineyard can be dug without labor and hardship. 3/ He himself, after having purified the sins of the people, showed them the paths of life and gave them the law that he had received from his father. 4/ (So you see," he said, "that he is lord of the people, having received power from his father.) But listen to how the lord took his son and the noble angels as advisors about the inheritance of the slave. 5/ The preexistent Holy Spirit, which created all that was created, God made to dwell in the chosen flesh. This flesh, in which the Holy Spirit dwelt, served the spirit well, living in a manner distinguished and pure, in no way defiling the spirit. 6/ Because it conducted itself well and with purity, cooperating with the spirit and working with it in every respect, acting stoutly and bravely, God chose it as partner for the Holy Spirit. For the behavior of this flesh pleased God because it was not defiled while it bore the Holy Spirit on earth. 7/ So he took the son and the noble angels as counselors, to the effect that this flesh, which had served the spirit without blame, should have some dwelling place, and not seem to have lost the reward for its service. For all flesh in which the Holy Spirit has dwelt, which is found to be undefiled and spotless, will receive its reward. 8/ You have the explanation of this parable, too."

Seeking Understanding

■ **4.1–5 [57]** In spite of having been given a perfectly good explanation of the parable in terms of true fasting, Hermas pushes for more—for particular explanations of the particular elements of the story. The parable has many different levels of interpretive possibility. Hermas' persistent questioning here forms the transition to the second of three interpretations. It and the Shepherd's resistance to the questioning (v. 2) are a regular feature of the dialogue, which serves to extend the narrative, offer some reprieve from moral instruction, and personalize the characters.[1] Without using the familiar word "doublemindedness" and its opposite, this is in fact the contrast in v. 3.[2] Those devoted to the interests of God have an understanding heart that can interpret parables, in contrast to those who hesitate ($\delta\iota\sigma\tau\acute{\alpha}\zeta\sigma\upsilon\sigma\iota\nu$)[3] and are torn between interests, lacking the courage to ask and receive from God—among whom Hermas must still apparently be counted.

By contrast, the compassionate[4] God does not hesitate

---

1   Compare *Vis.* 3.3.1–2; 6.5; 10.9–10. The closest parallel to this passage is *Vis.* 3.3.4, in which the woman church assures Hermas that what he is supposed to see, he will see. Hermas' most pert answer is *Sim.* 6.4.3, where he snaps back that he would not be asking if he understood.

2   Compare Jas 1:5–8, which does use $\delta\acute{\iota}\psi\upsilon\chi\sigma\varsigma$ ("doubleminded").

3   On the significance of this word group for the teaching on doublemindedness, see comment on *Man.* 9.2.

4   $\Pi\sigma\lambda\acute{\upsilon}\sigma\pi\lambda\alpha\gamma\chi\nu\sigma\varsigma$ M here and S at *Vis.* 1.3.2; 2.2.8; 4.2.3; $\pi\sigma\lambda\upsilon\epsilon\acute{\upsilon}\sigma\pi\lambda\alpha\gamma\chi\nu\sigma\varsigma$ or compound word in most places, A. The superior quality of S and M must establish the simpler form as the original: Bonner, *Papyrus Codex*, 55 n. 24.

(v. 4), but gives without question.[5] Hermas, now clothed with power by the great and glorious[6] angel, the mysterious character who sent the Shepherd and is not yet fully revealed,[7] is encouraged to ask for more and greater understanding. But Hermas responds cagily that he does not need to ask as long as the Shepherd is there to explain.

General Explanation of the Parable

■ **5.1 [58]** Once again, as in 4.2, the Shepherd seems to resist further explanation, a resistance that is clearly a literary device, for this resistance has totally disappeared by v. 5. This is not the first time Hermas has been called "mischievous" ($\pi\alpha\nu o\hat{\upsilon}\rho\gamma o\varsigma$)[8] or "brash" ($\alpha\hat{\upsilon}\vartheta\acute{\alpha}\delta\eta\varsigma$)[9] for his persistence. As clarified several times before,[10] the aim of the revelation and explanation to Hermas is so that he will communicate it to others. This is not private, but communal revelation mediated through one recipient.

■ **5.2** The next two verses lay out the second, allegorical interpretation of the parable in ten simple corresponding pairs. The planting of the vineyard, the people of God, in the field of the world calls on familiar biblical allegory,[11] even though the fact that the vineyard is situated in a field (2.2) is not important for either the original parable or this interpretation. It does, however, lend appropriateness to the identification of the lord of the field as the creator.[12] The next sentence, "The son is the Holy Spirit" ($\acute{o}$ $\delta\grave{e}$ $\upsilon\acute{\iota}o\varsigma$ $\tau\grave{o}$ $\pi\nu\epsilon\hat{\upsilon}\mu\alpha$ $\tau\grave{o}$ $\acute{\alpha}\gamma\iota\acute{o}\nu$ $\acute{e}\sigma\tau\iota\nu$) is a restoration accepted by most commentators.[13] Dibelius is probably correct that the sentence was omitted later for dogmatic reasons[14] by those who did not see or could not accept the complicated crossing of symbols with the next statement, and therefore found the statement in later centuries doctrinally unorthodox,[15] either by identifying the Son of God with the Holy Spirit or by positing two sons of God.[16] Contrary to normal expectation, the son of the parable (the Holy Spirit) is not the son of the allegorical interpretation, to whom the parabolic character of the slave corresponds.[17] This interpretation will become even more complicated in 6.1–3, where the son is the Son of God, not the Holy Spirit, only to return to being the Holy Spirit in 6.4.[18] The ambiguity results from awkward combining of different segments of interpretation and from later editing of different layers or

---

5 $\vec{A}\delta\iota\sigma\tau\acute{\alpha}\kappa\tau\omega\varsigma$ M, Whittaker, Joly ("without hesitation") is to be preferred, in contrast to $\delta\iota\sigma\tau\acute{\alpha}\zeta o\upsilon\sigma\iota\nu$ ("equivocate," "hesitate") in the previous verse and in *Man.* 9.2–6; see comment on *Man.* 9.2 Alternate reading $\acute{\alpha}\delta\iota\alpha\lambda\epsilon\acute{\iota}\pi\tau\omega\varsigma$ A, *sine intermissione* LL ("unceasingly"), which could be contrasted to the insecure and lazy, and is to be read at *Sim.* 9.11.7. Discussion in Bonner, *Papyrus Codex*, 55 n. 27.

6 $\vec{E}\nu\delta\acute{o}\xi o\upsilon$ ("glorious," "honorable") M; $\acute{\alpha}\gamma\acute{\iota}o\upsilon$ (holy) A; "*venerabili* LL, which probably represents $\grave{e}\nu\delta\acute{o}\xi o\upsilon$, although that word is usually rendered *honestus, praeclarus, dignitosus*. $\acute{\alpha}\gamma\iota o\varsigma$ is regularly *sanctus*" (Bonner, *Papyrus Codex*, 56 n. 29). $\acute{e}\nu\delta o\xi o\varsigma$ also *Sim.* 7.1; 9.1.3.

7 *Vis.* 5.2; *Sim.* 7.1; 9.1.3; 10.1.1, not to be confused with the angel of conversion, who is the Shepherd himself (*Vis.* 5.7; *Man.* 12.6.1). Cf. Introduction 3.3.3. For Henne (*L'unité*, 158–59), this angelic figure is really the son of God, who will be fully revealed only at the end.

8 *Vis.* 3.3.1, by the woman church; Hermas applies the same term adverbially to himself in *Man.* 3.3.3.

9 *Sim.* 5.4.2.

10 E.g., *Vis.* 2.4.3; 3.3.1.

11 Ps 80:8–13; Isaiah 5, etc.; and perhaps Matt 13:38.

12 Compare *Vis.* 1.1.6; 3.4; *Man.* 1.1. Cf. also Eph 3:9; Rev 4:11, etc.

13 Some documentation in Brox, 316. The sentence is missing in AL²E, part of a lacuna in M, but restored by Gebhardt-Harnack (152) from L¹ as *lectio difficilior* on the basis of its early dating.

14 Page 569.

15 Inasmuch as the sentence is original, Henne (*Christologie*, 189–90) sees in it the expression of trinitarian awareness, since the son plays so little role in the story that it is a gratuitous introduction of the Holy Spirit. Henne, however, doubts more than most that the sentence is original, arguing that it could be an attempted harmonization with 6.4–8, which would explain why 6.4 combines son and angels instead of holy spirit and angels.

16 Discussion of the literature in Pernveden, *Concept of the Church*, 43.

17 It is not clear why Henne (*Christologie*, 190) thinks the slave-son identification here has an entirely different import than in Phil 2:7 ("L'identification du Christ à l'esclave en Phil 2, 7 a une toute autre valeur"). The difference is the probable preexistence intended in Phil 2:6. In both cases, the slave-son is rewarded for fidelity even in suffering (6.2) by exaltation.

18 The identification of the Holy Spirit with the Son of God in *Sim.* 9.1.1 is deceptively different, for here

editions of the text, as the narrative developed and the interpretations became more complex.

■ **5.3–5** As in 2.2–3, οἱ χάρακες can be either the stockade walls, as translated here, or stakes supporting the vines.[19] The activity of the angels with regard to the people (οἱ συγκρατοῦντες τὸν λαὸν αὐτοῦ) likewise can mean either protecting from outside or supporting by propping up.[20] The food sent from the banquet to nourish the people is the food of the law. The association of food, wisdom, and law is traditional.[21] Contrary to the eschatological expectation of the return of Christ, here it is the absence and return of the Lord, that is, of God, that is awaited.[22] The question put forward by Hermas in v. 5 is really the introduction to the next chapter, and opens the christological crux.

Role of the Son of God

■ **6.1 [59]** The Shepherd's vehement denial of what seems obvious from the previous explanation (5.2) prompts the question whether the negative in the sentence is original. The interpretation is easier without it: the Shepherd affirms that indeed the correspondence between parable and interpretation matches the slave and Son of God, but that his fidelity was rewarded with the authority of adopted son and heir (2.7–8). Likewise, in the interpretation to follow, he is authorized as redeemer and lawgiver (6.2–3). Thus a humiliation-exaltation Christology could be suggested. But the manuscript evidence is in favor of retaining the negative,[23] and nearly all commentators accept it,[24] for it presents such a problem that it is unlikely to have been inserted later, and Hermas' subsequent lack of understanding fits better. A servant Christology is still implied in vv. 2, 4, 6.[25] A total emphasis on the slave identification is rejected by the Shepherd as inadequate.[26] The slave has had complete charge of the vineyard, but only in obedience, and this obedience results in his freedom, constituted by adoption as joint heir and companion with the son, the Holy Spirit.[27]

■ **6.2** The explanation given here uses not the characters of the parable, but their theological counterparts. The slave of the parable is the Son of God; that is who is referred to here. The reference to the son's cleansing of the people's sins by his own hard efforts is generally taken to be the one reference in *Hermas* to the redemptive suffering of Christ.[28] In keeping with the terms of

---

precisely, the Holy Spirit is *not* the Son of God (Brox, 316).

19 See note on 2.2 above.

20 Cf. BAGD *s.v.* The same verb is used elsewhere in *Hermas*: the old woman church sits in a chair for support, the second meaning (*Vis.* 3.11.4); larger stones support smaller ones in the tower by enclosing them, the first meaning (*Sim.* 9.7.5); the son of God is supported or surrounded on right and left by angels, either meaning (*Sim.* 9.12.8).

21 Neh 9:20; Prov 9:5; Sir 24:21; John 6:31–58. Cf. Peder Borgen, *Bread from Heaven: An Exegetical Study of the Concept of Manna in the Gospel of John and the Writings of Philo* (NovTSup 10; Leiden: Brill, 1965). *Sim.* 8.3.2–7 will later identify the Son of God with the law.

22 For a similar motif, see especially *2 Clem.* 12.1; 17.4. However, in NT eschatological parables of the householder returning from a trip (Matt 25:14–30 par. Luke 19:12–27; related saying in Mark 13:33–37), the parables are not allegorized, so the identification of the householder is ambiguous as well. Lake (165 n. 2) is mistaken that there is no mention of the lord's absence in the parable (see 2.2b).

23 Missing in A, but present in LLE. Unfortunately, fifteen lines are missing here in M. The οὐ ("not") is

bracketed by Whittaker (57); accepted by Joly (237), who surmises that the Shepherd wishes to teach Hermas that the slave-son connection does not correspond to Hermas' Christology to date.

24 Except Audet, "Affinités," 70–71.

25 Wilson (*Reassessment,* 125) notes that servant Christology, and especially a suffering messiah, is elsewhere absent from Hermas, and suggests that the author may introduce it to refute a servant Christology; but there is no critique of a servant Christology offered in the text.

26 Leutzsch (*Wahrnehmung,* 153) suggests a connection with the general despising of slavery, or even from Hermas' personal history of slavery (!).

27 Pernveden, *Concept of the Church,* 46, 49.

28 "Gemeint ist ganz offenbar das Leiden Christi" ("The suffering of Christ is obviously meant"), Dibelius, 570. Snyder (107) disagrees without further explanation: "There is no reference to the historical Jesus."

the parable about the vineyard, however, it is called not suffering but labor, as the final statement of the verse recalls. The cleansing or purifying from sin as work of Christ has not appeared before, but purity of heart and intention as avoidance of sin is a frequent concern in moral exhortation.[29]

■ **6.3** The paths of life ($\alpha i \ \tau \rho i \beta \alpha i \ \tau \tilde{\eta} \varsigma \ \zeta \omega \tilde{\eta} \varsigma$) is a biblical expression and forerunner of the "two ways" as ethical teaching.[30] The relationship of the son to the law (and what law?) is confusing. Later (*Sim.* 8.3.2), the Son of God will be identified with the law as the one preached throughout the world. The new law of Christ is undoubtedly meant,[31] but in continuity with Torah. The image of Christ as lawgiver is not typical of *Hermas,* but is perfectly consonant with the whole schema of the Shepherd's teachings presented as commandments and with the author's Jewish-Christian environment. Thus, the law received by Jesus and taught to the people most likely includes, but is not limited to, all the moral teaching in *Hermas* itself, especially as concentrated in the *Mandates.* That the son received the law "from his father" is also not typical and must reflect a previously known formula; it is strikingly similar to the end of John 10:18.[32]

■ **6.4** Still speaking of the Son of God as the slave of the parable, the text applies the Son's new, augmented authority over the vineyard as son and heir to the exaltation and lordship of Christ.[33] In v. 4b, the correspondence of characters suddenly shifts with brutal abruptness. We are back to the parable, and now the "lord" is the vineyard owner[34] and the son is the son in the parable, that is, the Holy Spirit.[35] This statement opens the crux of interpretation of the christological allegory, the most difficult part in the fifth *Similitude,* and one of the most problematic passages in the whole document.[36]

■ **6.5–8** The easiest way to understand these verses is to see them as teaching a pneumatic adoptionist Christology: the preexistent Holy Spirit[37] by coming to dwell in the historical, non-preexistent person of Jesus constituted him as holy (v. 5), and subsequently exalted him to heaven (v. 6), which is to say, in terms of the parable, that "this flesh," the human Christ, the slave of the parable, was rewarded for his faithful service, as all faithful servants will be (v. 7).[38] Yet if this unorthodox interpretation has been understood to be its primary meaning, it is strange that this immensely popular document of the

---

29   E.g., cleansing from sin: *Vis.* 2.3.1; from faults: 3.2.2; from evil deeds: 3.8.11; cleansing of hearts: 3.9.8; *Man.* 9.4, 7; 12.6.5; *Sim.* 5.1.5, 3.6; 6.5.2; of the church: 9.18.2–3. $K\alpha\theta\alpha\rho i\zeta\epsilon i\nu$ ("to cleanse," "purify") occurs twenty-seven times, $\kappa\alpha\theta\alpha\rho\delta\varsigma$ ("clean," "pure") twenty-three times in *Hermas*; see too its opposite, "defilement" ($\mu\iota\alpha\sigma\mu\delta\varsigma$) in 7.2–3. The cleansing is sometimes to be done by persons' effort, sometimes by the action of God. Cf. Acts 15:9; 2 Cor 7:1; especially Eph 5:26; Titus 2:14; Heb 9:14; 10:2; 1 John 1:7.

30   E.g., Ps 16:11; Prov 16:17; *Did.* 1.1–2. See Introduction 3.3.3.

31   Matt 28:20; *Barn.* 2.6; esp. John 10:18; 13:34; 14:15, 21; 15:10, 12.

32   Here $\tau\delta\nu \ \nu\delta\mu o\nu \ \delta\nu \ \xi\lambda\alpha\beta\epsilon\nu \ \pi\alpha\rho\grave{\alpha} \ \tau o\tilde{\upsilon} \ \pi\alpha\tau\rho\grave{o}\varsigma \ \alpha\grave{\upsilon}\tau o\tilde{\upsilon}$ ("the law which he received from his father"); John 10:18: $\tau\alpha\acute{\upsilon}\tau\eta\nu \ \tau\grave{\eta}\nu \ \xi\nu\tauo\lambda\grave{\eta}\nu \ \xi\lambda\alpha\beta o\nu \ \pi\alpha\rho\grave{\alpha} \ \tau o\tilde{\upsilon} \ \pi\alpha\tau\rho\acute{o}\varsigma \ \mu o\upsilon$ ("this commandment which I received from my father").

33   The first sentence, in parentheses, is omitted by A but restored from LLE, having been skipped by the A copyist by homoioteleuton, since both it and the preceding sentence have the same ending.

34   Who in the parable itself is consistently called not $\kappa\acute{\upsilon}\rho\iota o\varsigma$ ("lord") as here, but $\delta\epsilon\sigma\pi\acute{o}\tau\eta\varsigma$ ("master"). However, his title has shifted to "lord of the field"

($\kappa\acute{\upsilon}\rho\iota o\varsigma \ \tau o\tilde{\upsilon} \ \grave{\alpha}\gamma\rho o\tilde{\upsilon}$) in 5.2.

35   2.6, 11; 5.2. Rough edges such as these lead Nijendijk (*Christologie,* 93–97) to argue that in an original version, the son of the parable was the (heavenly) Son of God, who at a later stage was split off from the earthly son, who then became the slave, leaving the heavenly son to be identified with the Holy Spirit. Henne (*Christologie,* 206–8) suggests that the son in v. 4b is not the holy spirit, but the Son of God, partially because it corresponds better to principles of internal coherence established by himself, and because the Son of God appears with six angels in the ninth *Similitude.* "Cette identification est possible, sans être certaine" ("This identification is possible but not certain," 208).

36   For a history of interpretation, see Henne, *Christologie,* 157–71.

37   The Holy Spirit seems here to be associated with the figure of preexistent wisdom, agent of creation. Cf. Werner Bieder, "$\Pi\nu\epsilon\tilde{\upsilon}\mu\alpha, \ \pi\nu\epsilon\upsilon\mu\alpha\tau\iota\kappa\acute{o}\varsigma$," *TDNT* 6 (1968) 371–72.

38   For Dibelius, a "binitarian monotheism" (574).

early church was never condemned for christological heresy. Rather, it is modern interpreters who sometimes seek to explain away its unusual Christology. However, it is not totally clear that vv. 5–6 refer exclusively or even primarily to Christ, as most commentators assume. The relationship between the spirit and the "chosen flesh" (σὰρξ ἣν ἠβούλετο) could be about the relationship of humanity to the holy spirit, or the modification of a dualistic flesh-spirit anthropology in order to stress the importance, even immortality, of the flesh, sign of the whole person.[39] The Son of God is no longer referred to; the son in v. 7 is again the son of the parable, the Holy Spirit. That the flesh served the spirit (ἐδούλευσε) is peculiar; service to the spirit (=the son in the parable) rather than to the lord of the field is not part of the original story.

All of this leads Henne to propose that vv. 5–7 are not about Christology at all, but about the relationship of flesh and spirit.[40] Brox argues against him[41] that the christological exposition continues, citing as evidence that v. 4b signals the continuation of the interpretation of the parable by returning to the characters of the story, and that "flesh" in vv. 5–6 is singular as contrasted with the plural "all flesh," which signals a generalization in v. 6.[42] To these arguments could be added the past tense verbs throughout vv. 5–6, suggesting a historical referent, and the fact that between the other two interpretations of the parable, fasting and Christology, there was a clear break (chap. 4).

Yet, though v. 4b implies that the same interpretation is continuing, in fact these verses have moved off into

something different with not much by way of transition. It is likely that they speak of Christ as primary referent, but, as usual in *Hermas,* only for the sake of moral instruction and paraenesis, to which the consideration quickly moves. Thus, the humanity of Christ becomes the bridge to a third interpretation of the parable—one that departs substantially from the original story line. This interpretation is no longer allegory, but analogy, more along the lines of the first application on fasting (chap. 3). There the analogy of the fidelity of the slave, especially in going beyond what was commanded, was applied to the true spirit of fasting. Here faithful service to legitimate authority is seen as analogous to the submission of human flesh to the spirit of God, not of flesh to spirit in an anthroplogically dualistic sense.

Verses 5–6 are enclosed between two assertions that what lies between explains why the lord of the parable took his son and friends as advisors (vv. 4, 7). It is not immediately obvious how this is so. The answer comes in v. 7: just as the lord in the parable was concerned to honor the slave with a place in the family as reward for his fidelity, and gathered together the council of son and clients for approval of his decision (2.6), so God is concerned to honor the flesh with a (heavenly) dwelling place (τόπος τινὰ κατασκηνώσεως). Verse 7 says clearly that what applies to this particular flesh—to whomever it belongs—applies to all in whom the holy spirit dwells.[43] This makes a strictly adoptionist interpretation impossible, even though the "flesh" of vv. 5–6 probably does

---

39 See 7.2; Luigi Cirillo, "La christologie pneumatique de la cinquième parabole du 'Pasteur' d'Hermas," *Revue de l'histoire des religions* 184 (1973) 25–48 (28–29). There are two different anthropologies at work here, though they are not necessarily in conflict. The "flesh" here means the whole human person, which is biblical (e.g., Gen 6:12, 17; Deut 5:26; Ps 65:2; 145:21; Joel 2:28; Zech 2:13, etc.; compare *Man.* 3.1; 10.2.6); at other times, however, the author can speak of the flesh as an aspect of the person (e.g., 7.1; compare *Vis.* 3.9.3, 10.7). The same ambiguity is also biblical (Ps 16:9; 73:26; 119:120). Yet the spirit dwells in it as in a receptacle, an anthropology already taken for granted in the *Mandates.*

40 *Christologie,* 174–77.

41 "Henne . . . macht den gravierenden Fehler" ("Henne . . . makes the aggravating error"), 320.

42 But the singular is often used collectively in biblical literature, e.g., Ps 65:2; 145:21; Joel 2:28; Zech 2:13, etc. Robert J. Hauck ("The Great Fast: Christology in the Shepherd of Hermas" [*ATR* 75 (1993) 187–98]) also proposes Christology as the central point of the fifth *Similitude.* The most important assertion about Christ is that he did not defile the flesh. "In the Son of God, the Holy Spirit has completely conquered, and the flesh has taken up immortality" (197–98). Since this is salvific for all, it is not adoptionist but soteriological.

43 The dwelling of a holy spirit in persons is a theme familiar from the *Mandates* and the moral teaching on the two spirits: *Man.* 3.1; 5.1–2; 2.5–7; 10.2.5; Cirillo, "Christologie pneumatique," 29–39. Brox (320), for an unexplained reason, wants to distinguish between the Holy Spirit dwelling in Jesus and

refer to Christ by way of example of what is in store for all.[44] Thus, without using the familiar terms, the discussion as it extends into chapter 7 is really about the dignity of persons in view of the resurrection and exaltation of the faithful,[45] with Christ as firstfruits.[46] Yet the strictly christological perspective can be said to be adoptionist, since there is no indication of preexistence of the Son of God, and perhaps binitarian, since God and preexistent spirit belong to the same family. But the theology here is more accurately monotheistic with preexistent (but not necessarily divine) spirit and exalted

Son of God. Trinitarian in the orthodox sense it certainly is not. Eusebius notes the presence of various adoptionist theologies in Rome at this time.[47] We may have here a bit of popular belief that differed significantly from that of the theological authorities of the church.

Verse 8 seems like a simple conclusion,[48] but it is not clear to which parable it refers. Since the wording implies something additional to the original parable, perhaps it refers only to vv. 4–7, the lord's taking of his son and clients as advisors.

---

the holy spirit that dwells in others, but no such distinction is suggested in the text. The perils of capitalization in translation are evident here.

44 The spirit of God dwells in all flesh, and in the particular flesh of the servant Jesus; the difference is that he is the servant specially chosen (6.5), as the slave of the parable was chosen (2.2), thus evoking Isa 42:1: Cirillo, "Christologie pneumatique," 40–41.

45 Also Joly, 241 n. 3.

46 1 Cor 15:20.

47 *Hist. eccl.* 5.28.1–6. Eusebius is stressing the orthodoxy of teachers as early as Clement and Justin over against adoptionism as a late innovation, but by reporting that Victor excommunicated Theodotus the cobbler for such teaching, he implies that it was already in existence in Victor's time.

48 Compare *4 Ezra* 12.10; 13.53 (Joly, 240 n. 2), but the first introduces an interpretation, the second concludes one, as here.

5　　　Purity of the Flesh

7 [60]　　1/ "I rejoice, sir," I said, "to hear this explanation of the parable." "Now listen," he said. "Keep this flesh of yours pure and undefiled, so that the spirit that dwells in it may witness to it and your flesh be justified. 2/ See to it that it not enter your heart that this flesh of yours is perishable, and you misuse it in some kind of defilement. If you defile your flesh, you will defile the Holy Spirit, and if you defile your flesh, you will not live." 3/ "But sir," I said, "what if there was prior ignorance before these words were heard, how will such a person who defiles the flesh be saved?" "About former ignorance," he said, "the power to give healing belongs to God alone, who has all power. 4/ But for now, see to these things, and the Lord who is totally compassionate will heal them, if from now on you defile neither your flesh nor the spirit. They are together, and one cannot be defiled without the other. So keep both pure, and you will live to God."

■ **7.1 [60]** While flesh has previously meant the whole person, it can also be spoken of as an aspect of the person, as here. It is to be kept pure or clean (καθαρά) and undefiled (ἀμίαντος).[1] How this is done is not specified, and the idea is not necessarily connected to sexual purity. Certainly sexual irregularity is one way of incurring defilement,[2] but the terminology is remarkably absent in discussions of sexuality and frequent in other contexts: conversion, commandments, bitterness.[3] The indwelling spirit acts not only as power of relationship and inspiration to good, but also as witness to the integrity of the person in which it dwells.[4] In contrast to the meaning of δικαιοσύνη as just action in exhortatory contexts, here the action of God is meant, which renders capable of immortality the person who remains faithful to the indwelling spirit.[5]

■ **7.2** Of the several passages in *Hermas* in which some trace of the incipient Gnosticism already present in Rome might be detected, this is one of the best,[6] yet there is nothing in the text that would fit only, or even best, what we know of Gnosticism in Rome at this time.[7] The flesh is for Hermas the whole person, yet the per-

---

1　Also above at 6.7, undefiled and spotless (ἀμίαντος καὶ ἄσπιλος).
2　*Man.* 4.1.9.
3　*Man.* 2.7; 3.2; 5.2–6; *Sim.* 9.29.2.
4　Compare Rom 8:16.
5　Also at *Vis.* 3.9.1; *Man.* 5.1.7, where justification is the work of the most glorious angel.
6　The others are: *Vis.* 3.7.1; *Man.* 11.1; the parable, *Sim.* 5.2 (a Valentinian parable?); 8.6.5; 9.19.2–3; 22.1–3: Leutzsch, *Wahrnehmung*, 75–76, esp. n. 82 for those who agree. Louis Duchesne (*Histoire ancienne de l'église* [3d ed.; Paris: Fontemoing, 1907–1910] 1. 188–89) and others since have suggested that passages like this one and *Sim.* 9.22 were written with specific teachers like Marcion and Valentinus in mind; Hermas' solution was "simplicité de l'esprit et la droiture du coeur" ("simplicity of spirit and an upright heart"). Gnostic polemic is not

certain, but a counterpart may be the Coptic Gnostic *Apoc. Pet.* 78.15–19: "an imitation remnant in the name of a dead man, who is Hermas, of the firstborn of unrighteousness" (trans. J. Brashler and R. A. Bullard, *NHLE*, 376); discussion in Klaus Koschorke, *Die Polemik der Gnostiker gegen das kirchliche Christentum* (NHS 12; Leiden: Brill, 1978) 58–60.
7　On Roman Gnosticism, see Lampe, *Stadtrömische Christen*, 251–70; Carlo Cecchelli, *Monumenti Cristiano-Eretici di Roma* (Rome: Palombi, 1944).

son is also composed of spirit.[8] As in 6.5–6, though the language of resurrection is mysteriously absent, it is difficult to think that this concept is not behind the teaching on the incorruptibility of the flesh, and perhaps the thinking to which the Shepherd objects is as basic as that to which Paul objects in 1 Cor 15:12: "How can some of you say that there is no resurrection from the dead?"[9] In the last part of v. 2b, several commentators have accepted the emendation, "and if you defile the spirit, you will not live." The emendation creates better parallelism and would not be inconsistent,[10] but the manuscript evidence is universally as translated.[11]

■ **7.3–4** Verse 3a regards the transgressing of forbidden boundaries out of ignorance at an earlier time.[12] Verse 3b assures not of the innocence of those who sin in igno-

rance, but of the power of God to overcome the transgression with healing of sin.[13] In v. 4, God is again called fully compassionate ($\pi o\lambda \acute{v}\sigma\pi\lambda\alpha\gamma\chi\nu o\varsigma$), a frequent title.[14] Flesh and spirit belong together and share a common life ($\dot{\alpha}\mu\varphi\acute{o}\tau\epsilon\rho\alpha\ \gamma\grave{\alpha}\rho\ \kappa o\iota\nu\acute{\alpha}\ \dot{\epsilon}\sigma\tau\iota\nu$).[15] This is one of the clearest anthropological statements in *Hermas*, showing the close relationship of the nevertheless distinctive elements of the person, and must be kept in mind when attempting to understand any other passage that sounds dualistic. The chapter ends in the form of a commandment to live undefiled, and concludes with the formula that concludes many of the *Mandates*.

---

8   Cf. v. 4; Introduction 3.3.3.

9   A remarkably similar passage to this one is *2 Clem.* 9.1–5, where resurrection is explicit. It is inconceivable how, in light of this passage, Pernveden (*Concept of the Church,* 273) can say that in *Hermas* resurrection is replaced by direct ascension of the soul to heaven. For David Hill (*Regnum Caelorum: Patterns of Future Hope in Early Christianity* [Oxford: Clarendon, 1992] 80–81), resurrection in not explicit here because it does not fit well with the tower image, but is taken for granted: "The near silence of Hermas on the resurrection is thus due to the accepted and uncontroverted place which the doctrine had with Hermas and his readers."

10   See 5.6.5; *Man.* 10.2.5.

11   Emendation by Gebhardt-Harnack; Hilgenfeld, "the flesh and the spirit" (Dibelius, 577); emendation to spirit "in the supposed interests of the sense" (Lake,

168). List of those who accept the emendation in Brox, 326 n. 35. Both Whittaker (58) and Joly (240–41) are silent about it, and Dibelius (577) doubts it. For *2 Clem.* 14.3–5, abuse of the flesh is abuse of the church.

12   Compare *Man.* 4.1.5.

13   On God's forgiveness of sin as healing, see comment on *Vis.* 1.1.9.

14   See comment on *Vis.* 3.12.3. Most of the first sentence of v. 4 (until "[if] you defile") is missing in A, but present in MLLE, and PPrag 1, a recently published fragment of 7.3–4. This fragment exhibits a number of word-order changes that do not affect meaning.

15   PPrag 1 goes a little further by calling them $\kappa o\iota\nu\omega\nu\acute{\alpha}$ ("partners").

6

Shepherds of Luxury and Punishment

1 [61] 1/ While I was sitting in my house, glorifying the Lord because of everything I had seen, and meditating on how the commandments were attractive, powerful, joyous, honorable, and capable of saving the human spirit, I said to myself: "Happy would I be if I proceeded according to these commandments, and whoever does so will be happy." 2/ While I was saying this to myself, I suddenly saw him sitting next to me and saying: "Why are you doubleminded about the commandments I have mandated to you? They are beautiful. Do not be doubleminded at all, but clothe yourself in trust in the Lord and go forward in them. I will empower you in them. 3/ These commandments are helpful for those about to be converted. If they do not go forward in them, their conversion is in vain. 4/ So you [pl.] who are converted, reject the evils of this world which destroy you. By putting on the entire strength of justice, you will be able to keep these commandments and add no more to your sins. So by adding no more to your sins, you will eliminate many of your former sins. Therefore, go forward in my commandments, and you will live to God. All these things I have told you." 5/ After saying these things to me, he said, "Let us go into the country, and I will show you [sing.] the shepherds of the sheep." "Let us go, sir," I said. We came to a certain plain, and he showed me a young shepherd clothed in an ensemble of saffron-colored garments. 6/ He cared for a very large flock, and the sheep seemed to luxuriate and be dissipated and happy, ambling here and there, and the shepherd himself rejoiced over his flock. The face of the shepherd was very joyous and he ran about among the sheep. (And I saw other sheep relaxing and luxuriating in one place, not ambling around.)

2 [62] 1/ He said to me, "Do you see this shepherd?" "I do, sir," I said. "This is the angel of luxury and deceit," he said. "This one destroys the souls of the servants of God who are empty and turns them away from the truth by deceiving them with evil desires, in which they are lost. 2/ They forget the commandments of the living God and go off after crazy deceptions and luxuries and are destroyed by this angel, some to death, some to ruin." I said to him, "Sir, I do not know what this means: `some to death and some to ruin.' " "Listen," he said, "whatever sheep you see very happy and ambling around, these are the ones who are completely distanced from God and have given themselves up to the desires of this world. In these there is no conversion of life, because they have added on blasphemy against the name of the Lord. Death is for such as these. 4/ Those you saw not ambling around, but feeding in one place, are the ones who have given themselves over to luxuries and deceit, but have not blasphemed the Lord. These have been ruined to the truth. For them there is hope of conversion in which they will be able to live. For

184

ruin has some hope of rejuvenation, but death bears eternal destruction." 5/ When we had gone on a little further, he showed me a large shepherd, sort of wild in appearance, dressed in white goatskin, a bag on his shoulders, with a hard, knotty staff, and a large whip. He had a very severe look, so that I was afraid of him, he had such a look. 6/ This shepherd was receiving the sheep from the young shepherd, those that were dissipated and luxurious—but not ambling around—and he put them in a place that was steep, thorny, and full of thistles, so that the sheep could not disentangle themselves from the thorns and thistles, but were entangled in the thorns and thistles. 7/ They fed while entangled in the thorns and thistles and being beaten by him; they looked completely wretched. He drove them around here and there and gave them no rest, so they were not at all well off.

3 [63]   1/ Seeing them so beaten and miserable, I was sorry for them because they were so afflicted and had no relief at all. 2/ I said to the Shepherd who was speaking with me: "Sir, what kind of shepherd is this, so merciless and severe, who has no compassion at all on these sheep?" He said, "This is the angel of punishment. He is one of the just angels, but is in charge of punishment. 3/ He takes in those who have wandered away from God and have gone after the desires of this world, and he chastises them appropriately, with various and awful punishments." 4/ "I should like, sir," I said, "to know of what kinds are these various punishments." "Then listen," he said, "to the various torments and punishments. The torments are during life, for some are punished with losses, some with serious want, some with various illnesses, some with complete trauma, some are abused by unworthy persons, and suffer many other things. 5/ For some are unsettled about their decisions and throw themselves in many directions and nothing at all prospers for them. They say they do not succeed in what they do, and it never enters their heart that they have done evil deeds, but they blame the Lord. 6/ When they are afflicted with every affliction, then they are turned over to me for good discipline and are strengthened in trust in the Lord, and for the rest of the days of their life they serve the Lord with a pure heart. When they are converted, then it enters their heart about the evil deeds they did, and then they glorify the Lord as a just judge, knowing they have suffered justly, each according to one's own deeds. But from then on they will serve the Lord with their pure heart, and they do well in all their efforts, receiving from the Lord whatever they ask. Then they glorify the Lord that they were given over to me, and they no longer suffer anything bad."

4 [64]   1/ I said to him, "Sir, still explain this to me." "What do you want?" he said. "Whether, sir, those who luxuriate and live in deception are tormented for the same amount of time as they

have lived in luxury and deception?" He said to me: "They are tormented for the same amount of time." 2/ ["They are tormented for a short time, sir," I said.] "It is fitting that those who live in luxury and forgetfulness of God be punished sevenfold." 3/ He said to me: "You are stupid and do not know the power of the torment." "If I knew it, sir," I said, "I would not have asked you to explain it to me." "Listen," he said, "to the power of both. 4/ The time of luxury and deception is one hour, but the hour of torment has the power of thirty days. So if anyone lives in luxury and deception for just one day, and is tormented for one day, the day of torment is equal to a whole year. For as many days as someone has lived in luxury, that many years is the torment. So you see," he said, "that the time of luxury and deception is brief but the time of torment is long."

5 [65]   1/ "Sir," I said, "I still have not completely understood about the time of deception and luxury and torment. Explain it to me more clearly." 2/ He answered me, "Your stupidity is unending; you do not want to purify your heart and serve God. See to it," he said, "lest the time be completed and you be found to be still stupid. So listen," he said, "so as to understand it as you want. 3/ The one who luxuriates and is deceived for one day, doing just as one likes, is clothed with great stupidity and does not know what he or she is doing. That person forgets tomorrow what was done today. Luxury and deceit have no memory because of the stupidity in which they are clothed. When punishment and torment cling to someone for just one day, that one is punished and tormented for a whole year because punishment and torment have long memories. 4/ After being punished and tormented for a whole year, this person remembers the luxury and deceit and knows that the suffering of evil is because of this. Thus all people who live in luxury and deception are so tormented, because while still alive they have handed themselves over to death." 5/ "What luxuries are harmful, sir?" I asked. "Every act is luxury for a person that is done with pleasure. Even the bad-tempered person luxuriates by giving satisfaction to one's own vice. Likewise the adulterer, the drunkard, the slanderer, the liar, the avaricious, the robber, and the one who does similar things satisfies one's own disease; such a one lives in the luxury of one's own deeds. 6/ All these luxuries are harmful for the servants of God. Those who are punished and tormented suffer because of these. 7/ But there are also luxuries that save. Many luxuriate in doing good, carried away by their own pleasure. This luxury is helpful for the servants of God and brings life to that person. The harmful luxuries already discussed bring torment and punishment. If they remain this way and are not converted, they work death for themselves."

The sixth and seventh *Similitudes* offer an explanation of suffering: it is punishment for sin according to the measure of the seriousness of the sin. However, suffering is not retribution. It is the invitation to conversion of heart, a sign that should be recognizable to the spiritually alert that God is calling them to change their ways. With conversion of heart comes cessation of suffering.

■ **1.1–4 [61]** The sixth *Similitude* uses a vision of sheep with two kinds of shepherds to teach about the two kinds of luxury, as summarized at the end (5.5–7). This structure continues that of some of the *Mandates*,[1] and vv. 1–4 are in commandment genre.[2] For the second time, the location of Hermas' vision is his own house, where he is seated (v. 1), and where the Shepherd is suddenly beside him (v. 2).[3] Hermas is reflecting on the goodness of the commandments, even that they are sources of joy (they are ἱλαραί)[4] capable of saving the human person (καὶ δυνάμεναι σῶσαι ψυχὴν ἀνθρώπου).[5] Though Hermas' desire to participate in that happiness by observance of the commandments is expressed positively in the future tense (μακάριος ἔσομαι, "happy will I be"),[6] the sense of the statement is conditional,[7] as evidenced by the Shepherd's interpretation of the statement as doubt (v. 2). The concluding statement of v. 1 is a formula that occurs often in the *Mandates*.

Doublemindedness, a preoccupation of Hermas, has not been mentioned since *Sim.* 1.3 (v. 2). The change to the plural throughout v. 4 for general exhortation is also more frequent in the *Mandates,* as is the (usually concluding) formula, "you will live to God" (ζήσεσθε τῷ θεῷ). The "strength of justice," or more traditionally, "virtue of righteousness" (πᾶσα ἀρετὴ τῆς δικαιοσύνης), is a pleonastic, perhaps "hebraizing" expression.[8] The hearers are told that by observing the commandments they can break the cycle of sin, thus adding no more to its accumulation in their lives.[9] The next sentence[10] implies more: the forgiveness of former sins through the doing of good deeds according to the commandments. Though none of the manuscripts breaks here, there is a natural break in the flow of the text at the end of v. 4 with the Shepherd's own summarizing statement.

■ **1.5–6** Here begins the vision and explanation of the sheep herded by two kinds of shepherds. The scene shifts from Hermas' house to the countryside, or field (Ἄγομεν εἰς ἀγρόν), where other important revelations have already taken place,[11] as well as in an open field or plain (πεδίον).[12] The young shepherd is clothed in a σύνθεσις ἱματίων (an "ensemble" or matching outfit)[13] of a yellow color, probably of saffron dye, a luxury item[14] that already signals in this happy scene that all will not end well. Yet, for the moment, both sheep and shepherd in this first scene are happy.[15] The description of the sheep is positive, though warning signals are given by

---

1   Two kinds of fear (7.4); two kinds of restraint (8.1–11); two kinds of desire (12.1.1, 3.1).

2   Brox (332) aptly remarks that all three genres are brought together here, and that any attempt to outline the structure of the *Similitudes* or to isolate the genres is arbitrary.

3   See comment on *Vis.* 5.1.

4   Compare some of the commandments (*Man.* 12.3.4); of the service of fasting (*Sim.* 5.3.8b).

5   Cf. Jas 1:21.

6   Compare *Vis.* 1.1.2, μακάριος ἤμην ("happy would I be"), in a quite similar context.

7   BDF §362. Compare *Man.* 12.3.4–5, where the doubt is explicit.

8   Compare *Man.* 1.2; 6.2.3: πᾶσα ἀρετὴ ἐνδόξου ("every strength/virtue of glory"). Cf. Hilhorst, *Sémitismes,* 112.

9   See *Vis.* 5.5.7; the negative example at 2.3 below.

10   Missing in A, but present in MLLE.

11   *Vis.* 2.1.4; 3.1.2–4; 4.1.2; *Sim.* 2.1.

12   The plain or smooth ground (ὁμαλά) as place of revelation: *Vis.* 1.1.3 (see comment); *Sim.* 7.1 (Brox, 333–34).

13   Σύνθεσις (more usually, "compilation") is also used for clothing, attested a few times in the papyri during this period, e.g., *POxy* 496.4; *PHamb.* 10.13, 21; *Dig.* 34.2.38.1; but also Martial *Epig.* 2.46.4; 4.66.3–4; 5.79.2; 10.29.4 (of the clothing of a woman); Suetonius *Nero* 51; cf. BAGD, LSJ *s.v.* IV.1; PW *s.v.* 3. In some contexts, it seems to mean a luxurious dinner garment for attendance at private parties, which may be what leads Joly (245) to call it "un vêtement d'intérieur qui fait plus habillé que la tunique" ("an inside garment that makes one more dressed up than the tunic"), though he doubts this is its meaning here.

14   Collected and varied opinions of commentators on the meaning of the yellow garment in Brox, 334.

15   Brox (333) draws attention to "an interesting parallel" in *1 Enoch* 89.59–90.42, in which, however, there are many more shepherds and the whole scene is much more complicated.

the two present participles τρυφῶντα ("luxuriating") and σπαταλῶντα ("behaving riotously"). The final sentence of v. 6 in parentheses is preserved only in the Paris codex of Pseudo-Athanasius, but it describes the second category of sheep within the same flock, those who luxuriate but do not wander, and the information is presumed at 2.4, below.[16]

■ **2.1–4 [62]** The two groups of sheep are now explained allegorically in a manner not unlike that of the stones in the building of the tower in *Vis.* 3.5.1–7.6, but this whole explanation will be much less complicated. Here there are only two groups, and only sinners are included. The first group have only death in store for them because of their blasphemy (v. 3), while the second group, because they have not blasphemed, are destined for punishment and torture that leads eventually to their salvation (v. 4). Both at this point are led by a shepherd who is called an angel (v. 1), but is in fact a demonic figure who represents luxury and deceit, to be understood as self-deception. This figure can only destroy those who are empty,[17] that is, who have not filled themselves with the good things of God,[18] but rather with evil desires (v. 1). They demonstrate their emptiness by forsaking the commandments of the living God[19] (v. 2), but they depart in two different directions, whose difference is not clear: "death" (θάνατος) and ruin, destruction, or corruption (καταφθορά).

Appearances are deceiving. The sheep who look happiest, ironically, are the worst off (v. 3). Their constant movement does not mean that they enjoy a healthy spiritual freedom, but rather that they are restlessly looking for what they do not have by way of pleasure, and the well-dressed young shepherd encourages them at every step. These pleasures have previously been listed in detail and are not repeated here.[20] These sheep have no chance of conversion[21] because they have topped off their excesses with blasphemy, not in some kind of formal persecution,[22] but with their conscious daily choices of living according to their worldly desires and therefore in no way differently from unbelievers. By contrast, those sheep that seem less gregarious (v. 4) are in fact better off, for they have a chance for life that the first group do not. But first, they have some hard times ahead.[23] They are heading not for total destruction like the senseless hedonists before them, but for "ruin" (καταφθορά)[24] that carries through with hope of renewal (ἀνανέωσις).[25]

■ **2.5–7** The next part of the vision features a real shepherd, one unlike the luxuriously clothed youth of 1.5. This one is properly dressed in goatskin, with bag and staff.[26] But he is also a forbidding figure, in contrast to the major Shepherd, with savage face (ἄγριον τῇ ἰδέᾳ) and whip in hand. The second group of sheep, those from v. 4, are handed over to this fearful shepherd who

---

16   Most editors accept the sentence as genuine, except Lake (172–73), who makes no mention of it, and Whittaker (59), who relegates it to the apparatus.

17   The reference to being empty (τῶν κενῶν) is omitted by Ath²LLE, and on that basis by Lake (172) with no explanation, but it is attested in A and M, the latter not yet published when Lake wrote.

18   Compare the emphatic contempt of this kind of emptiness in *Man.* 5.2.2, 7; throughout 11; 12.2.1,4, where it is precisely τρυφή ("luxury") that is empty.

19   See *Vis.* 3.7.2.

20   *Man.* 6.2.5.

21   Like the stones of *Vis.* 3.6.1 that are smashed and thrown far from the tower. Joly (247 nn. 1, 2) raises the question whether Hermas believes that blasphemy is the unforgivable sin (Mark 3:28–29 parr. Matt 12:31–32; Luke 12:10) rather than that all sin can be forgiven in conversion, but he answers in the negative in the introduction (27–28): Hermas is contradictory on this point because he tries to balance both positions. Cf. *Vis.* 3.7.2; *Sim.* 8.6.2–4: there is no chance for some because they have hardened their own hearts.

22   So Dibelius (580), who appeals to *Sim.* 8.6.4; 9.19.1 as evidence for persecution, but even these passages can be explained differently: see comment on them below.

23   They correspond to the stones cast away—but not far away—from the tower in *Vis.* 3.5.5, so that they still have opportunity for conversion.

24   Dibelius (580) argues that this ruin, which really leads to life if there is conversion as a result, is different from the destruction to which foolishness (ἀφροσύνη) leads in *Tab. Ceb.* 3.3, because there it leads the one who does not understand eventually, but little by little, to death, like the fate of those destroyed slowly by the Sphinx, while here, ruin is less than death. The difference is only apparent, however, for here there is the hope, not the assurance, that suffering will lead to conversion and therefore to life.

25   Already understood as the effect of conversion in the rejuvenation of the woman church (*Vis.* 3.11.3; 12.1–3; 13.2; *Sim.* 9.14.3).

drives them into thorns and thistles, all the while beating them with his large whip (vv. 6–7). This description of their torments is consonant with the shepherding image used here. It corresponds to the description of the torments of the damned or punished in apocalyptic tours of hell. While the sheep are certainly miserable, in comparison with other contemporary examples of this developing genre the description is mightily restrained.[27]

■ **3.1–3 [63]** Hermas' compassion for the sheep does not keep him from his usual custom of asking many questions of the Shepherd. He is told that the punishing shepherd is not a demonic figure, as would be expected from the genre, but the angel of punishment (ὁ ἄγγελος τῆς τιμωρίας), one of the good angels,[28] in contrast to the deceptively attractive young angel who happily leads happy sheep to death in 1.5–6. Another angle on the Two Ways is being developed here: what is attractive to the insensitive leads to death, while what seems terrible leads to life.

■ **3.4–6** In answer to Hermas' question, the Shepherd enumerates a list of afflictions. This too corresponds somewhat to the description in the literature of torments suffered by those being punished.[29] What is remarkable, however, is that these punishments are not eschatological but rather βιωτικαί, meaning both in this mortal life and in everyday events, not planned or inflicted on purpose by human agents, but the ordinary setbacks that can happen to anyone. Thus Hermas avoids a natural opening for apocalyptic speculation in favor of a realistic theology of the redemptive significance of suffering in the life of the wavering believer. These afflictions are the means God uses to recall such recalcitrants to their true sense of direction. While still blinded by their own insensitivity, they blame God for everything that goes wrong in their lives (v. 5).[30] If, however, they can take advantage of their hard situation, being "afflicted with every affliction,"[31] to realize that their suffering is meant to lead to a change of heart, then the angel of punishment can do something constructive with them, ἀγαθὴ παιδεία ("good discipline," "education").[32] They turn to God with converted and grateful hearts, and their suffering ceases (v. 6b). Hermas here leaves untouched the problem of the suffering of the innocent, or continued suffering after conversion.

■ **4.1–4 [64]** Suitability of the punishment to fit the crime is an important component of contemporary ideas of retribution.[33] Here the question is compatibility of time, and it must be remembered that it is not other worldly but this-worldly torment (βάσανος)[34] that is envisioned (v. 1). Hermas shows himself to be more severe than the Shepherd by suggesting that one-to-one time correspondence should not be sufficient;[35] rather, sevenfold pun-

---

26 Compare the description of the main Shepherd-revealer in *Vis.* 5.1.

27 Some references in Brox, 337; cf. Martha Himmelfarb, *Tours of Hell: An Apocalyptic Form in Jewish and Christian Literature* (Philadelphia: Fortress, 1983).

28 Cf. ibid., 120–21. The idea occurs frequently, e.g., *Corp. Herm.* 1.23; 10.21; 13.7; *Tab. Ceb.* 10, but the agent is not always aligned with the power of good. See Peterson, "Kritische Analyse," 277 n. 26, for the speculation of the Jewish background of the two impulses in *Corp. Herm.* 13; A. D. Nock and A. J. Festugière, *Corpus Hermeticum* (Paris: Belles Lettres, 1945) 1. 24 n. 57, on Hellenistic counterparts.

29 See comment on 2.6–7 above.

30 The text here says that they do not do well ἐν ταῖς πράξεσιν αὐτῶν, which in other contexts could mean "in their business ventures," e.g., *Man.* 6.2.5; *Sim.* 4.5, 7. Here, however, the meaning is probably broader: in whatever they undertake.

31 A "Semitism," dative of association, already noticed by Dibelius (582).

32 Compare *Man.* 4.2.2. There are definite similarities here with *Tab. Ceb.* 10–11; there Punishment (τιμωρία) with whip, along with others, afflicts several figures who remain in unhappiness unless Conversion (μετάνοια) chooses to rescue them and lead them through intermediaries to True Education (ἀληθινή παιδεία), who saves them. Cf. Joly, 52.

33 Especially in the *Apoc. Pet.*; cf. Alan E. Bernstein, *The Formation of Hell: Death and Retribution in the Ancient and Early Christian Worlds* (Ithaca, NY/London: Cornell University Press, 1993) 282–91.

34 See comment on *Man.* 4.2.2.

35 The first sentence of v. 2 is omitted by A and probably by M, where the ms. is severely damaged at this point but is not likely to have had room (Bonner, *Papyrus Codex*, 72). A Greek sentence was reconstructed by Hollenberg, accepted by Joly (250), bracketed by Whittaker (62): Ἐλάχιστον, φημί, κύριε, βασανίζονται ("Sir, I said, they are tormented a little time"), from L¹: *et dixi ei: exiguum inquam cruciantur* ("and I said to him: they are tormented, I

ishment is more appropriate (v. 2).[36] The Shepherd's reproach prompts a saucy rejoinder from Hermas (v. 3).[37] Verse 4 gives a mathematical formula based on a twelve-hour day of activity,[38] and explains that the amount of suffering is appropriate to the amount of transgression, but since the sense of time passes very slowly during suffering, the time of torment seems much longer. This, however, is due to the perception of the sufferer, not to God's plan.

■ **5.1–4 [65]** Because of his apparent thickness about this point, Hermas is accused of not wanting to understand. The Shepherd's patience seems to be running short here,[39] and Hermas is hit with the threat of eschatological imminence to jolt his understanding (v. 2).[40] Just as those who put away evil are clothed with the strength of justice (1.4), so those who continue hard-hearted are clothed in stupidity (v. 3). Verses 3–4 repeat the lesson of 4.4, but more philosophically and with vivid observation of human experience. Enjoyment is present-oriented and would continue forever. It therefore neither has nor wants a memory of the past or a sense of the passing of time. Affliction, on the other hand, seems to last forever even if it really lasts only a short time. The sufferer has a sharp memory of what life was like before this terrible time, and an acute sense of the slow passing of time. Thus the paradox: those who choose the way of luxury

and deceit in the name of life have actually chosen death.

■ **5.5–7** These verses will trace a new development of the "Two Ways" teaching in Hermas. Just as there are both negative and positive aspects of many human affects,[41] so too with the notion of luxury. Deeds done for pure pleasure are harmful.[42] Harmful kinds of luxury involve the usual kinds of pleasures, but the catalog of vices includes a few unexpected ones, like giving in to bad temper,[43] and robbery. The allusion to all of them as symptoms of one's own disease (τῇ ἰδίᾳ νόσῳ) sounds strangely modern. There is, however, another kind of luxury (τρυφή) that is not harmful but salvific (v. 7). In contrast to the doublet teaching in the *Mandates,* here this good kind of luxury is not detailed, except to specify that it is the pleasure experienced by the servants of God in the doing of good: πολλοὶ γὰρ ἀγαθὸν ἐργαζόμενοι τρυφῶσιν, τῇ ἑαυτῶν ἡδονῇ φερόμενοι ("Many luxuriate in doing good, carried away by their own pleasure"). The Stoic suspicion of pleasure is neutralized here. Pleasure (ἡδονή) too can be good if it springs from the right source.

---

said, a little time"); L²: *et dixi, multum exiguum domine cruciantur* ("and I said, they are tormented, sir, a very little time").

36   Brox (339) rightly disagrees with Joly (250), who suggests that this comment argues in favor of the fictive character of Hermas' "family," since he would not wish more suffering on his own family. The comment says nothing one way or the other about this question.

37   Compare *Sim.* 5.4.2.

38   Twelve hours times thirty days = 360 days, or approximately a year. The figures are rhetorical estimates. The Roman day from sunup to sundown was divided into twelve hours (see Sontheimer "Tagezeiten 3," PW 24. 2020–21; also John 11:9; day-to-year correspondence for punishment, Num 14:34; Brox, 339–40; Joly, 250–51).

39   As in *Man.* 12.4.1, where the Shepherd also suspects that Hermas is doubting (12.3.4–6 above), or like that of the woman church in *Vis.* 3.8.9.

40   Of the parousia (Joly, 253); of the time for conversion (Brox, 340) in disagreement with Joly. But in the overall scheme of Hermas' eschatology, there is little difference between the two.

41   E.g., fear (*Mandate* 7), restraint (*Mandate* 8), desire (*Man.* 12.1–3).

42   A Stoic understanding of pleasure (Dibelius, 584; Brox, 340). The four Stoic categories of emotion are all dealt with by Hermas, though not according to Stoic thought: pleasure (ἡδονή, also as τρυφή ["luxury"]) throughout *Similitude* 6, esp. 6.4–5; pain (βάσανος ["torment"], θλῖψις ["affliction"], τιμωρία ["punishment"]), throughout *Similitude* 6; "fear" (φόβος), *Mandate* 7; "desire" (ἐπιθυμία), *Mandate* 12.1–3.1. In every case except pain, there are two kinds of this emotion, one good, one bad.

43   Ὀξυχολία, treated in the whole of *Mandate* 5.

7

Necessity of Penance for True Conversion

[66] 1/ A few days later, I saw him on the same plain where I had seen the shepherds, and he asked me: "What are you looking for?" "I am here, sir," I said, "to ask you to command the angel of punishment to leave my house, because he afflicts me greatly." "It is necessary for you to be afflicted," he said. "Thus the noble angel gave directives about you. He wants you to be tried." "What evil have I done, sir," I said, "to be handed over to this angel?" 2/ "Listen," he said, "your sins are many, but not so many that you should be handed over to this angel. But your household have committed great sin and lawlessness; the noble angel has become fed up with their deeds, and for this reason commanded that you be afflicted for a time, so that they will be converted and purify themselves from every desire of this world. When they are converted and purified, the angel of punishment will leave you." 3/ I said to him, "Sir, even if they have done such things as to frustrate the noble angel, what have I done?" "They cannot be afflicted in any other way," he said, "than if you, the head of the household, are afflicted. When you are afflicted, they are of necessity also afflicted, and when you fare well, they can suffer no affliction." 4/ "But see now, sir," I said, "they have accepted conversion with all their heart." "I know, too" he said, "that they have been converted with all their heart. But do you think that the sins of the converted are immediately forgiven? By no means. But the one who is converted must torment one's own soul and be mightily humbled in every deed and be afflicted with many various afflictions. And if that one endures the afflictions, the one who created everything and empowered them will surely have compassion and give some healing. 5/ Certainly this will happen if God sees the heart of the one converted, pure from every evil deed. So it is fitting that you and your household be afflicted now. But need I say more? You must be afflicted, as that angel of the Lord directed, who turned you over to me. And give thanks to the Lord for this, for considering you worthy to explain your affliction to you ahead of time, so that by knowing it in advance, you might endure mightily." 6/ I said to him, "Sir, be with me and I can bear any affliction." He said, "I will be with you, and I will ask the angel of punishment to afflict you more lightly. But you will be afflicted a little time, then you will be reestablished in your place. Only continue to be humbled and worshiping the Lord with a pure heart, you, your children, and your household, and go forward in my commandments which I commanded you, and your conversion will be able to be solid and pure. 7/ If you observe this with your household, all affliction will leave you. Affliction will depart from all," he said, "who proceed according to these my commandments."

■ 1 [66] The opening of v. 1 is intended to mark the passing of narrative time,[1] and a return to the setting of the initial vision, the plain,[2] in order to acquire better understanding, for Hermas has come there on purpose. Now we learn that it is as if the whole of *Similitude* 6 is a preparation[3] for this moment in which Hermas reveals his own investment in the question of suffering as punishment for sin. He is not only observer but victim. One can assume that the ϑλῖψις (affliction) that Hermas suffers is along the lines described in 6.3.4–5.[4] The noble or glorious angel (ὁ ἔνδοξος ἄγγελος), that is, the Son of God,[5] was the one who entrusted Hermas to the Shepherd in the first place (*Vis.* 5.2), for a purpose. Hermas' sufferings also have a purpose: the angel wishes that he be not only afflicted (ϑλιβόμενος) and tormented (βασανιζόμενος), but also wishes Hermas to be tried or tested (πειρασϑῆναι), to see if he has sufficient strength.[6] The final sentence of v. 1, Hermas' plaintive cry, is the cry of all who believe that suffering is the undeserved punishment of God.

■ 2–3 The Shepherd agrees with Hermas' complaint, that the severity of his sins does not equal the severity of his suffering, but there is another factor: his responsibility for the transgressions of his household, already raised in the *Visions*.[7] Because of them, the noble angel has become angered and annoyed to the point of exasperation (παρεπικράνϑη). Because of them, Hermas must bear the responsibility and the consequences,[8] and must therefore continue to suffer until they have a change of heart and a change of ways. There could be no clearer example of the social embeddedness of family members

in the head of the household.

Hermas' plea to be considered separately from the guilt of his household (v. 3) is therefore surprising, but he is desperate at this point. The Shepherd reinforces the usual understanding: his fate and their fate are bound up together, so that what happens to him is what happens to them, whether suffering or doing well (εὐσταϑοῦντος), the same expression used negatively for the unhappy sheep in 6.2.7.[9]

■ 4 The key elements of the narrative events underlying this passage unroll sequentially, so that the whole story is not known at the beginning, but only piece by piece. Now, it comes to light that some kind of conversion on the part of Hermas' household has already taken place. Even the Shepherd agrees with this judgment. But this element of the story introduces one of the most puzzling statements. It has already been established that the suffering inflicted on Hermas and his household is the result of their sin, as first demonstrated generally in the fate of the sheep in *Similitude* 6. Now we learn, however, that conversion has taken place, but the suffering has not lessened, and the Shepherd seems surprised that Hermas would expect it. This affliction, explains the Shepherd, cannot be alleviated immediately.[10] Rather, there is another piece to the story: the active involvement of the subject.[11] This is one of the few texts in *Hermas* that lends itself to the interpretation of conversion as doing penance: βασανίσαι τὴν ἑαυτοῦ ψυχήν ("torment one's own soul").[12] One component is fasting, usually associated with the terminology of humbling (ταπεινοφρονῆσαι),[13] which occurs here. But the aspect

---

1   As in *Vis.* 1.1.1–2; 2.1.1, 2.1; 3.1.2; 4.1.1.
2   6.1.5. See comment there and on *Vis.* 1.1.3.
3   Dibelius (584–85) considers this chapter an appendix to the previous *Similitude*. On the contrary, the previous teaching prepared for this discussion of Hermas' situation.
4   Also *Vis.* 1.3.1; 2.3.1; 3.6.7.
5   See Introduction 3.3.3, 3.3.4.
6   Used again in *Hermas* only in *Sim.* 8.2.7, in the same sense. Cf. BAGD *s.v.* πειράζω.
7   1.3.1–2; 2.3.1; 3.1.6. According to 2.2.2, their sin includes disrespect for their parents, which, if historical, would be part of the suffering Hermas endures. On the question of the historicity of these references, see Introduction 2.2.2; 2.2.3.
8   See comment on *Vis.* 1.3.1–2.
9   Noticed by Brox, 343.
10 Εὐϑύς, omitted by A, but confirmed by LLE and M

εὐϑυ[. Quantitative time, however, is not the issue here. The ejaculation that follows, "by no means," is either οὐ παντελῶς ("not completely," "not outright") A; L¹ *non proinde continuo* ("not immediately"); L² *nonne potius omnibus absolutis?*, an ambiguous expression that perhaps echoes the previous question itself. Bonner's reading of M (*Papyrus Codex,* 80 line 9), οὐ παντ[ ]ς in the middle of the line does not allow space for three letters in brackets, so he restores οὐ πάντως ("surely not"). The copyists were obviously confused by the text and tried to add their own interpretation.
11 The difficulty of the text has led to various interpretations, notably that different levels of sin require different levels of conversion or disciplinary penance, or that what is meant here is that sin has not been totally renounced; see further discussion in Brox, 344.

of discipline is mentioned only in passing as an essential component of suffering as atonement for sin. If the sufferer will endure, God, the creator and animator of all,[14] will surely[15] be compassionate[16] and extend forgiveness as healing[17] of the wounds caused by this affliction.

■ **5–7** Πάντως occurs again for a third time in close proximity at the beginning of v 5. Its meaning here depends on that assigned it at the end of v. 4. Hermas has been passed from hand to hand,[18] from the great angel to the Shepherd (who is the angel of conversion, *Vis.* 5.2, 7) to the shepherd-angel of punishment.[19] Presumably Hermas' foreknowledge of his fate, for which he is to be grateful, is the warning of God's displeasure given during the initial revelations (*Vis.* 1.3.1).

The accompaniment of his patron, the Shepherd who was sent to be present constantly (*Vis.* 5.2), gives Hermas the strength and reassurance to bear the suffering that is his lot for the moment (v. 6). Perhaps it is Hermas' acceptance and taking courage, signs of conversion, that prompt the Shepherd to intercede with the punishing angel for a mitigation of the sentence. He promises that the time of suffering will not last long. Soon Hermas will be restored to his prior place,[20] that is, his position of prosperity and success. Whereas Hermas' blood relatives are usually subsumed under reference to his "household" (οἶκος), here they are expressly distinguished, which supports the picture that Hermas is sufficiently prosperous to have an extended household.[21] The conclusion (v. 7) is in the form of a commandment, like that of the fifth *Similitude*. The cessation of suffering is dependent not only on the intercession of the Shepherd with the angel of punishment, but mostly on Hermas' further conversion and that of his household. Conversion for Hermas and for all means keeping the commandments, not in a legalistic sense, but in the true spirit of Jewish law observance, living according to their deepest meaning: acting in responsible relationship with God and with one another.[22]

---

12 Used in the active sense only here and *Man.* 4.2.2; see comment there.

13 See comment on *Vis.* 2.2.1; 3.10.6; *Sim.* 5.3.7.

14 A favorite description for God: *Vis.* 1.1.6; 3.4; *Man.* 1.1; *Sim.* 5.5.2.

15 A πάντως σπλαγχνισθήσεται ("will be compassionate"); L¹ *forsitan*; L² *fortasse* ("perhaps"), leading Dibelius (586) to emend to ποτε ("sometime"). But M according to Bonner (*Papyrus Codex,* 80) reads πα[at the end of line 17 with sufficient space for -ντως at the beginning of the next. Hilhorst (*Sémitismes,* 26) argues that in all three sections of *Hermas,* πάντως always means "maybe" ("Dans les trois parties, sans distinction, ce mot a en outre le sens exceptionnel de 'peut-être'") rather than the more usual "surely." This with appeal to Henry J. Cadbury, "Lexical Notes on Luke-Acts I" (*JBL* 44 [1925] 214–27 [223–27]), who argues for the same meaning in Luke 4:23; Acts 21:22; 28:4. This is not certain here, however: in *Vis.* 1.2.4; *Man.* 9.7; *Sim.* 1.5; 9.9.4 (with textual uncertainty and LL translation *forsitan*), the meaning could be either "surely" or "perhaps." The one other occurrence of the word is *Sim.* 5.7.4, with great similarity of situation and language to the present text. Kraft (*Clavis, s.v.*) gives both meanings; BAGD *s.v.* 2. gives "of course" as primary meaning for *Sim.* 5.7.4 and this text, with "perhaps" only as a possibility in parentheses. Joly (257) equivocates in the original translation: God "fera preuve d'une grande miséricorde" (God "will demonstrate great mercy"), but takes a stand in the notes of the revised edition (435) with "fera preuve

à coup sûr" ("will surely demonstrate mercy"). Snyder (115): "surely"; Brox (341): "mit Sicherheit."

16 On the σπλαγχνία word group, see comment on *Vis.* 3.12.3.

17 On this metaphor, see comment on *Vis.* 1.1.9.

18 As a client (Dibelius, 586).

19 Cf. a similar situation in *Act. Thom.* 54, 57, where a woman is entrusted by Jesus to his double, Thomas, for care, but Thomas has received no order to hand her over to demonic spirits of the underworld for torture; reference in Dibelius (586), but there need not be the contrast between the two modes of handing over, as he implies.

20 M τόπον ("place") to be preferred to A οἶκον ("house"); so Whittaker (65); Joly (258); οἶκον Lake (186), without access to M. Reading "house," and on the assumption that "house" is a metaphor for the church throughout, Wayne Meeks (*The Origins of Christian Morality: The First Two Centuries* [New Haven: Yale University Press, 1993] 125) suggests that Hermas, who had lost a leadership position in the church, hopes to be restored to it (insight attributed p. 234 n. 24 to unpublished paper of Craig Wansink). But see Introduction 2.2.2.

21 See comment on *Vis.* 1.3.1–2 and Introduction 2.2.2.

22 Throughout the Hebrew Scriptures, there is a close connection among fidelity to the covenant, keeping the law, humbling oneself in conversion, and forgiveness of sin, e.g., Deut 30:1–3; 2 Chr 7:14; Isa 55:6–7; Jer 31:33–34; Hos 6:6–7; Joel 2:13; Mic 6:6–8.

8

Cosmic Willow Tree

1 [67] 1/ He showed me a willow that shaded plains and mountains, and under the shade of the willow all those called in the name of the Lord had come. 2/ A splendid and very tall angel of the Lord stood next to the willow with a large pruning sickle, trimming branches from the willow and giving them to the people in the shade of the willow, and giving them little sticks about a cubit long. 3/ When everyone had received the sticks, the angel put down the sickle—and that tree was as healthy as when I had originally seen it! 4/ I marveled to myself, saying: "How can the tree be so healthy when so many branches were removed from it?" The Shepherd told me: "Don't marvel that this tree stays so healthy even though so many branches have been trimmed from it. Let be," he said, "until you see it all, and what it is will be explained to you." 5/ The angel who had given out the sticks to the people asked for them back. In the order in which they received them, they were called back to him, and each one gave back the sticks. The angel of the Lord took them and examined them. 6/ From some, he got the sticks back dry and sort of moth-eaten. The angel ordered those who had turned over the sticks in this condition to stand aside. 7/ Others handed over sticks that were dry but not moth-eaten. These too he ordered to stand aside. 8/ Others handed over sticks that were half-dried, and these were also ordered to stand aside. 9/ Others handed over their sticks half-dry and with cracks. These too stood aside. 10/ Others gave up their sticks green but cracked. These too stood aside. 11/ Others gave over sticks that were half-dry and half-green. These too stood aside. 12/ Others brought their sticks two-thirds green and one-third dry. These too stood aside. 13/ Others turned over sticks two-thirds dry and one-third green. These too stood aside. 14/ Others gave over their sticks almost completely green but just a little dry at the tip, and with cracks in them. These too stood aside. 15/ Others had sticks a little green but mostly dry. These too stood aside. 16/ Others came carrying sticks as green as they had received them from the angel; these were the majority, and the angel rejoiced greatly over them. They too stood aside. 17/ Many gave over their sticks green and with new growth. These too stood aside, and the angel rejoiced greatly over them. 18/ Others turned over their sticks green and with new growth, and the new growth even held some fruit. Those whose sticks were found like this were very happy. So the angel rejoiced over these, and the Shepherd along with him was very happy about them.

2 [68] 1/ The angel of the Lord ordered crowns to be brought. Crowns were brought, seemingly made of palm fronds, and he crowned the men who had turned over sticks with new growth and bearing fruit, and sent them off to the tower.

2/ He also sent off to the tower those with sticks with new growth but no fruit, giving them seals. 3/ All who went into the tower were clothed the same way, in garments white as snow. 4/ He sent off those who turned over sticks as green as they had received them, giving them a white garment and seals. 5/ When the angel had finished this, he said to the Shepherd: "I am leaving, but you, send them within the walls, according to each one's worthiness to dwell there. Examine their sticks carefully, and so send them on. Watch that not one get by you. But if anyone does get by you," he said, "I will try them before the altar." Having said this to the Shepherd, he left. 6/ After the angel left, the Shepherd said to me: "Let's take all the sticks and plant them, in case any of them might be able to live." I said to him: "Sir, how can these dry ones live?" 7/ He answered me: "This tree is a willow, a hardy species. If these sticks are planted and given a little moisture, many of them will live. So let's try it and water them. If any of them can live, I will rejoice with them; but if none can live, I will not prove careless." 8/ So the Shepherd ordered me to call them in the order in which they stood. They came in file and turned over their sticks to the Shepherd. The Shepherd took the sticks and planted them in rows. After planting them, he watered them so well that the sticks could not be seen above the water. 9/ After watering the sticks, he said to me: "Let's go, and come back after a few days to inspect all these sticks. The one who created this tree wants all who have received branches from it to live. I too hope that most of these sticks that have received moisture and have received water will live."

3 [69]   1/ I said to him: "Sir, explain this tree to me. I am confused about it, that it is so healthy; even though so many branches have been cut off, yet nothing seems to have been removed from it. This is what I am confused about." 2/ "Listen," he said. "This big tree that shades plains, mountains, and the whole earth is the law of God given to the whole world. But this law is the Son of God, preached to the ends of the earth. The people under its shade are those who have heard the proclamation and have come to believe in it. 3/ The great and honorable angel is Michael, who holds authority over this people and governs (them). This is the one who gives them the law, into the hearts of the believers. He watches those to whom it is given, to see if they have really kept it. 4/ You see the sticks of each: the sticks are the law. You see many sticks rendered unuseful; so you will know these as the ones who did not keep the law, and you will see the dwelling of each." 5/ I said to him: "Sir, why did he send some to the tower but left some with you?" He said, "All who have transgressed the law that they received from him, he left to my authority for conversion. But those who were

already happy with the law and have kept it, he keeps under his own authority." 6/ "Then who are those," I said, "who were crowned and went into the tower?" "Those crowned are they who contended with the devil and conquered him," he said. "They are the ones who have suffered for the law. 7/ Those who turned in their sticks green and budding but not bearing fruit are those who were persecuted because of the law but who did not suffer and did not deny their law. 8/ Those who turned in their sticks as green as they received them are distinguished and just, and have gone far with a pure heart, keeping the commandments of the Lord. You will find out the rest when I examine those sticks that were planted and watered."

4 [70]   1/ After several days, the Shepherd came back to the place and sat down in the angel's place, while I stood beside him. He said to me: "Gird yourself with a towel and minister to me." I girded myself with a clean sackcloth towel. 2/ Seeing me girded and ready to minister to him, he said: "Call the men whose sticks have been planted, in the order in which each handed over the sticks." I went to the plain and called them all, and they all stood in a row. 3/ He said to them, "Let each one pull out their own sticks [sic] and bring them to me." 4/ The first to turn them over were those who had them dry and chopped off, and since they remained dry and chopped, he ordered them to stand aside. 5/ Next to turn them over were those who had them dry but not chopped off. Some of them gave over the sticks green, some green and cut as if moth-eaten. Those who had given them over green he ordered to stand aside, and those who gave over dry chopped sticks, he ordered to stand with the first group. 6/ Then came those half-dry with cracks, and many of them gave them over green and without cracks, some green and budding, and with budding fruit, such were those who went crowned into the tower. But some handed them over dry and chewed up, some dry but not eaten, some still half-dry and cracked. He ordered each one of them to stand aside, some in their own ranks, some apart.

5 [71]   1/ Then those with sticks green but cracked turned them over; these were all green, and they stood in their own ranks. The Shepherd rejoiced over these because all were changed and had lost their cracks. 2/ Those that had been half-green and half-dry gave theirs over. Some were now completely green, some half-dry, some dry and moth-eaten, some green and budding. All of these were sent away, each in proper place. 3/ Then came those that had been two-thirds green and one-third dry. Many of them were turned in green, but many half-dry, others dry and moth-eaten. All of these remained in their proper ranking. 4/ Then came those with sticks two-thirds dry and one-third green. Many of

these gave them in half-dry, some dry [and eaten, some half-dry], and with cracks. The fewest gave them up green. All these stood in their own ranks. 5/ They gave up their sticks green, but a little dry and with cracks. Of those who gave them up green, some were green and budding. These too went into their ranks. 6/ Then those gave them up that had the least green and the rest dry. The sticks of these were found for the most part green and budding and with fruit on the buds, and others entirely green. The shepherd rejoiced exceedingly over these sticks, because they were found this way. And all of these went into their own ranks.

6 [72]   1/ After the Shepherd had observed all the sticks, he said to me: "I told you that this tree is hardy. See," he said, "how many have converted and have been saved." "I see, sir," I said. "This is so that you can see how great and glorious is the mercy of the Lord who has given the spirit to those worthy of conversion." 2/ "Then why are all not converted?" I said. "To those whose heart he saw would be pure and who would serve him with a whole heart, he gave conversion. But to those of whom he saw guile and evil, and that their conversion would be hypocritical, he did not give conversion, lest they again blaspheme his law." 3/ I said to him: "Sir, now unravel for me those who gave up sticks, what each of them is like, and their dwelling, so that the faithful who have received the seal and broken it and have not kept it whole might recognize their own deeds and be converted, and receive a seal from you [sing.], and glorify the Lord, who has had mercy on them and sent you for the renewal of their spirits." 4/ "Listen," he said. "Those whose sticks were found dry and moth-eaten are those who apostasize and betray the church and blaspheme the Lord in their sins, and are ashamed of the name of the Lord that has been invoked over them. These have ultimately died to God. Do you see that not a single one of them was converted, even though they heard the words you spoke to them, as I commanded you. From such as these, life has gone away. 5/ Those who gave them up dry and not moth-eaten are near them. They were hypocrites and proponents of strange teachings and deceivers of the servants of God—especially of those who sinned, not allowing them to be converted, but persuading them with their stupid teachings. They have hope of conversion. 6/ Do you see that many of them have been converted since you told them my commandments? They will still be converted. But as many as are not converted have lost their life. Those of them who were converted became good, and their dwelling was inside the first walls. Some of them even ascended the tower. Do you see, then," he said, "that turning from sin means life and not turning means death.

7 [73]   1/ "Those who gave them over half-dry and had

197

cracks in them—listen about them. Those whose sticks were half-dry are the doubleminded. They are neither living nor dead. 2/ Those who had them half-dry and with cracks in them are the doubleminded and those who speak evil, never at peace among themselves, but always causing dissension. But there is still conversion for them. You see," he said, "some of them have already been converted. And there is still hope for conversion in them. 3/ And," he said, "as many of them as have been converted have a dwelling place in the tower. Those who have undergone conversion more slowly will have a dwelling in the walls. Those who are not converted, but continue in their deeds will die the death. 4/ Those who gave over their sticks green and having cracks were always faithful and good but with some envy in them about prominence and honor. But all these are stupid who have envy toward each other about prominence. 5/ But these, too, when they heard my commandments, being good people, purified themselves and underwent conversion quickly. So their dwelling is in the tower. But any of them who returns to dissension will be thrown out of the tower with resulting loss of life. 6/ Life is for all who keep the Lord's commandments. But in the commandments there is nothing about prominence or honor, but about a man's patient endurance and humility. Life in the Lord consists of things like these, but for promoters of dissension and outlaws, there is death.

8 [74]   1/ "But those who gave over the sticks half-green and half-dry are those who are stuck in business concerns and do not adhere to the holy ones. This is why half of them lives and half is dead. 2/ Many of them, when they heard my commandments, were converted. For those who were converted, their dwelling is in the tower. But some were apostates to the end. There is no conversion for them, since because of their business concerns they blasphemed the Lord and denied him. So they lost their life because of the evil they did. 3/ Many of them were doubleminded. They can still have conversion if they do it quickly, and their dwelling will be in the tower. If they convert more slowly, they will dwell in the walls. But if they do not convert, they have lost their life. 4/ Those who gave them over two-thirds green and one-third dry are those who have denied with many denials. 5/ Many of them were converted, and went into the tower to dwell, but many distanced themselves from God to the end. These lost their life in the end. Some were doubleminded and dissenters. For these there is conversion if they convert quickly and do not stay in their pleasures. But if they stay in their deeds they are working out their own death.

9 [75]   1/ "Those who gave over the sticks two-thirds dry and one-third green are those who were faithful but who became rich and more honored among

198

the outsiders. They put on great arrogance, became haughty, and left the truth, and did not adhere to the just ones, but lived with the outsiders because this way of life was more pleasing to them. They separated from God but remained in faith though not acting like it. 2/ Many of them were converted and there was a place for them in the tower. 3/ Others, though, lived with the outsiders to the end, and, carried away by their empty honor, separated themselves from God and acted like them. These were counted as outsiders. 4/ Others of them were doubleminded, without hope of being saved because of the things they did. Others were doubleminded and made divisions among themselves. For these who were doubleminded because of their deeds, there is still the opportunity for conversion. But their conversion must be fast so that they may have a place in the tower. But for those who are not converted but stay in their pleasures, death is near.

10 [76] 1/ "Those who gave over the sticks green but with dry tips that had cracks were always good, faithful, and honorable before God, but sinned a little because of minor desires and had minor issues against each other. But upon hearing my words, most of them were quickly converted and they have a place in the tower. 2/ But some of them were doubleminded, and their doublemindedness caused greater dissent. In these there is hope of conversion because they were always good; only with difficulty will any of them die. 3/ Those who turned over their sticks dry but a little green are those who only believed but did the deeds of lawlessness, but they never separated from God, they bore the name willingly, and willingly gave hospitality in their houses to the servants of God. So when they heard about this conversion, they converted without hesitation and acted with every deed of justice. 4/ Some of them suffer and willingly endure affliction, knowing what they had done. All these have a place in the tower."

11 [77] 1/ After finishing the interpretations of all the sticks, he said to me: "Go and tell everyone to be converted and live to God, because the Lord had mercy and sent me to give the grace of conversion to all, even though some are unworthy because of their deeds. But the Lord, being patient, wants those called through his son to be saved." 2/ I said to him: "Sir, I hope that all who hear them will be converted, because I am convinced that each one who recognizes one's own actions and fears God will be converted." 3/ He answered me: "All who are converted wholeheartedly and purify themselves from their evil aspects as already described and add no more to their sins will receive healing of their earlier sins from the Lord, if they are not doubleminded about these commandments, and they will live to God. But," he said, "all who add to their sins and keep going in the desires of this world will

condemn themselves to death. 4/ But you [sing.], continue in my commandments and you will live to God. And whoever continues in them and acts correctly will live to God." 5/ Having shown me these things and said everything to me, he said: "I will show you the rest after a few days."

Structure

The whole eighth *Similitude* forms one unit, a story about the cosmic willow and the fate and meaning of its branches given to various sorts of people. It is a recasting with different images of the building of the tower. As there each kind of stone represents some class of believers, so here each kind of branch rendered corresponds to some group of believers.

The structure of the *Similitude* may be understood as follows.

1.1–4	introduction of the parable and the image of the tree
1.5–18	first report, of returned sticks, with different results
2.1–4	various rewards from the angel: crowns, seals, and garments
2.5–9	departure of the angel; planting of sticks by the Shepherd
3.1–3	explanation of tree and angel
3.4–5	general explanation of the sticks
3.6–8	explanation of the majority of sticks, returned completely green
4–5	second report, of planted sticks, with different results
6–10	explanation of the sticks
11	paraenetic conclusion[1]

The correspondence of various kinds of sticks with human conditions is as follows.

1.6; 4.4	dry and moth-eaten=6.4: apostates, betrayers, blasphemers: perished
1.7; 4.5	dry but not moth-eaten=6.5: hypocrites, false teachers: hope of conversion
1.8	half-dry
1.9; 4.6	half-dry with cracks=7.1-2: doubleminded
1.10; 5.1	green and cracked=7.4: jealous of honor
1.11; 5.2	half-dry, half-green=8.1-3: preoccupied with business
1.12; 5.3	two-thirds green, one-third dry=8.4-5: many denials
1.13; 5.4	two-thirds dry, one-third green=9.1-4: rich and honored among outsiders
1.14; 5.5	mostly green, dry tips, with cracks=10.1-2: with petty desires and quarrels
1.15; 5.6	mostly dry, a little green=10.3: belief without deeds, but hospitable

Into the tower:

1.16; 2.4	green=most of the people, holy, pure, keepers of the commandments
1.17; 2.2	green with buds=3.7: persecuted, faithful confessors
1.18; 2.1	green, with buds and fruit=3.6: martyrs who conquered the devil[2]

The Willow and the Sticks

■ **1.1–4 [67]** The willow (ἰτέα) is a bushy plant that grows near water sources.[3] In some MSS., its large size (ἰτέαν μεγάλην) is added.[4] The willow is a cosmic tree, covering not only plains and mountains, but the whole earth (3.2). Whereas the cosmic tree symbol usually unites zones of a layered universe (roots in the underworld, branches in the heavens),[5] this one serves an anthropo-

---

1 Alternative outlines in Cirillo, "Erma e il problema," 15–18; Brox, 352.

2 Differently constructed table given by Henne, *L'unité*, 118–19.

3 Ford ("Liturgical Background") suggests, within the context of a larger argument involving other Jewish holidays, that the willow here evokes the lulab of Sukkoth.

4 Adjective present in AE, but not MLL; not accepted by Whittaker, 65.

5 Tree of life: Genesis 3; cosmic tree: Ezek 17:22–24; 31:3–10 (with nations in its shade, v. 6); Dan 4:10–15; *1 Enoch* 24.4–6 (with Michael as revelatory angel; cf. *Sim.* 8.3.3 below); 26.1; *2 Enoch* 8.3–4; 2 Esdr 8.52; Rev 2:7; 22:2,4,19; *Teach. Silv.* 106.21–24. See also Prov 3:18; 11:30; 13:12; 15:4,

logical and ecclesiological function: it shelters all the faithful[6] called "in the name of Lord."[7] Frequently people or animals eat of its fruit; here, they take its branches. The tree also possesses a miraculous integrity: though the angel keeps pruning branches, its fullness remains (v. 3). Since the tree will later be identified as Law and Son of God, its remarkable resilience is appropriate. The tall distinguished angel[8] (v. 2) has appeared a number of times before, and will continue to appear.[9] He is the immediate representative of God, to whom the Shepherd is accountable. He will later (3.3) be identified as Michael, though his identity in other contexts is not that clear.

■ **1.5–18** With only the brief transition of an interchange between Hermas and the Shepherd, it is suddenly time for the sticks to be returned in v. 5. The impression of the scene is a military or judicial examination in which participants move forward in orderly groups. The thirteen different groups each have sticks in a slightly different condition, from hopeless to very encouraging. The moth-eaten sticks ($\beta\epsilon\beta\rho\omega\mu\acute{\epsilon}\nu\alpha\varsigma$ $\acute{\omega}\varsigma$ $\acute{\upsilon}\pi\grave{o}$ $\sigma\eta\tau\acute{o}\varsigma$, v. 6 and elsewhere) are of course not literally infested with moths—that is just what they look like—but with harmful beetles.[10] Two things are noticeable about this part of the story. First, these are not individuals, but groups or categories of persons who share the same situation; thus, while individuals each have their own fate, the teaching

is not at all individualistic. Second, the majority (v. 16) retain an integral record, returning their sticks just as green as they took them, and "many" even have new growth or fruit (vv. 17–18). The situation is not discouraging, in spite of the detailed differences among the ten groups that need improvement. In fact, the end result is cause for rejoicing on the part of the angel, the Shepherd, and the stick bearers (vv. 17–18), a typical response of those who live according to God.[11]

Crowning and Testing

■ **2.1–4 [68]** The last three groups mentioned in 1.16–18, namely, the majority with their green sticks, are examined and sent into the tower—the first mention of the tower since *Vis.* 4.3.4. They now receive their rewards from the angel, but in reverse order. Chapter 1 listed the different groups in ascending order, saving the best for last. Here, the best are rewarded first, so that those with buds and fruit on their green branches in 1.18 receive their reward of palm crowns in v. 1, a recognizable symbol of victory, based on athletic prizes.[12] In v. 1, it is $\acute{\alpha}\nu\delta\rho\alpha\varsigma$ ("men") who are crowned, as compared to $\acute{\alpha}\nu\theta\rho\omega\pi\omega\iota$ (generic "human beings") in 1.18. The vision is typological, not historical, and is cast in exclusively male form. Those with only buds[13] receive seals in v. 2; those whose branches had neither buds nor fruit, but remained green, receive seals and white garments (v. 4),

---

6   where other referents are compared to a tree of life. The cosmic tree is a favorite mythic symbol, stretching from the Ancient Near East through Judaism into early Christian literature and on into the Middle Ages, where it is transformed into the cross: Arnold Levin, "The Tree of Life: Genesis 2:9, 3:22–24 in Jewish, Gnostic, and Early Christian Texts" (Th.D. diss., Harvard University, 1966); Erwin R. Goodenough, *Jewish Symbols in the Greco-Roman Period* (New York: Pantheon, 1953) 7. 87–134; Moyo, "Angels and Christology," 66–74; Stephen J. Reno, *The Sacred Tree as an Early Christian Literary Symbol* (Forschungen zur Anthropologie und Religionsgeschichte 4; Saarbrücken: Alfred Rupp, 1978); Dronke, "Arbor Caritatis," 228–33.

6   Compare *1 Enoch* 26.1, where a tree at the center of the earth gives shade through branches that are cut yet live and bloom.

7   $\acute{E}\nu$ $\acute{o}\nu\acute{o}\mu\alpha\tau\iota$ $\kappa\upsilon\rho\acute{\iota}\upsilon$, LLE Pber; $\tau\tilde{\omega}$ $\acute{o}\nu\acute{o}\mu\alpha\tau\iota$ $\kappa\upsilon\rho\acute{\iota}\upsilon$ MA: cf. Isa 43:7; *Sim.* 9.14.3, but the meaning is the same.

8   On height as sign of greatness in Jewish and Christian angelology: *3 Enoch* 9.2–3; *4 Ezra* 2.43; *T. Reub.* 5.6; CD 2.19; Elchasai (Hippolytus *Ref.* 9.13; Epiphanius *Pan.* 30.17.6); *Gos. Pet.* 40; *Act. John* 90; Adam in *Apoc. Paul,* 51; *Acts of Perpetua and Felicitas* 10.4; Eusebius *Vit. Const.* 3.10; *Corp. Herm.* 1.1; cf. Introduction 3.3.3; Joly, 300–301, 438; Brox, 398.

9   *Vis.* 5.2; *Man.* 5.1.7; *Sim.* 5.4.4; 7.1–3, 5; 9.6.1.

10   A disease that causes rust or decay, as in Matt 6:19–20; cf. BAGD *s.v.* $\beta\rho\tilde{\omega}\sigma\iota\varsigma$ 2.

11   See comment on *Vis.* 1.4.3.

12   *Asc. Isa.* 9.8–9, 11, 18, 25–26, where crowns are in store for pre-Christian saints, but they cannot receive them until the coming of Christ; Jas 1:12; Rev 2:10; 3:11; 4:4, 10; *Martyrs of Lyon and Vienne* 36.

13   AE specify that the sticks are green: $\tau\grave{\alpha}\varsigma$ $\chi\lambda\omega\rho\acute{\alpha}\varsigma$ ("green") is added to $\tau\grave{\alpha}\varsigma$ $\acute{\rho}\acute{\alpha}\beta\delta\upsilon\varsigma$ ("the sticks"), but this can be understood from the context.

the same snow-white garments that the others also received (v. 3). The white garments, like the crowns, are recognizable signs of heavenly triumph.[14] Ἀπέλυσεν (he sent off) in v. 4 is to be understood as "into the tower," not sent away, because this group obviously shares the fate of the other two groups in vv. 1–2. The seals (σφραγῖδας) do not mean baptism here.[15] When this term is used for baptism, it is a collective singular,[16] and all of the groups spoken of here are baptized. Rather, this is an eschatological sign of acceptance into heaven or the kingdom,[17] especially for martyrs, which these groups are not. In the later explanation, those here crowned are martyrs, while the two groups who receive seals comprise those who were persecuted for God's sake but not killed, and those who were not persecuted but remained faithful (3.7–8). These seals are unlikely to be signet rings,[18] but rather the mark of a signet ring in a prominent place, such as the forehead,[19] so that it functions as a kind of "passport" into the tower.[20]

■ **2.5** As the angel leaves, he turns over the responsibility for screening to the Shepherd, instructing him to allow certain unspecified people through the checkpoint εἰς τὰ τείχη, which may have the same meaning here as in 6.6; 7.3; and 8.3, but more likely does not. Here it seems to mean "within the walls," rather than more literally *in* or *on* them, so that what is envisioned is a gate to a precinct surrounding the tower. Those whom the Shepherd admits will enter the area immediately surrounding the tower. But inasmuch as stones are symbols for various sorts of people in the original tower of *Vision* 3, what is meant later is a place in the actual construc-

tion of the building, but in the outer wall. It is clear in 7.3 and 8.3 that this is a position inferior to that of those who have actually entered the tower.[21] There, this position is reserved for those who have been slower to undergo conversion. In 6.6, the heterodox who change their strange teaching come to dwell within the first walls (εἰς τὰ τείχη τὰ πρῶτα)—in the foundations, perhaps? Neither situation seems to be the case here, for the angel's warning at the end of the verse is less about misplacement than about letting the unqualified slip by. It is typical of *Hermas* to introduce a new detail in the narrative and give it more than one meaning in succeeding chapters, as we have just seen with the use of the seal in vv. 2, 4, as compared with 8.6.3; 9.16.3–7. Since the Shepherd is the delegated angel of conversion, the great angel, after collecting those sticks that are "success stories," leaves the problems to be dealt with by the Shepherd, under whose authority they lie.[22] Even if some get past the Shepherd unworthily, however, they will still have to deal with the great angel,[23] who will test them at the heavenly altar, a motif newly introduced here and not sustained later in the narrative.[24] We will learn later that the great angel is Michael (3.3), who is otherwise known as the holder of the keys of heaven—*pace* Matt 16:19.[25]

■ **2.6–7** Since the Shepherd is in charge of conversion, he is acting in character, once the angel leaves, by offering a second chance to the dry sticks by planting them to see if they will prosper. Here the willow stick narrative is simply saying in another way what is one of the central messages of the whole work: there is another chance for

14 *Asc. Isa.* 9.2, 9, 11, 24–26 (both robes and crowns in the seventh heaven); *1 Enoch* 62.15–16; *2 Enoch* 22.8; *Sim.* 9.13.3.

15 In agreement with Dibelius, 591; Brox, 357.

16 E.g., *2 Clem.* 7.6; 8.6; *Act. Paul Thec.* 25; *Act. Thom.* 131; *Sim.* 8.6.3; 9.16.3–7; 17.4.

17 Cf. Rev 7:2; 9:4; Adalbert Hamman, "La signification de σφραγίς dans le Pasteur d'Hermas," *StPatr* 4=TU 79 (1961) 286–90.

18 Suggested by Brox, 357. Further discussion and references there.

19 Rev 7:3.

20 Dibelius' image, 591 ("der Pass, mit dem sie in den Turm gelangen"), with reference to the Naassene hymn in Hippolytus *Ref.* 5.10.2. Further references on all these uses in BAGD *s.v.*

21 It is also true there (with Brox, 359) that a third fate, in the walls, has been added to the two already

presented (in or out of the tower)—but not here. There is no evidence in any of these passages of an already established discipline of penance whereby penitents have a less desirable place in church; see Giet, "De trois expressions," 24–29.

22 *Vis.* 5.7; *Man.* 12.6.1; *Sim.* 8.3.5.

23 The grammatical number of translated pronouns here is exactly as found in the text: if anyone (τις, sing.) gets by, the angel will test them (αὐτούς, pl.) at the altar.

24 The altar of God in *Man.* 10.3.2–3; Rev 8:3 is a metaphor for the efficacy of prayer, whereas here, it is a place of testing and judgment. Cf. Rev 6:9; 9:13; 14:18; especially 16:7; Ignatius *Rom.* 2.2.

25 *3 Bar.* 11.2; *4 Bar.* 9.5.

26 Hilhorst, *Sémitismes*, 113–16. Cf. Matt 13:30 as cited by Origen *Hom. in Jer.* 1.15; Epiphanius *Pan.* 66.65.3

conversion. Besides, the Shepherd is concerned not to appear careless when he has to render an account to the returning angel. Hermas' question at the end of v. 6, "How can this be?" and the Shepherd's answer, "Let's give them another chance, and then I will not be liable for neglect," are paralleled at *Sim.* 9.7.4, 6 with stones in the tower. This is a different use of the word πειράζειν than in *Sim.* 7.1, where it has the more usual sense of testing. The hardiness of the willow (v. 7) is literally that it is a "lover of life" (φιλόζωον). This richness of life and the possibility for severed branches to sprout are images of the church's capacity not only to survive but to give life in abundance, like the expressed will of the tree's creator that all who receive from it will live (v. 9). The struggle between life and death will become the guiding metaphor in the later chapters.

■ **2.8–9** Hermas now as the Shepherd's assistant calls all the people who are still holding dry sticks. They come forward in orderly rows as if in procession or a military file (τάγματα τάγματα). The doubling of the adverbial expression instead of the more customary use of ἀνά or κατά as distributive is found more frequently in literature influenced by the LXX and may be a Semitism, but also occurs in other poetic and nonliterary Greek texts.[26] The sticks are then planted by the Shepherd, and severely overwatered. Though in the explanations later to follow, the important change factor will be, as usual, the response and change of heart of the stick bearers, here the image suggests something different: the change will come about through the agency of the Shepherd and the water, independently of the people involved. While there was no interlude in the narrative time of the first episode of the sticks (1.4–5), here the sticks are to be left for a few days before being inspected for change (v. 9). Abundant life-giving water is an image rich in bib-

lical connotations.[27] The poignant declaration and hope of the Shepherd that both God and he want all to live is another way of expressing in narrative form the repeated refrain of the promise of life to those who are converted in the *Mandates* and elsewhere, including the conclusion of the eighth *Similitude* (11.4).[28]

Explanation of the Willow and Acceptable Sticks

■ **3.1–2 [69]** After two episodes of the parable, the original acceptance of those with green sticks into the tower by the angel and the planting of the dry sticks by the Shepherd, the first explanation is now given, covering the meaning of the basic elements of the vision, and the action of the first episode (1.1–2.5). If the planting of the sticks is a later addition to the story, this explanation would have immediately followed the story it signifies.[29] This explanation fills in the time gap during the interlude of a few days after the planting of the sticks. Hermas, asking for his usual explanation, repeats his wonderment about the integrity of the tree after severe trimming (v. 1).[30] That the tree is God's law (v. 2), or rather, that the law is compared to a tree of life, is a common Jewish image.[31] Here it also carries the connotations of *Similitude* 1, and should be understood in that context. There the law of this land and the law of God's city, Christians' real homeland, are contrasted, and Christians are ultimately made to choose one or the other. But the introduction of the Son of God as the law in the next sentence adds a new twist, though not an entirely unknown connection.[32] The entire structure of the eighth *Similitude* would work very well without this identification, with the possible exception of 11.1. It is introduced gratuitously and probably secondarily, to add a christological interpretation, which takes another step beyond the Son as lawgiver in 5.6.3.[33]

(δήσατε δέσμας δέσμας); Mark 6:39–40; Mark 6:7 in some mss.; 6:39–40; *Act. Thom.* 8.

27 E.g., Ezek 47:1–12; Isa 44:3–4; 55:1; John 7:38, etc. The water is the law in Sir 24:23–31.

28 Cf. 1 Tim 2:4; 1 Pet 3:9.

29 For Dibelius (592), the first episode and most of the explanation is original Jewish material, while the second episode and the introduction of the Son of God in v. 1 are Christianized additions.

30 1.3–4; see comments there. Cirillo ("Erma e il problema," 18) calls attention to *1 Enoch* 24–26, where unusual trees and Michael are brought together. An intriguing parallel, certainly, though there the first

tree is noteworthy for its wonderful fragrance, not its size, and from the second, living, blooming branches are cut and provide shade.

31 E.g., *Pirqe 'Abot* 6.7.

32 Especially *Keryg. Pet.* as cited by Clement of Alexandria *Strom.* 1.29.182; 2.15.68; *Ecl. proph.* 58 (collected in *NTApoc* 2.39–40); also *Act. John* 112; Justin *Dial.* 11.2; 43.1; Christ as new covenant, 51.3; 118.3.

33 See *Teach. Silv.* 106.21–24, where Christ is wisdom, word, and tree of life. Brox (361) points to Rom 1:8; Col 1:6, 23; 1 Tim 3:16 on the universal preaching

■ **3.3** The angel Michael is guardian of nations, especially of Israel, sometimes in that capacity also functioning as judge.[34] Here he represents angelic mediation of the law, an idea already established in Christianity.[35] The great angel has already appeared as both mediator and chastiser.[36] Some commentators take this angelic figure in *Hermas* to be a Christ figure confused here with a traditional Jewish treatment of Michael, since he gives the law into the people's hearts, elsewhere sends the Shepherd to Hermas,[37] and seems to have a great deal of authority. The objection that the Son of God has already appeared here under a different guise does not hold, since the law is assigned as meaning to three different symbols, the tree, the Son of God (v. 1), and the sticks (v. 4). This polyvalence of symbols is not unusual in *Hermas*, and is part of the polysemy described by Henne.[38] But there is never an explicit connection between the great angel and the Son of God. The christological passage in *Sim.* 9.12.7–8 identifies the Son of God not as an angel but, using descriptions elsewhere applied to the chief angel, as the "honorable and great *man*" ($\check{\varepsilon}\nu\delta o\xi o\nu$ $\kappa\alpha\grave{\iota}$ $\mu\acute{\varepsilon}\gamma\alpha\nu$ $\check{\alpha}\nu\delta\rho\alpha$), surrounded by six other men, but the central figure is never called an angel, even though the other six later are (v. 8). Likewise in *4 Ezra* 2.42–48, adduced by Brox as a parallel, the Christ figure is a man surrounded by other people, identified by an angel as victorious confessors.[39] The objects of Michael's governance, "them" ($\alpha\mathring{v}\tau o\acute{v}\varsigma$), referring to the people, is missing in MA, restored from LLE, but the people are the obvious object, whether expressed or not.

■ **3.4–5** The law now takes on its third meaning in this chapter: the sticks given to the people (v. 4). While the tree and the Son of God are the law as given, as transcendent reality, here the sticks are the law as received, responded to, and lived. The rest of v. 4 forecasts the subject matter of chapters 4–10, the fate of those whose sticks had problems, those rendered useless ($\mathring{\eta}\chi\rho\varepsilon\iota\omega$-$\mu\acute{\varepsilon}\nu\alpha\varsigma$)[40] by their nonobservance. Hermas then asks why the separation between those accepted into the tower and those not. The Shepherd responds in his capacity as angel of conversion:[41] he has been given authority only over those who need improvement.

■ **3.6–8** Here begins the first part of the explanation of the sticks, beginning with the last mentioned in the original parable (1.18) and in the follow-up passage about their fate (2.1), and continuing in reverse order with the second and third last of the group (1.18=2.1=3.6; 1.17= 2.2=3.7; 1.16=2.3=3.8). The special place reserved for martyrs elsewhere[42] is reinforced here: those who contended with the devil[43] and suffered death ($\pi\alpha\vartheta\acute{o}\nu\tau\varepsilon\varsigma$) are crowned, having borne in their sticks the fruit (this is the condition of their sticks in 1.8) of martyrdom. The second group (v. 7) with green sticks and buds are the confessors whose ordeals carried the potential for the full fruitfulness of martyrdom, but through no fault of their own, did not fully develop. They suffered for the law of their true home, most evident in its identification with Christ (v. 1), and they endured faithfully without denial,[44] but did not actually die.[45] Finally, what is to be envisioned as the largest group are those whose sticks remained green (v. 8), and did not suffer any of the deterioration of the many groups not accepted by the angel,

---

of the gospel as context. Moyo ("Angels and Christology," 61, 85–90) argues that the Son of God is here a metaphor or personification of the law, rather than Christ, but the argument is partially based on the absence of the definite article before "son of God" in A. The article is, however, present in M.

34 Dan 12:5; *1 Enoch* 20.5; see John J. Collins, *Daniel: A Commentary on the Book of Daniel* (Hermeneia; Minneapolis: Fortress, 1993) 376, 390.

35 Gal 3:19; Heb 2:2; *Sim.* 5.6.2; also Josephus *Ant.* 15.136.

36 Usually as representative and agent of God to encourage or carry on the narrative: *Sim.* 5.4.4; 8.1.2, 5–6, 17–18; 2.1–5; but as messenger of punishment ($\check{\alpha}\gamma\gamma\varepsilon\lambda o\varsigma$ $\tau\mathring{\eta}\varsigma$ $\tau\iota\mu\omega\rho\acute{\iota}\alpha\varsigma$) in 6.3.2; 7.2, 5.

37 *Vis.* 5.2.

38 Henne, "Polysémie."

39 See further Introduction 3.3.4; Brox, 362–65. For Brox, either *Hermas* is careless with identifications or Michael has christological connotations.

40 Compare *Vis.* 3.6.7.

41 *Vis.* 5.7; *Man.* 12.6.1.

42 *Vis.* 3.1.9; 5.2; *Sim.* 9.28.2.

43 The martyr literature often depicts the suffering of the martyrs as a contest against diabolic power, e.g., Perpetua in prison dreams of contending in the arena as a man with a demonic antagonist of superhuman stature (*Acts of Perpetua and Felicitas* 10); cf. *Martyrs of Lyon and Vienne* 1.5; 2.6.

44 A frequent concern in these discussions: *Vis.* 2.2.8; 3.4; *Sim.* 9.26.3, 5–6; 28.4, 7–8, etc.

45 This category of people following times of persecution was specially revered and sometimes given special privileges, e.g., the rank of presbyter or

yet they did not have the opportunity to develop the buds or fruit of suffering. They did not have to endure persecution, yet they remained faithful and lived according to God's law. The chapter ends with a transition into the next section, which will deal with those sticks rejected by the angel but planted and nurtured by the Shepherd.

Results of Planting and Watering

■ **4.1 [70]** The interlude filled in by the explanation of the vision (chap. 3) is now past, and the Shepherd accompanied by Hermas returns to the place where the watered sticks are to be examined. The Shepherd sits in a position of authority, not previously alluded to, from where the great angel had previously presided over the scene. The Shepherd's full authorization to deal with the situation is symbolized by his willingness to occupy the same place. Hermas is assigned the role of "minister" or "assistant" ($\delta\iota\acute{\alpha}\kappa\circ\nu\circ\varsigma$), to stand beside the seated figure and to render service, even table service,[46] which seems to be envisioned here. To this end, he wraps around his waist a towel or apron of coarse linen.[47] The Shepherd assumes the pose of a wealthy patron carrying on business or receiving clients while at table. A similar situation occurs later at 9.10.2, though there Hermas does more direct physical work in his service.

■ **4.2–3** Hermas is not only table servant but manager or overseer for the Shepherd in this scene. He has now the task of calling up all the men ($\check{\alpha}\nu\delta\rho\alpha\varsigma$)[48] whose sticks had not been acceptably green, and were therefore placed under the authority of the Shepherd for planting. They have been planted on the plain, often a locus of revelatory activity.[49] The men answer when called, standing in order.[50] The specification that each man is personally to present his stick to the Shepherd stresses the

relationship between the new state of the stick and the personal responsibility of its bearer, yet the Greek text places together singular bearer, singular verbs, and plural sticks (Ἕκαστος ἐκτιλάτω τὰξ ῥάβδους τὰς ἰδίας καὶ φερέτω πρός με)—though it is to be assumed that each man has only one stick—perhaps to show the corporate aspect of the action, for they are arranged and present their sticks in groups.

■ **4.4–6** Now begins the presentation of the sticks, proceeding in the same order as they were given in the original parable: 4.4–5.6 parallels 1.6–15, after which in the first presentation come those with green sticks, and those with even buds and fruit, the three groups received by the great angel directly into the tower (1.16–18). The one exception to this parallelism is that those of 1.8 with simply half-dry sticks do not appear here, but will resurface in the explanation in 7.1b. While the word for an appearance like moth-eaten in 1.6, 7 is βεβρωμένος, here it is κεκομμένος ("chopped off"), in vv. 4–5 and βεβρωμένος and ἄβρωτος in v. 6, but the meaning is essentially the same.[51] The dry sticks of v. 5 that have now become green may recall other legends of flowering or leafing sticks.[52]

Continued Results of Planting and Watering

■ **5.1–6 [71]** The good report of the planted sticks continues. The first and last of this series have the best reports: the first, green but cracked (v. 1, corresponding to 1.10), are now entirely green; apparently the cracks have disappeared. The last group, those that had been mostly dry with only a little green (v. 6, corresponding to 1.15) are the greatest success story, for they are now mostly green, even with buds and fruit. Over both of these groups, at beginning and end, the Shepherd rejoices, a sign of connection to the central dynamic of the

---

deacon without ordination (presumably by this time limited to males) (Hippolytus *Ap. Trad.* 9 [10]).

46 For context, see John N. Collins, *Diakonia: Reinterpreting the Ancient Sources* (New York/Oxford: Oxford University Press, 1990) 149, 151.

47 Ὡμόλινον; cf. BAGD *s.v.* The sackcloth texture (ἐκ σάκκου) is omitted by *POxy* 3527.

48 See comment on 2.1.

49 See comment on *Vis.* 1.1.3.

50 The exact expression used for this idea is not clear in the mss.: ἔστησαν πάντα τὰ τάγματα A;]τα ταγματα M, which Bonner reconstructs as [πάν]τα τὰ τάγματα, now reinforced by *POxy* 3527]ντα τα

τάγμα[. Without knowledge of M or *POxy* 3527, Lake had reconstructed τάγματα τάγματα after 2.8.

51 Only *POxy* 3527 reads βεβρωμένας the first time in v. 4, thereafter agreeing with the other mss. See comment at 1.6.

52 Hercules' club (Pausanias 2.31.10; reference in Dibelius, 588), the fruitful rod of Aaron over against the other priests (Num 17:2–9; *1 Clem.* 43.5), and perhaps the miraculous rod of Joseph (*Prot. Jas.* 9.1).

book.[53] Those between vv. 1 and 6 yield mixed results: some are improved and others are worse. Verse 2 corresponds to 1.11; v. 3 to 1.12; v. 4 to 1.13, and v. 5 to 1.14. The full explanation of all the groups will come later, beginning at 6.4. Words in brackets in v. 4 are omitted by M.

Conversion to Those Who Will Accept It

■ **6.1–2 [72]** The Shepherd recalls to Hermas the tenacity of the willow[54] as the reason for the very encouraging results of the planting of the sticks. The next sentence can be understood on two levels as it passes from observation to metaphor: see how many branches of the tree have changed (μετενόησαν) and therefore have been saved rather than discarded (ἐσώθησαν). At the same time, of course, the comment applies to the people represented by the branches. Although conversion must be the work of each heart, it is only possible because of God's mercy.[55] The conclusion of the sentence can be understood as translated, or as "who has given the spirit of conversion to those who are worthy."[56] The meaning is not substantially altered either way. Hermas appropriately then asks (v. 2) in the language of the discussion under way the perennial question of grace and determinism: Why, if conversion is the gift of God, does not everyone receive it? The answer is divine foreknowledge: where God saw that conversion would be with a pure and sincere heart,[57] the gift was forthcoming, but where the response would be hypocritical, it was withheld, lest God's law be vilified.[58]

■ **6.3** Hermas gives his usual request for explanation of

the whole story. The reference to "the seal" (ἡ σφραγίς) in the first part of the sentence surely refers to baptism, after the analogy of the clay or wax impression made by a signet ring on an object to prevent interference by another party, or to mark the object as property or authentic document. This is one of the earliest references to the use of the word for baptism in early Christian literature.[59] To break the seal is to destroy the attestation of ownership. The second reference to a seal, however, cannot be baptism, which they have already received. Rather, this seal must refer to the *laissez-passer* or certificate of entrance given to at least two of the three groups with originally green sticks that were admitted immediately into the tower by the great angel (2.2, 4). The renewal of spirit is another way of speaking of the result of conversion, originally symbolized in the *Visions* as the rejuvenation of the woman church.[60]

■ **6.4** The explanation of the troublesome sticks now begins. The first group are the most serious, corresponding to 1.6 and 4.4. Here we are brought back into the realm of grave failure during persecution, a theme that occurs only sporadically in the text, with apostates, betrayers, and blasphemers.[61] Though the church has many forms in *Hermas*, it is spoken of in this manner, as an organization composed of people, only in a few other passages.[62] The invocation of the name of the Lord is an established theological and perhaps liturgical formula.[63] The finality of the destruction of these people is not a theological determinism but a moral judgment: it is not God who excludes them, but their own persistence in

---

53   On the function of joy, see comment on *Vis.* 1.4.3.
54   See comment on 2.7.
55   Πολυσπλαγχνίαν; on the word group, see comment on *Vis.* 3.12.3.
56   See discussion and references in Brox (368), who opts for the translation as given here in the text ("denen Geist geschenkt hat, die der Busse würdig sind") because the other seems strained, even though he notes that in 6.2 conversion is twice the object of God's gift. On worthiness, cf. 11.1.
57   On purity of heart, see note on *Sim.* 5.6.2.
58   Μήποτε πάλιν βλασφημήσωσιν τὸν νόμον αὐτοῦ MLL; βεβηλώσωσι τὸ ὄνομα αὐτοῦ ("profane his name") AEC². On the importance of the name of God, see *Vis.* 2.2.8 (with note); 3.5.3–4; 7.3, but the law of God with several meanings is also central here in chap. 3.
59   Together with *2 Clem.* 7.6; 8.6. Compare *Sim.*

9.16.3–7; 17.3, where the connection is explicit. Cf. *Act. Phil.* 134; *Mart. Matt.* 8, 27; *Act. Thom.* 26 (with oil), 49, 87, 118, 120, 150; but explicitly associated with water baptism in 121, 131–32, 152; *Act. Paul Thec.* 25; Clement of Alexandria *Quis Dives* 42.2; further refs. and bibliography, BAGD *s.v.* Cf. Adalbert Hamman, "La signification de σφραγίς dans le Pasteur d'Hermas," *StPatr* 4=TU 79 (1961) 286–90.
60   *Vis.* 3.13.2; cf. 8.9; *Sim.* 9.14.3; *Barn.* 6.11.
61   Cf. *Vis.* 3.7.2; *Sim.* 6.2.3; esp. *Sim.* 9.19.1 with the same three terms.
62   *Vis.* 2.4.3; 3.9.7; *Sim.* 9.18.2–4.
63   Gen 48:16; Deut 28:10; Jer 14:9; Amos 9:12; 2 Chron 7:14; 2 Macc 8:15; Jas 2:7; *4 Ezra* 4.25; *Sim.* 9.21.3; further references and comment, Michael E. Stone, *Fourth Ezra* (Hermeneia; Minneapolis: Fortress, 1990) 89. On the shame of bearing the name, see comment on *Sim.* 9.14.6.

evil and refusal to be converted.[64] The play on words between apostates and the departure of life in the last line of the verse is lost in translation: the first group mentioned at the beginning are apostates (ἀποστάται), who (etymologically) stand away or leave; in complementary manner, life stands away from or leaves them (ἀπέστη).

■ **6.5–6** The next worst group are those who corrupt others with their teaching, but do not go as far as outright apostasy and rejection of their baptismal commitment. The nature of their hypocrisy is vague; the term almost seems introduced gratuitously because of its familiar ring. Their hypocrisy consists not in false appearances and lack of sincerity, but in abandoning the truth. The real issue is not hypocrisy but heterodoxy—not in general, but specifically on the subject of repentance after sin. The problem seems to be not variant ideas about God so much as variant approaches to guilt and the moral life. Whether the persons in mind are the same as those responsible for other ideas that the author disagrees with is impossible to say. It does not seem that they have separated from the community, but that they are in fact very influential within it, especially since they are distinguished from those with cracks (σχίσματα) in 7.1.[65] Their fate is threefold. Some have not changed, and have lost their life (ἀπόλεσαν τὴν ζωὴν αὐτῶν), not literally, but spiritually: they have severed themselves from the source of life. Many have converted upon hearing the commandments preached, either by Hermas or by the Shepherd.[66] They became good (ἀγαθοὶ ἐγένετο)—a striking expression—and joined those who form part of the walls of the tower or its precinct.[67] Others went into the tower itself. Beginning with this verse, the guiding image through chapter 10 is the contrast between life and death. The final sentence sets this contrast within the central concern: "conversion of heart" (μετάνοια) is life, while the absence of conversion is death.

Fate of Those with Small Weaknesses

■ **7.1–3 [73]** The life-death contrast continues, and frames the discussion in chapter 7: see the end of v. 6. The simply half-dry sticks have not been mentioned since their initial appearance at 1.8. They reappear here in v. 1b as the "doubleminded" (δίψυχοι), the major term for troublesome people in *Hermas*.[68] As a substantive categorization of certain people, it has not been seen since *Man.* 11.13. *Hermas'* principal problem is with those who hesitate and cannot decide to which side they belong. They are a general group that, appropriately, exist somewhere in the vague middle between life and death. More specifically, the concern here is about the doubleminded who cause dissension, aptly assigned to sticks half-dry with cracks (σχίσμας). They correspond to the cracked stones of *Vis.* 3.6.3 and the believers from the cracked mountain in *Sim.* 9.23.1–3. Their inability to be at peace among themselves is another echo of 1 Thess 5:13, a favorite allusion of the author.[69] This group transgresses more seriously with their dissension than the green sticks with cracks (v. 4), and there is some question here whether it is simple dissension within the community or actual schism. The word σχίσμα is already understood in some quarters by this time as formal separation.[70] Those who undergo a change of heart can even have a place in the tower, or in the walls[71] (v. 3). But the grave pronouncement about those who do not undergo conversion suggests excommunication or mutual separation, sanctioned with a biblical expression, "to die the death" (θανάτῳ ἀποθνῄσκειν).[72]

■ **7.4–6** The interpretation of the green cracked sticks, which correspond to 1.10; 5.1, is of lesser consequence

---

64   Compare *Vis.* 3.7.2; *Sim.* 8.8.2, 5; 9.3; 9.14.2; cf. *Sim.* 6.2.3.

65   Compare *Sim.* 9.22. On the question of heterodox teachers and the possibility of Gnostic leanings, see comment on *Sim.* 5.7.2. Further discussion and references in Brox, 370–71.

66   Ἐλάλησα ("I spoke") A; but *pertulisti* ("you [sing.] announced") LL; missing in M; "you": Joly (277) and Snyder (123). If Hermas is the speaker, the passage must refer either to 4.2, where Hermas summons all holders of the planted sticks to appear before the Shepherd, or more generally, to Hermas' mandate to announce the message of conversion in the

church (*Vis.* 2.4.3).

67   See comment on 2.5.

68   See Introduction 3.3.1, 3.3.2.

69   See comment on *Vis.* 3.6.3.

70   See BAGD *s.v.* 2. Lake translates "schism" here and "schismatics" in v. 6, thus envisioning a more formal separation than Joly (279, 281), who translates "en dispute" and "querelleurs"; so too Snyder (124): "factious," "factionalism."

71   See comment on 2.5.

72   This construct of verb reinforced with its related noun in the dative is not unknown in Greek literature, but is more characteristic of the LXX, where it

for the most part. These people have not ceased to be faithful and good. Their only weakness is the typical Roman sensitivity about social status that was pervasive from the aristocracy down. Their concern is literally about prominent positions ($\pi\epsilon\rho\grave{\iota}\ \pi\rho\omega\tau\epsilon\acute{\iota}\omega\nu$).[73] Whether the problem is a general one in their life, or whether it concerns specifically rivalry about church leadership, is unclear. If the reference is to be associated with *Vis.* 3.9.7–10, church leaders are meant, and the situation is reminiscent of the Corinthian situation that prompted the writing of *1 Clement*. But there is nothing specific here to suggest that. If, rather, general vying for honor and status is meant, the text echoes the same concerns in *Man.* 5.2.2; 6.2.5; 10.1.5.[74] But if those who have changed their ways slip back again into habits of divisiveness, even those who had already been given entrance into the tower can be cast out of it. So acceptance into the tower is not final and only eschatological; there is the possibility of rejection due to relapse. Thus the image of the church as tower means not only its eschatological and transcendent reality, but also its earthly, historical existence, just as the church was rejuvenated through the conversion of its members in *Vis.* 3.11–13. Like the unrepentant heterodox teachers of 6.6, these relapsed dissidents will lose their life. The association of life with keeping the commandments is biblical (v. 6); "the commandments of the Lord" envision the decalogue and related matter, but also everything communicated by the Shepherd. The commandments speak not about concern for status, but the opposite, the countercultural values of the Gospel.[75] The chapter concludes as it opened, with the choice for life or death.

Fate of the Doubleminded and Deniers

■ **8.1–3 [74]** The guiding imagery of life and death continues. This chapter opens with the characterization of those half-alive and half-dead, thus putting the tension between life and death right into the context of one group of people. They lose their life in vv. 2 and 3, as do the next group in v. 5, who at the conclusion bring about their own death. First come those with sticks half-green and half-dry (as in 1.11, but the two aspects have been optimistically reversed in 5.2 and here). They intend to be good Christians, but are too immersed in their own business to associate as they should with believers who offer them no opportunity of advancement or gain. These people are one of *Hermas'* primary concerns.[76] Because of their divided hearts, they are half-alive and half-dead. They are divided into three types according to their response to the message: the success stories who convert and find a place in the tower; those who remained in apostasy ($\epsilon\grave{\iota}\varsigma\ \tau\acute{\epsilon}\lambda o\varsigma\ \grave{\alpha}\pi\acute{\epsilon}\sigma\tau\eta\sigma\alpha\nu$), whose denial of the values of God remains, and so they perished; and those who cannot make up their minds one way or another (v. 3), and so live in doublemindedness. They still have a chance for salvation, and the speed of their about-face will determine their place in the structure. The alternative, however, is disastrous.

■ **8.4–5** It is somewhat surprising that those with sticks two-thirds green and one-third dry, corresponding to 1.12 and 5.3, represent people with such serious charges against them: many denials, which in the context of other use of $\grave{\alpha}\rho\nu\acute{\epsilon}o\mu\alpha\iota$ ("to deny") can only mean denial of the faith through their actions at some level.[77] Yet the degree of greenness perhaps indicates the large number of them who were converted (v. 5) and went into the tower. An unspecified large number also were ultimately lost, not necessarily formally as apostates, but as failures to live authentically, some because of their doublemindedness, which prevented them from being wholly committed. Thus, as members of the community, they were a cause of dissension ($\delta\iota\chi o\sigma\tau\alpha\sigma\acute{\iota}\alpha$) because they could not be peaceful there, as in 7.2. The two aspects of their behavior, doublemindedness and dissension, must be closely related. The reason that they are doubleminded and troublemakers is that they cannot give up the pleasures to which they are accustomed.[78]

---

appears over two hundred times; also Luke 22:15; Acts 2:17; 5:28; 23:14; 28:26; Jas 5:17. Its frequency in the LXX qualifies the construction for Hilhorst (*Sémitismes*, 150–53) as a "secondary Semitism." The actual expression appears in Gen 2:17; 3:4; Num 26:65; 1 Sam 14:39, 44; Sir 14:17; Jer 33:8, etc.

73   Snyder (124): "questions of priority or particular status."

74   See comment and references on *Man.* 5.2.2.

75   Humility: $\tau\alpha\pi\epsilon\iota\nu o\phi\rho\acute{o}\nu\eta\sigma\iota\varsigma$ A; $\tau\alpha\pi\epsilon\iota\nu o\phi\rho o\sigma(\acute{v}\nu\eta\varsigma)$ M, but the meaning is the same.

76   See comment on *Vis.* 3.6.2; Introduction 2.2.2; Osiek, *Rich and Poor*, 121–27.

77   See comment on *Vis.* 2.2.8; also 2.3.8; *Sim.* 8.3.7.

78   Compare *Man.* 6.2.5; 11.12; *Sim.* 6.5.5; 8.9.4.

The Arrogant and Pleasure Seekers

■ **9.1 [75]** In this chapter, the language of life and death is slightly altered, but still present. The play is on the contrast between living with the outsiders, unbelievers (τὰ ἔϑνη, vv. 1, 3) and the death that awaits those who do so (v. 4). Here, those with sticks two-thirds dry and one-third green, corresponding to 1.13 and 5.4, would seem by the condition of their branches to be in a worse state than those of the preceding chapter. Their denial is more serious, for it is not only business concerns (8.1) and pleasures (8.5) that keep them in an uncommitted state, but wealth, status, and honor, the most seductive temptations to the root vice: pride.[79] There may be a contrast intended between those in *Vis.* 3.6.5–7, who formally deny their faith in persecution because of their wealth, and these who do not formally deny but continue to live as if they did.[80] Here as elsewhere where wealth and business concerns are criticized, we see one of the author's greatest preoccupations and catch a glimpse of the many problems and different viewpoints regarding early Christians' accommodation with their environment.[81]

■ **9.2–4** Four different outcomes are described for the above group. Many had a change of heart and were able to conquer their greed for status enhancement (v. 2). Still others (v. 3) went in the other direction into alienation from the faith, perhaps not formal verbal apostasy, but a complete retreat into a pagan life with deliberate severing of ties.[82] The ultimate Christian insult is reserved for them: they were counted among the "outsiders" (μετὰ τῶν ἐϑνῶν ἐλογίσϑησαν).[83] A third group of them remained indecisive about making a clean break with their former lifestyle, out of despair and guilt for what they had been (v. 4a).[84] A fourth outcome was to remain indecisive not because of guilt but because of the attraction of a pleasurable lifestyle, and therefore to be a cause of dissension in the community. For groups three and four, conversion is a possibility because their hearts are ready, more so group three, but conversion and salvation are not possible for the second group. The difference between the fourth group here and the second group in 8.5 is not at all clear. Probably the same concern is brought up twice.

Halfhearted Believers

■ **10.1–2 [76]** The picture begins to look brighter, for these are easier cases that will not have difficulty getting into the tower; they just need a little work. Those with green sticks with dry, cracked tips correspond to 1.14 and 5.5. That they were honorable in the sight of God (ἔνδοξοι παρὰ τῷ ϑεῷ) contrasts with those in 9.1 who gained status enhancement among the outsiders (ἐνδοξότεροι παρὰ τοῖς ἔϑνεσιν). Their petty desires and little quarrels did not hinder their conversion (v. 1). Even those whose doublemindedness caused them to be sources of trouble in the community (v. 2) have a very low chance of *not* getting in.[85]

■ **10.3–4** The description of the state of the last group of sticks, mostly dry with just a little green, would suggest people in a terrible state, but such is not the case. This group, corresponding to 1.15 and 5.6, have faith but not works.[86] Their lawless deeds (τὰ ἔργα τῆς ἀνομίας)[87] are actions not in conformity to the law of God. The difference here, the reason they are not condemned like so many other groups, is that they are ordinary sinners, who did nothing to separate themselves from God, never flinched from "bearing the name" of God, of which they were not ashamed,[88] and are also immediately capable of virtuous deeds, among them hospitality. In the network of house churches in this era, receiving traveling believ-

---

79   See comment on 7.4 and *Vis.* 3.6.2; *Man.* 10.1.4.
80   Dibelius, 599.
81   Crombie (42) inexplicably concludes that these references to "worldly Christians" are "inconsistent with the times of Clement" and so show the later dating of the book.
82   Though the A reading φϑειρόμενοι ("corrupted"; so Lake, 213) would be even more appropriate, they are in fact φερόμενοι ("carried away"; MLL) by empty honor (κενοδοξία).
83   Compare Matt 18:17.
84   Compare *Mandate* 9.

85   Δυσκόλως ("with difficulty"): see comment on *Man.* 4.3.6, where (along with other passages) it is used the opposite way, negatively.
86   Jas 2:18–25.
87   See Isa 59:6; 2 Pet 2:8; *Barn.* 4.1 (cited in Brox, 374).
88   See comment on 6.4, where, by contrast, another group is ashamed of the name invoked upon them.

ers, especially itinerant preachers and missionaries, was of crucial importance. Extending hospitality included more than generosity; it also created the bond of communion among churches. Refusal to grant hospitality was equivalent to breaking the bond of communion.[89] Upon hearing the message of conversion, they responded quickly, without hesitation (ἀδιστάκτως),[90] just the opposite of the doubleminded, who cannot get up the courage to act decisively in favor of God's interests. Their response is to do good deeds of justice (ἐργάζονται πᾶσαν ἀπρετὴν δικαιοσύνης),[91] just the opposite of their previous deeds of lawlessness. The opening sentence of v. 4 is textually uncertain. Most appropriate to the context would be "Some of them are afraid" because of their guilt over what they had done.[92] But the preferred manuscript renders the translation given here,[93] where their suffering is to be understood as redemptive against their sins (see *Sim.* 6.3).

Exhortation to Obey the Commandments

■ **11.1–5 [77]** The conclusion to the eighth *Similitude* summarizes once again the message of conversion using familiar language. Like many of the *Mandates,* the chapter opens with an appeal to "live to God," an appeal repeated in v. 3; it will also conclude with a similar appeal addressed to Hermas in the singular (v. 4). By contrast, those who do not change bring death upon themselves (v. 3). The message of conversion in response to God's mercy is addressed to all, regardless of worthiness (v. 1).[94] All who have received the call (κλῆσις) of baptism[95] are destined to be saved through God's son (διὰ τοῦ υἱοῦ αὐτοῦ σωθῆναι)—one of the few conventional Christian statements in the text. The original ending was undoubtedly v. 4. Verse 5 is a transition to the next section, added when the ninth *Similitude* was added to the text.

---

89 See *Man.* 8.10; Acts 10:23; 16:15; Heb 13:2; 3 John 5–9. Cf. A. J. Malherbe, "Hospitality and Inhospitality in the Church," *Social Aspects of Early Christianity* (2d ed.; Philadelphia: Fortress, 1983) 92–112.

90 On this expression, see comment on *Man.* 9.2.

91 Though the MSS. evidence is uncertain on the exactness of the last two words, "Mand. *1,* 2 and Sim. *6,* 1,4 [sic] argue for ἀρετὴν δικαιοσύνης" (Bonner, *Papyrus Codex,* 113).

92 Φοβοῦνται A, followed by Lake (215) without knowledge of M.

93 Τινὲς δὲ ἐξ αὐτῶν καὶ παθοῦνται κ[αὶ ἡδέως

θλίβον]ται Whittaker (75), following M, with bracketed material restored from LL *libenter patiuntur;* followed by Joly (284); Snyder (126). Fullest discussion in Bonner, *Papyrus Codex,* 113.

94 See 6.1.

95 Compare *Man.* 4.3.6.

9

The Twelve Mountains of Arcadia

1 [78]

1/ After I had written the commandments and parables of the Shepherd, who is the angel of conversion, he came and said to me: "I want to show you whatever the Holy Spirit showed you, who spoke with you in the form of the church, because that spirit is the Son of God. **2/** Since you were weaker in the flesh, it was not revealed to you through an angel. Then you were fortified by the spirit and strengthened in your own strength, so as to be able to see an angel. Then the building of the tower was revealed to you by the church. You have seen everything in a beautiful and seemly way, as it were, virginally. Now you are seeing through an angel, yet through the same spirit. **3/** But you must see everything more clearly from me. This is why I was assigned by the honored angel to stay in your house, that you might see everything boldly without being afraid of anything as you used to be." **4/** So he took me away to Arcadia to a breast-shaped mountain, sat me down at the top of the mountain, and showed me a large plain surrounded by twelve mountains, each of them different in appearance. **5/** The first was black as pitch, the second bald with no plants, and the third full of thorns and thistles. **6/** The fourth had plants that were half-dry, green on top but with dryness at the roots. Some of the plants were drying up as the sun burned them. **7/** The fifth mountain was very steep with green plants. The sixth mountain was completely full of cracks, some large, some small. The cracks had plants in them, but these plants were not doing well; rather, they were withering. **8/** The seventh mountain had joyful plants, and the entire mountain was thriving, and every kind of domestic animals and birds were feeding on that mountain. The more the cattle and birds fed, the more the plants of that mountain thrived. The eighth mountain was full of springs, and every kind of the Lord's creatures came to drink from the springs of that mountain. **9/** The ninth mountain had no water at all, but was entirely desert. In it there were wild animals and deadly snakes that could destroy people. The tenth mountain had large trees and was completely shady, and in the shade of the trees there were sheep lying down resting and ruminating. **10/** The eleventh mountain was heavily wooded and the trees bore fruit, each decked out with different fruits, so that anyone who saw them desired to eat of their fruits. The twelfth mountain was completely white, its appearance was full of joy, and the mountain was most beautiful in itself.

There is manuscript uncertainty about the place of this long section in the whole. A gives it no title; E entitles it the beginning of the *Similitudes*; C² simply "Beginning."

A clear break is envisioned within the text itself at this point. There is a familiar conclusion at *Sim.* 8.11.4, followed by a transition line into what follows. As the text stands, these comments (8.11.5) serve to link together two distinct sections of the book. The teaching on the different kinds of persons and different responses to the message of conversion has been conveyed through the image of stones used for the building of the tower in the third *Vision,* and through different conditions of willow sticks in the eighth *Similitude.* Here the same teaching will be conveyed via twelve mountains, to be taken up again in chapters 2–9, 12–16 with a reprise of the tower. For some, there is a contrast between the ideal church of the *Visions* and the historical, limited church[1] of especially this *Similitude.* Certainly both aspects of the church are presented in *Hermas,* but both aspects are present in both *Visions* and *Similitudes.* Here, the christological allusions will grow stronger, as will the detailed discussion of the shortcomings of church members.

After preliminary remarks in 1.1–3, the new vision of the twelve mountains is given. This vision begins a concentric pattern that extends through chap. 29 and highlights Hermas' encounter with the virtues.

9.1 Twelve mountains
  9.2–9 Tower revisited
    9.10–11 Hermas and the young women/virtues
    9.12–16 Explanation of the tower and the young women
9.17–29 Explanation of the twelve mountains

■ **1.1 [78]** The original directive to write down the commands and parables occurred in *Vis.* 5.5–6. Here the narrative direction indicates that that task has been completed and that a new section is beginning. The Shepherd is still the revelatory agent, and as usual, the Shepherd takes the initiative to show something new to Hermas. But now there is a new identification introduced. In *Vis.* 3.3 the woman church is the tower that is under construction, but now she is also the Holy Spirit; in another distinct and complementary statement that follows immediately, that spirit is also the Son of God. The first statement presupposes knowledge of the

Visions, but also takes the identification there considerably further. It is not correct to say that the church is therefore equated with the Son of God, any more than it is correct to say that the Son of God and the Holy Spirit are equated in *Sim.* 5.5.[2] Rather here, a deeper meaning is assigned to the apparition of the woman, beyond that of church.[3] Just as the incarnate Son is "the perfect dwelling of the Holy Spirit in flesh," so the church is the "perfect dwelling of the Spirit" in the human community.[4] The fact that this new meaning comes only here is typical of the additive style of the author, whereby new meanings are given to old images almost as an afterthought.

1.2–3 Verse 2 is difficult to interpret, and probably corrupt. M is mostly missing here, but what remains supports the reading of A. On the assumption that the reader is meant to know the content of the *Visions,* Hermas began the process of receiving visions in the weakened state of marital ambiguity, economic reversal, and fear.[5] He was encouraged to be strong as he began the task of writing the full revelation, and the process of revelation was also a process of coming to awareness of strength for Hermas,[6] so that as he progressed, strengthened by the spirit, he was able to strengthen his faith and resolve through his own human strength as well. Dibelius and Brox both suggest a period after "to be able to see an angel."[7] In this case, the clause that follows repeats the same idea already said in the first part of the verse: when Hermas was weaker, he could not see the revelations of the angel, but only of the church (vv. 1b–2a). Later, when he was stronger in the spirit, he was able to see an angel. In other words, the revelation by the woman church was preliminary to the more important revelation from an angel, namely, the Shepherd himself, that began at *Vision* 5. In this case, what is translated here as "You have seen . . . virginally" should be translated literally, "You have seen . . . as from a virgin" (ὡς ὑπὸ παρθένου ἑώρακας), that is, by means of the

1   Listed in Brox, 375–76.
2   There the son of the parable is the Holy Spirit; the slave of the parable is the Son of God.
3   Cirillo ("Erma e il problema," 30) suggests that, because of the rise of Montanism in Rome, Hermas wants to make a connection with the prominence of women in that community and even with feminine

images of the Holy Spirit and Christ (Epiphanius *Pan.* 49.1).
4   *Sim.* 5.6.5–7; Snyder, 128.
5   *Vis.* 1.3.1; 2.2.2–3; 3.1, 6.7.
6   *Vis.* 5.5; Young, "Being a Man."
7   Dibelius, 602; Brox, 380.

virgin church. This is how most commentators understand the phrase. The trouble with this interpretation is that the woman church is called "virgin" ($\pi\alpha\rho\vartheta\acute{\epsilon}\nu\sigma\varsigma$) only once, at the end of her appearances at *Vis.* 4.2.1. Since she has by that time undergone the transformation from old to young woman, and since bridal imagery is suggested only in that passage, it is unlikely that that is how she would be referred to here in this recapitulation of revelations given thus far.[8]

It does seem that a contrast is being made here between the revelation of the church in the *Visions* and the later revelation by the Shepherd/angel. The full stop suggested by Dibelius and Brox is helpful, so that the second half of the verse does repeat the sequence first stated in vv. 1b and 2a, first revelation of and by the church, then of and by the Shepherd/angel. But the reference to a virgin is more likely to Hermas himself, and to the change brought about in him by his contact with heavenly beings. Like the church in *Vision 3*, he has been rejuvenated spiritually.[9] The perfect tense used in this clause, in contrast to the aorist just before, also suggests Hermas' continuing involvement in the action. The continuation of the familiar pattern of insistent questions by Hermas to the Shepherd, however, does not suggest that the change has taught him anything.[10] Verse 3 reinforces the then/now contrast. The Shepherd, sent to Hermas to be accompanying spirit at the beginning of their rela-

tionship,[11] is the one from whom he must now see[12] everything.

■ **1.4** Here begins a new vision of twelve mountains that will be described succinctly in the rest of the chapter. The explanation will not begin until 9.17. Most of Hermas' visions come to him where he is. Here, as in *Vis.* 1.1.3 and 2.1, Hermas is transported to the vision—how, we are not told.[13] He is taken to the top of a mountain that is described as "breast-shaped" ($\mu\alpha\sigma\tau\tilde{\omega}\delta\epsilon\varsigma$)[14] so that he can survey the whole scene of the twelve mountains, which later in chapter 2 will surround the rock on which the tower is built.[15] The location of the vision in Arcadia has inspired numerous theories. This mountainous area of the central Peloponnesus, largely devoted to pastoral life, was home to both Hermes and Pan. The connection with a Shepherd/angel seems natural enough. Some have supposed that Hermas came originally from this area;[16] others that Hermas is really Hermes, so that the theosophical tractate *Poimandres* stands behind *Hermas* as Hellenistic source and prototype.[17] Arcadia has also been emended to Aricia, modern Ariccia, on the south side of Lago Albano at the foot of the Alban Hills southeast of Rome, thus an actual place in the surroundings of Rome.[18] Another emendation of the name is to the field of Ardat[19] in *4 Ezra* 9.26.[20] None of these theories has found favor, ingenious though they be.[21] Rather, the author uses "a reference to

---

8   Least satisfying is Lake's suggestion (217) that the revelation was "first sent in the form of a human being (the emphasis is on the humanity, not on the Virginity [*sic*]) and afterwards when he was stronger spiritually in the form of an angel."

9   The symbolism of virginity as wholeness is not limited to early Christianity; see, e.g., Philo *Cher.* 50; *Q. Exod.* 2.3: sexual union changes virgins to women, but divine union changes women to virgins. Contrast the virtues as "virgins" ($\pi\alpha\rho\vartheta\acute{\epsilon}\nu\sigma\iota$) in *Sim.* 9.2.3 and following chapters (identified as such in 9.15.1) with the black-clad "women" ($\gamma\upsilon\nu\alpha\tilde{\iota}\kappa\epsilon\varsigma$) who represent vices (9.15.3).

10   At 9.14.4, for instance, Hermas still protests that he does not understand anything.

11   *Vis.* 5.2; see comment there.

12   "See" ($\iota\delta\epsilon\tilde{\iota}\nu$) ML[1]; "learn" ($\mu\alpha\vartheta\epsilon\tilde{\iota}\nu$) AL[2](E).

13   This is common language for visionary experiences: compare Ezek 40:1–2; Matt 4:5, 8; Luke 4:5, 9; 2 Cor 12:2; Rev 17:3; 21:10, etc. Brox (382) lists commentators who assume flight, though no means of transportation is specified.

14   Cf. Strabo's description (14.6.3) of "breast-shaped Mount Olympus" ($\check{\sigma}\rho\sigma\varsigma$ $\mu\alpha\sigma\tau\sigma\epsilon\iota\delta\grave{\epsilon}\varsigma$ $\check{O}\lambda\upsilon\mu\pi\sigma\varsigma$) near Amathus in Syria (Dibelius, 603).

15   Compare Ezek 40:1–2; Rev 21:10.

16   Especially J. R. Harris, "Hermas in Arcadia," *JBL* 7 (1887) 69–83.

17   Reitzenstein, *Poimandres*, 33. Critics have drawn attention to major differences, especially that here Hermas is not revealer but recipient of revelation, whereas in *Poimandres* the opposite is true.

18   T. Zahn, *Der Hirt des Hermas* (Gotha: F. A. Perthes, 1868) 211–18.

19   Variations: Ardab (Armenian ms.); Arpad (Syriac and Ethiopic).

20   E.g., G. H. Box, *The Ezra Apocalypse* (London: SPCK, 1912) 212–13; Cirillo, "Erma e il problema," 14.

21   All are conveniently assembled and discussed in Snyder, 129.

a well-known literary figure of speech to create a bridge with Hellenistic culture."[22] Beyond this, however, the reference probably indicates familiarity with the name and its image in Greco-Roman popular culture.

■ **1.5–10** The twelve mountains are to some extent reminiscent of the seven mountains of *1 Enoch* 24–32, but there are considerable differences. There, all the mountains are beautiful and one extraordinary mountain is the throne of God. Here, at least seven of the mountains are potentially troublesome in their description, and the progression from bad to good is not completely clear, since the ninth mountain breaks the pattern. The mountains surround a large plain; as is shown in the next chapter, the plain is not empty, but contains the great white rock that is higher than the mountains, and this feature does resemble *1 Enoch* 25. The detailed description of the condition of the half-dry plants on the fourth mountain (v. 6) is reminiscent of some of the willow sticks in 8.4–5. The "cracks" ($\sigma\chi\acute{\iota}\sigma\mu\alpha\tau\alpha$) in the fifth mountain (v. 7) resemble the cracks in some of the stones destined for the tower in *Vis.* 3.2.8 and elsewhere, and by word association, though not by similarity of image, the cracks in some of the sticks in 8.9, 10, 14, and elsewhere. The seventh and twelfth mountains (vv. 8, 10) are characterized by "joy" ($\iota\lambda\alpha\rho\acute{o}\tau\eta\varsigma$), a favorite term.[23] The ninth mountain (v. 9) is the most dangerous and fearsome.

---

22   Snyder, 129.
23   See comment on *Vis.* 1.4.3.

9

The Tower Revisited

2 [79] 1/ In the middle of the plain he showed me a large white rock that had arisen out of the plain. The rock was higher than the mountains, four-cornered, so as to be able to contain the whole world. 2/ That rock was old, with a door cut into it. But the chiseling of the door was new, or so it seemed to me. The door so shimmered in the sun that I wondered at the brightness of the door. 3/ Twelve young women stood in a circle around the door. The four who stood at the corners seemed to me the most distinguished, though the others were also distinguished. They stood by the four sections of the door, each with two young women between them. 4/ They were clothed in linen garments, splendidly girded, with right shoulders uncovered as if ready to carry a load. In this way they were ready, very joyful and eager. 5/ When I had seen these things I was amazed because I saw things great and wonderful. I was still confused about the young women because they were so delicate, yet they stood courageously as though they were about to bear the whole of the heavens. 6/ The Shepherd said to me: "Why are you thinking to yourself and getting confused and making yourself sad? Whatever you cannot understand, have good sense and do not try, but ask the Lord to receive understanding and know them. 7/ You cannot see what is behind you, but you are seeing what lies ahead. Let go of what you cannot see and do not give yourself problems. Take control of what you do see and do not bother about the rest. Whatever I show you I will explain to you. Look to the rest."

3 [80] 1/ I saw six men who had come, tall, notable, and similar in appearance, and they called on a great number of men. Those who came were likewise tall, beautiful, and powerful, and the six men commanded them to build a certain tower upon the rock. There was a great crowd of these men who had come to build the tower, running back and forth around the door. 2/ The young women standing around the door told the men to hurry and build the tower. They extended their hands as if about to receive something from the men. 3/ The six men commanded stones to arise from a certain deep place and to go into the construction of the tower. Ten bright square unhewn stones came up. 4/ The six men called the young women and commanded them to carry through the door all the stones that were coming for building the tower, and to give them to the men who were going to build the tower. 5/ The young women took the ten stones that had first come from the deep, put them on one another, and carried them together like one single stone.

4 [81] 1/ Even as they had stood round the door, those who seemed strong were getting under the corners of the stone. The others were moving against the sides of the stone, and thus they all carried the stones. They brought them through the door as they had been ordered and gave them to the men in the tower, who took the stones and were building. 2/ The building of the tower was upon the great rock and above the door. Those ten stones were put in place [and filled the entire rock. They became] the foundation of the building of the tower, and the rock and the door were holding up the whole tower. 3/ After the ten stones came twenty-five other stones from the depth, which were placed into the building of the tower, carried by the young women like the first ones. After these came thirty-five, which were also placed in the tower. After these came another forty stones, which were all put into the building of the tower. [Thus there were four courses in the foundations of the tower.] 4/ They stopped coming up from the deep, and the builders stopped for a bit. Then the six men ordered the masses to bring stones from the mountains to build the tower. 5/ So stones of many different colors were brought from all the mountains, hewn by the men and given to the young women. The women carried them through the door and turned them over for the building of the tower. And when the variegated stones were put into the building, all alike became white and changed their many colors. 6/ But some stones that were turned over to the men for the building did not become bright, but were found to stay just as they were when inserted, for they had not been given over by the young women, nor had they been brought through the door. These stones were inappropriate in the building of the tower. 7/ The six men saw the inappropriate stones in the building and commanded that they be taken away and brought down to their own place from where they were taken. 8/ They said to the men who were carrying the stones in: "In no way must you put stones into the building, but put them next to the tower so that the young women can carry them in through the door and turn them over for the building. For if," they said, "they are not carried in by the hands of the young women through the door, they cannot change their colors. So do not labor in vain," they said.

5 [82] 1/ The building was finished on that day, but the tower was not completed, because its construction was to be extended, and there was a delay in the construction. The six men commanded all the builders to go apart a little distance and rest, but they told the young women not to leave the tower. It seemed to me that the young women had been left to guard it. 2/ But when all of them had gone away and were resting, I said to the Shepherd: "Why, sir, wasn't the construction of the tower finished?" He said: "The tower cannot be completed yet until its lord comes to inspect this building, lest if some of the stones are found to be crumbling, he can change them, since the tower is being constructed according to his wishes." 3/ I said: "Sir, I would like to know about the building of this tower, and about the rock, the door, the mountains, the young women, and the stones that arose from the depths unhewn, which went that way into the building; 4/ and why for the foundation ten stones were first laid, then twenty-five, then thirty-five, then forty, and about the stones that were placed in the building and then taken out again and returned to their own place. Give rest to my soul about all of this and let me know." 5/ He said: "If you do not turn out to be going after what does not matter, you will know everything. [After several days, we will come back here and you will see the rest of what will happen to the tower, and you will know all the parables clearly." 6/ And after several days] we returned to the place where we had sat, and he said to me: "Let's go alongside the tower, because the one responsible for the tower is coming to inspect it." So we came to the tower and there was absolutely no one around it except the young women. 7/ The shepherd asked the women if the ruler of the tower had arrived. They said that he was on his way to inspect the building.

6 [83]   1/ And behold, after a little while I saw ranks of many men coming, and in the middle a man so tall that his height exceeded that of the tower. 2/ The six men [set over the building walked to the right and left with him, and everyone who was working on the building] was with him, and many other distinguished figures circling around him. The young women who cared for the tower ran up to him and kissed him, and began to walk with him around the tower. 3/ The man inspected the building very closely, even touching each stone. With a stick he carried in his hand, he tapped every stone of the building [three times]. 4/ When he knocked them, some of them became black as pitch, some scaly, some cracked, some stunted, some neither white nor black, some rough so as not to fit with the other stones, and some with many stains. These were the different kinds of unsound stones found in the building. 5/ He commanded that all these should be removed from the tower and placed next to the tower, and that other stones should be brought and put in their place. 6/ [The builders asked him from which mountains he wanted stones to be brought and put in their place.] He commanded them not to bring them from the mountains, [but he commanded them to bring them from a certain plain nearby]. 7/ The plain was dug, and fine square stones were found, though some were round. Whatever stones were found in that plain were all brought and carried through the door by the young women. 8/ The square stones were trimmed and put in place of those removed, but the round ones were not placed in the building because they were hard to trim and time-consuming. They were placed next to the tower as if they would soon be trimmed and placed in the building, because they were fine indeed.

7 [84]   1/ When the honored man, lord of the whole

tower, finished this, he called over the Shepherd and turned over to him all the stones that were lying around the tower that had been removed from the building, and said to him: 2/ "Clean these stones with care and put into the building of the tower the ones that can fit in with the others, but the ones that do not fit, throw away far from the tower." 3/ [With this command to the Shepherd, he left the tower] with everyone with whom he had come. But the young women stood around the tower watching over it. 4/ I said to the Shepherd: "How can these stones come back into the building of the tower, once rejected?" He answered: "Do you see these stones?" "I see them, sir," I said. "I will trim most of these stones and place them into the building so as to fit with the other stones. 5/ "How, sir, can they fill the same place after they have been cut away?" He answered me: "The ones that come out little will be put in the center of the building, and the bigger ones on the outside to support them." 6/ Having said this, he said to me: "Let's go, and after two days let us come back and clean these stones and put them into the building. Everything around the tower must be cleaned up, lest the master come suddenly and find things not clean around the tower and become angry, and these stones will not get into the building of the tower, and I will appear to be careless in the master's sight." 7/ After two days we came back to the tower and he said to me: "Let's look at all the stones and see which ones can come into the building." "Let's look," I said.

8 [85] 1/ We began first to inspect the black stones, which were the same as when they had been removed from the building. The Shepherd commanded that they be taken away from the tower and put at a distance. 2/ Then he inspected the scaly ones, and took many of them and trimmed them, and commanded the young women to take them up and put them into the building. The young women picked them up and put them into the building, in the middle of the tower. The others he commanded to be put with the black ones, because they were also black. 3/ Next he inspected those with cracks. He trimmed many of them and commanded the young women to carry them to the building. But they were put on the outside because they were more sound. The rest he could not trim because they had too many cracks. This is why they were thrown away from the building of the tower. 4/ Then he inspected the stunted ones. Many of them were black, and some had big cracks. He commanded them to be placed with those thrown away. Most of them he cleaned and trimmed and commanded them to be placed in the building. The young women took them and fitted them into the middle of the tower because they were weaker. 5/ Next he inspected those that were half-white and half-black. Many of them were found to be black, and he commanded them to be taken away with those that were thrown out. The others were all taken up by the young women. Since they were white, they were fitted by the young women themselves into the building. They were placed on the outside because they were sound and could support those placed in the middle, because none of them were mutilated. 6/ Then he inspected those that were difficult and hardened, and some were rejected because they could not be trimmed, being too hard. The others were trimmed, taken up by the young women, and fitted into the middle of the building of the tower because they were weaker. 7/ Then he inspected those with stains, of which just a few were blackened, and he threw them away with the others. But most of them were fine and sound, and were fitted by the young women into the building. They were placed on the outside because of their strength.

9 [86]   1/ Next he came to examine the round white stones and said to me: "What shall we do about these stones?" "How should I know, sir," I said. "Then don't you notice anything about them?" 2/ "Sir," I said, "I do not have this skill, nor am I a stonecutter, nor can I understand." He said, "Don't you see how round they are? If I want to make them square, quite a bit will have to be cut off of them. Yet some of them will necessarily have to be placed in the building." 3/ I said, "Sir, if it must be, why do you torture yourself instead of just choosing the ones you want for the building and fitting them into it?" So he chose the biggest bright ones and trimmed them, and the young women took them up and fitted them into the outside of the building. 4/ The remnants were picked up and put back on the plain from which they were taken. But they were not rejected because, he said, "there is still a little of the tower to be built, and the master of the tower wants all the stones to be fitted into the building, because they are very brilliant." 5/ Twelve women were called, pleasing in appearance, clothed in black, [girded and with bare shoulders] and loosened hair. These women looked wild to me. The Shepherd commanded them to pick up the stones that had been rejected for the building and carry them to the mountains from which they had been taken. 6/ They were happy, and they carried all the stones and put them back from whence they had been taken. After all the stones had been removed and no stone remained around the tower, the Shepherd said to me: "Let's walk around the tower and see if there is any shortcoming in it." I circled it with him. 7/ When the Shepherd saw how lovely the building was, he was very happy, for the tower was so built that when I saw it, I desired it. It was built as if it were all one stone, without any joint in it, and the stone looked as if it had been cut out of rock. It seemed to me to be a single stone.

Vision of the Tower

■ **2.1–2 [79]** The two towers of *Vision* 3 and *Similitude* 9 are essentially the same, with some small changes, but mostly with further developments of the same images from the first to the second, supporting the theory of a single author who wrote in stages, and of an oral base in which stories are told and retold, with new elements added as they are thought of. Thus the second tower of *Similitude* 9 could represent the same initial idea reworked and expanded over a period of years. The major differences are as follows.[1]

The first tower is built on water, which is baptism (*Vis.* 3.2.4; 3.3.5); the second is built on a rock with a door, both of which are the Son of God (*Sim.* 9.3.1; 9.12.1–8). There is now no entry into the tower except through the door. In the first tower, the seven young women/virtues support the tower (*Vis.* 3.8.2). "Faith" ($\Pi\iota\sigma\tau\iota\varsigma$) and "Restraint" ($\dot{E}\gamma\kappa\rho\acute{\alpha}\tau\epsilon\iota\alpha$) have priority; the rest have mother-daughter relationships with each other (*Vis.* 3.8.2, 5, 7). In the second tower, the now twelve young women are spirits of the Son of God (*Sim.* 9.15.1) who must carry through the gate every stone that enters the tower. Five of the names from the first tower are repeated in the second, where four of the young women have some sort of priority: "Faith" ($\Pi\iota\sigma\tau\iota\varsigma$), "Restraint" ($\dot{E}\gamma\kappa\rho\acute{\alpha}\tau\epsilon\iota\alpha$), "Power" ($\Delta\acute{\upsilon}\nu\alpha\mu\iota\varsigma$), and "Endurance" ($M\alpha\kappa\rho\sigma\theta\upsilon\mu\acute{\iota}\alpha$). In the first tower, the seven young women have no negative counterparts; in the second tower, the twelve women in black garments are their opposites, not in a one-to-one correspondence, but as representatives of evil spirits (*Sim.* 9.9.5, 15.3).

In the first tower, the rejected stones never are able to enter, and once in the tower, no stones must be thrown out (*Vis.* 3.2.7–9). In the second, some entered the right way and were taken into the tower, but still were seduced by the evil women and put out (*Sim.* 9.13.6–9), so that access to the tower does not guarantee salvation. In the first tower, the foundation stones were the present and immediately past leaders of the church: apostles, overseers, teachers, and ministers (*Vis.* 3.5.1–2). In the second tower, the foundations go deeper, into the history of Israel: the first and second biblical generations, the prophets and servants of God, then only finally the apostles and teachers of the Son of God (*Sim.* 9.4.2–3, 5.4, 15.4).[2] Finally, the first tower seems to admit and even consider only the baptized, as the church is founded on the water of baptism and there is no discussion of nonbelievers, while in the second tower, the nonbaptized, the nations, are explicitly mentioned, in anticipation of their coming to faith (*Sim.* 9.17.1, 4).

The large white rock in the middle of the plain is the cosmic mountain that contains all within it. While called simply a "rock" ($\pi\acute{\epsilon}\tau\rho\alpha$), a familiar biblical image,[3] it is the highest mountain. It is not described as just being there, but as having risen up ($\dot{\alpha}\nu\alpha\beta\epsilon\beta\eta\kappa\upsilon\hat{\iota}\alpha\nu$) from the plain, hence, while located in one place, it also connotes the dynamic power of geological and thus cosmic forces. That it is "foursquare" ($\tau\epsilon\tau\rho\acute{\alpha}\gamma\omega\nu\sigma\varsigma$)[4] is an unusual description for a natural rock or mountain (perhaps cubic),[5] but not for a well-planned city.[6] That the rock is old (v. 2) but the door is new suggests a Christian adaptation. The door reflects the splendor of the new means of access to God.[7] It is interesting that nothing is made here of Matt 16:18 or a similar tradition about the church's foundation on a human rock, which is probably still at this time only an Eastern tradition.

■ **2.3** The seven young women, literally "virgins" ($\pi\alpha\rho$-$\theta\acute{\epsilon}\nu\sigma\iota$), of *Vis.* 3.8.2–8 have here increased to twelve. In 9.13.2 they will be called "holy spirits" ($\ddot{\alpha}\gamma\iota\alpha\ \pi\nu\epsilon\acute{\upsilon}\mu\alpha\tau\alpha$) without whom it is impossible to enter the reign of God.

---

1   Other discussions of differences in Snyder, 140; Brox, 375–77, 421.

2   Brox (377) opines a Jewish origin of the parable of the tower as Israel, built on the foundation of the patriarchs, the just, prophets, servants of God, and the twelve tribes, then the nations. But if this is so, it is curious that the biblical basis is not present in the first tower, which would presumably be closer to the source.

3   God as rock (Deut 32:4, 15; 2 Sam 22:47; Ps 18:46; 28:1; 62:6; 89:26; 94:22; 95:1; etc.); especially God's mountain (the Temple mount) as highest mountain: Isa 2:2; Mic 4:1; the church built on rock: Matt 16:18; the cornerstone (Isa 28:16), which becomes Christ (Rom 9:33; Eph 2:20; 1 Pet 2:6–8), the rejected cornerstone (Ps 118:22; Matt 21:42; Mark 12:10; Luke 20:17; Acts 4:11).

4   Also in *Vis.* 3.2.5.

5   Brox, 387.

6   Similarly in visionary literature, Rev. 21:16, but in city planning also said of Nicaea in Bithynia (Strabo *Geog.* 12.4.7); cf. BAGD *s.v.*

7   *Midrash Yalqut Shime'oni*, a tenth-century text incorporating earlier traditions, contains a parable (1.766 on Num 23:9) of a king who wanted to build a building, but when digging in the desired loca-

When they are later given names of virtues in 9.15.1, not all the seven names from the previous list will be repeated. Both seven and twelve are cosmically and religiously significant numbers for both Judaism and Christianity, but no significance is assigned to their numbers in the text. It is impossible to specify exactly what the author had in mind by using these numbers. In their earlier appearance in *Vision* 3, two were singled out for identification first. Here (15.2), four will be more important because of a special role they play, standing at the four corners of the gate. The exact placement of the twelve around a door in a rock is difficult to imagine from the description given. Lake imagines that the door "must have been a sort of porch, cut out of the rock" with the tower built directly above it, so that the young women stand in a square pattern. The general idea that the women surround the door is more important than exactly how they are standing.[8]

■ **2.4–5** In *Vis.* 3.8.2, the seven young women support the tower. Here the twelve women are also prepared to carry something heavy, stones for the tower. The marked contrast (v. 5) between their apparent delicacy and their robust readiness for carrying a heavy load sets the stage for their mythological power.

■ **2.6–7** This is not the first time the Shepherd reproaches Hermas for his curiosity. But this is more than just another stereotyped remark. These two verses are a wisdom meditation on the inadvisability of trying to know more than one can know. Thinking about divine mysteries is not discouraged, for elsewhere those who take no trouble to understand them because of their immersion in worldly concerns are criticized.[9] What is criticized here is the attitude of trying to figure out everything on one's own rather than in dependence on God, who alone can give understanding. Verse 7 teaches not to look back in regret to the past, but to look to what one can understand of the future.

Builders of the Tower

■ **3.1–3 [80]** The readiness of the young women to carry a load leads to the next part of the vision, in which the tower of *Vision* 3 reappears. The six men (ἄνδρες) are continuous from the original scene in *Vis.* 3.2.5. At 3.4.1, they were identified as angels, the first ones created. As in *Vis.* 3.2.5, they are again here assisted by a large crowd of other men (ἄνδρες) to build the tower, which this time, however, is not built on water but on the rock. Unlike the first vision, the stones now arise by themselves; they do not have to be brought up from the depths; contrast *Vis.* 3.2.5–6, 4.2, 5.2–3. Also in contrast to the first treatment of the tower, here there is a sense of urgency. The many male assistants are literally running (περιτρεχόντων) around the door, and the young women are cheering them on (v. 2) as they hold out their arms as if to receive something.[10] In reality, they will be giving stones to the men.

■ **3.4–5** The many men running around the tower have nothing to do until they are given stones by the women (vv. 4–5). At the angels' command (v. 3), ten good square stones come up by themselves from a deep place, which may or may not be the same as the water of *Vis.* 3.2.5, 6.[11] There, the contrast between that place and land makes the implication clear. Though not attested in any surviving manuscripts,[12] these stones must be unhewn to correspond to 9.5.3; 16.7, where the reading is sure. Here, as contrasted to the original vision of the tower, the young women receive the stones from the angels and must carry them through the door, then give them to the other men who are building the tower. It is useless to try to envision concretely how this is to happen through

---

tion, found only swamp. He kept looking until he found rock. Just so, God was discouraged over the generation of Enoch and the flood, but found the rock of Abraham (Isa 51:1–2) on which to build the world. M.-A. Chevalier, "Tu es Pierre, tu es le nouvel Abraham" (*EThR* 57 [1982] 375–87) argues that the midrash is a response to Matt 16:18–19, but G. Arnera, "Du rocher d'Esaïe au douze montagnes d'Hermas" (*EThR* 59 [1984] 215–220), argues that it is rather a response to Hermas' mountain. My thanks to Rabbi Hayim Perelmuter for help with this reference.

8   Lake, 221. For another conjunction of female alle-

gorization of virtues, rock, and gates, see *Tabula of Cebes*, especially 18–20.
9   *Man.* 10.1.4–5.
10   Lake's translation (225) misprints "tower" for "door" in vv. 1b and 2a.
11   Ἐκ βυθοῦ τινος, which Dibelius (607) takes to be the cosmic water.
12   Line missing in M; negative μή missing in AL[1]E; both words, μὴ λελατομημένοι, missing in L[2]. See note in Lake, 224.

a door carved in rock. The symbolism is the point. These primary stones are carried all together by the delicate-looking young women "as one single stone," corresponding to the outside appearance of the tower, as if built of one single stone, in *Vis.* 3.2.6.

Stones from the Depths

■ **4.1–3 [81]** Verse 1 continues the description of how the young women were able to carry the ten stones that seemed "like one single stone." They do it by putting the strongest at the corners to lift the stones, so that the others can then slip underneath along the sides. The text varies between "stone" and "stones" to convey the impression of a single stone, even though there are really ten carried together. The young women carry out the directives already given them in 3.4 above by carrying the stone(s) through the gate. The ten stones are then taken by the builders to become the foundation of the tower upon the great rock, above the gate. The bracketed words in vv. 2, 3 are restored[13] and in v. 2 make the reading smoother. The first number of stones in v. 3 varies in the manuscripts: twenty, twenty-five, or fifteen,[14] but the second and third numbers are sure.[15] The four groups of stones compose the four courses ($\sigma\tau o\hat{\iota}\chi o\iota$) of the foundations. The four cosmological elements are again invoked, though here the stability is horizontal rather than vertical.[16]

■ **4.4–8** Verse 4 serves as a transition between two aspects of the vision. Once the numbered stones have arisen, there is a pause in the flurry of activity that began at 3.1. But soon another phase of the building begins, as the six men turn to the hitherto unmentioned multitude to help in the effort by bringing more stones, this time not from the depths but from the mountains. An ancient prejudice in favor of white is revealed in v. 5c. The fact that "white" stones ($\lambda\epsilon\upsilon\kappa o\iota$) in v. 5c are equated with "bright" stones ($\lambda\alpha\mu\pi\rho o\iota$) in v. 6a indicates that white connotes cleansing here, not innate color. The placement of the stones in the building effects the transformation from color to whiteness, at least for most. Those for whom this is not the case (v. 6) prove to have come in the back way, or crashed the party. Since they are not brought in the correct way, they are shown to be counterfeit, and must be removed. The real reason for the problem is revealed in v. 8: these stones were not brought in by the hands of the young women through the gate.[17] The problem is not that they are presented by unacceptable people, but that they have been brought in the wrong—and perhaps deceitful—way. Since the women are "holy spirits" and virtues and the gate is the Son of God,[18] the allegorical meaning will come clear. These stones are to be placed near the tower ($\pi\alpha\rho\grave{\alpha}\ \tau\grave{o}\nu$ $\pi\acute{\upsilon}\rho\gamma o\nu$) in expectation of a changed status.[19]

Pause in the Construction

■ **5.1–2 [82]** The basic construction work is finished, but there is still more to do on the tower. It is essential to the narrative that the tower cannot yet be completely finished, because its completion brings the eschaton.[20] But from this time on, the end is nearer, and an interim period is established. This pause in construction is one of several extensions of time used in the narrative to

---

13 Omitted A; retranslated from LLE by Gebhardt-Harnack, 202; repeated in Whittaker, 79. Brox (391) questions the restoration, since otherwise the rock and gate are the foundation, not the ten stones. *Hermas,* however, is not known for such consistency.

14 Twenty in A; twenty-five in LL; fifteen in E. Normally A should be the preferred text, but in view of the agreement of ALL at *Sim.* 9.15.4, the twenty-five of LL is to be preferred here.

15 For discussion of the meaning of the numbers, see comment on 15.4 below.

16 Contrast *Vis.* 3.13.3; *Sim.* 9.2.1, etc.

17 They are similar to the unacceptable sticks that must be rejected in *Vis.* 8.2.5.

18 9.13.2, 15.2, 12.1.

19 As also in 9.6.5, 8; 7.1, with accusative of motion contrasted to their permanent position outside the tower or in a lesser place, signified by the dative ($\pi\alpha\rho\grave{\alpha}\ \tau\hat{\omega}\ \pi\acute{\upsilon}\rho\gamma\omega$) in *Vis.* 3.5.5 (Giet, "De trois expressions"; Brox, 392).

20 *Vis.* 3.8.9. Yet this pause in the building need not be equated with the classic "delay of the parousia" because, first, it is not at all certain that this was an interpretive category for early Christians or that this is the meaning of 2 Pet 3:9; and second, there is no anxiety expressed that the end will not come—quite the contrary. Joly (322) does equate the delay with the delay of the parousia, citing too Tertullian *Apol.* 32.1. To the point here is *Sim.* 10.4.4, in which the delay is for the sake of those who still need time for conversion. In *Hermas,* the delay is not a problem; the problem is that the end might come too quickly.

convey meaning to history.[21] The young women are the only ones left to guard the tower while the builders take a break.[22] Verse 2 gives the reason why the tower cannot yet be pronounced finished: it must first be inspected stone by stone by its lord. This is not the final judgment, for inferior stones will be replaced with good ones. It is rather a reflection on the imperfection of the historical church and the hope for its purification. The lord of the tower, who will appear in 6.1 as a tall man ($\dot{\alpha}\nu\dot{\eta}\rho$ $\dot{\upsilon}\psi\eta\lambda\acute{o}\varsigma$), is the same as the inspector of willow sticks in 8.2.5, who is there identified as Michael (8.3.3). In both cases, his role is to inspect ($\kappa\alpha\tau\alpha\nuο\epsilon\hat{\iota}\nu$).[23] But this role of inspection is also later delegated to the Shepherd with Hermas as assistant.[24]

■ **5.3–7**[25] Hermas here shows his usual curiosity, the literary device by which extensive explanations are introduced. No matter that early on he was chastised for his insatiable curiosity.[26] He will not get answers to his questions until chapter 12 because of the long process of inspection and replacement of the stones that comes in between. Hermas himself is being tried and inspected in the questioning process (v. 5): if he is found not to be concerned about worthless things ($\kappa\epsilon\nu\acute{o}\sigma\pi\omicron\upsilon\delta\omicron\varsigma$), he will get his answers. The sense of expectation for the arrival of the lord of the tower builds in vv. 6–7. In v. 2 the inspector is "lord" ($\kappa\acute{\upsilon}\rho\iota\omicron\varsigma$); in v. 6 source of "authority" ($\alpha\dot{\upsilon}\vartheta\acute{\epsilon}\nu\tau\eta\varsigma$);[27] in v. 7 "ruler" ($\delta\epsilon\sigma\pi\acute{o}\tau\eta\varsigma$).

In v. 4, the second number varies in the manuscripts; twenty-five is to be preferred on textual evidence.[28]

Visit by the Instructor

■ **6.1–3 [83]**[29] As is befitting a chief dignitary, the inspector is preceded by his court (v. 1) and is also joined by those waiting for him (v. 2). His exceeding height signals his importance.[30] Given the solemnity of the described arrival, the informality and affection of the young women are striking. The gesture of the kiss is apparently a normal way for males to greet males, even a male superior,[31] but perhaps the unusual feature here is that women (albeit allegorical figures) do so, as they will later to Hermas.[32] The inspector makes his rounds of the tower, tapping[33] each stone with a rod reminiscent of the magician's wand with which Jesus the miracle worker is so often depicted in early Christian art. The woman church also carried such a wand.[34]

■ **6.4–8**[35] The seven problem types of stone given here will be given again in the same order in chapter 8, but not in the later exposition of the twelve mountains. There the first black stones correspond to the first mountain (19.1), the third cracked group to the sixth mountain (23.1), the fifth group of indeterminate color perhaps to the doubleminded of the fourth mountain (21.1), and the rough sixth group to the fifth mountain (22.1). Nevertheless, as Dibelius points out,[36] there are

21 Some others are: *Vis.* 2.4.2, where the woman church has more to add to the book she has given Hermas; 3.12.2, where the rejuvenation of the woman church is compared to an elderly person facing death who gets a new lease on life by receiving an inheritance; 3.9.5, where there is still time for conversion before the tower is finished; and especially *Sim.* 10.4.4, where the building is delayed to allow time for conversion.

22 Not "the maidens had given up looking after the tower," mistranslated by Lake, 229. Cf. 7.3 below.

23 *Sim.* 8.1.5; 9.5.6–7, 7.7 (Brox, 396).

24 9.7.7, 8.1–2, 9.1, etc.

25 The words in brackets in vv. 5–6 are omitted by A and restored by Gebhardt-Harnack from L¹ in agreement with L²EC². They contain nothing essential to the narrative, but do enhance the extension of narrative time. Compare *Vis.* 2.2.1; 3.8.11; 4.1.1; *Sim.* 7.1; 8.2.9.

26 E.g., *Vis.* 3.2.1, 3.1, 5.2–5, etc. Chastisement: 3.6.5.

27 This is the first appearance of this term in Christian literature (cf. Josephus *Bell.* 2.5.240; BAGD *s.v.*).

28 See note on 4.3 above.

29 Words in brackets in v. 2 are omitted by A, restored by Gebhardt-Harnack from LLE.

30 See discussion at *Sim.* 8.1.2 and references there; here especially *Gos. Pet.* 40.

31 Josephus *Ant.* 7.7.284; 8.4.387. In the NT: Matt 26:48–49; Mark 14:45; Luke 7:45; 15:20; 22:47–48; Acts 20:37; in the letters, where it may refer to a ritual gesture during worship: Rom 16:16; 1 Cor 16:20; 2 Cor 13:12; 1 Thess 5:26; 1 Pet 5:14.

32 *Sim.* 9.11.4.

33 "Three times" ($\tau\rho\acute{\iota}\varsigma$) only in A.

34 *Vis.* 3.2.4.

35 Word in brackets in v. 6 are restored by Gebhardt-Harnack from LLE.

36 Page 611.

seven problematic types of stones here and seven problematic mountains later. This list is an expansion on the problematic stones of *Vis.* 3.6–7, where scaly, cracked, and stunted stones (3.6.2–4) are among other types of stones that must be rejected. All the unacceptable stones must be removed from the tower (v. 5), not to be finally rejected, but to be placed near the tower for future possibility of change. Though these original stones had come from the depths (9.3.3), their replacements (v. 6) will come from the nearby plain,[37] which produces fine stones for the building (v. 7) that are brought in the acceptable way, carried through the door by the young women.[38] Yet some of these stones are not square, but round (v. 8). They too are placed next to the tower for future work. They receive special attention here because of the potential difficulty of transforming them into acceptable square shape.[39] In the original description of problem round stones in *Vision* 3, their defect is the wealth to which they cling, and they cannot become useful until it is cut off. Later, in the final explanation, wealth is still the problem.[40] Though there are many kinds of behavior that Hermas attacks through these allegories, this one is foremost.

Cleaning of Imperfect Stones

■ **7.1–3 [84]**[41] The stones that have been tossed away near the tower[42] are now to have the opportunity of rehabilitation at the command of the authority figure, here called once more "lord of the (whole) tower" (κύριος ὅλου τοῦ πύργου) as in 5.2. The parallel to the narrative sequence of *Sim.* 8.2 is obvious: in both cases, first-rejected elements are given a second chance. There the sticks are watered by the Shepherd as agent of the great angel; here the Shepherd is directed by the great man to clean, or purify (καθάρισον), the stones removed from the original building and cast next to the tower temporarily.[43] Verse 2 is the testing point: those that can be reused are sorted out from those that must be refused once more and now thrown farther away, thus

definitively rejected. The great man leaves with his court (v. 3), leaving the young women still in charge of the tower (5.1).

■ **7.4–7** The Shepherd will trim the stones that need it, but his statement (v. 4) that he will put them into the tower does not mean that he will bypass the usual way of taking them into the tower—by the hands of the young women through the door.[44] Hermas' question in v. 4 is typical of his inquisitive attitude, but his question in v. 5 is logical: round stones that have been trimmed square will necessarily be smaller than they were before. They must therefore be fitted into a different place, in the center, which does not mean closer to the heart of the structure and therefore in an advantageous position. Rather, the larger stones on the outside are the more important ones that sustain the whole building. Probably what is envisioned is a circular tower, in which an inside course of stones could be smaller and would have to be placed in a tighter circle than those on the outside. How stones could be taken out of a supposedly completed structure and put back in on the inside is a question not to be pushed too far. The delay of two days (v. 6) once again indicates the giving of more time to those under test. The possible sudden arrival of the "master" (ὁ δεσπότης), now that he has already been there to inspect the tower (chap. 6), is probably here an eschatological image. Everything must be tidied up in anticipation for his final visitation. The Shepherd's concern not to appear careless is an honor issue: not his self-image, but his image before his patron is at stake. This is neither the first nor the last time that he expresses such a concern.[45]

Disposal of Unacceptable Stones

■ **8.1–7 [85]** The Shepherd with Hermas as observer examines all seven varieties of problematic stones, with the unspoken hope that the two days' delay has given them time for improvement. In some cases, that has

---

37 See comment on *Vis.* 1.1.3.
38 Those stones not brought in this way are not acceptable (9.4.8).
39 Also at 9.1–4.
40 *Vis.* 3.6.5–6; *Sim.* 30.
41 Words in brackets in v. 3 are omitted in A, restored from LLE.
42 9.4.8; 6.5, 8; see comment at 4.8; *Vis.* 3.5.5.

43 Παρὰ τὸν πύργον; see comment on 4.8; 6.5, 8.
44 Against Brox (400): in 9.8.2, 6, the stones are still brought in by the young women.
45 See 8.2.7; 9.10.4.
46 Dibelius, 614–15. Cf. Luke 1:34; John 3:4.

happened. In one case, the black stones (v. 1), there is no change, and they are definitively rejected by being cast far away. In others, however, some have gotten worse: among those too stunted (v. 4), many have turned black and/or cracked, and some of those of indeterminate color (v. 5) have also turned black and so must be rejected, as well as some with stains (v. 7). The majority, however, have passed the test and can be included in the inner wall of the tower (vv. 4, 7). How stones that were cracked could be found to be more sound ($ὑγιέστεροι$) than others that had never had cracks (v. 3) is not clear.

Round Stones and Blackrobed Women

■ **9.1–4 [86]** Again as in 6.8 the round white stones are saved for special attention. The usual dialogue between the Shepherd and Hermas leads to a pattern of misunderstanding (v. 2) on the part of Hermas, typical of the revelation dialogue, meant to emphasize human misunderstanding of divine things.[46] The Shepherd is worrying more about this group than any others. In v. 3 Hermas rather humorously becomes the advisor of the Shepherd, and the Shepherd seems to take his advice. This may be a humorous interlude, a charming piece to distract the listener during a multitude of monotonously similar episodes,[47] but it is also more: this group of round white stones that need extensive trimming are the wealthy—and Hermas is one of them![48] Besides, this is the only group of stones from which there are not some that are taken away for good. Here (v. 4), those taken away are not finally rejected, because the master of the tower will not give up on them. That they are bright ($λαμπροί$) is a puzzle, unless this is a way of expressing the hope of Hermas that they will still be converted.[49]

■ **9.5–6** From all the groups except the last, the round white stones, there have been some that still were not acceptable, and they have been cast away from the tower, but not definitively disposed of. That is the task of the twelve new women ($γυναῖκες$) who are now called onto the scene—by whom is not specified. Like the young women of the previous scenes, they too are girded and bare-shouldered, if the omission in A is to be restored.[50] The color of the garments of the young women and the condition of their hair were not specified. But the black clothing, loosened hair, and description of these "women" ($γυναῖκες$, not $παρθένοι$ like the others) suggest that they are different. Loosened hair can be a sign of mourning[51] (which is unlikely here), of ecstatic frenzy (like the maenads), or of questionable reputation,[52] the most likely here, given that they will later be identified as vices. Their wild look ($ἄγριαι$) also suggests the second and third reasons.[53] They have no intention of helping in the construction of the tower, for they are "happy" ($ἱλαραί$)[54] to have the task of carrying away all the rejected stones (v. 5), with the apparent exception of those mentioned in v. 4 for reasons given there. The stones are to be taken back to the mountains from which they came, that is to say, they are given over into the power of these women, who symbolize vices. They are not salvageable for the tower.

■ **9.7** Before returning to the harsh reality of the historical, imperfect church, the eschatological vision of the completed tower, the perfect church, can be briefly enjoyed. Like its counterpart in *Vis.* 3.2.6, it is seen as a single monolithic rock. This vision will even be improved upon later in 13.5, where the tower no longer "seems" to be a monolith, but has become one.

---

47 Joly, 308–9 note.

48 *Vis.* 3.6.5–7; *Sim.* 9.30.4–5; 31.1–2; Dibelius, 614.

49 Suggested by Dibelius, 615.

50 9.2.3–4. Words in brackets in v. 5 are omitted by A, restored by Gebhardt-Harnack from L¹ in agreement with L²E.

51 *Acts of Perpetua and Felicitas* 20.5.

52 E.g., Luke 7:37–38. Discussion in Brox, 403–4. Loose hair may mean unbound or uncovered; cf. J. Murphy-O'Connor, "Sex and Logic in 1 Corinthians 11:2–16," *CBQ* 42 (1980) 482–500 (489); Cynthia Thompson, "Portraits from Roman Corinth: Hairstyles, Headcoverings and St. Paul," *BA* 51

(1988) 99–115; Ross S. Kraemer, *Her Share of the Blessings: Women's Religions among Pagans, Jews, and Christians in the Graeco-Roman World* (New York/Oxford: Oxford University Press, 1992) 146–47; Howard Eilberg-Schwartz and Wendy Doniger, eds., *Off with Her Head! The Denial of Women's Identity in Myth, Religion, and Culture* (Berkeley: University of California Press, 1995).

53 In *Tab. Ceb.* 22–25, vices are beasts ($θηρία$) from which one is lucky to survive.

54 A word otherwise associated in *Hermas* with the goodness of believers and the works of God, as in v. 7 below; see note on *Vis.* 1.4.3.

9

Hermas and the Young Women

10 [87] 1/ As I walked around with him, I was joyful to see such good things. The Shepherd said to me: "Bring unslaked lime and small pottery sherds, so that I can fill in the marks of the stones that were taken up and placed in the building, because everything around the tower must be flat." 2/ I did what he commanded and brought them to him. "Assist me," he said, "and [the work will soon be finished]." He filled in the marks of the stones that had gone into the building and commanded that the surroundings of the tower be swept and cleaned. 3/ The young women took brooms and swept and removed all the dirt from the tower, and sprinkled water, and the location of the tower became joyful and attractive. 4/ The Shepherd said to me: "Everything has been cleaned. If the lord comes to inspect the tower, he cannot blame us in anything." After saying this, he intended to leave. 5/ But I took hold of him by his sack and began to adjure him by the Lord to interpret for me what he had shown me. He said to me: "I am occupied for a little while, and then I will interpret everything for you. Wait for me here until I return." 6/ I said to him: "Sir, what will I do here alone?" He said, "You are not alone. These young women are with you." "Then give me over to them," I said. The Shepherd called them over and said to them: "I hand him over to you until I come," and he left. 7/ So I was alone with the young women, who were most happy and treated me well, especially the four more distinguished ones.

11 [88] 1/ The young women said to me: "The shepherd will not come back here today." "So what shall I do?" I asked. "Wait for him [until evening], and if he comes, he will speak to you, and if he does not come, you will stay here with us until he does come." 2/ I said to them: "I will wait for him until evening, but if he does not come, I will go to my house and return early the next morning." But they answered me: "You were handed over to us. You cannot go away from us." 3/ "But where will I stay?" I said. They said: "You will sleep with us as a brother and not as a husband, because you are our brother, and besides, we are going to live with you because we love you so much." But I was ashamed to remain with them. 4/ The one who seemed most prominent among them began to kiss and embrace me, and when the others saw her embracing me, they too began to kiss me, lead me around the tower, and play with me. 5/ It was as if I had become young again, and I too began to play with them. Some were dancing, some moving rhythmically, some singing. Keeping silence, I walked with them around the tower and was very happy with them. 6/ When evening arrived, I wanted to go home, but they held on to me and did not let me go. I spent the night with them and slept next to the tower. 7/ They spread their own linen tunics on the ground and made me lie in the middle of them, and they did nothing but pray. So I also prayed with them unceasingly and no less than they did, and they were happy to see me praying in this way. I remained there with the young women until the second hour of the next day. 8/ Then the Shepherd came and said to the young women: "Have you dishonored him in any way?" They said, "Ask him." I said to him: "Sir, I was happy to stay with them." "What did you have for dinner?" he asked. I said, "Sir, I dined on the word of the Lord all night." "Did they receive you well?" he asked. "Yes, sir," I answered. 9/ "Now," he said, "what do you want to hear first?" "Sir," I said, "the way you showed me from the beginning, I ask you to show me as I ask you." "As you wish," he said, "I will interpret for you, and I will hide absolutely nothing from you."

Commendation to the Young Women

■ **10.1 [87]** The new theme introduced here, the need to patch up the holes left by the stones, is typical of the paratactic structure of the text, whereby a theme is completed and then a new aspect is brought in. The Shepherd wants to fill in the marks left by stones taken out, but out of what? Verse 1 by itself could mean spaces in the plain from which stones were put into the tower, or spaces in the tower itself from which unacceptable stones were removed. The plaster of lime powder and sherds[1] would suggest the latter, for this would be a strange way to fill in holes in the ground, but a recognizable, though cheap and unsturdy way to fill in holes in the wall of a building: cement and rubble, similar to the *opus caementicium* with which many poorly built Roman apartment houses were made. Yet the other positive connotations of ὁμαλός ("flat, level")[2] in the text and the language of v. 2 make it clear that it is holes in the plain surrounding the tower that are to be filled in.

■ **10.2–4[3]** This is the third time Hermas has functioned as the Shepherd's assistant.[4] The last time it was service at table (διακονία). This time it is help with remedial construction as "assistant" (ὑπηρέτης). Typically, the men, Hermas and the Shepherd, use building materials and the Shepherd commands, but the young women do the cleaning (v. 3), though they had also become part of the construction team at 8.2, 5–6. After sweeping, they sprinkle water on the ground to keep the dust down, a method still used in Mediterranean countries. The Shepherd's reputation with the great angel is at stake in his responsibility to keep the tower in order.[5] The possibility of a sudden visit by the lord of the tower is a preoccupation on his part.[6]

■ **10.5–7** As the Shepherd starts casually to go away, Hermas grabs him by his knapsack (πήρα), a bag for carrying things in lieu of pockets, which he has been carrying since his first apparition.[7] The delay before giving explanation is by now familiar. The presence of Hermas with the young women forms a creative interlude between revelation and explanation. It is also the centerpiece of a chiastic structure formed by the vision of the twelve mountains (9.1) and their explanation (9.17–29) enclosing the visions of the tower (9.2–9) and its explanation (9.12–16). Hermas' close encounter with the young women is thus highlighted. He seems at first to panic at the thought of being alone by the tower (v. 6)

---

1 Ὄστρακον taken as a collective by BAGD *s.v.*, or a single potsherd to use as a scoop (Edgar J. Goodspeed, "The Ostracon in Literature," *JBL* 73 [1954] 85–86).

2 See comment on *Vis.* 1.1.3.

3 Words in brackets in v. 2 are illegible in A; L² reads: *cito opus hoc efficitur.*

4 8.2.6; 4.1–2.

5 See comment on 7.6.

6 See 9.5.6, 7.6.

7 *Vis.* 5.1.

and is reassured by the presence of the young women, who do not need to forsake their responsibility to guard the tower in order to be with Hermas,[8] for they are still alongside it when night comes (11.6). The whole scene takes place next to the tower. Just as Hermas was entrusted to the Shepherd in *Vis.* 5.3, now the Shepherd delegates that responsibility temporarily to the young women, though they also let him know later that they will stay with him for an indefinite period of time (11.3). His first reaction to being with them is positive (v. 7). That four of them are more distinguished is a detail not followed up elsewhere, though later there will be one seeming leader (11.4).

Dances with Virtues: The Happy Overnight

■ **11.1–2 [88]** The statement of the young women in v. 1 reads literally: "Today the Shepherd does not come here" (Σήμερον ὁ ποιμὴν ὧδε οὐκ ἔρχεται), but since no night has passed between chapters 10 and 11, and the coming passing of night will be quite consequential, the sense of the sentence must be that the day is waning and they know that the Shepherd will not return until the next day, even though they suggest that Hermas wait[9] and see. By this point, Hermas is in a new panic: spending the night with the young women might be worse than spending it alone. They know their responsibility well (v. 2), and will not compromise: Hermas cannot

leave until the Shepherd, his tutelary spirit, returns.

■ **11.3–4** The following verses have been much discussed. Protective female heavenly figures and female personifications of virtues are Greco-Roman commonplaces. Even though the author probably drew the scene from Greco-Roman imagery,[10] the Jewish-Christian allegorical meaning cannot be lost to sight: in the absence of Hermas' patron angel, the Shepherd, the virtues protect him by not letting him out of their sight, and they lavish on him displays of emotional intimacy and affection. Verse 3 is full of erotic potential, which is why the young women are quick to explain that he will be to them "as a brother, not as a husband" (ὡς ἀδελφός, καὶ οὐχ ὡς ἀνήρ), as Hermas was early on directed to be with his wife as with a sister.[11] Their "love" (ἀγάπη) for him is sisterly and intense. Hermas' shame is the appropriate male reaction to being in a situation involving women that he cannot control. His sexual honor is at stake, with or without celibacy.

It was long ago suggested that this scene reflects the known early Christian practice of syneisaktism or *virgines subintroductae,* whereby a man and a woman would live together in celibacy in order to enjoy both companionship and the eschatological advantage of celibacy.[12] If 1 Cor 7:36–38 also speaks of this practice,[13] which is debated,[14] then the present passage would not be the earliest reference to the custom. Certainly the expression

---

8 So Brox, 406.

9 Μέχρις ὅτε . . . ἔλθη ("until . . . he comes") A; μέχρις ὀψέ ("until evening") restored by Gebhardt-Harnack from LLE.

10 Luschnat ("Jungfrauenszene," 57–60) offers a number of classical images that closely parallel some of the text, e.g., an inscription of the third century BCE from Paros that cites material of the seventh-sixth-century BCE poet Archilochos on poetic initiation by the Muses who play and laugh with him; *Corp. Herm. Asclepius* 9, in which the Muses are sent to humankind to inspire worship of God through songs of praise.

11 *Vis.* 2.2.3.

12 The literature includes: Pierre de Labriolle, "Le 'Mariage spirituel' dans l'antiquité chrétienne," *RH* 46 (1921) 204–25; Hans Achelis, "AGAPETAE" (*ERE* 1926; 1. 177–80); Henry Chadwick, "All Things to All Men," *NTS* 1 (1955) 261–75; Elizabeth A. Clark, "John Chrysostom and the Subintroductae," *CH* 46 (1977) 171–85; also in *Ascetic Piety and Women's Faith: Essays in Late Ancient Christianity* (Studies in Women and Religion 20;

Lewiston, NY/Queenston, Ontario: Edwin Mellen, 1986) 265–90; idem, *Jerome, Chrysostom, and Friends* (Studies in Women and Religion 1; New York/Toronto: Edwin Mellen, 1979).

13 First suggested by Eduard Grafe in 1899 and adopted by Hans Achelis, *Virgines subintroductae: Ein Beitrag zum VII Kapitel des I. Korintherbriefs* (Leipzig: Hinrichs, 1902).

14 One of the primary objections is that none of the Greek Fathers understood the passage in this way, but Clark counters that they were against it and so could not imagine their hero Paul being for it ("Subintroductae," 174–75). Whatever is going on in 1 Cor 7:36–38, however, it cannot be said that Paul enthusiastically endorses it.

"to live like brother and sister" here and in *Vis.* 2.2.3 already means a male-female relationship that is not characterized by regarding one another as sexual partners.[15] But whether either passage implies an already established custom of cohabitation under these circumstances is not certain.[16]

The erotic potential of sleeping together outdoors in v. 3 is apparent. That of the kissing and embracing in v. 4 is also apparent to the modern reader, but not necessarily to the ancient one in view of the same behavior of the young women toward the lord of the tower in 6.2, where eroticism is not suggested. The playfulness in which Hermas begins to engage with the young women is a childlike innocence of enjoyment.

■ **11.5–9** The young women seem to be having a great late afternoon party around the tower, in which Hermas enters fully. His rejuvenation, an image of conversion, mirrors that of the woman church in the third *Vision,* which was also the result of the conversion of members

of the church.[17] As evening comes, he makes one more unsuccessful attempt to escape (v. 6), but instead, finds himself on the ground praying all night (v. 7), until early morning at breakfast time, the second hour after sunrise. The Shepherd's first question upon his return (v. 8) is surprising but is again suggestive of preoccupation with sexual honor and the power relationship in which the young women, not Hermas, are in control. Finding food in prayer and the words of God is a biblical theme.[18] Finally (v. 9) the Shepherd is ready to answer Hermas' questions about the visions he has been enjoying.

---

15 Compare the apocryphal saying of Jesus in *Gos. Eg.* (Clement of Alexandria *Strom.* 3.92) with variant in *Gos. Thom.* 37, to the effect that revelation necessitates taking off clothes and regarding one another no longer as male and female.

16 Extensive discussion in Brox, 406–10, to which could be added: Lampe, *Stadtrömische Christen,* 191; Leutzsch, *Wahrnehmung,* 181–83; Will Deming, *Paul on Marriage and Celibacy: The Hellenistic Background in 1 Corinthians 7* (SNTSMS 83; Cambridge: Cambridge University Press, 1995) 45–46.

17 *Vis.* 3.11–13. Luschnat ("Jungfrauenszene," 54–56) cites parallel examples of rejuvenation through

dance: of Kadmos and Teiresias (Euripides *Bacchae* 188–90); others in Aristophanes *Ranae* 345; *Eirene* 860–62. For White ("Interaction," 147–48), Hermas' rejuvenation is like a return to infancy before the awakening of sexuality.

18 Deut 8:3; Amos 8:11; Wis 16:26; Matt 4:4; Luke 4:4; John 4:34; 6:27; *Apoc. Abr.* 12.1 (ref. in Brox, 412).

9

Explanation of the Tower and Young Women

12 [89] 1/ I said: "Sir, first of all, tell me this: who are the rock and the door?" He said: "This rock and the door are the Son of God." I said: "How can the rock be old but the door new?" "Listen," he said, "and understand, you who are without understanding. 2/ The Son of God was born before all his creation, so as to be counselor to the Father about creation. That is why the rock is old." "But why, sir, is the gate new?" I said. 3/ "Because," he said, "he was made known in the last days of the completion. That is why the gate is new, so that those who will be saved may through it enter the reign of God. 4/ Do you see the stones carried through the gate and [placed] in the building of the tower, but those not brought in thrown back to their original place?" "I saw it, sir," I said. "Just so," he said, "no one will enter the reign of God who does not receive the name of his son. 5/ If you want to enter a city that has been encircled with walls and has but one gate, can you enter the city any way but through the gate that it has?" "Sir, how can anyone do otherwise?" I said. "Well then, if you cannot enter the city except through the gate that it has, in the same way, one cannot enter the reign of God except through the name of the beloved son. 6/ Do you see the crowd building the tower?" he asked. "I see it, sir," I answered. "These are all honorable angels that have surrounded the Lord with walls. The gate is the Son of God, that one entrance to the presence of the Lord. No one can enter his presence any other way but by his son. 7/ Do you see the six men and the great and honorable one in the middle who is walking around the tower and who rejected the stones from the building?" he asked. "I see, sir," I said. 8/ He said, "The honored man is the Son of God, and the six honored angels are supporting him on the right and left. None of the honored angels can approach God without him. Whoever does not take his name will not enter the reign of God."

13 [90] 1/ "But who is the tower?" I asked. "The tower is the church," he answered. 2/ "Who are these young women?" He said, "These are holy spirits. One cannot be found in the reign of God unless they clothe you with their garments. If you only receive the name, but do not receive the clothing from them, it profits nothing. These young women are powers of the Son of God. If you bear the name but do not bear his power, you bear the name uselessly. 3/ The rejected stones that you see," he said, "these carried the name, but were not clothed with the garments of the young women." "What kind of garment is theirs, sir?" I asked. "Their own names are their clothing," he said. "Whoever wears the name of the Son of God must also wear their names. The son himself wears the names of these young women. 4/ Whatever stones you saw [coming into the tower, given over by their hands and staying in the building], have put on the power of these young women. 5/ This is why you see the tower

230

of rock as having become one single stone. Even so, those who believe in the Lord through his son and clothe themselves with these spirits will be one spirit, one body, and one color of garment. The habitation of those who wear the name of the young women is in the tower." 6/ "But sir," I said, "why were the rejected stones rejected? They came in through the gate and were placed into the building of the tower by the hands of the young women." "Since you care about everything," he said, "and ask pointedly, listen about the rejected stones. 7/ These all received the name of the Son of God, and they all received the power of these young women. They were strengthened by the reception of these spirits and were with the servants of God, and had one spirit and one body and one clothing. They thought alike and worked justice. 8/ But after some time, they became disobedient because of the women dressed in black that you saw, with bare shoulders, loosened hair, and attractive appearance. Seeing them, they desired them and put on their power, and took off the clothing and the power of the young women. 9/ So they were rejected from the house of God and turned over to those women. But those not deceived by the beauty of these women stayed in the house of God. This is the explanation of the rejected ones," he said.

14 [91]   1/ "So what then, sir," I said, "if these people, such as they are, are converted and reject the desires of these women, and return to the young women, proceeding according to their power and works—will they not enter the house of God?" 2/ "They will enter," he said, "if they reject the works of these women, take up the power of the young women, and proceed according to their works. This is why there was a stoppage in the construction of the tower, so that if these would be converted, they might go on into the construction of the tower. But if they are not converted, then others will enter, and they will be permanently cast out." 3/ I gave thanks to the Lord for all this, for being merciful to all those who call on his name, and sending the angel of conversion to us who sinned against him, and renewing our spirit; even of those of us already corrupted and having no hope of life, he gave us new life. 4/ "Now, sir," I said, "show me why the tower is not built on the ground, but on the rock and the gate." "Are you still senseless and dense?" he said. "I have to ask you everything, sir, because I can't understand a thing," I said. "Everything that is mighty and full of splendor is hard for people to understand." 5/ "Listen," he said, "the name of the Son of God is mighty and uncontained, and sustains the whole world. So if all creation is sustained by the Son of God, what do you think about those called by him, bearing the name of the Son of God, and proceeding according to his commandments? 6/ Do you see which ones he sustains? Those who bear his

name with all their heart. He became their foundation and sustains them gladly because they are not ashamed to bear his name."

15 [92]   1/ "Tell me, sir," I said, "the names of the young women and of the women clothed in black." "Listen," he said, "to the names of the stronger young women, those standing at the corners. 2/ The first is Faith, the second Restraint, the third Power, the fourth Endurance. The others standing in the middle of them have these names: Simplicity, Innocence, Purity, Joy, Truth, Understanding, Harmony, and Love. The one who bears these names and the name of the Son of God will enter the reign of God. 3/ Listen too," he said, "to the names of the women in black garments. Four of these are also more powerful: the first is Unbelief, the second Self-indulgence, the third Disobedience, and the fourth, Deceit. Those who follow them are called: Sadness, Evil, Sensuality, Bad Temper, Lie, Senselessness, Slander, and Hatred. The servant of God who bears these names will see the reign of God but will not enter it." 4/ "But, sir," I said, "which are the stones from the deep that were fashioned into the building?" "The first ones," he said, "the ten that were put into the foundation, are the first generation, the twenty-five are the second generation of just men, the thirty-five are the prophets and ministers of God, and the forty are apostles and teachers of the proclamation of the Son of God." 5/ "Then why, sir," I said, "did the young women hand over these stones for the building of the tower, bringing them through the gates?" 6/ "These first," he said, "bore these spirits and in no way distanced themselves from them, neither the spirits from the people nor the people from the spirits, but the spirits stayed with them until they fell asleep. But if they had not had these spirits with them, they would not have become useful for the building of the tower."

16 [93]   1/ "Show me still more, sir," I said. "What do you want now?" he said. "Why, sir," I said, "did the stones rise from the depth, and were placed into the building [of the tower], having borne these spirits?" 2/ "They had to rise through water," he said, "in order to be made alive. In no other way could they enter the reign of God, unless they put off the deadliness of their [first] life. 3/ So too, those who had fallen asleep received the seal and [entered the reign of God]. Before bearing the name of [the Son of] God," he said, "a person is dead. But upon receiving the seal, the person puts aside deadliness and takes on life. 4/ So the seal is the water. Into the water they go down dead and come up alive. The seal was proclaimed to them, and they profited from it to enter into the reign of God." 5/ "Why, sir," I said, "did the forty stones rise with them from the depth already having the seal?" "Because," he said, "these are the apostles and teachers who proclaimed the name of the Son of God, who,

having fallen asleep in power and faith of the
Son of God, even proclaimed to those who had
previously fallen asleep and gave them the seal
of the proclamation. 6/ They descended with
them into the water and came up again, except
that these descended alive and came up alive.
7/ Because of them, these others were enlivened
and came to know the name of the Son of God.
This is why these others also arose with them,
and together were fashioned into the building of
the tower, and were made to dwell with them
without needing trimming. They fell asleep in justice and great purity, except that they did not
have this seal. So you have the explanation of
these things." "Yes, sir, I have it," I said.

Rock, Door, and Proprietor

■ **12.1–3 [89]** Like *Sim.* 5.6–7, this chapter is a christological crux. Its all-embracing claims for the Son of God
belie any impression that the author does not have christological interests, even though they are put at the service of moral exigency. The explanation of the vision
related in chapter 2 begins with the old rock and the
new door (2.1). The question as Hermas poses it in v. 1
is already slanted to an expected anthropomorphic
answer, for he asks not "what" are rock and door, but
"who" ($\tau\acute{\iota}\varsigma$).[1] Both rock and door are the Son of God,
and in v. 8, the great man will be the same. This poses
considerable problem for a literalist and consistent interpretation of the parable, neither of which is helpful. The
images are determined by the initial vision in chapters
2–4, but their meaning is flexible. Assigning rock, door,
and inspector of the tower to the Son of God gives him
not only personal but also cosmic significance. Rock and
door have already established christological correspondences.[2] The tension between the old rock and the new
door expresses the christological tension between preexistence and historical incarnation. The preexistence
of the Son is clearly stated in v. 2, but he is in good company: previously the church and the great angel are also
said to be preexistent.[3] A wisdom background provides
the role of the Son as advisor ($\sigma\acute{\upsilon}\mu\beta\upsilon\lambda\upsilon\varsigma$) to the Father[4]
about creation.[5] The new gate is the manifestation of the
Son "in the last days of the completion" ($\grave{\epsilon}\pi\grave{\iota}\,\grave{\epsilon}\sigma\chi\acute{\alpha}\tau\omega\nu$[6]
$\tau\hat{\omega}\nu\,\grave{\eta}\mu\epsilon\rho\hat{\omega}\nu\,\tau\hat{\eta}\varsigma\,\sigma\upsilon\nu\tau\epsilon\lambda\epsilon\acute{\iota}\alpha\varsigma$), an eschatological phrase
that should be related to *Vis.* 3.8.9, where similar lan-

1   Noticed by Brox, 416; Snyder, 140; the same at 13.1.
2   Rock: 1 Cor 10:4 with sapiential background such as
    Wis 11:4; Rom 9:33; 1 Pet 2:6–8; Justin *Dial.* 113.6;
    probably *Barn.* 11.5; Ignatius *Pol.* 1.1. See discus-
    sion of wisdom connections in Pernveden, *Concept
    of the Church*, 66; Hans Conzelmann, *1 Corinthians*
    (Hermeneia; Philadelphia: Fortress, 1975) 166–67.
    Door: John 10:7, 9; Ignatius *Phld.* 9.1; perhaps *1
    Clem.* 48.2–4. No direct dependence on 1 Cor 10:4
    or John 10:7, 9 can be demonstrated, but in both
    cases the images must have had wider circulation in
    Christian spirituality.
3   *Vis.* 2.4.1 (church); 3.4.1 (great angel). But is the
    angel the same as the Son of God? This question is
    taken up below and in the Introduction 3.3.4.
4   Not a usual name for God in *Hermas*: used else-
    where only by the woman church once in *Vis.*
    3.9.10, and by the Shepherd in *Sim.* 5.6.3 in the

    parable of the son and servant, where the son of the
    parable is also, with the angels, counselor to the
    Father. But there the son in the parable does not
    correspond to the Son of God. See comment *ad loc.*
5   Prov 8:22–31; Wis 9:9; Sir 24:10.
6   So Whittaker, though the A reading $\grave{\epsilon}\sigma\chi\acute{\alpha}\tau\upsilon$ is also
    possible but awkward: "at the last of the days of the
    completion." It may have occurred under the influ-
    ence of 1 Pet 1:20: $\grave{\epsilon}\pi\grave{\iota}\,\grave{\epsilon}\sigma\chi\acute{\alpha}\tau\upsilon\,\tau\hat{\omega}\nu\,\chi\rho\acute{\upsilon}\nu\omega\nu$ (Nestle-
    Aland[26] with multiple variants similar to our text).

guage refers to the completion of the building of the tower as mark of the end time.[7] This idea, like the christological images, is already established in Christian tradition.[8] The reference here and the allusion to the redemptive work of Christ in *Sim.* 5.6.2 are, "however vague," the only historical references to Christ in the document.[9] Passageway into the kingdom of God through Christ or his requirements is also a well-established theme,[10] which is further developed in the next verses.

■ **12.4–6**[11] Verse 4a recalls the point in the narrative in which the normal mode for introducing new stones into the tower was to have them carried through the door by the young women. Some, however, were brought by the men directly into the tower without going through the door; for this the men were reprimanded by the six angelic supervisors (4.5–8). The meaning is now that they must bear the name of the Son of God.[12] Reception of the name here is probably to be understood as baptism, since it clearly is so at 16.3. The paratactic structure of the narrative is again evident in the development of the motif of entry through the gate. Here the added element is that entrance through the door means bearing the name of the Lord.[13] In 13.2, it will also mean acceptance of the virtues which the young women symbolize. The parable within a parable in v. 5 would be very familiar to inhabitants of ancient walled cities, though there was usually more than one gate.[14] The very unusualness of a single-gated city underscores the christological statement. In v. 6, Hermas sees a "crowd" (ὄχλος) building the tower. This must refer not only to

the six men and twelve women, but to the many, now identified as angels, who were helping to bring the stones (3.1). The third sentence of v. 6 momentarily switches the metaphor: if the Lord is rock and gate, but the tower is built upon the rock,[15] how do the angels form a wall surrounding the rock? Suggestions abound.[16] Probably the reference is not to the angels' activity of building the tower, but to their presence around the master of the tower when he visits, as in 6.1–2.[17]

■ **12.7–8** The six chief male builders are now identified as angels, too (v. 7), and the honorable figure, the master of the tower who had come to inspect it, as the Son of God (v. 8). Thus in the same explanation, the Son of God is rock, gate, and lord of the tower. If the parable is not pushed for logical consistency, this should be no more surprising than the double identification of Jesus as gate and Shepherd in John 10. The six angels are supporting (συγκρατοῦντες) him on both sides.[18] The importance of the central figure is enhanced one step more: it is not only believers who cannot enter the kingdom of God without passing through the Son, but the angels too cannot enter the presence of God without him. Though in other passages of *Hermas* it is tempting to equate the Son of God with Michael, here it seems that he is a much more enhanced figure.[19] Though his closest inner circle is composed of angels, nowhere does

---

7   See *Sim.* 9.5.1, where the major building phase of the tower is finished, though some work remains to be done. From that point, we seem to be in an interim period.

8   Eph 3:5, 9; Heb 1:2; 1 Pet 1:20; Ignatius *Mag.* 6.1; *2 Clem.* 14.2; *Sib. Or.* 8.456.

9   Brox, 417.

10 Matt 5:20; 7:21; 18:3; Mark 9:47; 10:23; John 3:3, 5; *2 Clem.* 9.6; 11.6. The expression "kingdom of God" occurs in *Hermas* here for the first time, and several times more only in *Similitude* 9.

11 The word in brackets in v. 4 is omitted in A, restored by Gebhardt-Harnack from LLEC[1].

12 This is the reading in one way or another of LLECC: LL *filii dei*; EC[1] of his son; C[2] of the son. It could be argued that A presents a distinctly different reading: τὸ ἅγιον αὐτοῦ ("his holy" [name]), which could be the name of God, not the Son. It is

only a question of what is the intended antecedent of "his," which, given the preponderant evidence of the translations, must refer to the Son.

13 See comment on *Vis.* 3.7.3.

14 "The gate that it has" (τῆς πύλης ἧς ἔχει) Pam L[1]; "the gate itself" (αὐτῆς) A.

15 Ἐπάνω τῆς πέτρας (9.3.1).

16 Many documented by Brox, 419. Among them, "the Lord is for the moment identified with the tower" (Lake, 251); the Lord is surrounded by a rampart which is the tower (Joly, 318).

17 So too Brox, 419–20.

18 Compare the resurrection scene with one angel on either side in *Gos. Pet.* 40.

19 Pernveden, *Concept of the Church* (63–64), and Moyo, "Angels and Christology" (116–18), offer helpful comparison and contrast of Michael in *Similitude* 8 and the Son of God in *Similitude* 9: both head

it say that the Son is an angel.[20] He is rather the means of access to God for persons and angels alike.

The Tower and Black-Robed Women

■ **13.1–2 [90]** Hermas asks who (not what) is the tower,[21] setting up the closest confluence so far with the tower in *Vision* 3, where it has the same identification (3.3.3). Another dimension of interpretation is added to entrance into the tower/reign of God (v. 1). The point raised here is a continuation and development of 12.4. Not only must the stones be carried through the door by the young women, but now (v. 2) the image has shifted to that of clothing with the holy spirits that will later (15.2) also be called by the names of virtues. The mention of good spirits takes us back to the world of the *Mandates* and their teaching on discernment of spirits.[22] The language of change of clothing to signify change of perspective occurs with some frequency in Jewish and Christian literature.[23] The language of clothing with virtues is common both in *Hermas* and in other early Christian texts.[24] In keeping with the christological centering of these chapters, the holy spirits/virtues are now essentially related to the Son of God as his "powers" (δυνάμεις).[25] Acknowledgment of the name and carrying the name, probably meaning baptism, are not sufficient; there is more to being a believer, and it has to do with the way of living one's life.[26]

■ **13.3** The rejected stones are those not brought through the door properly (4.6–8). A too literalist interpretation will force the details beyond their capacity: how can stones be brought through the door by the young women but not be clothed with them? Two different images are operating here, and they do not cohere perfectly. Meaning forces itself through the narrative and breaks down its consistency. The point is the same made at the end of v. 2: proper credentials are not sufficient. The young women have the capacity to communicate their being through their clothing, which symbolizes themselves. Since these qualities are essentials of the believers' life, the Son of God too is characterized by them. This is said with reference to the humanity of Christ, and need not be interpreted adoptionistically.[27]

■ **13.4–5**[28] The tower (v. 5), which has previously been described as a monolith in appearance,[29] is now augmented by another detail: it appears to be one stone with the rock upon which it is built.[30] Those who believe will become one spirit and one body with each other just as the individual stones carried by the young women became as one on their shoulders (3.5). The inverted allusion similar to Eph 4:4 testifies not so much to Hermas' knowledge of Ephesians as to the familiarity of

---

groups of angels; both have power and responsibility, Michael over the people, the Son over the tower; both delegate part of their task to the Shepherd; Michael inspects the sticks and the Son inspects the stones of the tower; Michael has and delegates authority to admit into the tower, and the Son implicitly delegates authority to the six men who oversee the building of the tower. On the other hand, the Son's power is considerably greater and more widely applicable.

20 Pointed out by Pernveden, *Concept of the Church*, 63.
21 See comment on 12.1.
22 Especially *Man.* 5.1; 6.2.
23 Snyder, 140, citing among others: Zech 3:3–5; *Apoc. Pet.* 17 (Akhmim frag.); *1 Enoch* 62:15–16; *2 Enoch* 22.8.
24 *Vis.* 4.1.8; *Man.* 1.2; 2.4; 5.2.8; 9.10; 10.3.1, 4; 11.4; 12.1, 2; especially the Pauline corpus: Rom 13:12; 2 Cor 5:3; Gal 3:27; Eph 4:24; 6:11, 14; Col 3:10, 12; 1 Thess 5:8; *T. Levi* 8.2; see comment in BAGD *s.v.* 2b. See also *Sim.* 8.2.3, where all who enter the tower are in white clothing.

25 See Philo *Fug.* 18.94–95, where five of the six cities of refuge for unintentional murder are "powers" (δυνάμεις), types of governing power, of the chief city, the divine logos.
26 Matt 7:21–24; Luke 6:46–49; Jas 2:18–19.
27 Against Brox (424) with reference to *Sim.* 5.6, 7.
28 Words in brackets in v. 4 are omitted in A, restored by Gebhardt-Harnack from LLE.
29 *Vis.* 3.2.6; *Sim.* 9.7.
30 The translation reflects the text as given in A and supported by Hilhorst (*Sémitismes,* 100) without Hilgenfeld's addition of μετά as third-to-last word, on the basis of LLE. The text is: διὰ τοῦτο βλέπεις τὸν πύργον μονόλιθον γεγονότα (μετὰ) τῆς πέτρας. Without the emendation, τῆς πέτρας ("of the rock") in Hilhorst's interpretation modifies τὸν πύργον (the tower) with two intervening words. He argues for the translation given in the text as comparable to *Sim.* 9.10.3b, where three words intervene between a noun and its genitive modifier. With the emendation, the sentence would translate:

the phrase in early Christianity. Its occurrence there in baptismal context strengthens the suspicion that the same is true here, even before the explicit introduction of baptism in 16.3. Here a different third element is added: the single color (white)[31] of the believers' garments, which may be another baptismal allusion.

■ **13.6–9** The question arises, how those who have entered the tower the right way and have clothed themselves with the power of the young women could still find themselves rejected, as for instance in chapter 18. The answer lies both here in vv. 8–9 and in 17.5: they defiled themselves (17.5), or, as explained here, they let themselves be led astray. As long as the tower is not fully completed, salvation is never absolutely assured. The possiblity of falling away is always present. In v. 7 a slightly different triad is presented than in v. 5, though in both cases the garment is the third element: here, one spirit, one body, and one garment ($\dot{\epsilon}\nu$ $\pi\nu\epsilon\hat{\upsilon}\mu\alpha$ $\kappa\alpha\grave{\iota}$ $\dot{\epsilon}\nu$ $\sigma\hat{\omega}\mu\alpha$ $\kappa\alpha\grave{\iota}$ $\dot{\epsilon}\nu$ $\ddot{\epsilon}\nu\delta\upsilon\mu\alpha$). Verse 7b contains a near-quotation of a favorite Pauline expression: $\tau\grave{o}$ $\alpha\dot{\upsilon}\tau\grave{o}$ $\varphi\rho\upsilon\nu\epsilon\hat{\iota}\nu$ ("to think the same way," "have the same attitude").[32] Only after some time as believers (v. 8) do some go astray through the persuasion of the other group of women first introduced at 9.5. With desire of them, some believers exchanged power for power, garment for garment, and so got what they wanted: full-time residence with them. But the consequence is being thrown out of the house of God[33] and they are handed over ($\pi\alpha\rho\epsilon\delta\acute{o}\vartheta\eta\sigma\alpha\nu$) to the authority of the wild women (v. 9), with dire consequences.[34] These women are beautiful (9.5) with a deceptive, destructive beauty that seduces into disaster, because they are really demonic spirits (18.3).

Necessity of Bearing the Name

■ **14.1–3 [91]** Hermas persists in his pursuit of the possibility of ultimate salvation even for those who have chosen a different path. He still asks if there can be conversion for them if they turn from following the wrong set of feminine figures to the true ones. Some translators understand "the desires of these women" ($\tau\grave{\alpha}\varsigma$ $\dot{\epsilon}\pi\iota\vartheta\upsilon\mu\acute{\iota}\alpha\varsigma$ $\tau\hat{\omega}\nu$ $\gamma\upsilon\nu\alpha\iota\kappa\hat{\omega}\nu$ $\tauο\acute{\upsilon}\tau\omega\nu$) as a subjective rather than objective genitive, as "the desire *for* these women."[35] This interpretation is well supported by 13.8, where the women are the object of desire of misguided believers, though the language of v. 2a here would suggest the opposite. The works of the women will be enumerated in the next chapter. The reason for the building stoppage (5.1) is now given: in order to allow still more time for conversion.[36] Verse 3 is an unusual transition piece in the form of a prayer of thanksgiving in the third person. It may reflect a familiar liturgical formulation. Neither here in v. 3b nor in 6.2.2–4 need the language of corruption be understood in a technical sense reflecting church discipline with regard to apostates.[37]

■ **14.4–6** In *Vis.* 3.2.4 the tower is built on water, a baptismal image (3.3.5), and sustained by the power of God. Here in the ninth *Similitude* (also 3.1; 12.1), that image shifts for christological purposes. Verse 5 is a logical argument that as goes the whole, so goes the most important part. The name of the Son of God is symbol of the person,[38] who is uncontained, an attribute otherwise ascribed to God,[39] and who bears ($\beta\alpha\sigma\tau\acute{\alpha}\zeta\epsilon\iota$) the cosmos.[40] Cosmological Christology quickly becomes ecclesiological Christology in vv. 5b–6a. The important statement is not so much the Son of God's sustaining the world as his sustaining of the faithful who with enthusi-

---

"This is why you see the tower as having become one single stone with the rock."

31   The color of the acceptable stones in 4.5; 9.1.

32   Rom 12:16; 2 Cor 13:11; Phil 2:2 (cf. v. 5); 4:2.

33   An unusual expression in *Hermas,* only here and 14.1; cf. Philo *Cher.* 52; 1 Tim 3:15; 1 Pet 4:17.

34   20.4; 21.4.

35   So Dibelius, 622 ("sich der Begierde nach diesen Weibern entschlagen"); Snyder, 143 ("throw off their desires for these women"); Joly (323) is ambiguous ("rejettent le désir de ces femmes"); more listed in Brox, 426. Lake's translation ("put away the lusts of these women," 257) by its use of the plural for desires ($\dot{\epsilon}\pi\iota\vartheta\upsilon\mu\acute{\iota}\alpha\iota$) seems to take it as a subjective genitive, but complicates the question

with the translation "lusts," which is not justified anyway on the basis of the use of $\dot{\epsilon}\pi\iota\vartheta\upsilon\mu\acute{\iota}\alpha$ in both positive and negative sense in *Man.* 12.1, 3.

36   Not the delay of the parousia; see comment on 5.1.

37   Discussion in Brox, 427.

38   The name of God is substitute for the presence of God, used as seal or breastplate, as in Rev 19:12: Margaret Barker, *The Great Angel: A Study of Israel's Second God* (London: SPCK, 1992) 208–10.

39   Ἀχώρητος: see comment on *Man.* 1.1, where the same expression occurs.

40   Col 1:17.

41   Compare *Sim.* 8.10.3. References to this expression and similar ones are frequent throughout the text. See comment on *Vis.* 2.2.8; 3.7.3; *Sim.* 8.6.4.

asm carry his name[41] and are not ashamed of it—an attitude with significant and specific social consequences. Shame is sensitivity to potentially violated honor. Believers who are ashamed to bear the name of the Son of God fear that their appropriate honor will be violated in the eyes of their peers and social superiors if they are known to be Christians. Thus they do not want to associate with other Christians or, especially, to be seen in their company.[42]

The Names of the Women

■ **15.1–3 [92]** The personification of virtues or qualities as women is commonplace in the literature and numismatics.[43] In *Vision* 3, seven such women assist in the building of the tower and sustain it; they are named in 3.8.3–8, with the first two singled out. Here there are twelve, four of whom have priority (v. 2) because they were the stronger in the construction scene (9.2.3; 4.1). They are followed by twelve vices (v. 3), personified as women in black clothing (9.5),[44] of whom the first four are also singled out. Any attempt to harmonize the three lists completely is doomed to failure. They do not match perfectly any more than do Pauline lists of virtues or spiritual gifts. In both lists of virtues, which are also proper names of the young women, "Faith" ($\Pi\acute{\iota}\sigma\tau\iota\varsigma$) and "Restraint" ($E\gamma\kappa\rho\acute{\alpha}\tau\epsilon\iota\alpha$) head the list, while the first two vices, "Unbelief" ($A\pi\iota\sigma\tau\acute{\iota}\alpha$) and "Indulgence" ($A\kappa\rho\alpha\sigma\acute{\iota}\alpha$), are their opposites. In the two lists of virtues, there are three others in common: "Simplicity" ($A\pi\lambda\acute{o}\tau\eta\varsigma$) and "Innocence" ($A\kappa\alpha\kappa\acute{\iota}\alpha$), and surprisingly in last place, "Love" ($A\gamma\acute{\alpha}\pi\eta$), with its opposite at the end of the list of vices: "Hatred" ($M\hat{\iota}\sigma o\varsigma$). Five of the seven virtues from *Vis.* 3.8 are repeated in the list of the twelve in *Sim.* 9.15.2. If $\epsilon\pi\iota\sigma\tau\acute{\eta}\mu\eta$ from *Vision* 3 is taken as the equivalent of $\sigma\acute{\upsilon}\nu\epsilon\sigma\iota\varsigma$ in *Similitude* 9, and $\sigma\epsilon\mu\nu\acute{o}\tau\eta\varsigma$ in *Vision* 3 of $\alpha\gamma\nu\epsilon\acute{\iota}\alpha$ in *Similitude* 9, then it could be said that all of the original list are represented in the new one.[45] If instead of bearing the name of the Son of God and the virtues, the believer adheres to the vices so as to substitute their names, such a one will be in the frustrating position of seeing the goal but finding it unattainable.[46]

■ **15.4–6** Whereas in *Vis.* 3.5.1–2 the white square foundation stones taken from the depths were apostles, overseers ($\epsilon\pi\acute{\iota}\sigma\kappa o\pi o\iota$), teachers, ministers ($\delta\iota\acute{\alpha}\kappa o\nu o\iota$), and those who have suffered for the name of the Lord, here the search for roots goes deeper. Verse 16.5 will make it clear that the intended people except for the forty are pre-Christian. The usual interpretation is that the ten are the patriarchal generation as recounted in Genesis 5 and Luke 3:36–38. The next group, the twenty-five of the "generation of just men"[47] ($\alpha\nu\delta\rho\hat{\omega}\nu\ \delta\iota\kappa\alpha\acute{\iota}\omega\nu$),[48] are then the generations from Noah to David in Luke 3:31–36. This is where the parallelism stops, however, for there are then forty-two generations from David to Christ, and no one has adequately explained the thirty-five prophets and forty apostles[49] of our text. One attempt is to take the first three numbers, ten, twenty-five, and thirty-five, for a total of the biblical number of seventy,[50] but this still does not explain the final forty, which is also, of course, a biblical number.[51] We are probably dealing here with local folk traditions. The biblical and therefore Jewish foundations of the tower are here evident. Even past generations lived by the spirits that represent the virtues, named in the first part of the chapter (v. 6). Since this tracing of ancestors goes much farther back than the one in *Vis.* 3.5.1–2, the people who represent it are all thought of as dead, in contrast to the previous text in which some have died but some are still alive.

---

42   *Sim.* 8.8.1; 9.20.2; Osiek, *Rich and Poor*, 41–49.

43   See comment on *Vis.* 3.8.3–8. In *Tab. Ceb.* 22–25, the vices are beasts, not women.

44   Ἰμάτια ("clothing") restored by Hilgenfeld from LLE; ὀνόματα ("names") A. The twelve in black clothing have been compared to the Erinye or Furies by Luschnat ("Jungfrauenszene," 61); cf. Aeschylus *Septem contra Thebas* 977, where they are called the black ones.

45   Further discussion on the relationships in Dibelius, 623; Snyder, 144.

46   Perhaps suggested by the plight of Moses in Deut 34:4 (suggested by Lake, 260). On the expression "kingdom of God," see comment on 12.3.

47   Here the number given by ALL; see MS. problems on 4.3; 5.4.

48   On this expression, see *Man.* 11.9.

49   Mistranslated "prophets" in Lake, 261.

50   Dibelius (625) suggests seventy shepherds of Israel (*1 Enoch* 89.59), who possibly become thirty-five in 90.1.

51   Further attempts by Dibelius, 624–25; bibliography in Brox, 397 n. 10. Not helpful is Joly's remark (327) that "Les 40 représentent les apôtres au sens large" ("The 40 represent the apostles in the broad sense").

Importance of the Seal

■ **16.1–4 [93]**[52] The association of passing through water with entering the kingdom of God (v. 2) and receiving the seal (σφραγίς)[53] is unmistakably a reference to baptism, more explicit than the original allusion in *Vis.* 3.3.5. The language of death and life is similar to Pauline language[54] but is not exactly the same: here, death is the pre-baptismal state, not the dying process that is symbolically enacted in the course of baptism. This passage is so consciously talking about baptism that it introduces the image of going down into the water dead in order to come up alive (v. 4), even though there is no mention in the parable of stones descending into the water, only being taken out. The absolute necessity of baptism is implicit here, and these verses, without saying so, present a good argument in favor of baptism in the name of the dead, apparently already an act of piety in first-century Corinth.[55] Here, though, it is actually deceased Christian preachers who accomplish this task.

■ **16.5–7** The forty already-baptized who have gone down into the water (v. 5) bring up the rest. This is a version of the tradition of the "harrowing of hell," usually said to be performed by Christ during the period of his burial.[56] Here, the apostles and teachers are sent to be the agents by which this soteriological mission is accomplished. Through their agency, those who were dead are restored to life, to become part of the foundation of the tower. Thus once again, two elements are necessary to belong to the structure of the tower: being brought up through the water (baptism) and thus bearing the name of the Son of God; and bearing the names of the young women (identification with the life of virtue). Whereas for the living, the problem has been to get the baptized to take on the life of virtue (13.1), here with the pre-Christian dead, the problem is the opposite: they practiced virtue in their lives (v. 7), but had not received baptism. Through the apostles and teachers, this problem is solved.

---

52   Words in brackets are omitted by A, restored by Hilgenfeld, Gebhardt-Harnack, or Whittaker from LLE.
53   On this terminology for baptism, see comment on *Sim.* 8.6.3. The term can mean other things in *Hermas* as well: cf. 8.6.3b and 2.4, where it is some kind of sign of recognition or stamp of approval.
54   Rom 6:1–11.
55   See Richard E. DeMaris, "Corinthian Religion and Baptism for the Dead (1 Corinthians 15:29): Insights from Archaeology and Anthropology," *JBL* 114 (1995) 661–82.
56   1 Pet 3:19–20; 4:6; *Ep. Apost.* 27; *Apoc. Pet.* 14; *Odes*

Sol. 42.11–20; Irenaeus *Adv. haer.* 1.27.3; Tertullian *Adv. Marc.* 4.24; done by John the Baptist in Hippolytus *Antichr.* 45. For Charles E. Hill (*Regnum Caelorum: Patterns of Future Hope in Early Christianity* [Oxford: Clarendon, 1992] 86), "The permutation [of *Vis.* 3.3.5] in *Similitudes* 9.15–16 probably represents an attempt to patch up a tired motif and stuff inside a theological concern (what has happened to the OT righteous?) neglected in the earlier presentation."

9   **Explanation of the Twelve Mountains**

17 [94]   1/ "So now, sir, explain to me about the mountains. Why is their appearance different from one another and variegated?" "Listen," he said, "these twelve mountains are twelve tribes that inhabit the whole world. The Son of God was proclaimed to them through the apostles."
2/ "But why are the mountains different and variegated? Explain it to me, sir." "Listen," he said. "These twelve tribes that inhabit the whole world are twelve peoples. They are various in understanding and thinking. As you saw the various mountains, so they are, and such are the differences of mind and way of thinking among the peoples. I will show you the way of each one."
3/ "First, sir," I said, "explain this: why though the mountains are so different, when their stones were placed in the building, did they became one bright color, like the ones that came up from the depths?" 4/ He said: "Because all the peoples living under heaven, when they heard and believed, were called by the name [of the Son] of God. When they received the seal, they took on one way of thinking and one mind, one faith and one love, and they bore the spirits of the young women with the name. This is why the construction of the tower became one color, bright as the sun. 5/ But after they came in together and became one body, some of them defiled themselves and were thrown out of the race of the just ones, and became again what they were before, only worse."

18 [95]   1/ "How, sir," I said, "did they become worse once they had known God?" He said, "the one who does not know God and does evil has some punishment for the evil done, but the one who knows God ought no longer do evil, but should do good. 2/ So if the one who should do good does evil, does it not seem like greater evil than from the one who does not know God? This is why those who have not known God and do evil are condemned to death, while those who have known God and have seen God's greatness yet do evil will be punished doubly and die forever. Thus the church of God will be cleansed. 3/ As you saw the stones taken away from the tower and handed over to the evil spirits and from there thrown out, even so there will be one body of the cleansed. Just as the tower came to be as if made from a single stone after it was cleansed, so will the church of God be after its cleansing and purging of evildoers, hypocrites, blasphemers, doubleminded, and doers of all kinds of evil. 4/ After these are thrown out, the church will be one body, one thinking, one mind, one faith, one love. Then the Son of God will be glad and rejoice in them, when he receives his cleansed people." "All this, sir," I said, "is great and wonderful. 5/ Still, sir," I said, "explain to me the meaning and deeds of each one of the mountains, so that every soul that is convinced by the Lord and hears may render honor to God's great, wonderful, and honorable name." He said, "Hear about the variety of mountains and the twelve nations.

19 [96]   1/ "From the first mountain, the black one, are believers such as: apostates, blasphemers against the Lord, and betrayers of the servants of God. For them there is no conversion, but there is death, and this is why they are black. Their race is outside the law. 2/ From the second mountain, the bare one, are believers like these: hypocrites and teachers of evil. These are like the first, with no fruit of justice. As their mountain is unfruitful, so these people have the name, but they are empty of faith and there is no fruit of truth in them. For these there is conversion if they turn quickly to convert. But if they delay, their death will be with the first group." 3/ "Why, sir," I said, "is there conversion for them but not for the first ones? Their deeds are about the same." "This is why there is conversion for them: because they have not blasphemed their Lord nor become betrayers of the servants of God. Because of the desire for profit they acted like hypocrites and each one taught [according to] the desires of sinful people. They will pay some just price, but there is conversion for them because they became neither blasphemers nor betrayers.

20 [97]   1/ "From the third mountain that has thorns and thistles are believers like these. Among them are the wealthy, those embroiled in many business affairs. The thistles are the wealthy and the thorns are those embroiled in many business affairs. 2/ These [then, the ones embroiled in many business affairs, do not] adhere to the servants of God but wander in error, choked by their deeds. The wealthy with difficulty adhere to the servants of God, afraid lest they be asked for something by them. Such as these will with difficulty enter the kingdom of God. 3/ Just as it is difficult to walk among thistles in naked feet, so it is difficult to such people to enter the kingdom of God. 4/ There is conversion for all of them, but quickly, so that they may now make up for those former times when they did nothing, and now do some good. [If they are converted and do some good] they will live to God. If they remain in their deeds, they will be turned over to these women, who will put them to death.

21 [98]   1/ "From the fourth mountain with many plants that are green above but dry near the roots, and some dried up by the sun, are believers such as these: some are doubleminded, and some have the Lord on their lips but not in their hearts. 2/ This is why their foundation is dry and without power, and their words alone are alive while their works are dead. Such ones are [neither alive nor] dead. The doubleminded are also like this. The doubleminded are neither green nor dry. They are neither alive nor dead. 3/ Just as the plants when they saw the sun dried up, so the doubleminded when they hear of affliction become idolaters through their cowardice and they are ashamed of the name of their Lord. 4/ Such ones

240

[neither live] nor die. But if they are converted quickly, [they will be able to live. If they are not converted,] they are already turned over to the women who take away their life.

22 [99] 1/ "From the fifth mountain with plants that are green and rough are believers like these: they are faithful, but slow learners, arrogant and self-centered, who want to know everything and know absolutely nothing. 2/ Because of their arrogance, understanding is far from them, and stupid silliness has entered them. They praise themselves as having understanding and want to be self-authenticating teachers though they are silly. 3/ Out of haughtiness many have become empty by exalting themselves, because arrogance [and empty pretense] are a great demon. Many of these were rejected, some were converted and became faithful and submitted themselves to those who have understanding, acknowledging their own silliness. 4/ For the rest there is conversion. They did not become evil, but only [stupid and foolish. If they] are converted, they will live to God. If they do not convert, they will dwell with the women who will do bad things to them.

23 [100] 1/ "Those from the sixth mountain that has large and small cracks and in the cracks withered plants are believers such as these. 2/ Those with small cracks are those who hold things against one another and are withered in faith because of their slanderous speech. But many of these were converted. The rest will be converted when they hear my commandments. Their slanders are small, and they will quickly be converted. 3/ But those with large cracks endure in their slander and maliciously fume against one another. These were thrown down from the tower and judged useless for its construction. This kind will live with difficulty. 4/ If God our Lord, ruler of all, who holds authority over all his creation, has no malice against those who acknowledge their sins, but is merciful, shall a mortal human being full of sin hold malice against another human person as though able to destroy or save that person? 5/ I, the angel of conversion, say to you [pl.]: whoever of you is of this faction, that you cleanse yourselves of this demon. If not, you will be handed over to him, for death.

24 [101] 1/ "From the seventh mountain in which are green, joyful plants, and the whole mountain is healthy, and all kinds of domestic animals and the birds of the air were feeding on the plants on this mountain, and the plants on which they were feeding were flourishing all the more, are believers such as these. 2/ They were always simple, without guile, and happy, holding nothing against each other, but always rejoicing in the servants of God, and clothed with the holy spirit of these young women, always filled with compassion for everyone, and supplied everyone with the result of their labors, without reproach or wariness. 3/ The Lord, seeing their simplicity

and real childlikeness, made the works of their hands flourish and bestowed favor on all their activities. 4/ I, the angel of conversion, say to you who are like this: stay the way you are, and your offspring will not be eliminated forever. The Lord has tested you and has inscribed you in our number, and all your offspring will dwell with the Son of God, because you have received something of his spirit.

25 [102]   1/ "From the eighth mountain which has many springs—and all the Lord's creation was drinking from the springs—are believers such as these: 2/ apostles and teachers who proclaimed to the whole world and who taught the word of the Lord with reverence and holiness, who held back absolutely nothing for evil desire but always went forward in justice and truth, as they received the Holy Spirit. Their passage is with the angels.

26 [103]   1/ "From the ninth mountain, the deserted one that has snakes and wild animals that devastate people, are believers such as these. 2/ Those with spots are ministers who minister badly and despoil the living of widows and orphans, and make profit for themselves off the ministry entrusted to them to do. If they keep on according to their own desire, they are dead and there is no hope of life for them. But if they turn and perform their ministry in a holy manner, they can live. 3/ Those with a scaly surface are the ones who denied and did not turn to their Lord, but have become like a dried-up wilderness, not adhering to the servants of God, but by going their own way they make their own souls to perish. 4/ Just as a vine left untended in an enclosure is ruined, overrun by weeds, and in time turns wild, and is no longer useful for its owner, so these people have given up on themselves and become useless to their Lord because they have gone wild. 5/ There is conversion for them if they are not found to have denied from the heart. But if they have denied from the heart, I do not know whether they can live. 6/ I do not say this for these days, that someone who denies now might receive conversion, for it is now impossible for someone who denies the Lord to be saved. But for those who denied previously, it seems there is conversion. If anyone is about to be converted, let it happen quickly before the tower is finished. Otherwise such a one will be devastated to death by the women. 7/ The stunted ones are the malicious and those who speak evil. They are the wild animals you saw on the mountain. Just as the snakes destroy and kill people with their own poison, so the words of these people destroy and kill others. 8/ These are stunted in their faith because of the behavior they have among themselves. Some were converted and saved. The rest who are this way can be saved if they will undergo conversion. If they will not be converted, they will be put to death by those women whose power they enjoy.

27 [104] 1/ "From the tenth mountain where there were trees giving shelter to some sheep are believers like these: 2/ overseers and hospitable people who always willingly received into their houses the servants of God without hypocrisy. The overseers always gave shelter unceasingly to the needy and widows as part of their ministry and always behaved in a holy manner. 3/ So all of them will always be sheltered by the Lord. Those who act this way will always be sheltered by the Lord, and their place is already with the angels, provided they remain until the end in the service of the Lord.

28 [105] 1/ "From the eleventh mountain with trees filled with fruit, each tree with a different fruit, are believers like these: 2/ those who suffered for the name of the Son of God, who eagerly suffered with their whole heart and gave over their lives." 3/ "Why, then, sir," I said, "do all the trees have fruit, but some fruit is more attractive?" "Listen," he said. "Those who suffered for the name are honorable before God and the sins of all of them have been removed because they suffered for the name of the Son of God. Listen to why their fruits are different and some are superior." 4/ He said, "Those who were summoned by authority and questioned and did not deny but suffered eagerly, these are more greatly honored before the Lord. This is the superior fruit. But those who were fearful and full of doubt and debated in their hearts whether to deny or confess, and they suffered, these are inferior fruit because this idea entered their heart. It is an evil idea, that a servant should deny one's own lord. 5/ So look out, you [pl.] who have these ideas, lest the idea stay in your hearts and you die to God. You who suffer for the sake of the name must give honor to God, because God has considered you worthy to bear the name and that all your sins might be healed. 6/ So consider yourselves fortunate, but think that you have done a great thing if any of you suffers for God. The Lord is bestowing life on you, and you do not know it, for your sins have weighed you down, and unless you had suffered for the name of the Lord, you would have died to God because of your sins. 7/ I am saying this to you who hesitate between denial and confession. Confess that you have a Lord, lest in denying you be handed over into prison. 8/ If the outsiders punish their slaves if one denies his or her own lord, what do you think the Lord, who is all-powerful, will do to you? Put out these ideas from your hearts, so that you might always live to God.

29 [106] 1/ "From the twelfth, white mountain are believers like these: they are like innocent babies, for whom no evil arises in their heart nor do they even know what evil is, but they remain always in innocence. 2/ People like these will dwell in the kingdom of God without hesitation because they did not defile the commandments of God in any way, but remained in innocence all the days of their life in the same attitude. 3/ Those who remain," he said, "and will be like babies, having no evil, will be held in greater honor than all those already mentioned. All babies are honored before God and hold first place with him. Blessed are you who have removed evil from yourselves and have put on innocence. You will live to God before all the rest." 4/ After he finished the parables of the mountains, I said to him: "Sir, now tell me about the stones taken from the plain and put into the building instead of the stones taken from the tower, and about the round ones put into the building and the ones that are still round."

Twelve Nations

The twelve mountains contain the following kinds of people:

1. Apostates, blasphemers, and betrayers (19.1)
2. Hypocrites and false teachers (19.2)
3. Wealthy and those choked with business concerns (20)
4. Doubleminded (21)
5. Slow learners and arrogant (22)
6. Quarrelers (23)
7. Simple, without guile (24)
8. Apostles and teachers (25)
9. Bad pastors and deniers (26)
10. Bishops and givers of hospitality (27)
11. Those who suffer for the name (28)
12. Innocent ones (29)

■ **17.1–2 [94]** The explanation of the twelve mountains, first introduced in *Sim.* 9.1, begins here and will continue through chapter 29. It will be similar to that of the sticks in the eighth *Similitude*. But a universal aspect is introduced here. The Shepherd seems no longer to be talking about believers alone, but about all people under the guise of twelve tribes ($\varphi\upsilon\lambda\alpha\acute{\iota}$),[1] indicating a probable Jewish origin of the story. They are no longer the components of Israel but represent twelve peoples ($\check{\epsilon}\vartheta\nu\eta$) who inhabit the world (v. 2), or the twelve tribes as having absorbed them. Yet v. 4 will return to belief in the name of the Son of God and baptism, making clear that what is envisioned here is membership in the church from all peoples, to whom the preaching of the apostles has gone forth[2] (v. 1). The foundation on the patriarchal generations of Israel, alluded to in 15.4, is never strongly developed, but a similar point is made here. The church is founded on its biblical and Jewish heritage, but has moved on further. The tower built on rock stands out in the center of, and higher than, the mountains (9.2.1).

■ **17.3–5** The natural diversity of the stones coming from different peoples is spoken of as different colors but the desirable end product is one same, bright white color for all the stones (9.4.5), so that the different colors should really be understood as discoloration. The discolored stones are transformed into unity in the one faith and one love (v. 4)[3] through acceptance of the name[4] in baptism[5] and acceptance of the virtues as way of life (13.7). Yet even after being fitted into the tower in the proper way, into the building that appears as a single stone and therefore as one body,[6] some made themselves unclean ($\grave{\epsilon}\mu\acute{\iota}\alpha\nu\alpha\nu$ $\grave{\epsilon}\alpha\upsilon\tauo\acute{\upsilon}\varsigma$). The language of purity stands out here in its context and is continued in the next chapter. Those who lapse into their former ways are worse than before they began their conversion process.

---

1   ALL, Joly (330) read in v. 1: $\tau\grave{\alpha}$ $\check{o}\rho\eta$ $\tau\alpha\hat{\upsilon}\tau\alpha$ $\tau\grave{\alpha}$ $\delta\acute{\omega}\delta\epsilon\kappa\alpha$ $\delta\acute{\omega}\delta\epsilon\kappa\acute{\alpha}$ $\epsilon\grave{\iota}\sigma\iota\nu$ $\varphi\upsilon\lambda\alpha\acute{\iota}$ ("these twelve mountains are the twelve tribes"). Pam E. Whittaker (90) read: $\tau\grave{\alpha}$ $\check{o}\rho\eta$ $\tau\alpha\hat{\upsilon}\tau\alpha$ $\delta\acute{\omega}\delta\epsilon\kappa\alpha$ $\varphi\upsilon\lambda\alpha\acute{\iota}$ $\epsilon\grave{\iota}\sigma\iota\nu$ ("these mountains are twelve tribes").

2   *Ep. Apost.* 1–2; *Ap. Const.* 1.1.1.

3   Compare 13.5.

4   Words in brackets in v. 4 omitted by A, restored by Gebhardt-Harnack from LLE.

5   Eph 4:4; compare 8.6.3; 9.16.3–5.

6   Here not a eucharistic (1 Cor 6:16; 10:17) but a baptismal allusion.

The Cleansing of the Church

■ **18.1–2 [95]** These verses continue the problem of the lapsed. Those with ignorance of the truth are less culpable than those who know.[7] By the final rejection of baptized offenders, the church will be cleansed. Here the tension between the call to all and the selection of the few, *Hermas'* habitual wide call to conversion and the purity of the church, is evident. Though there has been throughout a concern for purification of the church,[8] here there is a hardening of position that begins in v. 2 and continues in the next chapters, with the threat of eschatological death to those who finally cannot conform and so fit into the tower.

■ **18.3–5** The concern for cleansing and purification continues, to make way for a united community, one body.[9] Verse 3b enumerates in a list of vices some of those who cannot be tolerated in the church. It is a rather conventional list except for the expected doubleminded, *Hermas'* favorite villains.[10] Once more, the theme of unity of the purified church is stressed.[11] The joy of the Son of God (v. 4) at the final reception of his purified church contrasts with the serious tone of his first visit to inspect the tower (9.6–7) but parallels the rejoicing of the great angel who inspected the sticks in the eighth *Similitude.*[12] Verse 5 introduces what follows.

The First and Second Mountains

■ **19.1 [96]** The specific explanation of the twelve mountains, first listed at 9.1.5–10, begins with the worst and proceeds in a more or less direct way from worst to best,[13] in contrast to the description of the stones in *Vis.* 3.5–7, which proceeds from best to worst, and of the sticks in *Sim.* 8.3.6–8; 6–10 where there is little perceptible pattern. Here the movement from worst to best is also from black to white, utilizing the traditional stereo-

type of color preferences. The first mountain is black. Its inhabitants, apostates, blasphemers, and betrayers, traditionally the worst sinners, parallel one group of sticks, completely dry and moth-eaten.[14] For all three groups here there is no conversion—a strikingly harsh judgment of exclusion in this book so devoted to the idea that there is the opportunity of conversion for all. The counterpart of this passage in 8.6.5 says it a little differently: they heard the proclamation but refused to listen to it, so that exclusion was the result of their own decision. The third group there were betrayers of the church; here they are betrayers of the servants of God.[15] One wonders whether specific known instances are remembered.

■ **19.2** The same can be said for those from the second mountain, which is bare,[16] that is, without vegetation. Here again with hypocrites and false teachers there is a parallel with the sticks that were dry but not moth-eaten in 8.6.5.[17] The gardening image is applied: that the mountain is bare means that nothing can grow on it; so these people can grow no fruit of justice, but remain unfruitful. Here at least there is still the chance for conversion, however, and the threat that hangs over them is death with those of v. 1.

■ **19.3** Hermas catches what seems to be unfair with regard to the first group, that they have no conversion offered to them. The difference is that with the second group there is no blasphemy or betrayal of Christians. This surely indicates that we are not dealing here with formal heresy, which would receive a far more severe judgment, but with some who get carried away with their own ideas. The typical association of theological error and greed is present, but their teaching is not considered blasphemy or betrayal.[18] They are hypocrites only, professing the name but acting differently because of

---

7 See 2 Pet 2:20–22; cited by Brox, 443.

8 E.g., 8.2.5; 9.7.2, 6. See comment on 5.6.2.

9 There is editorial uncertainty about the punctuation in this section. Lake puts this statement and half of the next sentence into a parenthetical comment. See Dibelius, 627–28; Whittaker, 91.

10 See Introduction 3.3.1, 3.3.2; Osiek, *Rich and Poor,* 50.

11 Compare 13.5, 7; 17.4, 5.

12 8.1.16–18; 5.1.

13 The exception is the ninth mountain (chap. 26) in which three negative types are presented, perhaps because the first, bad pastors, appear there not in

an order of valuation but in the context of church leaders, who both precede them (apostles and teachers, chap. 25) and follow (bishops and givers of hospitality, chap. 27).

14 *Sim.* 8.6.4.

15 On this term, see comment on *Vis.* 1.2.4.

16 Not ὑψηλοῦ ("exalted," "raised up") AE, but ψιλοῦ ("bare") restored from L¹ *glabroso.*

17 See comment on *Sim.* 5.7.2.

18 Compare *Man.* 11.6, 12–13; Ignatius *Smyrn.* 6.2.

their disordered desires (τὰς ἐπιθυμίας τῶν ἀνθρώπων τῶν ἁμαρτανόντων).

The Third Mountain

■ **20.1–4 [97]**[19] This chapter and all subsequent chapters through 29 speak of one group only, in this case from the third, thorny mountain full of thistles, those whose business and wealth get in the way of their living according to their faith, in a way similar to two groups of sticks in the eighth *Similitude*: those with sticks half-dry and half-green, with too many business concerns (8.1–3), and those with sticks two-thirds dry, one-third green, who are rich (9.1–4). Both are combined here, and this group is very revealing of some of *Hermas'* major concerns: the dangers of wealth and responsibility of the wealthy, the distractions of business, lack of generosity, and disunity in the real church. By what can only be a careless slip or a manuscript problem in v. 1, not the distractions of wealth, etc., but the people are the thistles and thorns. This analogy does not continue in the rest of the explanation. Lying behind the whole imagery may be Mark 4:19 and its surrounding parable, or another version of the same allegory. Both wealth and overinvolvement in business are attacked here, and they are not exactly the same, though closely related through the connector of greed. The critique is a complement to Hermas' supposed advantage because of his reversal of fortune.[20] The stinginess of the rich in v. 2b rather than their shame is here blamed for their breaking of the unity of the community. Because they do not want to be asked for alms, they avoid other Christians. This behavior would be considered bad style not only in a Jewish or Christian community but elsewhere as well: the rich believers are shirking their responsibility as patrons, a social situation where an ostentatious display of generosity is necessary to retain one's honor among peers and subordinates.[21] Their admission into the kingdom of God, that is, into the tower, is in jeopardy, as with any wealthy persons according to the Synoptic tradition.[22] Conversion is liberally offered here (v. 4), but still with the threat of ultimate death at the hands of the black-clad women (15.3). If they do change their ways they will "live to God" (ζήσονται τῷ θεῷ), a familiar expression not seen since 8.11.4.

The Fourth Mountain

■ **21.1–4 [98]**[23] The fourth mountain contains plants whose very description connotes the problem it represents: they are pleasantly green on top but dry at the roots, plants that are dying from the roots up.[24] They represent the doubleminded who look good on the outside, but who are disintegrating from within, since their hearts are divided. They belong half to God and half to the world.[25] They have parallels both among the stones of *Vision* 3 and the sticks of *Similitude* 8.[26] The reference in v. 2 to their "foundations" (τὰ θεμέλια) is a term from the building rather than the immediate image of plants, but its use allows slippage between the metaphor at hand and the larger one of the stones and the tower. Verse 3 seems to refer to a habitual situation in which believers are on trial for the faith (θλῖψις). The word usually means some kind of suffering or difficulty connected with Christian identity, often but not always in an eschatological context.[27] To commit "idolatry" (εἰδωλολατρεῖν)[28] need not be thought of in a formal context of apostasy. In *Man.* 11.4 it means consulting a prophet who does not prophesy in the way approved by Hermas. Any kind of compromise with a lifestyle inimical to Christian belief could constitute idolatry, even acceptance of dinner invitations at which a sacrifice to another god is

19 Words in brackets in vv. 2 and 4 are omitted in A, restored by Gebhardt-Harnack from LLE.

20 *Vis.* 1.3.1; 3.6.5; *Man.* 5.2.2. See Osiek, *Rich and Poor,* 40, 43–44, 46–49, 124–25.

21 See Osiek, *Rich and Poor,* 121–25.

22 Matt 19:23; Mark 10:23; Luke 18:24. In all three texts the same word for "with difficulty" (δυσκόλως) appears as here in vv. 2–3; see further comment on *Man.* 4.3.6.

23 Words in brackets in vv. 2, 4 are omitted in A, restored by Gebhardt-Harnack from LLE.

24 Not at all an unrealistic description, against Brox, 446. It is exactly how certain plants die in drought or gradually colder autumn weather.

25 Dibelius, 629.

26 *Vis.* 3.7.1; *Sim.* 8.7.1–2.

27 Eschatological, e.g.: *Vis.* 2.2.7; 2.3.1; 4.1.1; but referring to present sufferings of a purificatory nature: *Sim.* 7.3–7.

28 The noun, a product of Hellenistic Judaism (e.g., *T. Jud.* 19), appears in Gal 5:20; Col 3:5; Polycarp *Phil.* 11.2; *Did.* 3.4; 5.1; *Barn.* 16.7; 20.1, but the verb in Christian literature to this point only in *Herm. Man.* 11.4 and here (cf. *T. Levi* 17.11.); BAGD *s.v.*

offered.[29] In *Hermas'* thinking, any departure from the integrity of living the faith could be idolatry. Here, it is through fear and shame[30] that it happens to those who cannot face the prospect of suffering because of their belief, a suffering that could take the form of social ostracism and public shame, not necessarily of arrest, torture, and death. The appeal to conversion is simultaneous with the process of their condemnation that is already under way: they are already handed over ($\check{\eta}\delta\eta$ $\pi\alpha\rho\alpha\delta\epsilon\delta o\mu\acute{\epsilon}\nu o\iota$ $\epsilon\mathring{\iota}\sigma\acute{\iota}$) to the death-dealing women.

The Fifth Mountain

■ **22.1–4 [99]** If fear and doubt are the keys to behavior on the previous mountain, on the fifth mountain it is complacency and arrogance. This chapter has no parallel in the previous visions of the stones or the sticks. The plants are green, signifying faith, but not pleasant to deal with. They are people who think they know everything, and therefore cannot learn anything even though they go through the appearances of learning. They want to be teachers (v. 2) on their own authority ($\dot{\epsilon}\vartheta\epsilon\lambda o\delta\iota$-$\delta\acute{\alpha}\sigma\kappa\alpha\lambda o\iota$).[31] Even the appeal to false knowledge and false understanding in vv. 1–2 is not sufficient evidence to assume full-blown Gnosticism as the culprit.[32] Yet there are some similarities, and the description given here could sound like a bad caricature of Gnostics. Arrogance about knowledge, however, has never been limited to Gnosticism. The author of *Hermas* is fed up with some people's opinions freely imposed.[33] He does not say that they are teachers, but that they wish to be, that is, they recognize themselves as teachers but at least

Hermas' segment of the community does not recognize them as such. Their arrogance[34] has made them empty[35] of anything good. The remedy is submission of judgment (v. 3) to those who have the true understanding. Some were able to accept this remedy: they experienced conversion and restoration of fidelity.[36] None of them is evil (v. 4), just stupid.[37] Perhaps because of this, the ultimate threat is not death at the hands of the black-clad women, just ambiguous disaster.

The Sixth Mountain

■ **23.1–5 [100]** Cracks have consistently been the very appropriate designation of causes of division within the community.[38] Here on the sixth mountain, the plants that attempt to grow in the cracks do not thrive (v. 1). A distinction is made between small and large cracks, to allow for greater nuance than in the previous discussions of community division (vv. 2, 3). The difference is one of degree. The people characterized by small cracks have minor resentments that can be overcome, while those with large cracks are tougher cases, people who are hardened in malicious resentment and anger. Their usefulness, to say nothing of their salvation, is in grave doubt.[39] The address for God in v. 4 could suggest that both God and Christ are intended: $\acute{o}$ $\vartheta\epsilon\grave{o}\varsigma$ $\kappa\alpha\grave{\iota}$ $\acute{o}$ $\kappa\acute{\upsilon}\rho\iota o\varsigma$ $\dot{\eta}\mu\hat{\omega}\nu$ (God and our Lord),[40] but the reference is to God under two titles.[41] The argument that follows is from greater to lesser: in the face of God's greater forgiveness and withholding of almighty vengeance, how can people who are not capable of such great vengeance think that they are authorized to hold grudges? Many NT passages

---

29 Cf. 1 Cor 8:10; 10:27–30 and the controversy about dining customs. Hermas, however, has nothing to say about this specific issue.

30 See comment on 14.6.

31 A *hapax legomenon*; cf. Col 2:23 $\dot{\epsilon}\vartheta\epsilon\lambda o\vartheta\rho\eta\sigma\kappa\acute{\iota}\alpha$ ("would-be worship"); they "wish to be teachers on an unofficial basis" (Snyder, 150); "a volunteer teacher in contrast to one authorized by the church" (BAGD *s.v.*); "a teacher who unduly magnifies his office" (Lake, 275 n.1).

32 With Brox, 447–48; against Dibelius (630) and a good number of others, given in Brox, 448. See comment on *Sim.* 5.7.2.

33 For a previous reference to teachers, see 19.2.

34 Words in brackets in v. 3 are omitted by A and restored by Whittaker from LLE.

35 See use of the idea of emptiness for a person devoid

of the good spirit in *Man.* 5.2.5, 7; for false prophets in *Man.* 11.3.

36 Literally, "they believed" ($\dot{\epsilon}\pi\acute{\iota}\sigma\tau\epsilon\upsilon\sigma\alpha\nu$), but since they are already believers (v. 1), here the verb must take the alternate sense of submitting to or trusting in the truth.

37 Words in brackets in v. 4 are illegible in A, restored by Whittaker from LLE.

38 *Vis.* 3.6.3; *Sim.* 8.7.2; 10.1–2.

39 They will live only with difficulty ($\delta\upsilon\sigma\kappa\acute{o}\lambda\omega\varsigma$); see comment on *Man.* 3.4.6.

40 This is the literal translation given by both Lake (277) and Snyder (151), but it is misleading; "our God and Lord," Crombie (51). See note in Joly, 340–41.

41 Dibelius, 631. On God as creator of all, see comment on *Sim.* 7.4.

leap to mind, especially the parable of the unforgiving servant (Matt 18:23–35).[42] Verse 5 begins with a solemn warning by the Shepherd in his capacity as angel of conversion.[43] Those who are "of this faction"[44] are to distance themselves from it. The teaching of the *Similitudes* does not usually refer explicitly to the two spirits as it does here, but that of the *Mandates* sets the context. Slander, malicious speech, and the holding of resentments are manifestations of possession by the evil spirit. A form of moral exorcism, of which all are capable, is called for.[45] The alternative is spiritual death.

The Seventh Mountain

■ **24.1–2 [101]** Those represented by the seventh mountain are the opposite of those on the sixth and correspond to the men with green sticks in 8.3.8, among those sent immediately into the tower. The mountain contains every good kind of plant that feeds animals and birds, and the plants grow all the more when fed upon (also at 9.1.8). Verse 2 describes their attitude, which is open to everyone, holding no resentments, the ideal way to be in community. By contrast to those from the sixth mountain who must rid themselves of the evil spirit, these have put on the holy spirit (singular) of the young women, so that the teaching on the two spirits from 23.5 is complemented. These people are a joy to be around, and their efforts support others as they give of themselves without holding anything back.[46] They are generous patrons of the needy, just the opposite of those in 20.2 who avoid their company lest they be asked for help.

■ **24.3–4** As a result, God rewards their efforts with generosity (v. 3) by making whatever they do (their πρᾶξις) flourish. This may be a general reference to activities, or, in view of the critique of business affairs as distractions in other passages,[47] it may refer specifically to their business, which God will make flourish because it does not prevent them from living a virtuous and generous life. For the third of three times,[48] the Shepherd identified as the angel of conversion (v. 4) solemnly gives an exhortation, this time not to change, but to stay the way they are—a rare command in this book so bent on changing people. If they endure as they are, they and their families will remain dear to God because they are inscribed in the book of life.[49] The unusual use of the first person plural in the mouth of the Shepherd ("inscribed you in our number") might be an unconscious slip on the part of the author that was never corrected in any of the surviving manuscripts. But it is more likely the Shepherd/angel speaking on his own to include these holy persons in their promised heavenly existence with the angels in the presence of the Son of God.[50] Since they have been clothed with the spirit of the young women, they also have the spirit of the Son of God, for it is the same spirit (13.3).

The Eighth Mountain

■ **25.1–2 [102]** The eighth mountain is a complement to the seventh; the seventh mountain provided food, through the generosity of the people represented there. The eighth contains wonderful springs that provide drink for all creatures through the ministry of the word preached by apostles and teachers, who have no explicit mention among the sticks of the eighth *Similitude,* but are among the white, square stones that go immediately into the tower in *Vis.* 3.5.1 and represent the forty stones taken from the depths in *Sim.* 15.4; 16.5. The possibility of their holding something back for evil desire (which they do not do) refers probably not to embezzlement nor to Gnostic mysteries, but to stinginess or lack of generos-

---

42 Also Jas 4:12; Matt 10:28.

43 First identified as such in *Vis.* 5.7. Other such solemn warnings: by the woman church to those who abuse leadership in the church, which also leads to community division as here (*Vis.* 3.9.7, 9); by the Shepherd to Hermas about keeping the commandments (*Man.* 12.3.6); also with his identification as angel of conversion as here in *Man.* 12.6.1; *Sim.* 24.4; cf. 28.7, 31.3, 33.1.

44 Literally, "who have this heresy" (ὅσοι ταύτην ἔχετε τὴν αἵρεσιν), but αἵρεσις cannot yet be translated as "heresy," nor is a doctrinal question at issue here.

45 See especially *Man.* 5.2.

46 Without reproach (ἀνονειδίστως) and without hesitation (ἀδιστάκτως). On the first, see Jas 1:5; on the second, comment on *Man.* 9.2.

47 Especially *Man.* 5.2.2; 6.2.5; *Sim.* 4.5, 7; 8.8.1–2; 9.20.2; Osiek, *Rich and Poor,* 47–49.

48 *Man.* 12.6.1; *Sim.* 24.4: see comment there.

49 Their seed will never be wiped out (οὐκ ἐξαλειφθήσεται τὸ σπέρμα ὑμῶν ἕως αἰῶνος): Ps 69:28 (contrast Ps 88:5); Rev 3:5; *1 Clem.* 53.4 (Exod 32:32). See comment on *Vis.* 1.2.1.

50 As also in 25.2; see comment on *Vis.* 2.2.7.

248

ity in their ministry.[51] Their heavenly destiny is therefore with the angels.[52]

The Ninth Mountain

■ **26.1–2 [103]** The ninth mountain, by contrast, is entirely without water (1.9). Here we are back to an undesirable locale with dangerous animals. It contains three kinds of stones: spotted (v. 2), rough or scaly (v. 3), and shortened or stunted (v. 7). All three kinds of stones are represented among those already built into the tower but found to be unacceptable in 6.4, 8.2, 4, 7.[53] Here they correspond to abusive ministers, deniers, and malicious speakers of evil, the last group identified with the wild animals. The length of this chapter compared to the brevity of those that immediately precede and follow is indicative of *Hermas'* tendency to accentuate problem areas and develop at more length the descriptions of people who need improvement. The "ministers" of v. 2 are διάκονοι who minister badly (κακῶς διακονήσαντες). The reference may be a general one here, to all kinds of ministers in the church. But given that διάκονοι are mentioned in *Vis.* 3.5.1 along with apostles, teachers, and "overseers" (ἐπίσκοποι), and given that their abuse of power here centers on relief services for widows and orphans,[54] the term could already be evolving in Rome as well as the East into a specific name for those who assist ἐπίσκοποι (here still a group of them, probably synonymous with

the presbyters of *Vis.* 2.4.3).[55] In contrast to the apostles and teachers of 25.2, where embezzlement is not the issue, that *is* the issue here: the corrupt ministers of this mountain have enriched themselves from church funds intended for the needy. Such a reference presupposes already some kind of centralized organization for distribution of relief, even though personal patronage for this purpose continued for some time.[56]

■ **26.3–5** The next group treated are those with rough and peeling surface. They have denied their faith in their Lord,[57] and their denial was made easier by their withdrawal from association with other believers. The expression used here, μὴ κολλώμενοι τοῖς δούλοις τοῦ θεοῦ ("not adhering to the servants of God"), appears elsewhere for those distracted by their wealth and business, and so may imply that here. The difference is that these people have been distracted all the way into denial of the faith.[58] They have therefore become like desolate land (ἐρημώδης), a term reserved in *Hermas* for the ninth mountain,[59] like an untended vine (v. 4) that turns wild and stops producing edible grapes,[60] and is thus no longer useful.[61] This chapter returns to the kinds of earthy comparisons more typical of the *Mandates,* here and in v. 7. *Hermas'* position on denial in v. 5 is curiously like that reported for Elchasai: that it is understandable that many will have to deny externally, which is even forgivable, as long as denial is not done from the heart.[62]

---

51 With Brox, 450–51, against Weinel (embezzlement, "Der Hirt des Hermas," in Edgar Hennecke, ed., *Neutestamentliche Apokryphen* [2d ed.; Tübingen: Mohr/Siebeck, 1924] 327–84), and Dibelius (gnostic teaching, 632).

52 Matt 22:30; see comment on *Vis.* 2.2.7.

53 Two of the three types (scaly and stunted) are among rejected stones in *Vis.* 3.2.8.

54 On the importance of these as objects of charity, see comment on *Man.* 8.10; Osiek, *Rich and Poor,* 62; also Justin *1 Apol.* 1.67.

55 Already with Ignatius, this role for deacons is set (*Magn.* 6.1; *Trall.* 2.3; 3.1; cf. *Pol.* 4.1; *Phil* 1:1; 1 Tim 3:8–13; *1 Clem.* 42.4; *Did.* 15.1; later, Hippolytus *Ap. Trad.* 34), though his form of governance by a single bishop will take at least another generation to reach Rome; see comment on *Vis.* 3.5.1; Introduction 2.2.2. On presbyter-bishops, see Eric G. Jay, "From Presbyter-Bishops to Bishops and Presbyters" *SecCent* 1 (1981) 125–72 (143).

56 See Bobertz, "Role of Patron."

57 For Brox (451), God is meant here, but given the

previous importance of baptism in the name of the Son of God (e.g., 9.16.7, 17.4), Christ is probably intended.

58 *Sim.* 8.8.1–2; 9.1, 20.2.

59 9.1.9, 26.1, 3; Dibelius, 633; Brox, 451–52.

60 In contrast to the careful care given the vineyard by the servant in *Sim.* 5.2.2–5.

61 See comment on *Vis.* 1.1.9; *Man.* 12.6.2.

62 Epiphanius *Pan.* 19.1.8–2.1; 3.1–3; Eusebius *Hist. eccl.* 6.38. This is not the same as the attitude toward persecution reported for the Valentinians, that external confession was all right for psychics but unnecessary for Gnostics: Antonio Orbe, *Los primeros herejes ante la persecución* (Estudios Valentianos 5; Analecta Gregoriana 83; Rome: Gregorian University, 1956).

The expression of doubt about the salvation of those who deny from the heart at the end of v. 4 is not a lack of knowledge on the part of the Shepherd, but the equivalent of salvation only with difficulty (δυσκόλως) elsewhere.[63]

■ **26.6** Verse 6 is a caveat regarding the very serious business of denial of the faith, lest anyone get the idea that "cheap grace" can be had after avoiding painful situations now.[64] Yet even the promise of forgiveness for denial in the past puts *Hermas* on a very different track than the position of many who later took the rigorist stance in the face of apostates during persecution who sought to be reinstated later. The very fact that the issue is raised here must mean that the situation and the question have already arisen.

■ **26.7–8** The stunted stones are among those also mentioned in *Vis.* 3.2.8 lying around the tower unusable.[65] The second homey analogy of the chapter compares the speech of evil speakers to poisonous snakes (v. 1).[66] They are aptly compared to stones that are too short because they are shortened or stunted in faith by reason of their loose tongues. They have the chance to escape from the death-dealing women whose δύναμις ("power") they possess, that is, they are characterized by the vices, especially καταλαλία ("malicious speech") (15.3).

The Tenth Mountain

■ **27.1–3 [104]** The tenth mountain presents an idyllic scene reminiscent of the original allusion to Arcadia (1.4). That the sheep are sheltered or shaded (σκεπάζειν) by trees is the guiding image, for this is also what the "overseers" (ἐπίσκοποι) do to the needy (v. 2b), and the reward they will have from God (v. 3). The people of this mountain correspond partially but not completely to the square white stones of *Vis.* 3.5.1 and the dry sticks with a little green in *Sim.* 8.10.3 who did some evil things but nevertheless were good at hospitality. Two kinds of hospitality are described in v. 2, reception of travelers and charity to the local needy. The overseers or elders and other ministers of hospitality (φιλόξενοι) performed a crucial function of providing the links and fostering union among churches, especially those at a distance. Many who acted as hosts of travelers were women, especially widows with room in their homes.[67] Christian travelers were the principal means of learning news about Christians in other cities and about members of their own communities who had moved elsewhere. They were also bearers of new theological ideas, and whether or not to receive them was also a question of authority and orthodoxy.[68] The other kind of hospitality alluded to here is that of coming to the aid of needy persons, especially widows devoid of any other support.[69] To the hospitable, God will give hospitality with the angels.[70]

The Eleventh Mountain

■ **28.1–2 [105]** With the eleventh mountain, we are again in a very desirable place full of fruit trees, each bearing a different fruit.[71] These are the people who have experienced some kind of persecution and have actually suffered (v. 2), to the point of imprisonment (v. 7) and perhaps to the point of death.[72] They are the same

---

63   *Man.* 4.3.6; 9.6; 12.1.2; *Sim.* 8.10.2; 9.20.2, 23.3; see comment on *Man.* 4.3.6.

64   Similar idea at *Vis.* 2.2.8; *Man.* 4.1.11 expresses the clarification lest the new opportunity for forgiveness be taken advantage of.

65   See note on v. 1 above.

66   The word for the poisonous animals here is τὰ θηρία, usually quadrupeds, used in v. 1 after τὰ ἑρπετά (snakes), but θηρίον does sometimes mean snake: Diodorus Siculus *Bibl. hist.* 20.42.2; Polyaenus *Strat.* 2.3.15; Acts 28:4–5. Of special interest is Josephus *Ant.* 17.117, where the two words are used in seeming apposition. Cf. BAGD *s.v.*

67   1 Tim 5:10; Osiek and Balch, *Families,* 208.

68   Phlm 22; Titus 1:8; Heb 13:2; 1 Pet 4:9; 3 John 9–10; *Didache* 11–13; *1 Clem.* 10.7–12.8; Abraham J. Malherbe, *Social Aspects of Early Christianity* (2d ed.; Philadelphia: Fortress, 1983) 92–112; Raymond E.

Brown, *The Epistles of John* (AB 30; Garden City, NY: Doubleday, 1982) 728–39; Osiek and Balch, *Families,* 206–14.

69   Rom 12:13; 1 Tim 5:4–5; *Man.* 8.10; Justin *1 Apol.* 1.67; Hippolytus *Ap. Trad.* 28; Bobertz, "Role of Patron."

70   On heavenly life with the angels, see comment on *Vis.* 2.2.7.

71   1.10; Rev 22:2.

72   Compare 1 Pet 4:12–19.

group as those for whom the right-hand place is reserved (*Vis.* 3.1.9), those brought up from the depths and fitting immediately into the tower in *Vis.* 3.5.2, and those who were crowned and passed immediately into the tower in *Sim.* 8.3.6. The situation of such suffering may be a past remembrance, perhaps of the bloody tragedy under Nero. But it is also possible that here and in the other passages mentioned, something less dramatic is envisioned: confiscation of property, loss of family, social disgrace. It is significant that among these passages only here in v. 2 is there explicit mention of loss of life, though the very term "to suffer" may be synonymous with death. Those who handed over their lives did so with all their heart.[73] Is *Hermas* talking about deaths he and his community know about, have heard about, or the biblical stories of the founding of the faith?

■ **28.3–5** Even within the ranks of those who suffered for the name of the Son of God, some are better than others. That suffering for the faith brings remission of sin was a common belief in the early church.[74] Hermas does know of some kind of situation in which Christians were arrested, interrogated,[75] and tortured by civil authority.[76] Since torture was required in the interrogation of slaves,[77] this may be an indirect reference to the plight of Christian slaves. Some of those tortured were courageous and sure of themselves, while others were less forthright in their convictions under pressure.[78] The solemn address to those who suffer (οἱ πάσχοντες) in v. 5 has a contemporary ring and suggests that some kind of pressure is being placed on Christians in the author's present or near future, for which *Hermas* wants

to offer strong encouragement.[79] Previously the language of "bearing" has been different for believers carrying the name and for the Son and the young women: believers have carried or worn the name as a long-term identity (φορεῖν),[80] while literary characters, the Son, the young women, and even the gate bear or support the weight of creation, the world, or the tower (βαστάζειν).[81] Now believers bear (βαστάζειν) the name because it has become a burden that brings on suffering.[82] Denial under pressure is equivalent to betrayal of loyalty to one's master or patron, a capital offense for a slave.

■ **28.6–7** Suffering for the name brings release from sin which otherwise would have been overwhelming; this is the way that the predicament of the unconverted has been presented throughout the text, so it comes as no surprise here. The second direct address of the chapter from the Shepherd to the whole listening audience (v. 7, the first was in v. 5) encourages the hesitant; though the explicit language of doublemindedness is not used here, that is the intent.[83] Listeners are exhorted to acknowledge their owner and patron and not be disloyal. The reference to imprisonment is puzzling, since one would think that those who did *not* deny would land in prison, while those who did deny would go free. The literature of Christian persecution generally indicates that denial or apostasy was in fact the principal goal of interrogators, who released those they were satisfied had renounced what they considered an aberration. Moreover, in the analogy of v. 8 it is the slave who *denies* loyalty who is punished. This leads to the probability that a

---

73 Acts 15:26; see comment on *Vis.* 2.2.4.
74 Also v. 5; on healing of sin, see comment on *Vis.* 1.1.9.
75 The verb ἐξετάζειν can mean legal inquiry with torture: Sir 23:10; Josephus *Ant.* 18.183; Polybius *Hist.* 15.27.7; BAGD *s.v.*
76 By ἡ ἐξουσία; on the use of this term for civil authority, compare Rom 13:1–3. Two mosaic medallions with portions of Rom 13:3b inscribed within wreaths were found in the floor of a Byzantine public building at Caesarea Maritima.
77 See Pliny *Ep.* 10.96.8; Justin *1 Apol.* 2.12.4.
78 Hesitation and retraction under torture and threat of death seem to have been fairly common: cf. *Mart. Pol.* 4 and the frequent mentions of apostates in *Hermas* (*Vis.* 1.4.2; *Sim.* 8.6.4; 9.19.1; etc.).
79 Matt 5:11; Luke 6:22; 1 Pet 4:14.
80 *Sim.* 9.13.2–3, 14.5–6, 15.2–3, 6, 16.1–3, 17.4.
81 E.g., 9.2.5, 4.2, 14.5. The Son supports (βαστάζει) those who bear (φοροῦντας) his name (9.14.6).
82 The only previous such usage is 8.10.3, where bearing the name is associated with hospitality and contrasted with apostasy (οὐδέποτε δὲ ἀπὸ τοῦ θεοῦ ἀπέστησαν καὶ τὸ ὄνομα ἡδέως ἐβάστασαν).
83 Here they are οἱ διστάζοντες ("the hesitaters").

literal imprisonment is not intended here, but rather a spiritual one as in *Vis.* 1.1.8 for those who imprison themselves by their own weaknesses.[84]

The Twelfth Mountain

■ **29.1–4 [106]** The twelfth mountain is all white and from it come the innocents, a vision of an ideal church and ideal believers with which *Hermas* is not dealing directly. It has a general parallel in *Vis.* 3.5.3. It is not clear what is the difference between them and the guileless ones of the seventh mountain (chap. 24) except that there the emphasis was on the peaceful and effective aspect of their social relationships, whereas here the emphasis is on their own personal innocence and the complete absence of any evil tendency in their hearts—sure evidence that here we are dealing with the strictly ideal. Verse 3a–b is addressed to a hypothetical group that probably finds no actual correspondence in the community: the completely innocent. It is something of a puzzle that Hermas would interject such an ideal at the end of a heartening portrayal of real people with real problems, except that perhaps he thought he had to say it under the influence of the Christian ideal of childlike innocence.[85] "Simplicity" ($\dot{\alpha}\pi\lambda\acute{o}\tau\eta\varsigma$) and "innocence" ($\dot{\alpha}\kappa\alpha\kappa\acute{\iota}\alpha$) are among the seven or twelve virtues symbolized by the young women who help build the tower,[86] but the term in vv. 1–2 is $\nu\eta\pi\iota\acute{o}\tau\eta\varsigma$ ("like a very small child"). The presentation serves no paraenetic purpose except to introduce v. 3c, the real message, a makarism on those who have distanced evil from themselves ($\check{o}\sigma o\iota$ $\check{\alpha}\nu$ $\check{\alpha}\rho\eta\tau\epsilon$ $\dot{\alpha}\varphi'\dot{\epsilon}\alpha\upsilon\tau\hat{\omega}\nu$ $\tau\grave{\eta}\nu$ $\pi o\nu\eta\rho\acute{\iota}\alpha\nu$) and put on innocence ($\dot{\alpha}\kappa\alpha\kappa\acute{\iota}\alpha$), a virtue that can be gained after falling. Then, surprisingly in view of the previous verses, such people will have first priority in heavenly life ($\pi\rho\hat{\omega}\tau o\iota$ $\pi\acute{\alpha}\nu\tau\omega\nu$ $\zeta\acute{\eta}\sigma\epsilon\sigma\vartheta\epsilon$ $\tau\hat{\omega}$ $\vartheta\epsilon\hat{\omega}$) rather than the martyrs of the previous chapter.[87] Verse 4 introduces the next discussion about the stones that were brought from the plain to replace those that were removed from the tower.[88]

---

84 Or perhaps the imprisonment after death to which those before Christ were subject: 1 Pet 3:19. Joly (81) too seems to think this with regard to *Vis.* 1.1.8.

85 Matt 18:3–6, 10; Mark 9:36–37; Luke 9:47–48; 1 Pet 2:1–2.

86 *Vis.* 3.8.3–8; *Sim.* 9.15.2.

87 For Joly (349) this is indicative that the author of *Hermas* does not write from the perspective of persecution. It could also simply be the result of the paratactic structure of the whole work.

88 6.5–8, 9.1–4.

9

Explanation of Stones from the Plain

30 [107] 1/ He said, "Listen about all of these. The stones that were taken from the plain and put into the building in place of those taken away are the base of the white mountain. 2/ Since all the believers from the white mountain were found to be without guile, the Lord of the tower commanded that these be brought from [the base of] the mountain to be placed in the building of the tower. He knew that if these stones go into the building of the tower they will remain bright, and not one of them will blacken.[1] 3/ But if he added those from the other mountains, he would have to return to the tower and cleanse it. These were all found to be white,[2] those who have believed and who will believe, because they are of the same race. Blessed is this race because it is without guile. 4/ Listen now about the round bright stones. They too are from the white mountain.[3] Listen to why they were found to be round. Their wealth hid them a little from the truth and made them dark, but they never departed from God, nor did an evil word come out of their mouth, but every justice and deed of truth. 5/ So when the Lord saw their minds, and that they were able to lean toward the truth and to remain with the good, he commanded that their wealth be cut away, but not completely so that they could accomplish some good with what was left. They will live to God because they are of a good kind. So they will be trimmed a little and placed in the building of this tower.

31 [108] 1/ "But the rest of them that stayed round and did not fit into the tower because they had not yet received the seal were put back in their original place. 2/ This world and the vanity of their wealth must be cut away, and then they will fit in the kingdom of God. They must enter the kingdom of God, for the Lord blessed this innocent kind. So from this kind no one will perish. Even if one of them be tempted by the very evil devil, such a one will quickly return to the Lord. 3/ I judge you [pl.] to be blessed—I the angel of conversion—whoever of you are innocent as babies, because your lot is good and honorable before God. 4/ But I say to all of you who have accepted the seal, hold to simplicity, do not remember offenses nor stay with evil deeds or bitter memories. Be of one spirit and do something about these evil divisions and get rid of them so that the lord of the sheep may rejoice in them. 5/ He will rejoice if he finds them all healthy. But if some are found to be scattered, woe to the shepherds! 6/ And if the shepherds themselves are found to be scattered, what will they have to say to the lord about his sheep? That they have given up because of the sheep? They will not be believed, because it is incredible that a shepherd should suffer by the hands of the sheep. They will be punished greatly for lying. I am a shepherd, and I must render account for you.

1 The Athos MS. ends here, and L[1] continues.
2 Text from Pam with some restored from LL follows.
3 Text to end of v. 31.6 is from L[1].

Replacement Stones

■ **30.1–3 [107]** Two distinct kinds of stones are treated here, though their origin is closely related: those taken from the plain and put into the tower, which differ little from the people described on the twelfth mountain (vv. 1–2), and those that are round and bright (vv. 4–5). Both have their origins in the twelfth, white mountain, but they are distinct. The first group, those brought from the plain to replace the stones already in the tower but then rejected (6.6–8), are the "foundation" or "base" (ῥίζαι, literally "roots") of the white mountain.[1] They match the general description of those already found on the twelfth mountain: they are completely innocent (v. 2; 29.1–2)[2] and thus the commander of the tower ordered that they go directly into the building, knowing that, unlike some of those used in the first construction, these will not discolor (6.4–5), necessitating another inspection on his part (v. 3). As in 17.1–2 and 31.1–2, here not only Christians are envisioned, but both those who are already believers as well as potential believers, all of whom have a common origin.[3] The makarism of v. 3 extends to both Christians and nonbelievers who are guileless, a revealing view of *Hermas'* attitude toward nonbelievers, though probably with a view to their conversion to the faith and baptism (31.1).

■ **30.4–5** The second group from the white mountain are the bright stones that are too round to go into the building directly.[4] They have meant consistently the same thing in the three references to them: they are the wealthy for whom their wealth is an obstacle. Like Hermas himself,[5] they must undergo a partial, but not complete, stripping of their wealth so that they can become useful for the tower. Not all their wealth should go (v. 5), because then they would not be able to accomplish something good with it. The plan for the rich is

that they understand the purpose for their wealth: using it generously for the poor.[6] This group has no other problem. They belong to the people of the white mountain, the bright stones, the innocent ones. They have no part with evildoers or evil speakers; no evil has come from their mouths.[7] Only their wealth stands in the way. Their being singled out demonstrates once more how preoccupied *Hermas* is with this question.

Round Stones with Too Much Wealth

■ **31.1–2 [108]** Not all of the previous group were acceptably trimmed. As in the original description (9.1–4), those easiest to trim were trimmed and placed in the tower, but those too hard to work with were taken back temporarily to the plain. Here, this last group was not accepted right away because they had not yet received the seal of baptism.[8] They are destined to enter the kingdom of God,[9] thus to be part of the tower and be saved, but they are still in process. The one thing that holds them back (v. 2) is the wealth to which they are too attached. If they accept baptism and become Christians, there will be demands on them for patronage and generosity within the Christian community that they hesitate to take on, like the wealthy resisters already within the community (20.2). If the autobiographical material in *Hermas* is historical, one senses here especially the identification of the author with those whose love of their fortune is the only thing that holds them back from full generosity. Again, the people whom the author of *Hermas* has in mind here are basically good and he holds out amazingly for their essential integrity. Their destiny is to be saved; the Lord has already blessed[10] them, and they will be able to withstand any kind of temptation. Whoever the people are whom *Hermas* has in mind here (perhaps friends or relatives?), they can do no wrong

---

1   Commentators puzzle over this use (e.g., Dibelius, 637; Brox, 458), but in fact, it is attested for the base of a hill: Polybius *Hist.* 2.66.10; Diodorus Siculus *Bibl. hist.* 20.41.3; Plutarch *Sulla* 16.1 (BAGD *s.v.*); or even the base of a pillar (LSJ *s.v.* 2).

2   Words in brackets in v. 2 are omitted in A, restored from LLE. The Athos ms. ends with the end of v. 2.

3   All are of the same γένος (Snyder: "type"). The idea of Christians as a γένος, an alternative to the Jew-Gentile tension, is first attested in just these years, perhaps influenced by 1 Pet 2:9: *Mart. Pol.* 3.2; *Diogn.* 1; Clement of Alexandria *Strom.* 6.5. The "race of the just" (τὸ γένος τῶν δικαίων, *Sim.* 17.5;

cf. *Mart. Pol.* 14.1; 17.1) is different since those who defile themselves after already being in the tower are ejected from it. Cf. BAGD, LPGL *s.v.*

4   *Vis.* 3.6.5–7; *Sim.* 9.9.1–3.

5   *Vis.* 3.6.7.

6   *Sim.* 2.10; Osiek, *Rich and Poor*, 78–90.

7   Eph 4:29.

8   On this expression, see comment on *Sim.* 8.6.3.

9   On this expression, see comment on 12.3, 20.2–3.

10   *Benedixit* L[1]; *probavit* L[2].

and it is only a matter of time in his thinking before they will come around.

■ **31.3–6**[11] As in 23.5 and 24.4, the Shepherd in his role as angel of conversion again makes a solemn pronouncement, this time a makarism on the innocent (v. 3) that, together with v. 4, is reminiscent of the sequence of 29.1–3: blessed are the innocent and blessed too are those who can become innocent by putting away guilty behavior with baptism. Rather than innocence referring to sexual purity as it usually does for modern readers, here the close proximity of exhortation about divisive social conduct in v. 4 suggests rather sins of resentment and factiousness that harm the unity of the community: they do not keep memory of offenses, or hang on to malice or hurtful memories (*neque offensarum memores esse neque in malitia vestra permanere aut in memoria offensarum amaritudinis*). The problem is forgiveness. Christians are to hold to one spirit,[12] because this unity will enable the "lord of the sheep" to rejoice. If not, the shepherds will be blamed, not the sheep (vv. 5–6): woe to the shepherds[13] if even they have fallen apart.[14] Though church leaders are not explicitly called shepherds in *Hermas*, perhaps in deference to the revelatory figure, the associations of shepherding with church leadership are early and unmistakable[15] and the connection is implicitly made in 27.1–2, where sheep are sheltered and church leaders are present. Church leaders have already been assailed for their failure to live up to their responsibility.[16] The concluding remark is a charming connector from the Shepherd: I know what I'm talking about because I am in the same situation.[17]

---

11 Most of vv. 3–6 is preserved in quotation from Antiochus (given in Whittaker, 101), which differs in many details. This translation continues to follow principally L[1].

12 See 9.13.5, 7, 17.5, 18.3 and especially v. 4.

13 On the woe formula, see comment on *Vis.* 4.2.6 (misprint in reference in Brox, 462).

14 *Dissipati* LL; διαπεπτωκότες Ant.

15 E.g., Matt 10:5–6; John 21:15–17; Eph 4:11; 1 Pet 2:25; 5:4.

16 *Vis.* 2.2.6; *Sim.* 9.26.2.

17 Compare Matt 8:9; Luke 7:8.

9   **Final Exhortations**

32 [109]   **1/** "Heal yourselves while the tower is still being built. **2/** The Lord lives among those who love peace because he loves peace. But he stays away from those who are evil, seditious, and ruined by their malice. Give back the spirit as whole as you received it. **3/** If you give a new, whole piece of clothing to the fuller and you get it back torn, will you take it? Will you not get excited and pursue him forcefully, saying: 'I gave you the clothing in one piece. Why did you tear it and render it useless? It cannot be used because of the large tear you put in it.' Won't you say all this to the fuller because of the tear he made in your clothing? **4/** If you mourn over your clothing because he did not give it back to you whole, what do you think the Lord will do to you, who gave you the spirit whole, but you gave it back useless so that it cannot be used by its Lord? It began to be useless as soon as it was ruined by you. So won't the Lord of this spirit put you to death?" **5/** "Yes," I said, "the Lord will punish everyone he finds still holding on to the memory of offenses." He said, "So do not presume on God's mercy, but honor him who is so patient with offenses, not like you. Be converted in a manner that will help you.

33 [110]   **1/** "Everything that has been written above, I, the Shepherd, the angel of conversion, have shown and said to the servant of God. If you hear and believe my words, and live according to them, and change your ways, you will be able to live. But if you remain in guile and malice, no one like this will live to God. I have said all these things to you." **2/** The Shepherd said to me: "Have you asked me everything?" I responded: "Yes, sir." "Why didn't you ask me about the places of the stones that were put into the building, of which we filled in the marks?" I said: "I forgot, sir." **3/** "Now listen about them. They are the ones who heard my commandments and were converted with their whole heart. The Lord saw how good and pure their conversion was, and that they could remain in it. So he ordered their former sins to be erased. These marks were their sins. They were filled in level so as not to appear."

Parable of the Cleaner

■ **32.1–5 [109]** The appeal is to a sense of healing from sin while there is still time (v. 1).[1] The dwelling of the Lord is with men[2] of peace, that is, with those who can let go

of malice and resentment. The whole chapter is reminiscent of the teaching in the *Mandates,* especially about the indwelling spirit.[3] To each believer a spirit is entrusted, which must be given back without damage (v. 2).[4] But it

---

1   *Remediate vos* LL. On healing from sin, see comment on *Vis.* 1.1.9.

2   Gender-specific *viris* LL. The androcentrism could be with the translations or, less likely, with the Greek, which most often uses generic ἄνθρωποι, but see *Man.* 6.2.7–8; 9.3.6; 10.3.1–2; 11.9, 13–14; *Sim.* 9.15.4.

3   *Man.* 5.1.; 10:2–3.

4   In *Man.* 5.1.3, a spirit of bad temper ruins the environment; in 10.1.2, sadness exasperates the good spirit.

is not certain whether a good spirit, the spirit of God (the Holy Spirit), or the human spirit is meant here. Comparison with *Man.* 5.1 and 10.1–2[5] and the allusion to the same as the Lord's spirit[6] in v. 4 suggest that the Spirit of God is envisioned here. The difference should not be pushed too far, for the spirit of God in *Mandate* 5 could also mean the particular holy spirit sent to inhabit a believer. The parable about expecting to get one's clothes back in one piece from the cleaners (vv. 3–4)[7] is still quite comprehensible, but the process through which woolen garments were put to clean them makes it doubtful that most survived intact.[8] The spirit is made useless (*inutilis*=ἄχρηστος,[9] v. 4) when the person in whom it dwells is not a person of peace, but of dissension and division, characterized by hanging on to resentful memories (v. 5). This is another reinforcement of the point already driven home in 24.2 and 31.4.

The Marks Left on the Plain

■ **33.1 [110]** Verse 1 is a formal ending, to which vv. 2–3 may have been added later as an afterthought. The author signals that the revelation is over, and the writing has been completed.[10] The revelation has been given to Hermas, but for dissemination to all.[11] Though there have been many references to life in God for those who keep the commandments of the Shepherd, and the threat of death at the hands either of the Lord[12] or of

the evil women,[13] here the teaching is set down in the formula of the Two Ways, introduced by another solemn statement of the Shepherd self-identified as the angel of conversion.[14] Those who believe and accept the commandments to do them will live to God; those who instead continue to act maliciously will not. That the doing of evil is summarized so succinctly in this kind of behavior speaks dramatically for the emphasis Hermas places upon conduct that fragments community unity.

■ **33.2–3**[15] These verses are typical of the aggregative structure of the text. Even after saying himself that everything has now been told (v. 1), the Shepherd playfully reverses roles and prompts Hermas to ask more, about a detail that he forgot to pursue: what about the marks on the surface of the plain where the stones were removed (10.1–2)? It is as if the Shepherd has by now identified with Hermas' insatiable curiosity and does him one better. There is a single image and a single point to be made, the effect of conversion for forgiveness of sin. Regardless of what they may have been previously, the stones taken from the plain are now those whose conversion was true, from the heart, and the filling in of the holes is the removal of the signs of their sins, so that the ground from which they came is again level.[16]

---

5   Both Lake (295) and Snyder (157) translate "your" spirit, though the possessive pronoun is not found in the Latin text; neither Dibelius (639) nor Brox (461) nor Crombie (54) adds the possessive. In *Man.* 5.1.2–3; 10:1–2, it is the particular holy spirit (τὸ πνεῦμα τὸ ἅγιον) sent to inhabit a believer who dwells there.

6   *Spiritus eius* ("his spirit") L[1]; *ipsius spiritus* ("his own spirit") L[2].

7   Greek κναφεύς, later γναφεύς, Latin *fullo*. The fullers' guilds were well known; at Pompeii, e.g., the aristocratic matron Eumachia was the patron of one of them.

8   Treatment included soaking in urine and beating with sticks; cf. Pliny *N. H.* 35.196–98 for kinds of earth used in the process; brief but colorful description in *OxCD s.v.* "Fulling."

9   *Vis.* 3.6.7; *Man.* 5.1.6 (caused by bad temper); *Sim.* 9.26.4.

10   The command to write is given in *Vis.* 5.5; the first completion is at *Sim.* 9.1.1, after which a new section is added. This, too, is now completed.

11   Τῷ δούλῳ τοῦ θεοῦ ("to the servant of God") F; *dei servis* ("to the servants of God") LL.

12   23.5, 32.4.

13   20.4, 21.4, 26.8.

14   23.5, 24.4, 31.3.

15   Translation of this chapter follows the Greek text preserved in F.

16   See comment on *Vis.* 1.1.3.

10

Conclusion

1 [111]   1/ After I had written this book, that angel who had handed me over to the Shepherd came to me in the house where I was and sat on the couch, and the Shepherd stood on the right. Then he called me and said to me: 2/ "I have handed over you and your household to this Shepherd so you can be protected by him." "Yes, sir," I said. "So if you want to be protected from all annoyance and trouble, and to have success in all your good deeds and words and in every truthful virtue, proceed according to these commandments that I gave you. 3/ If you [sing.] keep his commandments, every desire and sweetness of the world will be subject to you and success in every business undertaking will follow you. Take on his fullness and moderation and tell everyone about his honor and dignity with the Lord and his control of great power, and that he is mighty in his office. To him alone throughout the whole world conversion is entrusted. Do you not see how powerful he is? Yet you do not respect the fullness and forbearance he has toward you."

2 [112]   1/ I said: "Ask him, sir, if while he has been in my house I have done anything against his orders that would offend him." 2/ "I myself know," he said, "that you have not done anything nor will you do anything against his orders. I only talk this way with you so you will persevere, for he has given me a good report about you. But you will tell these things to others so that those who have undergone or who will undergo conversion will feel the same way you do, so he can give a good report about them to me, and I to the Lord." 3/ "Sir," I said, "I myself tell everyone about the wondrous acts of God. I hope that everyone who sinned previously, if they hear them, will willingly be converted and recover life." 4/ "Then stay in this ministry and complete it," he said. "Whoever does his commandments will have life and great honor before the Lord. But those who do not honor his commandments are fleeing from their own life and [are] against him. [But they have their own honor with the Lord. But those who oppose him] and do not follow his commandments deliver themselves to death and each one is guilty of his or her own blood. But I tell you to keep his commandments and you will have healing of your sins.

3 [113]   1/ "I sent these young women to live with you because I saw how congenial they were to you. You have them as assistants so that you can better keep his commandments, for it is not possible to keep these commandments without these young women. I also see how much they want to be with you, and I will tell them not to leave your house at all. 2/ But you, keep your house clean; they like to live in a clean house. They are clean, chaste, and industrious and have all found favor with the Lord. If they find your house pure they will stay with you; but if a little impurity comes into it they will leave right away. These young women do not in any way like impurity." 3/ I said

to him: "Sir, I hope to be pleasing to them so they will always want to stay in my house; [just as the one to whom you handed me over could not complain about anything with me, so they too will not be able to complain about anything in my regard." 4/ He said to the Shepherd: "I know that the servant of God wants to live and he will keep these commandments and will make this a clean dwelling for the young women." 5/ After saying this, he handed me over again to the Shepherd, called the young women, and said to them:] "Since I see that you like living in his house, I commend him and his household to you, and tell you not to leave his house at all." They gladly received his words.

4 [114] 1/ Then he said to me: "Conduct yourself manfully in this ministry, telling everyone about the mighty deeds of God, and you will find favor in this ministry. So all those who proceed according to these commandments will live and be happy in their life. But those who neglect them will not live and will be unhappy in their life. 2/ Tell everyone who can do right not to stop doing good deeds. It is helpful to them. But I say that everyone ought to be rescued from adversity. The one who is in need and suffers adversity in daily life is in great torment and deprivation. 3/ Whoever rescues such a person from deprivation acquires great joy for oneself. The one who is troubled by this kind of adversity suffers the same torment as one who is tortured in chains. For many bring death on themselves because of these kinds of calamities when they are not able to bear them. So the one who knows the calamity of such a person and does not come to the rescue commits a great sin and incurs blood guilt. 4/ So do good works, you [pl.] who have received from the Lord, lest while you delay, the tower be completed. The delay in the building was for your sake. Unless you hurry to do right, the tower will be finished and you will be excluded." 5/ After he said this he rose from the couch and went away, taking the Shepherd and the young women, but he said that he would send the Shepherd and the young women back to my house.

Hermas in Custody of the Shepherd

■ **1.1–2 [111]** Opinions are sharply divided over the importance and function of these last four chapters, whether they are a later addition as the beginning of v. 1 would indicate,[1] an original ending after the eighth *Similitude*,[2] whether they add nothing new[3] and are therefore totally dispensable or end the entire work with a flourish by bringing back the great angel as Son of God.[4] The scene is evocative of *Vision* 5, in which the Shepherd first appears in Hermas' house and sits down beside him to announce that he has been sent by the great angel for the rest of Hermas' life. Here the great angel and the Shepherd come together, and the great

---

1   Rejected by Joly (358).
2   Snyder, 158.
3   Dibelius, 641.

4   Joly, 359.

angel assumes the position of authority on the couch, while the Shepherd suitably, as agent of the great angel, stands at the right side.[5] Contrary to the scene in *Vision* 5, here Hermas is not on the couch, but is called to it as client. Verse 2 restates the commission given in *Vis.* 5.2, then continues into an apodictic blessing formula with promise not only of deliverance from temptation and evil, but also of prosperity and success in every undertaking in exchange for keeping the commandments.

■ **1.3** The formula is repeated but goes further: whereas such a formula would usually promise victory over spirits or the powers of evil, here worldly pleasures, major distracters from the faithful life, will be subject to Hermas. They are the demons to be conquered.[6] Again, as in the previous verse, success is promised, this time not only general success but, in the Latin translations, success in acceptable business (*in omni bono negotio*),[7] perhaps as a healing of the economic reversals Hermas is said to have suffered before the revelations began.[8] The promise is followed by an exhortation to Hermas to assume the characteristics of the Shepherd, about which the translations do not agree: his *maturitas* and *modestia* (perhaps translating τελείωσις and σωφροσύνη).[9] Besides making known the revelation and the glory and mercy of God, Hermas is also now to make known the wonderful qualities of the Shepherd: his *honor* and *dignitas*[10] (perhaps δόξα and σεμνότης in the lost Greek text),

and the authority he wields in the execution of his function (*officium*). As has often been stated thoughout the revelations, the Shepherd is the sole agent of conversion of sinners. The slight reproach at the end of the angel's speech is a rhetorical device, as becomes clear in v. 2 of the next chapter.

Strengthening of Hermas for His Task

■ **2.1–4 [112]** Hermas protests his innocence of behaving offensively against the Shepherd, as he protested at the beginning of the narrative his innocence of having behaved offensively toward Rhoda. There too the reason given by the heavenly revealer is not to make Hermas miserable but to make him a missionary of the message of conversion (v. 2).[11] Spreading this message is to be a special charge (*ministerium*) for Hermas, which need not indicate that he holds church office, but that he takes this responsibility very seriously.[12] Verse 4 contains the direst threat toward those who reject the commandments and the invitation to conversion. They have previously been threatened with death, especially at the hands of the fearsome women,[13] but now the responsibility for their death, the accusation of blood guilt,[14] is placed squarely upon themselves.[15] But the wish of the angel is conversion and healing of sin.[16]

---

5 Most modern translations read that the Shepherd stands at the *angel*'s right, which is not specified in L[1] *ad dexteram*, L[2] *ad dextram* (at the right side); he could also be to Hermas' right, therefore the angel's left. But given the relationships involved, the Shepherd as authorized representative would indeed stand at the angel's right hand.

6 See comment on *Vis.* 5.1–2 for Hellenistic background to the scene.

7 Probably translating either πρᾶξις or πραγματεία.

8 *Vis.* 3.6.7.

9 Thus L[1]; *modestia et veneratio* L[2]; "meekness and justice" E.

10 Thus L[1]. The two terms are replete with social connotations of rank and privilege in ways that the Greek words do not convey. The use of *honor* by both Latin translations confirms the viable equivalence of δόξα in the Roman world; compare *Vis.* 2.2.5, 6; 3.2.1; *Sim.* 5.3.3; 8.7.4, 6.

11 *Vis.* 1.1.5–8; 1.3.1.

12 His revelatory agent directs him to proclaim the message in company with the presbyters, thus from a leadership position (*Vis.* 2.4.3); *ministerium* here

may translate λειτουργία, used of fasting (*Sim.* 5.3.3, 8) and hospitality (*Sim.* 9.27.3). See Introduction 2.2.2.

13 *Sim.* 9.20.4, 26.8.

14 Responsibility for death, particularly a violent death. At 4.3 below, neglect of others in great need means blood guilt for another. Cf. especially Ezek 33:6–8; Acts 18:6 for guilt for one's own blood; also Num 35:33; Deut 21:7–9; 2 Sam 1:16; Jer 26:15; Dan 13:46, 62; Matt 27:4, 24–25; 1 Cor 11:27; S. David Sperling, "Bloodguilt," ABD 1 (1992) 764–65; H. Kosmala, "His Blood on Us and Our Children (The Background of Matt. 27,24–25)," ASTI 7 (1968–1969) 94–126; Henning G. Reventlow, "Sein Blut komme über sein Haupt," VT 10 (1960) 311–27.

15 Words in brackets are missing in L[1], restored by Hilgenfeld from L[2]. The first statement in brackets, *Hic autem apud deum habet honorem suam* ("This one has his own honor before God"), makes little sense in context and is probably corrupt.

16 On healing of sin, see comment on *Vis.* 1.1.9.

Hermas in Custody of the Young Women

■ **3.1–5 [113]**[17] In typical additive fashion, a new factor is introduced. Now not only the Shepherd will remain with Hermas, but also the young women who symbolize the virtues (9.15.1–2). Since they are holy spirits (9.13.2), they have the same general behavior as other good spirits who, like people with allergies, cannot abide that to which they are hypersensitive: uncleanness or competition from evil spirits.[18] The house must be kept well cleaned (*munda*) for them.[19] Bearing these good spirits has already often been held up as the only way to live a faithful life.[20] As in Hermas' first surprise encounter with the young women (9.10), they take delight in being with him, so their permanent assignment to stay with him now causes no problem but produces a very favorable response from them (v. 5). Their willingness to be with him signifies his susceptibility to their influence, that is, his ease and comfort with the virtuous life.

Real Meaning of Good Works: Compassion

■ **4.1–3 [114]** Finally one arrives at the real conclusion as the text now stands. Hermas is exhorted to act manfully (*viriliter*, translating $\dot{\alpha}\nu\delta\rho\epsilon\hat{\iota}\omega\varsigma$)[21] in the charge he has been given (*in ministerio hoc*).[22] The apodictic statement of v. 1b is one of the simplest restatements of the message of blessing and curse that informs so much of the moral instruction in the whole text. Verse 2 can be punctuated differently than given in the translation: "Tell everyone who can do right not to stop. Doing good deeds is useful to them."[23] But the meaning is not changed. The tone suddenly shifts in the next statement

of v. 2, and will continue through v. 3. The reason for doing good deeds is not so much self-improvement or salvation, but the imperative (*oportere*: "it ought to be") to relieve the suffering of others. The by-product, however, is joy (*gaudium*, translating $\dot{\iota}\lambda\alpha\rho\acute{o}\tau\eta\varsigma$,[24] v. 3). The motif of relieving the suffering of others has been integrated into the Christian sense of the mutual obligations of persons in community and especially into the ethic of community solidarity as Hermas has worked at it through the entire book: the need to share abundance with the needy, to spend money to "buy souls in distress," to understand this as the reason for wealth, and to continue community solidarity even though it may mean constant expectations of generosity on the part of those better off.[25] Such terrible suffering can lead even to suicide, the probable meaning of the unclear *mortem sibi adducunt* ("they bring death to themselves"), though other meanings are possible, such as doing something sinful out of desperation that leads to spiritual death, or sale of children or self-sale into slavery to escape debt.[26] The last statement of v. 3 is very clear and stark: anyone who knowingly ignores another in such a situation is guilty of that person's death (*reus fit sanguinis eius*).[27] That this strong language is placed so near the end of the entire text shows that the ethic of the book is not individualist but intensely communal and social.[28]

■ **4.4–5** Verse 4 returns to the more typical Greco-Roman self-interest as motive for doing good. The overriding image of the book is the building of the tower in anticipation of its completion, when human change will no longer be possible. Now the hearer is reminded that the

---

17 Words in brackets in vv. 3–5 are preserved in Greek in *POxy* 404, and given in true state of fragmentary preservation by Whittaker (109–11), and in full, largely restored text in Joly (362) and Lake (302).

18 *Man.* 5.1.2–4; 2.5–6.

19 On the necessity of purification, see comment on *Sim.* 5.6.2.

20 *Sim.* 9.13.2, 7; 15.2, 6; 17.4.

21 See comment on *Vis.* 1.4.3 and Young, "Being a Man."

22 See comment on 2.4.

23 As given here in the translation, Whittaker, 110–11; alternatively Joly, 362; Lake, 304–5; Brox, 467; Crombie, 55; Snyder, 160.

24 On the role of joy in the Christian life according to Hermas, see comment on *Vis.* 1.4.3.

25 *Vis.* 3.9.5; *Sim.* 1.8; 2.10; 8.10; 9.20.2. Full list of pas-

sages in Osiek, *Rich and Poor*, 41–45.

26 Rescuing others from such situations was a Christian act of heroic charity (*1 Clem.* 55.2); see Osiek, "Ransom."

27 On blood guilt, see comment on 2.4.

28 It is difficult to understand a judgment that *Hermas* ends in a quite prosaic and unspectacular manner ("völlig prosaisch und unspektakulär," Brox, 470). It is prosaic only if the bite of social conversion is not felt. See also Introduction 4.

tower is essentially finished, and a delay in its total completion allows one last opportunity for conversion before it is too late.[29] The end of v. 4 reminds us that in spite of what seems like a number of extra opportunities for the one conversion, exclusion remains a possibility—the very threat upon which the power of the call to conversion hangs. Verse 5 sounds like the connector to another episode, which perhaps the author intended but never succeeded in putting into writing.

---

29   9.9.5, 14.2.

Bibliography
Indices

Bibliography

1. Critical Editions, Commentaries, and Translations (listed in order of their publication)

Anger, Rudolph
  Hermae Pastor Graece (Leipzig: Weigl, 1856).

Tischendorf, A. F. C.
  Hermae Pastor Graece. Ex fragmentis Lipsiensibus instituta quaestione de vero Graeci textus Lipsiensis fonte (Leipzig: Hinrichs, 1856).

d'Abbadie, Antoine
  Hermae Pastor, Aethiopice primum edidit et Aethiopica Latine vertit Antonius d'Abbadie (Abhandlungen der Deutschen morgenländischen Gesellschaft 2.1; Leipzig: Brockhaus, 1860).

Dressel, Albert R. M.
  Patrum Apostolicorum Opera. Editio altera aucta supplementis ad Barnabae epistolam et Hermae Pastorem ex Tischendorfiana codicis Sinaitici editione haustis (Leipzig: Hinrichs, 1863).

Tischendorf, A. F. C.
  Novum Testamentum Sinaiticum sive N. T. cum epistula Barnabae et fragmentis Pastoris ex Sinaitico codice (Leipzig: Brockhaus, 1863).

Hilgenfeld, Adolph
  Hermae Pastor Graece (Leipzig: Weigl, 1866).

Crombie, F.
  "The Pastor of Hermas" (Introduction, translation, notes) (ANF; Edinburgh: T. & T. Clark, 1867) 2. 3–58. Introduction by A. Cleveland Coxe.

Hilgenfeld, Adolph
  Hermae Pastor. Veteram Latinam interpretationem e codicibus (Leipzig: Reisland, 1873).

Gebhardt, Oskar von, and Adolf von Harnack
  Hermae Pastor graece, addita versione latine recentiore e codice Palatino (Patrum Apostolicorum Opera 3; Leipzig: Hinrichs, 1877).

Lightfoot, James B.
  The Apostolic Fathers (London: Macmillan, 1889; reprinted Grand Rapids: Baker, 1981).

Funk, Francis X.
  "Hermae Pastor," *Patres Apostolici* (2 vols.; Tübingen: Laupp, 1901) 414–639.

Lake, Kirsopp
  Codex Sinaiticus Petropolitanus. The New Testament, the Epistle of Barnabas and the Shepherd of Hermas (Oxford: Clarendon, 1911). [facsimile edition]

Lelong, Auguste
  Le Pasteur d'Hermas (*Les Pères Apostoliques* 4; Paris: Picard, 1912).

Lake, Kirsopp
  "The Shepherd of Hermas," *Apostolic Fathers* (LCL; Cambridge, MA: Harvard University Press, 1913) 2. 1–305.

Dibelius, Martin
  Der Hirt des Hermas (HNT; Die Apostolischen Väter 4; Tübingen: Mohr/Siebeck, 1923).

Weinel, H.
  "Der Hirt des Hermas," in Edgar Hennecke, ed., *Neutestamentiche Apokryphen* (2d ed.; Tübingen: Mohr/Siebeck, 1924) 327–84.

Bonner, Campbell
  A Papyrus Codex of the Shepherd of Hermas (Similitudes 2–9) with a Fragment of the Mandates (University of Michigan Studies, Humanistic Series 22; Ann Arbor: University of Michigan Press, 1934).

Whittaker, Molly
  Der Hirt des Hermas (1956; 2d ed.; Die Apostolischen Väter 1; Berlin: Akademie-Verlag, 1967).

Joly, Robert
  Hermas le Pasteur (SC 53, 1958; 2d ed., SC 53bis; Paris: Éditions du Cerf, 1968; reprint 1986).

Snyder, Graydon
  The Shepherd of Hermas (ed. Robert M. Grant; Apostolic Fathers 6; Camden, NJ: T. Nelson, 1969).

Hellholm, David
  Das Visionenbuch des Hermas als Apokalypse (ConBNT 13.1; Lund: Gleerup, 1980).

Vezzoni, Anna
  "Un testimone testuale inedito della versione Palatina del *Pastore* di Erma," *SCO* 37 (1987) 241–65.

Brox, Norbert
  Der Hirt des Hermas (Kommentar zu den Apostolischen Vätern 7; Göttingen: Vandenhoeck & Ruprecht, 1991).

Carlini, Antonio
  Papyrus Bodmer XXXVIII. Erma: Il Pastore (Ia–IIIa visione) (Bibliotheca Bodmeriana; Cologny-Genève: Fondation Martin Bodmer, 1991).

Vezzoni, Anna
  Il Pastore di Erma: versione Palatina con testo a fronte (Il Nuovo Melograno 13; Florence: Casa Editrice Le Lettere, 1994).

Pickering, Stuart
  The Shepherd *of Hermas* (Papyrology and Historical Perspectives 4; Sydney: Ancient History Documentary Research, Macquarie University Press, forthcoming).

2. Select Monographs and Articles

Alfonsi, Luigi
  "La vite e l'olmo," *VC* 21 (1967) 81–86.

Audet, Jean-Paul
  "Affinités littéraires et doctrinales du Manuel de Discipline," *RB* 59 (1952) 219–38; 60 (1953) 41–82.

Barnard, L. W.
  "The Shepherd of Hermas in Recent Study," *Heythrop Journal* 9 (1968) 29–36.

Bauckham, Richard J.
  "The Great Tribulation in the Shepherd of Hermas," *JTS* 25 (1974) 27–40.

Bausone, Carla
"Aspetti dell'ecclesiologia del Pastore di Hermas," *StPatr* 11=TU 108 (1972) 101–6.

Bonner, Campbell
"A Papyrus Codex of the Shepherd of Hermas," *HTR* 18 (1925) 115–27.

Carlini, Antonio
"Un accusativo da difendere (*Hermae Pastor Vis.* III 1, 1; *Vis.* IV 1, 1)," *SCO* 38 (1988) 511–12.

Idem
"Due estratti del *Pastore* di Erma nella versione Palatina in *Par. Lat.* 3182," *SCO* 35 (1985) 311–12.

Idem
"Erma (*Vis.* II 3.1) testimone testuale de Paolo?" *SCO* 37 (1987) 235–39.

Idem
"ΜΕΤΑΝΟΕΙΝ e ΜΕΤΑΜΕΛΕΣΘΑΙ nelle visioni di Erma," in Sebastià Janeras, ed., *Miscellània papirologica Ramon Roca-Puig* (Barcelona: Fundacio Salvador Vives Casajuana, 1987) 97–102.

Idem
"Un nuovo testimone delle visioni di Erma," *Atene e Roma* n.s. 30 (1985) 197–202.

Idem
"Le passeggiate di Erma verso Cuma (su due luoghi controversi del *Pastore*)," in S. F. Bondi et al., eds., *Studi in onore di Edda Bresciani* (Pisa: Giardini, 1986) 105–9.

Idem
"La rappresentazione della ΠΙΣΤΙΣ personificata nella terza visione di Erma," *Civiltà classica e cristiana* 9 (1988) 85–84.

Idem
"Testimone e testo: Il problema della datazione di PIand I 4 del *Pastore* di Erma," *SCO* 42 (1992) 17–30.

Idem
"La tradizione manoscritta del *Pastor* di Hermas e il problema dell'unità dell'opera," *in Papyrus Erzherzog Rainer: Festschrift zum 100-Jährigen Bestehen der Papyrussammlung der Österreichischen Nationalbibliothek* (Textband; Vienna: Hollinek, 1983) 97–100.

Idem
"La tradizione testuale del Pastore di Erma e i nuovi papiri," in Guglielmo Cavallo, ed., *Le Strade del Testo* (Lecce: Adriatica Editrice, 1987) 23–43.

Idem
"Tradizione testuale e prescrizioni canoniche: Erma, Sesto, Origene," *Orpheus* 7 (1986) 40–52.

Chadwick, Henry
"The New Edition of Hermas," *JTS* 8 (1957) 274–80.

Cirillo, Luigi
"La christologie pneumatique de la cinquième parabole du 'Pasteur' d'Hermas," *Revue de l'histoire des religions* 184 (1973) 25–48.

Idem
"Erma e il problema dell'apocalittica a Roma," *Cristianesimo nella Storia* 4 (1983) 1–31.

Coleborne, W.
"A Linguistic Approach to the Problem of Structure and Composition of the Shepherd of Hermas," *Colloquium* 3 (1969) 133–42.

Idem
"The Shepherd of Hermas: A Case for Multiple Authorship and Some Implications," *StPatr* 10=TU 107 (1970) 65–70.

Demetz, Peter
"The Elm and the Vine: Notes toward the History of a Marriage Topos," *Proceedings of the Modern Language Association of America* 73 (1958) 521–32.

Ford, Josephine M.
"A Possible Liturgical Background to the Shepherd of Hermas," *RevQ* 6 (1969) 531–51.

Gamble, Harry Y.
Books and Readers in the Early Church: A History of Early Christian Texts (New Haven/London: Yale University Press, 1995).

Giet, Stanislas
"De trois expressions: 'Auprès de la tour,' 'la place inférieure,' et 'les premiers murs,' dans le *Pasteur d'Hermas*," *StPatr* 8=TU 93 (1966) 24–29.

Idem
Hermas et les pasteurs: les trois auteurs du Pasteur d'Hermas (Paris: Presses Universitaires de France, 1963).

Idem
"Les trois auteurs du *Pasteur d'Hermas*," *StPatr* 8= TU 93 (1966) 10–23.

Goldhahn-Müller, Ingrid
Die Grenze der Gemeinde: Studien zum Problem der zweiten Busse im Neuen Testament unter Berücksichtigung der Entwicklung im 2. Jh. bis Tertullian (GThA 39; Göttingen: Vandenhoeck & Ruprecht, 1989).

Grobel, Kendrick
"The Shepherd of Hermas, Parable II," in Richmond C. Beatty et al., eds., *Vanderbilt Studies in the Humanities* (Nashville: Vanderbilt University Press, 1951) 1. 50–55.

Hanson, A. T.
"Hodayoth vi and viii and Hermas Sim. VIII," *StPatr* 10=TU 107 (1970) 105–8.

Hauck, Robert J.
"The Great Fast: Christology in the Shepherd of Hermas," *ATR* 75 (1993) 187–98.

Henne, Philippe
"À propos de la christologie du *Pasteur* d'Hermas," *RSPhTh* 72 (1988) 569–78.

Idem
"Canonicité du 'Pasteur' d'Hermas," *Revue Thomiste* 90 (1990) 81–100.

Idem
La christologie chez Clément de Rome et dans le Pasteur d'Hermas (Paradosis, Études de littérature et de théologie anciennes 33; Fribourg: Éditions Universitaires, 1992).

Idem

"Hermas en Égypte: la tradition manuscrite et
l'unité rédactionnelle du *Pasteur*," *Cristianesimo
nella Storia* 11 (1990) 237–56.

Idem

"Le péché d'Hermas," *Revue Thomiste* 90 (1990)
640–51.

Idem

"La pénitence et la rédaction du *Pasteur*
d'Hermas," *RB* 98 (1991) 358–97.

Idem

"La polysémie allégorique dans le *Pasteur*
d'Hermas," *EThL* 65 (1989) 131–35.

Idem

L'unité du Pasteur *d'Hermas* (Cahiers Revue
Biblique 31; Paris: Gabalda, 1992).

Idem

"La véritable christologie de la *Cinquième Similitude*
du *Pasteur* d'Hermas," *RSPhTh* 74 (1990) 182–204.

Hilhorst, A.

"Hermas," *RAC* 108/109 (1988) 682–701.

Idem

Sémitismes et latinismes dans le Pasteur d'Hermas
(Graecitas Christianorum Primaeva 5; Nijmegen:
Dekker and Van de Vegt, 1976).

Humphrey, Edith McEwan

*The Ladies and the Cities: Transformation and
Apocalyptic Identity in Joseph and Aseneth, 4 Ezra, the
Apocalypse and the Shepherd of Hermas* (JSPSS 17;
Sheffield: Sheffield Academic Press, 1995).

Jeffers, James S.

*Conflict at Rome: Social Order and Hierarchy in Early
Christianity* (Minneapolis: Fortress, 1991).

Joly, Robert

"Hermas et le Pasteur," *VC* 21 (1967) 201–18.

Idem

"Le milieu complexe du 'Pasteur' d'Hermas,"
ANRW 2. 27.1 (1993) 524–51.

Idem

"Philologie et psychanalyse: C. G. Jung et le
'Pasteur' d'Hermas," *L'antiquité classique* 22 (1953)
422–28.

Kirkland, Alastair

"The Literary History of the Shepherd of Hermas
Visions I to IV," *SecCent* 9 (1992) 87–102.

Koester, Helmut

"Apocalyptic Ordering of Christian Life: The
Shepherd of Hermas," in idem, *Introduction to the
New Testament*, vol. 2: *History and Literature of Early
Christianity* (Berlin and New York: De Gruyter,
1982) 256–61.

Lake, Kirsopp

"The Shepherd of Hermas and Christian Life in
Rome in the Second Century," *HTR* 4 (1911)
25–47.

Lampe, Peter

*Die stadtrömischen Christen in den ersten beiden Jahr-
hunderten* (WUNT 2. 18; 2d ed.; Tübingen: Mohr/
Siebeck], 1989).

Leutzsch, Martin

*Die Wahrnehmung sozialer Wirklichkeit im "Hirten des
Hermas"* (FRLANT 150; Göttingen: Vandenhoeck
& Ruprecht, 1989).

Lucchesi, Enzo

"Le Pasteur d'Hermas en copte. Perspective nouvelle," *VC* 43 (1989) 393–96.

Luschnat, Otto

"Die Jungfrauenszene in der Arkadienvision des
Hermas," *Theologia Viatorum* 12 (1973–1974)
53–70.

Maier, Harry O.

*The Social Setting of the Ministry as Reflected in the
Writings of Hermas, Clement, and Ignatius* (Canadian
Corporation for Studies in Religion, Dissertations
SR 1; Waterloo, Ontario: Wilfrid Laurier Univer-
sity Press, 1991).

Martin, José P.

"Espíritu y dualismo de espíritus en el Pastor de
Hermas y su relación con el judaismo," *Vetera christianorum* 15 (1978) 295–345.

Michaels, J. Ramsey

"The 'Level Ground' in the Shepherd of Hermas,"
ZNW 59 (1968) 245–50.

Miller, Patricia Cox

"'All the Words Were Frightful': Salvation by
Dreams in the Shepherd of Hermas," *VC* 42 (1988)
327–38.

Idem

*Dreams in Late Antiquity: Studies in the Imagination
of a Culture* (Princeton, NJ: Princeton University
Press, 1994).

Mohrmann, Christine

"Statio," *VC* 7 (1953) 223–45.

Moxnes, Halvor

"God and His Angel in the *Shepherd of Hermas*,"
StTh 28 (1974) 49–56.

Moyo, Ambrose

"Angels and Christology in the Shepherd of
Hermas" (Ph.D. diss., Harvard University, 1978).

Musurillo, Herbert

"The Need of a New Edition of Hermas," *TS* 12
(1951) 382–87.

Nijendijk, Lambartus W.

"Die Christologie des Hirten des Hermas" (Th.D.
diss., Rijksuniversiteit Utrecht, 1986).

Opitz, Helmut

*Ursprünge frühkatolischer Pneumatologie. Ein Beitrag
zur Enstehung der Lehre vom heiligen Geist in der
römischen Gemeinde unter Zugrundlegung des I
Clemens-Briefes und des "Hirten" des Hermas* (Theologische Arbeiten 15; Berlin: Evangelische Verlagsanstalt, 1960).

Osiek, Carolyn

"The Early Second Century through the Eyes of
Hermas: Continuity and Change," *BTB* 20 (1990)
116–22.

Idem

"The Genre and Function of the Shepherd of

Hermas," in Adela Yarbro Collins, ed., *Early Christian Apocalypticism: Genre and Social Setting* (Semeia 36; Decatur, GA: Scholars Press, 1986) 113–21.

Idem

"The Oral World of Early Christianity in Rome: The Case of Hermas," in Karl P. Donfried and Peter Richardson, eds., *Judaism and Christianity in First-Century Rome* (Grand Rapids: Eerdmans, 1998) 151–72.

Idem

Rich and Poor in the Shepherd of Hermas: An Exegetical-Social Investigation (CBQMS 15; Washington, DC: Catholic Biblical Association, 1983).

Paramelle, E., and Pierre Adnès

"Hermas (Le Pasteur d')," *Dictionnaire de Spiritualité* (ed. M. Viller et al.; Paris: Beauchesne, 1969) 7. 316–34.

Pernveden, Lage

The Concept of the Church in the Shepherd of Hermas (Studia Theologica Lundensia 27; Lund: Gleerup, 1966).

Peterson, Erik

"Die Begegnung mit dem Ungeheuer," in idem, *Frühkirche, Judentum, und Gnosis* (Freiburg: Herder, 1959) 285–309.

Idem

"Beiträge zur Interpretation der Visionem im 'Pastor Hermae'," in idem, *Frühkirche, Judentum, und Gnosis* (Freiburg: Herder, 1959) 254–70.

Idem

"Kritische Analyse der fünften Vision des Hermas," in idem, *Frühkirche, Judentum, und Gnosis* (Freiburg: Herder, 1959) 271–84.

Reiling, J.

Hermas and Christian Prophecy: A Study of the Eleventh Mandate (NovTSup 37; Leiden: Brill, 1973).

Savignac, Jean de

"Quelques problèmes de l'ouvrage dit 'Le Pasteur' d'Hermas," *EThR* 35 (1960) 159–70.

Schwartz, J.

"Survivances littéraires païennes dans le 'Pasteur' d'Hermas," *RB* 72 (1965) 240–47.

Seitz, Oscar J. F.

"Afterthoughts on the Term Dipsychos," *NTS* 5 (1959–1960) 327–34.

Idem

"Antecedents and Signification of the Term ΔΙΨΥΧΟΣ," *JBL* 66 (1947) 211–19.

Idem

"Relationship of the Shepherd of Hermas to the Epistle of James," *JBL* 63 (1944) 131–40.

Idem

"Selected Subjects in the Thought and Terminology of Hermas" (Th.D. diss., Harvard University, 1945).

Idem

"Two Spirits in Man: An Essay in Biblical Exegesis," *NTS* 6 (1959–1960) 82–95.

Smith, Martha M.

"Feminine Images in the Shepherd of Hermas" (Ph.D. diss., Duke University, 1979).

Strock, Arthur W.

"The Shepherd of Hermas: A Study of His Anthropology as Seen in the Tension between Dipsychia and Hamartia" (Ph.D. diss., Emory University, 1984).

Ström, Ake von

Der Hirt des Hermas: Allegorie oder Wirklichkeit? (Arbeiten und Mitteilungen aus dem neutestamentlichen Seminar zu Uppsala 3; Uppsala: Wretmans, 1936).

White, John Carroll

"The Interaction of Language and World in the 'Shepherd of Hermas'" (Ph.D. diss., Temple University, 1973).

Wilson, J. Christian

Five Problems in the Interpretation of the Shepherd of Hermas: Authorship, Genre, Canonicity, Apocalyptic, and the Absence of the Name 'Jesus Christ' (Mellen Biblical Press Series 34; Lewiston/Queenston/Lampeter: Mellen, 1995).

Idem

Toward a Reassessment of the Shepherd of Hermas: Its Date and Pneumatology (Lewiston/Queenston/Lampeter: Mellen, 1993).

Wilson, William J.

"The Career of the Prophet Hermas," *HTR* 20 (1927) 21–62.

Young, Steve

"Being a Man: The Pursuit of Manliness in *The Shepherd of Hermas*," *JECS* 2 (1994) 237–55.

18:24	115[17], 246[22]	2:33	63[14]	6:19	138[17]
19:8	108[7]	2:38	74[49]	8:15	31[240]
19:12-27	178[22]	4:11	220[3]	8:17	87[25]
20:9-19	171[1]	5:28	207[72]	8:34	63[14]
20:17	220[3]	5:31	63[14]	9:33	220[3]
20:46	81[15]	7:23	44[28]	10:3	149[12]
21	95[57]	7:56	44	12:2	78[19]
21:23, 28	68	7:60	70[20]	12:8	55, 105[2]
22:15	207[72]	8:9	144[34]	12:9	72[31]
22:47-48	223[31]	9:5	100[15]	12:13	250[69]
24:31	100[20]	9:26	72[31]	12:16	236[32]
24:38	44[28]	9:31	104[5]	12:18	72[33]

John

1:6—2:2	29	10:11-16	100[18]	13:1-3	251[76]
2:25	115[12]	10:23	210[89]	13:1	149[12]
3:3, 5	234[10]	10:28	72[31]	13:3-4	127[6]
3:4	224[46]	10:48	74[49]	13:12	92[22], 235[24]
3:5	26[199]	12:12	59[12]	15:7	81[6]
3:12	134[25], 143[31]	12:15	100[16], 100[19]	16.1	22[172], 42
3:15	143[31]	13:2	54[2]	16.14	6, 8, 9, 18, 44[21]
3:31	143[31]	13:6	142[14]		
4:34	229[18]	14:23	55[11]	16:16	223[31]
5:15-18	29	15:8	115[12]		
6:27	229[18]	16:15	210[89]	**1 Corinthians**	
6:31-58	178[21]	16:16	142[15]	1:2	44[30]
8:35-36	171[8]	16:40	59[12]	1:28	104[4]
10:7, 9	233[2]	18:10	154[20]	2-3	33
10:9	26	19:5	74[49]	2:9	44[28]
10:11-16	100[18]	19:9, 23	74[44]	2.12	31[240]
10:18	179[31]	20:17	55[11], 71[22]	3:5	22[172]
12:28	92[14]	20:35	81[6], 106[6]	3:9-17	64[22]
13:1	74[47]	20:37	223[31]	3:15	96[65]
13:35	179[31]	21:9	142[13]	4:17	110[7]
14:2-3	158[5]	21:22	193[15]	5:6	119[12]
14:6	74[44]	22:4	74[44]	5:10-11	76[3]
14:13-14	132	23:14	207[72]	6:9	86[19]
14:15, 21	179[31]	24:14	74[44]	6:9-10	76[3]
15:7	132	24:25	129[4]	6:16	72[31], 244[6]
15:10	179[31]	28:4	193[15]	7	116
16:20-22	68	28:26	207[72]	7:8, 27, 40	54
20:14,16	100[20]	**Romans**		7:12-16	111[9]
21:15-17	255[15]	1:1	44[30]	7:17-24	115[15]

Acts

1:28	115[12]	1:20	167[5]	7:30-31	68
2:17	207[72]	3:18	104[5]	7:39	110[7]
2:28	74[44]	4:17	44[22], 103[3]	7:39-40	116
		6:1-11	238[54]	8:6	58[5]
		6:1	112[18]	8:10	247[29]
				9:13-14	145[48]

2. Names

Author's note: Since the two major commentaries of Martin Dibelius and Norbert Brox are cited on almost every page, full references are not given here. Citations under their names are of other works by them or places in which their work is especially discussed.

Achelis, H.
8[76, 77], 228[12, 13]

Adnès, P.
2[1]

Andreau, J.
21[163]

Anger, R.
3[19]

Arbesmann, R.
54[2]

Arnera, G.
221[7]

Ashby, T.
91[7]

Audet, J.-P.
23[176], 24[187], 25[190], 25[192], 27[209], 38[283], 56[14], 71[26], 74[49], 106[7], 178[24]

Aune, D.
1[1103], 55[10], 57[19], 71[22], 80[1], 82[23], 95[51], 96[59], 99[4, 7], 141[2], 142[11, 19], 144[32]

Azevedo, M. C. de 8[80]

Balch, D.
22[169], 49[1], 250[67, 68]

Barbel, J.
34[259]

Barberet, F.
104[10]

Bardy, G.
20[151], 33[247]

Barker, M.
35[260], 236[38]

Barnard, L. W.
29[220], 38[282]

Battifol, P.
29[224], 152[5]

Bauckham, J. R.
37[275], 94[37], 95

Bausone, C.
10[90], 71[31]

Beard, M.
13[111]

Belluci, A.
8[76]

Berstein, A. E.
189[33]

Betz, H. D.
77[3, 12]

Bieder, W.
179[37]

Bobertz, C. A.
164[21], 249[56], 250[69]

Bogdanos, T.
7[71]

Bonner, C.
1[2, 6], 3[27, 28], 4, 9[90], 98[2], 175[5, 6], 189[35], 192[10], 193[15], 205[50], 210[91, 93]

Boomershine, T. E.
14[114]

Borgen, P.
178[21]

Boring, E. M.
23[175]

Boswell, J.
42[1]

Bousett, W.
100[19]

Bowe, B. E.
59[9]

Box, G. H.
213[20]

Boyancé, P.
31[241]

Brown, P.
47[7]

Brown, R. E.
250[68]

Brox, N.
70[18], 74[52], passim

Bruce, F. F.
118[1]

Cadbury, H. J.
193[15]

Cameron, A.
42[1]

Carlini, A.
1[5], 2[8, 13, 15], 3[20, 26], 4[31], 5[50], 7[67, 68], 8[76], 19[44], 43[14], 45, 50[17], 56[16], 61[1], 62[4, 7], 72[30], 73[36, 38, 42], 77[12], 78[14], 88[33], 98[2]

Cecchelli, C.
182[7]

Chadwick, H.
5[50], 6[58], 228[12]

Chevalier, M.-A.
221[7]

Chevalier, R.
91[7]

Cirillo, L.
5[49], 6[58], 27[211], 64[23], 68[3], 180[39, 43], 181[44], 200[1], 203[30], 212[3, 20]

Clark, E. A.
228[12, 14]

Clark, K. W.
23[181]

Cody, A.
27[209]

Coleborne, W.
9

Collins, A. Yarbro
10[92], 12[105]

Collins, J. J.
10[93], 11[98], 12[106], 35[261], 58[3], 204[34]

Collins, J. N.
205[46]

Conzelmann, H.
100[19], 233[2]

Cotelier, J.
3

Cotterill, J. M.
25[194]

Cox, A. C.
19[145]

Crombie, F.
16[124], 19, 19[146], 94[41], 97[73], 118[1, 3], 124[8], 133[15], 141[3], 154[24], 209[81], 247[40], 257[5], 261[23]

Crook, J. A.
49[3]

Curtius, E. R.
85[7, 8]

D'Alès, A.
28[219], 29[223], 75[54], 115[10]

Daniélou, J.
33[247]

D'Arms, J.
21[158], 75[56]

DeMaris, R. E.
238[55]

Demetz, P.
8[77], 162[7]

Deming, W.
229[16]

Dewey, J.
13[110, 111]

Dexter, C.
21[163]

Dibelius, M.
24[186], 26[200, 204, 205], 31[236], 78[17], 81[12], 107[2], 129[7], 130[18], 132[2], 144[37], 148[3], 164[23], passim

Di Cristina, S.
9[81]

Dix, G.
86[15]
Donaldson, J.
16[124]
Dronke, P.
7[72], 100[16]
Duchesne, L.
4[36], 182[6]

Eilberg-Schwartz, H.
225[52]
Eitrem, S.
100[17]
Emmet, C. W.
111[9]
Eyben, E.
76[2], 86[18]

Fabre, G.
21[158]
Fasola, U.
8[76]
Ferguson, E.
6[57]
Festugière, A. J.
189[28]
Finley, M. I.
86[18], 171[3]
Finney, P. C.
9[81]
Fiorenza, E. Schüssler
12[104]
Fitzgerald, J. T.
25[193], 29[225], 45[32]
Florez, S. F.
36[272, 273], 37[280]
Ford, J. M.
25[190], 85[6], 200[3]
Fox, R. Lane
13[113], 23[177]
Frazer, J. G.
77[12]
Frei, H. A.
29[227]
Funk, F. X.
3[21, 22], 26[206], 44[24], 86[15], 129[6], 149[14]

Gamble, H.
2[10], 13[110], 14[116, 117]
Garnsey, P.
42[1], 120[22]
Garrett S.
95[46], 118[5], 144[41], 153[12]
Garrison, R.
174[12]
Gebhardt, O. von
2[15], 177[13], 183[11], 222[13], 223[25, 29, 35], 225[50], 228[9], 234[11], 235[28], 238[52], 244[4], 246[19, 23]
Geffcken, J.
77[6]
Giet, S.
9, 10[90], 33[258], 35[262], 75[54], 93[28], 111[11], 202[21], 222[19]
Gilliard, F. D.
14[116]
Gilmour, C.
30[232]
Goldhahn-Müller, I.
10[90], 28[218, 219], 29[221]
Goodenough, E. R.
201[5]
Goodspeed, E. J.
57[18], 227[1]
Goody, J.
13[111]
Grafe, E.
228[13]
Grant, R. M.
5[50], 57[18]
Greeven, H.
24[186], 26[200, 204, 205], 31[236], 78[17], 81[12], 107[2], 129[7], 130[18], 132[2], 144[37], 148[3], 164[23]
Grobel, K.
162[2, 7]
Gronewald, M.
2[12]

Grotz, J.
28[219], 69[13, 14], 70, 70[17, 19], 75[55], 110[6]
Grundmann, W.
149[11]

Haas, C.
31[241]
Hahneman, G. M.
6[57], 18[136], 27[313]
Hamman, A.
202[17], 206[59]
Hanson, A. T.
25[190]
Harnack, A. von
2[15], 4[43], 6[56], 13[110], 177[13], 183[11], 222[13], 223[25, 29, 35], 225[50], 228[9], 234[11], 235[28], 238[52], 244[4], 246[19, 23]
Harrill, J. A.
149[13]
Harris, J. R.
94[39], 213[16]
Harris, W. V.
13[110], 49[3]
Hauck, R. J.
180[42]
Havelock, E.
13[110], 14
Hay, D. M.
63[14]
Hellholm, D.
10[93], 12[105], 49[9], 61[1], 69[4], 71[26], 72[30], 97[75]
Hengel, M.
63[17]
Henne, P.
1[1], 3[29], 4, 4[32, 34, 39, 42], 4[43], 5[50, 51, 54], 6[57, 62], 10[90], 12, 29[223, 228], 43[19], 47[9], 50[16], 69[6], 69[13], 70, 70[17, 19], 75[53, 58], 79[20, 21], 85[17], 90, 90[1], 91[4], 110[3], 112[16], 114[7], 115[10], 168[1], 171[4, 6], 177[7, 15],

177[17], 179[35, 36], 180[41], 200[2], 204, 204[38]
Hermansen, G.
146[55]
Hilgenfeld, A.
2[14], 3[21], 9, 9[84], 50[14], 106[8], 235[30], 237[44], 238[52], 260[15]
Hilhorst, A.
1[3], 2[17], 3[25], 10[90], 21[153, 155, 161], 25[195], 26[197], 42[4], 44[28], 49[11], 55[6], 62[8], 69[4], 72[29], 92[15], 94[42], 96[60], 114[3], 114[6], 130[13], 134[22], 138[20], 149[5, 6], 162[7], 169[4, 6, 7], 187[8], 193[15], 202[26], 208[72], 235[30]
Hill, C.
56[12], 238[56]
Hill, D.
183[9]
Himmelfarb, M.
189[27]
Himmelman, N.
8[81], 16[127]
Hollenberg, G.
149[14], 189[35]
Hopkins, K.
13[111]
Horsley, G. H. R.
2[9]
Hüber, E.
88[31]
Humphrey, E. McEwan
28[117], 29[220], 36[274], 37[277]
Humphries-Brooks, S.
11[102]

Irmscher, J.
27[212]

Jackmann, K. R.
130[15]

In the design of the visual aspects of *Hermeneia*, consideration has been given to relating the form to the content by symbolic means.

The letters of the logotype *Hermeneia* are a fusion of forms alluding simultaneously to Hebrew (dotted vowel markings) and Greek (geometric round shapes) letter forms. In their modern treatment they remind us of the electronic age as well, the vantage point from which this investigation of the past begins.

The Lion of Judah used as visual identification for the series is based on the Seal of Shema. The version for *Hermeneia* is again a fusion of Hebrew calligraphic forms, especially the legs of the lion, and Greek elements characterized by the geometric. In the sequence of arcs, which can be understood as scroll-like images, the first is the lion's mouth. It is reasserted and accelerated in the whorl and returns in the aggressively arched tail: tradition is passed from one age to the next, rediscovered and re-formed.

"Who is worthy to open the scroll and break its
seals. . . ."
Then one of the elders said to me
"weep not; lo, the Lion of the tribe of David,
the Root of David, has conquered,
so that he can open the scroll and
its seven seals."
Rev. 5:2, 5

To celebrate the signal achievement in biblical scholarship which *Hermeneia* represents, the entire series will by its color constitute a signal on the theologian's bookshelf: the Old Testament will be bound in yellow and the New Testament in red, traceable to a commonly used color coding for synagogue and church in medieval painting; in pure color terms, varying degrees of intensity of the warm segment of the color spectrum. The colors interpenetrate when the binding color for the Old Testament is used to imprint volumes from the New and vice versa.

Wherever possible, a photograph of the oldest extant manuscript, or a historically significant document pertaining to the biblical sources, will be displayed on the end papers of each volume to give a feel for the tangible reality and beauty of the source material.

The title-page motifs are expressive derivations from the Hermeneia logotype, repeated seven times to form a matrix and debossed on the cover of each volume. These sifted-out elements will be seen to be in their exact positions within the parent matrix.

Horizontal markings at gradated levels on the spine will assist in grouping the volumes according to these conventional categories.

The type has been set with unjustified right margins so as to preserve the internal consistency of word spacing. This is a major factor in both legibility and aesthetic quality; the resultant uneven line endings are only slight impairments to legibility by comparison. In this respect the type resembles the handwritten manuscripts where the quality of the calligraphic writing is dependent on establishing and holding to integral spacing patterns.

All of the type faces in common use today have been designed between AD 1500 and the present. For the biblical text a face was chosen which does not arbitrarily date the text, but rather one which is uncompromisingly modern and unembellished so that its feel is of the universal. The type style is Univers 65 by Adrian Frutiger.

The expository texts and footnotes are set in Baskerville, chosen for its compatibility with the many brief Greek and Hebrew insertions. The double-column format and the shorter line length facilitate speed reading and the wide margins to the left of footnotes provide for the scholar's own notations.

Kenneth Hiebert